GROTIUS

RIGHTS OF WAR AND PEACE:

AN ABRIDGED TRANSLATION.

BY

WILLIAM WHEWELL, D.D.

MASTER OF TRINITY COLLEGE

AND PROFESSOR OF MORAL PHILOSOPHY IN THE UNIVERSITY OF CAMBRIDGE.

Edited for the Syndics of the University Press.

THE LAWBOOK EXCHANGE, LTD.
Clark, New Jersey

ISBN 9781584779421 (hardcover)
ISBN 978161619942X (paperback)

Lawbook Exchange edition 2011

The quality of this reprint is equivalent to the quality of the original work.

THE LAWBOOK EXCHANGE, LTD.

33 Terminal Avenue
Clark, New Jersey 07066-1321

Please see our website for a selection of our other publications
and fine facsimile reprints of classic works of legal history:
www.lawbookexchange.com

Library of Congress Cataloging-in-Publication Data

Grotius, Hugo, 1583-1645.
  [De jure belli ac pacis libris tres. English.]
  Grotius on the rights of war and peace : an abridged translation /
Edited for the Syndics of the University Press by William Whewell.
    p. cm.
  Originally published: Cambridge : J.W. Parker, 1853.
  ISBN-13: 978-1-58477-942-1 (cloth : alk. paper)
  ISBN-10: 1-58477-942-X (cloth : alk. paper)
  1. International law. 2. War (International law) 3. Natural law. I.
Whewell, William, 1794-1866. II. Title.
  KZ2093.A3J8813 2009
  341.6--dc22

                          2008043998

Printed in the United States of America on acid-free paper

GROTIUS

ON THE

RIGHTS OF WAR AND PEACE:

AN ABRIDGED TRANSLATION.

BY

WILLIAM WHEWELL, D.D.

MASTER OF TRINITY COLLEGE

AND PROFESSOR OF MORAL PHILOSOPHY IN THE UNIVERSITY OF CAMBRIDGE.

Edited for the Syndics of the University Press.

Cambridge:

AT THE UNIVERSITY PRESS.

1853

PREFACE TO THE TRANSLATION.

THE following translation of the celebrated work of Grotius, *De Jure Belli et Pacis,* was made with the intention of its being printed side by side with the original; and contains numerous references to quotations given in the original, but omitted in the translation for the sake of brevity and convenience. It has been thought that several persons might wish to have the translation alone, and therefore it is here so published. In doing this, the references have been retained unaltered; since, though the translation has thus necessarily an aspect of incompleteness, the reader has thereby an indication of what is omitted or abridged. It is hoped that, notwithstanding these omissions, the translation conveys a clear and correct view of the reasonings and discussions of the work.

The style of Grotius is concise, and in some degree technical, as the nature of the work requires: and this character it has not been attempted to avoid in the translation, except so far as to make it intelligible to ordinary Readers.

The Preface to the Edition, and the Latin Index to the Work, have been annexed to the translation, as likely to be useful to the English Reader. Even where they contain references to passages which do not appear in this volume, they will convey information respecting the original work.

EDITOR'S PREFACE.

"IT is acknowledged by every one," says Mr Hallam, "that the publication of this treatise made an epoch in the philosophical, and we might almost say in the political history of Europe." This opinion of the importance of Grotius's work *De Jure Belli et Pacis*, prevailed from the time of its first appearance, and was exemplified by all the marks of honour with which such a book can be greeted. Numerous editions in various forms circulated rapidly: copious comments of several annotators, translations into several languages, speedily appeared; the work was published in the author's life-time, *cum notis variorum*, a distinction hitherto reserved to the ancient classics: and it was put into the *Index Expurgatorius* at Rome. Gustavus Adolphus carried it about with him and kept it under his pillow: Oxenstiern appointed its author the ambassador of Sweden at Paris: the Elector Palatine Charles Louis established at Heidelberg a Professorship of the science thus created; and the science has been promoted by the like means in many other places up to the present time.

Nor has it, at this day, ceased to be a book of the first-rate importance in this science. It is spoken of with respect and admiration by the principal modern writers on International Law: a knowledge of it is taken for granted in the discussions of questions belonging to that subject; and it is quoted among the cardinal authorities on such questions. And treating, as it does, of the fundamental points of Philosophical Ethics, as well as of their application in the Laws of Nations, it has, in that department also, been always regarded as a primary work. It soon gave rise to Puffendorf's Treatise *On the Laws of Nature and Nations*, and to other books of the same kind; of which some, like our own Rutherforth's *Course of Lectures on Grotius*, show the celebrity of the work, by taking from it nothing but the name. Mackintosh, in more than one place, gives to the work the highest terms of his eloquent praise; and how Mr Hallam speaks of it has been mentioned above.

Several objections have, however, been made to the work; and among them, one which I shall especially notice, since an attempt is made in the present edition to remedy the inconvenience thus complained of. It has been said that Grotius's composition is so encumbered, in almost every page, with a multitude of quotations from ancient historians, orators, philosophers and poets, as to confuse the subject, obscure the reasoning, and weary the reader. I am not at all disposed to dissent from what several eminent men have said in answer to this; defending Grotius's quotations, as evidences of men's moral judgments, as appeals to general sympathy, and as graceful literary ornaments; but I am also ready to allow that these citations go to the extent of disturbing the didactic clearness and convenient brevity which we wish to find in a philosophical work. Hence, in the translation with which I have accompanied the text, I have omitted all the quotations except those which were necessary to carry on the argument. By this means, the bulk of the work has been reduced more than one half; while, the names of the authors quoted, being retained in the translation, the reader can, if he chooses, pass to the passages adduced, which he will find on the same page. The translation is thus rather a selective than an abridged translation; for the didactic and argumentative parts are, in general, so far from being here abridged, that explanatory expressions and clauses are introduced in a great number of passages where they seemed likely to make the meaning clearer.

It appears to me that the scheme and reasoning of Grotius's work are well worthy of being thus carefully presented to the reader. I agree with a former editor, Barbeyrac, that Grotius's learning, wonderful as it was, was far from being the greatest of his qualifications for the task which he undertook. His work is characterized throughout by solid philosophical principles consistently applied; by clear and orderly distinction of parts; by definite and exact notions, improved by the intellectual discipline of legal studies; by a pure and humane morality, always inclining to the higher side in disputed questions; and by a pervading though temperate spirit of religion. It may be doubted whether, even yet, we can place philosophical morality on any better basis than that which he lays down in his *Prolegomena;* namely, the social impulse by which man is actuated, in addition to the desire of his individual good. This social impulse is, he holds, the source of *Jus,* or Natural Law;—the basis of property and contract (Art. 8.) It is, he says, (Art. 16), too narrow a view to say that Utility is the Mother of Rights; the Mother of Rights is Human Nature, taken as a whole, with its impulses of kindness, pity, sociality, as well as its desire of individual pleasure and fear of pain. Human Nature is the Mother of Natural Law, and Natural Law is the Mother of Civil or Instituted Law.

By thus founding Morality and Law upon the whole compass of man's human and social, as well as animal and individual nature, Grotius, as I conceive, makes his system more true and philosophical than many of the more recent schemes of the philosophy of morals. He is thus favourably distinguished, not only from those who, like

Hobbes, found law and morality on the mutual fear of men, and from those who proclaim utility as the basis of their system; but also from later and celebrated dissertators upon Natural Law, such as Kant and Fichte, and other German philosophers. A recent writer* on this subject has justly remarked this distinction: that Grotius does not, as those philosophers do, seek the ground and basis of Rights in the insulated existence of the individual, but in the social relations of men. The critic remarks, also, that we do not find in him that strenuous attempt to separate jural from moral doctrines, which, in the Kantian period, was regarded as the essential condition for the proper development of jural philosophy: nor, again, do we meet in Grotius with that perpetual hammering upon the innate freedom of the Person as such; with the assumption that the Person, in virtue of his mere existence as a Person, is the bearer and possessor of an indefinite mass of Rights, all which may be asserted by force; while yet, on the other hand, the Person may, in cases of necessity, have to acquiesce in the mere possibility of acquiring Right, as the sole result of his Personality. And hence, as the writer just quoted further remarks, we do not find in him the harsh and startling propositions which occur so frequently in the jural speculations of the Kantian period.

The speculations on the subject of *Jus, the Doctrine of Rights and Obligations*, both in the hands of the German writers whom I have mentioned, in those of Grotius †, and in those of the Roman jurists from whom this strain of

---

* Hartenstein: Darstellung der Rechtsphilosophie des Hugo Grotius. In the *Transactions of the Royal Society of Saxony*, 1850.

† The title of the work in full is, *Hugonis Grotii De Jure Belli et Pacis Libri Tres, in quibus Jus Naturæ et Gentium, item Juris Publici præcipua explicantur.*

speculation was originally derived, proceed upon the sup-. position that there is a body of, Natural Law, *Jus Naturæ*, distinct from Instituted Law (*Jus Gentium* and *Jus Civile*), and belonging to man by his nature. I have elsewhere* endeavoured to shew that though man nowhere exists, and by his nature cannot exist, without Laws, there is no special body of Laws which can distinctively be called *Natural Law*, *Jus Naturæ*. I have noted (*Elements of Morality*, 1052) the inconsistencies into which Grotius, as well as others, is led, when he attempts to exemplify this distinction in particular cases. But I have also (1053, 1054) pointed out the truths which were often expressed by means of this distinction; namely, that the actual Law of any community might be worse than it is; and that it may be better. The *Jus Naturæ* may be the mere rudiments out of which the *Jus Gentium* is to be fashioned; or it may be the lofty ideal which the *Jus Gentium* never reaches. Both these lines of speculation are very interesting and instructive; and we may readily concede to the philosophical jurists the use of the phraseology which they have been accustomed to employ on such questions; and which is often convenient and useful for these and other purposes.

Jus Gentium is a phrase which, about the time of Grotius, was passing from its ancient Roman meaning, *the Law common to most Nations*, to its modern meaning, *the Law between Nations*. The prolix and multifarious character of Grotius's work arises, in a great measure, from his setting out from the first of these meanings, in order to discuss the second. He thus begins with the philosophy of ethics, and ends with exhortations to humanity, truth, and justice, even in the conduct of wars. The latter indeed, was more peculiarly his object than the former; for the narrow and

---

* *Elements of Morality*, Art. 650. Mr Bentham also denies the existence of such a body of Natural Rights.

savage view which derives law and justice from mutual fear, had not been prominently put forwards in that period, as it was soon afterwards by Hobbes; and Grotius, in debating the question, is driven to seek the opponents of his wider and humaner morality, in the ancient world, among the Grecian sophists. But the miseries arising from unregulated war pressed upon his thoughts with present and severe reality; for the Thirty Years' War had long been ravaging Europe. To this spectacle he himself ascribes the origin of his work. He says (*Proleg.* Art. 28), "I saw prevailing throughout the Christian world a license in making war, of which even barbarous nations would have been ashamed; recourse was had to arms for slight reasons, or for no reason; and when arms were once taken up, all reverence for divine and human law was thrown away; just as if men were thenceforth authorized to commit all crimes without restraint." The sight of these atrocities had led many men, he says, to hold all war to be unlawful to Christians; but he, more temperately, thought that the remedy was to bring it about that war itself should be subject to rules of humanity and decency. And he adds, that he conceived himself in some degree prepared for such a task by the practice of jurisprudence in his own country; and hoped, that, though unworthily ejected from that country, which had been honoured by so many of his works, he might still promote the science by the labours of his pen.

He claims (*Proleg.* 30), to be the first who had reduced International Law to the form of an Art or Science. Nor do I conceive that this claim goes beyond his due: though I am aware that certain writers have been recently brought to light and pointed out as his "Precursors*." The Precursors thus newly brought into notice are Johannes Oldendorp,

---

* Die Vorläufer des Hugo Grotius auf dem Gebiete des *Jus Naturæ et Gentium*. Von Carl von Kaltenborn, 1848.

whose *Isagoge Juris Naturalis, Gentium, et Civilis*, was published at Cologne in 1539; Nicolaus Hemming, who wrote *De Lege Naturæ Methodus Apodictica;* Benedict Winkler, whose *Principiorum Juris libri quinque* appeared in 1615, ten years before the publication of the work of Grotius. But I see no reason to think that these works did more to anticipate the work of Grotius than the works which he himself enumerates and criticizes, as bearing upon the subject; especially the work of the Oxford Professor of Law, Albericus Gentilis, *De Jure Belli*, Hanoviæ, 1598. In this work, as Mr Hallam has observed, the titles of the chapters run almost parallel to those of the first and third Books of Grotius; and Grotius himself mentions him (along with Balthasar Ayala), as a writer who had been of great use to him: "Cujus diligentia sicut alios adjuvari posse scio, et me adjutum profiteor," (*Prol.* 38). The work of Ayala, *De Jure et Officiis Bellicis*, published in 1582, is conceived by Mr Hallam to have been the first "that systematically reduced the practice of nations in the conduct of war to legitimate rules." But notwithstanding the labours of these authors, we may, I conceive, fully assent to Mr Hallam, when he says of Grotius's work: "The book may be considered as nearly original, in its general platform, as any work of man in an advanced stage of civilization and learning can be. It is more so, perhaps, than those of Montesquieu and [Adam] Smith."

Mr Dugald Stewart has, in his *Dissertation on the Progress of Philosophy*, spoken unfavourably, indeed contemptuously, of Grotius's great work. I am happily relieved from any necessity of replying to this criticism, by the admirable manner in which the task has already been performed by Mr Hallam. That judicious and temperate writer finds himself compelled to refer to Mr Stewart's attack in these terms: "That he should have spoken of a work so distinguished by fame, and so effective, as he himself admits, over the public mind of Europe, in terms of unmingled depreciation, without having done more than glanced at some of its pages, is an extraordinary symptom of that tendency towards prejudices, hasty but inveterate, of which that eminent man seems to have been not a little susceptible. The attack made by Stewart on those who have taken the law of nature and nations for their theme, and especially on Grotius, who stands forwards in that list, is protracted for several pages, and it would be tedious to examine every sentence in succession. Were I to do so, it is not, in my opinion, an exaggeration to say that almost every successive sentence would lie open to criticism." He then goes on to take the chief heads of accusation; and to his instructive discussion of them, I refer my reader*.

Paley also, in the Preface to his *Moral Philosophy*, censures Grotius for the profusion of his classical quotations; an objection of which I have already spoken, and which I have here tried to remedy; and for the forensic cast of his writings. That in the work of Grotius we see everywhere traces of the juristical training of his mind, is not to be denied; but it may be much doubted whether this is a disadvantage;—whether this legal discipline of the intellect have not given a precision to his divisions and reasonings which they would not have had without the habits so formed. Certainly a jurist would find, in Paley himself, great reason to complain that questions of morality and of law are mingled together in a very confused and arbitrary manner.

It was not the intention of Grotius to furnish a System of Ethics. But if we regard the work as to its bearing on ethical philosophy, it will, in many respects, sustain with advantage a comparison with the work of Paley. Grotius

---

* *Literature of Europe*, Part III. Chap. iv. § 83.

shews, satisfactorily as I conceive, that *utility* is a very narrow and perverse expression for the foundation of morality (*Proleg*. 16). And the foundation which he himself lays, is far broader and more philosophical (*Proleg*. 6). Man, he says, is an excellent animal, differing from other animals, not in degree only but in nature; and among his peculiar excellencies is a desire for society, a desire for a life spent in community with his fellow-men; and not merely spent somehow, but spent tranquilly and as a reasonable being; *communitatis non qualiscunque, sed tranquillæ, et pro sui intellectus modo ordinatæ*. This desire, or impulse, the Stoics called οἰκείωσις, *the Domestic Impulse*. We might be tempted to call it the Domestic *Instinct;* but then, we should have to recollect, that precisely one of the peculiarities which we have here to take into account, is, that man is not governed by Instinct, but by Reason; that in virtue of his human nature, the impulses which belong to him, analogous to the instincts of animals, become conscious and intelligent purposes: and thus personal security, property, contracts and the like, the necessary conditions of a tranquil and reasonable community of life, are necessary results of man's nature. And thus human nature is the source of Rights, as Grotius says, (*Proleg*. 16).

That man forms a judgment of actions, and tendencies to act, as being right or wrong; and that the adjective *right* has a wider range than the substantive *Rights;* are doctrines belonging to man's *moral* nature; and these doctrines lead us to a scheme of morality which has its foundations, as a sound scheme of morality must have, at once in the external conditions of man's being, and in the internal nature of his soul. The *Rights* which his outward circumstances necessarily establish, are recognized and made the cardinal points of *Rightness*, by his inward convictions. Among the convictions which belong to man, as a moral creature, is this; that not only his outward actions, but his inward purposes, volitions, affections, desires and habits, ought to be right. This consideration, however, leads us into a region of morality with which Grotius is not much concerned in the present work.

Many of the questions of International Law which are discussed by Grotius, have been the subject of much subsequent discussion; and in several cases, the opinions now generally accepted are different from those which he asserts. To have attempted to notice such cases, would have been, not to edit Grotius, but to compile a Treatise on the present state and past history of International Law. The student of such subjects will necessarily have to read many books; of which, however, this of Grotius is certainly one of the most indispensable. What is requisite in order to correct him, must be obtained by studying the best of his successors.

I hope that the deep and earnest love of Peace which inspired the design of this book, and which breathes so ardently through so many of its pages, will obtain a favourable reception for the work, in these days when the same sentiment is so strongly felt and so widely spread, and has shewn itself in so many remarkable ways. The progress of the study of International Law, on such principles as those of Grotius, and the increase of a regard for the authority of such Law, are among the most hopeful avenues to that noble Ideal of the lovers of mankind, a Perpetual Peace:—the most hopeful, because along this avenue, we can already see a long historical progress, as well as a great moral aim. Grotius himself, as was natural with his views, indulged the hope of such a consummation; as appears for instance, Book II. chap. xxiii. Sect. x. Art. 4, where he says: "It would be useful, and indeed it is almost necessary, that certain Congresses of Christian Powers should be held, in which controversies which arise among some of them may be decided by others who are not interested; and in which measures may be taken to compel the parties to accept peace on equitable terms." I trust that all Students and Professors of International Law will consider themselves as labouring upon a Problem which is still unsolved, while War exists; and in which all the approximate solutions must make wars more rare and more brief, as well as more orderly and more humane.

Notwithstanding the love of peace and the spirit of humanity which thus runs through the work of Grotius, it has been blamed by some, as sanctioning, by its doctrines, many of the most savage usages of war. But this objection can be made, I think, only by those who have not read the book with due attention. It is true, that in certain parts of the Third Book, he states the customary Rules, according to which wars have always been carried on; which Rules allow killing men, taking prisoners, capturing property, laying waste a country, and the like. And these he calls *the Rights of War;* and gives interpretations of the rules which may seem very severe. But this, he himself notes: and when he has performed this part of his task, he forthwith (in Chap. x.) proceeds to say, "I am now going to take from belligerents what I have seemed to grant to them, but have not really granted:" and then he goes on with a series of Chapters, which he calls *Temperamenta,* Restraints as to the exercise of these Rights of War, derived from considerations of humanity, justice, expedience and piety: and by these "temperaments," he divests war of all the cruelty and hardship which are separable from it. Still, some persons appear to be offended at violent and oppressive practices being called *Rights* in any sense. Upon this, I would remark, that there would be little use in a writer on this subject stating, as the Rights of War, Rules which never have been observed nor acknowledged in any actual war up to the present time. Killing, taking prisoners and making captures, besieging towns, and the like, are of the essence of war: and these are inevitably violent and painful inflictions. If at any time, the rules of such practices have been harsher than they now are, we may say that such Rules were the Rights of war in barbarous and ferocious times: but even in such times, those Rights imposed a certain restraint upon the victor; as for instance, the Right of making the conquered slaves, prevented his taking their lives. That such Rights are often morally wrong, Grotius himself repeatedly urges. The term *Rights*, like the term *Natural Law*, of which I have just spoken, may mean, either that which is secured to men by existing Rules, in every society, however rude; or that which it ought to be the aim of the most humane and pious men to secure by Rule, as the best condition of society. But this latter is not an ordinary nor convenient sense of the substantive *Rights*. If we were to adopt it, we should have a difficulty in establishing the Right of killing men at all for no crime; and therefore, there could be no Rights of War.

The translation may perhaps be welcome, even to the classical scholar, for Grotius's style is not only very concise and pregnant, but also full of expressions borrowed from the jurists and the schoolmen. But as the text will sufficiently explain these, I have not thought it necessary to translate the Notes, which besides, for the most part, refer to the quotations only.

There have already been published at least three translations of Grotius's work in English, besides a small and worthless abridgement, published in 1654 by C. B. (i. e.

Clement Barksdale, according to Watts). William Evats published a translation (in folio) in 1682, in which an attempt
was made (not very happily,) to improve the work, by introducing Grotius's Notes, and other matter, into the text.
And in 1738, a translation (also in folio), was published of
the text of the work, and of the Notes of Barbeyrac; not
only the smaller critical Notes which accompany the present
edition, but also of the larger Notes, generally of a juristical and historical kind, which Barbeyrac has appended to
his French translation. This edition is anonymous, but
bears traces of having been executed by a writer familiar
with the literature of jurisprudence. Besides these, there
is, I believe, a more modern translation, which I have not
seen.

I had no opportunity of consulting the translations of
1682 and 1738, till my own translation was completed;
and if this had been otherwise, the scheme of my translation is so different, that I should have had no temptation
to borrow from them. I have however taken a few Notes
from the edition of 1738.

Barbeyrac's critical notes, given in the present edition,
are excellent. They are mainly employed in verifying
Grotius's quotations: quotations, often, it would seem,
made by drawing upon a memory which appears to have
contained in its stores the whole mass of ancient literature.
Quotations so collected are often confused and imperfect,
as well as difficult to trace. The learning, acuteness, vigi-
lance and felicity, with which Barbeyrac has detected,
traced to their origin, and rectified, such mistakes as Grotius has committed, are such as may constantly excite the
admiration of the reader. Still, it would not have been
proper to publish a new edition of the work without again
verifying the references; and especially, enabling the reader
to refer to modern editions, instead of those which Bar-

beyrac employs. This task has been executed by the Rev. H. A. Holden, Fellow of Trinity College, who had before performed the same valuable service for the recent edition of Sanderson *De Obligatione Conscientiæ*.

The Notes of Gronovius, which occupy a considerable portion of the page of the most common editions of Grotius, are in reality of very little value. It is doubted by Tydman, a more recent editor, (Utrecht, 1773) whether they were intended for publication; and they may in general be omitted without loss. A few notices taken from them have been retained.

As further illustrating Barbeyrac's labours on this work, I have inserted his Preface, including the passage in which he expresses an unfavourable judgment of the value of the Notes of Gronovius. In this preface, the references to Barbeyrac's own Notes are here made according to the mode adopted in the present edition; namely, by means of the Arabic numerals from 1 to 9; the Notes of Grotius being marked by the letters of the alphabet, as in the earlier editions.

TRINITY LODGE, CAMBRIDGE,
August 23, 1853.

CONTENTS.

BOOK II.

BOOK III.

PRELIMINARY REMARKS.

1 THE Civil Law, both that of Rome, and that of each nation in particular, has been treated of, with a view either to illustrate it or to present it in a compendious form, by many. But International Law, that which regards the mutual relations of several Peoples, or Rulers of Peoples, whether it proceed from nature, or be instituted by divine command, or introduced by custom and tacit compact, has been touched on by few, and has been by no one treated as a whole in an orderly manner. And yet that this be done, concerns the human race.

2 For rightly did Cicero call that an excellent science which includes the alliances, treaties, and covenants of peoples, kings, and nations, and all the rights of war and peace. And Euripides prefers this science to the knowledge of things human and divine; for he makes Helen address Theonoe thus:

> 'twould be a base reproach
> That you, who know th' affairs of gods and men
> Present and future, know not what is just.

3 And such a work is the more necessary on this account; that there are not wanting persons in our own time, and there have been also in former times persons, who have despised what has been done in this province of jurisprudence, so far as to hold that no such thing existed, except as a mere name. Every one can quote the saying of Euphemius in Thucydides;—that for a king or a city which has an empire to maintain, nothing is unjust which is useful: and to the same effect is the saying, that for those who have supreme power, the equity is where the strength is: and that other, that state affairs cannot be carried on without doing some wrong. To this we must add that the controversies which arise between peoples and kings have commonly war for their arbiter. And that war is far from having anything to do with rights, is not only the opinion of the vulgar, but even learned and prudent men often let fall expressions which favour such an opinion. It is very usual to put *rights* and *arms* in opposition to each other. And accordingly Ennius says:

> They have recourse to arms, and not to rights.

And Horace describes Achilles thus:

> Rights he spurns
> As things not made for him, claims all by arms.

And another poet introduces a warrior, who when he enters on war, says:

> Now, Peace and Law, I bid you both farewell.

Antigonus laughed at a man, who, when he was besieging his enemies' cities, brought to him a Dissertation on Justice. And Marius said that the din of arms prevented his hearing the laws. Even Pompey, who was so modest that he blushed when he had to speak in public, had the face to say, *Am I who am in arms to think of the laws?*

4 In Christian writers many passages of a like sense occur: let that one of Tertullian suffice for all: *Deceit, cruelty, injustice, are the proper business of battles.* They who hold this opinion will undoubtedly meet our purpose, [of establishing the Rights of War,] with the expressions in Terence:

> You that attempt to fix by certain Rules
> Things so uncertain, may with like success
> Contrive a way of going mad by reason.

5 But since our discussion of Rights is worthless if there are no Rights, it will serve both to recommend our work, and to protect it from objections, if we refute briefly this very grave error. And that we may not have to deal with a mob of opponents, let us appoint them an advocate to speak for them. And whom can we select for this office, fitter than Carneades, who had made such wonderful progress in his suspension of opinion, the supreme aim of his Academical Philosophy, that he could work the machinery of his eloquence for falsehood as easily as for truth. He, then, undertook to argue against justice; and especially the kind of justice of which we here treat; and in doing so, he found no argument stronger than this:— that men had, as utility prompted, established Rights, different as their manners differed; and even in the same society, often changed with the change of times: but Natural Law there is none: for all creatures, men and animals alike, are impelled by nature to seek their own gratification: and thus, either there is no such thing as justice, or if it exist, it is the height of folly, since it does harm to itself in aiming at the good of others.

6 But what the philosopher here says, and what the poet (Horace) follows:—

> By naked nature ne'er was understood
> What's just and right:

must by no means be admitted. For man is an animal indeed, but an animal of an excellent kind, differing much more from all other tribes of animals than they differ from one another; which appears by the evidence of many actions peculiar to the human species. And among these properties which are peculiar to man, is a desire for society; that is, a desire for a life spent in common with fellow-men; and not merely spent somehow, but spent tranquilly, and in a manner corresponding to the character of his intellect. This desire the Stoics called οἰκείωσις, *the domestic instinct,* or *feeling of kindred.* And therefore the assertion, that, by nature, every animal is impelled only to seek its own advantage or good, if stated so generally as to include man, cannot be conceded.

7 And indeed even in other animals, as well as in man, their desire of their own individual good is tempered by a regard, partly for their offspring, partly for others of their own species; which in them, indeed, we perceive to proceed from some extrinsic intelligent principle*; because with regard to other acts not at all more difficult than those [thus directed towards the offspring, and the like,] an equal degree of intelligence does not appear. The same is to be said of infants, in which, previous to all teaching, we see a certain disposition to do good to others, as is sagaciously remarked by Plutarch: as for example, compassion breaks out spontaneously at that age. But inasmuch as a man of full age has the knowledge which enables him to act similarly in similar cases; and along with that, a peculiar and admirable appetite for society; and has also language, an instrument of this desire, given to him alone of all animals; it is reasonable to assume that he has a faculty of knowing and acting according to general principles; and such tendencies as agree with this faculty do not belong to all animals, but are peculiar attributes of human nature.

8 And this tendency to the conservation of society, which we have now expressed in a rude manner, and which tendency is in agreement with the nature of the human intellect, is the source of *Jus*, or Natural Law, properly so called. To this *Jus* belong the rule of abstaining from that which belongs to other persons; and if we have in our possession anything of another's, the restitution of it, or of any gain which we have made from it; the fulfilling of promises, and the reparation of damage done by fault; and the recognition of certain things as meriting punishment among men.

9 From this signification has flowed another larger sense of *Jus*: for, inasmuch as man is superior to other animals, not only in the social impulse of which we have spoken, but in his judgment and power of estimating advantages and disadvantages; and in these, not only present good and ill, but also future good and ill, and what may lead to each; we may understand that it is congruous to human nature to follow, in such matters also, [the estimate of future good and ill, and of the consequences of actions,] a judgment rightly framed; not to be misled by fear or by the temptation of present pleasure, nor to be carried away by blind and thoughtless impulse; and that what is plainly repugnant to such judgment, is also contrary to *Jus*, that is, to Natural Human Law.

10 And to this exercise of judgment pertains a reasonable and thoughtful assignment, to each individual and each body of men, of the things which peculiarly belong to them; by which exercise of judgment in some cases, the wiser man is preferred to the less wise; in others, our neighbour to a stranger; in others, a poor man to a

---

* In his Treatise *De Veritate Rel. Christ.* Lib. I. 7, Grotius notices the acts of animals, (as ants and bees,) which appear to proceed from some extrinsic Reason; *quæ quidem Ratio non aliud est quam quod Deus vocatur.* W.

c

rich man; according as the nature of each act and each thing requires. And this some persons have treated as a part of *Jus* properly and strictly so called; although *Jus* properly so called is really very different in its nature, and has this for its special office; to leave to another what is his, to give to him what we owe.

11 And what we have said would still have great weight, even if we were to grant, what we cannot grant without wickedness, that there is no God, or that he bestows no regard on human affairs. But inasmuch as we are assured of the contrary of this, partly by reason, partly by constant tradition, confirmed by many arguments and by miracles attested by all ages, it follows that God, as the author of our being, to whom we owe ourselves and all that we have, is to be obeyed by us without exception, especially since he has, in many ways, shewn himself both supremely good and supremely powerful: wherefore he is able to bestow upon those who obey him the highest rewards, even eternal ones, as being himself eternal; and he must be supposed to be willing as well as able to do this; and the more so, if he have promised such rewards in plain language; which we Christians believe, resting our belief on the indubitable faith of testimonies.

12 And here we are brought to another origin of Jus, besides that natural source; namely, the free will of God, to which, as our reason irresistibly tells us, we are bound to submit ourselves. But even that Natural Law of which we have spoken, whether it be that which binds together communities, or that looser kind [which enjoins duties,] although it do proceed from the internal principles of man, may yet be rightly ascribed to God; because it was by His will that such principles came to exist in us. And in this sense, Chrysippus and the Stoics said that the origin of *Jus* or Natural Law was not to be sought in any other quarter than in Jove himself; and it may be probably conjectured that the Latins took the word *Jus* from the name *Jove*.

13 To this we must add, that these principles God has made more manifest by the laws which he has given, so that they may be understood by those whose minds have a feebler power of drawing inferences: and he has prohibited the perverse aberrations of our affections which draw us this way and that, contrary to our own interest and the good of others; putting a bridle upon our more vehement passions, controlling and restraining them within due limits.

14 Further. The Sacred History, besides that part which consists in precepts, offers another view which in no small degree excites the social affection of which we have spoken; in that it teaches us that all men are sprung from the same parents. And thus we may rightly say, in this sense also, what Florentinus says in another sense, that there is a kindred established among us by nature: and in virtue of this relation it is wrong for man to intend mischief towards man.

Among men [all are not on the same footing towards us: as for instance,] our parents are a sort of Gods to us, to whom obedience is due; not infinite indeed, but an obedience of its own proper kind.

15 In the next place, since it is conformable to Natural Law to observe compacts, (for some mode of obliging themselves was necessary among men, and no other natural mode could be imagined,) Civil Rights were derived from this source, mutual compact. For those who had joined any community, or put themselves in subjection to any man or men, those either expressly promised, or from the nature of the case must have been understood to promise tacitly, that they would conform to that which either the majority of the community, or those to whom the power was assigned, should determine.

16 And therefore what Carneades said (as above), and what others also have said, as Horace,

Utility, Mother of just and right.

if we are to speak accurately, is not true. For the Mother of Right, that is, of Natural Law, is Human Nature; for this would lead us to desire mutual society, even if it were not required for the supply of other wants; and the Mother of Civil Laws, is Obligation by mutual compact; and since mutual compact derives its force from Natural Law, Nature may be said to be the Grandmother of Civil Laws. [The genealogy is, Human Nature: Natural Law: Civil Laws.] But Natural Law, [which impels us to society,] is *reinforced* by Utility. For the Author of Nature ordained that we should, as individuals, be weak, and in need of many things to make life comfortable, in order that we might be the more impelled to cling to society. But Utility is the *occasion* of Civil Laws; for the association or subjection by mutual compact, of which we have just spoken (15), was at the first instituted for the sake of some utility. And accordingly, they who prescribe laws for others, in doing this, aim, or ought to aim, at some Utility, to be produced to them for whom they legislate.

17 Further: as the Laws of each Community regard the Utility of that Community, so also between different Communities, all or most, Laws might be established, and it appears that Laws have been established, which enjoined the Utility, not of special communities, but of that great aggregate System of Communities. And this is what is called the Law of Nations, or International Law; when we distinguish it from Natural Law. And this part of Law is omitted by Carneades, who divides all Law into Natural Law, and the Civil Laws of special peoples; while yet, inasmuch as he was about to treat of that Law which obtains between one people and another, (for then follows an oration concerning war and acquisitions by war,) he was especially called upon to make mention of Law of this kind.

18 And it is without any good reason that Carneades maintains,

xxviii   PRELIMINARY REMARKS.

as we have said (5), that justice is folly. For since, by his own confession, that Citizen is not foolish who in a Civil Community obeys
the Civil Law, although, in consequence of such respect for the Law
he may lose something which is useful to himself: so too that People
is not foolish which does not so estimate its own utility, as, on account
of *that*, to neglect the common Laws between People and People. The
reason of the thing is the same in both cases. For as a citizen who
violates the Civil Law for the sake of present utility, destroys that
institution in which the perpetual utility of himself and his posterity
is bound up; so too a people which violates the Laws of Nature and
Nations, beats down the bulwark of its own tranquillity for future
time. And even if no utility were to arise from the observation of
Law, it would be a point, not of folly, but of wisdom, to which we
feel ourselves drawn by nature.

19 And therefore neither is that other saying of Horace [i Sat. iii.]
universally true:

'Twas fear of wrong that made us make our laws;

an opinion which one of the interlocutors in Plato's *Republic* explains
in this way: that Laws were introduced from the fear of receiving
wrong, and that men are driven to practise justice by a certain compulsion. For that applies to those institutions and laws only which
were devised for the more easy maintenance of rights: as when
many, individually feeble, fearing to be oppressed by those who were
stronger, combined to establish judicial authorities, and to uphold
them by their common strength; that those whom they could not
resist singly, they might, united, control. And we may accept in this
sense, and in no other, what is also said in Plato, that Right is that
which the stronger party likes: namely, that we are to understand that
Rights do not attain their external end, except they have force to back
them. Thus Solon did great things, as he himself boasted,

By linking Force in the same yoke with Law.

20 But still Rights, even unsupported by force, are not destitute of
all effect: for Justice, the observance of Rights, brings security to the
conscience; while injustice inflicts on it tortures and wounds, such as
Plato describes as assaulting the bosoms of tyrants. The conscience
of honest men approves justice, condemns injustice. And what is the
greatest point, injustice has for its enemy, and justice has for its friend,
God, who reserves his judgments for another life, yet in such a manner
that he often exhibits their power in this life; of which we have many
examples in history.

21 The reason why many persons, while they require justice as
necessary in private citizens, commit the error of thinking it superfluous in a People or the Ruler of a People, is this: in the first place,
that in their regard to rights they look at nothing but the utility
which arises from rights, which in the case of private citizens is evident, since they are separately too weak to protect themselves: while

great States, which seem to embrace within them all that is requisite to support life in comfort, do not appear to have need of that virtue which regards extraneous parties, and is called justice.

22 But, not to repeat what I have already said, that Rights are not established for the sake of utility alone, there is no State so strong that it may not, at some time, need the aid of others external to itself: either in the way of commerce, or in order to repel the force of many foreign nations combined against it. And hence we see that Leagues of alliance are sought even by the most powerful Peoples and Kings; which can have no force according to the principles of those who confine rights within the boundary of the State alone. It is most true [as Cicero says,] that everything loses its certainty at once, if we give up the belief in rights.

23 If no society whatever can be preserved without the recognition of mutual rights, which Aristotle [rather Plato, J. B.] proves by the strong instance of a society of robbers; assuredly that society which includes the whole human race, or at any rate, the greater part of nations, has need of the recognition of rights : as Cicero saw when he said that some things are so bad that they are not to be done even for the sake of saving our country (*Off.* 1. 45). Aristotle speaks with strong condemnation of those, who, while they will allow no one to hold rule among themselves, except him who has the right to do so, yet in their dealings with strangers have no care of rights, or the violation of rights.

24 A little while ago we quoted Pompey for his expression on the other side; yet on the other hand, when a certain Spartan king had said, Happy that republic which has for its boundaries the spear and the sword, Pompey corrected him, and said, Happy rather that which has justice for its boundary*. And to this effect he might have used the authority of another Spartan king, who gave justice the preference over military courage, on this ground; that courage is to be regulated by justice, but if all men were just, they would have no need of courage. Courage itself was defined by the Stoics, Virtue exercised in defence of Justice. Themistius, in an Oration to Valens, eloquently urges, that kings such as the rule of wisdom requires them to be, ought not to care for the single nation only which is committed to them, but for the whole human race; they should be, as he expresses it, not *philo-macedonian* only, or *philo-roman*, but

---

* Barbeyrac conjectures that this anecdote of Pompey, for which he cannot find any other authority, was produced, by Grotius mixing together in his memory two stories, both told in Plutarch's *Apophthegmata :* one, of a saying of Agesilaus, (or Archidamus,) who, when asked how far the Lacedemonian territory extended, swung his spear and said, *So far :* the other story, that when Phraates sent to Pompey and begged that the Parthians might have, for their boundary towards the Romans, the Euphrates; Pompey replied that the boundary should be Justice. Tydman (in his Preface) defends Grotius from Barbeyrac's charge of confusion in this quotation.

philanthropic. The name of Minos became hateful to posterity in no other way than this : that he terminated his equity at the boundaries of his own government.

25 It is so far from being proper to admit, what some choose to say, that in war all rights cease, that war is never to be undertaken except to assert rights; and when undertaken, is never to be carried on except within the limits of rights and of good faith. Demosthenes well said, that war was the mode of dealing with those who could not be kept in order by judicial proceedings. For judicial proceedings are of force against those who feel themselves to be the weaker party : but against those who make themselves or think themselves equals, war is the proceeding; yet this too, in order to be justifiable, to be carried on in a no less scrupulous manner than judicial proceedings are.

26 Be it so then, that, in the conflict of arms, laws must be silent : but let this be understood of laws civil, judicial, proper to peace; not of those laws which are perpetual and accommodated to all time. For it is excellently said by Dio Prusæensis, that between enemies, written laws, that is, Civil Laws, are not in force ; but that unwritten laws are, namely, those which nature dictates, or the consent of nations institutes. We may learn this from the old Formula of the Romans ; *I decide that those things may be sought by a pure and pious war.* The same old Romans, as Varro remarked, undertook war tardily, and without allowing themselves any licence, because they thought that no war except a pious one ought to be undertaken. Camillus said that wars were to be carried on no less justly than bravely. Africanus said, that the Romans began just wars, and ended them. Again, in Livy we read, *War has its laws no less than peace.* And Seneca admires Fabricius as a great man, and, what is most difficult, a man innocent even in war, and who thought that there were wrongs even towards an enemy.

27 How great the power of the conscience of justice is, the writers of histories everywhere shew, often ascribing victory to this cause mainly. Hence have arisen these proverbs ; That it is the Cause which makes the soldier brave or base : that he rarely comes safe back who goes out on the bad side : that Hope is the ally of the good Cause : and others to the same effect. Nor ought any persons to be moved by the occasional success of unjust designs; for it is enough if the equity of the cause has an efficacy, and that a great one, in action ; even though this efficacy, as happens in human affairs, is often prevented from taking effect, being counteracted by other causes. And further; in conciliating friendships, which nations, as well as individuals, need, on many accounts, a great effect must be assigned to an opinion that we do not hastily or unjustly undertake war, and that we carry it on religiously. For no one readily joins himself to those whom he believes to think lightly of right laws and good faith.

28 I, for the reasons which I have stated, holding it to be most

certain that there is among nations a common law of Rights which is of force with regard to war, and in war, saw many and grave causes why I should write a work on that subject. For I saw prevailing throughout the Christian world a license in making war of which even barbarous nations would have been ashamed; recourse being had to arms for slight reasons or no reason; and when arms were once taken up, all reverence for divine and human law was thrown away, just as if men were thenceforth authorized to commit all crimes without restraint.

29 And the sight of these atrocities has led many men, and these, estimable persons, to declare arms forbidden to the Christian, whose rule of life mainly consists in love to all men: and to this party sometimes John Ferus and our countryman Erasmus seem to approximate, men much devoted to peace, both ecclesiastical and civil: but they take this course, as I conceive, with the purpose with which, when things have been twisted one way, we bend them the other, in order to make them straight. But this attempt to drive things too far, is often so far from succeeding, that it does harm; because the excess which it involves is easily detected; and then, detracts from the authority of what is said, even within the limits of truth. We are to provide a remedy for both disorders; both for thinking that nothing is allowable, and that everything is.

30 Moreover, having practised jurisprudence in public situations in my country with the best integrity I could give, I would now, as what remains to me, unworthily ejected from that country graced by so many of my labours, promote the same subject, jurisprudence, by the exertion of my private diligence. Many, in preceding times, have designed to invest the subject with the form of an Art or Science; but no one has done this. Nor can it be done, except care be taken in that point which has never yet been properly attended to;—to separate Instituted Law from Natural Law. For Natural Law, as being always the same, can be easily collected into an Art: but that which depends upon institution, since it is often changed, and is different in different places, is out of the domain of Art; as the perceptions of individual things in other cases also is.

31 If, then, those who have devoted themselves to the study of true justice would separately undertake to treat of separate parts of Natural and Permanent Jurisprudence, omitting all which derives its origin from the will of man alone:—if one would treat of Laws; another, of Tributes; another, of the Office of Judges; another, of the mode of determining the Will of parties; another, of the Evidence of facts; we might, by collecting all these parts, form a complete body of such Jurisprudence.

32 What course we think ought to be followed in the execution of such a task, we shew by act rather than by words, in this present work; in which is contained by far the noblest part of Jurisprudence.

33 For in the First Book, (after a Preface concerning the origin of Rights and Laws,) we have examined the question whether any war be just: next, in order to distinguish between public and private war, we have to explain the nature of sovereignty; what Peoples, what Kings, have it entire; what, partial; who, with a right of alienation; who, otherwise; and afterwards we have to speak of the duty of subjects to superiors.

34 The Second Book, undertaking to expound all the causes from which war may arise, examines what things are common, what are property, what is the right of persons over persons, what obligation arises from ownership, what is the rule of royal succession, what right is obtained by pact or contract, what is the force and interpretation of treaties, of oaths private and public, what is due for damage done, what is the sacredness of ambassadors, the right of burying the dead, and the nature of punishments.

35 The Third Book has for its subject, in the first place, what is lawful in war; and when it has drawn a distinction between that which is done with impunity, or may even, in dealing with foreigners, be defended as consistent with Rights; and that which is really free from fault; it then descends to the kinds of Peace and to Conventions in War.

36 The undertaking such a work appeared to me the more worthy of the labour which it must cost, because, as I have said, no one has treated the whole of the argument; and those who have treated parts thereof, have so treated them that they have left much to the industry of others. Of the old philosophers nothing is extant of this kind, neither of the Greeks, among whom Aristotle is said to have written a book called the *Laws of War**, nor of those (the Fathers) who wrote as Christians in the early period of the Church; which is much to be regretted; and even of the books of the ancient Romans concerning the Law recognized by their *Feciales*, or *Heralds' College*, we have received nothing but the name. [See *Cic. Off.* i. 11; iii. 29.] Those who have made what they call *Summæ* of *Cases of Conscience*, have introduced chapters, as concerning other things, so concerning war, concerning promises, concerning oaths, concerning reprisals.

37 I have also seen special books concerning the Laws of War, written partly by theologians, as Francis Victoria†, Henry Gorichem‡, William Matthæi [Mathison?], Johannes de Carthagena§; some by

---

* But the true reading is Δικαιώματα πόλεων, the *Laws of States.* J. B.

† A Spanish Dominican who lived in the 16th century. The treatise here mentioned is *De Indis et Jure Belli*, and appears among his twelve theological lectures.

‡ A Dutchman so named from the place of his birth, and chancellor of Cologne. He lived about the middle of the fifteenth century, and wrote a treatise *De Bello Justo.*

§ His book was printed at Rome in 1609.

Doctors of Law, as Johannes Lupus*, Francis Arias †, Joannes à Lignano ‡, Martinus Laudensis §. But all these have said very little, considering the copiousness of the argument; and said it in such a way that they have mingled and confounded law natural, law divine, law of nations, civil law, and canon law.

38 What was most wanting in all these, namely, illustrations from history, the learned Faber ‖ has undertaken to supply in some chapters of his *Semestria*: but no further than served his own special purpose, and only giving references. The same has been done more largely, and that, by applying a multitude of examples to certain maxims laid down, by Balthazar Ayala ¶, and still more largely by Albericus Gentilis**; whose labour, as I know it may be serviceable to others, and confess it has been to me, so what may be faulty in his style, in his arrangement, in his distinctions of questions, and of the different kinds of Law, I leave to the judgment of the reader. I will only say, that in the decision of controversies he is often wont to follow, either a few examples that are not always to be approved of, or else the authority of modern lawyers in opinions given, not a few of which are accommodated to the interest of those that consult them, and not founded upon the nature of equity and justice. The causes for which a war is denominated just or unjust, Ayala has not so much as touched upon: Gentilis has indeed described, after his manner, some of the general heads; but many prominent and frequent cases of controversy he has not even touched upon.

39 We have been careful that nothing of this kind be passed over in silence; having also indicated the sources from which we derive our judgments, so that it may be easy to determine any question that may happen to be omitted by us. It remains now that I briefly explain with what aids, and with what care, I undertook this work.

In the first place, it was my object to refer the truth of the things which belong to Natural Law to some notions, so certain, that no

---

* A native of Segovia. His Treatise *De Bello et Bellatoribus* may be found in a large collection called *Tractatus Tractatuum.* Tom. xvi, of the Venice edition, 1584.

† A Spaniard. His book is in the same volume of the same collection, under the title *De Bello et ejus Justitia.*

‡ A native of Bologna. His Treatise *De Bello* is in the same volume.

§ His name was Garat. His Treatise *De Bello* appears in the same volume of the Collection. It was reprinted at Louvain in 1648, with the Treatise of Ayala, spoken of afterwards.

‖ Peter du Faur of St Jori, Councillor of the Grand Council, afterwards Master of Requests, and at last First President of the Parliament of Thoulouse. He was scholar to Cujas. His work entitled *Semestrium Libri Tres* has been several times printed at Paris, Lyons, and Geneva.

¶ He was a native of Antwerp, of Spanish extraction. His Treatise *De Jure et Officiis Bellicis* was printed at that city in 1597.

** Professor at Oxford about 1600. His book is *De Jure Belli.*

one can deny them, without doing violence to his own nature. For the principles of such Natural Law, if you attend to them rightly, are of themselves patent and evident, almost in the same way as things which are perceived by the external senses; which do not deceive us, if the organs are rightly disposed, and if other things necessary are not wanting. Therefore Euripides in his *Phœnissœ* makes Polynices, whose cause he would have to be represented manifestly just, express himself thus:

> I speak not things hard to be understood,
> But such as, founded on the rules of good
> And just, are known alike to learn'd and rude.

And he immediately adds the judgment of the chorus, (which consisted of women, and these too barbarians,) approving what he said.

40 In order to give proofs on questions respecting this Natural Law, I have made use of the testimonies of philosophers, historians, poets, and finally orators. Not that I regard these as judges from whose decision there is no appeal: for they are warped by their party, their argument, their cause: but I quote them as witnesses whose conspiring testimony, proceeding from innumerable different times and places, must be referred to some universal cause; which, in the questions with which we are here concerned, can be no other than a right deduction proceeding from the principles of reason, or some common consent. The former cause of agreement points to the Law of Nature; the latter, to the Law of Nations: though the difference of these two is not to be collected from the testimonies themselves, (for writers everywhere confound the Law of Nature and the Law of Nations,) but from the quality of the matter. For what cannot be deduced from certain principles by solid reasoning, and yet is seen and observed everywhere, must have its origin from the will and consent of all.

41 I have, therefore, taken pains to distinguish Natural Law from the Law of Nations, as well as both from the Civil Law. I have even distinguished, in the Law of Nations, that which is truly and universally lawful, true Rights; and *quasi*-Rights, which only produce some external effect similar to that of the true Rights: for instance, this effect; that they may not be resisted by force, or may even be defended by force, in order to avoid grave inconvenience. [Such *quasi*-Rights are those of a Master over his slave, where slavery is established by Law. W.] How necessary this observation is in many instances, will appear in the course of the work. No less careful have I been to separate those things which belong to *Jus*, or *Right*, properly and strictly so called, (out of which arises the obligation of restitution,) and those which are more laxly described by *right*, adjectively; because to act otherwise is at variance with some dictate of right reason; concerning which diversity of *Jus* or Right we have already said something above.

42 Among the philosophers, the first place is deservedly assigned

to Aristotle; whether we regard the order of his treatment of these subjects, or the acuteness of his distinctions, or the weight of his reasons. Only it were to be wished that his authority had not, some ages ago, been converted into a tyranny by others; so that Truth, in the pursuit of which Aristotle faithfully spent his life, suffers no oppression so great as that which is inflicted in Aristotle's name. I, both here and in other places, follow the liberty of the old Christians, who did not pin their faith to any sect of philosophers; not that they agreed with those who say that nothing can be known; than which nothing is more foolish; but that they thought that there was no sect which had seen the whole of the truth, and none which had not seen some part of the truth. They therefore aimed at collecting the truth which was diffused among individual philosophers, and among sects, into one body: and they thought that this result could be nothing else but the true Christian doctrine.

43 Among other points, to mention this in passing, as not foreign to our purpose, it appears to me that both some of the Platonists and the ancient Christians had good reason to depart from Aristotle's doctrine, in which he placed the very nature of Virtue in a *medium* of the affections and actions: which having once laid down, carried him so far, that he compounded Liberality and Frugality, two very different virtues, into one virtue; and assigned to Truth, two opposites which are by no means co-ordinate, Boasting and Dissimulation; and fastened upon some things the name of vices, which either do not exist, or are not, of themselves, vices; as the contempt of pleasure, and of honour, and a lack of irascibility towards men.

44 That this foundation of virtue, [that it is the *medium* between two extremes,] is not a right one, appears from the example of Justice itself; for the *too much* and *too little* which are opposed to this, since he cannot find in the affections and the consequent actions, he seeks them in the things with which justice deals; which proceeding is, in the first place, a transition to another genus; a fault which he justly blames in others. And in the next place, to take less than is one's own, may indeed have a vice adventitiously connected with it, growing out of a consideration of what a person, under the circumstances, owes to himself and those who depend on him; but certainly cannot be repugnant to justice, which resides entirely in abstaining from what is another's. And to this mistake that other is similar, that adultery as the fruit of lust, and homicide arising from anger, he will not allow to belong properly to injustice; though injustice is nothing else in its nature than the usurpation of what is another's; nor does it make any difference whether that proceeds from avarice, or from lust, or from anger, or from thoughtless compassion; or on the other hand, from the desire of superiority, in which the greatest examples of unjust aggressions originate. For to resist all impulses on this account only, that human society may not be violated, is what is really the proper character of justice.

45 To return to the point from which I started, it is true that it belongs to the character of certain virtues, that the affections are kept in moderation; but it does not follow that this is the proper and universal character of all virtue; but that Right Reason, which virtue everywhere follows, dictates that in some things a medium course is to be followed, in others, the highest degree of the affection is to be aimed at. Thus for instance, we cannot love God too much; for superstition does not err in this, that it loves God too much; but that its love acts perversely. We cannot desire eternal happiness too much, nor fear eternal misery too much, nor hate sin too much. It is therefore truly said by Gellius, that there are some things of which the range is not to be bounded by any limits; such that the larger and fuller they are, the more praiseworthy are they. So Lactantius, after discoursing much concerning the affections, says, *The procedure of wisdom is not shewn in moderating them, but their causes; since they arise from external incitements: nor are we to make it our business to restrain such affections, since they may be feeble in the greatest crimes, and vehement without any crime.* It is our purpose to place Aristotle very high, but with the same liberty which he allowed himself, with reference to his own master, actuated by his love of truth.

46 Passages of history are of twofold use to us; they supply both examples of our arguments, and judgments upon them. With regard to examples, in proportion as they belong to better times and better nations, they have the more authority; and therefore we have preferred those taken from the Greeks and the Romans. Nor are the judgments delivered in such histories to be despised, especially when many of them agree: for Natural Law, as we have said, is in a certain measure, to be proved by such consent; and as to the Law of Nations, there is no other way of proving it.

47 The opinions of poets and orators have not so much weight; and these we often use, not so much in order to claim assent to what they say, as that we may give to what we say something of ornament from their modes of expression.

48 The books written by men inspired by God, or approved by them, I often use as authority, with a distinction between the Old and the New Law. There are writers who allege the Old Law as a proof of the Law of Nature; but undoubtedly, without sufficient reason; for many parts of that Law proceed from the free will of God; which, however, is never at variance with the true Law of Nature: and so far, an argument may rightly be drawn from it; provided we distinguish accurately the Command and Will of God, which God sometimes executes by means of men, and the Rights of men towards one another. We have therefore shunned, as far as we could, both that error, and the error contrary to that, of those who think that, after the promulgation of the New Covenant, there is no longer any use for the old one. We hold the contrary; both for the reasons which we have now alleged; and because the nature of the

New Covenant is such, that with relation to the precepts which are given in the Old Testament pertaining to the moral virtues, the New Testament commands the same, or greater virtues of the same kind; and we see that the ancient Christian writers have used the testimony of the Old Covenant in this manner.

49 But in order to see what is the knowledge which the books of the Old Testament contain, the Hebrew writers may help us no little; and especially those who were best acquainted with the discourses and manners of their countrymen.

50 I use the New Testament for this purpose; that I may shew, what cannot be shewn in any other way, what is lawful for Christians; which however, contrary to what most writers have done, I have distinguished from the Law of Nature: holding it for certain that in that more holy Law, a greater holiness is enjoined upon us than the Law of Nature of itself requires. Nor have I omitted to note, where there are matters which are rather recommended to us than commanded; that we may understand that to deviate from the commands is wicked, and makes us liable to punishment: to aim at the highest excellence, is the work of a nobler and more generous spirit, which will not want its reward.

51 The Synodical Canons which are authentic, are collections from the general precepts of the Divine Law, adapted to special occurrences. And these either shew what the Divine Law commands, or exhort us to that which God enjoins. And this is the office of a truly Christian Church: to deliver to Christians the precepts which God has delivered to it, and in the manner in which God has delivered them.

Also the customs which were received or commanded among those ancient Christians who were truly worthy of that great name, may, with reason, have the force of Canons.

Next to these, is the authority of those who, each in his own time, flourished among the Christians, with the reputation of piety and learning, and who were never charged with gross error. What these assert with great positiveness, as matters of which they are convinced, must be allowed to have no small weight in the interpretation of what is obscure in the sacred writings: and this the more, in proportion as we have the assent of a greater number, and as they approach nearer to the times of original purity, when neither the domination of one, nor the combination of several, had operated to adulterate primitive truth.

52. The Schoolmen, who succeeded them, often shew no ordinary powers of intellect; but they fell upon evil times, ignorant of good literature; and therefore it is the less wonderful, if, among many things which merit praise, there are some which need excuse. Yet when they agree in points of morals, they are not likely to be wrong: since they are very clearsighted in discerning what may be found fault with in the doctrines of others: while, in their mode of maintaining opposite sides of a question, they afford a laudable

example of moderation; contending against each other with arguments; and not, as the custom has been of late, to the dishonour of
learning, with railing and abuse, the foul offspring of ill-regulated
minds.

53 Of the teachers of the Roman Law, there are three kinds:
the first, those whose works appear in the Pandects, the Codex of
Theodosius, and that of Justinian, and the laws called Novells. The
second class contains those who succeeded Irnerius; namely Accur-
sius, Bartolus, and so many others, who have long borne supreme
sway in the Courts of Law. The third class includes those who
have combined the study of elegant literature with the study of the
law. For the first I have great deference; for they often supply
the best reasons to prove what belongs to the nature of Jus; and give
their testimony both to Natural Law and to the Law of Nations: yet
in such a way that they, no less than others, often confound these
provinces: indeed they often call that *Jus Gentium*, the Law of Nations, which is only the law of certain peoples; and that, not even
by consent, but what one nation has received by imitation of another, or by accident. Also what truly belongs to *Jus Gentium* they
often treat promiscuously and indiscriminately with points which
belong to the Roman Law; as appears in the titles concerning Captives, and Postliminium. We have endeavoured to keep these subjects distinct.

54 The second of these classes, regardless of divine law and of
ancient history, attempted to define all the controversies of kings
and peoples on the grounds of the Roman Law, sometimes taking
into account the Canons. But these writers, too, were prevented, by
the unhappiness of their times, from understanding those laws
rightly; being, in other respects, sufficiently intelligent in investigating
the nature of right and equity: whence it comes to pass, that they,
while they are good authorities for making new laws, are bad interpreters of laws already made. They are to be listened to with most
attention, when they give their testimony to such customs as make the
Law of Nations in our time.

55 The masters of the third class, who include themselves within
the limits of the Roman Law, and either never, or in a very slight
degree, travel into that common or Natural Law, have scarcely any
use in reference to our argument. They join the subtilty of the
schoolmen with a knowledge of the laws and canons; so that two of
them, Spaniards, Covarruvias and Vasquius, did not abstain from the
controversies even of peoples and of kings: the latter, very freely;
the former, more modestly, and not without shewing some exactness
of judgment. The French have introduced the practice of connecting
history more with the study of the law: among whom Bodin and
Hotoman have a great name: the former, in the general scheme of
his work; the latter, in questions scattered through the progress
of his. Both the opinions and the arguments of these writers will

often require our consideration, and will supply us with materials for truths.

56 In the whole course of my work I have had in view these things especially: to make my definitions and reasons as clear as I could: to arrange in due order the matters I had to treat of: and to distinguish clearly things which were really different, though they seemed identical.

57 I have refrained from discussing points which belong to another subject; as the Utility of this or that course; for these belong to a special Art, namely, the Art Political; which Aristotle rightly treats as a separate subject, mixing with it nothing of any other kind; thus differing from Bodinus, in whom this Art is confounded with *Jus* in our sense. In some cases, however, I have made mention of the Utility of acts; but collaterally only, and in order to distinguish that question the more plainly from the question of Right.

58 The reader will do me injustice, if he judges me to have written with a regard to any controversies of our own time; either such as already exist, or such as can be foreseen as likely to arise. I profess, in all sincerity, that, as mathematicians consider their figures as abstracted from body, so did I, in treating of Rights, abstract my mind from every particular fact.

59 As to the style, I was unwilling, by adding prolixity of language to the multitude of the matters treated of, to weary the reader whom I wished to benefit. I therefore have followed a concise and didactic mode of treatment: that they who have to manage public affairs, may see, at one view, the kinds of controversies which are wont to arise, and the principles by which they are to be decided: this being known, it will be easy to accommodate their own discourses to the subject, and to expand the discussion as much as they please.

60 I have adduced the words of the authors themselves, when they were such as either carried with them authority, or exhibited especial elegance: and this I have sometimes done in Greek authors; but mostly, when either the quotation was short, or one of which I despaired of imitating the grace in a Latin translation: such a translation I have however added in every instance, for the benefit of those who find the Greek difficult.

61 I beg all readers into whose hands my work may come, to take the same liberty in judging of my opinions and expressions which I have taken with regard to those of others. They cannot be more ready to admonish me when I am in error, than I shall be to attend to their admonition.

And now, if I have said anything which is at variance with sound piety, with good morals, with holy scripture, with the unity of the Christian Church, with truth in any form;—let that be as unsaid.

RIGHTS OF WAR AND PEACE.
BOOK I.

CHAPTER I.

What is War. What are Rights.

I. [QUESTIONS of Rights among citizens of the same State are settled by the instituted Law of the State; and therefore do not belong to our subject, which is, Rights by nature, not Rights by institution.]

Between persons who are not bound by a common instituted Right, as those who have not yet formed a State; or between those who belong to different States—whether private persons, or kings, or those whose mutual Rights [and Obligations] resemble those of kings, such as Rulers of peoples, or free Peoples themselves—questions of Rights pertain either to time of war or time of peace. But war is undertaken for the sake of peace; and, on the other hand, there is no question of Rights which may not issue in war: hence we shall begin by Rights in war, or, as they are termed, Rights of War: and the consideration of War will lead us to the consideration of Peace, the end of war.

II. 1 We have then to treat of War, and of the Rights of War. We must then ask, What is War? What are Rights?

Cicero says that War is a contest or contention carried on by force. But usage applies the term, not to an action, [a contest,] but to a

B

state or condition: and thus we may say, War is the state of persons, contending by force, as such.

Hence we do not exclude *private** wars, which preceded public wars, and have the same origin as those.

2 The name, (*Bellum*,) comes from an old word *Duellum*, and implies the separation of two, (*duo;*) as peace is *unity*, when two are made one. So the Greek πόλεμος from πολύς, *many*.

3 The common use of the word *War* allows us to include Private War, though, used generally, it often means specifically *public* War.

We do not say that war is a state of *just* contention, because precisely the point to be examined is, Whether there be just war, and What war is just. And therefore we must distinguish the subject, War, from the question which we examine concerning it.

III. 1 By entitling our Treatise, *Of the Rights of War*, we mean, in the first place, to imply the discussion of the questions just stated, Whether any war is just, and What is just in war. For *Rights*, *Jus*, in this case, means only what is right, that is, just; and that, rather with a negative than a positive sense; so that *that* comes within the substantive *Right*, which is not unjust, or wrong.

That is unjust which is contrary to the nature of a society of rational creatures. Cicero, Seneca, Florentinus, reason on the ground of man being intended by nature for society. [See the quotations.]

2 Society is either that of equals, as brothers, friends, allies; or it is unequal, as that of parent and child, master and servant, king and subjects, God and men: and what is just, is different in the two cases. We may call them respectively Equatorial Rights and Rectorial Rights.

IV. *Jus*, *Right*, has another signification, derived from the former, as when we say *my* Right. In this sense Right is a moral Quality by which a person is competent to have or to do a certain thing justly.

Right in this sense belongs to a person, though sometimes it follows a thing: as one piece of land may have a right of way, or other easement, over another piece of land. In this case the Right still belongs to a person, namely, to the person who possesses the first piece. Such rights are called *real* Rights in comparison with others which are merely personal.

This moral quality, when perfect, is called *facultas*, a jural claim; when less perfect, *aptitudo*, a fitness, or moral claim.

V. A Jural Claim, belonging to any one, the jurists call *suum*, his own thing. We shall call this hereafter a *Right* strictly speaking, or a *Right proper*.

---

* In including *private*, and excluding *just*, in his definition of war, Grotius seems to have in view the definition of Albericus Gentilis; "Bellum est contentio, publica, armata, justa." For reasons for preferring the latter definition, see *Elements of Morality*, Art. 1058. The rights of War, as understood in modern times, exclude private wars, or wars among subjects, and include the *assertion* of justice. If they did not, there would be no question of *Rights*. W. W.

It includes, Power; whether over one's self, which is Liberty;
 or over another, which is Authority, for example,
paternal, dominical (that of a master over a servant;)
  Ownership; whether full, as of Property;
   or less full, as of Compact, Pledge, Credit, to which
corresponds Debt on the other side.

VI. But this Right is again twofold: Vulgar, which exists for the
purpose of private use; and Eminent, which is superior to vulgar Right,
and is the right which the community has over persons and things
for the sake of the common good.

Thus the Royal authority has under it the paternal and dominical.
So the power of ownership of the Sovereign over private property
for the common good is greater than that of the private owners: so
every one is more bound to the state in regard to public uses than to
his private creditor.

VII. A Fitness is what Aristotle calls ἀξίαν, a moral desert, or claim.

VIII. 1 A Jural Claim, or Right proper, belongs to Expletory
Justice, or Justice proper. This is what Aristotle calls *Contractual
Justice*; but the term is too narrow; for that the possessor of my
thing should restore it to me, is not a matter of contract; and yet it
belongs to this division. Elsewhere he calls it by a better name,
Corrective Justice.

A Moral Claim [sometimes called an Imperfect Right] belongs to
Attributive Justice, which Aristotle calls Distributive Justice, the companion of the virtues which are useful to our neighbours, as liberality,
mercy, directive prudence.

2 Aristotle says that Expletory Justice proceeds by arithmetical
proportion, Attributive, by geometrical proportion; but this is not
always true. The two differ, not in their rules, but in the matter
about which they are concerned. A contract of partnership is ruled
by expletory justice, but according to geometrical proportion; if there
is only one person fit for an office, it is by attributive justice given
to him alone, instead of reckoning proportion.

3 Equally erroneous is what others say, that Attributive Justice
concerns things common or public; Expletory, private possessions.
For if a man bestow his private property in legacies, he uses attributive justice; and the state, in paying what it owes to private
citizens, uses expletory justice*.

See the story in the Cyropædia, in which Cyrus is blamed for giving
the big boy the larger coat, which belonged to the little boy: because
his business was expletory, not attributive justice.

IX. 1 *Jus* has a third signification, meaning Law in its largest
sense, namely, "a Rule of moral acts obliging to what is right."

"*Obliging*" is necessary to this signification: for mere Counsel or

---

* The remarks in the text go far to prove that the distinction of Contractual,
Corrective, or Expletory justice, on the one hand, from Distributive or Attributive
Justice on the other, is not tenable. W. W.

Advice is not included in *Jus* or Law; and Permission is not Law, but the absence of Law, except so far as it obliges other persons not to impede.

"Obliging to what is *right*," not to what is just; for *Jus* in this signification does not include strict Justice merely, but the matter of other virtues. Yet what is right is sometimes loosely called *just.*

2 The best distinction of Law in this general sense, is that of Aristotle, into Natural Law, and Voluntary or Legal Law [or Positive Law; δίκαιον φυσικὸν and δίκαιον νομικόν, *Eth. Nicom.* v. 10,] or Instituted Law, τὸ ἐν τάξει. The Hebrew has a like distinction.

X. 1 Natural Law is the Dictate of Right Reason, indicating that any act, from its agreement or disagreement with the rational [and social*] nature [of man] has in it a moral turpitude or a moral necessity; and consequently that such act is forbidden or commanded by God, the author of nature.

2 Acts concerning which there is such a Dictate, are obligatory, [morally necessary,] or are unlawful, in themselves, and are therefore understood as necessarily commanded or forbidden by God; and in this character, Natural Law differs, not only from Human Law, but from Positive Divine Law, which does not forbid or command acts which, in themselves and by their own nature, are either obligatory or unlawful; but, by forbidding them makes them unlawful, by commanding them makes them obligatory.

3 In order to understand Natural Law, we must remark that some things are said to be according to Natural Law, which are not so properly, but, as the schools love to speak, reductively, Natural Law not opposing them; as we have said [III. 1] that some things are called just, which are not unjust. And again, by an abuse of expression, some things are said to be according to Natural Law which reason shews to be decent, or better than their opposites, though not obligatory. [As monogamy is better, though we cannot strictly say that polygamy is contrary to Natural Law. Concerning the use of the term *Natural Law,* or *Law of Nature,* in such cases, see *E. M.* 1054.]

4 It is to be remarked also that Natural Law deals not only with things made by nature herself, but with things produced by the act of man. Thus property, as it now exists, is the result of human will: but being once introduced, Natural Law itself shews that it is unlawful for me to take what is yours against your will. And thus Paulus says that theft is prohibited *naturali jure;* Ulpian says that it is *naturâ turpe,* bad by nature: Euripides says it is displeasing to God.

5 Natural Law is so immutable that it cannot be changed by God himself. For though the power of God be immense, there are some things to which it does not extend: because if we speak of those things being done, the words are mere words, and have no meaning, being self-contradictory. Thus God himself cannot make twice two

* Added by Barbeyrac, from what follows XII. 1. See also above, III. 1.

not be four; and in like manner, he cannot make that which is intrinsically bad, not be bad. For as the essence of things, when they exist, and by which they exist, does not depend on anything else, so is it with the properties which follow that essence: and such a property is the baseness of certain actions, when compared with the nature of rational beings. And God himself allows himself to be judged of by this rule. [See the quotations. The passage from Aristotle, *Eth. Nicom.* II. 6, is misapplied, as Barbeyrac observes.]

6 Yet sometimes, in acts directed by Natural Law, there is a seeming of change, which may mislead the unwary; when in fact it is not Natural Law which is changed, but the thing about which that Law is concerned. Thus if a creditor gives me a receipt for my debt, I am no longer bound to pay him; not that Natural Law has ceased to command me to pay what I owe, but because I have ceased to owe it. So if God command any one to be slain or his goods to be taken, this does not make lawful homicide or theft, which words involve crime: but the act will no longer be homicide or theft, being authorized by the supreme Lord of life and of goods.

7 Further; some things are according to Natural Law, not simply, but in a certain state of things. Thus a community in the use of things was natural till property was established; and the right of getting possession of one's own by force existed before instituted law.

XI. 1 What the Roman lawbooks say of a law of nature which we have in common with animals, which they call more peculiarly *jus naturæ*, besides the natural law which we have in common with men, which they often call *jus gentium*, is of little or no use. For no creature is properly capable of *Jus*, which does not by nature use general precepts: as has been remarked by Hesiod, Cicero, Lactantius, Polybius. [See the quotations.]

2 If we ever assign justice to brute animals, it is improperly, when we see in them some shadow or vestige of reason. There being acts which we have in common with brutes, as the rearing of offspring, and others which are peculiar to us, as the worship of God, has no bearing on the nature of *Jus*.

XII. 1 That there is such a thing as Natural Law, is commonly proved both *a priori* and *a posteriori;* the former the more subtle, the latter, the more popular proof. It is proved *a priori* by shewing the agreement or disagreement of anything with the rational and social nature of man. It is proved *a posteriori* when by certain or very probable accounts we find anything accepted as Natural Law among all nations, or at least the more civilized. For a universal effect requires a universal cause: now such a universal belief can hardly have any cause except the common sense of mankind.

Hesiod, Heraclitus, Aristotle, Cicero, Seneca, Quintilian, agree that the consent of all nations is evidence of the truth. And Porphyry, Andronicus of Rhodes, Plutarch, Aristotle, agree that the more savage nations are of less weight in such an estimate. [See the quotations.]

XIII. Thus much of Natural Law; next of Positive or Instituted Law. [See Sect. x. 2.] And this is either Human or Divine.

XIV. 1 Of Human [instituted] Law, first, as more widely known. This is either the Civil Law, [that is, the National Law,] or Law in a narrower, or in a wider sphere.

The Civil Law is that which governs the State, (*Civitas*).

The State, (*Civitas*) is a perfect [that is, independent] collection of free men, associated for the sake of enjoying the advantages of *jus*, and for common utility.

Law in a narrow sphere, and not derived from the State, though subject to it, is various, as paternal precepts, the commands of a master, and the like.

Law in a wider sphere is *Jus Gentium*, the Law of Nations, that Law which has received an obligatory force from the will of all nations, or of many.

I have added "*or of many*," because scarce any Law is found, except Natural Law, (which also is often called *Jus Gentium*,) common to *all* nations. Indeed that is often *Jus Gentium* in one part of the world which is not so in another; as we shall shew when we come to speak of captivity and of *postliminium*.

2 This *Jus Gentium*, Law of Nations, is proved in the same manner as the unwritten Civil Law, by constant usage, and the testimony of those who have made it their study. It is, as Dio Chrysostom says, the invention of life and of time. And here the best historians are a great help to us*.

XV. 1 What is Divine [instituted] Law is sufficiently apparent from the term itself; namely, that which has its origin from the Divine Will; by which character it is distinguished from Natural Law, which also may be called Divine, [but which is independent: see § x. 5]. In such Law it may be said, but with reserve, that God did not command the act because it was just, but that it was just because God commanded it.

2 This Law is given either to the whole human race, or to one nation. To the human race, the Law has thrice been given by God; at the Creation; immediately after the Deluge, and at the coming of Christ. These three sets of Laws oblige all men, as soon as they acquire a sufficient knowledge of them.

XVI. 1 There is one nation in particular to which God has especially given his Laws, namely, the Hebrew People. See Deut. iv. 7; Psalm cxlvii.

2 It is erroneous to suppose (as some Jews have done) that those of other nations, in order to be saved, must submit to the Jewish law. For the law does not oblige those to whom it is not given; and it tells us itself to whom it is given, by saying, "Hear, O Israel." And the

---

* Concerning the distinction of the two senses of *Jus Gentium*, that of the Romans, with whom it means the Law common to all nations, and that of the moderns, with whom it means the Law between nations, see *Elements of Morality*, 1051.

Jews are perpetually spoken of as under a special covenant, and chosen to be a peculiar people of God; as Maimonides proves from Deut. xxxiii. 4.

3 There were however always living among the Jews certain "devout persons," as the Syrophœnician woman, Cornelius, the "devout Greeks" (Acts xvii. 4), who are also spoken of in various passages of the Old Testament [see the references]. These, as the Jewish doctors teach, were bound to obey the laws given to Adam and to Noah, to abstain from idols and from blood, and some other matters; but not to observe the peculiar Jewish laws: except that some laws expressly direct that not only the Jew, but the stranger within his gate should be bound by them: [as the law of the Sabbath: Exod. xx. 10].

4 It was also permitted to strangers to worship and to sacrifice in the temple; but standing in a peculiar place, separate from the place of the Israelites.

The prophets speaking to strangers; Elisha to Naaman, Jonah to the Ninevites, Daniel to Nebuchadnezzar, and other prophets to the Tyrians, Moabites, and Egyptians; never say that they were required to submit to the Law of Moses.

5 The same is true of circumcision; with this difference, that the Law of Moses bound the Israelites only, the law of circumcision, all the posterity of Abraham; whence the Jews imposed circumcision on the Idumeans. Therefore the other peoples who used circumcision were probably descended from Ishmael or from Esau, or from Keturah [Abraham's wife, Gen. xxv. 1].

6 In all other cases, the reasoning of St Paul, Rom. ii. 14, applies. The Gentiles are a law to themselves: the uncircumcision, keeping this law, is counted for circumcision [v. 26]. And this was acknowledged [see the example]. But circumcision was sometimes undergone by strangers for special objects [see the text]. Yet some in later times perversely held that there was no salvation out of the pale of Judaism.

7 Hence we learn that we are not bound by any part of the Jewish law, peculiarly so called; because all obligation extraneous to Natural Law comes from the will of the Lawgiver; and there is no indication that it was the will of God that others besides the Israelites should be bound by that law. We have therefore no occasion to prove the abrogation of this law; for it could not be abrogated with regard to those who were never bound by it. With regard to the Jews, the obligation of the Ritual Law was removed on the promulgation of the Gospel, as was revealed to St Peter, Acts x. 15. The rest of the Jewish Law was abolished by the dispersion of the Jewish nation.

8 What we Gentiles have gained by the coming of Christ is, not that we are freed from the law of Moses: but that, wherever formerly we could only have an obscure hope founded on the goodness of God, we now have a Covenant, and may be gathered into one Church with the descendants of the Patriarchs, the Law being taken away, which was the partition-wall between us; Eph. ii. 14.

XVII.   1 Since then the law of Moses cannot impose any direct obligation upon us, let us see if it can be of any other use in questions of the Rights of War, and the like.

2 (1) In the first place, the Jewish Law shews that what is commanded by that law is not contrary to Natural Law. For Natural Law being, as we have said [x. 5] perpetual and immutable, God, who is never unjust, could not command anything against that Law. Add that the Law is called right, pure, holy, just, and good. [See the quotations].

This is true of precepts : with regard to permissions, we must distinguish. Permission, as a mere fact, [that is, by saying nothing, as the law does concerning actions altogether indifferent,] need not be considered.   Permission legal, is either plenary, which gives a right to do a thing entirely lawfully; or less full, which only gives impunity among men, and a Right not to be impeded by any other person.   Permission of the former kind, no less than Precept, proves that the matter so stated is not against Natural Law.   With regard to permission of the latter kind, the case is different.   But this inference [from the Law of Moses to the Natural Law] rarely occurs : because when the words of permission are ambiguous, it is more convenient to infer, from the Natural Law, the kind of the permission, than from the kind of the permission, to infer the agreement with Natural Law.

3 (2) We remark also : that it is now lawful for the Rulers of Christian states to make laws of the same purport as the laws of Moses ; except those Mosaic Laws of which the whole substance belonged to the time when Christ was expected, and the Gospel not yet revealed; or except Christ has commanded the contrary generally; or specially.   With these three exceptions, there cannot be devised any case in which that which was formerly instituted by the Law of Moses should not be within the lawful sphere of instituted law at present.

4 (3) In the third place : whatever is commanded by the law of Moses, connected with the virtues which Christ requires from his disciples, that, at least, if not more, is due from Christians.   The foundation of this remark is this : that the virtues which are required of Christians, as humility, patience, kindness, are required in a greater degree than they were under the Jewish Law: and that with good reason ; because the heavenly promises are more and more clearly given in the Gospel.   And hence, the Old Law is declared not to have been *perfect*, nor *faultless* : and Christ is called *the end of the Law;* and the Law *a schoolmaster to lead us to Christ.* [See the references in the text.]

For example, the Old Law concerning the Sabbath, and the Law concerning Tithes, shew that Christians are obliged to give up not less than a seventh part of their time to divine worship ; and not less than a tenth part of their goods for the support of those who minister in sacred things, and the like pious uses.

CHAPTER II.

Whether War ever be just.

HAVING seen what are the fountains of *Jus* or of Law, let us come to the first and more general question, which is this: Whether any war be just; or, Whether it ever be lawful to make war.

I. 1 This question, and others which will follow, are first to be treated with reference to Natural Law. Cicero repeatedly speaks of certain First Principles, and certain other truths, the consequences of these, but of higher value than those. There is, according to him, a First Principle of Self-preservation. An animal, from its birth, is urged to care for and preserve itself, to choose the means of preserving its good condition, to shun destruction, and every thing which leads to its destruction. Thus there is no one who does not prefer to have the parts of his body sound and whole, rather than maimed and distorted. The first business of each is to preserve himself in the state of nature; the next, to retain what is according to nature, and to reject what is contrary to it.

2 After this Principle, there follows a notion of the Agreement of things with Reason, which is superior to the body; and this Agreement, in which what is reasonable (*honestum*) becomes our object, is seen to be of more importance than those things to which alone the first impulse of appetite tended. The first Principle [of self-preservation] commends us to Right Reason; but Right Reason ought to be dearer to us than those things by which we were first led to use it.

This is allowed by all who are of sound mind, without demonstration. Hence in examining what agrees with Natural Law, we must first see what agrees with that first principle of Self-preservation; and afterwards proceed to that which, though subsequent in origin, is of greater dignity; and must not only accept it, if it be offered, but seek it with all care.

3 This object, what is reasonable, (*honestum*,) has different ranges in different cases, according to the diversity of the matter. Sometimes it lies (as it were) in a point, so that if you depart from it by the

smallest space, you fall into a fault: sometimes it has a wider field, so that the thing in question may be either done laudably, or omitted or done otherwise without pravity, according as we pass from the existence to the non-existence of certain conditions*. Between black and white, we find intermediate and mixed degrees, which approach the one or the other. And it is in this latter class of cases that laws, both divine and human, are mainly occupied; aiming at this, that what of itself was only laudable, may become a duty. As we have said above, that when we examine concerning Natural Law, we inquire whether anything can be done not unjustly; and then that is understood to be unjust, which has a necessary repugnance with a rational and social nature.

4 In the first principle of nature [Self-preservation] there is nothing which is repugnant to war: indeed all things rather favour it: for the end of war, the preservation of life and limb, and the retention or acquisition of things useful to life, agrees entirely with that principle. And if force be requisite for this purpose, still there is in this nothing at variance with nature; for all animals are provided by nature with means for the very purpose of self-defence. So Xenophon, Ovid, Horace, Lucretius. Galen observes that man is an animal born for peace and war, not born with weapons, but with hands by which weapons can be acquired. And we see infants, without teaching, use their hands for weapons. So also Aristotle. [See the passages in the text.]

5 Again, Right Reason and the nature of Society, which are next to be considered, do not prohibit all force, but that only which is repugnant to Society; that is, that which is used to attack the Rights of others. For Society has for its object, that every one may have what is his own in safety, by the common help and agreement. Which consideration would still have place, even if property were not introduced: for even then, each one would have a property in his life, limbs, liberty; and these could not be attacked without wrong done to him. And also to use things which lay in common, and to take as much of them as nature should require, would be the right of the person who first took occupation of them; and he who should prevent the exercise of this Right, would do the occupier wrong. And this is much more easily understood now, when property has taken a shape by law or usage: as Cicero says. [See the passage in the text.]

6 Therefore it is not contrary to the nature of Society to take care of the future for one's self, so that the Rights of others be not infringed: and thus, even force, which does not violate the Right of another, is not unjust. So Cicero, Ulpian, Ovid. [See the passages.]

II. 1 Our doctrine, that all war is not contrary to Natural Law,

* Thus polygamy may be blameless, permitted, or criminal, according to the state of law. Monogamy may be laudable when polygamy is permitted; but may be elevated into a duty in a better state of society. W. W.

is further proved from the sacred history.   Abraham made war upon
the four kings who had plundered Sodom, and was thereupon blessed
by Melchisedec.   This he did without the special mandate of God, as
appears by the history: he must therefore have been justified by the
Law of Nature: for he was a most holy and wise man, as even heathen
authors declare.   I do not use the history of the seven people, whom
God gave up to be rooted out by the Israelites: for the Jews had a
special command for thus dealing with people guilty of enormous
crimes; whence these wars are in Scripture called the wars of the
Lord, as being undertaken by the command of God, and not by the
will of man.   An example more to the purpose is that in which the
Jews, under Moses and Joshua, resisted the attack of the Amalekites:
(Exod. xvii. 8), which God did not command beforehand, but approved
when it was done.

2 But further, God prescribed to his people general and perpetual laws concerning the mode of carrying on war (Deut. xx. 10.
15): shewing plainly by this that a war may be just, without a special
mandate: for the case of the nations of Canaan is here expressly distinguished from the case of other nations.   And inasmuch as nothing
is there said as to what are just causes of war, this shews that they
are assumed to be known by the light of nature.   Thus we have
Jephthah's war against the Ammonites concerning the occupation of
land (Judges xi. 13): David's war against the same people for the
insult done to his ambassadors (2 Sam. x. 4): so the Apostle to the
Hebrews (xi. 32) speaks of Gideon and Barak and Samson and
Jephthah and David and Samuel and others, who through faith subdued kingdoms, waxed valiant in fight, turned to flight the armies of
the aliens: when, as the context shews, "faith" includes the belief that
what is done is pleasing to God.   [The quotation 1 Sam. xxv. 28
should have come in earlier.]

III.   1 What we say is proved by the consent of all nations, and
especially of wise men.   There are the noted passages in Cicero's
Oration for Milo, in which he appeals to the testimony of nature for
the right of self-defence.   To the same purpose Josephus the historian, Caius and Florentinus the jurists.   [See the quotations.]

2 The equity of this is so manifest, that even in brute animals,
among which, as we have said, there are no rights, but only a shadow
of them, we still distinguish between force used in committing injury,
and in repelling it.   Thus Ulpian, after saying that an animal which is
devoid of reason cannot commit wrong, still adds, that if rams or bulls
fight, Q. Mutius had ruled that a distinction was to be made, and that
if the one who had been the aggressor was killed, the action would not
lie; but if the one who had given no provocation was killed, the action
was good.   [The *misquotation* from Pliny adds nothing to the argument.]

IV.   1 By Natural Law, then, [*Jure naturali* or *Jure gentium*] it
is plain that all wars are not condemned.

2 That by the voluntary or instituted Law of nations [see Chap. I. § ix. 2] wars are not condemned, we have evidence enough in the histories, laws and customs of all nations. Indeed Hermogenianus has said that wars were introduced *Jure gentium*, by Natural Law: which we are to understand thus: that by the *Jus gentium* a certain form of war was introduced, so that wars which take this form, have, *jure gentium*, certain effects. And hence we have a distinction, of which we shall afterwards make use, into a war formal according to *Jus gentium*, which is also called a just or legitimate war, a complete war; and informal war, which may still be legitimate or just [in a more general sense,] that is, agreeable to justice. Informal wars, if there be a reasonable cause for them, are not supported by *Jus gentium*, but neither are they resisted by it, as will hereafter be shewn. Livy and Florentinus say that *Jus gentium* directs us to repel force by force. [See the passages.]

V. 1 Concerning Instituted Divine Law [Chap. I. § xv. 1] there is more difficulty. Nor is the objection valid, that Natural Law is immutable, and therefore cannot be changed, even by God: for this is true as to what is commanded or forbidden by Natural Law, but not as to what is only permitted. Things of that kind are not properly under Natural Law, but extraneous to it, and may be forbidden or commanded [by Instituted Law].

2 The first passage usually brought from Scripture, to shew that wars are unlawful, is the law given to Noah (Gen. ix. 5, 6). What is there said, *Your blood of your lives I will require, at the hand of man will I require it,* some understood in the most general sense; and what is said afterwards, *Whoso sheddeth man's blood, by man shall his blood be shed,* they regard as a threatening, not an approval. I cannot assent to either opinion. The interdict concerning the shedding of blood is not of wider extent than the command, *Thou shalt not kill:* and this, it is plain, does not prohibit either capital punishment or wars. And the one law, as well as the other, does not constitute any new offence, but only declares and repeats the Natural Law, obliterated by evil custom. Whence the words [*sheddeth man's blood*] are to be understood as including criminality in the act: as the word *homicide* does not mean *any* killing of a man, but the intentional killing of an innocent man. What is added, *his blood shall be shed* in turn, appears to me to imply, not the mere fact, but the Law of justice.

3 My explanation of the matter is this. It is naturally equitable that whatever evil any one has inflicted, the same he shall suffer, according to what is called the Law of Rhadamanthus. So Seneca. Cain, with a sense of this natural equity said (Gen. iv. 14), *Every one that findeth me shall slay me.* In the earliest times, however, for various reasons, this was not enforced; the manslayer was indeed shunned by men, but not put to death: as Plato directs in his *Laws:* and as Euripides states the usage of Greece in his *Orestes.* So Thucydides ; Lactantius.

4 The example of Cain was regarded as establishing a law, so that Lamech (Gen. iv. 24) promised himself impunity, from this example, after the like deed.

5 But since before the deluge, in the age of the giants, violence had become general, when after the deluge, God restored the race of man, he provided by increased severity against the recurrence of the evil: and repressing the lenity of the former time, he gave his permission to that which was naturally equitable, that he who slew a homicide should be blameless. Which afterwards, when tribunals for high crimes were instituted, was confined to the judges. Yet a vestige of the ancient usage remained in the Right of the avenger of blood, even under the Law of Moses, of which we shall hereafter speak.

6 We have a strong confirmation of this interpretation in Abraham, who, though he must have known the law given to Noah, took arms against the four kings. So Moses directed the Israelites to fight against the Amalekites, not specially consulting God on this point. Add to this, that capital punishments are applied not only to homicides, but to other criminals, not only among other nations, but in the chosen people of God. Gen. xxxviii. 24.

7 In fact men had proceeded from like to like, by the light of reason, in their conjecture of the divine will, and had judged that what was the appointed punishment of homicides was equitable also towards other great criminals. For there are things which are to man of no less value than life, as good fame, virginity, conjugal fidelity: and things without which life cannot be safe, as a reverence for the sovereign authority which holds society together: so that those who assail these objects are held as no better than homicides.

8 Connected with this is the tradition extant among the Jews, that there were given by God to the sons of Noah several laws; which are not all recorded by Moses, because it was enough for his purpose to give them afterwards as included in the particular law of the Hebrews. Thus it appears, Lev. xviii. 6, that there was an ancient law against marrying persons near of kin, though no such law is previously mentioned by Moses. And the Jews say that among the laws given to Noah, were precepts that not only homicide, but adultery, incest, and robbery should be punished with death. And this is confirmed by Job, xxxi. 11; *This is an heinous crime: yet it is an iniquity to be punished by the judges.*

9 Moreover the law given by Moses gives reasons for capital punishments, which are valid among other nations as well as the Jews: as Lev. xviii. 24, &c., *Defile not yourselves, &c.* Psal. ci. 5, *Whoso privily slandereth his neighbour, him will I cut off.* Prov. xx. 8, *A king that sitteth in the throne of judgment scattereth away all evil with his eyes.* And especially concerning homicide, it is said, Num. xxxv. 33, that *the land cannot be cleansed of the blood that is shed therein but by the blood of him that shed it.*

Further, it is absurd to suppose that the Hebrew people were indulged with the privilege of protecting public and private interests by capital punishments, and defending themselves by war, and that other kings and nations at that time had no such privilege: and that, this being so, those kings and nations were yet never rebuked by God for the practice of capital punishment and of war, as they were often rebuked for other offences.

10 On the contrary, we must suppose that, as the law of Moses was the expression of the divine Will, the other nations would do well and piously to take example by that law: which it is probable that the Greeks, and especially the Athenians, did: whence arises the so great similarity of the old Attic Law, and the Laws of the Twelve Tribes therefrom derived, with the Laws of the Hebrews.

VI. 1 The arguments adduced against war from the Gospel are more specious: and in examining these, I shall not assume, as many do, that there is in the Gospel nothing, besides the precepts of belief and institution of the sacraments, which is not matter of Natural Law: for that, in the sense in which it is commonly understood, I do not believe.

2 I willingly acknowledge that nothing is commanded us in the Gospel which has not a natural reasonableness: but I do not see why I should grant that we are bound to nothing by the Laws of Christ beyond what we are bound to by the Law of Nature. And when men maintain the contrary, it is wonderful to see what pains they are compelled to take to prove that some things which are forbidden by the Gospel, are also unlawful by the Law of Nature; as concubinage, divorce, plurality of wives. These things are such that reason itself dictates that it is better to avoid them; but not such that they are seen to be criminal without the divine law.

Again, who can say that such a Precept as that, 1 Joh. iii. 16, We ought to lay down our lives for the brethren: is binding by the Law of Nature? Justin Martyr says that to live according to nature is the condition of him who has not yet come to believe.

3 Nor shall I follow those who make another large assumption, that Christ in delivering the precepts, Matt. v. et sqq. is only speaking as the interpreter of the law given by Moses. For a different notion is suggested by the words so often repeated: *Ye have heard it said by them of old time: But I say unto you.* Where the apposition shews, what the Syriac and other versions express, that *veteribus* rather means *to them of old time* than *by them;* as *vobis* means *to you,* not *by you.* And these men of old time were those who lived at the time of Moses: for what is ascribed to them is not the dogmas of doctors of the law, but the doctrines of Moses, either in words or in sense: as appears by the examples. *Thou shalt not kill, &c. An eye for an eye, and a tooth for a tooth. Thou shalt love thy neighbour* (the Israelite), *and hate thine enemy,* the seven expelled nations, to whom the Jews were forbidden to shew mercy: to whom are to be added the Amalekites. [See the references.]

4 To the understanding of the words of Christ, it is to be observed that the Law given by Moses is taken in two senses : first, according to that which it has in common with other laws established by men, as restraining grave crimes by visible punishments, and keeping the Hebrew people in a state of civil society; in which sense, by it, *every transgression and disobedience received a just reward*, Heb. ii. 2 ; and in which sense, Heb. vii. 16, it is called *the law of a carnal commandment;* and Rom. iii. 27, *the law of works:* and secondly, as requiring also purity of mind, and some acts which may be omitted without temporal punishment, in which sense it is called *the spiritual law*, Rom. vii. 14, *rejoicing the heart*, Psalm xix. The Lawyers and Pharisees, contented with the former part, regarded not the second part, which is better, nor inculcated it on the people. That this is true, we learn not only from the New Testament, but also from Josephus and the Hebrew doctors.

5 Yet even with regard to this second part, it is to be observed that the virtues which are required of Christians were either recommended or enjoined to the Hebrews ; but they were not enjoined in the same degree and with the same breadth as to the Christians. And in both these respects [degree and breadth] Christ opposes his interpretation to that of the ancients ; whence it appears that his words do not contain a bare interpretation.

It is useful to know this, not only with reference to the point now in hand, but also to many other points, that we may not exaggerate the authority of the Hebrew law.

VII. 1 To proceed then to the passages which shew that war is not made unlawful by the law of Christ.

(1) The first is 1 Tim. ii. 1, 2, 3, *I exhort, therefore, that first of all supplications, &c.* We are here taught three things: that it is agreeable to God that kings be made Christians; that kings when made Christians continue kings; and that Christian kings enable other Christians to lead a quiet and peaceable life. So Justin Martyr mentions prayer for kings and princes ; and in the Constitutions of Clement the Church prays for Christian Magistrates.

2 But how do kings secure peace and tranquillity to their subjects? This he teaches, Rom. xiii. 4, *He is the minister of God to thee for good, &c.* The *sword* implies all controlling power, as also sometimes among the Jurists; but still, in such a manner that the highest kind of that power, the actual use of the sword, [that is, capital punishment and war,] is not excluded. This place is illustrated by Psalm ii., which though verified in David has a fuller accomplishment in Christ. [See the passages in Acts and Hebrews.] That Psalm exhorts the kings of the earth to *kiss the Son lest he be angry :* that is, to do him service in their capacity of kings. [See the passages quoted from Augustine.]

3 (2) The second passage is, that already partly cited, Rom. xiii. *There is no power but of God. The powers that be are ordained of God, &c. :* whence the apostle infers that we are to obey and honour the

powers that are ordained; and that, from our hearts; and that he who resisteth the power resisteth the ordinance of God. By *ordinance* we cannot understand merely what God will not prevent, as he permits bad actions: for such permission would not impose any obligation of honour or heartfelt obedience. On this supposition the Apostle, in speaking so highly of the powers that be, would give a reason which is equally true of thefts and robberies. It follows then that the powers thus ordained, are approved by God; and since God cannot approve contradictory things, that this power is not at variance with the will of God revealed by the Gospel, and obligatory on all men.

4 Nor is this argument refuted by the consideration, that the powers that be in St Paul's time, were not Christian. For in the first place, this is not universally true. Sergius Paulus, the Proprætor of Cyprus, had become a Christian; not to mention the ancient story concerning the king of Edessa, perhaps distorted, but yet with a foundation of truth*.

But in the next place, the question is not whether the persons were impious, but whether their office was impious; which the Apostle denies, when he says that even at that time it was ordained of God, and therefore was to be honoured from the heart, which is God's peculiar dominion. And thus Nero and king Agrippa might have submitted themselves to Christ, and have retained respectively the imperial and the royal power; which could not have subsisted without the power of the sword and of arms. And thus as under the Old Law, sacrifices were pious, though celebrated by impious priests, so government is a pious office, though it be held by an impious man.

5 (3) The third argument is taken from the words of John the Baptist; who, when he was asked by the Jewish soldiers, (of which nation there were many thousands in the Roman army, as is manifest from Josephus and other writers,) What they should do, to avoid the wrath of God; did not tell them to cease to be soldiers, which he ought to have done if such were the will of God; but told them to abstain from extortion, and to be content with their wages.

Since the words of the Baptist contain a manifest approval of a military life, many answer, that the exhortations of the Baptist and the precepts of Christ are widely different; so that the one might teach one thing, the other, another. This I cannot admit; for

John and Christ announced their doctrine in the same manner; *Repent, for the kingdom of heaven is at hand*, Matth. iii. 2; iv. 17. Christ says that the kingdom of heaven, (that is the new law, for it is the Hebrew manner to call a law a kingdom,) is taken by force, from the times of John the Baptist, Matth. xi. 12. John is said to have preached the baptism of repentance for the remission of sins: Mark i. 4. The Apostles are said to have done the same in the name of Christ, Acts ii. 38. John requires fruits worthy of repentance, and threatens them with destruction who do not bring forth

* Barbeyrac remarks that the learned hold the story of Abgarus a 'mera fabula.'

such, Matth. iii. 8 and 10. He requires works of love beyond the law, Luke iii. 11; *He that hath two coats, &c.* The law is said to have endured until John, that is, a more perfect doctrine began with him, Matth. xi. 13. The beginning of the Gospel narrative is John: Mark i. 1. Luke i. 77. John was on this account greater than the prophets, Matth. xi. 9, Luke vii. 26; being sent to give knowledge of salvation unto the people, Luke i. 77; and to preach the Gospel, Luke iii. 18. Nor does John anywhere distinguish Jesus from himself by the difference of their precepts, (though what is indicated in a more general and confused and rudimentary manner by John, Christ, the true light, delivers clearly,) but by Jesus being the Messiah that was to come, Acts xix. 4, John i. 29; that is, the king of the kingdom of heaven, who was to give the Holy Spirit to them that believed on him, Matth. iii. 11. Mark i. 8. Luke iii. 16.

6 (4) In the fourth place, there is this argument, which appears to me to have no small weight. If the right of inflicting capital punishments, and of defending the citizens by arms against robbers and plunderers, was taken away, there would follow a vast license of crime and a deluge of evils; since even now, while criminal judgments are administered, violence is hardly repressed. Wherefore if the mind of Christ had been to induce such a state of things as never was heard of, undoubtedly he would have set it forth in the clearest and most special words, and would have commanded that none should pronounce a capital sentence, none should wear arms: which we nowhere read that he did: for what is adduced to this effect is either very general or obscure. Equity and common sense teach us that, in order to avoid that sense of passages which would lead to extreme inconveniences, we may limit the range of general terms, and explain ambiguities, and even depart in some degree from the propriety and received use of words.

7 (5) In the fifth place, it cannot be shewn by any argument that the law of Moses concerning the judgments of tribunals ceased to be in force before the city of Jerusalem was destroyed, and with it, the existence and the hope of the Jewish nation ceased. For there is neither in the law of Moses any term appointed for the force of the law, nor do Christ or his Apostles anywhere speak of the cessation of that law, except in so far as such an event may, as we have said, be comprehended in the destruction of the Jewish State: on the contrary, Paul says that the high priest was appointed to judge persons according to the law, Acts xxiii. 3. Christ himself, in the preface to his precepts, says, that he was not come to destroy the law, but to fulfil it, Matth. v. 17. Now in what sense this is to be understood of the Ritual Law, is plain enough; for the lineaments which shadow out an object are fulfilled when the perfect form of the thing is exhibited. But how can this be true of the Judicial Law, if Christ, as some hold, took it away by his coming? But if the obligation of the Law remained as long as the Jewish State continued, it follows that Jews,

C

even though converted to Christianity, if they were summoned before a magistrate, could not refuse, and ought not to judge otherwise than Moses had commanded.

8 Weighing the whole case, I do not see the slightest reason for thinking that any pious men, at that time hearing the words of Christ, could think otherwise. I acknowledge that before the time of Christ some things were permitted, either as matters of impunity, or as not destroying purity of mind, (a distinction which we need not dwell upon here,) which Christ did not permit to his followers; as, to put away a wife for every cause, to sue one at law for satisfaction; but between the precepts of Christ and those permissions, there is a diversity, not a repugnance. For he who does not put away his wife, or who remits a satisfaction due to him, does nothing against the law: on the contrary, he conforms to the Law in the highest degree. But the case of a judge is altogether different; for him the Law does not permit, but commands him to punish the homicide with death; and he himself is guilty before God if he does not do this. And if Christ forbids him to punish the homicide with death, he commands what is altogether contrary to the Law; he destroys the Law.

9 (6) The sixth argument shall be from the example of Cornelius the Centurion, who both received from Christ the Holy Ghost, the undoubted sign of justification, and was baptized in the name of Christ by the apostle Peter: but we do not read that he gave up the military life, nor was exhorted by Peter to do so.

Some reply that when he was instructed by Peter in the Christian religion, he was also instructed of the unchristian character of his military life. This would be to the purpose, if there were any plain and certain interdiction of a military life in the precepts of Christ. But when there is nowhere such a thing in any clear form, it was plainly necessary that something should have been said on the subject in this place, where it was specially required; in order that the ages to come might not be ignorant of the rules of its duty. And that Luke, when conversion led to any special change in the occupation of the converts, did not omit to state it, we see elsewhere, Acts xix. 19, *Many of them also which used curious arts brought their books, &c.*

10 (7) A seventh argument of a like kind we draw from what is said of Sergius Paulus, as already partly noticed. For in the history of that convert there is no indication of his having abdicated the office of magistrate, or having been admonished to abdicate. Now what is not narrated, when, as we have said, it was highly important that it should be narrated, must be supposed not to have happened.

11 (8) An eighth argument is, that the Apostle Paul, when he was apprized of the Jews lying in wait for him, directed the fact to be made known to the captain, and when the captain had furnished soldiers, as a guard for him in his journey, he made no opposition, and did not warn the captain or the soldiers that it was displeasing to God to repel force by force. And yet Paul was one who neither

omitted nor allowed others to omit any occasion of teaching men their duty, 2 Tim. iv. 2.

12 (9) A ninth argument is, that if a thing be good and right, the end to which it tends cannot be otherwise than good and right. Now to pay taxes is right, and is a thing even binding on the conscience, as the Apostle Paul explains: but the end to which taxes are subservient, [that is, one end among others,] is that the government may be able to maintain forces for the purpose of defending good citizens and restraining bad men, Rom. xiii. 3, 4, 6. Tacitus and Augustine both make this remark. [See the text.]

13 (10) We have a tenth argument from Acts xxv. 11, where Paul says, *If I be an offender, or have committed anything worthy of death, I refuse not to die.* Whence I collect Paul to have been of the opinion, that even after the publication of the Gospel-law, there are some crimes which equity allows, or even requires, to be punished with death; which also Peter teaches, 1 Epist. ii. 19, 20, *If when ye be buffeted for your faults ye shall take it patiently.* If the will of God had then been that there should no longer be capital punishments, Paul might have cleared himself indeed; but he ought not to have left men to think that then, no less than previously, it was lawful to put criminals to death. But when we have proved that capital punishment may lawfully be practised after the coming of Christ, we have also proved, as I conceive, that war may be made lawfully, for example against an armed multitude of evildoers; who must be overcome in battle that they may be dealt with by justice*. For the power and the number of the evildoers, though it may have its weight in prudential deliberation, does not affect the question of what is right.

14 (11) An eleventh argument is, that in the Revelation, wars of the righteous against the wicked are predicted with manifest approval, xviii. 6, and elsewhere.

15 (12) A twelfth argument may be this: that the law of Christ took away only the law of Moses in so far as it separated the Gentiles from the Jews: Ephes. ii. 14. But such things as are reckoned good by nature and the assent of the most civilized nations, it was so far from taking away, that it comprehends them under the general precept of all virtue, everything of good report, Phil. iv. 8. 1 Cor. xi. 13, 14. Now the punishment of criminals, and defensive war, are held praiseworthy by their nature, and come under the virtues of justice and beneficence.

And hence, in passing, we may note the error of those who deduce the right of the Israelites to make war from the fact alone, that God had given them the land of Canaan. That indeed was a just cause, but not the only cause. For before that time pious men, acting by the

---

* We may however remark that to treat the army of an enemy as a body of evildoers, is not the true view of war, nor necessary to its justification. War is a relation between two *States*; and the Right of making war is a necessary Right of a State. See *Elements of Morality*, 775.

light of reason, had made war; and the Israelites themselves did so for other causes, as David, for the insult done to his ambassadors. For the possessions which any one has by human right are his no less than if God had given him them: and this right is not taken away by the Gospel.

VIII. Let us now see what arguments are offered in support of the opposite opinion, that the pious reader, judging fairly, may see which side preponderates.

1 (1) First, it is usual to adduce the prophecy of Isaiah, ii. 4; that the people shall beat their swords into plowshares, and their spears into pruning-hooks; that nation shall not lift up sword against nation, neither shall they learn war any more. But either this prophecy is to be received conditionally, like many others;—namely, that we are to understand that this would be the state of things, if all nations should receive and fulfil the law of Christ; to which end God declares that nothing is wanting on his part. For it is certain that if all be Christians, and live as Christians, there will be no wars: as Arnobius and Lactantius remark. [See the text.]

Or it may be understood absolutely; in which case the facts shew that it is not yet fulfilled, and that its fulfilment, like the conversion of the Jews, is still to be looked for. But in whichever way you take it, nothing can be inferred from it against the justice of wars; so long as there are persons who do not allow the lovers of peace to live in peace, but use force against them.

2 From the fifth chapter of Matthew, many arguments are usually drawn; and in order to estimate the value of these, we must repeat what has been said already; That if the intention of Christ had been to take away all capital punishment, and the right of making war, he would have done this in the most express and special words, in consideration of the magnitude and novelty of the thing: and all the more on that account, that no Jew could think otherwise than that the laws of Moses which concerned the Jewish State and tribunals were to retain their authority over Jews, as long as the State existed. With this previous remark, let us consider in order the force of the particular passages.

3 (2) The second argument, then, in favour of the opposite opinion is taken from these words: *Ye have heard that it hath been said, An eye for an eye, and a tooth for a tooth: but I say unto you, that ye resist not the evil man: but whosoever shall smite thee on thy right cheek, turn to him the other also.* Hence some infer that no injury is to be resisted or satisfaction for it to be required, either publicly or privately. But this is not what the words say: for Christ is not here addressing magistrates, but those who are assailed: nor does he speak of wrongs of all kinds, but of such as a blow on the cheek; for the subsequent words restrict the generality of the preceding.

4 So in the following precept, *If any man will sue thee at law, and take away thy coat, let him have thy cloke also:* it is not every appeal

to a judge or an umpire which is forbidden, according to the interpretation of Paul, who does not forbid men having matters at law,
1 Cor. vi. 4: only he forbids the Christians to go to law before the heathen tribunals: and this he does by the example of the Jews, among
whom this maxim was current; He who refers the concerns of the Israelites to the judgment of strangers, pollutes the name of God: but
Christ, in order to exercise our patience, directs us that with regard to
matters which may easily be replaced, as our coat, or if need be, our
cloke along with our coat, we should not contend at law; but though
our right be indisputable, abstain from prosecuting it judicially. Apollonius Tyanæus said that a philosopher ought not to quarrel about
paltry pelf. Ulpian says, *The prætor does not disapprove the act of
him who thought it a good thing to have nothing, that he might have
nothing to go to law about. For this temperate notion of those who hate
lawsuits is not to be condemned.* What Ulpian here says is approved by
good men, is what Christ makes his command, choosing the matter of
his precepts from the most approved and becoming examples. But
you cannot infer from this that even a parent or a guardian is not to
defend before the judge, if he be compelled, the means of subsistence
of a child or a ward. A coat and a cloke are one thing, but the necessary means of subsistence another. In the Clementine Constitutions
it is said of a Christian, *If he have a lawsuit, let him try to bring it to an
end, even if he have thereby to suffer loss.* What is commonly said of
moral rules applies here also, that right dealing does not lie in a point,
but has a certain appropriate latitude.

5 So in what follows, *Whosoever will impose service as for one mile,
go with him two:* our Lord does not speak of a hundred miles, a distance that would carry a man quite away from his business, but of one,
and if need be, two; which is a trifling amount of walking. The
meaning then is this; That in matters which are not very inconvenient to us, we are not to insist upon our right, but to give up even more
than is asked, that our patience and kindness may appear to all.

6 It is added, *Give to him that asketh thee, and from him that would
borrow of thee turn not thou away.* If you carry this to an indefinite
extent, nothing can be more harsh. He who does not care for his own
is worse than an infidel, says St Paul, 1 Tim. v. 8. Let us then follow
Paul, the best interpreter of his master's law, who, when exciting the
Corinthians to beneficence towards those of Jerusalem, says, 2 Cor.
viii. 13, *Not that other men may be eased and ye burdened, but that your
abundance may be a supply for their want.* The like expressions are
used by heathen authors, as Livy, Xenophon. [See the text.]

7 As the Hebrew law allowed a liberty of divorce, to moderate the
harshness of men towards their wives; so to restrain private revenge,
to which the nation was very prone, the law allowed the injured man
to require from the injurer compensation or satisfaction, not with
his own hand, but before the judge. This was followed in the law of
the Twelve Tables, which authorized retaliation. But Christ, a teacher

of a better patience, is so far from approving the injured man who demands such satisfaction, that he will have some injuries not even repelled either by force or judicially. But what injuries? Such as are tolerable: not that the same course of action may not be laudable in more atrocious attacks: but because he contents himself with a patience within certain limits. And thus he takes as his example a blow on the cheek, which does not endanger the life or maim the body, but only expresses a contempt which does us no harm.

In like manner Seneca, Pacuvius, Cæcilius, Demosthenes, distinguish between contumely and injury. [See the text.] And Seneca says·that the pain of contumely is the feeling of the humiliated mind recoiling from an act or deed which assails our honour.

8 In such circumstances Christ commands patience: and that he may not be met by the common objection that *By bearing one injury you incite another*, he adds, that we are rather to bear a second injury than to repel the first; since we thereby receive no evil except what has its seat in a foolish persuasion.

To give the cheek to the smiter, is a Hebraism implying to bear patiently, as appears, Isaiah l. 6, Jerem. iii. 3. Tacitus uses a similar expression.

9 (3) A third argument is usually drawn from that which follows in St Matthew, *Ye have heard that it hath been said, Thou shalt love thy neighbour, and hate thine enemy; But I say unto you, Love your enemies, bless them that curse you, do good to them that hate you, and pray for them that despitefully use you, and persecute you.* There are who think that such love to enemies and assailants is inconsistent both with capital punishments and with war.

But this is easily refuted if we consider this precept of the Hebrew law more nearly. The Hebrews were commanded to love their neighbour, that is, the Hebrew; for so the word *neighbour* is there taken, as we see, Levit. xix. 17, *Thou shalt not hate thy brother in thy heart: thou shalt in anywise rebuke thy neighbour;* compared with verse 18, *Thou shalt not avenge nor bear any grudge against the children of thy people, but thou shalt love thy neighbour as thyself.* But notwithstanding this, the magistrate was commanded to put to death the manslayer and other great criminals: notwithstanding this, the eleven tribes justly made war upon the tribe of Benjamin for a heinous crime, Judg. xx.: notwithstanding this, David who fought the battles of the Lord, rightly won by arms from Ishbosheth the kingdom promised to him. [2 Sam. iii. 1.]

10 Let it be granted then that the word *neighbour* is now to be extended more widely so as to include all men: for all nations are now received under one common rule of grace; no people is cut off from God; still there will be the same permission for all nations which there then was for the Israelites, who were then commanded mutual love, as all men now are.

But if you allege that a greater degree of love is enjoined in the

Gospel-law, this also may be conceded, provided we make this reserve, that all are not to be loved equally, but, for example, a father more than a stranger: and thus, the good of the innocent is to be preferred to the good of the guilty, public good to private good. Now capital punishments and just wars arise from our love of the innocent. See Prov. xxiv. 11, *If thou forbear to deliver them that are drawn unto death, and those that are ready to be slain, &c.* And thus the precepts of Christ respecting loving and helping all are to be fulfilled in such a way that a greater and juster love do not interfere. There is a noted ancient saying, *It is as great a cruelty to be indulgent to all as to none.*

11 Add that we are commanded to love our enemies by the example of God, who makes his sun to rise on the unjust. Yet the same God punishes some evil deeds in this life, and will hereafter punish them in the heaviest manner. And the same argument solves what is said on this subject about the injunction to Christians to be merciful. For God is called merciful, gracious, longsuffering, Jonah iv. 2, Exod. xxxiv. 6; and yet Scripture everywhere speaks of his wrath, that is, of his intention to punish, in reference to the rebellious, Num. xiv. 18, Rom. ii. 8. And of this wrath, the magistrate is constituted minister, Rom. xiii. 4. Moses is praised for his extreme gentleness; yet Moses inflicted punishment, even capital punishment, on the guilty. We are everywhere commanded to imitate the gentleness and patience of Christ. Yet Christ it was who inflicted the most severe punishment on the disobedient Jews; Matth. xxii. 7. [In the parable, *He destroyed those murderers, and burnt up their city.*] The Apostles imitated the gentleness of their master; and yet they used their divinely-given power for the punishment of evil-doers: 1 Cor. iv. 21, *Shall I come unto you with a rod?* v. 5, *To deliver such a one unto Satan for the destruction of the flesh;* 1 Tim. i. 20, *Whom I have delivered unto Satan.*

12 (4) The fourth passage which is objected is Rom. xii. 17, *Recompense no man evil for evil, &c.* But here too the same answer as above is evidently applicable. For at the very time at which God said, [as here quoted by St Paul,] *Vengeance is mine, I will repay,* [Deut. xxxii. 35] capital punishments were practised and laws concerning war were given. So again they are commanded to do good to their enemies, Exod. xxiii. 5: *If thou meet thine enemy's ox or his ass going astray, &c.* (that is, among their fellow-citizens;) and yet this did not prevent, as we have said, either capital punishments, or wars among the Israelites themselves. And therefore the same words, or similar precepts, though at present having a wider application, are not now to be wrested to such a sense. And this the less, because the division of chapters, as we now have it, was not made by the Apostles, nor in their age, but much later, for convenience of reading and reference: and therefore what now begins chapter xiii. *Let every soul be subject to the higher powers,* and what follows, must be taken in connexion with the precepts against recompensing evil for evil.

13 In this part of his teaching, St Paul says that the public authorities are the ministers of God, and avengers to execute wrath (that
is to inflict punishment,) upon evil-doers. And thus he already distinguishes between punishment for the sake of the public good, which the
magistrate inflicts in the place of God, and which is to be referred to
the vengeance reserved to God; and the vengeance of the passion of
revenge, which he had before interdicted. For if that punishment
which is inflicted for the sake of the public good is to be comprehended in that interdict, what would be more absurd than, that when
he had said that capital punishments are not to be inflicted, he should
add, in this the public powers are ordained by God, to require punishment in God's place?

14 (5) A fifth passage alleged by some is 2 Cor. x. 3, *For though
we walk after the flesh, we do not war after the flesh; for the weapons
of our warfare are not carnal, &c.* But this passage is nothing to
the purpose. For both what precedes and what follows shews that
St Paul intends by the term *flesh* the weak condition of his own body,
as it appeared to the eye, and on account of which he was despised.
To this he puts in opposition his weapons, that is, the power given
him to coerce the refractory, such as he had used against Elymas, the
incestuous person at Corinth, Hymenæus and Alexander. This is the
power which he says is not carnal, that is, weak, but on the contrary,
most mighty. What has this to do with the right of capital punishment or of war? Rather on the contrary, because the Church at that
time was destitute of the aid of the public authorities, therefore God
had raised up for its defence that miraculous power; and this accordingly began to fail as soon as there were given to the Church Christian Emperors; as the manna failed when the Jews came into a land
that bore fruit.

15 (6) The passage adduced from Eph. vi. 11, *Put on the whole
armour of God, that ye may be able to stand against the wiles of the devil.
For we wrestle not against flesh and blood,* (supply *only,* after the Hebrew usage,) *but against principalities, &c.*: refers to the warfare which
Christians have to carry on as being Christians; not that which they
may have in common with other men under certain circumstances.

16 (7) The passage of St James which is adduced in the seventh
place, iv. 1, *Whence are wars and fightings among you, &c.*: contains
nothing universal. It only says that the mutual wars and fightings,
by which the Hebrews were then universally plagued, (a part of which
history we may see in Josephus,) arose from causes not laudable;
which is the case even now, as we grieve to know. That avarice and
ambition are the causes of wars, has often been remarked. [See the
passages from Tibullus, Strabo, Lucan, Plutarch, Justin, Cicero, Maximus Tyrius, Jamblichus.]

17 (8) What was said to Peter, *He that smiteth with the sword shall
perish with the sword,* since it does not properly refer to war in its
common aspect, but to private war, (for Christ himself gives this reason

for prohibiting or neglecting his defence, that his kingdom was not of this world, Joh. xviii. 36,) will be better discussed in its own place.

IX. 1 When we have to inquire into the sense of any writing, we commonly assign great weight both to subsequent usage, and to the authority of the learned: and this is to be attended to also in the sacred writings. For it is not probable that the Churches, which were constituted by the Apostles, should either suddenly or universally have gone astray from the precepts which, being briefly expressed in writing, the Apostles had more fully explained in their oral instructions, or by the usages which they had established. Now those who argue against war are accustomed to adduce some sayings of the ancient Christians; on which I have three remarks to make.

2 (1) The first is, that from these passages, nothing more can be collected than the private opinion of certain individuals, not the public judgment of the Church: add to which, that the persons whose sayings are quoted are mostly writers who like to go in a path of their own, and to teach in a very high strain; such are Origen and Tertullian. But even these writers are not consistent with themselves. For the same Origen says that bees are an example appointed by God to shew that just wars may be carried on if it be necessary: the same Tertullian who in other places seems to disapprove of capital punishment, says also, *Nobody but a criminal will deny that it is a good thing when criminals are punished.* And as to a military life, he hesitates. In the treatise *De Idololatria,* he seems to incline against it; but in the treatise *De Corona Militis* he distinguishes in favour of the condition of those who were soldiers before they were Christians. He knew that such had continued soldiers, which they would not have done if they had understood that a military life was forbidden by Christ; any more than soothsayers, magicians, and other professors of forbidden arts were permitted to practise their art after baptism. In the same book he addresses a certain Christian soldier, *O glorious soldier in God.*

3 (2) The second observation is, that the Christians often avoided or disparaged a military life on account of the circumstances of the time, which scarcely permitted a soldier's life to go on without some acts inconsistent with the Christian law. We see in Josephus that the Jews asked, and in some cases, received excuse from military duties on the ground of their interfering with their national usages. [See the passages in the text.] Very similar are the difficulties which Tertullian objects to the military profession of his time; as in the book *De Idololatria, There is no consistency between the military oath (sacramentum) and the divine sacrament:* namely, because the soldiers had to swear by the heathen gods, Jupiter, Mars and others; and in the book *De Corona Militis,* he says, *Shall he keep guard in front of the temples which he has renounced, and sit in places such as the Apostle condemns, and be the defender by night of those powers which his exorcisms have driven away in the day?* And again, *How many other things are there in the duties of a soldier which the Christian must interpret as transgressions!*

4 (3) The third remark which I make is this, that the Christians of the first times were animated by so ardent a desire to do what was best, that they often accepted the divine *counsels* as if they had been commands. Thus Athenagoras says that the Christians do not resist by the law those who plunder them; Salvian says that we are commanded to give up that which is the subject of a suit, that we may be rid of litigation. And, speaking generally, such is perhaps the tendency of Christian counsel, and the scheme of the highest Christian life; still it is no command. In like manner, many of the early fathers disapprove of oaths altogether, without making any exception; though Paul himself on an important occasion used an oath. In this way Lactantius says that a righteous man (by which he means a Christian) will not be a soldier; but he also asserts that he will not be a sailor. How many of the ancient Christian writers exhort their followers against second marriages! And all these things are laudable, excellent, very agreeable to God, but are not required of us by any law of necessity. And these remarks will suffice for solving the objections to the lawfulness of war taken from the early Christian writers.

X. 1 But now to confirm our case, in the first place there are not wanting writers on our side, more ancient than those just quoted, who assume that both capital punishments and wars may be lawfully used by Christians. Clemens Alexandrinus says that the Christian, if he is called to empire, will be like Moses, a living law to his subjects, will reward the good and punish the bad. And in another place, describing the dress of the Christian, he says he will go barefoot, except he happen to be a soldier. And in the Constitutions which bear the name of Clemens Romanus, it is said that, *Not all putting to death is unlawful, but only that of an innocent man: but that which is right in this case, it is for the magistrates alone to judge.*

2 But setting aside private authorities, let us come to the public authority of the Church, which ought to be of the greatest weight. I say then that soldiers were never rejected from baptism, or excommunicated, on that account; which should have been done and would have been done, if a military life had been at variance with the Christian covenant. In the Constitutions already quoted we read, *A soldier seeking baptism is to be taught to abstain from violence and extortion, and to be content with his wages. If he conform to this, let him be admitted.* Tertullian, in his *Apology*, speaking in the character of the Christians, says, *We act with you as sailors, as soldiers.* A little before he had said: *We are strangers to you, and yet we have filled all the departments of your society; your cities, islands, castles, towns, councils, even your camps.* In the same book he had narrated that a shower was sent in answer to the prayers of Christian soldiers in the army of M. Aurelius. In the *de Corona*, he says that the soldier who had cast off the crown was a more stedfast man than his brethren, and he shews that he had many Christian fellow-soldiers.

3 Add to this, that some soldiers, who suffered torments and death for Christ, received from the Church the same honour as the other

martyrs: among these are recorded three companions of St Paul; Cerialis under Decius; Marinus under Valerian; fifty persons under Aurelian; Victor, Maurus, and Valentinus, soldier-master under Maximian; about the same time Marcellus the Centurion, and Severianus under Licinius. Cyprian writing concerning Laurentinus and Ignatius, two African Christians, says, *They formerly served in the armies of men, but being true and spiritual soldiers of God, they overthrew the devil by the confession of Christ, and by their suffering obtained as their reward, the palms and immortal crowns given by their divine Master.* And hence it appears what the Christian community thought of a soldier's profession, even before the emperors were Christians.

4 That the Christians at that time did not like to be present at capital punishments, ought not to seem strange, since Christians were often the subjects of such punishments. Add to this that the Roman laws were too harsh to agree with Christian kindness, as the Silanian Law may serve to shew*. But after Constantine had begun to favour and encourage the Christian religion, capital punishments were still not discontinued. Constantine himself established a capital punishment of a peculiar kind for parricides and child-murderers; though in other respects very merciful, so that he was blamed by many for his excessive lenity. Also he had in his army many Christians, as history teaches us, and inscribed his banner with the name of Christ. From that time also the military oath was changed into the form, which is extant in Vegetius, *By God, and Christ, and the Holy Ghost, and by the majesty of the Emperor, which next to God is to be reverenced and beloved by mankind.*

5 Moreover, out of so many bishops who had braved the extremest sufferings for religion, there was not at that time a single one, who tried to scare Constantine from capital punishments and war, or Christians from military service, by the prospect of the divine anger: though many of them were most strenuous guardians of religious discipline, and not at all given to pass over what concerned the duty, either of the Emperor, or of others: such as was Ambrose in the time of Theodosius, who in his seventh Sermon says: *It is not soldiering which is a sin, but soldiering for plunder:* and in his *Duties: The courage which defends our country from barbarians abroad, or the helpless from harm at home, or society from robbers, is mere justice.* This argument seems to me so strong that I require nothing more.

6 Not that I am ignorant that bishops and Christian men often interposed with their instructions to avert punishment, especially capital punishment; nor that a practice was introduced that those who had taken refuge in the Church, should not be given up except on the assurance that their lives would be spared; and also that at the time of Easter, criminals who were in prison were set free. But any one who examines these circumstances with care will see that they are the marks of Christian kindness, seizing every occasion of clemency; not

* [The Law that when a man was killed in his own house, all his slaves should be put to death. See Tacit. *Ann.* XIV. 42.]

manifestations of an opinion condemning all capital punishments; and accordingly the places and times and interposition which procured such indulgence were limited by certain exceptions.

7 (1) Here some object to us the twelfth Canon of the Council of Nicæa, which directs that, *If persons called by grace, have first renounced the military profession* (cingulum militiæ deposuerunt,) *and then returned to it, as dogs to their vomit; let them, after being Hearers for three years, be Penitents for ten years*[*]; *with power in the bishop to modify their sentence according to the evidence of their repentance.*

Here the mention of a penitence of thirteen years indicates at once that there is question not of some slight and ambiguous, but of some grave and undoubted crime.

8 And in fact there is no doubt that *Idolatry* is the crime in question; for what had been said before in the eleventh Canon, must be understood as tacitly repeated here: as is customary in Canons. Now Licinius, as we learn from Eusebius, made men quit the military profession except they would sacrifice to the heathen gods, which Julian afterwards imitated; on which account Victricius and others are said to have given up the military profession (*cingulum abjecisse*) for Christ. The same thing had before been done in Armenia under Diocletian by one thousand one hundred and four persons, of whom there is mention in the Martyrologies; and by Menna and Hesychius in Egypt. And thus at the time of Licinius many renounced the military profession; among whom was Arsacius, who is named among the Confessors, and Auxentius, who was afterwards bishop of Mopsuesta. And thus those who, pricked by conscience, had once left the military profession, could not return to it under Licinius, except by renouncing the faith of Christ; and this transgression was the more grievous, inasmuch as their former act shewed that they had knowledge of the divine law; wherefore those defaulters are punished even more severely than they who are mentioned in the preceding Canon, who, without danger to their life or fortune, had renounced Christianity. But to interpret the Canon which we have quoted as referring to a military life in general, is contrary to common reason. For history clearly testifies that those who under Licinius had renounced military life and had not returned to it under Licinius, in order that they might not violate the Christian faith, had the option given them by Constantine, whether they would be excused military service or enter the army; and no doubt many of them did the latter.

9 (2) Some object to us the epistle of Leo, which says, *It is contrary to ecclesiastical Rule, to return to a military life after act of penitence.* But we are to recollect that penitents, no less than clerical persons and ascetics, were required to lead a life not only Christian, but of eminent purity, that as great an example might be given for correction as had been given for sin. In like manner in the record of the ancient usages of the Church, which, to give it authority, is com-

[* There were four degrees of Penitence in the early Church, Πρόσκλαυσις, Ἀκρόασις, Ὑπόπτωσις, Σύστασις. *Gronovius.*]

monly called the Apostolic Canons, it is directed: *No Bishop, Priest, or Deacon, shall be a soldier, or shall have the characters of a Roman officer, along with his sacred function.* The things which are Cæsar's are for Cæsar; those which are God's are for God. Which passage shews that those who did not seek the honour of the clerical profession were not forbidden to be soldiers.

10 More than this; those were forbidden to be admitted to the clerical order who after baptism had either held a magistrate's office, or a command in war; as we may see in the epistles of Syricius and Innocentius and in the Council of Toledo. In fact, clerical persons were taken not from Christians of every kind, but from those who had given an example of a most correct life. Add to this, that the obligations of military service and of some magistracies was not perpetual; but those who were devoted to the sacred ministry, were not allowed to be drawn from it by any other daily care and labour. On which account the sixth Canon also directs that No Bishop, Priest, or Deacon should administer secular cases, and the eightieth, that he shall not even involve himself in public administration; and the sixth of the African Canons, directs that he shall not undertake a trust or advocacy in the affairs of others; as Cyprian thinks that they should not even undertake the office of guardian.

11 We have the express judgment of the Church on our side in the council of Arles, held under Constantine: for the third Canon of the Council says thus: *Those who cast away their arms in peace shall abstain from the communion:* that is, those who leave the army in a time when there is no persecution raging; for that is what the Christians meant by peace, as appears in Cyprian and others. Add to this the example of the soldiers under the Emperor Julian, Christians of no common proficiency, who were ready to render testimony to Christ by their deaths: they were willing to fight in defence of the State, but when commanded to use their weapons against Christians, they acknowledged the Emperor of Heaven. Of like character had before been the Theban Legion under Diocletian, of which we shall speak hereafter.

12 At present it may suffice to quote their expressions, which describe the office of the Christian soldier with compact brevity: *We offer to you our arms as ready to use them against any enemy, though we refuse to stain them with the blood of the innocent. Our right hands know the way to fight against the impious and the adversary, but they have not the art of butchering the good man and the fellow-citizen. We recollect that we have taken arms for our citizens rather than against them. We have always fought for justice, piety, the protection of the innocent; those have hitherto been the rewards of our labours. We have fought for our faith: and how shall we preserve our faith towards thee* (meaning the Emperor), *if we do not shew our faith towards God?*

[The quotation from Basil seems an after-thought.]

CHAPTER III.

Of War public and private.   Of Sovereignty.

I. 1 The first and most necessary partition of War is this, that War is private, public, or mixed. Public war is that which it carried on under the authority of him who has jurisdiction; private, that which is not so; mixed, that which is public on one side and private on the other. Let us speak of private war first, as the more ancient.

2 That private war may be lawful, so far as Natural Law goes, I conceive is sufficiently apparent from what has been said above, when it was shewn, that for any one to repel injury, even by force, is not repugnant to Natural Law [Chap. II.]. But perhaps some may think that after judicial tribunals have been established, this is no longer lawful: for though public tribunals do not proceed from nature, but from the act of man, yet equity and natural reason dictate to us that we must conform to so laudable an institution; since it is much more decent and more conducive to tranquillity among men, that a matter should be decided by a disinterested judge, than that men, under the influence of self-love, should right themselves according to their notions of right. So Paulus the Jurist, and king Theodoric. [See the passages.]

II. 1 It is not to be doubted, indeed, that the licence which existed before the establishment of public justice is much restricted. Yet still it continues to exist; namely when public justice ends: for the law which forbids us to seek our own by other than judicial proceedings, must be understood to apply only when judicial aid can be had. Now judicial aid ceases either momentarily or continuously. It ceases momentarily when the judge cannot be waited for without certain danger or loss. It ceases continuously either *de jure* or *de facto*: *de jure*, if any one be in an unsettled place, as at sea, in a desert, in an uninhabited island, or in any other place where there is no political government: *de facto*, if the subjects do not obey the judge, or if the judge openly refuses to take cognizance.

2 What we have said, that even after judicial tribunals are established, all private war is not repugnant to Natural Law, may also be understood from the Jewish Law, in which God thus speaks by Moses, Exod. xxii. 2: *If a thief be found breaking up, and be smitten that he die, there shall no blood be shed for him: if the sun be risen upon him, there shall blood be shed for him.* For this law, making so nice a distinction, appears not only to give impunity to the slayer, but to explain Natural Law: and not to be founded in any peculiar divine mandate, but in common equity; and accordingly we find that other nations have followed the same. The Law of the Twelve Tables is well known, doubtless taken from the old Attic Law: *If a man commits a robbery by night, and if any one kill him, it is justifiable homicide.* And thus, by the laws of all nations which we know, he is deemed innocent who defends himself being in peril of life; which manifest consent is a proof that such a course is not at variance with Natural Law.

III. 1 Concerning the more perfect Instituted Divine Law (Chap. I. § xv.), namely the Evangelical Law, there is more difficulty. That God, who has more Right over our lives than we ourselves have, might have demanded from us forbearance to such an extent, that even when brought privately into danger, we should be bound to allow ourselves to be killed rather than kill another, I do not doubt. The question is, whether he did intend to bind us to this. It is usual to adduce for the affirmative two passages which I have already quoted with reference to the general question: *I say unto you that ye resist not evil,* Matth. v. 39, and Rom. xii. 19, *Avenge not yourselves, dearly beloved.* A third passage is those words of Christ to Peter, (Matth. xxvi. 52), *Put up thy sword within the sheath, for all they that take the sword shall perish with the sword.* Some add to these the example of Christ, who died for his enemies, Rom. v. 8, 10.

2 Nor are there wanting among the ancient Christians, those who though they did not condemn public wars, thought that private self-defense was forbidden. We have already (Chap. II. § 10, No. 5) adduced the passages of Ambrose in defense of war: there are passages in Augustine more numerous and more clear, known to all. Yet the same Ambrose says, Perhaps when he said to Peter, who offered him two swords, *It is enough; it was as if he said, that the use of such weapons was lawful till the Gospel: the Law was a teacher of equity, the Gospel, of truth.* And the same writer in another place: *A Christian, if he should come in the way of an armed robber, may not return his blows; lest in defending his safety he should stain his piety.* And Augustine, *As to the law which permits such* (robbers and other violent transgressors) *to be put to death, I reprehend it not; but how I am to defend those who*

put men to death, I do not see. And in another place, *As to putting men to death that other men may not be killed by them, I cannot approve of such deeds ; except the agent be a soldier, or a public officer, or do this, not for himself, but for others, having received legitimate authority.* And Basil was of the same opinion.

3 But the opposite opinion, as it is the more common, so does it seem to us the more true, that such forbearance is not obligatory : for in the Gospel, we are told to love our neighbour as ourselves, but not better than ourselves ; nay even, when an equal evil impends over ourselves and another, we are not forbidden to consult our own safety rather than that of others, as we have shewn above from St Paul, when he explains the law of kindness. Perhaps some one may urge in reply, that though I may prefer my own good to the good of my neighbour, this does not hold of unequal goods : and that I must rather give up my life than that the aggressor should be permitted to fall into eternal damnation. But we may answer that the person attacked may also need time for repentance before he dies, or may think so on probable grounds, and that the aggressor may possibly have time for repentance before his death. But in truth we are not to estimate the moral consequences of a danger into which a man throws himself, and from which he can relieve himself.

4 Certainly the Apostles, even to the last, with the knowledge and under the eye of Christ, travelled armed with sword, which also other Galileans, travelling from their country to Jerusalem, did for fear of robbers, as we learn from Josephus ; who says also that the Essenes, most blameless men, did the same. Hence when Christ said that a time was at hand such that men should sell a garment to buy a sword, Luke xxii. 36, the Apostles answered that they had two in that company : which company consisted of the Apostles alone. And though what was said by Christ, was in truth, not a command but a proverbial expression, signifying that most grave perils were impending, as clearly appears from the opposition of the former time, which had been safe and prosperous, verse 35, *When I sent you without purse, &c. ;* yet it shews what was customary, and what the Apostles thought lawful.

Now it is rightly said by Cicero, that *It would not be lawful to carry a sword if it were not lawful under any circumstances to use it.*

5 The other passage, *Resist not evil,* is more universal than that which follows, *Give to every one that asketh :* which nevertheless admits of exception, namely, that we are not to overburthen ourselves. Nay more : This precept concerning giving has nothing added to it of a restrictive force, but is limited only by the sense of equity : whereas the precept, not to resist, has the explanation added in the example of a buffet on the cheek ; that it may be understood to oblige us precisely then when we are assailed by an injury such as a buffet, or something of the same kind : for otherwise it would have been more suitable to say, *Resist not an injurious aggressor, but give up your lives rather than use arms.*

6 In the words to the Romans, *Avenge not yourselves*, the Greek word means to *avenge*, not to *defend*. [See the passages.] And this is plain from the context: for he had just said, Rom. xii. 17, *Recompense no man evil for evil;* which is a description of vindictive, not of self-defensive conduct. And Paul supports himself by reference to Deut. xxxii. 35, where the meaning of the word, and the sense of the passage, shews that self-defense cannot be intended.

7 What is said to Peter does contain a prohibition of using the sword, but not in self-defense: for he had no reason to defend himself; since Christ had just said concerning his disciples, *Suffer them to depart;* and that, in order that the words which he had uttered might be fulfilled: *Of those whom thou hast given me 1 have lost none:* John xviii. 8, 9: nor to defend Christ, for he would not allow himself to be defended. And hence in St John he adds the reason for this prohibition: *The cup which my Father has given me, shall I not drink it?* verse 11; and in Matthew he says, *How then shall the Scriptures be fulfilled, which say that so it must be?* St Peter then, according to his fervid temper, was moved by the desire of revenge, not of defense. Add to this, that he was using weapons against those who came in the name of the public authorities: and whether these may in any case be resisted, is a peculiar question, to be specially treated hereafter. What the Lord adds, *All they that take the sword shall perish by the sword,* is either a proverb borrowed from common usage, which meant that blood leads to blood, and therefore that the use of arms is always full of peril; or, as is the opinion of Origen, Theophylact, Titus, and Euthemius, it denotes that we are not to take vengeance out of the hands of God, since it is what he will fully exact in his own time: and this is plainly expressed, Revelation xiii. 10, *He that killeth with the sword must be killed with the sword. Here is the patience and the faith of the saints.* And this agrees with what Tertullian says, *So sufficient is God, as one in whom our patience may trust: if we leave our injuries to him, he is our avenger; if our losses, our recompenser; if our pains, our physician; if our death, our restorer to life. What a privilege of patience it is to make God our debtor!* And at the same time the words of Christ seem to contain a prophecy of the punishment which the Roman sword was to exact from the sanguinary Jews.

8 With regard to the example of Christ, who is alleged to have died for his enemies, it may be answered, that all the acts of Christ are full of virtue, and such as may be laudably imitated, as far as is possible, and will not fail of their reward; but they are not all such as proceed from a law, or make a law for us. For that Christ died for his enemies and for the ungodly, was what he did, not in pursuance of any law, but from a special covenant with his Father; who promised, on that condition, not only eternal glory, but also an endless offspring, Isaiah liii. 10. And so Paul describes this as a special and exceptional and unparalleled act, Rom. v. 7: *Scarcely for a righteous man will one die.*

D

And Christ commands us to put our life in peril, not for any one, but for *the brethren*, 1 John iii. 16.

9 As to the opinions adduced from Christian writers, partly they appear to be rather counsels, and the recommendation of an elevated purpose, partly they are the private opinions of those writers, not the common judgment of the Church. For in the very ancient Canons which are called Apostolic, he especially is excluded from the communion, who in a quarrel had slain his adversary at once, in heat of blood. And this opinion Augustine, whom we have quoted on the opposite side [§ II. Art. 2], appears to approve.

IV. [And now of Public War.] 1 Public War is either formal, according to the Law of Nations, or less formal. What I here call formal, is commonly called legitimate, in that sense in which a legitimate will is opposed to a codicil, and a legitimate marriage, to the cohabitation of slaves: not that a man may not lawfully make codicils, or a slave cohabit with a woman; but because a Will and a Marriage have peculiar effects by the Civil Law, which it is important to note. For many, not understanding the word *legitimate*, think that all wars which are not legitimate are unlawful and unjust. In order that a war may be formal according to the Law of Nations, two things are required; first, that it be carried on on both sides by the authority of those who have a political sovereignty; next, that certain formalities be employed, of which we shall speak in their place. Since both these conditions are requisite, one alone without the other is not sufficient.

2 An informal public war may both want those formalities, and be made against private persons, and by the authority of any magistrate. And if we look at the matter without reference to civil laws, it would seem that every magistrate has the right of making war, both to protect the subjects committed to his charge, and to exercise his jurisdiction, if opposed by force. But because by war the whole State is brought into danger, therefore it is provided by the laws of almost every nation, that war is not to be made except by the authority of the Sovereign Power. Plato has such a provision in the last book of his *Laws*. And in the Roman Law, he was held guilty of high treason who without the authority *of the Sovereign* made war, levied troops, or formed an army: the Cornelian law said, without authority *of the People*. So it is in the Codex of Justinian: and so argues Augustine. [See the text.]

3 But as all precepts, however universal, are to be interpreted according to equity, so is this law. For in the first place, there can be no doubt that he who is at the head of any jurisdiction may, through the officers of his court, compel by force a few contumacious persons to obey him, when there is no need of major force for the purpose. And again, if the danger be present and pressing, so that there is no time to consult the Sovereign, here also necessity makes an exemption. On the ground of such a right as this, L. Pinarius, the commander

of the garrison of Enna, being aware that the townsmen had the intention to revolt and join the Carthaginians, by a sudden onslaught on
them kept possession of the town.   And even without great necessity,
in order to obtain satisfaction for injuries which the king neglects to
prosecute, Francis Victoria gave the citizens of towns the right of
making war.   But this opinion is deservedly repudiated by others.

V. 1 In what events the right of using arms is to be allowed to
subordinate magistrates, and whether such a war is to be called a
public war, the Jurists differ.   Some affirm, some deny.   If indeed we
call that *public* which is done by the authority of the magistrate, there
can be no doubt that such wars are public wars; and that therefore those
who in such cases oppose the magistrates, incur the punishment of
contumacy against their superiors.   But if *public* be taken in a higher
sense, for that which is formal, as beyond controversy it often is, those
are not public wars; for the full right of public war requires both the
authority of the Sovereign and other conditions.   Nor is this disproved
by the fact that in such struggles men have their goods taken from
them, and licence is granted to soldiers: for those features are not so
peculiar to public war that they may not have place in other cases.

2 But this too may happen; that in an extensive empire, the subordinate powers may have, as a matter conceded to them, the right of
making war: and if this be the case, the war must then be considered
as made by authority of the Sovereign power; for when a superior
gives another the right of doing anything, it is held to be done by
the authority of the giver.

3 A more difficult controversy is, whether, when there is no such
mandate, a conjecture of the will of the Sovereign be sufficient.   To
me it seems that this is not to be admitted.   For in this state of things,
it is not enough to consider, What would be the wish of the Sovereign
if he were consulted: but rather this: What the Sovereign, in the
case when the business admits of delay, or is of doubtful prudence,
would wish to be done without consulting him, if a general rule on
this subject were to be established.   For however in any particular
case the reason [for consulting the Sovereign] may seem to vanish on
examination, the general rule of not incurring the dangers [which
arise from not doing so] does not cease to have weight: and this
cannot be done, if every [subordinate] magistrate judges for himself
in such cases.

4 [Examples.] Thus Cn. Manlius was rightly accused by his officers
of having made war on the Gallo-Grecians without the command of
the Roman people: for though there had been legions of those Galli
in the army of Antiochus, yet, peace being concluded with Antiochus,
the question, whether that offence was to be further visited upon the
Gallo-Grecians, was to be decided by the Roman people, not by Cn.
Manlius.   [Again] because Cæsar had made war on the Germans, Cato
advised that he should be given up to the Germans: but in this, I
conceive that he did not think of Right, so much as wish the city to

be delivered from the fear of a master. For the Germans had assisted the Gauls, the enemies of the Romans, and therefore there was an injury to complain of, if the Romans had just cause for their war against the Gauls. But Cæsar, when he had had Gaul assigned him as a province, ought to have been content to expel the Germans from it, and ought not, without having any danger on that side, to have followed the Germans within their own frontier, without first consulting the Roman people. Hence the Germans had not the right of demanding that Cæsar should be surrendered to them, but the Romans had the right of calling Cæsar to account. So the Carthaginians answered the Romans in a similar case; [when Hannibal had besieged Saguntum.] *I do not conceive that the question between us is whether Saguntum was besieged by private or by public authority, but whether the siege was justifiable or not. For it is a question between us and our officer whether he acted by our authority or his own; our dispute with you is, whether the treaty allowed the act.*

5 Cicero defends the act both of Octavius and of Decimus Brutus who of their own motion made war upon Antony. But, even if Antony had deserved to be treated hostilely, the decision of the Senate and the people should have been waited for, whether it was for the interest of the State to overlook the act [of Antony] or to avenge it; to treat for peace, or to rush into arms. For no one is bound to use his Right to his own loss. And if Antony was judged a public enemy, it was for the Senate and people to determine by whom the war was to be conducted. So when Cassius asked the Rhodians for soldiers to help him according to their treaty, they replied that they would send them if the Senate ordered them.

6 Warned by this and other examples, we must recollect not to give our approval to everything which is said by authors, even of great name; for they are often governed by the time, or by partial affections, and stretch their measure to their block. We must endeavour to form a clear and unbiassed judgment, and avoid setting up as examples cases which ought to be excused rather than praised.

7 Since then it is said that a public war must not be carried on except by the authority of the person in whom the Sovereignty resides; it will be necessary, for the understanding of this question, and in order to decide other points concerning war, that we should understand what this Sovereignty is, and who has it; and this all the more, inasmuch as learned men, in our time, arguing the question rather with a view to some present object than according to the truth, have made a subject, in itself not simple, still more entangled.

VI. [Of Sovereignty.] 1 The Moral Faculty or Attribute of governing a state, which is commonly called the Civil Power, is described in Thucydides by three characters, when he says that a city is αὐτόνομος, αὐτόδικος, αὐτοτελῆς; has its own laws, tribunals, and magistrates. Aristotle makes three parts of the administration of the State; consultation concerning public affairs, election of magistrates, and

administration of justice. To the first part he refers deliberation concerning peace, war, treaties, laws; he adds the infliction of death, or
exile, forfeiture, bribery; that is, as I interpret him, public offences,
having before spoken of the administration of justice in private cases.
Dionysius of Halicarnassus notes three points especially; the Right of
creating magistrates, the Right of making and abrogating laws, and the
Right of deciding on war and peace : and again in another place, he
adds the case of sacred things, and the convocation of the assemblies.

2 We may easily divide this subject in such a way that there shall
be neither defect nor redundance. He who rules the State rules it
partly by himself, partly by others. By himself, he is either employed
about general matters, or about particular. He is employed about
general matters, in making laws and in rescinding them; both with
regard to sacred subjects (so far as the care of those belongs to the
State) and secular. The particular matters about which he is employed are either directly public, or private, but with a reference to the
public. Directly public, are public acts, as making war, peace, treaties; or money matters, as taxes and commercial duties, and the like;
among which is comprehended that *dominium eminens* which the State
has for public uses, over its citizens and the property of its citizens.
This art is by Aristotle called by the general name πολιτικὴ, that is
civil, and βουλευτικὴ, *deliberative*. Private matters are controversies
between individuals which the public interest requires to be settled by
public authority. The art which deals with them is called δικαστικὴ,
judicial. The part of government which is executed by others, is
executed either by magistrates, or by other commissioned persons,
among whom are ambassadors. And in these things consists the Civil
Power.

VII. 1 That Power is called *Sovereign*, whose acts are not subject to the control of another, so that they can be rendered void by
the act of any other human will. When I say *any other*, I exclude the
Sovereign himself, who may change his determination, as may his successor who has the same authority, and therefore the same power, not
another power. Let us see then in what *subject* this Sovereign power
resides. The subject in which a power resides is either common or
special; as the common subject in which the sight resides is the body,
but the special subject is the eye. And in like manner the common
subject in which the Sovereignty resides is the State, which we have
before described as a perfect [independent] community.

2 We exclude therefore peoples which have put themselves in subjection to another people, such as were the provinces of the Romans.
Such peoples are not by themselves a State, as we now take that word,
but the inferior members of a great State, as servants are members
of a family. Again, it sometimes happens that several peoples have
the same head, though each of these peoples constitutes a perfect
community; for though several bodies cannot have one head in the
natural body, they may in the moral body; for there, the same per-

son may be separately regarded as the head in his relation to different bodies. Of which there may be a certain indication in this, that when the reigning house is extinct, the right of government reverts to each people separately. And thus it may happen that several States are combined in a close federal connexion, and make one *System*, and yet each is a separate State. [Strabo, Aristotle.]

3 Therefore the common subject of Sovereignty is the State, understood in the way we have described. The special subject is one or more persons according to the laws and customs of each nation.

VIII. 1 And here we must first reject their opinion who say that the Sovereignty everywhere belongs to the People; so that *it* has the power of controlling kings, and of punishing them if they abuse their power. What evil this opinion has caused, and may cause, any wise man may see. We refute it with these arguments.

A man may by his own act make himself the slave of any one: as appears by the Hebrew and the Roman law. Why then may not a people do the same, so as to transfer the whole Right of governing it to one or more persons? And it is not to the purpose to say that we are not to presume such a fact; for this question is not, what is to be presumed in a case of doubt, but what may lawfully be done. Nor is it to the purpose to allege the inconveniences which follow or may follow from such a course: for whatever form of government you take, you will never escape all inconvenience.

2 But as there are many ways of living, one better than another, and each man is free to choose which of them he pleases; so each nation may choose what form of government it will: and its right in this matter is not to be measured by the excellence of this or that form, concerning which opinions may be various, but by its choice.

3 Nor is it difficult to conceive causes why a people may resign the whole power of its own government, and transfer it to another; as for example, if it be in great peril and cannot find a defender on other conditions: or if it be in want and cannot otherwise obtain sustenance. So the Campanians of old submitted themselves to the Romans, [see the text from Livy] and some peoples, which wished to do so, were not accepted. What then prevents a people from giving itself up to some powerful man in the same manner? Or again, it may happen that a large landowner will not allow persons to dwell on his land on any other condition: or if any one have a large body of slaves, he may manumit them on condition of being his subjects and paying his taxes. So the Germans did. [See the text from Tacitus.]

4 Add to this that, as Aristotle says that some men are slaves by nature, so some nations are more prone to be governed than to govern. So the Cappadocians, when the Romans offered them their liberty, refused it, and declared they could not live without a king. So it was said that it was absurd to give freedom to Thracians, Mysians, Getans, because they had no heart for it.

5 Also many may be moved by the examples of nations which have

lived happily for many generations under the rule of kings; as the cities of Asia under Eumenes. And sometimes the condition of the State is such that it cannot be safe except under the rule of one; as many prudent men have thought was the case with the Roman State at the time of Augustus. On these and other accounts, it not only may, but does often happen, that many subject themselves to the rule and power of another.

6 Moreover civil authority, or the right of governing, may also be acquired by legitimate war. And all this applies to a government by a body of Nobles, as well as by a single Ruler: and no State was ever so popular, that some were not excluded from public voting; as strangers, paupers, women and children.

7 Some peoples have other peoples under them, not less subject than if they were under kings: and thus that interrogation, *Is the Collatine people its own master?* And the Campanians, when they had given themselves up to the Romans, are spoken of as not being their own masters. Acarnania and Amphilochia are described subjects of the Etolians; Peræa and Caunus, as dependencies of the Rhodians; Pydna, as given by Philip to Olynthus. The towns which had been under the Spartans, after they were taken from their rule, had the name of Eleutherolacones, Free Laconians. Cotyora is spoken of by Xenophon as a city of the Sinopians. Nicæa in Italy was adjudged to the Massilians, as we read in Strabo, and the island Pithecusa to the Neapolitans. So in Frontinus we read that the town Calatia was adjudged to Capua, Caudium to the colony of Beneventum, with their territories. Otho gave the cities of the Mauri to the province of Bætica, as it is recorded in Tacitus. All which acts must be rejected, if we are to hold the doctrine that the right of governing is always subject to the judgment and will of those who are governed.

8 That there are Kings who are not subject to the will of the People, even taken in its totality, both sacred and profane history testify. The kings of Israel were appointed by God, and were said to be anointed over the people, over the Lord's inheritance, over all Israel. [See the passages quoted O. T. : and also Horace.]

9 Seneca described three forms of government;—by the people, by a senate, or by a monarch: [and the latter is considered as absolute.] So Plutarch speaks of those who have authority not only from the laws, but over the laws. Otanes in Herodotus speaks of irresponsible authority. So Dio Prusæensis and Pausanias oppose kingly power to responsible power.

10 Aristotle says that some kings have the power which, in other places, the nation has over itself. So when the Roman rulers had acquired a really royal power, the People is said to have transferred to them all its authority and power. Hence Antoninus said that *God alone is the judge of the Prince.* Dio says, of such a Prince, that *he is free to do and not to do what he pleases.* Such a power was that in

ancient Greece of the Inachidæ at Argos. [See the Chorus in the *Supplices* of Æschylus.]

11 Very different was the power of the kings at Athens, as Theseus speaks in the *Supplices* of Euripides. [See the passage.] For Theseus, as Plutarch explains, was only a Leader in war, and Guardian of the laws, being in other respects on a level with the citizens. Hence kings who are subject to the people are only improperly called kings. So after Lycurgus, the kings of the Lacedæmonians are said to be kings in name, not in reality, by Polybius, Plutarch, and Cornelius Nepos. And this example was followed in other parts of Greece, as at Argos. [See the passage from Pausanias.] And so the senate judged of the kings at Cuma, as Plutarch notes. Aristotle denies that such kingly government is a peculiar form of government, since it is only a part in an aristocratical or democratical constitution.

12 Sometimes we find, in peoples not generally governed by kings, examples of a temporary kingly authority, not subject to the people. Such was the authority of the Amymones among the Cnidians, and of the Dictators in the early times of Rome, when there was no appeal to the People: whence Livy says that the edict of the Dictator was obeyed as a divine law, there being no choice but to obey. And Cicero speaks of the Dictature as controlling the regal power.

13 The arguments on the other side [that all kings are responsible to the people] are not difficult to answer: for

(1) First, the assertion that he who constitutes any authority is superior to the person so constituted, is only true in that constitution which depends perpetually on the will of the constituent body: not in that which, though voluntary at first, afterwards becomes compulsory: thus a woman constitutes a person her husband, whom afterwards she is obliged for ever to obey. And in this strain is the speech of Valentinian to his soldiers. [See the passage.]

Nor is it true, as is assumed, that all kings are constituted by the people; which we have already shewn by the example of a landowner accepting tenants on condition of their obeying him; and of nations conquered in war.

14 (2) The other argument is taken from the maxim of the philosophers, that all government exists for the sake of the governed, not of the governors; whence they conceive it follows that, the end being more noble than the means, the governed are superior to the governors.

But it is not universally true that all government is for the sake of the governed: for some kinds of government are for the sake of the governor, as that of the master in his family; for there the advantage of the servant is extrinsic and adventitious; as the gain of the physician is extrinsic to the art of medicine. Other kinds of government are for the sake of common utility, as the marital. So some kingly governments may be established for the good of the kings, as those which are won by victory: and these are not therefore to be called tyrannies; since *tyranny*, as we now understand it, implies injustice. Some governments too may have respect to the utility both of the governor and the governed; as when a people in distress places a powerful king over it to defend it.

But I do not deny that in most governments, the good of the governed is the object; and that, as Hesiod, Herodotus and Cicero say, kings are constituted for the sake of justice. But it does not follow, as our opponents infer, that peoples are superior to kings: for guardianship is for the sake of the ward, and yet the guardian has authority over the ward. And we are not to allow them to urge that if a guardian neglects his duty to his ward, he may be superseded; and that therefore kings may be so. For this is the case with a guardian, because he has a superior, (the State); but in political government, because we cannot have an infinite gradation of superiors, we must stop at some person or body, whose transgressions, having no superior judge, are the province of God; as he himself declares. And he punishes them, if he deem fit to do so; or tolerates them, in order to punish or to try the people.

15 So Tacitus says that the vices of Princes are to be tolerated like bad seasons; and may alternate with better. And M. Aurelius said that the magistrates judge private men; Princes, the magistrates; God, Princes. In Gregory of Tours is a passage to the same effect. So the Essenes hold, in Porphyry: so Irenæus, and the Clementine Constitutions. [See the text.]

16 Nor is it an objection to this, that peoples are described as being punished for the faults of kings: for that does not happen because the people did not punish the king or control him, but because it consented, at least tacitly, to his transgressions*. Although indeed, God might punish the King by his supreme power without the help of the people.

IX. 1 Some assert that there is a mutual subjection, so that the whole people ought to obey the king when he rules rightly, but when a king rules ill, he is subject to the people. If these reasoners were to say that those things which are manifestly iniquitous are not to be done, though commanded by the king, they would say what is true, and confessed by all good men: but this [resistance or disobedience] does not include any authority, or right of control.

If any people intended to share the power of government with the king, (on which point we shall have something to say hereafter,) such limits ought to be assigned to the power on each side as might easily be recognized by distinctions of places, persons, and matters.

2 But the goodness and badness of an act, [the allegation that the king rules well or ill,] which are often matters of great doubt, especially in political affairs, are not fit marks to make such distinctions. Whence

---

* I suppose the opponent would ask, how the people could shew that it did not tacitly consent to the king's transgressions, otherwise than by controlling or punishing him. W. W.

the most extreme confusion must follow, if the king and the people claim cognisance of the same matter by the allegation of good and evil conduct. Such a disturbed state of things no people, so far as I know, ever thought of introducing.

X. 1 Having thus removed the opinions which are false, it remains that we lay down some cautions, which may shew us how to judge rightly in whom the Sovereign authority in each nation resides.

The first caution is this: that we are not to be deceived by ambiguous names or mere external appearances. For example, in the Latin there is a customary opposition of Governor (*Princeps,*) and King; as where Cæsar says that the father of Vincetorex acquired the government of Gaul, but was put to death because he aimed at the kingly power; and where Piso, in Tacitus, says that Germanicus was the son of a Roman governor, not of a Parthian king; and where Suetonius says that Caligula was within a little of converting the office of a Governor into a royal estate; and where in Velleius, Maroboduus is said to have imagined to himself, not a government constituted by the choice of subjects, but royal authority.

2 Yet we often find these two names confounded: for the Lacedæmonian governors of the posterity of Hercules, after they were subjected to the Ephori, were called nevertheless Kings, as we have seen. And in ancient Germany there were Kings whom Tacitus asserts to have held their authority by force of persuasion, not of command: and Livy says that King Evander governed more by personal might than by legal office; and Aristotle and Polybius call the Suffete of the Carthaginians, *King;* as also Diodorus; so likewise Solinus calls Hanno King of the Carthaginians: and Strabo says of Scepsis in the Troad, when, joining the Milesians, they formed a republic, that the posterity of the old Kings retained the royal name and something of the royal honour.

3 On the other hand, the Roman emperors, when they had acquired unquestioned and unconcealed absolute powers, continued to be called *Principes*, not Kings.

Also the ensigns of royal power are assigned to the Governor in some cities which are free; [as to the Doge at Venice. *Gronovius.*]

4 The Estates of the Realm, or assemblies which represent the various classes of the community, "Prelates, Nobles, and Burgesses," are sometimes only a Great Council of the King, serving to make him acquainted with the complaints of the people, which are often not urged in the Privy Council; and to enable him to decide what is best on such subjects. But in other places these Estates have the right of taking cognisance of the acts of the Prince, and even of prescribing laws by which he is bound.

5 Many think that the distinction of Sovereignty and subordinate authority is to be found in the difference of succession and election: what comes by succession they hold to be sovereign; not what comes by election. But this is certainly not universally true. For succession is not a charter which determines the force of authority, but a con-

tinuation of authority already existing. The authority bestowed by the election of the family is continued by succession: whatever amount of right the first election gives, the succession transmits the same. So the Lacedæmonian kings, though not absolute, were hereditary. The distinction is noted by Aristotle and Thucydides. On the other hand, the Roman empire was absolute, yet elective.

XI. 1 A second caution is this. We must distinguish between what a thing is, and what is the kind of possession of it. A thing is, for example, a piece of land; also, in this sense, a road, an act, a right of way. Now such a thing may be held *pleno jure*, in full right of property; or *jure usufructuario*, as tenant for life; or *jure temporario*, as tenant for a time only. Thus the Roman Dictator held his authority as temporary tenant; most kings, both elected and hereditary, by usufructuary right; but some kings, in full right of property; as those who have acquired their power in a legitimate war, or in whose power any people has put itself absolutely, for some sufficient motive.

2 The Dictator was Sovereign, though temporary. For the nature of moral things [such as power] is known from their operations, and those faculties or powers which have the same effect must be called by the same name. Now the Dictator, during his office, performed all the acts which the most absolute king can perform; nor could his acts be rendered void by any one. And the duration of a thing does not alter its nature. If indeed you ask concerning the dignity, the *majesty* of the office, undoubtedly it is greater in a perpetual office. In the same manner those Regents are Sovereigns for the time, who govern during the nonage, insanity, or captivity of the king, and whose power is not revocable before a certain legitimate period.

3 The case is different with governors whose authority may be revoked at any time; as the kings of the Goths and the Vandals. These are not sovereign.

XII. [There are monarchies *pleno jure*.]

1 Some oppose this, because, they say, men are not things, and cannot be possessed *pleno jure*, as things. But personal liberty is one thing, civil liberty, another. Men may have personal liberty, so as not to be slaves; and yet not have civil liberty, so as to be free citizens. *Libertas* and *regnum* are constantly opposed in the Roman writers. [See the passages.] The question is not concerning the liberty of individuals, but of a people: and a people which is not thus free, is said to be *non sui juris, non suæ potestatis.* [See the passages.]

2 When a people is transferred from one Sovereign to another, it is properly, not the persons, but the right of governing them, which is transferred; as a freedman (*libertus*) may be assigned by his patron to one of his sons.

3 Again, they object that if the king has conquered another nation [and so made them his, *pleno jure*,] he has won them by the dangers and labours of his citizens, and therefore the acquisition is theirs. But this will not hold. For the king may have supported the army out of

his own property or patrimony. For though he has only the usufruct of his patrimony, he may do what he likes with that. So in the Civil Law, when a property is adjudged from a tenant to the heir, the yearly fruit is not refunded, because that belongs not to the heir, but to the property.

A king then may have authority over a people *proprio jure*, so that he can even alienate the kingdom to another. This has even been done: as by Solomon to Hiram (or Hierom) king of Tyre.

4 And often in Grecian history. [See the examples.]

5 And in Roman history. Attalus left his kingdom, Asia, to the Romans by will: so did Nicomedes, Bithynia; so did Appion, Cyrenaica.

6 [Other examples.]

XIII. 1 Some sovereignties are not held *pleno jure*: namely, those which are bestowed by the will of the people. In this case, the king is not to be presumed to have the right of alienation. So Crantzius notes, as a thing without precedent, Unguin giving Norway by testament. The bequests of kingdoms by Charlemagne, Louis, and others, were to be taken rather as a commendation than an alienation: and accordingly Charlemagne desired to have his testament confirmed by the Frankish nobles. So Philip, king of Macedon, commended his nephew as king to the cities of Macedonia.

2 Louis restoring the city of Rome to Pope Paschal is not to the point; for the Franks might properly restore to the Roman people that authority over the city of Rome which they had received from the Roman people; and the Pope might be considered as representing the people.

XIV. Some powers lower than sovereignty are held *pleno jure*: as marquisates, counties, baronies, are sold, bequeathed, or otherwise alienated, much more commonly than kingdoms.

XV. 1 The distinction between patrimonial and non-patrimonial kingdoms is seen in the mode of appointing a Regent or Guardian, when the king, from age or disease, cannot act. In non-patrimonial kingdoms this is done by public law, or that failing, by consent of the people: in patrimonial kingdoms, by the father, or the family. Thus in Epirus, the Regents were appointed by the consent of the people: in the kingdom of Asia, by the will or testament of the sovereign.

2 Whether the king be, in addition, the owner of the land, as the king of Egypt after Joseph, and the kings of the Indian nations, makes no difference in this matter.

XVI. [Sovereignty is not destroyed by grants of rights from the Sovereign.]

1 The third observation is, that the authority does not cease to be sovereign, although the Ruler makes certain promises to his subjects, or to God, even of matters relating to the government. I do not now speak of promises to observe Natural Law and Divine Law, or the *Jus gentium*, to which all kings are bound, even without promise; but of

the concession of rules to which they could not be bound without promise. The truth of this appears from the analogy of the master of a family, who, though he should have promised to do something which pertains to the government of the family, does not thereby cease to have the supreme power in the family, so far as family matters are concerned. Nor does a husband lose his marital power, by making certain promises to his wife.

2 But still it must be confessed, that when this is done, the sovereignty is in some degree limited, whether the obligations respect the exercise of certain acts, or directly affect the power. In the first case, an act done against the promise becomes unjust, because, as we shall elsewhere shew, a legitimate promise gives a Right to the promisee: in the second case, the promise is null by reason of defect of the power of making it. But it does not follow from this that the person so promising has a superior; for the promise is null, in this case, not by the act of superior power, but by Natural Law.

3 Thus the Persian king was absolute and irresponsible; yet he took an oath on his accession, and could not change laws duly made. [See the examples.] So the kings of the Ethiopians. So the kings of the Egyptians, who were absolute, were obliged to many observances: if they violated these, they could not be accused in their lifetime; but after their death they were accused, and buried with certain solemnities. So those Hebrew kings who had reigned ill were buried in places out of the Royal burial-ground. 2 Chron. xxiv. 25; xxviii. 27. And this was an excellent institution, preserving the sacredness of the kingly power, and yet restraining kings from violating their faith by the fear of a future judgment. So the kings of Epirus swore to reign according to the Laws.

4 But suppose the condition to be added, that if the king violate his promise he should lose his kingdom? Even so, his sovereignty does not cease; it becomes a mode of possessing the kingdom, narrowed by the condition, and not unlike to a temporary sovereignty. So the king of the Sabæans, as Agatharcides related, was completely absolute, but if he quitted his palace, was liable to be stoned.

5 So an estate which we enjoy by a trustee is ours no less than if it were possessed in full property; but it ceases to be ours when the conditions of the trust direct. Such conditions belong to other contracts, as well as to the tenure of government. Some leagues with neighbours seem to have been made with such a sanction.

XVII. 1 The Sovereignty may be divided according to its *potential* or its *subjective* parts.

The Sovereignty consists of the parts which we have mentioned [see § VI.], with the addition of irresponsibility: but it may be divided either according to the powers [deliberative, judicial, &c.] or the subjects who are governed. Thus the Roman Empire, though one, was often divided, so that one Ruler had the East, another the West; or into three parts. So too it may happen that a people when it chooses a king, may reserve certain acts to itself, and may commit others to the king, *pleno jure*. This is not the case whenever the king is bound by certain promises, as we have shewn; [§ xvi.] but is to be understood to happen then, when either the partition of power is expressly instituted, concerning which we have already spoken; or if a people, hitherto free, lay upon the king some perpetual precept; or if anything be added to the compact, by which it is understood that the king can be compelled or punished. For a precept is the act of a superior, at least in the thing commanded: to compel, is not always the act of a superior; for by Natural Law every creditor has the Right of compelling his debtor to pay; but to compel is at variance with the nature of an inferior. Therefore in the case of such compulsion, a parity of powers at least follows, and the Sovereignty is divided.

2 Many persons allege many inconveniences against such a two-headed Sovereignty; but in political matters nothing is quite free from inconveniences; and Rights arise, not from what seems to one or another convenient, but from the will of him who is the origin of Rights. For example, the kings established by the Heraclidæ in Argos, Messena, and Sparta, were bound to govern within the rules of the law; and so long as they did so, the people were bound to preserve the throne to them.

Also such engagements have been made, not only between the king and his people, but among different kings, and among different peoples; and between kings and neighbouring peoples; each giving such a *guarantee* to the other.

XVIII. 1 There is no partition of the Sovereignty, in cases when kings allow their own acts not to be valid except when approved by some assembly*. For acts which are thus rescinded are to be understood to be rescinded by the authority of the king; who provided such a caution against fallacious representations. So Antiochus the Third sent a rescript to the magistrates, that if he commanded anything contrary to the Laws, they should not obey him: and Constantine directed that widows and orphans should not be compelled to come to the Emperor's court for judgment, though a rescript of the Emperor to that effect should be produced.

2 The case is like that of a testament in which it is added that no subsequent testament shall be valid; for this clause has the effect of making a later testament presumed not to be the real will of the testator. But as this clause may be rescinded by an express and special signification of the will of the writer, so may that direction of the king.

XIX. I do not here use the authority of Polybius, who refers the Roman State to the class of mixed Sovereignty. For at that time, if we look, not at the acts, but at the right of acting, it was merely democratical: for both the authority of the Senate, which he regards as an aristocracy, and that of the Consuls, whom he considers as kings, was

* As the king of France has his edicts registered by the Parliament. *Gronovius.*

subject to the People. And the same is to be said with respect to other political writers, who regard external appearances and daily administration, rather than the question of Rights.

XX. Examples of mixed Sovereignty. [See the text.]

1 The Hebrew kings were absolute, like other oriental monarchs:

2 The Hebrew king had peculiar exceptions from the law:

3 Yet some cases were reserved to the Sanhedrim.

4 Mixed sovereignty among the Macedonians: the Gothones; the Pheacians:

5 Under the Roman kings:

6 In Rome under the early Consuls:

7 In Athens at the time of Solon.

These points being settled, let us examine certain questions which often occur in this matter.

XXI. 1 First, Whether one who is bound by an unequal alliance can have sovereign power.

By an unequal alliance, or unequal league, I do not mean one in which the parties have a different amount of power; as the league of the Thebans with the Persians at the time of Pelopidas; and of the Romans with the Massilians, and afterwards with king Masanissa; nor a league which has a transient operation, as when he who was an enemy is received into amity, on condition of paying the expences of the war, or any other consideration; but a league which by the force of the compact gives a permanent precedence to one of the parties: when for instance, the one party is bound to preserve the authority and majesty of the other, as was the case in the league of the Etolians with the Romans. [See the explanation in the text.] To this relation are referred what are called the Rights of Protectorate, Advocacy, Patronage, and the Rights of the Mother-cities in Greece over their Colonies. [See Thucydides.] So the league between Alba and Rome.

2 This is the characteristic of an alliance between unequals; that the greater share of power goes to the stronger, the greater share of advantage to the weaker. [Andronicus Rhodius.] And a people is free which is not under the power of any other, even though there be a league in which it is stipulated that it shall preserve the majesty of another people: [as Proculus pronounced.] Since therefore a people bound by such a league is free, it follows that it preserves its sovereignty.

The same may be said of a king; for there is an entire analogy between a free people, and a king who is truly a king. Proculus adds, that though one of the peoples be superior, both are free; *superior* is here understood not of power, but of authority and dignity. So Clients are free, yet inferior to Patrons.

3 Clients are under the protection of their Patrons (*in fide patronorum*); so in an unequal alliance, the inferior people is under the protection of the people superior in dignity. They are under their patronship, not under their authority, *sub patrocinio, non sub ditione.* There are many examples of this distinction, in Appian, Livy, Cicero,

Strabo. [See the text.] As private patronship does not take away personal liberty, so public patronship does not take away public liberty,
which cannot exist without sovereignty. Other kings, on the contrary,
were really subjects of the superior power, as the kings of Armenia to
the Romans, the kings of Cyprus to the Persian king. [See the authorities: Gronovius adds, for the Armenians, *Florus*, 4, 12.]

4 Proculus adds that *We* (the Romans) *take cognisance of criminals
in the federate cities;* which seems at variance with what we have said.
To understand this, we must know that there may be four kinds of
controversies in such cases. First, if the subjects of the people or
king which is under the protection of another, be charged with violation of the terms of the league: secondly, if the peoples or kings
themselves be so charged: thirdly, if the allies, who are under the
protection of the same people or king, have a dispute among themselves: fourthly, if the subjects complain of wrong done them by those
under whose authority they are.

In the first case, if the offence be apparent, the king or people is
bound either to punish the offender, or to give him up to the party
whom he has wronged; but this holds good, not only in unequal, but
in equal alliances, and even when there is no league in existence, as
we shall hereafter shew. They are also bound to see that compensation be made, which was the office of the *Recuperatores* at Rome. [See
the definition of *Recuperatio* from Festus.] But one of the allied states
has not a direct Right of seizing or punishing the subject of another.
So when Annibal seized Decius Magius the Campanian, he pleaded
against this as contrary to the federal Rights, and was set at liberty.

5 In the second case, one ally has the power of compelling another
to abide by the terms of the league, and even of punishing, if this be
not done. But this also is not peculiar to unequal alliances; for the
same holds in an equal alliance. For in order to justify any party in
doing himself justice upon a wrong-doer, it is sufficient that he be
not himself the subject of the offender; a case elsewhere to be
treated. And therefore this is practised between kings and peoples
not federate.

6 In the third case, as, in equal alliances, the dispute is commonly
referred to a convention of the allies who are not interested in the
dispute, as we read that the Greeks, antient Latins, and Germans used
to do; or otherwise, to arbiters, or to the Head of the League as a
common arbiter: so, in unequal alliances, it is commonly agreed that
disputes are to be settled by reference to him who is the superior in
the alliance. But this also does not prove superior authority; for
even kings are accustomed to have pleas before judges appointed by
themselves.

7 In the fourth case, the allies have no Right of Cognisance. So
when Herod made accusations against his sons to Augustus, they
pleaded that he himself, both as father and as king, had cognisance of
them. So when some of the Carthaginians complained to Rome

against Annibal, Scipio said that the Senate ought not to interfere in the interior matters of Carthage. And so Aristotle says that an Alliance differs from a single State in this; that Allies provide against their own mutual injuries, but not against the mutual injuries of the citizens of one of the Allied States.

8 In unequal alliances, the words *command* and *obedience* are sometimes used with reference to transactions between the superior and inferior: but this does not refute what we have said. Such terms are either used of things tending to the common good of the alliance, or to the private advantage of the superior.

In common things, at times when the common convention is not assembled, the Head of the League usually gives commands to the allies; as Agamemnon to the Greek kings; and the Lacedæmonians, and afterwards the Athenians, to the Greek States. [See Thucydides and Isocrates.] The Latins call this *commanding;* (*imperare;*) the Greeks, more modestly, *ordering;* (τάσσειν.) [See Thucydides, Pliny.] This being done by the Head of an equal Alliance, may naturally be done by the Superior in an unequal Alliance. This kind of *imperium*, ἡγεμόνια, does not take away liberty. So the Rhodians say in Livy: so the Greek cities are described in Diodorus; so Dio Prusæensis says of the Athenians; so Cæsar of the Suevi.

9 In matters relating to the utility of the Superior in an unequal alliance, his requirements are called *commands*, not of Right, but as producing the effect of commands: as the requests of kings are often called commands; [so Livy] and as the patient is said to command his physician: [more commonly the physician is said to command the patient. *J. B.*]

10 But yet, true it is, that he who is superior in an alliance, if he be much the more powerful, often gradually obtains a real *imperium*, especially if the alliance be perpetual, with the Right of introducing garrisons into the towns; as the Athenians did when they allowed appeals to be made to them by their allies, which the Lacedæmonians never did; at which time Isocrates compares the power of the Athenians to an empire. So the Latins complained that under the figment of an alliance with Rome they were in slavery. So the Etolians spoke of the vain pretence and empty name of liberty; and the Achæans afterwards, that the alliance was a slavery, having no security of liberty. So Civilis, in Tacitus, complains that it was not an alliance, as formerly, but that they were treated like slaves; and again, that their wretched slavery was falsely called peace. Eumenes, in Livy, says that the allies of the Rhodians were allies in name only; in reality, subjects and under command: and the Magnesians say that Demetrias, free in appearance, is really at the beck of the Romans; and Polybius says that the Thessalians, in pretence free, were really under the power of the Macedonians.

11 When this happens, and such Power becomes a Right, a case which we shall have to treat hereafter, then those who had been Allies

E

become Subjects; or at least there is a partition of the Sovereignty; which, as we have above said, may take place in certain circumstances.

XXII. The payment of money to the Superior does not destroy Sovereignty; whether it be a compensation for injury done, or a consideration for protection. Such cases happened among the Greeks; and to the kings of the Hebrews and of the neighbouring nations after the time of Antonius: but such payment is a confession of weakness, and may derogate something from the dignity of the State which makes it.

XXIII. 1 The question of the Feudal Relation is more difficult; but it may be easily solved by what precedes. This contract is peculiar to the German nations, and is nowhere found except where the Germans have established themselves. In it two things are to be considered, the Personal Obligation, and the Right of Real Property.

2 The Personal Obligation is the same, whether any one [the Superior Lord] by the Feudal Law possesses the Right of Lordship, or any other Right, over a thing situated at a distance from him. As such an Obligation would not take away the Right of personal liberty [in the person subject to such command], so neither does it take away from a king or a people the Right of Sovereignty, which is civil liberty. This is most apparent in those Free Fiefs which are called *Frank Fiefs*, which consist solely in the Personal Obligation, without any Right to Real Property. For these are only a kind of unequal alliance, such as we have spoken of; in which one party promises to the other aid, [for instance, Military Service,] and the other party promises Protection and Guardianship. Even if the condition be aid promised [by the Vassal] against *every* other party, which is what is now called a *Liege Fief*, that does not detract anything from his [the Vassal's] sovereignty; not to mention that there is always included a tacit condition, that the war be just; which we shall treat of elsewhere.

3 As to the Right of Real Property [belonging to the Feudal Vassal], that is doubtless such, that the Right of Lordship, if it be held in virtue of the Fief, may be lost by the extinction of the Tenant's family, and also for certain crimes. But in the mean time it does not cease to be Sovereign; for, as we have repeatedly said, (§ XI. 1) we must distinguish between what a thing is, and the kind of possession of it. And we find that many kings were established by the Romans on that condition, that if their family failed, the authority should revert to the Romans; as in Paphlagonia.

XXIV. And thus in political authority, as in private property, we must distinguish Right from the use of Right; or [in the language of the Schoolmen] the *actus primus* from the *actus secundus*. A king who is an infant has the Right, but cannot exercise it; so one who is insane, captive, or who lives in the territory of another so that his actions with regard to the exercise of his remote kingdom are not freely done. In all these cases there are to be established Guardians or Regents. So Demetrius, when he was living under constraint in the power of Seleucus, forbad that credence should be given to his Seal or his Letters, and directed every thing to be administered as if he were dead.

CHAPTER IV.

Of Wars of Subjects against Superiors.

I. 1 WAR may be carried on by private persons against private persons, as by a traveller against a robber; and by sovereigns against sovereigns, as by David against the king of the Ammonites ; and by private persons against those who are sovereigns of others, but not of them, as by Abraham against the king of Babylon and his neighbours; and by sovereigns against private persons, either their own subjects, as by David against the party of Ishbosheth, or not their own subjects, as by the Romans against the pirates.

2 But we have now to inquire only whether it be lawful either for private or for public persons to carry on war against those who have over them an authority either sovereign or subordinate.

And in the first place, it is not controverted that those who are armed with the authority of the supreme power may take arms against inferior authorities; as was the case when Nehemiah was armed with the edict of Artaxerxes against the chiefs of the neighbouring country. So the Roman emperors concede to the owner of the soil the liberty to expel those who would lay down the lines of a camp there.

But we inquire what is lawful against the supreme power, or in-ferior powers acting under the authority of the supreme power.

3 It is beyond controversy among all good men, that if the persons in authority command any thing contrary to Natural Law or the Divine Precepts, it is not to be done. For the Apostles, in saying that we must obey God rather than man, appealed to an undoubted rule, written in the minds of all, which you may find, almost in the same words, in Plato. But if we receive any injury from such a cause,

or in any other way from the will of the Supreme Power, we are to bear it rather than resist by force.

II. 1 By Natural Law, all have the Right of repelling wrong. But civil society being instituted to secure public tranquillity, the State acquires a Superior Right over us and ours, as far as is necessary for that end. Therefore the State may prohibit that promiscuous Right of resisting, for the sake of public peace and order: and it is to be presumed to have intended this, since it cannot otherwise attain its end. If this prohibition does not exist, there is no State, but a multitude without the tie of society. So the Cyclops are described by Homer and Euripides; so the [hypothetical] Aborigines, and the Getuli, by Sallust. [See the references.]

2 Such a prohibition of force, then, is the usage of all society. *It is the general pact of human society*, says Augustine, *to obey kings*. So Æschylus, Sophocles, Euripides, Tacitus, Seneca, who took it from Sophocles, and Sallust. [See the passages. The line *Indigna digna habenda sunt, rex quæ facit*, is a parody of a line in Plautus, *rex* being put for *herus*. *Captiv.* II. 1. 6. *J. B.*]

3 Hence the majesty, that is, the dignity of the Sovereign, whether he be king or people, is defended by so many laws, so many penalties. The soldier, who, when the centurion has to scourge him, resists and seizes the vine-stalk (the instrument of punishment), is cashiered; if he breaks it on purpose, or lays a hand on the centurion, his offence is capital. And Aristotle says, *If a magistrate strikes any one, the blow is not to be returned.*

III. So in the Hebrew law, he was condemned to death who was disobedient either to the high priest, or to a Ruler of the people, appointed by God in an extraordinary manner. The passage 1 Sam. viii. 11, [*This will be the manner of the king over you: He will take your sons, &c.*] if carefully examined, appears not to imply a true Right, (for a very different course of conduct is prescribed in the law when the duty of the king is spoken of;) nor a mere Fact; (for the fact of a king doing this would not be peculiar, since some private persons also do injuries to others;) but a Fact which has a peculiar effect, that this being done by the king, there is an obligation of not resisting. And therefore it is added that the people so oppressed shall cry out to God for help, namely, because no help of man is to be had. So that this exercise of power is called the king's *Right*, as the judge is said to *do Right* to the parties, even when he judges wrong.

IV. 1 In the New Testament, Christ, when he commands us to give to Cesar the things that are Cesar's, gives it to be understood that his disciples must pay as much obedience to the powers that be as was due from the Hebrews to the Hebrew kings; if not more; and this, joined (if need be) with endurance of evil. Paul interprets this excellently, Rom. xiii. 2 et seqq. In the subjection which he recommends, he includes the obligation of not resisting; and not only the obligation to this which arises from fear, but that which flows from a sense of duty, and is an obligation, not towards man only, but towards God. He adds two reasons; first, that God has approved the order of command and obedience, both formerly in the Hebrew Law and now in the Gospel; wherefore the public powers are to be regarded by us as if they were ordained of God; for a person makes that his act to which he imparts his authority. The other reason is, that this order promotes our good.

2 But some will say it is not for our good to suffer injuries. Here some reply, with more truth than pertinence to the apostle's meaning, that these injuries also are for our good, because our endurance of them will not lose its reward. To me it appears that the Apostle considered the general end which is proposed in such order, namely, the public tranquillity, in which that of individuals is comprehended. And it cannot be doubted that, for the most part, we gain this good by the public powers; for they further the happiness of the subjects for the sake of their own happiness. Hence the wish, *May there be those whom you may rule* [as Furfidius says to Sulla, Florus 3, 21]. It is a Hebrew proverb that *If there were no public power, one man would swallow another alive:* of which also Chrysostom gives the sense.

3 If the Rulers at any time are misled by excessive fear or anger, or other passions, so as to deviate from the road that leads to tranquillity, this is to be held as the less usual case, and compensated by the alternation of better times. And Laws are content to respect what commonly happens; as Theophrastus and Cato remark. [See.] Exceptional cases must submit to the general rule; for though the reason of the rule does not specially hold in that special case, yet the general reason of the rule remains; and to this special facts must be subjected. This is better than living without a rule, or leaving the rule to every one's will. So Seneca. [See.]

4 To this effect is the memorable passage in the speech of Pericles, as stated by Thucydides. Livy expresses it more briefly. So Plato, Xenophon, Jamblichus. [See.]

5 This public order of command and obedience is inconsistent with the private license of resisting. See Dio Cassius.

6 St Peter speaks to the same effect as St Paul. So the Clementine Constitutions. We are taught that subjection is due to masters, even to the harsh; and the same is to be referred to kings; for the reason [in St Peter] holds equally good of kings. And we are taught also that the subjection required of us includes endurance of evil. So of parents in Publius Syrus, Elian, Justin, Livy: of kings, in Tacitus, Claudian. [See.]

V. 1 The custom of the early Christians, the best interpreters of the law of our Lord, did not deviate from this rule. For though very wicked men held the Roman empire, and there were not wanting persons who opposed them on pretence of relieving the State, the Christians never took part in their attempts. And so the Clementine Constitutions enjoin; and Tertullian boasts that the Christians had no share in the murder of the Roman Emperors. [See the passages.]

2 Ambrose, though fearing harm not only to himself but to his flock from Valentinian, would not use the excitement of the people as a means of resistance; as he says in his Epistles. [See.] The same Ambrose would not use the forces of Maximus against the Emperor, though both an Arian and an oppressor of the Church. So when Julian the Apostate was pursuing the most destructive counsels, he was repressed only by the tears [not the arms] of the Christians. And yet his army consisted almost entirely of Christians. Add to this that Julian's cruelty was not only a wrong to the Christians, but brought the State into great danger. So Augustine.

VI. 1 Some learned men of our time, yielding too much to the influences of time and place, have persuaded first themselves (for so I believe) and then others, that this, though true of private persons, is not true of inferior magistrates; that they have a right of resistance, and ought to use it; which opinion is not to be admitted. For those inferior magistrates, though public persons with regard to their inferiors, are private persons with regard to their superiors. All authority is subject to the Sovereign authority; and what is not done by that authority is a private act. [See the Scholastic reasons.]

2 The state of things thus defended is like that fabled in heaven, when the minor Deities rebelled against Jove. The subordination of all to the Supreme Power is recognized by common sense; in Seneca; Papinius; Augustine. [See.]

3 And also by Divine Authority; expressed by Peter, Paul, Samuel.

4 And so also the state of public religion depends on the will of the King and the Council. (Synedrium.) The engagement of the magistrates and the people to be faithful to God, after the king, is to be understood, as far as is in their power. We do not read of the images of false gods being thrown down, except by command either of kings, or of the people when free. When this is done by force against the consent of the kings, it is related as a testimony of Divine Providence so permitting; not in approval of the human act.

5 On the contrary is urged Trajan's saying when he gave the dagger to the Prætorian Prefect: *Use it for me if I rule rightly; if ill, against me.* But Trajan wished to avoid assuming kingly authority, and to be a true Governor (Princeps), and as such was subject to the will of the Senate and people; whose commands the Prefect was to execute, even against the Prince. So M. Antoninus would not touch the public money without consent of the Senate.

VII. 1 Whether in a very grave and certain danger the rule of non-resistance holds, is a more difficult question. For the laws of God may admit of exemption in cases of extreme necessity. So the Hebrew law of the Sabbath did; and this exception is approved by Christ; as also in the case of the shew-bread. And so other laws of the Hebrews did. Not that God has not the Right of our obedience under certain death; but that some laws are of such a nature that it is not credible that they were given with so rigid an intention: still more in human laws.

2 Yet even human laws may command some acts of virtue with certain danger of death; as the military rule of not quitting our post. But this is not lightly to be supposed the intention of the lawgiver; nor do men appear to have accepted it so, unless extreme necessity require. For laws are and ought to be made, with a sense of human weakness. The law of which we speak (that of non-resistance) seems to depend on those who first formed civil society, and from whom the Rights of Rulers are derived. And if these could be asked whether they would impose on all this burthen, that they should prefer to die rather than in any case resist a superior by force, it is probable they would answer that they would not: unless perhaps with this addition; except resistance would involve extreme disturbance of the State, and the death of many innocent persons. And what benevolence would recommend in such circumstances, we may confidently ascribe to human law.

3 It may be said that the rigid obligation of bearing death rather than resisting a superior, proceeds not from human, but from Divine Law. But it is to be noted that Civil Society is the result, not of Divine precept, but of the experience of the weakness of separate families to protect themselves; and is thus called by Peter an *ordinance of man*, though it is also an ordinance of God, because He approves it. And God, approving a human law, must be conceived approving it as human, and in a human manner.

4 Barclay, the most strenuous asserter of royal authority, yet allows that the people, or a *considerable part* of it, has the Right of protecting itself against extreme cruelty, though he asserts the whole people to be subject to the king. I can understand, that in proportion as what is preserved [by the rule of non-resistance] is more valuable, so much the more serious a matter is the equitable construction, which allows an exception to the words of the law. But still, I do not venture indiscriminately to condemn, either *individuals* or a *minority* of the people who thus have recourse to the ultimate means of necessity, provided they do not desert a respect for the common good. So David gathered the discontented to him, and had above four hundred armed men; of course, to repel violence. But this was not till David knew that Saul sought his life. And he did not seize upon cities, but hid himself in desert places or in foreign countries, avoiding to do harm to those of his nation.

5 So the Maccabees were not justified by the general right of resistance; for Antiochus was king, and they had no legal right of resistance. They were justified by extreme danger.

6 And even in such a case, the person of the king is to be respected; as was done by David.

7 Nor are those who resist to throw false reproaches on any one;

but on the king, not even true ones. Still more are they to abstain from laying hands on him. [See the heathen authorities.]

8 Whether what was lawful for David and for the Maccabees be lawful for Christians, is a graver question, since their Master, commanding them to bear their cross, seems to require a more exact patience. And certainly Christ counsels flight to Christians who are in danger of death, (that is, those who are not bound to their place by duty,) but nothing beyond flight. So Peter says that Christ *has left us an example*, 1 Pet. ii. 21, and that we are to rejoice if we suffer as Christians, 1 Pet. iv. 12, 13, 14. And by such patience the Christian religion grew strong.

9 And so the ancient Christians teach: Tertullian; Cyprian; Lactantius; Augustine. [See the passages.]

10 So Cyril holds concerning the sword of Peter. So the Theban legion did not resist when decimated for refusing to sacrifice.

11 [The speeches of Mauritius the captain of the Theban legion, and of the soldiers, are to the same effect.]

12 [As also the speech of Exuperius their standard-bearer.]

13 Then the butchery followed. The old martyrology tells the story of their suffering without resisting.*

14 Those who professed the ὁμοούσιον (*the Son of one substance with the Father*) were put to death without resistance by Valens.

15 He who follows such examples, if he so lose his life, saves it, as Christ has declared.

VIII. But on this rule of non-resistance there are some remarks to be made.

First, those Rulers who are subject to the people, whether by original institution or by subsequent convention, if they transgress against the laws and the State, may not only be resisted, but put to death, as Pausanias at Lacedæmon. So Mezentius in Virgil is resisted.

IX. Secondly, if the king or other ruler has abdicated his power, or manifestly regards it as *derelict*, lost to him, he may thenceforth be treated as a private person. But he is not to be regarded as possessing it as derelict, merely because he uses it negligently.

X. Thirdly, says Barclay, if the king alienates the kingdom or brings it into subjection to another, he forfeits it. At this I stop. Such an act, if the kingdom be elective or hereditary, is null; and an act which is null, cannot have any effect in law. I think that the law of the jurists concerning tenants for life, which tenants, as we have said, such kings resemble, is more applicable; namely, that if they transfer their right to another, the act has no effect. And when it is said that the tenant's interest reverts to the lord, it is to be understood that it does so at the legal time.

But if the king take measures to transfer or subject his kingdom to another, I do not doubt that he may be resisted in that design. The authority is one thing, the manner of holding it another; and the

* But Barbeyrac says the story is 'mera fabula.'

people may resist the latter being changed: for that is not compre-hended in the authority. As Seneca says in a similar case; *We are to obey a father; but not in his wish to become not a father.*

XI. Fourthly, if the king act, with a really hostile mind, with a view to the destruction of the whole people, Barclay says that the kingdom is forfeited; for the purpose of governing and the purpose of destroying cannot subsist together: so that he who professes him-self the enemy of the whole people, *ipso facto*, abdicates his kingdom. But this can hardly happen in a person of sound mind, who governs one people only. If he govern several peoples, he may wish to destroy one of them for the sake of another, that he may found colonies there.

XII. Fifthly, if the kingdom be bestowed by commission from a superior; and if the king either commit felony against the lord of the fief, or if there be a clause in the grant, that if the king do so and so, his subjects are released from the tie of obedience; then also the king falls back into a private person.

XIII. Sixthly, if the king have a part only of the Sovereignty, another part being in the Senate or the people, and if the king invade the part which is not his, he may justly be opposed by force, because in that part he has not authority. And this I conceive may be, although the law directs that the power of making war be in the king. For this must be understood of external war. And since each party has its portion of the Sovereignty, it must also have the right of defending that part. When this is the case, the king may lose his portion of the Sovereignty by the right of war.

XIV. Seventhly, if in conferring the royal authority, it be stated that in a certain event, the king may be resisted; although by that means there is not a part of the Sovereignty withheld, yet a certain natural liberty is retained by the subjects and exempted from the royal authority. He who alienates his right [as the people here does] may limit by compact the right so alienated.

XV. Next concerning Usurpers.

1 We speak now of an Usurper of the kingdom, not after he has by long possession or treaty acquired a Right, but so long as his pos-session remains illegitimate. And during such possession, the acts of government which he exercises may have an obligatory force, not from his Right, which is null, but because it is probable that the legi-timate governor would wish that it should be so, rather than that laws and tribunals should be abolished and confusion ensue. Cicero says that the laws of Sylla were highly cruel, yet he thought it necessary to preserve them. So also Florus judges.

2 But in matters which are not thus necessary, and which tend to strengthen the unjust possession of the Invader, he is not to be obeyed, if he can be disobeyed without extreme danger.

XVI. But whether such an Usurper may be put down by [private] force, or put to death, is a question.

And first, if he have seized the kingdom by an unjust war, not legitimate according to the Law of nations, and no treaty has followed, it appears that the Right of War remains; and that everything is lawful against him which is lawful against an enemy, who may be slain even by a private person*. *Against traitors and public enemies*, says Tertullian, *every man is a soldier*. So every one is allowed to do justice on those who desert the army.

XVII. The same may be true in virtue of a law, existing before the usurpation, which gave every one the right of killing him who did this or that before his eyes: for instance, surrounded himself with a body-guard, seized a fort, put a person to death without lawful judgment, made magistrates without the regular choice. Such laws existed at Athens and Rome.

XVIII. To kill the usurper will be lawful for one who has authority from the legitimate power: and along with such we must reckon the guardians of royal wards, as Jehoiada was to Joash, when they put down Athaliah, 2 Chron. xxiii.

XIX. 1 In other cases than these, I cannot grant that it is allowable to a private person to put down by force, or to put to death, the usurper of a kingdom: for it may be that the legitimate governor would rather that the usurper should be left in possession, than that occasion should be given to dangerous and bloody movements, which generally follow, when those are killed who have a strong faction in the people, or have friends in other nations. Whether the legitimate government would wish that peril to be incurred, is uncertain; and without knowing their will, force is not justified. Cicero said, *To me any peace with my fellow-citizens seems better than civil war*. So Favonius, T. Quintius, in Livy: so Aristophanes. [See.]

2 Whether liberty or peace be better, is a most difficult point; on which individuals ought not to assume the office of judges. [See Tacitus, Cicero, Lucan (I. 351), Sylla (in Plutarch *de Genio Socrat.* p. 576.)]

3 So Plato says we are not to do violence to our country, or to our parents. So Sallust, Plutarch, Ambrose, Thomas Aquinas.

4 The killing of Eglon king of Moab by Ehud, Judg. iii. 15, is no precedent; he had a special mandate from God. So God in other cases exercised his judgments, as by Jehu against Joram, 2 Kings ix.

XX. As a general consideration, a private person should not assume the judgment of a controverted point, but follow possession. So Christ commanded tribute to be paid to Cæsar because his image was on the coin, that is, because he was in possession of the empire.

---

* This is not the modern Law of War, which makes a distinction between *Combatants* and *Non-Combatants*. See *Elements of Morality*, VI. 1060.

CHAPTER V.

Who may lawfully make War.

I. AS in other things, so in the actions of the will, there are commonly three kinds of efficient causes; the principal, the auxiliary, and the instruments. The principal effective cause in war is commonly he whose interest is concerned; in private war, a private person; in public war, a public power, generally a sovereign power. Whether war may be made by another, for those who do not themselves stir in it, we shall see elsewhere. In the mean time we hold by this maxim; that by Natural Law, every one is the vindicator of his own right: this is what hands were given for.

II. 1 But further: to help another when we can, is not only lawful but proper. Those who have written of Duties, rightly say that nothing is so useful to man as other men. But there are various ties of men to men, which invite them to mutual aid. Relatives in blood unite for mutual help, and neighbours are called upon for aid, and fellow-citizens. Hence the Roman cry in sudden distress, *Porro Quirites, et quiritari. Up Romans, for Romans.* Aristotle says that every one ought to use arms for himself, if he has received an injury, or to help relatives, benefactors, allies who are injured. And Solon taught that a State was fortunate, in which every one thinks the injuries of others his own.

2 If other ties are wanting, the tie of a common human nature is sufficient. Nothing belonging to mankind is indifferent to man. So Menander, Democritus, Lactantius.

III. When we speak of Instruments, we do not here mean weapons or the like, but voluntary agents, whose will is moved by the will of another. Such an Instrument is a son to a father, a servant to a master: So Democritus. So a subject in a State is the instrument of the Ruler.

IV. By Natural Law all subjects may take part in war; but some are excluded by special law, as slaves formerly among the Romans, and clerical persons now. Which law, like all of that kind, is to be understood with an exception of extreme necessity.

And so much generally of auxiliaries and subjects: special considerations will be treated in their own place.

RIGHTS OF WAR AND PEACE.

BOOK II.

CHAPTER I.

Of the Causes of War; and first, of Self-Defense and the Defense of our Property.

I. 1 LET us come to the causes of war; I mean justificatory causes; for there are causes which operate on the ground of utility, distinct from those which depend on justice; and these again may be distinguished from occasional causes, or the first collision, as the stag in the war of Turnus and Æneas. These are sometimes confounded. [See Polybius, Livy, Elian, Diodorus.]

2 These justificatory causes are properly our subject. The necessity of just causes for war is acknowledged. [See Dionysius, Demosthenes, Dio Cassius, Cicero.]

3 Just cause is requisite for public no less than for private war. Seneca complains that the State forbids homicide on a small scale, but commands it on a large one. It is true that wars undertaken

by public authority have peculiar jural effects, as public sentences have; but they are not therefore blameless, except there be a reason for them.   If Alexander made war on the Persians without cause, he was rightly called a robber by the Scythians, by Seneca, by Lucan, by the Indians; and treated as an equal by a pirate.   Philip his father did the like.   Augustine says, *Without justice what is empire, but robbery on a great scale?*   So Lactantius.

4 A just cause of War is injury done us, and nothing else.   Augustine says, *The Injustice* (that is the injury) *of the adverse party makes a war just.*   The formula of the Roman Heralds [in declaring war] was, *I call you to witness that that people is unjust, and does not perform its obligations.*

II. 1 There are evidently as many sources of war as there are of Actions at law; for when the judgments of tribunals cease to be of force, war begins.   Now Actions are either on account of injury done, or not yet done: Actions for injury not yet done, are when security is sought that an offence shall not be committed, or that reparation shall be made for an incumbent loss, or an injunction that no force be used.   Actions for injury done, are either that it be repaired, or punished; injury to be repaired regards either what is or was ours, as when we reclaim our property, or claim an obligation; or it regards what is owing to us, either by contract, or for wrong done us, or by appointment of law.   An act regarded as punishable gives rise to accusation and public trial.

2 Most writers state three just causes of war; defense, recovery of property, and punishment of wrong; which three we find mentioned in the proclamation of Camillus against the Gauls: *All that we may lawfully defend, recover, revenge.*   [Compare this with Plato and Seneca.]   The formula of the Roman Heralds was, *What things were to be given, done, and discharged, they have not given, done, and discharged.* [See Sallust; Augustine.]

3 Such is the natural feeling of Justice among nations.   [See Diodorus, Livy, Aristotle, Curtius.]

Therefore the first cause of a just war is an injury not yet done which menaces body or goods.

III. If the body be menaced by present force with danger of life not otherwise evitable, war is lawful, even to the slaying of the aggressor, as we have before said, in proving some private war to be lawful.   And this right of defense arises from the natural right of self-protection, not from .the injustice or fault of another who makes the danger.   And therefore this right of self-protection is not taken away, even if the aggressor be blameless; if, for instance, he be a soldier acting *bonâ fide;* or if he take me for another than I am, or if he be insane or a sleepwalker, such as we read of; it is sufficient that I am not bound to suffer what he attempts to inflict; just as if a wild beast were to attack me.

IV. 1 Whether innocent persons, who, interposing prevent the defense or flight without which death cannot be avoided may be cut down or trampled down, is a question. There are who think it lawful, even Divines. And certainly if we only look at Natural Law, that cares much less for ties of society, than for the defense of the individual. But the law of love, especially the Evangelical law, which commands us to regard another as ourselves, plainly does not permit this.

2 Thomas Aquinas well says, if it be rightly taken, that a man killed in self-defense is not killed by intention: not that sometimes, if no other way of safety appear, it may not be lawful to do that of set purpose, which will cause the death of the aggressor; but that such death is not chosen as something primarily intended, as in judicial punishment it is, but it is chosen as the only thing which is then possible; since he who is attacked, even then, ought to do anything by which the assailant may be scared away, or deprived of power, rather than by which he may be killed.

V. 1 Present danger is here required, and imminent in a point of time. I confess indeed that if the aggressor be taking up weapons, and in such a way that he manifestly does so with the intent to kill, the deed may be anticipated; for in moral things, as in natural, there is no point without a certain latitude: but they are in great error who allow any fear [however slight] as a right of killing for prevention. It is well said by Cicero that most injuries proceed from fear, he who meditates hurting another, fearing that if he do not do so, he will suffer some evil. So Clearchus in Xenophon, Cato for the Rhodians. [Sec.] Gellius says, a man is not to act like a gladiator, who must kill or be killed. So Cicero, quoted by Quintilian: Euripides, Thucydides, Livy. Quintilian quotes, *Who allowed you such fear?* And so Livia in Dio. [See.]

2 If any one direct against us violence not present; as if he make a conspiracy, or lay an ambush, or put poison in our way, or assail us with a false accusation, false testimony, or iniquitous judgment; I deny that he may be lawfully slain, if either the danger may be otherwise avoided, or it be not certain that it cannot be otherwise avoided. For delay allows recourse to many remedies and many chances; as we say, between the cup and the lip. Although there are not wanting both Jurists and Divines who extend the indulgence further. But the other opinion, which is the better and safer, is also not without its authorities.

VI. What shall we say of peril of mutilation of limb? Since the loss of a limb, especially of a principal one, is very grievous, and nearly equal to loss of life; and since, moreover, it can hardly be known whether it do not bring in its train loss of life; if it cannot otherwise be avoided, I think the author of such danger may be slain.

VII. Whether the same be lawful in defense of chastity, can scarcely be doubted, since not only common estimation, but the divine law, makes chastity of the same value as life. [He refers to Deut. xxii. 25, *If a man find a betrothed damsel in the field*, &c., the *man shall die;* which J. B. observes, hardly justifies his saying that chastity is on a par with life.] And so Paulus the Jurist decided. An example occurs in a Tribune of Marius, killed by a soldier, in Cicero and Quintilian. There are also examples of men in such cases killed by women. Such Chariclea in Hierocles justifies. [See.]

VIII. Though, as we have said, it be lawful to kill him who is preparing to kill, yet he acts more laudably who would rather be killed than kill; this is granted by some, making the exception of a person whose life is important to many. But to impose this rule, contrary to forbearance, on all whose lives concern other persons, seems very unsafe. It must, I think, be restricted to those whose duty it is to protect others from force; such as companies on the road, who are under such an engagement, and public Rulers: as Lucan says. [See.]

IX. 1 On the other hand, it may happen that because the life of the aggressor is useful to many, he cannot be killed without sin; and that, not only by the divine law, but by Natural Law. For Natural Law not only respects what corrective justice dictates, but also contains in itself acts of other virtues, as temperance, fortitude, prudence, as in certain circumstances not only good but obligatory. Now benevolence binds to act as we have said.

2 Vasquius says that a prince, when he insults an innocent man, ceases to be a prince: but nothing can be less true or more dangerous. For as ownership, so political authority, is not lost by delinquency, except the law so direct. But there never was a law that such authority should cease by an offence against a private person; and I believe, never will be. And what Vasquius lays down as the foundation of this and many other inferences, that all authority looks to the good of those who obey, not of those who command, even if it were universally true, is nothing to the purpose. For a thing does not fail because its utility in some one point fails. What he adds, that the safety of the community is desired by each for his own sake, and therefore each must prefer his own safety to that of the community, does not hang together. For we desire the safety of the community for our own sake, but not our own sake only, but that of others also. [J. B. doubts whether this be conclusive.]

3 The opinion of those who think that friendship arises from need only, is false, and rejected by the soundest philosophers; for we have a natural tendency to friendship. And that I should prefer to my sole good the good of many, benevolence often counsels, sometimes commands. So Seneca and Ambrose. [See.]

X. 1 If any one be in danger of receiving a buffet, or the like evil, some hold that he has a right to protect himself by killing his enemy. If merely corrective justice be regarded, I do not dissent. For though a buffet and death are very unequal, yet he who is about to do me an injury, thereby gives me a Right, that is a moral claim against him, *in infinitum,* so far as I cannot otherwise repel the evil.

And even benevolence *per se* does not appear to bind us to the advantage of him who does us wrong. But the Gospel law has made every such act unlawful: for Christ commands us to take a buffet, rather than hurt our adversary; how much less may we kill him? We must therefore beware of the doctrine of Covarruvias, that with Natural Law in our minds, we cannot conceive anything permitted by natural reason which is not permitted by God, since God is Nature itself. For God, who is the Author of nature in such a way that he is above Nature, has a right to prescribe laws to us concerning the things which by nature are free and undetermined; much more, that that be duty which by nature is good, though not duty.

2 It is wonderful, since the will of God appears so clearly in the Gospel, that there should be found Theologians, and Christian Theologians, who not only think killing may be permitted to avoid a buffet, but even when a buffet has been received, if the striker flies, for the recovery of honour, as it is called. This seems to me very far removed from reason and piety. For honour is an opinion of one's own excellence; and he who bears such an injury shews himself excellently patient, and so increases his honour rather than diminishes. Nor does it make any difference if some of corrupt judgment turn this virtue into a disgrace by artificial names: for those perverse judgments neither change the fact nor its value. And not only the ancient Christians said this, but also the philosophers, who said it was the part of a little mind not to be able to bear contumely, as we shall shew elsewhere.

3 Hence it appears also that that is wrong which is delivered by most writers, that defense with slaying is lawful, that is by Divine Law, (for I do not dispute that it is by Natural Law,) when flight without danger is possible: namely, because flight is ignominious, especially in a man of noble family. In truth there is, then, no ignominy, but a false opinion of ignominy, to be despised by those who follow virtue and wisdom. In this matter I rejoice that I have with me the opinion, among the Jurists, of Molinæus.

What I have said of a buffet and of flight, is to be understood of other things, by which our true estimation is not damaged.

But if any one say something of us, which if believed, would detract from our reputation among good men, what then? There are who teach that he also may be slain: very wrongly, and even contrary to Natural Law; for such slaying is not a course fitted to protect our reputation.

XI. Let us come to injuries by which our property is attacked.

If we regard corrective justice, I do not deny that in order to preserve our goods, the robber, if need be, may be killed; for the difference that there is between things and life, is compensated by the preference to be given to the innocent, and the condemnation incurred by the robber, as we have said. Whence it follows that if we regard Natural Law alone, the thief flying with his plunder may, if the goods cannot otherwise be recovered, be slain with a missile. So

F

Demosthenes against Aristocrates.   [See.]   Nor does benevolence oppose this as a command; setting aside human and divine law; except the thing stolen be a trifle which may be contemned; an exception rightly added by some.

XII.   1 Let us look at the sense of the Hebrew Law, (Exod. xxii. 2) with which agrees the law of Solon, and of the Twelve Tables, and Plato's *Laws*. These laws all agree in distinguishing the nocturnal from the diurnal thief*. Some think that this is because by night we cannot tell whether he is a thief or a murderer, and therefore may kill him as a murderer. Others think it is because by night we have less chance of recovering the property. I think that neither is the true ground; but this; that no one ought to be slain directly for the sake of mere things, which would be done if I were to kill an unarmed flying thief with a missile, and so recover my goods: but if I am myself in danger of life, then I may repel the danger even with danger to the life of another; nor does this cease to hold, however I have come into that danger, whether by trying to retain my property, or to recover it, or to capture the thief; for in all these cases I am acting lawfully according to my right.

2 The difference depends then on this; that by night there is no testimony to be had; and therefore if the thief be found slain, credit is to be given to him who says that he slew him in defending his life: that is, if he be found with any hurtful instrument. Deut. xxii. 2: *If a thief be found breaking up*, should be translated, *with a weapon for breaking through*. So Jer. ii. 34.

So the law of the Twelve Tables forbids the diurnal thief to be killed, except he defended himself with a weapon. On the other hand, Ulpian teaches that a man who kills a nocturnal thief does it with impunity, if he could not without peril avoid it.

3 And therefore, as I have said, the presumption is in favour of him who kills the nocturnal thief; but if there be testimony by which it appears that the slayer was not in danger of his life, the presumption ceases, and he is guilty of homicide. Add to this, that the law of the Twelve Tables required him who discovered a thief, either diurnal or nocturnal, to cry out aloud; namely, that neighbours or magistrates might come together for help and testimony. And as such concourse is easier by day than by night, therefore more credence is given in the case of the nocturnal danger.

The case is similar with regard to the Hebrew law, Deut. xxii. 23, which directs that a maid who has been forced in the field is to be believed, but in the city, not, *because she cried not being in the city*.

4 To this is to be added, that in what happens by night, we have no means of knowing the extent of the danger, therefore it is more terrible.

And therefore the Hebrew, like the Roman law, directs that which benevolence recommends, that no one should be slain only because

* See *Elements of Morality*, 665.

he takes a thing, but only if he who defends it comes into danger. Maimonides says, that the slaying of a man is permitted to a private person only to preserve what, lost, cannot be recovered, life and chastity.

XIII. 1 What shall we say of the Gospel law? That it permits what the Mosaic law permitted; or that in this, as in other cases, the Gospel is more perfect than the Law, and requires more of us? I do not doubt that it does require more; for if Christ direct us to give up our coat and cloak, and Paul, to suffer unjust loss, rather than have recourse to the bloodless contest of law; they would have directed us to give up things of greater value, rather than put to death a man, the image of God, and sprung of the same blood with ourselves. Wherefore if our property can be preserved without peril of slaying, it is well; but if not, it is to be given up: except it be something on which our life and that of our family depends, and which cannot be recovered at law: as for instance, if the thief be unknown, and we have some hope that the matter will end without fatal consequences.

2 And though almost all, both Jurists and Theologians, hold that we may not only kill a man in defense of our property, but beyond that limit; as, if he be running off with what he has taken; yet we have no doubt that the opinion which we have stated was that of the early Christians. So Augustine. But this discipline has been relaxed by time.

XIV. It is made a question whether the civil law, when it permits us to kill a thief with impunity, does not give us a Right to do so; since the civil law has the Right of life and death. But this is not so. In the first place, the Civil Law has not the Right of life and death in all cases, but only in cases of great crimes. The opinion of Scotus is probable, that we have no right to condemn any one to death except for the crimes so visited in the Mosaic Law, or those which are of the same atrocity. In fact, in so grave a case, we cannot have a knowledge of the divine will which can satisfy our minds, except from that law; which certainly does not punish theft with death. And moreover, the law neither does nor ought to give the Right of privately putting to death those who deserve death, except in very atrocious crimes; otherwise tribunals would be useless. Wherefore if the law allows us in any case to kill a thief with impunity, it takes away the punishment, but does not give the Right.

XV. It follows, from what has been said, that private persons may join in single combat in two cases; first, if an assailant gives us the choice of single combat, being ready to kill us otherwise without combat; and secondly, if the king or magistrate set two condemned persons to fight in such a combat; in which case they may take their chance of surviving. But he who gives such command does not seem to do his duty well; for if the death of one was enough, it was better that he who should die should be chosen by lot.

XVI. What has been said of the right of defending ourselves and our property, more peculiarly relates to private war, but so that it may be adapted to public war, attending to the diversity of conditions. For in private war the Right is momentary, and ceases as soon as the judge can be referred to. But public war does not arise, except when the judge's authority does not exist, or ends, has a prolonged character, and is constantly sustained by the accession of new losses and injuries. Besides in private war, defense alone is considered; but the public powers have the right not only of defending, but also of obtaining satisfaction. Hence they may prevent force not present, and threatening from afar; not directly (for that, as we have taught, is unjust,) but indirectly, by taking satisfaction for a delinquency begun, but not consummated *: of which we shall treat elsewhere.

XVII.   There is an intolerable doctrine in some writers, that by the Law of Nations we may rightly take arms against a power which is increasing, and may increase, so as to be dangerous. Undoubtedly, in deliberating of war, this may come into consideration, not as a matter of justice, but as a matter of utility; so that if the war be just on other accounts, it may, on this account, be prudent; and this is what the arguments of authors come to. But that the possibility of suffering force gives us the right of using force, is contrary to all notion of equity. Such is human life, that we are never in complete security. We must seek protection against uncertain fears from Divine Providence, and from blameless caution, not from force.

XVIII.   1 Nor do we agree that those who have deserved war, have a Right to defend themselves; namely, because few persons are content with taking satisfaction to the mere extent of the injury. For that fear of an uncertainty cannot give a Right to force: and so, a person accused of a crime has not a right of forcibly resisting the ministers of justice, for fear of being over-punished.

2 He who has injured another ought first to offer him satisfaction at the arbitration of a good man; and if this fail, his warfare will be righteous. So Hezekiah acted, 2 Kings xviii. 7, 14, and xix. 1. So Pontius the Samnite urged that this was all that could be required. [See Livy.]   So when the Thebans had done this, Aristides says that justice had passed over to their side.

* The broad differences marked in this article between public war and private self-defense shew how improperly the latter is called *war*. W. W.

CHAPTER II.

Of the Common Rights of Men.

I. WE treat now of the Causes of War; and first, of Injury done us with respect to what is ours. Some things are *ours* by the Common Right of mankind; others by our own Special Right. We will begin with the Common Right of mankind. This Right either directly regards corporal things, or certain acts. Corporal things are either unappropriated, or the property of some one. Unappropriated things are either such as cannot be appropriated, or such as can. Hence we must consider the origin of Property, or Ownership, which the jurists call *Dominium.*

II. 1 God gave the human race generally a right to the things of a lower nature, at the Creation, and again, after the Deluge. Every thing was common and undivided, as if all had one patrimony. Hence each man might take for his use what he would, and consume what he could. Such a Universal Use was then a Right, as Property is now. What each one had taken, another could not take from him by force without wrong. Cicero compares this state of things to the theatre, which though it be common, yet when a man has taken any place, it is his.

And this state might have continued, if men had remained in great simplicity, or had lived in great mutual good will. One of these two conditions, a community of goods arising from extreme simplicity, we may see in some of the peoples of America, who have lived for many generations in that state without inconvenience. The other, a community of goods from mutual charity, was exhibited formerly among the

Essenes, and then among the first Christians at Jerusalem, and now in many places among Ascetics. The simplicity of the first races of men was proved by their nakedness. They were rather ignorant of vices than acquainted with virtue: as Trogus says of the Scythians. So Tacitus, Macrobius, the Book of Wisdom, St Paul. Their business was the worship of God, of which the Tree of Life was a symbol, (see Revelation xxii. 2). They lived easily on what the earth, without labour, spontaneously produced.

2 But men did not continue in this simple and innocent life, but applied their minds to various arts, of which the symbol was the Tree of the Knowledge of good and evil; that is, of those things which may be used ill or well. So Philo, Solomon, Dio Prusæensis. [See.] The oldest arts, agriculture and pasture, appeared in the first brothers (Cain and Abel); not without a division of possessions already shew-ing itself, and even not without bloodshed. And at length when the good were corrupted by intercourse with the bad, came the life of the Giants, that is, times of violence. And when the world was cleared by the Deluge, instead of that ferine life, followed the pursuit of plea-sure, with wine and lawless love.

3 But the concord was especially broken by a more generous vice, ambition: of which the Tower of Babel was the sign; and then different men divided the earth among them and possessed it. Yet still there remained among neighbours a community, not of their flocks and herds, but of their pastures; for there was enough for all for a time: until, cattle increasing, the land was divided, not according to nations as before, but according to families. And some made and occupied their own wells, things most necessary in a thirsty region, and not sufficing for many. This is the account of the sacred history, sufficiently agreeing with the account given by philosophers and poets.

4 There we learn what was the cause why men departed from the community of things, first of moveables, then of immoveables: namely, because when they were not content to feed on spontaneous produce, to dwell in caves, to go naked, or clothed in bark or in skins, but had sought a more exquisite kind of living, there was need of industry, which particular persons might employ on particular things. And as to the common use of the fruits of the earth, it was prevented by the dispersion of men into different localities, and by the want of justice and kindness which interfered with a fair division of labour and sus-tenance.

5 And thus we learn how things became Property; not by an act of the mind alone: for one party could not know what another party wished to have for its own, so as to abstain from that; and several parties might wish for the same thing; but by a certain pact, either express, as by division, or tacit, as by occupation: for as soon as com-munity was given up, and while division was not instituted, it must be supposed to have been a matter of agreement among all, that what

each had occupied he should have as his own. So Cicero, Quintilian. And the ancients when they called Ceres *the Author of Laws*, and her festival *Thesmophoria, Law-bearing*, had this meaning; that from the division of land arose a new origin of Rights.

III. 1 This being laid down, we say that the sea, whether taken as a whole, or as to its principal parts, could not become property. And as some concede this with regard to private persons, but not with regard to peoples, we prove it first from a moral reason; namely, that the cause why community was given up, here ceases. For the magnitude of the sea is so great that it is sufficient for all peoples for every use, either of drawing water, fishing, or navigation. The same might be said of the air, if there was any use of it to which the use of the earth is not also necessary, as in bird-catching it is; and therefore this employment is governed by the ownership of the land.

The same is true of sandy bays, where there is nothing which can be cultivated, and the only use, procuring sand, is inexhaustible.

2 There is also a natural reason which prevents the sea from being made property; namely, because occupation can only be applied to a thing which is bounded. [Thucydides, Isocrates.] Now fluids are in themselves unbounded, as Aristotle says; and cannot be occupied except as they are contained in something else; as lakes and ponds are occupied, and rivers as far as their banks go. But the sea is not contained by the land, being equal to the land or greater, so that the ancients say the land is bounded by the sea. [Apollonius, Sulpicius Apollinaris, Livy, Seneca, Lucan.] Nor are we to feign a division of the sea: for when the earth was first divided, the sea was for the most part unknown; and therefore we cannot imagine any way in which distant nations could agree as to such division.

3 Therefore those things which were common to all, and were not divided in the first division, now do not become property by division, but by occupation, and are divided only after they have become property.

IV. Let us come to those things which may become property, but are not yet so. Such are many places hitherto uncultivated, uninhabited islands, wild beasts, fishes, birds. But here two remarks are to be made: first, that there are two kinds of occupation, in totality, and in particular shares. The former kind is commonly made by the people or the Ruler of the people; the other by individuals, but rather by assignation than by free occupation. And if anything occupied in totality is not assigned to special owners, that is not free of ownership, but belongs to the ownership of the first occupier, say, the people or the king. Such are rivers, lakes, marshes, woods, rocky mountains.

V. Concerning wild beasts, fishes, birds, this also is to be remarked; that he who has the ownership of the land and water, may, on that ground, prevent any one from taking those creatures, and thus acquiring property in them. The reason is, that it is morally necessary to the government of a people that they who mingle with the people even for a time, which is done by entering the territory, must conform to its institutions. Nor is this disproved by what we often read in the Roman Law, that *jure naturæ* or *jure gentium* men are free to pursue animals of chase. For this is true as long as no Civil Law interferes: as the Roman Law left many things in that primeval state which other nations settled otherwise. And when the Civil Law has settled anything otherwise, the Natural Law itself directs that it be obeyed. For though the Civil Law cannot ordain anything which the Natural Law prohibits, nor prohibit what that ordains: yet it may circumscribe natural liberty, and forbid what was lawful by Natural Law; and even interfere to prevent an ownership which might be acquired by Natural Law.

VI. 1 Let us consider whether men have any Common Right to those things which are already made private property. Some may think that this is a strange question, since property seems to have absorbed all the Right which flowed from the common state of things. But this is not so. For we must consider what was the intention of those who introduced private property: which we must suppose to have been, to recede as little as possible from natural equity. For if even written laws are to be construed in that sense as far as possible, much more is mere usage, which is not fettered by written words.

2 Hence it follows, that in extreme necessity, the pristine right of using things revives, as if they had remained common: for in all laws, and thus in the law of ownership, extreme necessity is excepted.

3 Hence the rule, that in a voyage, if the provisions run short, what each one has must be thrown into the common stock. So to preserve my house from a conflagration which is raging, my neighbour's house may be pulled down: and ropes or nets may be cut, of which any ship has run foul, if it cannot be extricated otherwise. All which rules are not introduced by the Civil Law, but by the interpretations of it.

4 For among Theologians also, it is a received opinion, that in such a necessity, if any one take what is necessary to his life from any other's property, he does not commit theft: of which rule the reason is, not that which some allege, that the owner of the property is bound to give so much to him that needs it, out of charity: but this, that all things must be understood to be assigned to owners with some such benevolent exception of the Right thus primitively assigned. For if the first dividers had been asked what was their intention, they would have given such a one as we have stated. [Of necessity, see Seneca, Cicero, Curtius.]

VII. But cautions are to be applied, that this liberty go not too far.

First, that we must first endeavour in every way to avoid this necessity in some other manner, as by applying to the magistrate, or by trying whether we cannot obtain the use of things from the owner by entreaty. Plato allows a man to take water from his neighbour's well if in his own he has dug down to the chalk, seeking water; and Solon, if he has dug in his own ground forty cubits. For as Plutarch says, he thought that necessity was to be relieved, not idleness encouraged; and Xenophon says to the Sinopians, If we are not allowed to buy, we must take; not from contempt of Rights, but from necessity.

VIII. Secondly, such liberty is not granted, if the possessor be in like necessity; for *cœteris paribus*, the case of the possessor is the better. Lactantius says, that he does not do amiss who abstains to thrust a drowning man from a plank, or a wounded man from his horse, even for the sake of his own preservation. So Cicero: and Curtius.

IX. Thirdly, that when it is possible, restitution be made. There are some who think otherwise on this point, and consider that, as the man used his own Right, he is not bound to restitution. But it is more true that this Right was not plenary, but limited by the burthen of restoring what was taken, when the necessity was over: for such a Right suffices to preserve the natural equity of the case against the rigour of ownership.

X. Hence we may collect how he who carries on a righteous war may lawfully seize a place situate in a land which is not at war; namely, if there be a danger, not imaginary, but certain, that the enemy will seize that place, and thence do irreparable damage: and next, on condition that nothing be taken which is not necessary for this purpose of caution, for example, the mere custody of the place, leaving to the true owner the jurisdiction and the revenues: finally, if it be done with the intention of restoring the custody to the true owner as soon as the necessity is over: Livy says, *Enna retained by a step necessary, or unjustifiable;* because in such a case every thing is unjustifiable which is not necessary. So the Greeks who were with Xenophon, in their need took the ships which they found passing, spared the lading for its owners, fed and paid the sailors. This then is the first Right which, when ownership has been established, remains out of the old community of goods; namely, the Right of Necessity.

XI. Another Right is the Right of Harmless Use. *Why,* says Cicero, *when a man can without any loss to himself, should he not impart what is useful to the receiver, and not inconvenient to the giver?* So Seneca denies that we have a Right to refuse a man permission to light his fire at ours. So in Plutarch, we are not to destroy meat when we have more than we need, nor to conceal or to muddy a spring of water, when we have used it, nor to pull down guide-posts or sea-marks which have done their service to us: they are to be left to be of use to others.

XII. So a river, as it is a river, is the property of the people within whose boundary it flows, or of him under whose authority the people is. He may run a pier into the river; and what is produced in the river is his. But the same river, as it is flowing water, remains common, for drawing or drinking: so Ovid. Water is in this way public property. So Virgil.

XIII. 1 And so land, and rivers, and any part of the sea which is become the property of any people, ought not to be shut against those who have need of transit for just cause; say, because being expelled from their own country they seek a place to settle; or because they seek traffic with a remote nation; or because they seek their own in a just war. The reason is the same as above; that ownership might be introduced with the reservation of such a use, which is of great advantage to the one party and of no disadvantage to the other; and the authors of ownership are to be supposed to have intended this*.

2 We have a valuable example of this in the history of Moses, who applied first to the Edomites, and then to the Amorites (Numb. xx. and xxi.), for leave to pass through the land on condition of going by the king's high way, and paying for what they took. And when these conditions were rejected, he on that account made war on the Amorites; justly, as Augustine says.

3 The Greeks, of the ten thousand under Clearchus, claimed the same Right; so Agesilaus, Lysander, the Batavi, Cimon. The middle opinion is the true one; that a transit is first to be requested; but if denied, may be asserted by force. So Agesilaus, when the king of Macedon, thus applied to, said he would consult, replied, *Let him consult, meantime we shall pass through.*

4 Nor can any one properly object that he is afraid of the multitude of those who make the transit. For my Right is not taken away by your fear; and this the less, because there are ways of providing against danger; as by sending the body of persons in small parties, and without arms, as the Colognese proposed to the Germans; by placing guards at the expense of the transit-seekers; by taking hostages. So too fear of war from him against whom the transit-seeker makes a righteous war, does not justify him in refusing. Nor is it enough to say that he may pass another way: for every one might say the same, and thus the Right of Transit be destroyed. It is enough if he pass *bonâ fide* by the shortest and most convenient way. If indeed he who seeks transit makes an unjust war, or brings my enemies with him, I may deny the transit; for in such a case I might meet him on his own ground and stop his way.

5 Transit is to be granted not only to persons, but to merchandize; for no one has a right to impede one nation in cultivating trade with another remote nation; for it is of advantage to the human race that such intercourse should be permitted: nor is that a damage to any one; for if any one misses some gain which he had reckoned

---

* Gronovius in a long note gives very strong reasons why this Right of Transit cannot be held, and cases in which it has been negatived.

upon but never had, that is not to be reckoned loss*. So Philo, Plutarch, Libanius, Euripides, Florus.

XIV. 1 It is made a question whether, when merchandize thus passes through a country, the Rulers of that country may impose a transit-duty. And certainly whatever taxes have no respect to the articles of merchandize, cannot equitably be imposed on them. So neither a capitation tax, nor taxes for the general purposes of the State, can be required of foreigners passing through.

2 But if, either to provide security for the merchandize, or for this along with other objects, a burthen fall on the country, a tax may be imposed on the merchandize, if it do not go beyond the measure of the cause. That is the measure of the equity, as of other taxes, so of duties on merchandize. Thus Solomon (1 Kings x. 28) had a tax upon horses and linen yarn which passed the isthmus of Suez. So transit duty was demanded by the Gebanites, Massilians, Corinthians, Romans. And the jurists have much to say of the passage of rivers.

3 But this limit is often transgressed; as by the Arabian chiefs.

XV. 1 It ought also be permitted to those that travel through the land, to tarry there for a short time for the sake of health or other just cause; for this also is a harmless use. So Ilioneus in Virgil; and when the Megareans complained that the Athenians excluded them from their ports *contrary to the known rules of justice,* their complaint was approved by the Greeks.

2 It is consequent upon this, that the transit-maker may erect a momentary hut, on the shore for instance, though the shore be occupied already. For the rule that it requires the order of a judge to build on the shore or in the sea, refers to permanent structures.

XVI. Further, a place of settlement is not to be denied to foreigners who are expelled from their own country; provided that they submit to the constituted government, and such other regulations as are requisite to avoid confusion. So Virgil, Dionysius of Halicarnassus, Eratosthenes, the Eolians, Rhodians, Carians, Lacedæmonians, Cumæans. But when the Minyans coming thus, asked the Lacedæmonians to share their power with them, they were injurious aggressors, as Herodotus speaks; and Valerius says that they turned a benefit into an injury.

XVII. And if there be any portion of the soil of a territory desert and barren, that also is to be given up to immigrants who ask for it; or even may be rightly occupied by them; because that which is not cultivated, is not to be conceived as occupied, except as to the ownership, which continues to be in the old people. So the Latin Aborigines granted land to the Romans; so Dio Prusæensis says; so the Ansibarii in Tacitus held: though their general doctrine was wrongly

---

* Gronovius notes that this is much too lax and liberal, and contrary to the practice of nations, as he shews by examples.

applied in that case; for the lands were occupied: so the Romans rightly resisted the Senones on the same ground.

XVIII. After the Common Right to things follows the Common Right to acts; and this is given either simply or hypothetically. There is given *simply* a Right to those acts without which life cannot conveniently be sustained, and others which may be compared with these. The same necessity is not required here, as in taking what belongs to another; for here we do not speak of what may be done, the owner being unwilling; but of the mode of acquiring things with the owner's consent; asserting only, that he may not prevent the acquisition either by law or by conspiracy. For such impediment in such matters is contrary to the nature of human society. This is, as Ambrose says, to separate ourselves from the intercourse of our common parent; to deny what is given for all; to tear up the root of our common life. For we do not now speak of superfluities, the mere instruments of pleasure; but of the necessaries of life, food, clothing, medicaments.

XIX. We say then that these things, all men have a Right to purchase at a fair price; excepting when they from whom they are asked, themselves need them: as in a great scarcity of corn, it is forbidden to be sold. And yet even in such a necessity, foreigners once admitted cannot be expelled, but the common evil is to be borne in common, as Ambrose says.

XX. We have not the same Right to sell what we have; for every one is free to decide what he will acquire, and what not. Thus formerly the Belgians would not admit wine and other foreign merchandize: and the Arabians admitted some articles and not others.

XXI. 1 In the Right of which we speak is included, we conceive, the Right of seeking and making marriages with neighbouring nations: if for instance, a population entirely male expelled from some other place come thither. For to live without marriage, though not entirely repugnant to human nature, is repugnant to the nature of most men. Celibacy suits only superior minds: therefore men ought not to be deprived of the means of getting wives. So Romulus in Livy: so Canuleius. So Augustine.

2 The Laws of some nations, which deny marriage to strangers, either depend on this ground, that at the time when they were made there was no people which had not a sufficient supply of women; or they do not treat of marriage in general, but of that marriage which is legitimate in a peculiar sense, that is, which produces some special kind of legal effects.

XXII. The Right *hypothetical* to acts, refers to acts which any nation has permitted to strangers generally: in this case, if one people be excluded from such acts, it is wronged. Thus if it be permitted to strangers to catch beasts, fish, birds, in certain places, or to get pearls; to take legacies, to sell goods, to contract marriages, even without the plea of want of women, that cannot be denied to one particular people, except on account of a delinquency; on which account the rest of the Hebrews took away from the Benjamites the right of intermarriage with them.

XXIII. But what is said of such permissions, is to be understood of such things as are permitted in virtue of natural liberty not taken away by law; not of those things which are permitted by indulgence, as a relaxation of law: for there is no wrong in denying an indulgence. And thus Francis Victoria and Molina may be reconciled.

XXIV. I recollect a question raised, Whether it be lawful for one people to make an agreement with another, that they will sell to them alone fruits of a certain kind, which grew nowhere else. I conceive it to be lawful, if the buying people be ready to sell them to others at an equitable price: for it makes no difference to other nations, from whom they buy what gratifies their natural desires. And one party may anticipate another in a gainful trade; especially if the people making this bargain have taken the other people under its protection, and have incurred expense on that account. Such forestalling and monopoly, made with the intention which I have described, is not contrary to Natural Law; although sometimes it is prohibited by Civil Law, on account of public utility.

CHAPTER III.

Of the original acquisition of Things. The Sea, Rivers.

I. A THING may become our property by acquisition, original or derivative. Original acquisition formerly, when the human race could meet together and agree, might be made by division; at present it is only made by occupation.

II. It may be said perhaps that property may be originally acquired by being given on conditions, as a farm; or deposited as a pledge: but on consideration, it will appear that such ownership is not new, except in its form; by its own virtue, it resided in the ownership of the former owner.

III. Paulus the Jurist adds, to the enumeration of the causes of acquisition, this, if we have made anything, so as to cause it to exist. But since, in the course of nature, nothing can be made except out of pre-existing matter, if that matter was ours, the ownership continues when it assumes a new form; if the matter was no one's property, this acquisition comes under occupation; if the matter belonged to another, the thing made is not ours alone, as will appear below.

IV. 1 Therefore we have to consider occupation; which, after that primitive time, is the only natural and original mode of acquisition. In things which are properly no one's, two things are occupable; the lordship, and the ownership, so far as it is distinguished from the lordship. Kings have power over all things (the lordship); individuals have property (ownership.) The city is the king's; but nevertheless in the city each has his own. Lordship has two kinds of matter subject to it; primary, persons, which matter alone sometimes suffices; as in the case of a body of people (men, women, and children,) seeking a new settlement; and secondary, a place, which is called a *territory*.

2 Therefore, though lordship and ownership are commonly acquired by one act, they are really distinct. The ownership may pass not only to citizens, but to strangers; while the lordship remains in the same hands as before. So Siculus *De Conditionibus Agrorum.* Demosthenes uses different words for landed property in our own territory and in another.

V. In a place in which the lordship is already occupied, the right of occupying moveable things (as wild beasts, birds, &c.) may be barred by the Civil Law, as we have said (B. II. c. ii. § v.). For the right to take such things is from a permission of Natural Law; not from a command, directing that there shall always be such liberty. Nor does human society require that it should be so. If any one should say that it appears to be a part of *jus gentium* that such a liberty should exist; I reply, that although in any part of the earth this be or should be so received, yet it has not the force of a general compact among nations: but is the Civil Law of several nations distributively, which may be taken away by nations singly. There are several such points which the jurists say are *juris gentium*, in what relates to the division and acquisition of property.

VI. It is to be observed also, if we regard Natural Law alone, that there is no ownership except in a creature endowed with reason. But the *jus gentium* has introduced an assumption, on the ground of common utility, that infants and insane persons can receive and retain ownership, the human race, as it were, performing their parts for them. And in fact many things besides nature may constitute Rights, though nothing can constitute Rights against nature. Therefore this ownership which is thus introduced in favour of infants and the like by the custom of civilized nations, stops at the *primus actus,* the potential fact of having; and does not go on to the *actus secundus,* the operative fact of using. For alienation and similar processes in their very nature include the use of reason, which cannot exist in such agents. To which we may refer, Gal. iv. 1, *the heir, so long as he is a child, &c.*

VII. We have above begun to speak of the sea; we must now finish what we have to say on the subject.

Rivers may be held as by occupation, though neither their upper nor lower extremity be included in the territory; but cohere with superior or inferior water, or with the sea. It is sufficient that the greater part, that is, the sides, are inclosed with banks, and that a river is something small in comparison with the land.

VIII. By this it appears that a portion of the sea also may be occupied by him who possesses the land on each side: although it be open at one end, as a bay, or at both, as a strait; provided it be not such a portion of the sea as is too large to appear part of the land. And what is lawful to one people or king, seems also to be lawful to two or three, if they, in like manner, wish to occupy the sea which lies among their dominions. And thus two rivers which flow between two peoples are occupied by both, and thus are divided.

IX. 1 It must be confessed, however, that in the parts of the earth known to the Roman empire from the earliest times down to Justinian, it was a part of the Law of Nations that the sea could not be occupied by any people, even for purposes of fishery. Nor are they to be attended to who say, that since, in the Roman Law, the sea is called *commune omnium*, common to all, it is to be understood as common to Roman citizens. For, in the first place, the expressions are too general; as in Theophilus, Ulpian, Celsus. [See.] And next, the jurists distinguish these *publica populi*, public property of one people, from things common to all. So in the Institutions and Theophilus. [See.]

2 As to shores of the sea, Neratius said that they are not public as belonging to any one people, but as still in a state of nature, never having come to belong to any, not even any people. This seems to be contradicted by what Celsus says, that the shore within the bounds of the Roman authority belongs to the Roman people; but that the sea is common. The two may be reconciled, if we suppose that Neratius meant the use of the shore as far as it is used by navigators or travellers; but Celsus, so far as it is taken up for some permanent use, as for a building. For this, as Pomponius teaches us, was obtained only by application to the judge, as also the right of building in the sea.

X. 1 Though this is so, yet that the sea, in the sense which we have spoken of, is not occupied, nor can lawfully be occupied, is a result of institution, not of natural reason. For a river is public property, as we know; and yet the right of fishing in a certain bend of the river may belong to a private person by occupation: and Paulus pronounced, that if any one could have property in the sea, he might obtain a sentence of the court in the usual form, *uti possidetis*, since the case would be a private, not a public one; but in this he speaks, doubtless, of a small part of the sea, such as can be taken into private grounds, as was done by Lucullus and others. C. Sergius Orata *made seas of his own by shutting up estuaries*, as Valerius says. And this authority was used by Leo the Emperor, for appropriating the entrance of the Bosphorus by shutting it with piers.

2 Since a portion of the sea may become part of a private estate, namely, if it be included in the estate, and so small as to seem part of it, and if Natural Law does not prohibit this; why should not a portion of the sea included within the territory of a people or of several peoples be the property of those whose the shores are? provided that the size of that portion of the sea compared with the territory be not larger than the creek of the sea compared with the estate. And it is not a reason against this, that the sea is not included on all sides, as we may understand by the example of a river, and of the sea admitted into the heart of a city.

3 But many things which are permitted by nature, the Law of Nations, by a bond of common consent, has prohibited. Wherefore in those places in which such a Law of Nations is in force, and is not

suspended by common consent, any portion of the sea, even though small and mostly included by shores, is not the property of any people.

XI. It is further to be noted, that since, in those places in which that Law of Nations concerning the sea is not received, or is abolished, it is not to be inferred from the mere occupation of the land, that the sea is occupied: so also, that a mere mental act does not suffice for the occupation of the sea; but that there is need of some external act [as the presence of ships] by which the occupation may be understood to take place. And again, that if the possession which arose from occupation be given up by desertion, the sea forthwith returns to a state of nature; that is, to community of use; which was declared by Papinian to be the law respecting a shore not built on, and a fishery in a river.

XII. This is certain, that even he who holds the sea by occupation cannot prevent an unarmed and harmless navigation upon it; since even a transit of this character over land cannot be prohibited, which nevertheless is both less necessary, and more noxious*.

XIII. 1 The empire of the sea, claimed over a portion of it without any other property [on which it depends] might easily proceed from such claims as we have spoken of, nor do I conceive that the Law of Nations, of which we have spoken, would stand in the way. It has often been asserted and conceded; thus the Argives expostulated with the Athenians for allowing the Spartans to pass over the sea, whereas the treaty was that neither party should allow the enemies of the other to pass *through their domain.*

And in the truce, in the Peloponnesian war, the Megareans are permitted to navigate the sea contiguous to their and their allies' shores. So the sea is spoken of as part of the Roman empire, by Dio Cassius, Themistius, Appian, Dio Prusæensis, Virgil, Gellius. So the Massilians and the Sinopians.

2 The empire of a portion of the sea is, it would seem, acquired in the same way as other lordship; that is, as above stated, as belonging to a person, or as belonging to a territory : belonging to a person, when he has a fleet which commands that part of the sea; belonging to a territory, in so far as those who sail in that part of the sea can be compelled from the shore as if they were on land.

XIV. Hence he does nothing contrary to the Law of Nature and Nations, who, undertaking the care of assisting navigation by providing lighthouses and buoying sand-banks, imposes an equitable tax upon navigators; like the Roman Erythræan tax to meet the expense of the expedition against the pirates; and the passage dues which were levied by the Byzantines in their sea; and those which the Athenians levied in the same sea when they occupied Chrysopolis: [See Polybius.]

* The right of transit by land, which is here described as "more noxious," and used as an argument, was proved by assuming it to be absolutely innoxious. See B. II. c. ii. § xiii. W. W.

G

and what the Athenians formerly had levied in the Hellespont, as Demosthenes shews; and the Roman emperors, as Procopius mentions, in his time.

XV. 1 There are examples of treaties by which one people bound itself to another not to navigate beyond certain boundaries. Thus the kings of the region on the Red Sea, and the Egyptians, had a convention that the Egyptians should not come upon that sea with any ship of war, nor with more than one merchant-vessel. So the Athenians and Persians at the time of Cimon agreed that no armed Median ship should sail within the Cyanean and Chelidonian islands; and after the battle of Salamis, within the Cyaneans and Phaselis. In the truce of the Peloponnesian war, it was agreed that the Lacedæmonians should not send to sea ships of war, but only merchant-ships of not above 500 talents burthen. In the First Treaty of the Romans with the Carthaginians, it was agreed that the Romans and their allies should not navigate beyond Cape Fair (*Pulchrum Promontorium*), except compelled by tempest or hostile force; and that those who had come under such compulsion should only take necessaries, and should depart within five days: and in the Second Treaty it was agreed that the Romans should not plunder nor traffic beyond Cape Fair, Mastia, and Tarseium. In the peace with the Illyrians it was agreed that they should not navigate beyond Lissus with more than two barks, and those unarmed: in the peace with Antiochus, that he should not navigate beyond the promontories of Calycadnus and Sarpedon (in Cilicia), except with the ships which carried his subsidy, ambassadors, or hostages.

2 But these examples do not prove possession of the sea, or of the right of navigating, by occupation. For peoples as well as individuals may, by compact, concede to another not only the Rights which are theirs specially, but also those which they have in common with all men: and when this is done, we may say, what Ulpian said when an estate was sold on condition that the purchaser should not carry on a thunny fishery to the prejudice of the seller;—namely, that there could not be a servitude over the sea, but that the *bona fides* of the contract required that the rule of the sale should be observed; and therefore that the possessors and their successors were under a personal obligation to observe the condition.

XVI. 1 When a river changes its course, a question often arises between neighbouring peoples whether the boundary of the territory also changes, and whether the additions which the river makes to one side belong to the land to which they are added; which controversies are to be solved by regarding the nature and mode of the acquisition.

Those who write concerning land, tell us that there are three kinds, the *limitatus*, which is limited by an artificial boundary; the *assignatus per universitatem*, which is determined by its measured quantity, and the *arcifinius*, which is defined by natural boundaries,

as rivers or mountains.*   In the two former kinds, if the river changes
its course, the territory is not changed, and if any alluvial addition is
made to it, it is an accession to the property of the occupier of the
land.

2 In land defined by a river, its natural boundary, if the river
changes its course gradually, it changes also the boundary of the territory; and whatever the river adds to one side belongs to him to whose
land it is added; because each people must be supposed to have settled
their claims on the understanding that the river, as a natural terminus,
should divide them by a line drawn along its middle.   So Tacitus
speaks of the Rhine as a boundary, so Diodorus of another river; and
Xenophon calls such a river simply the *Horizont*, the boundary.

3 The ancients relate that the Achelous, perpetually changing its
course, was the constant cause of war between the Etolians and Acarnanians; and that Hercules confined it within banks, and thus put an
end to the quarrel.

XVII. 1 But this is only true if the river has not *at once* changed
its channel. For a river, as bounding territories, is not considered
simply as water, but as water flowing in a certain channel and bounded
by certain banks.   And therefore any addition or subtraction of particles which leaves to the whole the same general aspect, allows the
thing to be taken for the same.   But if the aspect of the whole be
changed at once, it becomes another thing.   If a river is dammed up
in the upper part, and turned into a new cut made by hand, it ceases
to be that river; and in like manner if the river leave its old bed and
break its way by a new channel, it is not the same river as before, but
a new river, the old one being extinguished.   And since, if the river
had dried up, the boundary of the territory would remain the middle
of the channel as it was just before; so, because the intention of the
peoples must be supposed to have been that their lands were to be
naturally divided by the river, but that if the river ceased to be, then
each should hold what he had held; therefore when the channel is
thus changed the same rule must be observed.

2 In doubtful cases, the territories which border on the river are
to be supposed to have that for their boundary: because nothing is
more suitable for separating the lands of different nations than a river
which is not easily crossed.

That national territories are defined by the rules of *ager limitatus*†
or *ager mensura comprehensus* more rarely happens; and then, not
from primeval occupation, but from concession, [or by treaty.]

XVIII. But though in doubtful cases, as we have said, national
territory extends to the middle of the river, it may happen, and some-

---

* Gronovius says that these distinctions are wrongly given by Grotius, and
wrongly applied; but Barbeyrac defends him.

† In modern times, national territories have frequently been defined by boundaries entirely artificial, as parallels of latitude, and meridians; of which the map
of America affords many examples. W. W.

times does, that the whole of the river belongs to one party; as when the second bank has been taken possession of at a later period, after the first bank and the river had been already occupied; or because the matter was so settled by compact.

XIX. 1 This also is worth observing; that there may be an original acquisition of those things which have had an owner, but have ceased to have one; as being derelict, or because the owners have been removed; for then things return into the state of nature in which they were at first.

2 This also is to be noted; that sometimes the first acquisitions of property are made by a people or its head in such a manner that not only the lordship, including that *jus eminens* of which we have spoken, (B. I. c. iii. § vi;) but that also the private ownership, was acquired at first generally for the people or its head; and then the property was distributed particularly in special lots to private persons, in such a manner that their ownership depended on that former ownership; if not in the same way as the ownership of a Vassal from that of Seignior, or the ownership of the tenant-farmer from that of the landlord, yet in some slighter way; as in fact there are many species of ownership: among which is the ownership of a trustee. So Seneca and Dio Prussæensis, Strabo, Tacitus, speak of various ways in which a thing may be mine. [See.]

3 And since private properties thus depend on the general proprietorship, if any portion of property ceases to have a special owner, it does not then become the property of the *occupier*, but reverts to the community, or to the superior lord. And a rule similar to this of Natural Law, might be introduced by Civil Law, without the reason we have given.

CHAPTER IV.

Of presumed Dereliction of Property, and the Occupation which follows; and how it differs from Usucaption and Prescription.

I. HERE arises a great difficulty concerning the right of usucaption, [by which a thing long used becomes the property of the possessor.] This Right is introduced by the Civil Law,[not by Natural Law,] for time, of its own nature, has no effective power; for nothing is done by time, though everything is done in time. Hence this right, as Vasquius thinks, cannot have place between two free peoples, or kings, or a people and a king; nor even between a king and a private person who is not his subject, nor between the subjects of two different kings or peoples: which appears to be true, except so far as things and acts are governed by the laws of the territory: [for a person in one territory, knowing the laws of another territory as to usucaption, may act accordingly, in questions of right between him and another person in the stranger territory.] Yet if we admit this, there seems to follow this very inconvenient conclusion, that controversies concerning kingdoms and their boundaries are not extinguished by any lapse of time; which not only tends to disturb the minds of many and to perpetuate wars, but is also repugnant to the common sense of mankind.

II. For [the authority of time and usage has been generally acknowledged in disputes on such subjects]. So in Judges xi. 13, 26, when the king of the Ammonites claimed the land from Arnon to Jabbok and Jordan, Joshua said that Israel had dwelt there 300 years; *why therefore did ye not recover them in that time?* And the Lacedæmonians in Isocrates lay it down as a rule most certain, and acknowledged by all nations, that public possessions, as well as private, are so confirmed by length of time that they cannot be taken away; on this ground they repel those who demand Messena. [See.] So Philip the Second of Macedon told Quintius that he would give up the cities which he had himself taken, but not those which had legitimately descended to him from his ancestors. Sulpitius in Livy, disputing against Antiochus, shews it to be unjust that because the Greeks in Asia had at one time been in subjection, he should make that the ground of an asserted right of reducing them to subjection again after several ages. The historians speak of the claim of ancient possessions as idle talk, mythical stories. See also Cicero.

III. In truth, the effects, as to Rights, which depend on man's will, still do not follow the mere internal act of the mind, except that act be indicated by some external signs. For to assign a jural efficiency to mere acts of the mind, would not be congruous to human nature, which cannot know the acts of the mind, except from outward signs. Yet signs denoting the acts of the mind have never a mathematical, but only a probable certainty; for men may express in words something different from what they feel and will, and may simulate in their acts. But the nature of human society does not suffer that the acts of the mind, sufficiently indicated, should have no efficacy: therefore what is sufficiently indicated in words, is to be held true, as against him who so indicates it.

This doctrine of the force of words is to be applied to derelicts.

IV. 1 A derelict may also be indicated by the fact; thus, that is a derelict which is thrown away; unless the circumstances of the case be such that it may be supposed to be put away for a time and with the intention of taking it again. Thus a debt is supposed to be remitted by giving up the note of hand which acknowledges it. An inheritance, as Paulus says, may be refused, not only by words, but by deed, and by any indication of will. So if he who is the owner of anything, knowingly contracts with another person in whose possession it is, as with the owner, he must be held to lose his right: and there is no reason why this should not hold also between kings and peoples.

2 In like manner a superior, making a concession to an inferior, or giving him a command which he cannot lawfully perform, except he be relieved from the tie of the law, is supposed to have loosed that tie. This rule flows, not only from the Civil Law, but from Natural Law, according to which any one may abdicate what is his; and from the natural presumption by which every one is supposed to intend what he has sufficiently indicated. And in this sense may be accepted what Ulpian said, that the acknowledgment in court of the payment of a debt*, is a part of *jus gentium;* (it being really a part of *jus civile*).

V. 1 Among "facts" we must also understand what is left un-

---

* Heinec. *Elem. Jur. Civ.* § 1022. Est ergo *acceptilatio* actus legitimus quo interrogatione debitoris et congrua creditoris responsione obligatio per stipulationem contracta dissolvitur. Formula erat *Quod ego tibi promisi, habesne acceptum? Habeo acceptum.* ·

done, considered with due circumstances. If any one, present and knowing, is silent, he may be assumed to assent; as also the Hebrew Law recognizes, Num. xxx. 4, 5, 11, 12: *If a woman vow a vow, &c.;* except circumstances shew that he was prevented from speaking by fear or other cause. Thus that is supposed to be lost, with regard to which the hope of recovering it is given up; as Ulpian says, that pigs carried off by wolves, and goods lost in shipwreck, cease to be ours, not at once, but when they cannot be recovered; that is, when there is no reason to believe that they keep any hold on the mind of the owner; when there is no indication of a purpose of recovering. For if persons have been sent to seek what is lost, or if a reward for finding it is offered, we must judge differently. If any one knows a thing which is his to be held by another, and in the course of a long time says nothing against it, he, except some other reason manifestly appear, must be supposed to have acted with the purpose of no longer having that thing as his. And so Ulpian says, that a house may, by long silence, be understood to be derelict by the owner. And Pius, the Emperor, in a rescript says, You have no right to ask for the interest of your money for the past period, for the length of time shews that you had given it up. You did not require this payment from your debtor, in order to gain favour with him.

2 Similar to this is the case of Custom. For Custom, without referring to the Civil Law, which fixes a certain time and manner for introducing it, may be introduced by a subject people, in virtue of its being tolerated by the Ruler. But the time in which such Custom receives the effect of Law, is not defined, but arbitrary; namely, as much as is necessary to signify the consent of the party.

3 But in order that silence may be valid for the presumption of derelict, two things are required; that it be the silence of a party knowing, and freely willing; for the inaction of a party which is in ignorance, has no effect; and when there is another cause known which influences the will, conjecture as to what it is ceases.

VI. To establish the assumption of these two conditions, other conjectures are of force: but for the most part, the effect of time, in both points, is great. For in the first place, it can hardly happen that in a long time, a thing pertaining to any one should not come to his knowledge, since time supplies many occasions. And a shorter time is sufficient for this purpose in a case between persons present, than absent, even without referring to the Civil Law. So fear once impressed is understood to last for a certain time, but not for ever, since a long time affords many occasions of taking counsel against the danger, either by one's own means or by means of others; as by going out of the bounds of the authority of him who inspires the fear; or at least, it affords the means of renewing our right by protest, or, what is better, of referring to judges or arbitrators.

VII. Since time beyond the memory of man is morally, as it were, infinite, a silence for such a time will always suffice to esta-

blish derelict, except there are very strong reasons on the other side.
It is well remarked by the more prudent jurists, that time beyond the
memory of man is not the same thing as a century, though the two
periods are often not very different; because the common term of
human life is a hundred years; which period commonly includes three
generations of men; as the Romans objected to Antiochus, when they
pointed out that he asked for cities which neither he, nor his father
nor his grandfather, had ever had.

VIII. 1 It may be objected that men are fond of their property,
and that negative acts, even in a great length of time, ought not to be
taken as proving that they throw it away. But, on the other hand,
we ought to think well of men, and not to suppose that they would
allow another man to be perpetually in the wrong, for the sake of a
perishable thing.

2 And as to political authority, though highly valued, it has also
heavy burthens, and such as bring divine wrath on those who administer them ill: and as it would be cruel for different asserted
guardians to litigate, at the expense of the ward, which has a right to
manage his affairs; or, to use Plato's comparison, for the crew of a
vessel to contend, with much danger to the vessel, who should steer;
so are they not always to be praised who with great loss, and much
effusion of the innocent people's blood, are ready to fight who shall
govern the people. The ancients praise Antiochus for expressing
his thanks to the Romans who had reduced his kingdom within
manageable limits. So Lucan implies that a rivalry for empire is
absurd.

3 Then again, it is for the good of human society that governments should at some time be placed beyond the risk and doubt of
controversy; and the modes of settling the matter which have this
tendency are to be preferred. If Aratus thought it hard that private
possession of 50 years should be disturbed, we must still more hold
by the saying of Augustus, that a good citizen does not wish the present state of the republic to be changed. So Alcibiades in Thucydides,
Isocrates, Cicero, Livy.

4 And even if these arguments were wanting, the presumption that
each man wishes to keep what he has, may be met by another presumption, that no man will stay a very long time without giving some
indication what his wishes are.

IX. And perhaps we may say that this is not merely a matter of
presumption, but that this law was introduced by an instituted law of
nations, that a possession going beyond memory uninterrupted, and
not accompanied with any appeal to justice, absolutely transfers
ownership. It is credible that nations have agreed upon this, since
such a rule tends greatly to peace. But it is essential to require uninterrupted possession, as stated in Livy. For a desultory possession is
of no efficacy, as the Numidians urge against the Carthaginians, also
in Livy. [See.]

X. 1 But another and an important question arises here: whether those not yet born may tacitly lose their rights by such *dereliction*. If we say they cannot, the definition just given is of no avail for the tranquillity of authority and ownership, since most kinds of these are such that they belong to posterity. If we say that they can, it will appear strange how silence can prejudice those who cannot speak because they do not exist; and how the act of others can be allowed to harm them.

2 For the solution of this difficulty, it is to be observed, that he who is not yet born has no rights, as a thing not existing has no attributes. Wherefore if the people, from whose will the right of reigning proceeds, changes its will, it does no injury to those who are not yet born, and who have not yet acquired any right. And as the people may change its will expressly, it may also tacitly be presumed to have changed it. If then the will of the people be changed, and since the right of the expected progeny does not yet exist, and the parents from whom they are to be born relinquish their right, nothing prevents its being *occupied* by another as a derelict.

3 In this we speak of Natural Law: for by the Civil Law, as other fictions may be introduced, so this also, that the law may represent the part of the persons who do not yet exist, and may thus prevent adverse occupation being a prejudice to them: which purpose of the law, however, is not lightly to be assumed, because *that* private advantage is much at variance with public utility. Whence those fiefs which [by law] are conveyed, not by the right of the last possessor, but by a primitive investiture in each vacancy, may, by a sufficiently long usage, be acquired [as territory], as the best jurists hold. Covarruvias has asserted this with strong reasons, respecting rights of primogeniture and entailed estates.

4 For nothing prevents the Civil Law from introducing such a Right as cannot be alienated by one act, but yet, in order to avoid the uncertainty of ownership, may be lost by neglect after a certain time: but in such a way that future claimants shall retain a right of personal action against those who have committed the neglect, or their heirs.

XI. From what we have said, it appears that both a king as against a king, and a free people as against a free people, may acquire a right, not only by express consent, but by dereliction and possession following this, or taking a new force from it. For as to what is said, that what is not legally valid at first cannot become valid by the subsequent fact, it is to be taken with this exception, except a new cause intervene, fit of itself to produce such validity. And thus [by the course of usage] the king of any people may lose his authority and become subject to the people; and he who was not king, but only governor, may become king with absolute authority; and the sovereign authority, which at first was in the king or in the people wholly, may be shared between them.

XII. 1 This also is a question worth examining*: Whether the law of usucaption or prescription, made by the sovereign, may affect the right of sovereign authority, and its necessary parts, which we have elsewhere explained (B. I. c. iii. § vi.). Not a few of the Jurists seem to think that it may, treating this question of the sovereignty as a matter of Civil Law. We think otherwise. For in order that any one may be bound by a law, there is required both power and will, at least presumed, in the author of the law. But no one can bind himself in the manner of a law, that is, in the character of a superior: and hence it is that the authors of laws have the right of changing their laws. However, a person may be bound by his own law, not directly, but by reflexion; namely as being a part of the community, in virtue of natural equity, which requires the component parts to follow the analogy of the whole. So Saul put himself and his son Jonathan on the same footing as the rest of the people, 1 Sam. xiv. 40. But this does not apply in the case which we are now treating; for we consider the author of the law, not as a part of the community, but as him in whom the whole legislative virtue resides; for we speak of the sovereignty as such. [Therefore the sovereign has not the power of binding himself by such laws.] But neither can he be presumed to have the will; for the authors of laws are not supposed to include themselves, except both the matter and the reason of the law are universal; as in settling prices by law. But the sovereignty has not parity of reason with other things; on the contrary, it is a matter of a higher order than other things.

Nor have I ever seen a civil law treating of prescription, which comprehended in its sphere the sovereign power, or could be probably supposed to have comprehended it.

2 Whence it follows that the time defined by law is not sufficient to acquire the sovereignty or any necessary part of it, if there are wanting those natural conjectures of which we have before spoken; and that if those conjectures exist to a satisfactory extent, so great a space of time is not required; and that the Civil Law, which prohibits a possession being acquired in a certain time [by prescription], does not apply to the Sovereignty.

* Gronovius treats this as the question whether any rights belonging to the sovereignty can be matter of prescription; and says that Grotius's opinion, that they cannot, is both servile, and dangerous to princes; for the power of princes has in many cases been increased by prescription; and where the power of the people rests upon prescription, if kings refuse to allow it, they are involved in seditions and troubles, like Charles I. in England.

But Barbeyrac remarks that Grotius is speaking of Usucaption and Præscription as defined according to the rules of Civil Law; and that he allows in Art. 2 of this section, that parts of the sovereignty may be established by usage, even in shorter times than the Civil Law requires for prescription. To which we may add, that Gronovius in another note ([61]), asserts that the people cannot be supposed to give up its "most just, certain and eternal possession," namely its sovereign rights; thus going much beyond Grotius on one side of the question. W. W.

It would however be possible that the people, in conferring the sovereignty, should express its will in what way and in what time the supreme authority might be lost by disuse; which will would undoubtedly be to be followed, and could not be infringed, even by a king possessed of the sovereign power; because it pertains, not to the sovereignty itself, but to the mode of holding it; of which difference we have elsewhere spoken.

XIII.   But [though the sovereignty is thus exempt from the Rules of the Civil Law] those things which are not of the nature of the sovereignty, and do not belong to it as natural properties, but can either be naturally separated from it, or communicated to others, are altogether subject to the rules of Civil Law concerning Usucaption and Prescription. So we see that there are subjects who have by prescription acquired the Right that there is no appeal from them; but yet so that there is always some mode of carrying the matter to a higher tribunal, by petition, or in some other way. For that there should not be in any way an appeal from a person, is at variance with the notion of a subject: it belongs to a sovereignty or a part of it; and cannot be acquired otherwise than according to Natural Law, which regulates the sovereignty.

XIV.   1 Hence it appears how far we are to receive the doctrine which some put forth, that it is always lawful for subjects, if they can, to obtain their liberty, that is, Civil liberty; because the authority which was gained by force may be taken away by force; and in regard to that which was given voluntarily, they may repent and change their mind. [But this goes too far.] For authority gained at first by force may by tacit consent receive firm right: and the will exercised, either in the original institution of a government, or at an after period, may be such as to give a right which afterwards does not depend upon the will. King Agrippa said to the Zealots who were clamorous for liberty, It is now out of season to demand liberty. You should have fought formerly, not to lose it. For submission is a hard lot, and it is honourable to fight in order to avoid it. But when a person has once been overcome in such a struggle, if he shake off the yoke, he is no longer a lover of liberty, but an insurgent slave. And so Josephus himself said; and Cyrus to the king of Armenia. [See.]

2 But that a long forbearance of the king, such as we have before described, may be a sufficient ground of the people obtaining its liberty from a presumed relinquishment of imperial authority, is not to be doubted.

XV.   But rights which do not involve daily exercise, but are exercised, once for all, at a convenient time, as the loosing of a pledge; also freely used rights*, to which the act exercised is not directly contrary,

---

* In the table of contents at the head of the chapter, the subject of this section is thus given: *Rights which are meræ facultatis, are not lost in any course of time; Jura meræ facultatis* are Rights which a man possesses but is not bound to exercise.

but is contained in it as a part in the whole;—as if any one should for a hundred years have alliance with one only of his neighbours, when he might have it with others also;—are not lost, except for the time when prohibition or coaction intervenes, and obedience is rendered to it with a sufficient signification of consent; and since this agrees, not only with Civil Law, but with natural reason, it will properly have place also among the most exalted persons. [Such persons will not attempt to control the exercise of those rights.]

CHAPTER V.

Of the original acquisition of Rights over Persons; wherein of the Rights of Parents; of Marriage; of Corporations; of Rights over Subjects, and over Slaves.

I. THERE are rights over persons as well as over things; and these may be acquired by generation, consent, or delinquency.

Parents acquire a right over their children by generation; both parents, the father and the mother; but if there be a contention between the authorities, the authority of the father is preferred, as superior in sex.

II. 1 In Children, three periods of life are to be distinguished; first the period previous to years of discretion; next, the period when they have come to years of discretion, but remain part of the parents' family; third, the period when they have gone out of the family. [See Aristotle.]

In the first period, all the actions of the children are under the dominion of the parents; for he who cannnot govern himself must be governed by another; and the parents are the natural governors. [See Eschylus.]

2 Yet even in this period, a son or daughter is capable of ownership over things *jure gentium;* but the exercise of this right is impeded

by their imperfection of reason. They have the right to have, but not to use. Therefore that whatever becomes the property of the child becomes the property of the parents, is not Natural Law, but is an institution of the laws of certain peoples; which also in this matter distinguish the father from the mother, and sons not yet emancipated from paternal control, from those who are emancipated, and natural children from legitimate; which distinctions are unknown to nature; except the superiority of sex, when the authorities interfere, as we have mentioned.

III. In the second period, when the reason is matured by time, those actions only are subject to the authority of the parents which have some important bearing upon the state of the paternal or maternal family: for it is equitable that a part should follow the analogy of the whole. In other actions, the children have, at that period, the moral right to act; but are bound, even in those, to endeavour to please their parents. But since this obligation is not founded in a jural right, like the above obligations [at the earlier period], but in piety, reverence, and the duty of repaying the benefits they have received, it does not render void what is done in transgression of it; as a donation made contrary to the rules of prudence by the owner is not void.

IV. In both these periods, the parents' right of governing includes also the right of coercing, so far as children require to be compelled to their duty or amended. What is to be done concerning greater punishments, we shall discuss elsewhere.

V. But although the paternal authority so far follows the person and position of the father, that it cannot be taken from him and transferred to another, yet by the Law of Nature, and where the Civil Law does not impede, the father may put his son in pledge, and if necessary, even sell him, when there is no other means of providing for him; which appears to have passed to other nations from an old law of the Thebans: as the Theban law came from the Phœnicians, and higher still, from the Hebrews [Exod. xxi. 7, *And if a man shall sell his daughter to be a maidservant*, &c. Romulus made the same law. Dionys. Halic. 2, 28. *Gronovius.*] The same held with the Phrygians. Nature is conceived to give a right to do every thing without which that cannot be obtained which nature demands: [as the sustenance of children.]

VI. In the third period, the son is independent and *sui juris*, the duty of piety and reverence still remaining, as its cause is perpetual. Whence it follows that the acts of kings are not void because they have parents alive.

VII. Whatever goes beyond this, proceeds from instituted law, which is different in different places. Thus the right which God gave to the Hebrews, of making void the vow of a son or a daughter, was not perpetual, but lasted as long as they were part of the father's house. Thus the Romans had a *patria potestas* over sons, even those

who were themselves heads of families, so long as they were not emancipated.   This power over their children the Romans themselves
remark that other nations had not.   So Sextus Empiricus, Simplicius.
[See.]   Aristotle notes a similar right among the Persians as tyran-
nical. Where we are to distinguish accurately Civil Law from Natural
Law.

VIII.   1 The right over persons which arises *ex consensu*, from
consent, flows either from partnership or from subjection.   The most
natural form of partnership appears in marriage ; but on account of the
difference of sex, the authority is not common to the two ; the husband
is the head of the wife (Eph. v. 23) ; namely, in matters relating to the
marriage union and to the family : for the wife is part of the husband's family.   Thus to determine the place of domicile, is the husband's office.   If any further rights are given to the husband, as by
the Hebrew law, the right of disallowing the vows of the wife, and in
some nations, the right of selling the wife's goods, this is not by Natural
Law, but by institution.

The subject requires that we consider the nature of the marriage union.

2 Marriage, by Natural Law, we conceive to be such a cohabitation of the male and female, as places the female under the protection
and custody of the male ; for such a union we see in some cases in
mute animals.   But in man, as being a rational creature, to this is
added a vow of fidelity by which the woman binds herself to the
man.

IX.   1 Nor does nature appear to require any thing more for the
existence of marriage.   Nor does the divine law seem to have required more, before the propagation of the gospel.   For holy men,
before the law, had more than one wife ; and in the law, precepts are
given to those who have more than one ; and the king is commanded
not to have many wives, or horses ; whence the Hebrew commentators
note that the king might have eighteen wives or concubines ; and God
says to David that he had given him many wives.

2 And in like manner a process is appointed for him who wishes
to put away his wife ; and no one is prohibited from marrying her
who is put away, except him who put her away, and a priest.   But
this liberty of going to another husband is to be so restricted, even
by Natural Law, that no confusion of offspring shall arise.   Hence
the question of pontifical law in Tacitus ; *whether after the conception
and before the birth of the child a woman might lawfully marry.* By
the Hebrew law three months must be interposed between the marriages.

But the law of Christ refers, as other things, so this, to a more
perfect rule ; and by this, pronounces him who had put away a wife,
except an adulteress, and him who married one thus put away, as
guilty of adultery ; and Paul, his Apostle and Interpreter, not only gives
the man a right over the body of the woman, which also was the

Natural Law, [see Artemidorus] but also gives the woman right over the body of the man. So Lactantius says that each party may be guilty of adultery.

3 I know that most hold that, in both these places, Christ did not establish a new law, but restored that which God had established in the beginning of things; and to this opinion they are led by the words of Christ, where he speaks of what was *in the beginning*. But to this it may be answered, that doubtless, from that first condition, in which God gave one woman to only one man, it does sufficiently appear what is best and most agreeable to God; and hence it follows that such a condition was always excellent and laudable; but it does not follow that it was sinful to do otherwise; for where there is no law, there is no transgression; and at that time, there was no law, on that point, in existence. Thus when God said, either through Adam or through Moses, that the marriage union was so close that a man must leave the family of his parent to make a new family with his wife, it is nearly the same as what is said to Pharaoh's daughter, Psal. xlv. *Forget also thy people, and thy father's house.* From this institution of so close a union, it appears sufficiently that it is most agreeable to God that that conjunction should be perpetual; but it does not thence follow that God had then commanded that the tie should not be loosed on any account. But Christ forbade that man should put asunder what God had joined together; thus taking, from that condition which is best and most agreeable to God, matter most worthy of the new law.

4 It is certain that in ancient times most nations used both the liberty of divorce and also plurality of wives. Tacitus notices that the Germans were, in his time, almost the only barbarians who were content with single wives: and that appears constantly in the histories of the Persians and the Indians. Among the Egyptians, the priests alone had only one wife. In Greece, Cecrops was the first who gave one wife to one husband. And if any peoples had a more continent practice, as the Romans always abstained from two wives, and long from divorce, they are to be praised as having made an advance to what was best. Hence also the wife of the Flamen Dialis, the priestess of Jupiter, could not have her marriage dissolved but by death. Yet still it does not follow that they sinned, who did otherwise before the promulgation of the Gospel.

X. 1 Let us now see what marriages are valid by Natural Law: in deciding which, we are to recollect that not everything which is contrary to the Law of Nature [that is to the moral nature of man] is void by Natural Law; as appears by the example of a prodigal donation: [which is contrary to the natural virtue of prudence, and yet valid.] Those acts only are invalid, in which there is wanting a principle giving validity to the act, or in which the vice continues in its effect. The Principle, both here and in other human acts in which Right is created, is, that which we have called a moral Faculty or jural claim, joined with a sufficient Will.

What sort of will is sufficient to create a Right, will be better treated further on, where we speak of promises in general. With regard to the jural claim, a question arises concerning the consent of parents, which some require as naturally requisite to the validity of marriage. But in this they are wrong; for the arguments which they adduce only prove how suitable it is to the duty of sons to obtain the consent of their parents: which we concede without hesitation, with this limitation only, that the will of the parents be not manifestly unjust. For if sons owe in all things a reverence to parents, they do so especially in a matter which has a national bearing, as is the case with marriage. But this does not shew that the right which we call a jural claim is not possessed by the son. For he who marries a wife ought to be of mature age; and he goes out of the family, so that in this matter he is not subjected to the family government. And the duty of reverence alone does not make null an act which is contrary to it.

2 The rule established by the Romans and others, that certain marriages, because the consent of the father is wanting, shall be void, is not a rule of Natural Law, but depends on the will of the lawgiver. For under the same rule, the mother does not make the marriage void by her dissent; though the children by nature owe obedience to her; nor does the father, after his son is emancipated; and if the father be still under the authority of *his* father, both the father and the grandfather must consent to the nuptials of the son, while for the daughter, the authority of the grandfather is sufficient; which differences, unknown to Natural Law, shew sufficiently that these rules come from the Civil Law.

3 In the Scripture we see indeed that pious men, and much more women, (whose modesty makes it suitable for them to act on another's will in this matter; to which view also pertains what is said 1 Cor. vii. 38, *He that giveth her in marriage, &c.*) have, in contracting matrimony, conformed to the authority of their parents. Yet Esau's marriage [who took his wives of the daughters of Canaan, in spite of his father's disapprobation, Gen. xxviii. 8; xxxvi. 2] is not pronounced void, or his children illegitimate. So Quintilian, looking at strict Natural Law. [See.]

XI. Marriage with a woman already married to another, is doubtless void by Natural Law, except her former husband have dismissed her; for so long his authority over her continues. It is void because the jural claim is wanting, being taken away by the former marriage, and the whole effect [of the second marriage] is vicious. Every act connected with it is a trespass on what belongs to another.

On the other hand, by the law of Christ, marriage with him who is the husband of another woman is void, on account of the right which Christ has given a virtuous wife over her husband.

XII. 1 The question concerning the marriage of those who are connected by blood or affinity is sufficiently grave, and not unfre-

H

quently stirred with great vehemence. For if any one tries to assign certain and natural causes why such unions, in the cases in which they are forbidden by law or by usage, are unlawful, he will find that that is difficult, and indeed impossible. For the reasons given by Plutarch and Augustine [see], that social ties are to be extended more widely by diffusing our relationships, is not of such weight that what is done against it can be deemed void or unlawful. For that which is the less useful of two courses, is not thereby forthwith unlawful. Add, that it may happen that whatever the amount of utility on this side be, it may be outweighed by a greater utility on the other side; and that, not only in the case of exception mentioned in the Hebrew Law, when a man dies without offspring, (which is of the same kind as the rule about heiresses in the Hebrew and Attic law,) namely to preserve the property of the family in the family; but also in many other cases, which occur or may be imagined.

2 From this general remark, I except the union of parents of any degree with their children; for, if I am not deceived, the reason why such unions are unlawful is apparent. For the husband, who is the superior by the law of matrimony, could not pay to his mother (being his wife) the reverence which nature requires; nor could a daughter to a father; for though she is inferior in the marriage union, yet the marriage introduces a companionship which excludes filial reverence. Paulus the Jurist says that Natural Law and modesty are to be regarded in contracting marriage, and adds, that it is against modesty for one to have his own daughter to wife. Such marriages, then, are both unlawful, and also void, because the vice has a perpetual effect.

3 Nor need we be moved by the argument of Diogenes and Chrysippus, taken from cocks and hens, and other animals ; by which they try to prove that such unions are not against Natural Law. For, as we have said in the beginning of this Book, it is enough, if anything is contrary to *human* nature, to prove it unlawful. And Incest between ascending and descending degrees is so. So Paulus, Xenophon, Michael Ephesius, Hippodamus, Lucan, Dio Prusæensis.

4 And here we cannot but wonder at the reasoning of Socrates in Xenophon, who finds nothing to blame in such marriages but the disparity of years, whence must follow either barrenness, or an ill-formed progeny. If this reason alone were the obstacle, certainly such unions would be neither unlawful nor void; any more than between other persons whose ages are as different as those of parents and their children usually are.

5 We are rather to consider whether, in men not depraved by education, there is not, besides the reason given by the understanding, a certain horror of such union with parents and offspring, residing in the affections themselves; since even some animals have such a horror. So many have thought: Arnobius; Aristotle of the camel, and the Scythian horse; Oppian; Seneca in the Hippolytus.

XIII. 1 We must next consider the question concerning the degrees of affinity, and the degrees of consanguinity in a transverse line; especially those which are expressly mentioned, Levit. xviii. For though we should grant that these interdicts do not proceed from the mere Law of Nature, yet in virtue of the Divine precept, these unions may pass among forbidden things. And that the precept is one which does not bind the Hebrews only, but all men, seems to be collected from the words of God, Lev. xviii. 24, 25, 27, *Do not ye pollute yourselves, &c.*

2 For if the Canaanites and their neighbours sinned in doing such things, it follows that some law of God on that subject must have gone before; and as this is not merely a Natural Law, it remains that it was from God, either given to those nations peculiarly, (which is less probable, nor do the words carry that meaning,) or to the human race; either at the Creation, or at the restoration of things after the Deluge. And such laws, which were given to the whole human race, were not, it appears, abrogated by Christ; but those laws only which separated the Jews from other nations. Add to this, that Paul speaks of the marriage of a man with his father's wife as something shocking, though there is no special precept of Christ on that subject; nor does he use any other argument than that such a union is held to be impure even by the heathen. And that it is so appears in ancient authors. So Charondas; Lysias; Cicero; Plutarch; Virgil. And if this common opinion was not drawn from a dictate of nature, it follows that it descends from an old tradition originating in a divine precept.

3 *The ancient Hebrews, who are not to be thought slightly of as commentators on this part of the divine law, and especially Maimonides, the greatest of them, says that there are two reasons for these laws, given Lev. xviii., concerning marriage: First, a natural modesty which does not permit persons to mingle with their own offspring, either in themselves, or in persons closely connected by blood or by marriage union: Second, lest the daily and confidential intercourse of certain persons should give occasion to sexual union, if such union could be confirmed by marriage. Which two causes if we judiciously apply to the laws given in Leviticus, it will easily appear that in the first transverse degree of blood, (brothers and sisters,) on account of the very recent image of the parents in the children, the first cause holds, as proceeding from that which, if nature does not command, at least she points out as more becoming: as there are many such things, which make the matter of divine and human laws.

4 Hence the Hebrews say that in the direct line the degrees not named in the law are comprehended, from the manifest parity of reason. These degrees they thus reckon: mother's mother; mother's father's mother; father's mother; father's father's mother; father's father's wife; mother's father's wife; son's daughter-in-law; son's

* For the reasons against marriages of near relations, see *Elements of Morality*, 749 and 980.

son's daughter-in-law; daughter's daughter-in-law; son's daughter's daughter; son's son's daughter; daughter's daughter's daughter; daughter's son's daughter; wife's son's daughter's daughter; wife's daughter's daughter's daughter; wife's father's mother's mother; wife's mother's father's mother: which the Romans express in a different way. And so *in infinitum* if it could be necessary.

5 These laws, and the law against the marriage of brother and sister, the Hebrews think were given to Adam at the same time with the laws, to worship God, not to shed blood, to worship no false gods, not to take what is another's. But they think that the laws concerning the conjugal union were given so that they should not be in force till the human race was to a certain extent multiplied; which could not take place at first without the marriage of brothers and sisters. Nor do they think it any objection to this account, that it is not given in the narration of Moses; for he held it sufficient to indicate this tacitly, by condemning other nations on that ground: For that there are many things in the Law which are not told in the order of time, but as occasion offers; whence that noted maxim of the Hebrews, that in the Law there is no before and after.

6 On the union of brothers and sisters, see Michael Ephesius, Diodorus Siculus, Dio Prusæensis, Seneca, Plato.

7 All which passages shew the ancient opinion of a divine law against such marriages; whence we see they are called *nefas*.

XIV. 1 These manifest expressions shew what a difference there is between these and remoter degrees. For to marry a father's sister is forbidden; but a brother's daughter, who is in the same degree, it is not forbidden to marry; and there are examples of it among the Hebrews. So this was done at Rome and at Athens: See Tacitus, Isæus, Plutarch. The Hebrews give a reason, that young men usually frequent the houses of their grandfathers and grandmothers, or even live in them along with their aunts; but they have not the same access to the houses of their brothers, nor so much freedom there. If we accept this, as indeed it seems to be reasonable, we must confess that the law of not marrying relations in the right line, and sisters, since the human race was multiplied, is perpetual; and common to all men, as depending on natural decency; so that whatever is done against this law is void on account of the abiding vice of condition: but that the other laws are not so; but contain rather a caution than a law, which caution may also be applied in other ways.

2 Certainly in the ancient (so called) Apostolical Canons, he who married two sisters successively, or his niece (the daughter of his brother or sister) was only excluded from the clerical office. Nor is it difficult to answer what was said concerning the sin imputed to the Canaanites and the neighbouring peoples. For the universal terms may be restricted to the principal heads: the *pollutions* of the Canaanites may be those which are mentioned Lev. xviii. 22, 23;

and the other laws, concerning incest, are added as an outwork to these.

That the expressions cannot be understood of every part, we may see by the prohibition of having to wife at the same time two sisters, which we cannot suppose was a universal rule, since Jacob transgressed it. So Amram the father of Moses married his aunt, and among the Greeks, Diomedes married his mother's sister; Iphidamas, the same; Alcinus, his brother's daughter.

3 But the early Christians did well, who spontaneously observed, not only those Laws which were given as common to all, but also those peculiarly given to the Hebrew people; and even extended their modesty to other ulterior limits, so as to surpass the Hebrews in this virtue, as in other things. And it appears from the Canons that this was done. So Augustine says, that what was not forbidden, as marriage of cousins, was avoided, as approaching forbidden ground. And this feeling was followed by the laws. Theodosius forbade the marriage of cousins, and Ambrose praised him for doing so.

4 But it is to be understood that what is forbidden by human law is not necessarily void when it is done, except the Law so directs. The Canon LX. of Seville says, if any one after the death of his wife shall marry her sister, he shall be excluded from the Communion five years; thus shewing that the tie of matrimony remains. And as we have said, in the Apostolical Canons, he who married two sisters, or a niece, was only excluded from the Clergy.

XV. 1 To proceed to other matters, we may observe that, in some cases, concubinage is a true and valid marriage, although it be deprived of some of the peculiar effects of the Civil Law, and even lose some of its natural effects by the impediment of the Civil Law. For example, the union of a slave with a maid servant is, by the Roman Law, cohabitation, not marriage; but yet, in such a union, there is nothing wanting to the nature of marriage, which accordingly, in the old Canons, is called γάμος, marriage. And so the union between a free man and a female slave is called concubinage, not marriage; and this name was afterwards extended to other persons of unequal quality; as at Athens, to a union between a citizen and a foreigner. So in Virgil, Aristophanes, Ælian, the child of a foreign mother by a citizen is called *nothus*, illegitimate. [See.]

' 2 But as in a state of nature, such unions as we have spoken of might be true marriage, if the woman was under marital custody, and had vowed fidelity to the husband; so also in the state of the Christian Law, a union between a slave and a male servant, or between a free man and a female slave, will be a true marriage; much more a union between a citizen and a foreigner, or a senator and a freed woman; if the conditions which are necessary by instituted Christian Law are present, namely, the indissoluble conjunction of one man and one woman; although some effects of the Civil Law may not follow this union, or some which would spontaneously follow may be impeded,

In this sense are to be understood the words of the first Council of Toledo: *He who, not having a wife, has a concubine, is not to be rejected from the Communion; so only that he be content with the society of one woman, whether wife or concubine.* Add to this, the passage in the Clementine Constitutions. So Theodosius and Valentinian call certain cases of concubinage unequal marriages, and say that a charge of adultery may arise out of them.

XVI. 1 And even if human Law forbid marriages between certain persons, it does not follow that the marriage is void, if it be really contracted. For these are two different operations, to prohibit, and to annul what is done. For prohibition may exert its force by a penalty either express or arbitrary. Ulpian calls this kind of Laws imperfect, which forbid a thing to be done, but do not rescind it if done. Such was the Cincian Law.

2 Afterwards there was a law of Theodosius made, that if the law had only prohibited a thing, and had not specially said that what was done in contradiction of it was void, yet that the thing so done was null, void, and of no effect; that is, if the matter came into a court of justice. But this was not in virtue of the prohibition alone, but of the new Law; and such a rule other nations are not bound to follow. For often the indecency in the act is greater than in the subsequent effect; and often the inconveniences which follow the rescinding of the act are greater than the indecency or inconvenience of the act itself.

XVII. Besides marriage, the most natural of partnerships, there are others, both private and public; and these latter, either partnerships *in populum* or *ex populis*. All partnerships have this in common, that in those matters for which the partnership was instituted, the whole body, and the majority as representing the whole, bind the special members of the partnership. For it must be supposed to have been the intention of those who united to make the society, that there should be some way of promoting business; and it is manifestly unjust that the greater part should follow the less; wherefore by Natural Law, not taking into account pacts and laws which prescribe a form for conducting business, the majority has a right to act for the whole. So Thucydides, Appian, Dionysius Halicarnassensis, Aristotle, Curtius, Prudentius, Xenophon. [See.]

XVIII. If the opinions are equally divided, nothing must be done; for then there is not so much power of movement as is requisite for a change. And for this reason, if the opinions of the judges are equally divided, the accused is acquitted; by what the Greeks call Minerva's vote. [See Æschylus and Euripides.] So too the person in possession keeps the property. [See Aristotle and Seneca.]

XIX. Here a question often arises how the votes are to be taken, together or separate. And here, so far as Natural Law goes, that is, if there be no pact nor precept of Law, there is to be a difference made between the opinions which are altogether different, and those of which one contains a part of another; and these latter are to be conjoined in the point in which they agree. Thus if one party of the judges would fine a man in 20 pounds, and one in 10, they are to be joined, as to the 10, against the party which would acquit. But those who vote for the death of the accused, and those who vote for his exile, are not to be conjoined; for death does not include exile. But also those that acquit must not be joined with those who vote for exile; because although they agree not to put the accused to death, that is not precisely what the vote expresses, but is deduced from it by a consequence, for he who exiles does not acquit. Whereupon Pliny, when something of this kind had happened in the senate, said that the diversity of opinions was so great that they must be taken singly; and that it made little difference that several rejected the same thing, if they could not all accept the same thing. So Polybius notes that Postumius the Prætor took an unfair course with regard to the Greeks, when he took the votes, and put together those who condemned them to slavery, and those who thought they should be kept for a limited time, against those who absolved them. So other cases in Gellius and in Quintilian.

XX. This also is to be added, that if any members are absent, or otherwise prevented from using their vote, their right devolves on those who are present. [See Seneca.]

XXI. The natural order of precedence in a partnership is the order in which the members have come into it. So the eldest brother always retains his superior privileges. See Aristotle. So Theodosius and Valens, of precedence between the Consuls. So in the general association of Christian kings and nations, formerly those had precedence in the councils who had first professed Christianity.

XXII. It is to be added however, that when a partnership has its foundation in property which all do not equally share in; as if, in an inheritance or other estate, one person has a half, one a third, one a fourth; then, not only is the order of precedence to follow the order of shares, but also the weight of the votes must be proportional to the shares. And as this is the rule of natural equity, so is it also the rule of the Roman Law. So Strabo mentions a league between Cibyra and those neighbouring cities, in which Cibyra had two votes, (as contributing more,) the others, one each. And again, in Lycia, he says there were 23 cities of which some had 3 votes, some, 2, some, one only, and bore the burthens in the same proportion. But, as Aristotle says, this is right, if the partnership be formed for the sake of possession.

XXIII. An association in which many fathers of families coalesce into one people and state, gives the greatest right to the body over its parts; for this is the most perfect society; nor is there any external act of man which either does not regard this society of itself, or may not regard it from circumstances. It may, as Aristotle says, make laws on all subjects.

XXIV. 1 It is often asked, whether citizens may quit the State without leave obtained. We know that there are peoples where this is not permitted, as the Muscovites; nor do we deny that civil society may be formed on such a pact, and that usage may take the force of a pact. By the Roman Laws, at least in their later forms, a person was allowed to remove his domicile; but he who had done so, was still bound by the obligations of the town to which he belonged. Those who were under such rule remained within the limits of the Roman empire, and the rule referred specially to the interests of the tributary collection.

2 But the question for us is, What ought to be the rule by Natural Law, if no agreement has been made; and this, as relates, not to any part only, but the whole of the state or the whole body of a sovereign empire. And that the subjects may not depart in large bodies, is evident enough from the necessity of the end, which gives a right in moral matters; for if that were permitted, Civil Society could no longer subsist. With regard to the emigration of individuals, the case is different; as it is one thing to take water out of a river in a vessel, another thing to turn off a part of the river by a side cut. Some hold that each ought to be at liberty to choose his own city: so Tryphoninus; Cicero. But here the rule of natural equity is to be observed, which the Romans followed in winding up the affairs of private societies; that it should not be done, if the interests of the society forbade: That is to be done, said Proculus, not which is the interest of one member, but of the whole society. And it is for the interest of the society that a citizen should not leave the country, if the country be greatly in debt, except the citizen is prepared to pay his part; and again, if the country have undertaken war, relying upon its population, especially if a siege be likely; except that citizen be willing to find a substitute to take his place in defending the country.

3 Except in these cases, it is to be supposed that a people agree to the free departure of citizens; for they derive advantages from it in other ways.

XXV. The State has no authority over exiles. So say the Heraclidæ in Euripides; so the son of Alcibiades in Isocrates.

The association of several peoples, either by themselves or by their heads, is a League: and we shall hereafter treat of such, when we come to obligations by compact.

XXVI. [Next of Subjection by Consent, as a kind of Association.]

Subjection by consent is either private or public. Private subjection by consent may be manifold, as there are many kinds of [private] government. The noblest species of this is *Arrogatio*, by which a person who is his own master, gives himself into the family of another, to be subject to him, in the same manner that a son of mature age is subject to a father. But a father cannot give his son to another, in such a manner that the paternal power passes fully to him, and that he should discharge the office of father; for this, nature does not suffer.

But he may commend his son to another, and give him to the other to be brought up as an adopted son.

XXVII. 1 The most ignoble species of subjection is that in which a person gives himself into perfect slavery; as those among the Germans who played the last throw of the dice for their own liberty, as Tacitus says. So Dio Prusæensis.

2 That is perfect slavery, when a man gives his whole labour for ever for the sustenance and other necessaries of life. If the matter is thus taken in natural terms, there is nothing shocking in this; for the perpetual obligation to labour is compensated by the perpetual certainty of food; which often those have not who work for daily wages. See Eubulus; Posidonius.

XXVIII. Masters have not over slaves the power of life and death, (I speak of plenary and internal jurisdiction,) nor can any one lawfully put a man to death, except he have committed a capital offense. But by the laws of some peoples, the master, if for any cause he has killed his slave, meets with impunity, as absolute kings do. Seneca before us had used this comparison. And yet undoubtedly a slave may receive a Wrong from his master, as Seneca also affirms; but impunity is not properly called a Right. The like right Solon gave parents over children, as did the old Law of Rome. See Sextus Empiricus and Dio.

XXIX. 1 The question concerning those who are born slaves, is more difficult. By the Roman Law, and by the Law of Nations respecting captives, as we shall explain elsewhere, as in beasts, so in men of servile condition, the offspring follows the mother; which however is not sufficiently congruous to Natural Law, when the father may be known by sufficient evidence. For since in dumb animals the father, no less than the mother, shares the care of the offspring, we have, in this, an evidence that the progeny belongs to both. And thus, if the Civil Law had been silent on this point, the progeny would follow the father no less than the mother. Let us suppose then, to make the difficulty less, that both the parents are in slavery; and let us see whether the offspring would be of servile condition by Natural Law. Certainly if there were no other means of bringing up the offspring, the parents might give their future progeny along with themselves into slavery: since on such grounds, parents may even sell their children.

2 But since this Right by Natural Law flows from necessity only, it is not the right of the parents, in any other case, to give their children into slavery. And therefore the right of the owners over the progeny of slaves arises, in this case, from their supplying sustenance and the other necessaries of life. And thus, when the children born of slaves are to be supported for a long time, and the subsequent labour corresponds to the aliment afterwards supplied, it is not lawful for those thus born to escape slavery.

But if the cruelty of the owner be extreme, it is a probable opinion that even those who have given themselves into slavery may seek refuge in flight. For what the Apostles and the ancient Canons prescribe to slaves, that they are not to withdraw themselves from their masters, is a general rule only, and delivered in opposition to the error of those who rejected all subjection both private and public, as contrary to Christian liberty.

XXX. Besides complete slavery, of which we have now spoken, there are imperfect kinds of slavery; as those which are for a time; or under a condition; or to perform certain work. Such is the state of *liberti,* freedmen; *statu liberorum**, manumitted by testament under a pendent condition; *nexi,* slaves for debt; *addicti,* slaves by sentence of a judge; *ascripti glebæ,* serfs conveyed with the land; and the slavery among the Hebrews for seven years, and that which lasted till the Jubilee. So the *Penestæ* of Thessaly; so what are called *mortuæ manus,* villein tenants; and finally, mercenaries; which differences depend on law or on compacts. Also by the Natural Law the condition of those, one of whose parents is of free and the other of servile condition, seems to be an imperfect slavery, for the reasons given above.

XXXI. That is public subjection, in which a people gives itself into subjection to one man, or to many, or to another people. We have above given the formula of such a subjection, in the case of Capua. (B. i. c. iii. § viii.) So the formula used in the case of the Collatine people: See Livy: to which Plautus alludes. The Persians call this presenting earth and water. There are other modes of public subjection less perfect, either as to the mode of possessing such subjects, or as to the plenitude of authority; the degrees of which may be sought in what we have said above (B. i. c. iii.).

XXXII. Subjection from delict or delinquency, may arise without preceding consent, when he who has deserved to lose his liberty is reduced by force into the power of him who has a right to punish him. Who has the right to punish, we shall hereafter see. (B. ii. c. xx. § iii.) And in this way, not only may individuals be reduced into private subjection; (as at Rome those who did not appear to answer to a charge of delict, and those who had made a false return of their property; and afterwards, women who had married the slave of another master.) but also peoples might be reduced into public subjection for a public delict. There is this difference, that the slavery of a people is of itself perpetual, because the succession of parts does not prevent its continuing to be one people. But the slavery of individuals does not go beyond the person; because the consequences of the crime follow the criminal. But both kinds of slavery, public and private, may be penal, whether it be perfect or imperfect, according to the nature of the crime and the punishment.

Of the slavery both private and public which arises from the instituted Law of Nations, we shall have an opportunity of speaking hereafter, when we come to the effects of war. (B. iii. c. vii.)

* I have taken Gronovius's explanations of these various kinds of imperfect slavery. W. W.

CHAPTER VI.

Of acquisition derivative, by the act of man; and herein of the alienation of the Sovereignty, and of its accompaniments.

I. 1 THINGS become ours by derivative acquisition, by the act of man, or by the act of the law. That those who are the owners of things may transfer the ownership, either the whole or in part, is a part of Natural Law, when ownership has been introduced: for this is a part of the nature of plenary ownership. So Aristotle.

But two things are to be noticed; one, in the giver, one, in the receiver. In the giver an internal act of the will does not suffice; but there are required besides, either words or external acts; because a mere internal act, as we have said elsewhere, is not congruous to the nature of human society.

2 That tradition (delivery) also is required, is a matter of Civil Law; which, because it is received by many nations, is improperly called a part of *Jus Gentium*. So in other places we find the usage to be, that a declaration before the people or the magistrate, or a registry of the gift, is required; which it is quite certain are matters of the Civil Law.

An act of the will expressed by a sign must be understood to mean, of a rational will.

II. On* the other side, in him to whom the thing is given, there is required, setting aside the Civil Law, by Natural Law, the will of accepting, with its sign: which will ordinarily follow the giving; but may precede it; as for instance if the receiver had asked that the thing be given, or granted: for such a will is supposed to continue to exist, except some change appear.

The other things which are required for the conveyance of a right and for acceptance of it, and how each may be done, we shall treat of below, in the Chapter on Promises: for the right of alienating and of promising are the same, at least by Natural Law.

* See *E. M.* 699.

III. As other things may be alienated, so may Sovereign authority, by him who is really the owner, that is, as we have said above
(I. iii. § xii.), by the king, if the authority is patrimonial: otherwise, by
the people, but with the consent of the king; because he too has his
right, as tenant for life, which is not to be taken away against his will.
And so much of the whole sovereign authority.

IV. In the alienation of a part of the sovereignty, it is also required that the part which is to be alienated consent to the act. For
those who unite to form a State, contract a certain perpetual and
immortal society, in virtue of their being integrant parts of the
same; whence it follows that these parts are not under the body in
such a way as the parts of a natural body, which cannot live without
the life of the body, and therefore may rightly be cut away for the
utility of the body. The body of which we speak is of another kind,
namely a voluntary combination. And thus its right over its parts is
to be measured by its primeval will; and this must not be supposed
to have been such that the body should have the right of cutting
off parts from itself, and giving them into the authority of another.

V. And in like manner on the other hand, a part has not a right
to withdraw from the body, except evidently it cannot otherwise preserve itself: for, as we have said, in every thing of human institution
the case of extreme necessity is to be excepted, which reduces the matter
to mere Natural Law. So Augustine. So in the oath of the Greeks,
in which those who had submitted to the Persians were devoted to
severe punishment, with the reservation, *Except they had been plainly
compelled.*

VI. And hence it may be sufficiently understood, why, in this
matter, the part has a greater right to protect itself than the body has
over a part*; because the part uses a right which it had before the
society was formed, and the body does not. Nor must any one say
to me that the sovereignty resides in the body as an attribute in its
subject, and therefore may be alienated by it as ownership may. For it
resides in the body as in an adequate subject, not divisible into several bodies, as the soul or life resides in perfect bodies. But the
necessity which reduces the thing to Natural Law cannot have place
with regard to the body: for in Natural Law, some things are comprehended, as consuming a thing by eating, and retaining possession
of a thing, which are natural operations; but not alienation, which is
introduced by the act of man, and takes its measure from that.

VII. But sovereignty over a locality, that is, a part of the territory, say an uninhabited or deserted part, may, so far as I see, be alienated by a free people, or by the king with the consent of the people.
For a part of the people, because it has free will, has also the right of

* Gronovius, in his Notes, is very impatient of this discussion of Grotius, and
says that it tends to make the claims to kingdoms eternal: as when the French
deny that Francis the First, as a captive, could cede to Charles the Fifth the kingdom of Naples, the dukedom of Savoy, and the Belgian provinces.

refusing consent; but the territory, both the whole and its parts, are common to the people, *pro indiviso*, as a whole, and therefore subject to its will. But if a people cannot alienate the sovereignty of a part of the people, as we have said, much less can a king, though having full sovereignty, but not in a full manner, according to the distinction explained above.

VIII. Wherefore we cannot agree with jurists who, to the rule of not alienating the parts of the empire, add two exceptions, public utility, and necessity; except in this sense, that when the common utility of the body and of the part is the same, the consent both of the people and of the part may seem, even by a silence of no long time, to be given; and more easily still, if necessity appear. But when the will, either of the body or of a part, is manifestly on the contrary side, nothing ought to be understood as done, except, as we have said, when a part is compelled to secede from the body.

IX. Under alienation is rightly comprehended also *infeudation*, giving the kingdom as a fief to a superior, with the power of taking possession of it if the holder commit felony, or if his family fail*. And hence we see that by most peoples, infeudations, as well as alienations, are held void when made by the kings without consulting the people. The consent of the people is understood to be given, whether it meet as a whole, which was formerly the usage among the Germans and Gauls, or by certain representatives of the integrant parts, invested with sufficient powers. For what we do by others we do ourselves. Nor can a part of the empire be *oppignerated* or put in pawn, except with similar consent; not only because oppigneration is commonly followed by alienation, but also, because the king is bound to the people to exercise the sovereign authority himself, and the people is bound to its parts to preserve this exercise in its integrity; for which purpose the members of the civil society came together.

X. To concede subordinate civil functions to persons, even with the right of hereditary succession, is what a people may do; since such concessions do not trench upon the integrity of the body politic and the sovereignty. But the king cannot do this without consulting the people, if we confine ourselves within the limits of Natural Law: for a temporary right, such as that of an elective or hereditary king, can only have temporary effects. But this right may be given to kings, not only by express consent, but by tacit assent introduced by usage, such as we now see commonly prevail. And so we perpetually read in history of the Median and Persian kings giving towns or provinces as possessions to be held for ever.

XI. The patrimony of a people, the produce of which is destined to support the burthens of the republic or of the royal dignity, may not be alienated by kings, neither in the whole nor in part. For in this too they have only a life interest. Nor do I admit the exception, If it

* As king John of England executed an infeudation of his kingdom to the Pope. *Gronov.*

be a thing of small amount; for of what is not mine, I may not alienate even a small part. But in things of small amount, the consent of the people may be presumed from its knowledge and silence, rather than in great matters. In which sense we may also apply what we have said above on the subject of alienating the parts of the sovereignty, to the case of the public patrimony; and the more, inasmuch as a matter of smaller amount is here involved: for the patrimony is constituted [not on its own account but] for the sake of the State.

XII. But many persons run into error by confounding the annual income of the patrimony with the patrimony itself. Thus the right to alluvial accession generally belongs to the patrimony; the things alluvially added are part of income; the right of receiving the taxes is in the patrimony; the annual produce of the taxes is income; the right of confiscation is in the patrimony; the property confiscated is income.

XIII. But the parts of the patrimony may be oppignerated, for cause arising, by kings who have plenary sovereignty; that is who have the right, for cause arising, of imposing new taxes. As the people is bound to pay taxes imposed for good cause, so is it to loose a thing pawned for good cause: for such loosing of a thing pawned is a sort of tax. And the patrimony of the people is [in this case] pledged to the king for the debts of the people. And I may oppignerate things pledged to me.

What we have hitherto said holds, except there be a law, besides the general condition of sovereignty, either enlarging or contracting the authority of the people or of the king.

XIV. 1 Also we must observe that when we speak of alienation, we include, in that class of processes, testamentary dispositions. For though a testament, like other acts, may assume a certain form by the Civil Law; yet its substance has a close affinity with ownership, and thus, is under Natural Law. For I may alienate my possession, not only simply, but also under condition; not only irrevocably, but revocably, and even retaining in the mean time possession and the fullest power of enjoying it. But alienation under condition, namely the condition of my death, and revocable before that event, while I retain possession and enjoyment in the mean time, is a Testament. So Plutarch, speaking of Solon's granting the Athenians permission to make a will, adds, in order that every one might have full ownership over his own property. So Quintilian. So Abraham if he had died without children, would have left his property to Eliezer. Gen. xv. 2.

2 The law that in some places strangers are not allowed to make Wills, is not a part of *Jus gentium*, but of the peculiar law of such States; and if I am not mistaken, proceeding from that period when strangers were looked upon as enemies; and therefore it has deservedly fallen into disuse among the most civilized nations.

CHAPTER VII.

Of the derivative acquisition which takes place by Law; and herein of succession to intestate property.

I. THE derivative acquisition or alienation which takes place by Law, takes place either by the Law of Nature, or by the instituted Law of Nations, or by the Civil Law. Of the Civil Law we do not treat, for to do so would be an infinite task; and the principal controversies concerning war are not defined by the Civil Law. Only this we may note, that some civil laws are manifestly unjust: as those which confiscate goods thrown on shore by shipwreck. For without any probable preceding cause, to take away from any one his right to his own property is mere wrong. So Euripides, Constantine, Dio Prusæensis. [See.]

II. 1 By the Law of Nature, which follows from the nature and force of ownership, alienation is made in two ways, by legal compensation and by succession.

Alienation takes place by legal compensation, as often as, in the place of a thing which is mine or is owing to me, when I cannot obtain the thing itself, I receive another thing of the same value from him who detains or owes what is mine. For expletory justice, when she cannot restore the same thing, has recourse to a thing of the same value, which is in moral estimation the same. That the owner-ship is transferred in such cases, is proved by the end of the pro-cedure, which in moral cases is' the best proof. For I cannot obtain compensation for my right, except I become the owner. My detention of the thing is of no use, if I cannot use it as I choose. So in Diodorus, Hesioneus took the horses of Ixion, as compensation for what he promised his daughter and did not give.

2 By the Civil Law indeed, it is, as we know, forbidden to execute justice for one's self; so that it is called violence, if any one take by act what is owing to him; and in many places he loses the right of a creditor who does so. And indeed if the Civil Law did not directly prohibit this, it would follow from the institution of judicial tribunals that it is unlawful. Therefore the rule that we have laid down holds, when the course of regular justice is *con-tinuously* interrupted, as we have explained above, (I. iii. 2). When the interruption is momentary, the taking of the thing will be lawful, in case you cannot otherwise recover what is yours; for example, if your debtor be running away. But the establishment of ownership must be waited for till the judge assigns it, as is usual in *reprisals;* of which we shall hereafter treat. But if the right be certain, and at the same time it be morally certain that compensa-tion cannot be obtained from the judge; for example, for want of proof; the truer opinion is, that under the circumstances, the law concerning the tribunals ceases, and the matter reverts to the pris-tine rule.

III. Succession to intestate property, setting aside the Civil Law, has its natural origin in the conjecture of the will of the last possessor. For inasmuch as the force of ownership was such that the property might, by the will of the owner, be transferred to another, even on account of approaching death, and with possession retained, as we have said before; if any one has made no manifesta-tion of his will, and yet it be not credible that he was so minded that his property should after his death come into the hands of any one who should take possession of it; it followed that the pro-perty should belong to him to whom it was most probable that the defunct person wished it to belong. As Pliny says, It is a rule of law to understand the will of persons defunct. And in a doubt-ful case, every one is supposed to have willed that which is most equitable and proper. And in this case, the first claim is that which is strictly due; the next that which, though not strictly due, is con-formable to duty.

IV. 1 Jurists dispute whether children have a right to aliment from their parents. For some are of opinion that it is indeed agreeable to natural reason that children should be supported by their parents, but that it is not a debt or due. We make a distinction as to the word *debt* or *due;* which strictly taken, is sometimes taken for the obligation introduced by expletory *jus;* but sometimes, more laxly, that which cannot be decently omitted, though that decency proceeds not from expletory justice, but from some other source. Now what we here speak of is (except there be in addition some human law) a debt or due in the laxer sense. So Valerius Maximus, Plutarch. [See.] That he who gives *the form* gives what is requisite to the form, is a dictum of Aristotle. Therefore he who is the cause of a man's existence, ought, as far as he can and as far as is necessary, to provide him with the things necessary to human life, that is, natural and social life.

2 So other animals by natural instinct provide for their offspring. Hence Apollonius Tyanæus so amends Euripides, and gives many arguments, which see in Philostratus; and so Appian: and Euripides in the *Dictys.*

Hence the old jurists refer the bringing up of children to Natural Law; that is, to that class of things which Instinct recommends to animals, and Reason to man. So Justinian, Diodorus Siculus, Quintilian. Sallust calls a testament in which the son is excluded, *impious.* And since this is a natural due, the mother ought to support her children of which the father is uncertain.

3 And though the Roman Laws directed that those born of a cohabitation condemned by the laws should have no legal inheritance, as the law of Solon provided that it was not necessary to leave anything to natural children; the rules of Christian piety corrected this rigour, and teach that all children may rightly have that left them by their parents, and if need be, should have that left them, which is sufficient to support them. And thus is to be taken what is usually said; that the lawful share of the inheritance (*legitima*) cannot be taken away by human laws: that is, so far as this lawful share implies necessary aliment. For what is more than this may be taken away without transgressing Natural Law.

4 Not only descendants in the first degree, but in the second, if necessary, and in ulterior degrees, ought to be supported. So Justinian. And this extends to those who are descendants through females, if they have no other source of support.

V. 1 Also aliment to parents is due from their children: which is not only a matter of law, but expressed by a proverbial term referring to the supposed filial piety of the stork. And Solon is praised for marking with infamy those who do not discharge this due. But this is not so ordinarily applicable as the rule concerning children; for children, when they are born, bring with them nothing on which to live: add to which, that they have to live longer than the parents have. Therefore as honour and obedience are due to parents, not to children, so support is due to children more than to parents. So Lucian and Aristotle.

I

2 Hence, even without the aid of the Civil Law, the first rule of succession is, that the goods go to the children; because the parents are believed to have intended to provide for them, as for parts of their own bodies, not only necessaries, but all things which pertain to an agreeable and decent life, and especially after they cease to be able to enjoy their property. So the Jurists Paulus, Papinian. So Valerius Maximus says of Hortensius, when he made his son his heir, though disapproving his character, that *He rendered the due honour to the tie of blood*. So St Paul, 2 Cor. xii. 14.

VI. It is ordinarily the case, that the father and mother provide for their children, and therefore, so long as they are alive, the grandfather and grandmother are not bound to furnish them aliment; but when the parents, or one of them, fails, it is equitable that the grandfather and grandmother should undertake the care of the grandchildren for their defunct son and daughter: and this goes on in like manner to parents still further removed. And hence is the origin of that right by which the grandson succeeds in the place of the son, as Ulpian speaks. See Modestinus, Justinian, Isæus, Philo Judæus, Demosthenes. This vicarious succession by family branches, the more recent Jurists call *Representation*. This prevailed among the Hebrews also, as the division of the promised land among the sons of Jacob, plainly shews. [Ephraim and Manasseh, the sons of Joseph, having a lot; but in fact they had *each* a lot, being adopted. *J. B.*]

VII. What we have said of the conjectured will, holds only if there be no evidence to the contrary. Amongst such evidence, the first place belongs to *abdication* of a son, which was practised by the Greeks, as *exheredation* [disinheriting] was by the Romans: but this rejection or disinheriting of a son, if he had not merited death by his crimes, was to be so limited that he was to be provided with aliment, as we have stated above.

VIII. 1 To the rule of a man providing for a son, this exception also is to be added; if it be not sufficiently certain that he is really his son. Things which are done in the sight of men have a certain degree of certainty from testimony; and as persons are usually present at the birth of a child, the mother is known, but the father cannot be known with the same certainty. So Homer, Menander.

Hence it was necessary to find some other way in which it might be known who was the father of a child: and the way is, marriage in its natural state, that is cohabitation, the woman being in the custody of the man. But if it be known in any other way who is the father, or the father have ascertained the fact, such offspring, as well as any other, does by Natural Law succeed. Why not? Since a stranger, adopted as a son, also succeeds from the conjectured will.

2 Natural children, even after the law has made a difference between them and legitimate children, [see Euripides,] may be adopted [by the father], except the law interpose. This was formerly permitted by the Roman Law of Anastasius: but afterwards, in order to favour

legitimate marriage, a more difficult way of putting them on a footing of equality with legitimate children was introduced, *per curiæ oblatio-nem,* by offering them to be *Curiales* [a burthensome condition], or by subsequent marriage [of the parents]. An example of the old adoption of natural children we have in the sons of Jacob, who were by their father made equal to the sons of free women, and received equal parts in the inheritance.

3 On the other hand, it may happen, not only by law but by compact, that children born in marriage may receive aliment alone, or at least may be excluded from the principal inheritance. A marriage contracted on such a compact, even with a free woman, the Hebrews called concubinage; such was the marriage of Abraham with Keturah, whose children, like Ishmael the son of Hagar, received certain gifts or legacies, but did not succeed to the inheritance of their father. Such is the marriage which is called *morgengabe:* and not very different from this is the law of second marriages among the Brabanters: for the landed property which existed when the former marriage was dissolved passes to the children of the first marriage.

IX. 1 Where there are no children to whom the succession may naturally fall, the case is less clear; nor is there any point in which Laws are more various. The whole variety however may be referred mainly to two sources; one of which respects the proximity of degree, the other directs the property to return to the quarter from which it came; as the phrase is, the father's goods to the father's house, the mother's to the mother's. We find it necessary to make a distinction between the property of the father and grandfather, (as it was expressed in the formula* in which the prodigal was interdicted from the control of property,) that is, the old inheritance, and new acquisitions. The former are to be regulated by Plato's rule; who directs the *patrimonial lot* to be kept inviolate for the family to which it belongs. Which we are not so to accept as if it were not lawful to dispose by testament of property received from father or grandfather, (for that is often not only laudable but necessary,) but that it may appear what is to be supposed the will of an intestate person in a doubtful case. For we grant that the person of whom we speak has in him plenary ownership †.

2 But since he cannot retain his ownership after death, and it must be held for certain that he would not lose the means of doing a favour to some one; let us consider what is the most natural order of such favours ‡. Aristotle says that we are to repay obligations before

---

* The formula was this: Quando tua bona paterna avitaque nequitia tua dispendis, liberosque tuos ad egestatem perducis, ob eam rem tibi ea re commercioque interdico. Paulus 3. Sent. tit. 4. § 7. *Gronovius.*

† It is plain that Plato's law withholds plenary ownership. W.

‡ The making the owner so completely the master of his property even after his death, that it is to be disposed of by conjecture as to what he would have wished, rather than by any other rule, is an extreme view of ownership. W.

we confer favours; and so Cicero, Ambrose. But obligations may be repaid to the living or to the dead: to the dead, in their children who are a part of them; and whom if they were alive they would wish to have benefited. See Lysias.

3 And this equity has been recognized by the careful framers of Justinian's code, in the question between full brothers, and brothers by the father's side, and by the mother's; and in some other cases. See Aristotle: Valerius Maximus. In Justin it is called *gentium commune jus* for brother to succeed to brother.

4 When he is not to be found from whom the property came, nor his children, it remains that the obligation be repaid to those to whom it is due in the next degree, though less due; that is, to a parent of superior degree and his children; especially since by that means it remains among the nearest relatives, both of the deceased owner, and of the person from whom the property came. So Aristotle.

X. 1 In newly acquired property, (the surplus beyond the patrimonial lot, of Plato) when the rule of repaying obligations fails, it remains that the succession fall to him who is believed to have been most dear to the deceased: and this is he who comes nearest to the deceased in the degree of relationship. So Isæus, Aristotle, Cicero, Tacitus, Ambrose. [This however is a moral claim, not a jural claim.]

2 The succession to intestate property, of which we here speak, is nothing but a tacit testament made out by conjecture of the late owner's will. So Quintilian. And what we have said of property newly acquired, will hold also of inherited property, if neither the persons from whom it came nor their children are extant.

XI. 1 The rules which we have given, though most consentaneous to natural conjecture, are, however, not necessary by Natural Law; and therefore by different causes, moving the human will, they vary by compacts, laws, customs. These in some cases allow one person to succeed in the place of another; in other cases, do not permit it; in others, make a distinction as to whom the property came from; in others, disregard this. In some cases the first-born take more than those born later, as among the Hebrews; in others, the shares are equal. In some cases the father's relatives only are reckoned; in others, the mother's relatives share equally with the father's. Sometimes the sex has its effect, sometimes it has not; sometimes account is had of cognation within the nearer degrees, in other cases it is extended further. It would be tedious and foreign to our purpose to follow these differences.

2 This rule we must hold by: that when there are no more express indications of will, it must be supposed that every one intended, with respect to his own succession, that which the law or custom of the people directs: and this, not only from the force of the authority of the State, but from conjecture of what the person's will was. And this is to be held good also of the persons who have the sovereign authority. For they are probably believed to have judged in their own

case that which is most equitable, which is what they have established as law or sanctioned as custom.

XII. In the Succession to kingdoms, we must distinguish the kingdoms which are held by plenary possession and which are patrimonial, from those which are held in some way involving the consent of the people. Of which difference we have spoken above.

Kingdoms of the former kind may be held by males or females: as formerly in Egypt and in Britain. See Lucan and Tacitus. And adopted as well as real children succeed in such cases, from presumption of the will. So Hyllus the adopted son of Hercules succeeded Æpalius; Molossus succeeded Pyrrhus; Atheas [Ateas, *Gronov.*] would have taken Philip for his successor; Jugurtha succeeded to the kingdom of Numidia; and so in the kingdoms of the Goths and Lombards adoption prevailed. Even the kingdom shall pass to those relatives of the last possessor who have no connexion by blood with the first king (the source of the royal stock), if such succession be received in the country in question. Thus Mithridates, in Justin, says that his father received Paphlagonia by inheritance, the line of domestic kings being extinguished.

XIII. If it be directed that the kingdom is to pass undivided, but not to whom it is to go, the eldest child, male or female, will take it. See the Talmud on kings, Herodotus, Livy, Trogus Pompeius. This is called *jus gentium*, the order of age and of nature. But he or she who succeeds in such a kingdom is bound to provide a satisfaction for the coheirs, instead of their share of the power, if, as and as far as, it can be done.

XIV. Those kingdoms which have become hereditary by the free consent of the people, are transferred according to the presumed will of the people. The people are presumed to will what is most expedient. Hence it follows, in the first place, that the kingdom passes undivided, because that arrangement is of great use to preserve the state and the concord of the citizens. So Justin: except law or custom ordain otherwise, as at Thebes, the kingdom was divided between the males; and ancient Attica among the sons of Pandion; and Rhodes; and Argos. [See.]

XV. Another rule is, that the succession remains among those who are descended from the first king: for that family is conceived to be elected for its nobility, and when it fails, the kingdom to return to the people. So Curtius. [See.]

XVI. In the third place, that none succeed except those who are born according to the laws of the country: not natural children, who are open to contempt, since their father did not deem their mother worthy of a legitimate marriage, and besides, as being less certain. For in kingdoms it is expedient for the people that there should be the greatest possible certainty, to avoid controversies. So Demetrius in Macedon was taken, rather than Perseus. So says Ovid. Also not adoptive children, because the nobility of the race makes kings more reverenced, and turns more hope to them. So Horace. [See.]

XVII. In the fourth place, that among those who are admitted alike into the inheritance, whether as being of the same degree, or as succeeding in the place of their parents, males are preferred to females; because males are more fitted both for war and for other parts of government.

XVIII. 1 Fifthly, that among males, and among females when the males fail, the elder is preferred, because he is either more mature in judgment, or will sooner be so. So Cyrus in Xenophon. But because this superiority of age is only temporary, while that of sex is perpetual, the prerogative of sex is stronger than that of age. So Herodotus, Diodorus, Trogus, Xenophon, Virgil. So at Lacedæmon, Sparte the daughter of Eurotas succeeded, and her children; and the children of Helen, to Tyndareus, because there were no male children. And Eurystheus was succeeded by his uncle Atreus. By the same right the kingdom of Athens passed to Creusa, that of Thebes to Antigone, because the males failed: and the kingdom of Argos went to Argus the grandson of Phoroneus through his daughter.

2 Whence it is to be understood that although children in some degrees fill the place of parents who have died, that is to be understood, so as that they are capable of ruling compared with others, and saving the prerogative, first of sex, and then of age. For the quality of sex and of age, so far as in this matter they are considered by the people, adheres to the person, so that it cannot be separated from it.

XIX. It is made a question whether a kingdom, when thus transferred, is a part of the inheritance. And the more true opinion is that it is a certain kind of inheritance, but distinct from the inheritance of other property; such an inheritance as is seen in some fiefs, in leases, in the right of patronage, in priority of legacy. Whence it follows that the kingdom pertains to him who may take the property as heir if he choose to do so; but in such a way that it may be taken without the property and its burthens. The reason is, because the people is supposed to wish that the kingdom should be transferred by the best right possible; nor is it their concern, whether the king accept the inheritance of the property or not; since they chose the hereditary order of succession, not that the heir of the ordinary property should have it, but that the order might be certain, and might carry with it the reverence given to the blood; and also that from the habits of the race and their education, there might be the hope of good moral qualities: and that the possessor of the kingdom might bestow more care on the kingdom, and defend it with more energy, since he was to leave it to those whom he most wished to benefit for benefits received, or from natural affection.

XX. But when the rule of succession is different in *allodial* and in *feudal* property, if the kingdom be not a fief, or certainly was not so at first, even though *homage* have been done for it; the succession is by the law which regulated allodial property when the kingdom was instituted.

XXI. But in those kingdoms which were given as fiefs by a person who had plenary ownership, the law of feudal succession is to be followed: not however always the Lombardic law which we have in the law-books, but that which was received in each nation at the time of the first investiture. For the Goths, Vandals, Huns, Franks, Burgundians, Angles, Saxons, all the Germanic nations which occupied the best parts of the Roman empire, had each their own laws or customs concerning fiefs, as well as the Lombards.

XXII. 1 But there is another succession frequent in kingdoms, called *Lineal;* in this, the rule observed is, not that of the representation of the heir by his progeny, but the heir transmits the future succession, [even if he die before he succeed himself] the law founding a true right upon an expectancy which of itself produces no effect; [see the illustration from the Civil Law;] so that this right passes to his posterity who are descended from the first king: but according to a certain order; so that there are first called in the children of the last possessor of the first degree, both those who are alive and those who are dead: and among those alive and dead account is had, first of sex, then of age: and if the right of the dead be superior, it passes to those who descend from them, with the like prerogative, first of sex, and then of age; and preserving at every step the right of transmission from the dead to the living, and from the living to the dead. If the children of any branch fail, the succession passes to the next who are nearest of kin, or would be if they were alive, by a similar transmission, and observing in those of the same branch the same distinction of sex and age; so that transition is never made, on account of sex or age, from one line to another. It follows from this, that a son's daughter is preferred to a daughter's son, and a brother's son to a sister's son, and an elder brother's son to a younger brother, and so in other cases. This is the succession of the kingdom of Castile: and the same rule holds with regard to *majorats* in that kingdom.

2 An argument for this lineal succession, if law and example be wanting, may be taken from the order of public assemblies; [such as a House of Peers.] For if in such cases also account is had of lines of descent, that will be a sign that expectancy [is by the law vivified into a Right, so that the succession passes from the dead to the survivors.

This is a *Cognatic* lineal succession, in which women and the sons of women are not excluded, but are postponed in their own line; but yet so that there is a regress to them, if there be a failure of claimants nearer, or equal in other things, who are males, or from males.

The foundation of this succession, so far as it differs from the hereditary, is the hope entertained by the people as to the good education of those who have the legitimate hope of the kingdom : and such are they whose parents, if they had lived, would have succeeded.

XXIII. There is also an *Agnatic* lineal succession, of males to males only; which, obtaining in a certain noble kingdom, is called *Frank* Law [or *Salic* Law.]   This, so far as it differs from the cognatic, was introduced mainly with this view, that the empire might not pass to foreign blood by the marriages of the female branches.

In both these lineal successions, those are admitted who are distant even in the most remote degree from the last possessor, provided they descend from the first king.

There are some cases when, failing the agnatic succession, the cognatic is substituted.

XXIV. Other modes of succession also may be introduced according to the will of the people, or by the will of the patrimonial sovereign. For instance, he may settle that those who on each occasion are nearest to himself, [see Grotius's note] should succeed to the kingdom : as amongst the Numidians formerly, I suppose by some such rule, the brothers of the last possessor were preferred.   So in Arabia Felix, the Tauric Chersonese, and the Africans of Morocco and Fez. And this rule is, in doubtful cases, followed in choosing trustees for family property, as is the sounder opinion, agreeing also with the Roman laws, though the commentators wrest them another way.

These rules being well known, it will be easy to answer the controversies concerning the right of succession, which are thought very difficult in consequence of the different opinions of jurists.

XXV. It is made a question, whether a son can be disinherited by his father so as to be prevented from succeeding to the kingdom. Here we must distinguish alienable, that is, patrimonial kingdoms, from those which are inalienable.   In alienable cases, there is no doubt that disinheritance takes its effect, since the kingdom cannot differ from other property; and therefore the rules which by law or custom obtain as to *exheredation* will have place here.   And if there are no laws or customs, by Natural Law exheredation is lawful, except as to aliment; and even without that exception, if the son have committed a crime worthy of death, or otherwise greatly offended.   Thus Reuben was deprived of his right as first-born by Jacob for his offense, and Adonijah, of the kingdom, by David.   And he is held for tacitly disinherited who has committed a grave crime against his father, if there are no tokens of *condonation* or pardon*.

But in inalienable kingdoms, though hereditary, the same does not hold : because the people chose indeed the hereditary way ; but the hereditary way with the usual succession to intestates.

Still less will exheredation hold good in a lineal succession, when the kingdom comes to each person by the gift of the people, without attempting to imitate the hereditary rule.

XXVI. Similar is the question whether the kingdom, or the right

* This is rejected by Barbeyrac as too severe.

of succeeding to it, can be abdicated. And that each person for himself may abdicate, there is no doubt: whether he can do so for his children also, is more controverted, but is to be solved by the same distinction. For in hereditary kingdoms, he who abdicates for himself can transfer nothing to his children. But in a lineal succession, the act of the father cannot be allowed to prejudice sons already born; because as soon as they began to exist, they acquired a right by law; nor sons not yet born, because it cannot prevent that the right should descend to them also by the gift of the people. Nor does the difficulty of transmitting the right make any obstacle: for the transmission is necessary, not voluntary, so far as the parents are concerned. There is this difference between children born, and to be born; that those not yet born have not yet acquired any right, and therefore their rights may be cut off by the will of the people, if the parents whose interest it is that the right should pass to the sons have given up that right: and to this pertains what we have said above of dereliction.

XXVII. 1 This also is made a question, Whether the reigning king, or the people, or judges appointed by them, can judge concerning the succession. And we must deny that they can pronounce a judgment as if they had jurisdiction in such a case. For jurisdiction belongs only to a superior, not merely taking account of the person, but of the cause also, which is to be regarded with its circumstances. But the cause of the succession is not subject to the reigning king: which appears from this, that the reigning king cannot bind his successor. For the succession to the sovereignty is not under the authority of the sovereign, and therefore remains in the natural state in which there was no jurisdiction*.

2 If however the right of succession be controverted, they who claim the right, will do rightly and piously if they agree to appoint arbitrators. The people has transferred all the jurisdiction from itself to the king and the royal family; and so long as that lasts, it has no relicks of it. I speak of a true kingdom, not merely of a government. But if a question arise concerning the primeval will of the people, it will be much to the purpose to ask the people now existing, which is conceived to be the same with the former people, to express its opinion upon that matter, which is to be followed, except it appear certainly that the will of the people formerly was different, and that a right was thence acquired. Thus Euphaes, as king, permitted the Messenians to determine who of the royal family of the Egyptidæ should reign; and in the controversy of Xerxes and Artabazanes the people decided.

XXVIII. To come to other questions; that a son who was born before his father's accession to the kingdom is, in an indivisible kingdom, to be preferred to one born during the enjoyment of power, is true in every form of succession. In a divisible kingdom he will doubtless have his share; as is the case with other property, in which

* Gronovius argues against this doctrine, but rather in the manner of a rhetorician than a jurist. W.

no difference is ever made as to the time when it was acquired. Now he who would take a share in a divisible inheritance, will, in a matter indivisible, be preferred on the ground of age; and thus the fief follows the son who was born before investiture. But in a case of lineal succession also, as soon as the kingdom is acquired, there is some expectancy given to the children born previously; for suppose that none were born afterwards, nobody will say that the former children were to be excluded. But in this kind of succession, an expectancy once given to any one gives him a right, and does not cease by any subsequent event; except that in a cognatic succession it is suspended by the privilege of sex. The opinion which we are stating obtained in Persia between Cyrus and Arsica; in Judea between Antipater, the son of Herod the Great, and his brothers; in Hungary, when Geissa took the kingdom; and in Germany, though not without recourse to war, between Otho I. and Henry.

XXIX. The fact that a different rule was followed at Sparta, proceeded from a peculiar law of that people, which on account of their education, preferred those that were born in the reign. The same may take place by a peculiar Law of the primitive investiture, if the government be given as a fief to a vassal and his offspring: on which argument Ludovico seems to have relied against Galeazzo his brother, in the controversy respecting the dukedom of Milan. For in Persia, Xerxes who obtained the kingdom against his brother Artabazanes owed his success to the power of his mother Atossa, rather than to his right, as Herodotus notes. And in the same kingdom of Persia, when afterwards the same controversy arose between Artaxerxes Mnemon and Cyrus, Artaxerxes as the eldest, though born in a private station, was made king.

XXX. 1 It has also been a matter of contest, discussed by means of wars and single combats, whether the grandson of the former son be to take precedence of the later son. This, in a lineal succession, can have no difficulty; for there the dead are held as living, in this respect, that they transmit their right to their children: wherefore in such a succession the son of the first-born is preferred without any regard to age; and in cognatic kingdoms, the daughter also: for neither age nor sex lead them to desert the line. In divisible hereditary kingdoms, the claimants share the inheritance according to the shares of the sons; except in those countries in which the substitution of the son for the parent is observed, as among most peoples in Germany. For it was only at a later period that grandsons were admitted along with sons to the inheritance. But in a doubtful case, we are rather to suppose that that vicarious succession has place, because nature favours it.

2 If the substitution of the son in the place of his deceased parent be plainly introduced by the Civil Law, it will have place, although, in any law, *proximus*, "the nearest relation," be mentioned as the successor. The reasons which are drawn from the Roman Laws to this effect, are insecure; as will appear to any one who examines these laws themselves. But this is the best reason; that in a

favourable matter, the signification of words is to be extended to every property, not common only, but artificial also; so that under the name of sons are to be comprehended adoptive sons; and under the name of death, civil death, because the laws have been accustomed so to speak. Therefore he may justly come in the name of *proximus* whom the law has put in the nearest place to the succession. But in hereditary indivisible kingdoms, in which substitution of one person into the place of another is not excluded, we cannot say that either the grandson always, or the second son always, is preferred; but as being equal in claim, by the effect of law in equalizing their degrees of relationship, he is preferable who is the elder; for in hereditary kingdoms, as we have said, the privilege of age is not transferred by succession. At Corinth the eldest of the descendants of the deceased king succeeded. So among the Vandals it was provided that the heir should be he who was nearest and oldest; and the second son, being older, was preferred to the son of the first son. So in Sicily, Robert was preferred to the son of his elder brother Charles Martel, not exactly for the reason which Bartolus devised, because Sicily was a fief; but because the kingdom was hereditary.

3 We have a similar succession exemplified in the Frank kingdom, in Guntram; but that happened rather by the election of the people, which at that time had not quite fallen into disuse. But since the agnatic lineal succession without any election is introduced, the matter is clear of controversy: as formerly at Sparta, where, when the kingdom passed to the Heraclidæ, there was a similar agnatic lineal succession. And thus Areus was preferred to his uncle Cleonymus. But in the cognatic lineal succession also the grandson is preferred; as in England, Richard* the grandson of Edward III. by his first-born [the Black Prince] was preferred to Edmund and Thomas [and others], sons of the same Edward III.: which also is the rule in the kingdom of Castile.

XXXI. By a like distinction we reply to the question between the surviving brother of the last king, and the son of his elder brother: except that we must know that in many places succession into the place of a person deceased is received, as among the children, when it is not received in the transverse line. When the law is not manifest, we are rather to incline to that rule which puts children in the place of their parents, because natural equity points that way, that is, in things which have descended from the grandfather. Nor is it any objection that Justinian calls the right existing in the sons of brothers a *privilege*; for that he does, not with reference to Natural Law, but to the old Roman Law.

Let us run over some other questions which Emanuel Costa proposes.

XXXII. He says, that the son of the brother of the deceased, or even his daughter, is to be preferred to their uncle; rightly, not only in a lineal succession, but also in a hereditary one, in kingdoms where

* Barbeyrac has corrected Grotius's mistakes in the English royal genealogy.

substitution in the place of the deceased is observed: but not in king-doms which in precise words respect the natural degree; for there he will be preferred who is superior in sex or age.

XXXIII. He adds, that a grandson through a son is preferred to a daughter; rightly; namely, on account of sex: with this excep-tion, unless the question be in a country which, even among children, regards only the degree [the order, not the sex].

XXXIV. He adds, that a younger grandson by a son, is pre-ferred to an older grandson by a daughter; which is true in a cognatic lineal succession, but not in a hereditary, except a special law be produced. Nor is the alleged reason sufficient, that the father of the first would have excluded the mother of the second; for that would have happened on account of a mere personal preference, which is not transferred.

XXXV. What he adds as probable in his opinion, that the grand-daughter by the first-born excludes a younger son, cannot be received in hereditary kingdoms, even if we admit substitution in the place of the deceased: for that does indeed make the granddaughter capable of the succession; but among those capable, the privilege of sex must have its weight.

XXXVI. And therefore in the kingdom of Arragon, the son of a sister is preferred to the daughter of a brother.

XXXVII. In the same manner, in hereditary kingdoms, the younger brother of the king is preferred to the daughter of his elder brother.

CHAPTER VIII.

Of Acquisitions commonly said to be Jure Gentium.

I. 1 THE order of our subject has led us to that acquisition which takes place *jure gentium*, as distinct from *jus naturale*, Natural Law; which we have above called Instituted *Jus Gentium*. Such are the things done by the Laws of War; but we shall treat of these hereafter.

The Roman Jurists, when they speak of acquiring the ownership of things, reckon many ways of such acquisition, which they say are *juris gentium;* but if we duly attend, we shall see that they all, if we except the Laws of War, do not pertain to that *jus gentium* of which we now speak; but are either to be referred to Natural Law (not mere Natural Law, but that which follows the introduction of ownership, and precedes all Civil Law,) or to the Civil Law, not of the Roman People alone, but of many other nations: I suppose, because the origin of such Law or custom came from the Greeks, whose Institutions, as Dionysius Halicarnassensis and others note, the peoples of Italy and the neighbourhood followed.

2 But this is not the *jus gentium* properly: for that does not pertain to the mutual society of nations amongst themselves, but to the tranquillity of each people: whence it might be changed by one people without consulting others; and also it might happen that in various places and times, very different usages, and thus, different *jus gentium* improperly so termed, might be introduced: which, we see, happened, in fact, from the time that the Germanic nations invaded almost the whole of Europe. For as the laws of Greece formerly, so now Germanic Institutions are everywhere received, and are still in authority.

The first mode of acquiring ownership which is called by the Romans *juris gentium*, is the occupation of things which belong to no one (*res nullius*) : which mode is, doubtless, natural in the sense which I have mentioned; ownership being supposed to be introduced, and as long as the law has made no other appointment. For ownership may also take place by the Civil Law.

II. To this head is referred, first, the capture of wild beasts, birds, fishes. But how long these are *res nullius*, belong to no one, is not without question. Nerva says, that fishes in a pond are ours, fishes in a lake are not; beasts which are in a park are ours, not those which range in the woods, though surrounded by a fence. But fishes are included in a lake, which is private property, as much as in a pond; and a well-fenced wood shuts in beasts, no less than a park : these things differ only in that one is a narrower, the other a wider custody. And accordingly, in our time, the contrary opinion more rightly prevails : and beasts in private woods, and fishes in private lakes, as they can be possessed, so can they be owned.

III. The Roman jurists say, that when beasts recover their natural liberty they cease to be ours : but in all other things the ownership which begins with possession is not lost when we lose the possession; but, on the contrary, gives a right to recover possession. And it cannot make much difference whether it be a fugitive slave that takes them away, or that they take themselves away. Therefore the sounder opinion is, that the ownership is not lost because the beasts escape from our custody, but that it is lost from the probable conjecture, that we may be supposed to let them go as derelicts, on account of the difficulty of pursuing them; especially as it is impossible to know our beasts from others. But this conjecture may be refuted by other evidence : as if the beast be *marked*, or have a bell hung to it; as we know that deer and hawks have sometimes had, and thereby have been restored to the owners.

Some corporeal possession is required to make the ownership complete; and therefore it is not enough to have wounded them, as is rightly held, in opposition to Trebatius. Hence the proverb, *You started the hare for him to catch*. And so Ovid.

IV. But a possession which gives ownership may be acquired, not by the hands alone, but by instruments, as traps, snares, nets; on two conditions; first, that the instruments be in our power; next, that the creature be so caught that he cannot escape. And by this rule is to be decided the question of the boar which fell into the snare.

V. This is the rule, if no Civil Law intervene : for jurists are much mistaken who think that it is so decidedly Natural Law that it cannot be changed. It is Natural Law, not simply, but in a certain state of things, that is, if it be not otherwise provided. But the peoples of Germany, when they wished to assign to their princes and kings some rights to sustain their dignity, wisely thought that they might best begin with those things which can be given without damage

to any one; of which kind are the things which have not yet become
the property of any; [and thence they gave them a right to the game].
And this too was what the Egyptians did. For there the king's proc-
tor claimed things of that kind. The law might transfer the ownership of these things even before occupation, since the law alone is sufficient to produce ownership.

VI.   Other ἀδέσποτα, ownerless things, are acquired in the same
way as game. For these too, if we follow nature alone, belong to him
who finds them and takes possession. Thus Acanthos was adjudged
to the Chalcideans who entered it first, not to the Andrians who first
cast a javelin into it: for the beginning of possession is the contact of
body with body, which, with regard to moveables, is mostly performed
with our hands, with regard to the soil, with our feet.

VII.   Among ownerless things is *treasure trove*, that is, money of
which the owner is unknown; for what does not appear is, so far, as if
it did not exist. Hence by Natural Law such treasure belongs to the
finder, that is, him who took hold of it or took it up. Nor is it an
objection, that by laws and customs other rules may be established.
Plato directs that the fact shall be reported to the magistrates, and the
oracle consulted; and Apollonius adjudged it, as a boon of the gods,
to him whom he thought the best man. That among the Hebrews
the received rule was that the treasure should go to the owner of the
soil, appears to follow from the parable, Matth. xiii. The same was
the case in Syria. See Philostratus. The Laws of the Roman Emperors varied much on this point; as appears partly by the constitutions, and partly by the histories of Lampridius, Zonaras and Cedrenus.
The peoples of Germany gave treasure trove, like other ownerless
things, to the prince; and that is now the common law, as a sort of *jus
gentium*. For it is observed in Germany, France, England, Spain, and
Denmark. And that there is in this no wrong done, we have sufficiently explained.

VIII.   Let us now come to the additions made to land by rivers;
on which subject there are very many rescripts [opinions on cases] of
the old jurists, and of the moderns, whole books. But the rules delivered on this subject by them are, for the most part, instituted rules
of certain nations, not Natural Law; although they often give their
rules as Natural Laws. For many of their determinations rest on this
foundation, that the banks belong to the nearest landowners, and also
the bed of the river when deserted by the stream: from which it follows
that the islands which make their appearance in the river belong to
the same persons. Thus in the inundation of a river they make a
distinction that a small inundation does not take away ownership, a
large one does; but so that if the river retires by a single impulse, the
ground which was flooded returns to the owner by *postliminium*, [a
resumption of the previous condition of property:] if the river recedes
gradually, it is not so; but, on the contrary, passes to the nearest landowners. That all this might be established by law, and defended by

the consideration of its being a useful rule for the preservation of the banks, I do not deny: that it is Natural Law, which they seem to think, I by no means concede.

IX. 1 For if we look at the general case, peoples occupied the land, not only as lords, but as owners, before it was assigned to private proprietors*. Seneca, Cicero, Dio Prusæensis, Tacitus, speak of the occupation of land by peoples. [See.] What was thus occupied by peoples, and was not afterwards distributed, is to be considered as belonging to the people; and as in a river which is private property, an island which makes its appearance, or a deserted river-bed, is the property of the private person; so in a public river, both of these belong to the people, or to him to whom the people has given them.

2 What we have said of the bed of the river, is true also of the bank, which is only the extreme portion of the bed, that is, where the river naturally stops. And we find that this is now the general usage. In Holland, and the neighbouring countries, where of old these controversies were more frequent on account of the lowness of the land, the magnitude of the rivers, and the neighbourhood of the sea, which receives the mud carried down, and brings it back by the reflux of the tide, it was always settled that islands which were true islands were the public property; and in like manner, the deserted beds of the Rhine and the Meuse; which has often been adjudged, and rests on the soundest reasons.

3 For even the Roman jurists allow that an island which floats in a river, for instance, one resting on roots and branches, is public property; because the party who has a right to the river has a right also to an island produced in the river. But the same reason holds for the bed as for the river: not only in the way in which the Roman jurists take it, because the bed is covered by the river, but for another, which we have mentioned above; that the bed and the river were occupied at the same time by the people, and have not since passed into private ownership. And therefore we do not accept as Natural Law what they say, that if the lands are marked by boundaries, the island belongs to him who takes possession of it. That would be so, only if the river and the bed of the river were not already occupied by the people; as an island which rises in the sea belongs to him who takes possession of it.

X. 1 Nor can we admit that doctrine above stated concerning a very grave inundation, if we only follow natural reason. For mostly, though the surface part of the ground is dissolved into sand, the lower solid part of the soil remains; and though it may in some measure change the quality, it does not change the substance, any more than a part of the land from which a lake is drained, the right to which is not changed by such a process, as the Romans rightly decide. Nor is that Natural Law which they say, that the rivers, like the collectors of a land-tax [who have to seize and sell the property

* As Barbeyrac says, the contrary is more nearly true. W.

of defaulters, *Gron.*] increase private property by public, and public by private. The Egyptians judged better, who made a measurement and division of the land, which was independent of the inundations.

2 There is nothing contrary to this opinion in what the Roman writers have delivered, that what is ours does not cease to be ours except by our own act; add, or by law. But among our acts are included also the things which we do not do, so far as they supply a conjecture of the will. Wherefore we grant this, that if the inundation be very grave, and if there are no other signs which imply an intention of retaining the ownership, the land may easily be presumed to be a derelict; and this estimation, as it is naturally indefinite from the variety of circumstances, and one of those things which must be left to the judgment of a fair man, so is it often defined by the Civil Law. Thus in Holland land is held to be derelict, if it has been under water for ten years, and there are no signs of continuation of possession: and in this case we reasonably accept a rule which the Romans reject; that if you can do nothing else, you may be supposed to retain possession by fishing over it. So princes were accustomed to appoint a time within which the ancient possessors were bound to free their lands from water: and if they did not do this, warning was given, first to those who had mortgages upon the land, next to those who had jurisdiction, either civil only, or criminal also; and if all these parties were behindhand in doing what the law required, the whole right of the property passed to the prince: and he either drained the lands himself, and added them to his patrimony, or gave them to others to be drained, retaining a part of the profit.

XI. Concerning alluvium, that is, the addition of particles which cannot be claimed by any one, because it is unknown whence they come, (for otherwise the part would not, by Natural Law, change its owner,) it should be considered as certain that this also belongs to the people, if the people have assumed possession of the river as owner, which in a case of doubt is to be supposed; otherwise, the property of him who takes possession of it.

XII. 1 But as the people may concede this right to others, so undoubtedly it may concede it to the possessors of the adjacent lands; and it is supposed to have done so, if those lands have no other boundary on that side than the natural boundary, that is, the river. Wherefore we are not to despise the laborious discussion of this subject by the Romans; in which they have distinguished *limitatum*, land bounded by artificial limits, from other lands; provided we recollect that land *mensurâ comprehensum*, determined by its measured quantity, (see II. iii. xvi.) is governed by the same rule as *limitate* land. For what we said before of ownership, when we spoke of occupation, obtains also with regard to private lands: adding this difference, that lordships (*imperia*) are, in a doubtful case, to be supposed to be *arcifinial*, bounded by natural limits, because that best agrees with the nature of the territory: but private lands are rather supposed not to be

K

naturally bounded, but either limitate, or determined by measure; for this is more congruous to the nature of private possession.

2 We do not deny that it may be that a people assigns land to a private person by the same rule by which it had itself occupied it, that is, up to the river; and if that is the case, the possessor has a right to the alluvium: which, in Holland, was some generations ago adjudged to be the case with the lands between the Meuse and the Yssel, because these, both in the leases and in the records of the land-tax, are always said to reach to the river. And if such lands be sold, although, in the articles of sale, some measure be mentioned, yet since they are sold, not by measure but bodily, they retain their nature and right of alluvium: which is also declared in the Roman Law, and everywhere acted on as usage.

XIII. What we have said of alluvium, is also to be considered to apply to a deserted river-bank and a part of the bed dried up; namely that, in places not occupied, they belong to him who takes possession; in occupied rivers, to the people; and to private persons only if they have received from the people, or from one who derives right from the people, land running on to the river, as such.

XIV. But since we have said that the rule respecting an island is different from the rule for alluvium, a controversy often arises which of the two a piece of ground is, when there is an elevated promontory connected with the nearest land by a plain which is under water: which perpetually happens with us on account of the inequality of the ground. Here usages vary. In Gueldres it becomes part of the land, provided it be occupied and can be visited with a loaded cart: in the land of Putten, as far as a man on foot with a sword in his hand can reach. The most natural rule is, that an island should be considered as separate from the land when there is a strait through which a ship can commonly pass.

XV. 1 No less frequent is the question between the sovereign prince, and his vassals who have subordinate authority. That the mere concession of sovereignty does not carry with it the increase made by rivers, is plain enough. But it is to be noted that some vassals have received, with their definite authority, the right to the whole land, saving what belongs to private persons; it may be, because the land formerly belonged to the prince or to the people, or was drained by the people. In this case it is not doubtful that the vassals have the same rights which the prince or the people had. And thus we see in Zealand, vassals who have only civil jurisdiction, [not criminal,] still pay the land-taxes for the whole of the land; of which they in return claim a part from private possessors according to their holdings. And in such cases there is no question about the right of alluvium.

In some cases, the river is given to a person, and then of course he rightly claims the islands that are produced, whether arising from accumulated mud, or parts of the bed which the river leaves.

2 There are other persons whose grant does not comprehend either the one or the other of these things : and these have no case against the public; except either the custom of that country favours them, or a long possession, with due circumstances, have generated a right.

But if it be not the authority or lordship, but the land which is granted as a fief, we must see what is the nature of the land, as above stated. If it is *arcifinial*, the alluvium is to be considered as compre- hended in the grant, not by the peculiar right of the prince, but by the nature of the land: for a tenant for a term would in such case also enjoy the profits of alluvium.

XVI. The Romans, in order to prove their own Law to be Natu- ral Law, are wont to adduce that trite maxim : It is according to nature that he should have the advantages of anything who has the disadvantages: wherefore, as the river may often carry away a part of my land, it is reasonable that I should take what it gives. But that rule does not hold, except when the advantages come from a thing which is ours; but here they come from the river, which belongs to another party. But that what is destroyed is lost to the owner, *is* Natural Law. And that what they allege is not universally applicable, appears by the exception, admitted by themselves, of limitate land. The river enriches some, impoverishes others, as Lucan says.

XVII. What they further say, that even a public road [passing along the river-bank] does not bar the right of alluvium, is a doctrine for which there is no natural reason; except the private land be bound to keep up the road.

XVIII. There is another mode of acquisition, amongst those which are reckoned *juris gentium*, by the generation of animals: in which that which has been ruled by the Romans and some other nations, that the offspring follows the mother (as to property) is not Natural Law, as we have said above, (II. v. xxix.) except so far that the father is unknown in most cases. But if there were any probable cer- tainty concerning him, no reason could be assigned why the offspring should not belong partly to him. For that what is born is part of the father is certain. Whether it derive more from the father or the mother is disputed among physiologists. So Plutarch. [See.] And this view was followed in the old laws of the Franks and Lom- bards.

XIX. 1 [There is a question concerning property in which mate- rials and labour are mixed.]

If I make a new article of materials belonging to another, the Sabinians* determined it to be the property of him to whom the materials belonged; Proculus, the property of me who gave it the new form, by which the article began to be what it is. But at last the medium opinion was accepted: that if the matter could return to its former shape, the owner of the material should have it; if it could not, then the person who was the author of the new form. But

* The followers of Massurius Sabinus. *Gronov.*

Connanus condemns this, and is for having this point alone considered; whether there be a greater amount of value in the workmanship or in the material; and for directing that that which is the more valuable should prevail, and draw to it that which is of less value; arguing by reference to the doctrines of the Roman jurists concerning value added to a thing.

2 But if we look at Natural Law merely, as the Roman jurists decided that when materials of two kinds belonging to two persons are indistinguishably mixed, there is a common property produced, in proportion to each person's share, because otherwise there could be no natural termination of the question: so when things consist of matter and form as their parts, if the matter belong to one, the form to another, it follows by Natural Law that the article is common property, according to the share of value which belongs to each. For the form is part of the substance, but not the whole substance: which Ulpian saw, when he said that by the change of form the substance was *almost* destroyed.

XX. But that they who with fraudulent intent meddle with matter that belongs to another, lose their right to the form which they have given it, is indeed a rule not otherwise than equitable; but it is a penal Law, and therefore not a Natural Law; for Nature does not determine punishment, nor does she take away ownership for a delinquency *per se;* though by Natural Law delinquents are worthy of some punishment.

XXI. But that the minor thing becomes an appendage to the major thing, which is the ground on which Connanus rests, is a natural rule in fact, but not in law. He who is part-owner of an estate, for a twentieth part only, is as much part-owner as he who has the nineteen parts. Wherefore all that is settled in the Roman Law, or may further be settled, about one part becoming an appendage to the other on account of the prevalence of value, is not Natural Law, but Civil Law, introduced for the convenience of business; nature not repugning, because the law has the right of giving ownership. But there is scarce any part of law in which the opinions and errors of jurists are so various. For who will allow that if copper and gold are mixed together they cannot be separated, as Ulpian writes; or that in welding, [*ferruminatio*] there is an indistinguishable mixture, as Paulus; or that the rule is different for a written paper and a picture; the canvas being an appendage to the picture, but the writing to the paper?

XXII. That plantations and crops are appendages to the soil is similarly an established rule of law; of which the reason is, that they are nourished by the soil. On this account a distinction is made in a tree, according to whether it has shot out roots. But aliment makes only a part of a thing already existing: and therefore, as the owner of the soil acquires some right from the aliment supplied, so the owner of the seed, plant, or tree planted, does not thereby lose his right according to Natural Law.   Therefore this too will be a case of common property: and in the same way in a house, of which the parts are the ground and the superstructure; for if the building be moveable, the owner of the soil haś no right in it, as Scævola also decided.

XXIII.   That a *bona fide* possessor, [one who believes that he has a right,] acquires a property in all the fruit or income which he draws from the property, is not Natural Law: but only so far as this; that he has a right to charge the expenses which he has bestowed upon the property, and his useful labour, and of deducting them from the income received: and even of retaining the rising crop if repayment is not otherwise made.

XXIV.   The same may be said of a possessor *male fide,* [who knows that he has not a right,] when the penal law does not interfere. *It is more considerate,* says Paulus the jurist, *that even in a man who has robbed us we should take account of his expenses; for the complainant ought not to derive gain from another's loss.*

XXV.   The last mode of acquisition which is called *juris gentium* is by tradition or delivery.   But we have said above that delivery is not required by Natural Law for the transfer of ownership; as indeed the Jurists themselves in some cases acknowledge: as in a thing which is given to another, while the present enjoyment of it is retained by the donor, or which is made over to a person who already holds it, or has it as a loan, or in things thrown among a crowd for them to catch.   And in some cases, even now, a man may transfer the ownership before he is owner himself; as [by a certain Roman law,] in inheritances, legacies, things given to churches or pious places, or to communities, or for the sake of aliment, or in cases when a joint property in the goods is established.

XXVI.   We have noted these things, in order that when any one finds the term *juris gentium* in the Roman jurists, he may not, as a matter of course, understand that *jus* which is immutable: but may carefully distinguish precepts of Natural Law from those which, in a certain state, are natural; and rights which are common to many peoples independently, from those which contain the bond of human society, [and therefore are truly *juris gentium*].

But this is to be noted, that if by this *jus gentium* improperly so called, or by the law of one people, a mode of acquiring property be introduced without any distinction of citizen and stranger, this, of course, gives a right to foreigners also: and if the person be prevented from taking possession of the right, there may arise a wrong which gives a just occasion of war.

CHAPTER IX.

When Lordship and Ownership cease.

I. WE have sufficiently explained how both private ownership and public authority is acquired, and how it is transferred; let us now consider how it ceases.

That it ceases by derelict, is above shewn in passing; because the will ceasing, the ownership does not remain. There is also another mode of its ending: the subject or person in whom the lordship or ownership resides being removed, that is, before alienation either express at least, or tacit, such as there is in successions to intestates. Wherefore if any person die without giving any indication of his will, and without leaving any relative, every right which he had perishes, and therefore his slaves (except some human law prevent it) will be free; the peoples who had been under his authority will be their own masters, because these things (slaves and governments) are not things which can be taken possession of by the first comer; but his other property may be so *occupied.*

II. The same which we have said of a person may be said of a Family which fails, and which had any rights.

III. 1 The same, if a People fails. Isocrates, and after him the Emperor Julian said, that states are immortal; that is, that they may be so; because a People is that kind of body which consists of separate elements, but is subject to one name, and has *one habit,* as Plutarch says, one spirit, as Paulus. This spirit or habit in a people is the full and perfect common participation of civil life; the first production of which is the sovereignty, the bond by which the State is held together, the vital breath drawn by so many thousands, as Seneca speaks. And these artificial bodies have plainly an analogy with natural bodies. A natural body does not cease to be the same, though the particles are gradually changed, the *Form* remaining the same, as Alphenus, after the philosophers, discourses.

2 And thus we can explain what Seneca says, that no one of us is

the same in age which he was in youth, this being understood of the matter of which we consist; as Heraclitus said, according to the quotation of Plato in the *Cratylus*, and Seneca in the above cited place, that we cannot bathe twice in the same river: which Seneca rightly corrects, by saying the name of the river remains, the water passes. So Aristotle, comparing a river to a people, says, that rivers are called the same, though new water is constantly coming in, old water going out. Nor is it the empty name which remains; but that habit, which Conon defines as a *habit holding the body together*, and Philo, as a *spiritual bond*, and which the Latins also call *the spirit* of the thing. Thus a People, as Alphenus and Plutarch say, is reckoned the same now as it was a hundred years ago, though none of those who lived then is alive now, *As long as that communion which makes a people and binds it together with mutual bonds preserves its unity*, as Plutarch expresses it. And hence arises the mode of speaking, that when we address a people now existing, we attribute to it what happened to the same People several generations ago; as we may see both in the historians, and in the Scriptures. [See the passages.] So in Tacitus, Antonius Primus reminds the veterans of the Third Legion, that, *Under M. Antonius, they had repelled the Parthians, under Corbulo, the Armenians.*

3 It is therefore through spite, and not as speaking truly, that in the same Tacitus, Piso denies that the Athenians of his time are the Athenians, those being extinct by a succession of calamities; and says, that they are a mixture of the dregs of nations. For that accession of strangers had perhaps detracted something from the dignity of the people, but had not made it another people. Nor was he ignorant of this, since on those very Athenians of his time he charged the old faults which they had committed, their failures against the Macedonians, their violence against their own citizens.

But while the change of component parts does not make a people cease to be what it was, even for above a thousand years; it cannot be denied that a people may cease to be: and this may happen in two ways; by the destruction of the body, or by the departure of the *form* or spirit of which I have spoken.

IV. The body is destroyed, either by the simultaneous removal of the parts, without which the body cannot subsist, or by taking away their connexion as a body. To the former mode, you must refer peoples swept away by the sea, as the peoples of the island of Atlantis, of whom Plato speaks, and others whom Tertullian mentions. Also such as have been swallowed up by an earthquake or a chasm opened in the ground, of which there are examples in Seneca and Ammianus Marcellinus, and elsewhere: and those who voluntarily destroyed themselves, as the Sidonians and the Saguntines. Pliny says that fifty-three Peoples of ancient Latium perished, leaving no trace.

If, of such a people, so few survive that they cannot make a People, what are we to say? In that case, the ownership which the people had in the way of private persons may subsist; but not anything which belongs to a people as a people : and the same may be said of a College or Corporation.

V. The connexion of the parts of the body is taken away, if the citizens either break up their society spontaneously on account of pestilence or sedition ; or be so distracted by force that they cannot come together; which happens sometimes in war.

VI. The *form* of a People is taken away, when the participation in common rights no longer subsists, either at all, or at least, perfectly : whether individuals are reduced into a state of personal slavery, as the Myceneans sold by the Argives, the Olynthians by Philip, the Thebans by Alexander, the Bruttians sentenced to slavery at public works by the Romans ; or retaining their liberty* are deprived of their political power.   Thus Livy relates of Capua, that the Romans determined that it should be inhabited as a hamlet merely, with no municipal body, no senate, no assembly of the people, no magistrates; a collection of individuals without authority, among whom a judge sent from Rome should administer justice; and accordingly Cicero says, that there was no image of a State left at Capua.   The same is to be said of peoples reduced into the form of a province, and of those who are brought under the authority of another people.   Thus Byzantium was put under Perinthus by Severus, and Antiochia under Laodicea by Theodosius.

VII. If the People migrate from its place, either of its own will, on account of famine, or other calamity; or under compulsion, as the Carthaginian people in the third Punic war, if the form of which I have spoken remain, the people does not cease to be; still less, if the walls of the city only are thrown down.   Therefore when the Lacedæmonians would have excluded the Messenians from being admitted among those who were to swear to the peace of Greece, because their city-walls were destroyed, the matter was decided against them by the common council of the allies.

VIII. 1 Nor does it make any difference how the people is governed, whether by the authority of a king, or that of a number, or that of the multitude.   The Roman people was the same under kings, consuls, emperors.   Even if the king govern with the most absolute power, the people will be the same which it was before, when it was its own master; provided the king is set over it as the head of that people, not as the head of another people.   For the authority which is in the king as the head, is in the people as the whole body, of which the head is a part : and therefore when the king, if he be elective, or the king's family, is extinct, the supreme authority reverts to the people, as we have shewn above.

Nor is the objection from Aristotle valid; when he says that the *form* of the State being changed, the State is no longer the same; as, says he, the harmony is not the same when we modulate out of the Dorian mood into the Phrygian [though the notes may be the same].

---

* *Ea retenta* is plainly to be understood as *libertate retenta*. W.

2 For it is to be understood that an artificial thing may have several *forms;* thus, one *form* of a legion (or regiment) is its government by
legati, tribuni, centuriones; (colonels, captains, serjeants, &c.): another
form of the same body is its order of march or of battle. Thus one
form of a State is the common participation of right and authority;
and another is the relation of the parts governing and governed. The
politician looks at the latter form, the jurist at the former: and Aristotle was aware of this, when he subjoins, *Whether the name* (of the
State) *is to be changed when the form of government is changed, is another
inquiry:* that is, it belongs to another science [*Jus*], which Aristotle
does not confound with Political Science (*Politica*), that he may not
commit the fault which he blames in others, of *passing to another
genus.*

3 When a People has a king placed over it, it does not cease to
owe the moneys which it ˙owed being free: for it is the same people,
and retains the ownership of the things which had belonged to the
people; and also authority over itself, though this authority is not
now to be exercised by the body, but by the head. And hence we see
what answer is to be made to a controversy which sometimes arises
from circumstances; In what place in a convention ought he to sit who
has acquired the sovereignty over a people free before: as in the
Amphictyonic council, Philip of Macedon had the place which the
Phoceans had had. And so on the other hand, the place which had
belonged to the king, shall be filled by the people, made free.

IX. If at any time two Peoples are united, their rights will not be
lost, but imparted by each to the other; as the rights, first of the
Sabines, and afterwards of the Albans, were imparted to the Romans,
and they were made one republic, as Livy speaks. The same is to be
conceived of kingdoms which are united, not by league, nor only
because they have a common king, but joined by a real union.

X. It may happen, on the contrary, that what had been one State
is divided, either by mutual consent, or by war; as the body of the
Persian empire was divided among the successors of Alexander. When
this happens, there are several sovereignties in the place of one, each
having its rights over the separate parts. If there was anything
which they had in common, that is either to be administered in common, or to be divided proportionally.

To this head also is to be referred the separation of a Colony from
the mother-country. For in this case also there is produced a new
people which is its own master: *They are sent out not to be slaves, but
to have equal rights,* says Thucydides. And so he says that the second
Colony was sent by the Corinthians to Epidamnus *to have fair and equal
rights.* Tullus in Dionysius of Halicarnassus says, *That the mother-
country should govern her colonies, as a necessary law of nature, we do
not think either true or just.*

XI. 1 There is a very celebrated question among historians and jurists, To whom now belong the Rights which did belong to the Roman Empire?

Many hold that these rights belong to the German Kingdom, as it was formerly called, or the German Empire; (it makes no difference which name you adopt:) and they conceive that, in some way or other, one Empire was put in the place of the other. And yet it is well known that Great Germany, that is, Germany beyond the Rhine, was, for the greater part of the time, entirely without the circle of the Roman Empire. It appears to me that such a change or translation is not to be presumed, except it be proved by certain documents. I therefore hold that the Roman people is still the same people as formerly, before it received the admixture of strangers; and that the Roman Empire remained in it, as in the body in which it existed and lived. For what the Roman people had formerly a right to do, before the Emperors reigned, it had the right of doing the same, when one Emperor was dead, and another not yet created. And even the election of the Emperor belonged to the people; and was sometimes made by the people, by itself, or by the Senate. And the elections which were made by the Legions, sometimes by one and sometimes by another, were not valid by any rights which the Legions had; (for in so vague a name there could be no certain right;) but through the approbation of the people.

2 It does not make any objection to this view, that by a constitution of Antonine, all the inhabitants of the Roman Empire were made Roman citizens. For by that constitution, the subjects of the Roman Empire obtained those rights which the Colonies formerly had, and the Municipalities (*Municipia,*) and the Togate Provinces, (*Provinciæ Togatæ;*) namely, that they should participate in the honours of the state, and use the Roman Law (*jus Quiritium;*) but not that the source of Empire should be in other peoples, as it was in the people of the city of Rome; which to do, was not in the power of the Emperors, because they could not change the manner and cause of holding the imperial authority*.

Nor did it detract any thing from the right of the Roman people, that the Emperors chose to live at Constantinople rather than Rome. It must be supposed that the election was made by that part of the Roman people which lived at Constantinople (whence Claudian calls the Byzantines *Quirites,*) and confirmed by the whole people. And the Roman people preserved no small monument of its right, in the prerogatives of the city, in the honour of the consulship, and in other things. And therefore all the right that those who lived at Con-

---

* Grotius here sets up one fiction, that, under the Emperors, the right of election was in the people of Rome; and then another fiction, that this first fiction is not to be extended to persons not belonging to the city of Rome, though they had been made Roman citizens. We cannot wonder that he has found opponents in this view, as Gronovius in his Notes.

stantinople had to elect the Roman Emperor, depended on the will of the People of Rome. And when the Byzantines had, contrary to the desire and practice of the Roman people, elected a woman, Irene, to the empire, to omit other reasons, the Roman people revoked that concession, express or tacit, and elected an emperor itself; and declared its election by the voice of its First Citizen, that is, its Bishop*; (as in the Judaic republic before the kings existed, the High-priest was the first person.)

3 This election was a personal election in the case of Charlemagne and some of his successors: who themselves carefully distinguished the right of authority which they had over the Franks and Lombards, from their right over the Romans, as obtained on new grounds. But afterwards, when the Frank people were divided into a western people, which now holds France, or Gallia, and an eastern, which holds Germany or Alemannia; and when the eastern Franks, (the Germans) had begun to elect kings, (for at that time the succession of Frankish kings was *quasi* agnatic, but depended more on popular suffrage than on certain right,) it was agreed by the people of Rome, in order that they might be sure of a protector, not to have a king of their own, but the king whom the Germans had elected: yet so that they might retain some power of confirming or annulling the election, so far as they were concerned.

4 This approbation was wont to be proclaimed by the Bishop, and solemnly celebrated by a special coronation, [that of King of the Romans.] Wherefore he who is elected by the Seven Princes who represent Germany, has authority to rule over the Germans according to their usages. But the same person is, by the approbation of the Roman people, made Roman Emperor, or King, or, as historians often speak, King of the kingdom of Italy. And by that title, he has under him whatever belonged to the people of Rome, and that has not passed under the authority of other peoples by compact, or by occupation of derelict, or by the right of conquest.

And hence we easily understand by what right the Bishop of Rome, during the vacancy of the Empire, gives the investitures of the fiefs of the Roman Empire; namely, because he is the first person in the Roman people, which at that time is free. For whatever

---

* Here we have a third fiction, that the election of the Byzantine Emperors was made by the Roman citizens at Byzantium, (though the Roman citizens in other cities had not such power of election, by the second fiction;) and a fourth fiction, that it was confirmed by the Roman citizens at Rome: which last fiction is slightly countenanced by the protest against Irene: and a fifth fiction, that the Pope, as the first citizen of Rome, declared the election made by the Roman People according to their ancient right; which is probably, as Gronovius says, not a view which would have pleased the Pope.

Grotius's scheme does however explain the relation of the Emperor of Germany, the kings of the Romans, and the Pope; and thus makes a jural transition from the ancient to the modern world. W.

office belongs to any body, is wont to be discharged by the first person of that body, as we have elsewhere said.

Nor is that unsound which Cynus and Raynerius have laid down, that if the Roman Emperor were prevented from discharging his office by disease or captivity, there might be a substitute for him appointed by the Roman People.

XII.   That the person of the heir, as to the continuation both of public and private ownership, is to be conceived as the same with the person deceased, is undoubted law.

XIII.   How far the Conqueror succeeds to the Conquered, will be explained below in speaking of the effects of war.

––––––––––

CHAPTER X.

Of the Obligation arising from Ownership.

I. 1 HAVING explained, as far as is requisite for our purpose, the Right which we may have over persons or things, we must now see what obligation upon us arises therefrom. Now such obligation arises either from things extant, (including in *things*, persons,) or from things not extant.

2 From things extant, this obligation arises; that he who has a thing of mine in his power is bound to do so as much as he can that it may come into my power. I say, as much as he can: for he is not obliged to what is impossible, nor to restore the thing to me at his own expense; but he is bound to indicate it, that another may recover what is his. For as in the state of community of things, a certain equality came to be observed, so that one might be able to use those common things not less than another; so when ownership is introduced, there is a sort of association established among owners, that he who has in his power a thing belonging to another, is to restore it to the owner. For if ownership were only so far effective, that the thing is to be restored to the owner if he asks for it, ownership would be too feeble, and custody too expensive.

3 Nor is it here considered whether a person has obtained possession of the thing *bona fide* or *mala fide*, believing that he has a right, or not: for the obligation from delict (*mala fides*) is one matter, but the thing (and possession of it) is another. The Lacedæmonians tried to free themselves from the delict by condemning Phœbidas who had seized Cadmea, the citadel of the Thebans, in violation of the treaty; but as they, nevertheless, retained the citadel, they were charged with injustice: and this injustice, as being flagrant, was avenged by a singular providence of God, as Xenophon notes. So Cicero blames M. Crassus and Q. Hortensius who had kept possession of legacies by a will which was false, though fabricated without fault of theirs.

4 But because this obligation binds all men, as by a universal

contract, and gives a certain right to the owner: hence it comes that special contracts, as later in time, are subject to exception. Hence light is thrown on the case put by Tryphoninus. *A robber took my property and deposited it in the hands of Seius, who was ignorant of the crime: ought Seius to restore it to the robber or to me? If we look only at the giver and receiver,* bona fides *requires that the thing deposited should be restored to him who gave it. If we look at the equity of the whole matter, taking into account all the persons concerned, the property must be restored to me, from whom it was most wrongfully taken.* And he rightly adds: *I am of opinion that justice requires to give to each man his own in such a way, that it be not again to be transferred by the more just demand of another person.* In fact, the claim of the owner is more just, in virtue of that right which we have spoken of as contemporary with ownership. And hence it follows, as we find in the same Tryphoninus, that he who in ignorance has received, as a deposit, a thing which is his own, is not bound to restore it: and the question discussed a little before, concerning things deposited by him whose property had been forfeited, is to be decided on these grounds, rather than by the consideration which Tryphoninus adduces, of the utility of the punishment.

5 It makes no difference in the nature of ownership whether it arise *jure gentium* or *jure civili:* for it always has along with it the accompaniments which are natural to it: among which is the obligation of every possessor to restore a thing to its owner. And this is what Martinus says, that, *jure gentium,* things may be sued for from him who possesses them without just cause.

From this source arises that which is delivered by Ulpian, that he who finds anything is so far bound to restore it to the owner, that he cannot demand a reward for finding it. Also the produce of the thing found is to be restored, saving the expense.

II. 1 Concerning things not extant, this is the rule established by mankind (the *jus gentium*), that if you are made richer by something which is mine, and which I am deprived of, you are bound to make restitution to the extent of your gain. For by what you have gained from my property, you have so much the more, and I the less. But ownership was introduced to preserve equality, that is, each having his own. So Cicero. [See.]

2 This rule of equity extends so far that the jurists define many points by means of it, without applying rules of law, referring to equity as the plainest ground. Thus a person is held responsible for the acts of a servant whom he has set over a shop, except he have warned people against trusting him. And even when he has given warning, if the servant have only a share in the business, and if the surplus of profit go to the master, his warning is not held good. *For,* says Proculus, *he appears to act fraudulently* (dolo malo) *who tries to get gain by the loss of others* (the servant's creditors); where *dolus malus* means anything contrary to natural right and equity.

If a friend, at the request of the mother, have advanced money for the son's agent, he has not properly an action against the agent, for commission discharged or work done; nor was it properly the agent's work which he did; for it was in regard to the mother that he gave his money; yet, according to Papinian, there will lie an (indirect) action for work done, against the agent, because he has been liberated from responsibility by the money of the friend.

If a wife have given money to her husband, which she could by law call back again, she has an action establishing her claim to that which has been bought with the money: for, says Ulpian, it cannot be denied that the husband is the richer by the proceeding: and there is to be an inquiry what he possesses which is his wife's.

If money, which my servant stole from me, you have spent, thinking that it was his own property, I have an action against you, as if my property had come into your hands without any just title to it.

Wards are not bound to repay loans according to the Roman Law; yet, if the ward thereby become richer, an indirect action will lie.

If a debtor pledge a thing belonging to another, and it be sold by the creditor, the debtor is relieved, in respect to the creditor, to the extent of the price received for the thing: because, says Tryphoninus, whatever be the kind of obligation which the debtor has, the price paid in consequence of the debtor's proceeding, may more equitably go to the debtor's profit, than to that of the creditor. But the debtor will be bound to the buyer, because he is not to gain by another's loss. If the creditor had taken a greater part of the produce than would pay him, he would have to account for the whole which he had received.

In like manner, if you dealt with my debtor, not as thinking him indebted to me, but to another person, and borrowed money of him, you are bound to me; not because I have entrusted money to you; (for this cannot be done without mutual consent;) but because my money, which has made its way to you, it is fair and equitable that you should render to me.

3 The later jurists extend these principles to other similar cases: for instance, that if a person have absconded and his goods have been sold, when he had a case which would have protected them, he is to be admitted to the money raised by the sale: and he who has lent money to support the son, if the father be insolvent, and the son have maternal property, has an action against the son.

These two rules being rightly understood (for extant and non-extant property), the answer will not be difficult to the questions which are wont to be proposed by Jurists and by Theologians, writing for the instruction of the internal tribunal of the mind.

III.　In the first place, it appears that a *bona fide* possessor is not bound to any restitution, if the thing be destroyed; for he neither has the thing nor any gain from the thing: [a *mala fide* possessor is bound by his own act, besides the consequences of wrong doing.]

IV.   Secondly, a *bona fide* possessor is bound to restore also the still extant produce of the thing: I say the produce of the *thing;* for the produce of industry, even if it would not take place without the thing, is not due to the thing.   The cause of this obligation is ownership: for he who is owner of a thing is naturally owner of the fruits of the thing.

V.   Thirdly, that a *bona fide* possessor is bound to restitution both of the thing and of the produce of it consumed by him, if in any case he would have consumed as much: for by so much he is held to be richer.   And accordingly Caligula is praised for having, in the beginning of his reign, when he restored governments to persons, given them also the income of the interval elapsed.

VI.   Fourthly, a *bona fide* possessor is not bound to restore the produce which he neglected to take; for he neither has the thing, nor anything which has come into its place.

VII.   Fifthly, if a *bona fide* possessor has given to another a thing given to himself, he is not bound to restitution, except, in any case, without having this thing, he would have given something of equal value: for then he has gained by sparing his own property.

VIII.   Sixthly, if he sell a thing which he have bought (belonging to another), he is not bound*, except in so far as he sold it for more than he gave for it.   If he have sold a thing given to him (belonging to another) he is held to restore the price; except it happen that he have spent the price, and would not otherwise have spent the money.

IX.   1 Seventhly, a thing belonging to another which has been *bona fide* bought, is to be restored, and the price paid cannot be demanded back*.   To which rule it seems to me that this exception should be made;—except in so far as the owner could not probably recover possession of his thing without some expense; as, for example, if it were in the hands of pirates: for then we may deduct as much as the owner would willingly have expended on it.   For the actual possession of a thing, especially of a thing difficult to recover, is of itself a valuable matter, and in this the owner, after he has lost the thing [and recovered it] is richer than he was before.   And therefore though the buying of a thing which is one's own is not valid by ordinary law, yet Paulus says that it is valid, if it be agreed from the first that the possession which another has of it may be bought.   Nor do I here require that the thing should be bought with a purpose of restoring it to the owner, in which case an action for agency would lie.   Some hold one way, some the other.   For the action for agency is the creation of the Civil Law, and has none of those foun-

* These two Rules do not agree well together: according to the seventh, a thing belonging to another, which we have bought *bona fide*, we must restore to the owner, not requiring the price from him; according to the sixth, if we have bought it, and then sold it, we are not bound to restore the price. It appears to be assumed, in the seventh Rule, that we have a remedy against the seller. W.

dations by means of which nature induces obligation. And we are here inquiring what is Natural Law.

2 Ulpian's opinion respecting funeral expenses is of the same kind; that a just judge in such cases does not merely imitate the effect of an action for agency, but follows equity in a larger manner, the nature of the action allowing him to do so. And so, what the same writer elsewhere says, if any one has transacted business for me, not having a regard to me, but for the sake of his own gain, he may have an action, not for all that he has expended, but for the amount by which I am richer. And so the owners of goods which are thrown overboard to lighten the ship, recover a part from the others whose goods are saved by that proceeding; for a person who preserves, by any step, his property which was in danger of perishing, is by so much the richer.

X. Eighthly; the person who has bought a thing belonging to another, cannot restore it to the seller to save himself the price: because, as soon as the thing is in his possession, the obligation of restoring it has begun.

XI. Ninthly; he who has a thing the owner of which is unknown, is not naturally bound to give it to the poor: although this is a very pious course, in many places properly ordered. The reason is, because, in virtue of ownership, no one has a right except the owner. But that there is no owner, and no apparent owner, is the same thing to him to whom he is not apparent.

XII. Tenthly, by Natural Law, what is received either for a shameful cause, or for an honest cause to which any one was bound, [without reward,] is not to be restored: though such a rule is not unreasonably introduced by some laws. The reason is, that no one is bound by the reason for which the thing is given, except it be a thing belonging to another: but in the case now supposed, the ownership passes in virtue of the will of the former owner. It is another matter if there be something wrong in the mode of acquisition; for instance, extortion: for this is another principle of obligation, concerning which we do not now speak.

XIII. Let us add also this, erroneously ruled by Medina: that the ownership of things belonging to others may pass to us without the consent of the owner, if they are such things as are commonly valued according to number, weight, and measure. Things of this kind are said *functionem recipere*, to be such that one portion may pass for another, so that they may be restored by means of that which is not identical, but only the same in kind. But this can be done only when consent has preceded, or may, by law or usage, be understood to have preceded, as in lending; or if the thing, being consumed, cannot be exhibited. But without such consent, express or presumed, and without necessity, that *function* has no place.

L

CHAPTER XI.

Of Promises.

I. 1 THE order of our work has led us to the obligation which arises from promises. And here we at once find opposed to us a man of no ordinary erudition, Francis Connanus. For he maintains this opinion, that, *jure naturæ ac gentium*, those pacts which have not a consideration (συνάλλαγμα), do not induce any obligation; though no doubt they may be properly fulfilled, if the matter be such as it would have been, without promise, proper and congruent to some virtue to perform.

2 He adduces for his opinion not only the *dicta* of jurists, but also these reasons: (1) That there is a fault no less in him who rashly trusts a person who makes a promise for no cause: (2) That there is a great danger thrown upon the fortunes of all, if men be judged to be bound by a promise, which often proceeds more from ostentation than from real purpose; or from a purpose, but a light and inconsiderate one: (3) That it is right to leave something to each person's honesty, and not to bind men to the necessity of an obligation:—that it is disgraceful not to fulfil promises, not because such a course is unjust, but because thereby the levity of the promise is detected.

He also uses the authority of Cicero, who says, that promises are not to be kept when they are useless to those to whom they are made; nor if they do more harm to you than good to those to whom you made them. (*De Off.* i. 10.)

If the matter be no longer open, in consequence of some step having been taken, he pronounces that what you ought to do, is, not what is promised, but what is for the interest of the promisee:—that the pacts, not having any force of themselves, receive force from the contracts of which they are parts or additions, or from the delivery of the thing in question; whence arise, partly actions, partly exceptions to actions, and prohibitions of suit.

But pacts which have an obligatory force according to the Laws, as pacts with stipulations and some others, have, he holds, this force by the help of the laws, which have this efficacy, that what of itself is proper, they make to be necessary.

3 But this opinion cannot stand, in the general form in which he propounds it. For, in the first place, it follows therefrom that pacts between kings and different peoples, so long as nothing thereof is performed (*re integrâ*) have no force; [the parties being bound by no common instituted law;] especially in those places in which no regular form of treaties and engagements has been introduced.

And again, no reason can be found why laws, which are in a certain way a common pact of the people, and are so called by Aristotle and Demosthenes, should be able to give obligatory force to pacts; while the will of a person, directed especially, and by every means, to put himself under an obligation, should not be able to do so; especially when the Civil Law offers no impediment.

Add to this, that when the will is sufficiently signified, the ownership of a thing may be transferred, as we have already said: why then may there not also be a transfer of a *jus in personam*, a right to the performance of a person's promise, or a right to transfer ownership, (which is a less thing than ownership itself,) or a right to do anything; since we have the same right over our actions as over the things which belong to us?

4 To this is to be added the consent of wise men; for as it is said by jurists, that nothing is so natural as that the will of the owner when he wishes to transfer to another a thing which is his, should be held valid; in the same way it is said that nothing is so congruous to the mutual confidence of mankind, as to perform the agreements which have been made among men. Thus the edict concerning paying money agreed to be paid at a certain time, when in the person so agreeing no cause had preceded except consent, is said to favour natural equity. Paulus also says, that a man owes us a debt, when, *jure gentium*, he ought to give it us, we relying upon his good faith; in which place, first, the word *ought* implies a certain moral necessity: nor can we admit what Connanus says, that we rely upon a man's good faith, only when some step has been taken in agreement with the promise: for in that place Paulus was speaking of an action for recovering what has been paid and was not owing; which falls to the ground, if the money be paid in virtue of a compact of any kind whatever: for then, even before any step had been taken (*re adhuc integra,*) by Natural Law and *jure gentium*, it ought to be paid; even if the Civil Law did not lend its aid, to cut off occasions of litigation [by stopping the action after it has been paid].

5 Cicero, in his *Offices*, gives so much weight to promises, that he

L 2

calls Good Faith the foundation of Justice. So Horace: and the Platonists often call Justice, *Truth*, or *Truthfulness*, which Apuleius translates *Fidelitas*. Simonides, as quoted in Plato's *Republic*, says that justice is, to return what is entrusted to us, and to speak the truth.

6 But in order that the thing may be well understood, there are three ways of speaking concerning the future, which must be carefully distinguished.

II. The first degree is an assertion explaining our present purpose with respect to some future action: [*I intend to give you:*] and that this may be free from fault, a requisite is, a truth of the thought for the present time, but not that the thought be persevered in. For the human mind has not only a natural power of changing its purpose, but also a right. And if there be any fault in the change, or accessory to it, that is not intrinsic to the change, as a change, but belongs to the matter; for instance, if the first intention was the better of the two.

III. The second degree is, when the will determines itself for a future time, with a sufficient sign to indicate the necessity of persevering; [*I will give you*]. This may be called *pollicitation;* it is obligatory without the Civil Law, either absolutely or conditionally, but it does not give to another person a proper right. For in many cases it happens that there is an Obligation in us, and no corresponding Right in another*: as appears in the duties of mercy and gratitude; and to these, the duty of constancy or fidelity is similar. Therefore in virtue of such pollicitation, the thing so promised cannot be retained, or he who made the promise be compelled by Natural Law to fulfil it.

IV. 1 The third degree is, when to such a determination is added a sign of wishing to confer a proper right upon another: [*I promise you:*] which is a perfect promise, with the same effects as alienation of ownership. For it is either a way to the alienation of the thing, or it is an alienation of some portion of our liberty. To the former head belong promises to give, to the latter, promises to do.

A strong example of what we say is furnished by the Scriptures, which teach us that God himself, who cannot be compelled by any instituted law, would act contrary to his nature, except he performed his promises. [See the passages.] Whence it follows, that the performance of promises proceeds from the nature of immutable justice, which is, in a certain way, common to God and to all rational creatures. So Prov. vi. 1. A promise is spoken of as indissoluble: and a vow. Numb. xxx. 4, 5, 6. So the word ὑπόσχεσις is explained by Eustathius. So Ovid. [See.]

2 This being understood, we shall have no difficulty in replying to Connanus's arguments. For the *dicta* of jurists respecting nude pacts regard the rule which was introduced by the Roman laws, which

* It is better to use *Obligation* only as correlative to *Right*, and *Duty* when there is no such correlative Right, but a moral claim. *E. M.* 84, 89.

made *stipulation* the certain sign of a deliberate purpose. Nor do we deny that similar laws existed in other nations. *What law obliges us to perform what we have promised to any one?* says Seneca, speaking of human law [Natural Law], and a promise not made with formal solemnity.

3 There may, however, by Natural Law, be other signs of a deliberate purpose, besides the formality of *stipulation*, or anything else which the Civil Law requires as a ground for an action. But what is done not of deliberate intention, we also do not hold to have the force of obligation, as Theophrastus also had noted. And even as to that which is done with deliberate intention, but not with a purpose of conceding a proper right to another, we deny that it gives to any one a right of demanding the performance by Natural Law: though, in this case, we allow that not only a propriety, but even a moral necessity arises.

As to what is adduced from Cicero, we shall treat below, when we have to speak of the interpretation of pacts.

V.   But let us see what conditions are required to produce the force of a perfect promise.

1 First there is required the use of reason: and therefore madmen, and idiots, and children, cannot make a promise. With regard to minors, the case is different; for although these are conceived not to have a sufficiently stable judgment, as also women are not, yet this state is not perpetual, nor is it of itself sufficient to nullify the force of a promise.

2 When a boy begins to have the use of his reason, cannot be defined with certainty: but the inference is to be made from his daily acts, or from that which commonly happens in each country. So among the Hebrews, a promise was valid which was made by a boy after he was thirteen years old, or a girl after twelve. Elsewhere, the Civil Laws, moved by good reasons, pronounce certain promises of wards or minors to be void, not only among the Romans, but also among the Greeks, as Dio Chrysostom notes; and against some such promises, they introduce the benefit of restitution. But these are properly effects of Civil Law, and therefore have nothing to do with Natural Law and *jus gentium;* except that when they obtain, it is agreeable to Natural Law that they be observed.

Hence even if a stranger make an agreement with a citizen, he is bound by the same laws: because he who makes a contract in any place, is under the laws of the place as a temporary subject*.

3 It is plainly another matter if the compact be made at sea, or in a desert island, or by letter between persons absent. For such pacts are governed by Natural Law only; as also the pacts of sovereigns as such. For in the private acts of sovereigns, those laws have place which make the act void, when it is in their favour, not to their detriment.

* *Lex loci contractus: E. M.* 1106.

VI. 1 The discussion of pacts made in error* is sufficiently per-
plexed.   For a distinction is commonly made between an error as to
the substance of a thing, and an error not about the substance: as,
whether fraud was the occasion of the contract: whether the person
with whom the contract was made was a party to the fraud: whether
it be an action *stricti juris* or *bonæ fidei†*.   For, according to these
variations, writers pronounce some acts void, others, valid, but open to
be rescinded or remodelled at the choice of him who is injured.   But
the greater part of these distinctions come from the Roman Law,
both the old Civil Law, and the decisions of Prætors; and some of
them are not sufficiently true or accurate.

2 But the way to find the natural truth, is opened to us by a principle concerning the force and efficacy of laws, which is received by
an almost universal consent:—that if the law be founded on the presumption of some fact, which fact is really not so, then that law does
not oblige: because, the truth of the fact failing, the whole foundation of the law is wanting.   But *when* the law *is* founded on such a
presumption, is to be collected from the matter, words, and circumstances of the law.   In like manner then we shall say, that when a
promise is founded on the presumption of some fact which is not really
so, that by Natural Law it has no force: because the Promiser does
not agree to the promise except on a certain condition which in reality
did not exist: to which we must refer Cicero's question concerning
the person who, falsely believing his son to be dead, made another
person his heir.   [*De Oratore*, i. 38.]

3 But if the promiser has been negligent in inquiring into the
matter, or in expressing his intention, and another person has thereby
suffered loss, the promiser will be bound to make that loss good; not
by the force of his promise, but as having done damage by his fault;
of which head we shall hereafter treat.   But if there was indeed an
error, but one on which the promise was not founded, the act will be
valid, a true consent being there not wanting.   But in this case also,
if he to whom the promise is made, fraudulently give occasion to the
error, *he* will be bound to make good whatever damage the promiser
has done from that error, from that other head of obligation.   If the
promise was founded partly in error, it will be valid as to the remaining part.

VII. 1 Of promises made through fear‡, the treatment is no
less entangled.   For here too a distinction is commonly made between a fear which is grave, either absolutely, or with reference to the
person who fears, and a slight fear; between fear impressed justly
and unjustly; by the promisee, or by another: also between acts of
liberality, and acts of mutual promise. And according to these diversi-
ties, some acts are declared void; others, revocable at the choice of the

---

* Of Erroneous Promises, see *E. M.* 281.   † *E. M.* 717, 718.
‡ Of Extorted Promises, see *E. M.* 292.

promisee; others, cases for entire restitution; not without great variety of opinion on these particular cases.

2 I am entirely of the opinion of those who think that, setting aside the Civil Law, which may either take away or diminish an obligation, he who has promised any thing under fear, is bound *: for here was consent, not conditional, as in the case of erroneous promises, but absolute. For as Aristotle says, he, who in fear of shipwreck, throws his goods overboard, would wish to keep them, conditionally, if there was not the danger of shipwreck; but, absolutely, he is willing to lose them, considering the circumstances of time and place.

But I also think that this is certainly true; that if the promisee has produced a fear, not just, but unjust, even though slight, and if the promise was occasioned by this, he is bound to liberate the promiser if the promiser desires it; not because the promise was invalid, but on account of the damage wrongfully done: what exception to a demand this gives rise to, we shall explain in its own place below.

3 That some of our acts are rescinded on account of fear impressed on us by another person than the one with whom we treat, is a matter of Civil Law, which often also makes either void or revocable acts freely done; on account of infirmity of judgment. And what we have said above, of the force and efficacy of Civil Laws, is to be understood as repeated here.

What is the efficacy of an Oath in making promises hold, we shall see below.

VIII. 1 As to what concerns the *matter* of promises, a condition to produce a perfect promise is, that it is, or may be, in the rightful disposal of the promiser. Whence, first, promises are not valid, to do an act in itself unlawful; for such a right no one has nor can have. But a promise, as we have said above, receives its force from the right of the promiser, and cannot be extended further. When Agesilaus was interrogated concerning a promise which he had made, he said: *If it be just, well and good: if not, I said, but I did not promise.*

2 If the matter be not now in the power of the promiser, but may at some time be so, the efficacy of the promise will be suspended: because then, the promise must be supposed to be made under the condition, if the thing come into his power. But if the condition under which the thing may come into the power of the promiser, be also *potestative* [such as he can himself bring about or accelerate], the promiser is bound to do whatever is morally equitable, in order that the condition may be fulfilled.

3 But in such cases also, the Civil Law is wont to make many things void for the sake of utility, which by Natural Law would be obligatory; as a promise of future marriage, made by a man or woman who has a spouse alive; and not a few things done by minors or sons of families.

---

* *Obligatur*, says Grotius: *minime obligatur*, says Barbeyrac, and refers to his notes on Puffendorf. See for the reasons why he is bound, *E. M.* 295.

IX. It is commonly made a question, whether a promise made for a cause naturally vicious is valid by Natural Law; as if any thing be promised for committing homicide. Here it is evident enough that the promise itself is vicious, for it is made that another person may be induced to commit a crime. But what is done viciously, is not necessarily void, as to its jural effects; as appears by the case of a prodigal donation. There is however this difference; that when the donation is made, the viciousness ceases: for there is no vice in the thing being left in the hands of the donatary. But in promises made for a vicious cause, the vice remains as long as the crime is not perpetrated: so long, the fulfilment of the promise, as a stimulus to evil, has a taint in it, which ceases when the crime is committed. Whence it follows, that up to that time, the efficacy of such a promise is suspended, as we said above, in speaking of promising a thing which is not ours to give: but the crime being perpetrated, the force of the obligation comes into play, having been intrinsically in existence from the first, but barred by the vice which was connected with it. We have an example of this in Judah, who paid to Thamar her hire, deeming her a harlot.

But if the wrong of the promisee gave occasion to the promise, or there be an inequality in the contract, how these things are to be remedied, is another question, hereafter to be considered.

X. What is promised, for a consideration which was due without the promise, is still to be paid, if we look at Natural Law, according to what we have said above of the acceptance of a thing belonging to another. (II. x. 11 and 12.) But here also the damage produced by extortion, or the inequality of the contract, will require to be repaired, according to rules hereafter to be given.

XI. As to what concerns the mode of making the promise, that, as we said of the transfer of ownership, requires an external act; that is, a sufficient sign of the will, which sometimes may be a nod, but more frequently, the voice or writing.

XII. We may also be bound by means of another man, if there be clear evidence of our purpose in appointing him as our instrument either for this special purpose, or in a general manner. And in a general appointment, it may happen that the person appointed binds us, when he acts contrary to our will signified to him alone. For here there are two distinct acts of willing: one by which we obliged ourselves to hold valid whatever he does in this kind of business; another, in which we put him under an obligation to us, not to act except according to our directions, known to him and not to others, which is to be noted in those things which Envoys promise for kings in virtue of their written powers, when they go beyond their secret instructions.

XIII. Hence we may understand that an *exercitorian* action (one against ship-owners for the contracts of the captain,) and an *institorian* action, (one against the owner of a trading concern for the contracts of the acting agent,) depend on Natural Law, being, not so much distinct kinds of action, as qualities of actions. But it has been improperly added by the Roman Law, that all the ship-owners are bound severally, as well as jointly, by the acts of the captain. This is neither in accordance with natural equity, which is satisfied if each owner is responsible for his own share; nor useful to the public; for persons are deterred from sending adventures in ships, if they are in fear that they may be indefinitely involved by the acts of the captain. And therefore in Holland, where commerce has long flourished, that Roman law neither prevailed formerly, nor does now; on the contrary, it is the law that, in an exercitorian action, even the whole body of owners are not held responsible, beyond the value of the ship and cargo.

XIV. In order that a promise may transfer a right, acceptance is required here no less than in the transfer of ownership; but in such a way that here also a precedent asking is understood to remain in force, and to have the effect of acceptance. Nor is this contradicted by what is appointed in the Civil Law, that offers made to the Public are binding; which reason has induced some persons to judge that by the Law of Nature, the act of the promiser alone suffices: for the Roman Law does not say this, that the force of such an offer or *pollicitation* is complete before acceptance; but it forbids it to be recalled, so that it may always be accepted: which effect is not a result of Natural Law, but of Civil Law; very similar to what the *jus gentium* has introduced concerning infants and idiots. For with regard to such persons, both the purpose of taking possession of things which require such a step, and the purpose of acceptance when that is required, are supplied by the law.

XV. The question is also raised, whether it is sufficient that acceptance is made, or whether it must be notified to the promiser before the promise receives its full effect. And it is certain that a promise may be made either way: and also in this way: I desire that it be valid, if accepted: or in this manner: I desire that it be valid, if I shall understand that it has been accepted. And in matters which regard mutual obligation, the latter sense is presumed: but in promises merely liberal, the former meaning rather is supposed to prevail, except the contrary appear. [Barbeyrac dissents from this.]

XVI. Hence it follows, that before acceptance, since the right has not yet been transferred, a promise can be recalled without injustice, and even without inconstancy, if it were really made with the intention that it should begin to be valid on acceptance. Also a promise may be revoked, if the promisee die before acceptance: because the acceptance seemed to be referred to the promiser himself, not his heirs. For it is one thing to wish to give a right which will pass to the heirs; another thing to wish to give it to the heirs: for it makes a great difference on whom the benefit is conferred. And this was Nerat's answer, that he did not think that the prince had conceded to a person defunct what he had conceded to him supposing him alive.

XVII. 1 A promise may also be revoked by the death of him who was chosen to declare to the promisee the promiser's will; for the obligation ended in his words. The case is different in a messenger who carries letters merely, and who is not the instrument of the obligation, but the carrier of the obligatory instrument; therefore letters indicating consent may be carried by any one. We must distinguish also between a minister who is elected to make known the promise, and him who is elected to make the promise. In the former case, the revocation will have its force, even if it do not become known to the minister: in the other case, the revocation is void, because the right of promising was dependent on the will of the minister or agent, which will, the revocation not being yet known, was free from all fault. So also in the former case, the donation may be accepted, even the donor being dead; as being perfect on one side, although revocably: as may be seen on a large scale in ambassadors: in the other case, the donation cannot be accepted, because it was not really made, but only ordered to be made.

2 But in a doubtful case, the will of the person who gives the order is understood to be, that the order be fulfilled, except some great change take place, as the death of the person ordering. But there may be conjectures which may favour another judgment, which are readily to be admitted, in order that a donation which was directed to be made for a pious cause may subsist. And in like manner may a controversy be decided which was once agitated, whether an action will hold against the heir of a person entrusted with such a charge, on which subject M. Drusus the prætor and Sextus Julius gave different edicts.

XVIII. 1 Also controversies often occur respecting acceptance made for another: in which a distinction is to be made between a promise made to me, to give a thing to another, and a promise conveyed in the name of him to whom the thing is to be given. If the promise is made to me, omitting the consideration whether the performance of the promise is to my private interest, (which was introduced by the Roman law,) it seems, by the Law of Nature, that I acquire the right of effecting, by my acceptance, that the right promised pass to the other person: so that in the intermediate time the promise cannot be revoked by the promiser; but I, to whom the promise was made, have power to remit it. For that sense is not repugnant to Natural Law, and agrees best with the words of such a promise: nor is it a matter uninteresting to me, that a person should acquire a benefit through me.

2 But if the promise be conveyed in his name to whom the thing is to be given, it is to be distinguished whether he who accepts has either a special mandate to accept, or a commission so general that such acceptance may be included in it; or have not such commission. When such a mandate has proceeded, I do not think that any further distinction is to be made, (as the Roman Laws direct,)

whether the person be his own master or not, but that by such
acceptance the promise becomes perfect: because consent may be
given and signified by a minister. For I am supposed to wish
what I have put in the power of another, if he too wishes it. But,
failing such a mandate, if another, to whom the promise was not made,
accepts, the promiser being willing, the effect will then be this; that
the promiser will not have power to revoke his promise, before he
whom the promise concerns, has determined that it shall be valid
or invalid: but so that, in the intermediate time, he who has accepted
the promise cannot remit it, because he was not employed to receive
any right, but to bind the good faith of the promiser in maintaining
a proposed benefit: so that the promiser, if he revoke, acts against
good faith, but not against the right of any one.

XIX. From what has been said, it may be collected what is
to be decided concerning a burthen added to a promise. For this
may be done, so long as the promise is not yet completed by acceptance, nor made irrevocable by an especial engagement. But a burthen, added for the convenience of a third party, may be revoked, as
long as it is not accepted by that third party: although there are
not wanting, in this as in other questions, those who think otherwise.
But to a person who looks rightly at the matter, the natural equity
will appear evident, so that it will not need many proofs.

XX. This also is often disputed, how a promise founded in
error can recover its force, if the promiser wishes to stand by his
promise. And the same question may be asked concerning promises, which are void by the Civil Law on account of fear or other
causes, if the cause afterwards have ceased. For to confirm these,
they require only an internal act, which, conjoined with the former
external act, they think suffices to produce an obligation. Others,
not satisfied with this, because an external act cannot be a sign of
a *subsequent* internal act, require a new promise expressed and accepted. The middle opinion is the true one: that an external act
is required, but not expressed in words, when the retention of the
thing promised by the promisee, and its relinquishment on the part
of the promiser, or any similar event, may suffice to signify consent.

XXI. This also is not to be omitted, in order that Civil Law
and Natural Law may not be confounded; that promises which have
no cause expressed, are not void by Natural Law, any more than
donations of property.

XXII. Also that he who has promised an act on the part of
another, is not bound to the extent of the interest of the promisee,
provided he has not omitted to do what he could on his own part,
to obtain the doing of the thing promised; except there be words,
or the nature of the business, such as to induce a stricter obligation.
As if he had performed his engagement, says Livy, *because it did not
depend on him that it was not performed.*

CHAPTER XII.

Of Contracts.

I. OF human acts which tend to the utility of others, some are simple, some are compound.

II. Of simple acts, some are gratuitously *beneficial*, others are of the nature of exchange of one act for another, *permutatorial*. Beneficial acts are either merely so, or with some mutual obligation. Mere beneficial acts are either discharged in the present time, or stand over for the future. A useful good office is performed in the present time, and of this it is not necessary to speak, since it produces advantage indeed by the recipient, but no effect as of right: so also a donation, by which ownership is transferred, of which we treated above, when we spoke of acquisitions of ownership. As acts standing over for the future, we reckon promises both of giving and of doing; concerning which we have already spoken.

Beneficial acts with a mutual obligation, are those which dispose of any thing without alienation, or so dispose of an act that some effect survives. Such is a concession of the use of a thing, which is called a Loan; and of acts, the undertaking of an office expensive or obligatory, which we may call a Commission; of which kind is a Deposit, namely, the office of keeping a thing in custody. Similar to these acts are the promises of acts, except that, as we have said, these stand over for the future; which also we desire to have understood of the acts now to be explained.

III. 1 Permutatorial acts either separate the parties or produce a community between them. Those acts which separate, *diremtorial* acts, the Roman jurists rightly divide into these: *do ut des: facio ut facias: facio ut des.* See Paulus and the Digests. [Dig. xix. 5.]

2 But the Romans except from this division certain contracts which they call *nominate* contracts*; not so much because they have proper names, (for *permutation* or exchange, which they exclude from nominate contracts, has also a proper name,) as because, from their more frequent use, they have received a certain force and nature, which may be sufficiently understood by the name, although nothing be said specially. Whence also with regard to them there were certain established formulæ of actions. While in other contracts, which are less frequent, that only was implied which was expressed; and therefore there was not any common and usual form of action, but a form accommodated to the fact, which was therefore called a form *in prescript words*.

For the same reason, of a more frequent use in the nominate contracts, if certain requisites were present, the necessity of fulfilling the contract was held as the rule; as in *sale*, if the price had been agreed upon, the contract was good, even *re integrâ*, that is, though nothing had been performed on either side: while in the rarer contracts, *re integrâ*, there was allowed the liberty of retracting, that is, impunity, because the Civil Law withheld coactive force from those contracts, leaving them to stand on the good faith of the contracting parties only.

3 Natural Law does not recognize these distinctions: for the contracts which are called by men *innominate*, are neither less natural nor less ancient than the nominate. Nay Exchange, which is reckoned among the innominate, is both older and simpler than Buying. Eustathius, where in the *Iliad* (B. x.) a public contest is mentioned with a prize appointed, which in Homer is said to be *earned*, interprets it, *taken in exchange*, adding, *for it is a sort of contract;* namely, *facio ut des,* I work that you may pay. We therefore, following nature, shall refer all diremtory contracts to the three kinds which we have mentioned, making no distinction of nominate and innominate.

4 Hence we shall say that *do ut des, I give that you may give,* either one thing for another, which is specially called Permutation or Exchange, and is doubtless the oldest kind of commerce: or money for money, to which the merchants give the technical name of *Exchange:* (*Cambium:*) or a thing for money, as in Buying and Selling: or the use of a thing for a thing: or the use of a thing for the use of a thing: or the use of a thing for money, which is Letting and Hiring. By *use*, we here mean both the naked use, and that which is combined with the enjoyment of the produce, whether temporary, or personal, or hereditary, or circumscribed in any other way; as that which among the Hebrews continued to the year of the Jubilee. In a Loan, the thing is given, in order that after the lapse of a certain time, the same in quantity and kind may be returned, of things which

* See *E. M.* 708, &c.

are estimated in weight, measure, and number, both other things and money.

5 The exchange of act for act may have innumerable kinds according to the diversity of the acts. But *facio ut des*, is, *I act that you may give*, either money, (and this includes Letting and Hiring, and Assurance against risk, a contract formerly hardly known, now among the most common,) or that you may give a thing, or the use of a thing.

IV. Acts communicatory, either establish a community of acts, or of property, or property on the one side, acts on the other for the common utility; all which are called Partnership. In which class are included associations for the mutual Protection of ships in time of war, against pirates or other enemies, which is called *an Admiralty*.

V. Acts are mixed (or compound, § 1) either as principal, or by the accession of another act. [First as principal.] Thus if I knowingly buy a thing for more than it is worth, and give the seller the excess of price, it is partly buying, partly donation. If I promise money to a goldsmith for making rings for me of his own gold, it is partly buying (of material), partly hire (of labour). So in Partnerships it happens that one person contributes acts and money, another money only. And in the Feudal Contract, the concession of the fief is a benefice, but the pact of military service for protection is *facio ut facias*. And if the fief be burthened with an annual payment, it is, so far, a letting for a money-rent. So money lent to shipowners is partly a Loan and partly Insurance.

VI. Acts are mixed by the accession of another act, as in giving security, and in pledge. For suretiship, if you regard the business which takes place between the surety-giver and the principal debtor, is for the most part a commission: if you regard the business between the creditor and the surety-giver, who receives nothing, it is an act merely liberal: but because this liberal act is added to an onerose contract, it is reckoned with such contracts. So the giving of a pledge seems to be a liberal act, by which the detention of a thing is conceded; but this also takes its nature from the contract which is thus supplied with a security.

VII. All acts useful to others, with the exception of merely beneficial acts, are called Contracts.

VIII. In Contracts, nature requires equality, and in such a way that, from inequality, he who has the worse share, acquires a right. This equality consists partly in the act, partly in the matter concerning which the act is, and in the acts both precedent and principal.

IX. 1 It belongs to the preceding acts, that he who makes a contract about any thing, ought to make known the faults of the thing so far as he knows them, which is not only the usual rule of Civil Laws, but also agreeable to the nature of the act. For between the contracting parties, there is a connexion closer than the common society of mankind. And in this way we answer the argument of Diogenes of Babylon on this subject, who says that all that is untold is not therefore concealed: and that it is not necessary for me to say all that it is useful for you to hear: thus I need not tell you how the heavens move. For the nature of Contract, having for its object common utility, requires some closer union. So Ambrose and Lactantius. [See.]

2 The same does not apply to circumstances which do not affect the thing itself: as if any one know that there are many ships on their way bringing corn. To tell this is kind and laudable; often so far, that it cannot be omitted without violating the rule of charity : but the omission is not unjust; that is, it is not repugnant to the right of him with whom I deal: so that here that may hold which the same Diogenes said, as Cicero reports *, *I bring my wares to market: I offer them for sale: I sell what is my own: not dearer than others; perhaps cheaper, as I have a larger stock. Whom do I wrong?* Therefore we are not in general to follow the rule which Cicero lays down, that it is concealment, if those whose interest it is to know anything, you would have ignorant of it for the sake of your gain. That holds with regard only to points which affect the thing itself: as if a house which is to be sold is unhealthy; if it has been ordered by the magistrate to be pulled down : where see the examples which he gives.

3 The faults which are known to the person with whom you deal, need not be mentioned ; as the *servitude* to which the house was subject which Gratidianus sold to Oratas, having bought it of him before : for both parties, having equal knowledge, are on an equality. So Horace ; Plato.

X. Nor is it only in the understanding with respect to the matter, but also in the use of the will, that there ought to be a certain equality between the contracting parties : not indeed that if there have gone before any fear justly impressed, that must be removed, for that is extrinsic to the contract: but that no fear is to be unjustly impressed with a view to the contract; or if it be impressed, that it be put away. Looking at this rule, the Lacedæmonians rescinded the purchase of the land which the Thebans had extorted from the possessors by fear. See Xenophon. What exception there is to this in the Law of Nations, we shall see in its own place.

XI. 1 In the principal act of a contract this equality is required, that more be not demanded than is equitable. Which, in beneficial contracts, can hardly have place. For if any one demands some payment for a loan, or for executing a commission, or keeping a deposit, he does no wrong, but he alters the nature of the contract, and makes it, from being gratuitous, become semipermutatory. But in all permutatory contracts this is carefully to be observed. Nor is it enough for any one to say that what the other party has promised

* See *E. M.* 716.

more than equality, is to be regarded as a donation. For such is not the intention of contracting parties, and is not to be presumed so, except it appear. For what they promise or give, they are to be supposed to promise or give as equivalent to what they are to receive, and as what is done on the ground of such equivalence.

2 Authorities of Chrysostom, Hermias, Levit. xxv. 14 and 17.

XII. 1 There remains to be considered, equality in the thing itself, consisting in this, that though nothing was concealed which ought to have been told, nor more exacted than was thought to be due; yet if there be an inequality in the thing itself, though without any fault of the parties; if for instance there was some latent defect, or some error about the price, that also is to be made good, and the difference paid to him who suffers by it; because, in a contract, there was intended, or ought to have been, that each party should have the same value.

2 The Roman law appointed this as the rule, not in every inequality, (for the law does not follow matters to their smallest dimensions, and also wishes to obviate the multitude of lawsuits,) but in a grave inequality, as for instance, one which exceeds the half of the fair price. In fact, laws, as Cicero says, remove what is not equitable, in cases when you can take hold of it with your hand; the philosophers, so far as you can grasp it by reason and intelligence. But those who are not subject to Civil Laws ought to follow that which right reason dictates to them as equitable; and even those who are subject to laws, whenever the question is what is right and pious; since the laws do not create or destroy right, but only deny their support to some rights for certain causes.

XIII. 1 It is to be noted that a certain equality of matter is to be regarded even in beneficial contracts; not a complete equality, as in commutatorial, but one according to the nature of the transaction: so that a person may not be damaged by a benefit which he bestows: for which reason a commissioner or agent is to be indemnified for the expense and loss which he incurs by his agency: and a *loanee* is bound to make good the thing lent if it be destroyed; because he is bound to the owner, not in respect to the thing alone, that is, by virtue of ownership, as any possessor of it would be bound, (as above said,) but also in virtue of the benefit received: which holds true, except the thing would have perished also, if it had remained with the owner. For in this case, the owner loses nothing by the loan. On the other hand, a depositary receives nothing but a reliance on his good faith: therefore if the thing perish he is not bound; not by reason of the thing, for it no longer exists, and he is no better off for it; nor by reason of his having accepted it, for by accepting it, he bestowed, not received, a benefit. In a pledge, and in a thing hired, a middle way is to be followed: so that he who has accepted the thing is not bound to make it good like a loanee, and yet is bound to use more diligence than a depositary: because the acceptance of a pledge is gratuitous indeed, but is usually an accompaniment of an onerose contract.

2 All which rules agree indeed with the Roman Laws, but appear not to come originally from them, but from natural equity. And hence the same rules are to be found also among other nations. So Maimonides, Seneca. And according to these principles we must judge also of other contracts. But having finished the general discussion so far as our purpose requires it, let us run over certain special questions of contracts.

XIV. 1 The most natural measure of the value of any thing is the need for it, as Aristotle rightly shews : which is seen most clearly in the exchange of things amongst barbarians. Yet this is not the only measure. For the will of men, which is the master of things, desires many things more than are necessary. *Pearls*, says Pliny, *derive their value from luxury.* And so Cicero of pictures : *the measure of man's desires in these things is the measure of value.* And, on the other hand, it comes to pass that the most necessary things are of small value for their abundance. So Seneca shews by many examples, and adds, *The price of any thing is a temporary accident : however much good you may say of them, they are worth just so much as they will fetch when sold.* So Paulus, *The prices of things are not from the opinion or utility of individuals, but are a common function ;* that is, as he explains elsewhere, *what they would be worth to people in general.* Hence it comes to pass that a thing is supposed to be of such value as is given or offered for it commonly ; which cannot help having a certain latitude, within which more or less may be given or asked, except when the law has appointed a certain *point* of price for things, as Aristotle speaks.

2 For that common price, account is commonly taken of the labour and expense of the sellers, and it undergoes sudden changes according to the excess or defect of buyers, money, and wares. There may also be certain accidents of the things, capable of an estimation, on account of which the things may be lawfully bought or sold above or below the common price ; suppose, on account of loss to be incurred, cessation of gain, particular tastes, or if they are bought or sold to oblige a person, being otherwise not to be bought or sold. Also account may be taken of the loss or cessation of gain which arises from the payment deferred or anticipated.

XV. 1 With regard to Buying and Selling, it is to be noted that the ownership may be transferred at the moment of contract, without delivery, and that this is the simplest process. So Seneca says, that selling is the alienation of the thing, and the transfer of one's property and one's right to another : as exchange also is. And if this be the case, if the ownership be not to pass immediately, the seller is obliged to give the ownership [at an appointed time]. And in the meanwhile, the thing is in the possession and at the risk of the seller.

M

Wherefore that selling and buying consist in giving the means of having the thing sold, and remedy if the title to it prove bad, and that the thing is necessarily forthwith at the risk of the buyer, and also that the produce belongs to the buyer even before the ownership passes, are all fictions of the Civil Law, and are not everywhere observed. Indeed most legislators have provided that up to delivery the possession and risk are the seller's, as Theophrastus holds: and as we find in Stobæus, where you find many other rules about the formalities of sale, about *earnest* of sale, about retraction, very different from the Roman Law: as also that among the Rhodians sale was to be completed, as well as some other contracts, by public registry, as Dio Prusæensis notes.

2 This also is to be observed, that if a thing be sold twice over, that sale of the two is valid which included a present transfer of the ownership either by delivery or otherwise. For by this means the jural claim passes from the seller, which it does not by a mere promise.

XVI. It is not all monopolies which are at variance with Natural Law. Monopolies may sometimes be permitted by the government for just cause, and at a settled price; of which we have a remarkable example in the account of Joseph's administration of Egypt. So under the Romans the Alexandrians had the monopoly of Indian and Ethiopian wares. Monopolies may also be established by private persons, provided they be on equitable terms. But if persons, like the Velabrian oil-merchants, enter into a combination to raise the price above the common price, or prevent by fraud or force the importation of a larger quantity, that they may buy up the article and sell it at a price which at the time of sale is unreasonable, they are guilty of a wrong, and are bound to repair it. If in any other way they prevent the importation of wares, in order to sell them at a higher price, though in the state of the market not an unreasonable one, they offend against the law of charity; as Ambrose shews; but they do not properly violate the rights of others.

XVII. Concerning Money, it is to be noted that it naturally operates *functionally*, that is, one portion of it may do the office of another; and this, not only as to the material [gold for silver and reciprocally], nor in its special appellation and form [crowns for dollars], but in a more general sense, in its relation to all other things, or at least to the most necessary; and the estimation of this relation, if no other agreement is made, is to be made with reference to the time and place of payment. So Michael Ephesius says that money, though not in itself immutable, is the measure of all other things: the sense of which is this: that whatever is taken in order to be the measure of other things ought to be such that of itself it is least subject to change: and of this kind are gold, silver, brass: for their value is nearly the same at all times and everywhere: and as other things which men need are plentiful or scarce, the same money of the same material and weight, is sometimes worth more of those things, sometimes less.

XVIII. Letting and Hiring, as Caius rightly says, come nearest to selling and buying, and are governed by the same rules; the price corresponds to the rent or wages, and the ownership to the use of the thing hired or service rendered. Wherefore as, when a thing is destroyed, the loss falls on the owner, so by Natural Law barrenness of land hired, and other accidents which impede the use, are at the loss of the Hirer; and nevertheless the Letter has a right to the rent promised, because he gave up the power of using the thing himself, which at the time of letting was worth so much; though this may be changed by laws and covenants. But if the Letter, when the first Hirer is prevented making use of the thing, lets it to another, whatever he receives from that bargain he must pay to the first Hirer, that he may not become richer by what belongs to another.

XIX. And what we said above of Selling, that a thing may be bought or sold for more or less if it be done to gratify a person, being otherwise not open to be bought or sold, is to be understood also of a thing or of service let and hired. Or if one service may be useful to many persons, as, for instance, a journey undertaken by an agent, and if the latter (the agent) have engaged himself to several persons jointly, he may demand from each the payment which he would require from one, if the law do not forbid. For the same labour being useful to a second person as well as to the first, is something extrinsic to the contract entered into with the first, and does not diminish the value of his services to the first.

XX. 1 As to Lending Money, it is commonly made a question by what kind of law usury is forbidden. And although the more received opinion is that it is forbidden by Natural Law, Abulensis is of a contrary opinion. And in truth the arguments on the other side are not such as compel assent. For when it is said (1) That money lent is a gratuitous benefit, the same may be said of any other thing lent, and yet it is not unlawful to demand payment for the loan of a thing; this only makes the contract take another name, *letting* instead of *lending*.

Nor is it more convincing to say (2) That money is barren by its nature; for houses and other things which produce no fruits by nature, the industry of man makes fruitful.

The other arguments are more specious, (3) That here, a thing of the same kind is repaid for a thing, and that the use of the thing, money, cannot be distinguished from the thing itself, since it consists *in abusu*, in getting rid of it: and therefore nothing ought to be demanded for it.

2 (4) It is said in the decree of the Senate*, That though there cannot be properly usufruct of a thing which perishes in the using,

* Under Tiberius. Heinecc. *Elem. Jur. Civ.* 419.

M 2

yet there may be *quasi usufruct* of such a thing, but that it does not thereby become the property of the tenant. But this merely defines the word *usufruct*. Certainly that word does not properly agree with the right of usury. But it does not follow that there is no such right: since, on the contrary, it is certain that if any one were to grant a proprietor such a right, money might be paid for it.

And the right of not having to repay anything, whether money or wine, till after a certain time, is something which has an estimable value. For he who pays later, pays less. And therefore, in the way of exchange the use of money may be paid for by the use of land.

As to what Cato, Cicero, Plutarch, and others say against usury, it does not touch its intrinsic nature, but its ordinary accompaniments and consequences.

3 But whatever may be our opinion of such arguments, it ought to suffice for us that there was a law given by God to the Hebrews, which forbad Hebrew to lend Hebrew money on usury. For the matter of this law, if not necessary, is certainly morally good; and so is assumed in Ps. xv. 5. Ezek. xviii. 8. And precepts of this kind bind Christians also, as being called to higher pitches of virtue than others; and what was then the duty towards a Jew, is now a duty to all men, the separation being taken away by the Gospel, and the term *neighbour* more widely extended. So Lactantius and Ambrosius condemn usury. And Augustus noted for rebuke some who borrowed money at low interest and lent it at high.

XXI. It is to be observed, however, that there are some things which approach to the nature of usury, and commonly are held to be usury, which are pacts of another kind: as pacts for making good the loss which he suffers who lends money, by being kept out of his money so long: and on account of the gain which the money-lender loses by lending, deducting what corresponds to the uncertainty of his hopes, and the labour he would have had to undergo. And again, if anything be demanded on account of expenses incurred by him who lends money to many, and has it ready for that purpose; and for the danger of losing the principal, where due security is not taken; this is not usury. So Demosthenes in his oration against Pantænetus, denies that he is to be stigmatized as an usurer because, what money he gained by commerce or manufacture, he lent out at moderate interest, partly to keep the capital, partly to gratify another.

XXII. Human Laws which allow something to be covenanted for the use of money, if the rate lie within a due compensation, are not opposed to Natural or Divine Laws, as in Holland it has long been granted to persons in general to require 8 per cent. per annum, and to Merchants 12. If they exceed that standard, laws may afford impunity, but they cannot give a right.

XXIII. Contracts for averting risk, which are called Insurance, are void if either of the contracting parties know that the thing insured has either reached its destination safely, or is lost: not only on account of the parity which the nature of permutatorial contracts requires, but also because the proper matter of this contract is loss *uncertain*. The value of such danger is to be sought in common estimation.

XXIV. 1 In Partnerships in trade, where money and money are contributed by the parties, if the sums are equal, the gain and loss ought to be equally shared: if unequal, proportionally to the shares: Aristotle's rule. The same will hold if equal or unequal shares of labour are contributed. But money may be compared with labour, and labour with money. See Plautus.

2 But this joint contribution may be made in various ways: for either labour may be supplied by one party and the use of money (annual payment) by the other: in which case if the money-share be lost, the loss is the owner's, and if it be saved the gain is his: or labour and the ownership of money (capital) are the relative contributions; in which case he who supplies the labour partakes in the money-share. In the first case that which is compared with the labour is not the money-share, but the risk of losing it, and the gain which might be expected from it. In the other case the value of the labour is considered as something added to the money-share, and according to such value, he who supplies the labour has a share in the capital. What we have said of labour is also to be understood of the labour and risk of navigation, and the like.

3 That any one of the partners shall share the profit and not suffer by the loss, is against the nature of partnership; but such an agreement may be made without wrong. For then the contract will be a mixture of Partnership and Insurance; and the equality will be preserved, if he who in case of loss has taken the risk of loss, receives more of the profits in proportion. But that any one should bear the loss without profit, is not to be admitted, because in partnerships the community of interests is so natural, that without it partnership cannot subsist. What the Jurists say, that when the shares are not mentioned they must be understood to be equal, is true only if the contributions are equal. And in the common undertakings of good men, we must compare, not what happens here or there, but what may be probably hoped.

XXV. In associations of shipowners for mutual protection against pirates, the common utility aimed at is the protection; sometimes also the taking of prizes (privateering). The custom is to value the ships and cargo and to make up a sum in this way, and to apportion the losses which take place, among which are the expenses of the wounded men, among the owners of the ships and cargoes according to their proportion of that sum. And what we have hitherto said on this subject is agreeable to Natural Law.

XXVI. 1 Nor in these matters is anything changed by the instituted Law of Nations; excepting this only, that if an inequality of the contributions be agreed upon, this, where there is neither false declaration nor reticence of what ought to have been said, is in exterior actions held for equality. And thus, as by the Civil Law before Diocletian there was no action before a court of law for such inequality, so now among those who are connected only by the Law of Nations, there is no demand or compulsion allowed on that account. This agrees with what Pomponius says, that in the price of selling and buying, it is naturally allowed to men to circumvent one another: where *allowed* means, not that it is right, but that there is such permission that no remedy exists against him who offers such a defense.

2 *Naturally*, in this place, as in some others, is put for what is everywhere a received custom: as St Paul says that nature herself teaches us that it is shameful for a man to have long hair; though it is not repugnant to nature, and is the usage among many peoples. (1 Cor. xi. 14.) So the Author of the Book of Wisdom calls the worshippers of idols (not all men) vain by nature (xiii. 1), and St Paul, *by nature the children of wrath* (Eph. ii. 3), not speaking so much in his own character, as in that of the Romans, among whom he was then living. So Euenus, Galen, Thucydides, Diodorus: and so the Greeks spoke of *naturalized* virtues and vices. So Pomponius, when he says that a civilian could not die both testate and intestate, adds that the two things are naturally at variance: although that rule depends solely on the customs of the Romans, and has no place among other peoples, and not even among the Romans in soldiers' testaments.

3 The utility of introducing such rules as I have mentioned is evident, in order to obviate infinite controversies, which could not have been put on clear grounds in consequence of the uncertain prices of things among those who have no common judge, and which would have occurred if it had been reckoned lawful to depart from pacts on account of the inequality of conditions. So the Imperial Laws recognize Buying and Selling as being the result of long haggling and final agreement. So Seneca, and Andronicus Rhodius.

4 The writer of the life of Isidore calls this, injustice allowed by law.

CHAPTER XIII.

Of Oaths.

I. 1 AMONG all peoples, and in every age, the force of Oaths in proposals, promises, and contracts, has always been very great. So Sophocles in the Hippodamia ; Cicero.

2 And a heavy punishment was understood to await the perjured : so Hesiod. So that the posterity would have to expiate the crime of their ancestors, which was only believed in the case of the greatest crimes : and it was believed that even the will to commit perjury, without the deed, would bring down punishment. See Herodotus in the story of Glaucus, and Juvenal.

3 Cicero says well, *An Oath is a religious affirmation : what you promise solemnly, God being referred to as witness, is to be kept.* What he adds, *For then the matter pertains, not to the anger of the gods, for there is no such feeling, but to justice and good faith,* is not to be rejected, if by *anger* he understands a perturbation, a passion : but if a purpose or will of punishing, is by no means to be received, as Lactantius proves.

Let us now see whence the force of an Oath arises, and to what it tends.

II. First, that has place here, which we said of promises and contracts, that there is required a mind master of its reason and deliberate. Hence if any one, not thinking to swear, utters the words of an oath, it is not swearing. See in Ovid the story of Cydippe, [who read aloud on an apple which Acontius her lover had thrown at her, *I swear that I will marry Acontius.*] So Euripides in the Hippolytus.

But if any one, willingly swearing, wished not to bind himself, he is not the less obliged, because obligation is the necessary effect of an oath, and inseparable from it.

III. 1 But if any one utters the words of an oath, but with a purpose of not swearing, there are writers who hold that he is not bound, but that he sins by swearing rashly. But the sounder opinion is, that he is bound to make true the words to which he took God to witness: for that act, which is of itself obligatory, proceeded from a deliberate mind. And hence it follows that, as Cicero says, not to do what you intentionally swear is perjury. See Homer.

2 This is so, with the exception of the case in which you who swear, know or believe that he with whom you have to do takes your words otherwise: for in taking God to witness his words, he ought to perform them as he supposes them to be understood. So Cicero regulates an oath by the *mens deferentis*, the mind of the proposer. Tacitus speaks of men in fear changing the words of the oath: Augustine, of men keeping the words and balking the expectation. So Isidore. To swear without reserve is *liquido jurare*. So Metellus, rightly, would not swear to the Apuleian law, though it was void, as being informally passed.

3 For though in promises some tacit condition may be understood which absolves the promiser, that is not so in an Oath. So St Paul, Heb. vi. 18, That by *two* immutable things, in which it was impossible for God to *deceive:* speaking after the manner of men.

4 For God does not really change his decrees. He is said to change and to repent, when he acts otherwise than the words seem to imply, which he does on account of a condition tacitly understood, which has ceased. See the passages. And in this sense God may improperly be said to *deceive* us; the word often meaning to *frustrate hope*. See the passages. And this appears more plainly in threats, because they give no right: sometimes in promises, where there is a tacit condition.

5 Therefore the Apostle speaks of two things which mark immutability; the promise, which gives the promisee a right; and the oath, for that repels tacit and latent conditions. See the Psalms as quoted. For it is another thing if any conditions are openly indicated by the nature of the transaction. And to this some refer Numb. xiv. 30: *Ye shall not come into the land concerning which I sware to make you dwell therein.* But it is more exact to say that the land was sworn, not to the individuals, but to the People, namely, the posterity of those to whom God had sworn, as ver. 23. Such a promise may be fulfilled at any time, and is not restricted to certain persons.

IV. 1 From what has been said, it may be understood what is to be judged of an oath obtained by fraud. For if it be certain that the swearer supposed some fact which is not so, and would not have sworn except he had so believed, then the oath is not binding. But if it be doubtful whether, even without that fact, he would not have sworn the same, he must stand by his words, because simplicity in the highest degree is suitable in swearing.

2 To this I refer the oath of Joshua and the elders of Israel to the Gibeonites, Josh. ix. They were deceived by the simulation of the Gibeonites, but it did not follow that Joshua and the Israelites, if they knew that they were neighbours, would not have spared them. For what they said, ver. 7, *Peradventure ye dwell among us, and how shall we make a league with you?* may be understood as an inquiry whether the Gibeonites asked for a league of equality or of submission; or that they might shew that it was not lawful for the Hebrews to make leagues with certain peoples; not to imply that they would not spare their lives if they surrendered. For the divine law, which devoted those peoples to destruction, was to be understood by comparison with the rest of the law, in such sense that it was to take its course except any one attended to the warning, and did what was commanded them. This appears in the history of Rahab, who was spared; and of Solomon, who put the remainder of the Canaanites under a tribute of bond-service.

3 And to this view belongs what is said in the book of Joshua, xi. 19, 20, that none of the seven cities of Canaan made peace, for God had hardened their hearts that they might have no favour; wherefore it is probable that if the Gibeonites had stated the actual fact, they would have obtained their lives on condition of submission; the oath therefore was good. So much so, that God inflicted heavy punishment for the violation of it. 2 Sam. xxi. 6. So Ambrose maintains this oath. And the Gibeonites were punished for their deceit with personal servitude, whereas, if they had acted openly, they might have escaped on condition of paying a tribute.

V. But the signification of an oath is not to be extended beyond the received usage of speech. Therefore those were not perjured, Judges xxi. 7, who, when they had sworn that they would not give their daughters to wife to the tribe of Benjamin, still permitted them to live with those who had taken them by violence. For it is one thing to give, another, not to ask back rigorously. So Ambrose. Not dissimilarly the Achæans, when the Romans were dissatisfied with something which they had done and sworn to, requested the Romans to change it themselves, and not to ask them to make void what they had sworn to uphold.

VI. That an oath may be valid, the obligation must be lawful. Wherefore there is no force in a sworn promise concerning a thing unlawful, either by Natural Law, or Divine Prohibition, or Human, of which we shall speak afterwards. So Philo Judæus. Thus David spared Nabal, whom he had sworn to kill. Cicero mentions, as an example, Agamemnon's vow; Dionysius, the conspiracy of the decemvirs. So Seneca, Ambrose, Augustine, Basil.

VII. 1 Even if the thing promised be not unlawful, but something impeding a greater moral good, the oath will not be valid: because we are bound by God to aim at a moral progress; so that we may not take this liberty for ourselves. So Philo Judæus, of persons who in anger, &c. swear that they will not change their minds, or do good to this or that man. The forms of such oaths occur in Hebrew. [See.]

2 A vow of anything to God that another might not have it, was held valid by the Hebrew masters, even against parents; which Christ condemns. Even if the vow be against others it is not binding, because it is opposed to our moral progress.

VIII. Oaths concerning things impossible we need not speak of: for no one can be compelled to do what is impossible.

IX. As to what is for the time or by supposition impossible, the obligation is suspended; so that he who has sworn on the supposition, ought to do all that he can, that he may render possible what he has sworn.

X. The Forms of Oaths differ in words, agree in substance. They ought to have this meaning, that God is called upon, suppose in this way: *May God be my witness;* or, *May God be my Judge;* which two forms come to the same thing. For when a superior, having the right of punishing, is called in as a witness, he is also called upon to punish perfidy: and He who knows all things is the Avenger, because he is the Witness. Plutarch says every Oath ends in imprecations on the false swearer. To this view belonged the ancient forms of leagues, in which victims were slain: of which see the meaning in the passages quoted. So Abram's sacrifice, Gen. **xv.** 9.

XI. 1 But it is also an old custom to swear, mentioning other things or persons, either as imprecating harm from them, as the sun, the earth, heaven, the prince; or as calling to be punished in them, as one's head, children, country, prince. And this was done not only by the heathen, but by the Jews; as Philo shews. He says that those who are going to swear, ought not forthwith to go up to the Creator and Father of all, but to swear by parents, heaven, earth, the universe. And so Eustathius notes that the ancient Greeks did not commonly swear by the Gods, but by other things present; as by the sceptre; and this was instituted by Rhadamanthus. [See.] So Joseph swore by the life of Pharaoh, following the Egyptian custom; and Elisha to Elijah, *As thy soul liveth,* 2 Kings ii. 2.

And Christ, in Matth. v., does not, as some suppose, teach that these oaths are less lawful than those in which God's name is expressed, but that they were true oaths, though the Hebrews thought more lightly of them. As Ulpian says, that he who swears by his own salvation, swears by God; so Christ taught that he who swears by the temple, or by heaven, swears by God.

2 The Hebrew teachers of that time held that men were not bound in oaths in which they had sworn by created things, except the thing sworn by, were, as a penalty, vowed to God. This is the oath of *Corban,* which is not only mentioned in Matthew, but also was known to the Tyrians, as we learn from Josephus against Appion. And hence

I suppose the oriental peoples were called *Korbani*, as in Æschylus and Euripides*. Christ refutes this error.

Tertullian says that the ancient Christians swore by the Safety of the Prince. In Vegetius, as above stated, the formula is, By God and the Majesty of the Emperor, which, after God, is to be reverenced and honoured by men.

XII. Moreover he who swears by false gods is bound; because, though under false notions, he refers to the general idea of Godhead: and therefore the true God will interpret it as a wrong to himself if perjury be committed. We do not find that holy men ever proposed an oath in that way, much less that they swore such an oath, which I wonder that Duarenus permits†. But if those with whom they were dealing could not be brought to swear otherwise, they contracted with them, taking such an oath as was to be had, as Jacob from Laban, Gen. xxxi. 51. So Augustine says, He who swears by a stone, if he swear falsely, is perjured: not that the stone hears the speaker, but that God punishes the perjurer.

XIII. 1 The principal effect of an oath is to put an end to strife, as the writer to the Hebrews, vi. 16. So Philo, Dionysius, Diodorus.

2 Therefore the swearer must *swear sincerely*, so that his words agree with his thoughts, and *swear faithfully*, so that his deeds agree with his words: the violations of these duties we might call *false swearing* and *perjury*, but the distinction is not adhered to. [See the Greek words.]

XIV. And if the matter be such, and the words so conceived, that they refer not to God only but to a man also, [as if I swear to give you a thing,] then, undoubtedly, the man acquires a right by the oath, as from a promise or contract simply. But if the words do not regard a man as conferring on him a right, or regard him, but have something opposed to them; then the effect of the oath will be that the man will acquire no right; but he who has sworn to God will be obliged to stand by his oath. This is exemplified when one, by inspiring unjust fear, has given occasion to a sworn promise. So we see the Hebrew kings rebuked by the prophets, and punished by God, for not keeping their faith with the Babylonian kings. Cicero lauds Pomponius, who kept an oath given under terror: *such*, he says, *was the force of an oath at that time.* And hence Regulus was bound to return to his imprisonment, though unjust; and those ten whom Cicero mentions, to return to Annibal.

XV. 1 And this is not only true between public enemies, but any parties: for respect is not had to the person to whom the oath is made, but to God by whom we swear; and this is sufficient to produce

---

* Barbeyrac says, not in Euripides, but in Lycophron; and he questions the etymology of *Korbani*.

† Duarenus does not permit men to swear, but only to *accept*, an oath by *Mahomet*. J. B.

an obligation. Therefore Cicero is to be repudiated when he says that it is no perjury if we do not pay the price which we have promised to robbers for sparing our life, not even if we have sworn: because a robber is not an open enemy, having the rights of war, but a common enemy of all men: which also the same Cicero says elsewhere of tyrants, as does Brutus in Appian.

2 But though, in the Instituted Law of Nations, it is true that an enemy differs from a robber, as we shall shew below; yet this difference cannot have place when, though the right of the person fail, our business is with God: on which account an oath is called *a vow*. Nor is that true which Cicero assumes, that we have no common ground of rights with robbers: for that a deposit is to be restored when made by a robber, if the owner do not appear, is rightly ruled by Tryphoninus.

3 Wherefore I cannot approve what is delivered by some writers, that he who has promised anything to a robber may discharge his duty by a momentary payment, and be allowed forthwith to take back what he has paid. For words used in an oath, and so, towards God, are to be understood with entire simplicity; and therefore, so as to have effect. And therefore, he who returned to the enemy clandestinely and came away again, did not satisfy his oath that he would return, as was rightly judged by the Roman Senate.

XVI. 1 Are oaths to a faithless person not to be kept: as Accius, quoted in Cicero's *Offices*, holds?

Not if the sworn promise had evidently respect to another promise which was a sort of implied condition. But they are to be kept, if the promises are of a diverse kind, and without mutual reference: for then each must observe what he has sworn. And thus Regulus is praised by Silius for keeping faith with the faithless.

2 That inequality in contracts, by Natural Law, gives ground either for rescinding or remodelling them, we have said above. And though the Law of Nations has changed something in this matter, we are often allowed by the Civil Law, which is of force over those who are parts of the same people, to return to the Natural Law. But here if an oath have been introduced, although nothing, or less than the contract, may be due to the person, our faith to God is to be kept. So Ps. xv. 4, *He that sweareth to his neighbour, and disappointeth him not, though it were to his own hinderance.*

XVII. But it is to be observed, that when there is no right of a person produced, in consequence of some of these defects, but only our faith engaged to God; the heir of the swearer is not bound. Because as the goods pass to the heir, that is, the things about which men deal, so do the burthens upon them: but not the obligations which any one was liable to, as duties of piety, kindness, or good faith. For these do not belong to what is strictly called *jus* or right, as we have shewn.

XVIII. So when a right is not acquired by a person, in virtue of another's oath, yet if the oath respect the utility of any one, and he will not have this utility, the swearer is not bound. Also he is not bound if the quality under which he swore has ceased. So in Cesar, Curio addresses those who had been Domitius's soldiers: *Who could hold you by an oath, when he himself, throwing away the ensigns of authority, and laying down his command, as a private man and a captive, has himself become subject to others?* And afterwards he says that their oath is rescinded by his degradation.

XIX. It is made a question whether that which is contrary to an oath is only unlawful, or also void.

For this we must distinguish: if good faith alone be engaged, an act done against the oath is valid; as a testament, a sale. But not, if the oath be so expressed that it contains at the same time a full abdication of power to do the act.

And these are the natural consequences of oaths; from which we must form a judgment of the oaths of kings, and the oaths which foreigners swear to foreigners, when the act is not necessarily subjected to the laws of the place.

XX. 1 Let us now consider what the authority of superiors, that is of kings, fathers, masters, husbands (in marital matters), can do [in modifying the effect of oaths]. The act of a superior cannot effect that an oath, so far as it was obligatory, is not to be performed; for that it is to be so, is a matter both of Natural and of Divine Law. But because our acts are not fully in our power, but in such a way that they depend on superiors, therefore there may be a double act of a superior as to the matter sworn; one direct, on the person of the swearer, the other, on the person to whom the oath is made.

2 The act of the superior may be directed on the person of the swearer, either before swearing, rendering the oath void, in so far as the right of the inferior is subject to the superior; or after the swearing, forbidding that it be fulfilled. For the inferior, as inferior, was not able to bind himself except so far as it should please his superior; he had no further power. And thus by the Hebrew Law the husband might make void the vows of his wife. Seneca proposes this question: *If a law be made that no one shall do what I had promised my friend I would do, what then?* And he solves it, saying, The same law which *forbids me defends me.* But there may be a mixed act of both parties; as if the superior should direct that what the inferior shall swear in this or that case, say from fear or from weakness of judgment, shall be valid, only if he himself approves of it. And on this ground may be defended the absolutions from oaths which were formerly granted by princes; and are now, by the consent of princes, for the sake of piety, granted by the governors of the Church.

3 The act of the superior may be directed on the person of him to whom the oath is made, by taking from him the right which he has thus acquired: or even, if he have no right, by forbidding that

he receive anything in virtue of such oath: and that, in two ways, either as a penalty, or for public utility, in virtue of his Eminent Dominion. And hence it may be understood, if the swearer be not under the same subjection as the person sworn to, what the governor of each may do in respect to the oath.

*He who on oath has promised anything to a mischievous person, as such, as for instance a robber, cannot take from him the promised right on the ground of penalty: for then his words would have no effect, which is by all means to be avoided.

In like manner what is promised cannot be given as a compensation for a right which was in controversy before, if the agreement took place after the controversy began.

4 Human Law may take away the impediment which it had thrown in the way of certain acts, if an oath, either in general, or in a particular form, be introduced: which the Roman Law did in the case of those impediments which regard, not directly public utility, but the private utility of the swearer. And if this be done, the act so sworn will be valid in the same manner as it would, without the Human Law, have been valid by Natural Law; either only by binding good faith, or by giving a right to another, according to the different nature of such acts, as already explained.

XXI. 1 It is here to be noted in passing, that what is said in the precepts of Christ, and in St James, of not swearing, does not properly apply to an oath of assertion, of which there are some examples in St Paul himself, but to an oath of promise with regard to an uncertain future. This plainly appears in the words of Christ, Matth. v: and in the reason which St James adds, v. 12, *lest ye fall into condemnation,* ὑπόκρισιν, is, *lest ye be found fallacious.* See the passages.

2 The same is proved by the words of Christ, *Let your words be yea, yea, and nay, nay*: which St James explains, *Let your yea be yea, and your nay, nay*: that is, let your *yea* mean a sincere consent, and your *nay* a resolute refusal. See the illustrations.

3 On the contrary, those whose acts are at variance with their words are those whose word is *yea and nay,* 1 Cor. i. 18, 19, that is, their *yea* is *nay,* and their *nay* is *yea*: as St Paul himself explains. See Festus's etymology of *naucum.*

4 Therefore Christ said the same thing as Philo, that the best thing is that our word should be as our oath. So the Essenes, according to Josephus.

5 Pythagoras seems to have taken this from the Essenes, or those who followed the Essenes. His precept is, *Not to swear by the gods, for you ought to act so that men believe you without an oath*: so the Scythians in Curtius: so Cicero for Roscius; Solon; Clemens Alexandrinus; Alexis the Comic Poet. Cicero relates that at Athens, when a certain man, noted for his holiness and gravity, had to give his testimony, and approached the altar to swear, the judges with one

---

* These two rules refer to promises rather than oaths. W.

voice refused to have the oath administered, his character being guarantee sufficient.

6 The maxims of Hierocles on the Golden Poem are not different, *He who said, Reverence an oath, by that very precept enjoined you to abstain from swearing with regard to future uncertain matters. About such it is neither worthy nor safe to swear.* So Libanius in praising the Christian Emperors: Eustathius on the Odyssee.

XXII. Hence, in many cases, instead of an oath, was introduced a practice that good faith should be confirmed by giving the right hand, or some other sign; with this implication, that if the promise was not fulfilled, the promiser was held no less detestable than if he had perjured himself. Especially it is a common saying, concerning kings and princes, that their word goes for their oath. For they ought to be such that they can say with Augustus: I am a man of good faith: and with Eumenes, that they would sooner forfeit their life than their word: as also Gunter says to Ligurinus.

Cicero in his oration for Deiotarus, praises Cesar by saying that his hand was as firm in pledging truth as in fighting battles. And in the heroic times, a sceptre was set up as the king's oath, as Aristotle notes.

CHAPTER XIV.

Of the Promises, Contracts, and Oaths of Sovereigns.

I. 1 THE Promises, Contracts, and Oaths of Kings, and other persons who have like authority, give rise to peculiar questions, both as to the lawful power they have over themselves and their own actions, and that which they have over their subjects, and that which they have over their successors.

As to the first head, it is made a question whether the king, as he can relieve his subjects from an oath, can do the same to himself, and put himself back into his original condition. Bodinus thinks that the king may be so reinstated, on the same grounds as a subject would be so ; whether he have been circumvented by the fraud and deception of another party, or by his own error, or fear; and this, both in matters which affect the rights of the sovereignty, and those which pertain to private advantage. He adds, that the king is not even bound by an oath, if the conventions made are of that kind from which the law permits parties to recede, even though the agreement is conformable to propriety ; for (he holds) he is not therefore bound, because he has sworn, but because every one is bound by just conventions, so far as the interest of another is concerned.

2 We make a distinction here, as we have done in other places, between the acts of the king which are royal acts, and acts of the same person which are private acts. For in royal acts, what the king does is to be held as if it were done by the community : and as laws made by the community itself would have no force over such acts, because the community is not superior to itself, so neither have laws made by the king any such force. Therefore against such contracts, restitution will not hold : for this restitution is a creature of the Civil Law. And thus kings are not relieved from contracts which they had made as minors.

II. 1 If a people have established a king who has not plenary rights, but is under additional legal constraints, acts contrary to these laws may be by them made void; either altogether, or in part; because to this extent the people had retained a right to itself. In the case of kings who reign with plenary rights, but have not the kingdom as their own property, such acts of theirs as alienate the kingdom or a part thereof, or its revenues, have been discussed above; and we have shewn that such acts are by Natural Law void, as being acts done to the property of another.

2 But the private acts of the king are to be considered, not as the acts of the community, but as acts of a private party, and consequently, done with the intention of following the common rule of law. Wherefore the laws which make some acts void, either absolutely, or if the person injured by them demands that they should be so, hold here also; as if the contract had been made under that condition. And accordingly we have seen certain kings protect themselves in this way against the evil of usury*. But the king may release his own acts, as he may those of others, from these laws: and whether he intends to do this, is to be estimated from the circumstances. If he does, the matter must then be judged by mere Natural Law. This is to be added; that if any law make an act void, not in favour of the doer, but as a penalty on him, this does not hold against the acts of kings; as in other matters also, penal laws, and all which has a power of coercion do not apply to them. For punishment and coercion can only proceed from diversity of will: the coercer and the coerced require distinct persons; distinct relations [of the same person] are not sufficient.

III. A king, as a private person, may nullify an oath, *antecedently*, if by a prior oath he deprive himself of the power of swearing to such an effect; but *consequently*, [after the act,] he cannot do this [by his royal authority:] for here too a distinction of persons is required. For the oaths which are nullified subsequently to the act, were already understood to be made with the exception, "except a superior refuse his consent;" but to swear in such a sense, that you are bound, except you yourself refuse consent, is absurd, and contrary to the nature of an oath. But although a right may not be acquired by another person in virtue of the oath, on account of some defect in the person who swears, yet that he is bound to God, we have shewn above: and this applies to kings no less than to others; contrary to the sentiments of Bodinus in the place cited.

IV. Also Promises, when full, absolute, and accepted, naturally transfer a right, as we have shewn above; and this likewise applies to kings, no less than to others: so that we condemn, in this sense, the

---

* Gronovius says that Grotius is here making an excuse for Philip II. of Spain, who repudiated a portion of his debts in 1596: and refers to Mezeray, B. xviii. Barbeyrac adds, on the same authority, that two years after, Philip revoked this act, and acknowledged his debts.

N

opinion of those who say that a king is never bound by the promises which he made without a cause. In what sense this may be truly held, we shall hereafter see.

V. What we have said above, that the Civil Law of the kingdom does not hold in the compacts and contracts of kings, Vasquius also has rightly seen. But his inferences, that buying and selling without a certain price, letting and hiring without stating the hire, a lease without a writing, are valid if done on the part of kings, is not to be conceded: because these acts are not done by the king as king, but by him as by any other person. In this class of acts, it is so far from being true, that the common laws of the kingdom have no force, that we maintain that even the laws of the town in which the king lives are of force: inasmuch as the king abides there in a special manner, as a member of that society. Which, however, is as we say, except circumstances shew that it pleases the king to make his act free from the authority of those laws. Another example which Vasquius gives, of a promise made in any way [informally], agrees well with this rule, and may be explained by what we have said above.

VI. 1 Almost all jurists deliver an opinion that by contracts which the king enters into with his subjects, he is obliged naturally only, not civilly: which is a very obscure way of speaking. For juristical writers sometimes by an abuse of language call that, *natural obligation*, which it is by nature a handsome thing to do, though it is not truly due: as for an executor to pay legacies entire without the deduction which the Falcidian law allows; to pay a just debt when the creditor has been deprived of his legal right by a penal sentence; to return a benefit for a benefit; none of which, [when done,] can be recovered by an action of false debt. But sometimes, more properly, they use the term for that which truly *obliges* or binds us; whether another person thereby acquire a right, as in pacts, or does not, as in a full and firm *pollicitation* or proffer. Maimonides distinguishes these three cases; things which are not due, he calls *kindnesses;* things due by strict law, *judgments;* things due by propriety, *justice.* So Matth. xxiii. 23, *mercy, judgment, and faith,* are by some interpreted, as if *faith* were put for *righteousness: judgment* means what is strictly due: see 1 Macc. vii. 18, and viii. 32.

2 Again; a person may be said to be civilly obliged by his own act, either in this sense,—that the obligation does not proceed from mere Natural Law, but from the Civil Law, or from both;—or in this sense, that it gives ground for an action in a Court of Law.

We say then that by the promise and contract of a king, which he enters into with his subjects, there arises a true and proper obligation, which confers a right upon the subjects: for this is the nature of promises and contracts, as we have shewn above, even between God and men. But if the acts be such as are done by the king, but done by him, only as by any other man, the Civil Laws also will be valid in that case: but if the act be an act of the king as king, the Civil Laws do not apply to that; which distinction has not been sufficiently attended to by Vasquius. But notwithstanding this distinction, in either case a legal action will arise from the act; namely, to the end that the right of the creditor may be declared: but coaction cannot follow, on account of the condition of those with whom the business is. For it is not allowable for subjects to compel him whose subjects they are: equals have such a right towards equals, by nature; superiors have it over subjects by law only.

VII. This also is to be noted, that a right, even when it has been acquired by subjects, may be taken away by the king in two modes; either as a Penalty, or by the force of Eminent Dominion. But to do this by the force of Eminent Dominion, there is required, in the first place, public utility; and next, that, if possible, compensation be made, to him who has lost what was his, at the common expense. And as this holds with regard to other matters, so does it with regard to rights which are acquired by promise or contract.

VIII. Nor may we, in this matter, in any way admit the distinction which some make, between rights acquired by force of Natural Law, and those which come from the Civil Law. For the right of the king over the one class and the other is equal, and the latter cannot, any more than the former, be taken away without cause. For when ownership, or any other right, has been legitimately acquired by any one, that it may not be taken away from him without cause, is a matter of Natural Law. If the king act in any other way, he is without doubt bound to repair the damage done: for he acts against the true right of the subject. In this therefore the rights of subjects and the rights of foreigners differ;—that the rights of foreigners, (that is, of those who are not subjects in any way,) are by no means subject to the right of Eminent Dominion; (whether they are subject to Penalty, we shall hereafter see;) but the rights of subjects are liable to that right, so far as public utility demands.

IX. From what we have said, this also appears:—how false that is which some deliver, that the Contracts of Kings are Laws. For, from laws, no one acquires a right against the king; therefore, if he revokes them, he does wrong to no one. (He sins, however, if he do so without just cause.) But from his promises and contracts, rights arise. By contracts, the contracting parties only are bound; to laws, all are subject. But yet some transactions may be mixed of contracts and laws, as a treaty made with a neighbouring king, or with a farmer of the revenues, which is at the same time published as a Law, so far as it contains things to be observed by the subjects.

X. Let us proceed to the case of Successors: and with regard to them, we must make a distinction, whether they are heirs to the whole property of the deceased as well as to the kingdom; as those are who receive a patrimonial kingdom by testament, or by intestacy; or whether they are only successors to the kingdom; suppose by a new election, or by the law of the land, or by some imitation of the common rule of inheritance, or otherwise: or whether, finally, they succeed by mixed right. For with regard to those who are heirs of all the property as well as of the kingdom, there can be no doubt that they are bound by the promises and contracts of their predecessor. For the rule, that the property of the deceased is bound for debts, even for personal debts, is a rule coeval with property itself.

XI.   1 But of those who succeed only to the kingdom; or to the property as sharers only, but to the kingdom, alone; how far they are bound, is a matter worthy of inquiry, especially as it has hitherto been treated very confusedly. That the successors of the kingdom, as such, are not directly and *immediately* bound [by those contracts,] is evident enough; because they receive their rights, not from him who has lately deceased, but from the people; whether the rule of succession approach more nearly to the rule of common inheritance, or recede further from it; of which difference we have treated above.

2 But *mediately*, that is, by the mediate effect of the State, such successors also are bound; which will be thus understood. Every society, no less than individual persons, has the right of binding itself, by its own act, or that of the majority. And this right it may transfer, either expressly, or by necessary consequence; suppose, by transferring the government: for in moral matters, he who gives the end, gives the means which lead to the end.

XII.   1 But this does not go to an infinite extent. For an infinite power of imposing such obligations is not necessary, in order rightly to exercise the government: as such power also is not necessary for a guardian or a *Tutor;* but only so much as the nature of the office requires. The *Tutor is reckoned in the place of the owner,* says Julian, *when he administers his pupil's affairs, not when he plunders him:* and in this sense we are to understand what Ulpian says, that the contract of the master of a society, may not only bring advantage to the society, but also disadvantage. But yet we are not, as some hold, to reduce the engagements of a king to the rules of one man undertaking another's business; namely, that his acts are then only valid when they turn out to the advantage of the principal party. For to put the Ruler of the State to such a strait, would be dangerous to the State itself. And accordingly, the community is to be supposed to have held this opinion, when it bestowed the government upon him. And what the Roman Emperors declared, in a Rescript with respect to the corporation of a town,—that what was transacted by the magistrates should be of force in a doubtful case, but not, if what was unquestionably due was given away,—may be and ought to be applied to our question, relative to the whole People, observing a due proportion in the application.

2 As the subjects are not bound by every law; for there may be laws, (even without going to those which command something unlawful,) which are evidently foolish and absurd;—so too the contracts of Governors then bind their subjects, when they have a probable reason;

and in a doubtful case, this may be presumed, on the authority of the Governors. And this distinction is much better than that which is put forth by many, governed by the result, according as it is a moderate or an immoderate damage. For it is not the result which is to be regarded in such a case, but the probable reason for doing the thing; if there be such a reason, the People itself will be bound, if by any event it should become its own master; and the successors to the government, as the heads of the People. For, in like manner, if a free People had made any engagement, he who afterwards should receive the sovereignty, in the fullest manner, would be bound by the engagement.

3 The emperor Titus is praised on this account, that he would not allow himself to be petitioned to confirm any thing which his predecessors had granted, [holding the grants valid without such process;] while Tiberius and those emperors who followed him, did not recognize the grants of their predecessors as valid, till they had themselves repeated them. The excellent emperor Nerva, following the example of Titus, says, in an edict which is extant in Pliny, *Let no man suppose that what he has obtained from another Prince, either privately or publicly, shall be by me revoked, that so, if I confirm those grants, he may be the more obliged to me; no man's congratulation need be accompanied by such petitions.* But on the other hand, when Tacitus had related of Vitellius, that he had torn the empire in pieces, reckless of the interests of posterity, the common world flocking about him to catch his extravagant gifts, and some even purchasing his favour with money; he adds: *Wise men held those grants to be void, which could be neither given nor received without damage to the State.*

4 That must also here be added; that if in any case a contract begins to tend, not only to some loss, but to the ruin of the community, so that, from the beginning, the contract in its extension to that case would have been unjust and unlawful; then that contract may, not so much be revoked, as declared not to be binding any longer, as being made without the condition without which it could not justly be made.

5 What we have said of contracts, holds also of the alienation of the People's money, and of any other things which the king has by law a power to alienate for the public good. For here too a similar distinction is to be applied, whether there was a probable reason for giving or otherwise alienating.

6 But if the engagements have reference to the alienation of the kingdom or its parts, or of the royal patrimony, they will be invalid, as being a contract about that which is another's. The same will hold in limited monarchies, if there be any matter or kind of act which the people has excepted from the royal power. For in order to give validity to such acts, there is required the consent of the People, either by itself, or by those who legitimately represent the People; as may be understood by what we have said above respect-

ing alienation. By the application of these distinctions, it will be easy to judge whether the pleas of kings who refuse to pay their predecessors' debts, not being their heirs, are just or unjust : of which examples may be seen in Bodinus.

XIII. Nor is that which many have delivered, that the favours of Princes, granted out of pure liberality, may at any time be revoked, to be allowed to pass on without distinction. For there are some grants which the king makes out of his own property, and which, except they are granted expressly during pleasure only, have the force of a complete donation. And these cannot be revoked, except, in the case of subjects, in the way of penalty, or for the sake of public utility, and then with compensation if it may be. There are other grants which merely remove legal restrictions, without any contract. These are revocable. Because, as the law which is relaxed universally may always be re-established universally, so, that which is relaxed particularly may be re-established particularly. For in this case no right against the author of the law is acquired.

XIV. By contracts made by those who without right have usurped the government, the People, or the Legitimate Sovereign are not bound. For Usurpers have no authority to bind the People.

However, the People are bound by what has been expended for their benefit [by an Usurper;] that is, so far as they are the richer for it.

CHAPTER XV.

Of Treaties and Sponsions*.

I. COMPACTS or Conventions are divided by Ulpian into public and private : and public, he expounds, not by definition, but by examples which he gives ; a *treaty of peace,* which is the first example; or *when the generals in a war make some convention,* which is the second. By public compacts or conventions, therefore, he understands those which can only be made by the supreme government or some public governor ; by which character they differ, not only from the contracts of private persons, but from the contracts of kings about their private concerns. For though causes of war arise from the latter also, they proceed more commonly from public questions. Therefore, since we have discussed many points with regard to compacts in general, we must add some remarks belonging to this more eminent kind of compact.

II. These public agreements we may divide into Public Treaties, Sponsions, and other Compacts†.

III. 1 With regard to the difference of Public Treaties (*Fœdera*) and Conventions made on personal responsibility (*Sponsiones*), we may take Livy's view, in which he says that *fœdera* are treaties made by the sovereign power of the State, in which the people is liable to the Divine wrath if it do not make good its engagements. Among the

---

* Mr Wheaton adopts the term *Sponsions,* exactly in the sense in which Grotius uses it in this Chapter, as denoting engagements made without full authority. *International Law,* Part III. Chap. 11, § 3. (1836).

† See *E. M.* 1124.

Romans they were formally made by the *Feciales*, with the *Pater Patratus* at their head. *Sponsions* is the term which we may use when persons not having a commission from the Supreme Authority make any engagement which properly touches that authority. Sallust says, *The Senate, as was to be expected, decreed that no Treaty (foedus) could be made without its direction and that of the people.* Hieronymus, king of Syracuse, made a Convention of alliance with Annibal; but afterwards sent to Carthage to convert the Convention into a Treaty. So that when Seneca says, *The Treaty made by the General was held as made by the People,* he must mean the generals of the old time, who had such a commission. In kingdoms, it is the king's office to make Treaties. See Euripides.

2 As a Magistrate's acts do not bind the People, so neither do those of the smaller part of the people: which justifies the Romans in breaking their convention with the Galli Senones; for the greater part of the people was with the Dictator Camillus; and as Gellius says, the People cannot be treated with in two bodies.

3 But when they who have not authority from the people have made a convention respecting something which belongs to the rights of the people, let us see to what they are bound. It may be thought perhaps that, in this case, the party who made the convention have performed their engagement, if they have done all that was possible for them, that the terms of the convention on their part should be fulfilled; according to what we have said in speaking of promises. But the nature of these affairs, which involve a contract and not a mere promise, requires a much stricter obligation. For he who in a contract gives anything of his own, or promises it, expects something to be done for him by the other side: whence by the Civil Law also, which repudiates promises for the acts of others, yet a promise of the agent binds and is valid so far as he is concerned.

IV. In Livy, Menippus, rather for his purpose than scientifically, divides Treaties between Kings and States into three kinds; treaties of a conqueror in war with the conquered, and in these the terms depend on the will of the victor: treaties of peace between parties who end a war with equal success; and here the terms are equal, and possessions which had been disturbed by war are restored by agreement; and these treaties are constructed either on the ancient forms, or according to the convenience of the parties: and the third kind, when those who have never been enemies make a treaty of friendship and alliance; neither party giving and neither receiving the law.

V. 1 We must make a more accurate division. We say then that some treaties establish that which is conformable to Natural Law; others add something to it. Treaties of the former kind are not only commonly made by hostile parties ending a war, but formerly were both frequent, and in a certain way necessary, between those who had before had nothing to do with each other. Which arose from this, that the rule of Natural Law, that there is a certain natural relationship among men, and that therefore it is unlawful for one man to harm another, as it was obliterated by vicious habits before the deluge, so was it again after the deluge: so that robbery and plunder of strangers without declaring war, was held lawful: a *Scythism*, as Epiphanius calls it.

2 Hence we have that question in Homer, Are ye Pirates? asked as an inoffensive inquiry, as Thucydides notices: and in an old law of Solon there are mentioned companies of Freebooters; since, as Justin says, up to the time of Tarquin, Sea Rovers were objects of admiration: and again, in the old Roman law, If there be any nation with which the Romans have neither friendship, nor friendly intercourse, nor alliance, they are not enemies indeed; but that what belonging to the Romans goes into their power is theirs, and a free Roman taken by them becomes a captive; and the same if any come from them to the Romans. [*Dig.* XLIX. 15.] Thus the Corcyreans, before the Peloponnesian war, were not enemies of the Athenians, but had neither peace nor truce with them, as appears by the oration of the Corinthians in Thucydides. Sallust says of Bocchus, *not known to us either in war or in peace.* Hence Aristotle praises those who plunder barbarians: and the old Latin word *hostis* meant only stranger.

3 In this class are comprehended treaties in which it is provided that there shall be on both sides the right of hospitality and of intercourse, so far as they come under Natural Law, of which we have treated elsewhere. This distinction is referred to by Arcus in Livy, where he says, that the question is not concerning alliance but intercharge of rights; namely, that they should not let the Macedonian slaves find a refuge among them. The whole of this class of conventions the Greeks call *Peace*, and oppose to *Truce*. See Andocides.

VI. 1 Conventions which add something to Natural Law are either equal or unequal. Those are equal, which bear equally and commonly on both parties, as Isocrates says. So Virgil. The Greeks distinguish them from Unequal Compacts and Conventions of Command, which are less dignified, and, as Demosthenes says, to be avoided by those who love liberty, as approaching to servitude.

2 Conventions of both kinds are made for peace, or some alliance: equal treaties of peace are those which stipulate restitutions of captives and captures on both sides, and mutual security. Equal treaties of alliance either pertain to commerce, or to alliance in war, or to other matters. Equal treaties on the subject of commerce may be various, for instance, that no import duties be paid on either side, which was the agreement in the old treaty of the Romans and Carthaginians, except what was paid to the harbour-master and the public crier; or that no duties be paid greater than at present, or greater than a certain rate.

3 In alliances for war, the terms may be, that each side supply equal forces of infantry, cavalry, and ships: either for the whole war,

which the Greeks called *Symmachia,* and which Thucydides explains, *to have the same friends and the same enemies:* as also in Livy; or for defensive purposes only, which was *Epimachia;* or for a certain war, or against certain enemies; or against all, excepting allies, as in the league between the Carthaginians and Macedonians, in Polybius; so also the Rhodians by treaty promised aid to Antigonus and Demetrius against all, except Ptolemy.

An equal treaty may also, as we have said, pertain to other matters; as, that neither shall have fortresses within the boundaries of the other; that neither shall defend the subjects of the other; that neither shall give passage to the enemies of the other.

VII.   1 From the explanation of what are equal conventions, it is easily understood what are unequal.   Unusual Treaties are either proposed by the superior party, or by the inferior.   By the superior, as if he promises assistance without any reciprocal stipulation: by the inferior, when there is an inferiority of claim, are what we have spoken of as Conventions of Command.   And these are either without infringement of the sovereignty of the inferior, or such as infringe it.

2 Such as infringe the sovereignty, as in the second treaty of the Romans with the Carthaginians, that the latter should not make war without the permission of Rome: from that time, as Appian says, the Carthaginians were by treaty submiss to Rome.

To this class we might add surrender on conditions, except that this contains, not an infringement, but a transfer of the sovereignty, of which we have spoken elsewhere.   Such a convention Livy calls *fœdus* in the case of the Apulian Theates.

3 In unequal treaties made without infringement of the sovereignty, the burthens imposed on the inferior are either transitory or permanent: Transitory, as the payment of a subsidy, the dismantling of strong towns, the withdrawing from certain places; the giving up hostages, ships, elephants: Permanent, as the paying deference to the authority and majesty of the superior; of which engagement I have elsewhere spoken.   Nearly of the same kind is the engagement to have for enemies and for friends those whom the other party shall prescribe; not giving passage or provisions to a party with whom the other is at war.   And the smaller matters; not building forts in certain places, not having a moveable army, not having ships beyond a certain number, not founding a city; not navigating; not raising soldiers in certain places, not attacking allies, not supplying provisions to the enemy; rescinding treaties before made with other parties: of all which we may find examples in Polybius, Livy, and others.

4 Unequal treaties may be made, not only between the conqueror and the conquered, as Menippus thought, but between the more and the less powerful who have never been at war.

VIII.   It is often made a question whether it is lawful to make treaties with those who are strangers to the true Religion; which point, in Natural Law, is open to no doubt. For that Law is so far common to all men that it recognizes no distinction of Religion. But the question is put on the ground of the Divine Law, and so treated, not only by Theologians but by Jurists, and among them, by Oldradus and Decianus.

IX. 1 First of Divine Law. We have examples of covenants for mutual forbearance, with strangers to true Religion, before the law of Moses, as Jacob with Laban, not to speak of Abimelech. The law of Moses did not change this : for example, the Hebrews are forbidden to treat the Egyptians as enemies. The seven Peoples of Canaan are an exception, on account of their obstinate idolatry.

2 Treaties of commerce, and the like, may be made with such persons: so David and Solomon with Hirom king of Tyre.

3 The Law of Moses separates the Jews from the rest of mankind. But that the Jews were not to do good to other nations, was a perverse interpretation of later masters. See Juvenal, Cicero, Seneca, Apollonius Molo, Diodorus, Philostratus, Josephus.

4 This was not Christ's interpretation. Also, see David's intercourse with strangers : and Solomon's.

5 Besides the exception of the Peoples of Canaan,·the Ammonites and Moabites also are excepted. Beneficial leagues with them are forbidden, but war is not authorized. See the passages.

6 See also the example of Abraham and his league with the king of Sodom. And the Maccabees made leagues with Greeks and Romans.

7 If any kings or peoples were condemned to destruction by God, doubtless it was then unlawful to protect them or to join with them. So 2 Chron. xix. 2, Jehu the prophet says to Jehoshaphat, *Shouldest thou help the ungodly, &c.* So 2 Chron. xxv. 7 to Amaziah. But this was on account of personal considerations, not the nature of the treaty, as appears by the circumstances: [which see.]

8 Observe that the case was worse with the Ten Tribes, who, though descended from Jacob, had deserted God, than with others.

9 Sometimes also treaties are condemned on account of the bad motive from which they proceeded. Thus, 2 Chron. xvi. 2, Asa's league with the Syrians. So other kings sinned. And trust in Egypt is condemned; but Solomon made a league with Egypt.

10 Moreover the Hebrews had a promise of success if they obeyed the law, and so, did not need human aid. Solomon's precepts in the Proverbs about shunning the fellowship of the wicked belong to private prudence, not to public policy, and admit of many exceptions.

X. 1 The Gospel changed nothing in this matter: it rather favours conventions with all men that we may do them good : as God makes his sun to rise on the just and on the unjust. So Tertullian.

2 Which must be taken with a difference, that we are to do good

to all, but specially to those who are our partakers in religion. See the Clementine Constitutions, Ambrose, Aristotle.

3 Familiar intercourse is not forbidden with strangers to Religion, nor even those who have gone back from religion; but only unnecessary familiarity. St Paul's warnings, 2 Cor. vi. 14, &c. refer to idolatry, as appears by what follows, and by 1 Cor. x. 21.

4 Nor does the proof follow, [that we are not to make treaties with them,] because we are not willingly to come under the authority of the impious, or to contract marriage with them. For such steps produce much more danger to religion, and are more permanent, and more free; while treaties depend on occasion of time and place. And as we may benefit the profane, so we may ask their help, as Paul claimed the help of Cæsar and of the chief Centurion.

XI. 1 Hence in an alliance with those of a false religion, there is no inherent or universal pravity: the case is to be judged by the circumstances. But care is to be had that too much mixture with them do not taint the weak. For which purpose, separate habitation is good, like that of the Israelites in Egypt. So Anaxandrides. And to this pertains what we have said of Jews and Christians serving as soldiers with heathens.

2 But if the strength of the profane is likely thus to be much increased, we must abstain from such alliances, except in case of necessity: such as Thucydides speaks of. [See.] For it is not mere right which justifies men in doing what may indirectly harm religion. We must seek first the kingdom of God, that is, the propagation of the Gospel.

3 It were to be wished that many princes and peoples would lay to heart that liberal and pious saying of Fulk, Archbishop of Rheims, who thus admonished Charles the Simple: *Who is not alarmed when you seek the friendship of the enemies of God; and invite the co-operation and the arms of pagans for the calamity and ruin of the Christian name? It makes no difference whether any one joins himself with pagans, or denies God and worships idols.* There is in Arrian a saying of Alexander, that *Those grievously offend who enter the service of Barbarians to fight against Greeks and Grecian rights.*

XII. Add that all Christians are members of one body; are commanded to bear each other's sufferings and sorrows: and as this applies to individuals, so does it to peoples, as peoples, and to kings, as kings. Each must serve Christ according to the power given him. But this they cannot do, when the infidel is powerful, except they help each other: and this cannot well be done except a general league be made with that view. Such a league has been made, and the head of it created by common consent Roman Emperor*. Therefore all Christians ought to aid in this cause according to their power with men or money: nor do I see how they can be excused,

* Frederic III., A.D. 1461, says Gronovius; and refers to *Boecleri* Disputatio *de Passagiis.*

except they be detained at home by an inevitable war or some similar evil.

XIII.   1 The question often arises, if several parties carry on a war, to which of two in preference ought he to give assistance who is under agreement with both. This is first to be understood, as we have said above, that no one is bound to unjust wars. Therefore that one of the allies who has a just cause is to be preferred, if the transaction is with a stranger: and also if it be with another of the allies. Thus Demosthenes, in the oration concerning Megalopolis, shews that the Athenians ought to assist the Messenians, who are their allies, against the Lacedæmonians, who are also their allies, if the wrong be on the side of the latter. In the treaty of Hannibal with the Macedonians, it stood, *We will be the enemies of your enemies, except the kings, states and ports with which we are in league and friendship.*

2 If two allies quarrel, being both in the wrong, which may happen, we are to take part on neither side. So Aristides.

3 But if two allies make war on others for just cause, if we can send aid to both, soldiers or money for example, we are to do so ; as we are to pay several personal creditors. But if our individual presence, as having promised, be required, reason requires that he be preferred with whom the league is oldest: so the answer of the consul to the Campanians.

4 But an exception is to be added, if the later league contain, besides a promise, anything which contains a transfer of ownership, or a subjection to the other party. For thus in selling also, we say that the prior sale is valid, except the later sale transfer the ownership. So in Livy the Nepesini held their surrender more binding than their alliance. Others make more subtle distinctions, but I believe this, as most simple, to be also most true.

XIV.   When the time is ended, the treaty ought not to be tacitly supposed renewed, except by acts which receive no other interpretation : for a new obligation is not lightly presumed.

XV.   If one party violate the league, the other may withdraw from the agreement : for every article of the agreement has the force of a condition. Take two examples from Thucydides. [See.] But this is only true if it be not otherwise agreed, as is sometimes done; that a withdrawal from the league is not to be justified by every slight offense taken.

XVI.   1 Sponsions, that is, conventions made on personal responsibility (see c. III.) may be as various in their subject-matter as public treaties. They differ in the power of those who make them. But there are two common questions concerning such conventions: First, if the convention be rejected by the king or the state, to what are the responsible parties bound? To give an equivalent; or to restore things into the state in which they were before the convention; or to give up their persons? The first course appears to be conformable to the Roman Civil Law; the second, to equity, as was urged by the Tribunes in the Caudine controversy; the third, to usage, as the conspicuous examples of the Caudine and the Numantian conventions shew*.

But the important point is, that the supreme authority is not bound to any one course. As Posthumius says: *You* (the people) *have made no convention with the enemy; you have not authorized any citizen to make a convention for you: you have nothing to do with us, to whom you gave no commission, nor with the Samnites, with whom you have had no transaction.* He adds well: *I deny that without the permission of the people, any engagement can be made which binds the people:* and, also well: *If the people can be bound to anything* [by the acts of others] *it may be bound to all things.*

2 Therefore the People was not bound either to compensation or to restitution. If the Samnites wished to deal with the People, they ought to have kept the army at the Caudine Forks, and to have sent ambassadors to Rome, to treat with the Senate and People concerning peace, leaving them to estimate the safety of the army at what value they might. And then they might have said, what Velleius reports that they and the Numantines said, that the violation of public faith ought not to be deemed expiated by the blood of an individual.

3 With greater speciousness it might be said, that all the soldiers were bound by the treaty. And that would have been equitable, if the treaty had been negociated in their name, and under their direction, by the acting parties, as was done in the treaty of Hannibal with the Macedonians. But if the Samnites were content with the engagement of the persons negociating, and of the 600 hostages whom they demanded, they had themselves to blame. On the other hand, if the negociators pretended that they had the power of making a convention in the name of the public, they were bound to restitution, as having done damage by fraud. If that does not appear, they were bound to a reasonable compensation to the Samnites, according to the purport of the negociations. And in this case, not only the bodies, but also the goods of the negociators, were bound to the Samnites, except they had paid such a compensation as we have spoken of. For, with regard to the hostages, it was agreed that if the engagement did not stand, their lives were to be forfeited. Whether the same penalty was agreed upon for the negociators, does not appear. But the stipulation of a penalty affects what is done, in this way: that if the thing to be done cannot be performed, there is nothing else in the obligation [but the penalty]: for the penalty is introduced as something certain into the place of an uncertain compensation. And at that time the common opinion was, that a man's life might be seriously given as a pledge.

4 But with us who think differently, I am of opinion that by such

* Flor. i. 16, and ii. 18. *Gronov.*

a convention, first, the party's goods are liable for compensation of the interest affected, and if they are not sufficient, that his body is forfeited to slavery.   When Fabius Maximus had made an agreement with the enemy, which the Senate repudiated, he sold his landed property for 200,000 sesterces, and made good the loss.   And the Samnites rightly conceived that Brutulus Papius, who broke a truce, should be given up along with his property.

XVII.   1 Another question is, whether a convention made by a subordinate person, on his own responsibility, binds the supreme power, by knowledge and silence on their part.   Here we must first distinguish whether the convention is made simply, or under condition of being ratified by the supreme power.   For if so, this condition, not fulfilled, (for conditions must be expressly fulfilled,) nullifies the convention; which applies to the convention of Lutatius with the Carthaginians; to which was to be added, that the people, because that convention was made without its authority, denied that it was bound thereby: and therefore another treaty was made on a fresh footing by the public authority.

2   We must next see whether, besides silence, any other circumstance has been added.   For silence, without some thing or act, does not supply a sufficiently probable conjecture of the will; as may be understood by what we have said above, of the dereliction of ownership.   But if any act have been added which cannot be probably referred to another cause, then the act of convention is rightly understood to be accepted as valid.   And so the convention with the Gaditani was proved valid, as Cicero notes.

3   The Romans urged silence against the Carthaginians in reference to the convention made with Asdrubal.   But since that convention was conceived in negative expressions—that the Carthaginians should not pass the Ebro—it was scarcely a case in which silence alone could establish a ratification of the act of another: since no act of theirs had followed, except it might be that some Carthaginians, wishing to pass the Ebro, had been prevented by the Romans, and the Carthaginians had acquiesced: for such an act has the force of a positive act, and is not merely negative.   But if the pact of Lutatius had had more parts, and it appeared that the other parts, though dissenting from common rule, had been observed by the Romans, then there would be a sufficient proof of the confirmation of the convention.

4   It remains for us to treat of the conventions which generals and commanders of armies make, not concerning political matters, but their own proceedings and business: but we shall have a better opportunity of discussing this in treating of the rules of War.

CHAPTER XVI.

Of Interpretation.

I. 1 IF we merely consider him who has promised, he is bound to perform, without compulsion, that to which he was willing to be bound. *In good faith, what you thought, not what you said, is to be considered,* says Cicero. But because internal acts of themselves are not an object of sense, and some certain rule must be established, in order that obligations may not be frustrated, as they might be, if any one, by pretending any sense of his words which he chose to assign, could free himself; natural reason dictates that what is promised to any one, compels the promiser to that which a right interpretation suggests; for otherwise the matter would have no determinate result; which in moral matters is held to be impossible. Perhaps it was in this sense that Isocrates, treating of pacts, spoke of *the common rule which all observe.* So Livy: *sine dolo malo intellecta.*

2 The measure of right interpretation, is the purpose, as inferred from the most probable signs. These signs are of two kinds, words, and other conjectures; which are considered either separately or conjointly.

II. If there is no conjecture which points another away, the words are to be understood, not according to grammatical and etymological, but popular propriety, as regulated by usage. That was a foolish evasion therefore of the Locrians, who, when they had sworn that they would keep their compact as long as they stood upon the earth and carried heads on their shoulders, put earth in their shoes, and heads of garlick on their shoulders, and then threw them away; as if they could in that way free themselves from their oath: as the story is in Polybius. There are some examples of similar bad faith in Polyænus, which it is not necessary to transcribe, because there is no controversy in such cases. Cicero rightly says, that such artifices do not extenuate, but establish perfidy.

III.   In Terms of Art, however, which are popularly hardly intelligible, the definition of the meaning by persons learned in the Art is to be taken: as, what is Treason, what is Parricide; in which writers on Oratory refer to definitions. As Cicero says, *The words of the Dialecticians are not those of common language, but of their own art, and the same is the case in every art.* Thus if in pacts mention be made of an Army, we shall define an Army to be a body of soldiers which openly invades an enemy's territory; for historians perpetually put in opposition what is done stealthily in the manner of robbers, and that which is done with a regular army. And therefore what numbers make an army, must be judged according to the force of the enemy. Cicero calls six legions with auxiliaries an army. Polybius says, the Roman army consisted commonly of 16,000 Romans and 20,000 allies: but a smaller number may satisfy the name. For Ulpian says, that he commands an army who commands a single legion with the auxiliaries; that is, as Vegetius explains, 10,000 foot and 2000 horse. And Livy makes the force of a regular army 8000 men. In the same way we must judge of a Fleet. So a Fort is a place strong enough to be held against the enemy for a time.

IV.   1 It is necessary to have recourse to conjectures, when the words or the connexion of the words is ambiguous, admitting of numerous significations, which the Rhetoricians call an *Amphiboly**. The Dialecticians, more subtly, distinguish *Homonymy*, in which these several senses are in one word, from *Amphiboly*, in which they are in a connexion of words. The like conjectures are necessary when there is in pacts an *Enantiophany*, an appearance of contradiction. For the conjectures are to be sought which may reconcile one part with another, if it may be done. For if the contradiction be real, the latter agreement of the contracting parties must supersede the former: because nobody can will two opposite things at the same time: and the nature of acts which depends on the will is, that by a new act of the will they may be changed, either in one part only, as in a law, and a testament, or in several parts at the same time, as in contracts and pacts. Here they speak of *Antinomies**. In these cases, then, the evident obscurity of the word compels us to recur to conjectures.

2 Sometimes the conjectures are so evident, that they spontaneously suggest themselves, even contrary to the more received

* Ad Herenn. i. 11, and 12; Quintil. vii. 7 and 9.

O

signification of words. This is the received distinction of What is said, and what is meant. The topics, from which conjectures of the meaning are collected, are principally, the Matter, the Effect, and the conjoined Circumstances.

V. From the Matter; as if a truce of 30 days is made, the word *Day* is to be understood, not of natural days but of civil days; for that agrees with the matter: so the word *donare*, for giving up one's rights conditionally: so the word *arms*, which sometimes means the instruments of war, sometimes armed soldiers, must, according to the matter, be interpreted one way or the other: so he who promises to give up men, must give them up alive, not dead, as the Platæans quibbled. So when persons are to lay down their steel, this is to be satisfied by laying down their swords, not their steel buckles, as Pericles ingeniously suggested; and when men are to be allowed to depart from a city, they are to do so freely and in safety, contrary to Alexander's proceeding: so to give up the half of the ships, is half the number of whole ships, not each ship cut in halves: as the Romans did to Antiochus. And the like cases must be judged in the same manner.

VI. From the Effect; in which the main case is, when a word taken from ordinary use draws with it an absurd effect. For if the word be ambiguous, the interpretation is rather to be taken which involves no absurdity. Hence the quibble of Brasidas was not to be admitted, who, having promised that he would depart from the Bœotian territory, denied that that was Bœotian territory which he occupied with his army; as if the term were to be understood of warlike possessions, not of the ancient boundaries; in which sense the compact was unmeaning.

VII. Things are conjoined in their origin, or in place. Those are conjoined in their origin which proceed from the same will, although uttered at a different place and time; whence a conjecture is drawn, because in doubtful cases the will is supposed to be in agreement with itself. Thus in Homer, the agreement between Paris and Menelaus, that Helena should be given to the victor, must, from what follows, be so expounded, that he is victor who kills the other. Plutarch gives the reason, that judges take the view which is least ambiguous.

VIII. Of things conjoined in place, that which has the greatest force, is the reason of the law, which many confound with the intention, though in fact it is one of the indications by which we trace the intention. But among conjectures, this is the strongest, if it appear certainly that the will was moved by any reason as a sole cause; for there are often several reasons; and sometimes the will determines itself by its liberty and without regard to reason, which suffices for producing an obligation. Thus a donation made in contemplation of a marriage has no power if the marriage does not follow.

IX. But it is to be remarked, that many words have several significations, one, stricter, one, laxer; which happens for many causes: either because the name of the genus is appropriated to one species, as in the word *cognation*, which, meaning any relationship, is used for one kind; and *adoption*, which meaning any assumption of a child, is used for one with certain formalities: and so in masculine words which are used as common to both genders, when common words are wanting; or because the usage of art is more wide than popular usage; as death, in Civil Law, includes civil death, transportation for life, though it does not mean this in popular language.

X. It is also to be observed, that of the things which are promised, some are promises of favour, others of *odium*, others mixed, others medium. Those are of favour, which are equal to both parties, and regard the common utility. In proportion as this is greater and more extensive, the greater is the favour included in the promise; as greater, thus, in things which make for peace than for war; and greater for defensive than for other war. Those are promises of odium which lay a burthen on one party only, or on one more than another, and which impose penalties, and nullify acts, and change former promises. If any thing be mixed, as for instance, what changes former agreements, but for the sake of peace, that must be held favourable or odious as the one or the other may predominate, leaning to favourable, *cœteris paribus*.

XI. The distinction of acts *bonæ fidei* and *stricti juris*, so far as it flows from the Roman Law, does not pertain to the *Jus Gentium*. Yet in a certain sense it may be adapted here: so far as this for instance, that if in any place certain acts have a certain common form, that, so far as it is not changed, is understood to be inherent in the act: in other acts, more indefinite in kind, such as donative, and promise made of mere liberality, we must stand more by the words.

XII. 1 This being understood, the following rules are to be observed: In *non-odious* promises, the words are to be taken according to the general propriety of popular usage, and if such usage is manifold, according to that which is widest; as that the masculine gender goes for the common gender, and an indefinite for an universal locution. So the words [in the form of the Interdict for recovering possession] *Unde quis dejectus est*, will apply to restore him who was not ejected, but forbidden to return to his property, as Cicero rightly argued.

2 In *favourable* promises, if he who speaks understands the law, or if he have had the advice of persons skilled in the law, the words are to be taken more laxly, so that they may include a technical or a legal signification. But we must not recur to significations plainly improper, except otherwise some absurdity or the inutility of the pact would follow. On the other hand, words are to be taken more strictly even than propriety requires, if that be necessary to avoid injustice or absurdity; but if the necessity be not such, but a manifest justice

and utility in the restriction, we must confine ourselves within the narrowest boundaries of propriety, except circumstances counsel another course.

3 In *odious* promises, figurative language is in some small measure admitted, to avoid the odium. Therefore in a donation and grant of any right, words, however general, are usually restricted to that which was probably thought of. And in this class, that is sometimes spoken of as occupied, which there is hope of retaining. Thus auxiliaries promised on one side only, are understood to be at the expense of him who asks for them.

XIII. 1 It is a noted question, whether under the title of Allies, those are included only who were so at the time of the league being made, or those who became so afterwards; as in the league between the Romans and Carthaginians after the war about Sicily: *The allies of each People shall be unharmed by each People.* Hence the Romans inferred, that though the league struck with Asdrubal, that he should not pass the Ebro, was not available to them, because the Carthaginians had not ratified it; yet that if the Carthaginians gave their sanction to the act of Annibal who besieged the Saguntines, who had become allies of the Romans after the treaty, war might be declared against them as having violated the treaty. Livy gives the reasons, which are taken almost word for word from Polybius.

How shall we pronounce on this point? That the word *allies* may mean, in a reasonable usage, both those who were so at the time of making the treaty, and a larger signification including future allies, is indubitable. Which interpretation is to be preferred, we must consider, on the preceding principles: and according to them, we say that it does not comprehend future allies, because it treats of breaking the league, which is a matter of odium, and of taking away the liberty of the Carthaginians, to punish with arms those who had wronged them; which is a natural liberty, not likely to be supposed abdicated.

2 Was it then not lawful for the Romans to take the Saguntines into alliance, or when allied, to defend them? Certainly this was lawful, not in virtue of the league, but in virtue of Natural Law, which they had not abdicated by the treaty: so that the Saguntines should be in the same situation as if no convention had been made about allies: in which case the Carthaginians would not be acting against the league, if they made what they conceived to be a just war against the Saguntines; nor the Romans, if they defended them: just as at the time of Pyrrhus, an agreement was made between the Carthaginians and Romans, that if either of those Peoples made a league with Pyrrhus, it should be lawful for the other to do so likewise. I do not say the war could have been just on both sides; but I deny that this point had to do with the violation of the league: as in the question concerning the Mamertines, Polybius distinguishes the points, whether it was just, and whether it was consistent with the league.

3 And this is exactly what the Corcyreans in Thucydides say to the Athenians, that it is lawful for them to send aid to them, and that it is not an objection, that the Athenians had a league with the Lacedæmonians, since by that league it was lawful to acquire new allies. And this opinion the Athenians themselves afterwards followed; for they gave command to their officers that they should not fight against the Corinthians, except they attacked Corcyra, or invaded its soil, in order not to break the league. For it is not at variance with a league, that they who are attacked by one party should be defended by the other, peace remaining as to other matters. Justin says, of these events, that *The treaty which they had made in their own name, they broke in the person of their allies, &c.* So in the Oration on Halonesus, it appears that, by the peace between the Athenians and Philip, it was provided that the cities of Greece, not comprehended in that treaty, should be free; and if any one attacked them, those comprehended in the peace might defend them. And this is an example in an equal league.

XIV. In an unequal league we shall suppose other terms: that it is agreed that neither of the allies shall make war without permission of the other: which were the terms of the league of the Romans and Carthaginians, after the second Punic war, as mentioned above: as also in the league of the Macedonians and Romans before the reign of Perseus. Since "making war" may include all kinds of war, both offensive and defensive, we must suppose this to be taken in the narrower sense, and to mean offensive war, that the liberty of the parties be not too much restricted.

XV. Of the same nature is that promise of the Romans, that Carthage should be free: which, although, from the nature of the act, it could not be understood of full sovereign power, (for they had already lost the right of making war and other rights,) yet it left some liberty to them, and at least so much, that they should not be compelled to remove the seat of their government by extraneous command. It was in vain, then, that the Romans laid stress on the word *Carthage* [shall be free,] as if it meant the population, not the city; (which, though an improper expression, might be conceded, the attribute *free* belonging to the population rather than the city). For in the word, *free*, αὐτόνομον, as Appian says, there was a mere quibble.

XVI. 1 To this is to be referred that frequent question concerning personal and real pacts. If the transaction be with a free people, it is not doubtful that what is promised is by its nature real, because the subject (the People) is a permanent thing. And even if the state be converted into a kingdom, the league will remain, because the body remains, though the head is changed; and, as we have said, authority exercised by the king does not cease to be the authority of the people. Exception is to be made, if it appears that the cause of the treaty was peculiar to the republican state, as if free cities make a league in defense of their liberty.

2 Even if the compact be made with the king, it is not necessarily personal: for as Pedius and Ulpian say, commonly the person is inserted in the compact, not that it may be a personal compact, but that it may appear on the face of it with whom it was made. And if it be added to the treaty, that it is to be perpetual, that it is made for the good of the kingdom, or with him and his successors, as is commonly added in treaties, or for a definite time, it is plainly real. Such appears to have been the treaty of the Romans with king Philip, which, when Perseus his son refused to acknowledge as pertaining to him, war arose on that ground. But other words also, and the matter itself, sometimes supply probable conjecture on this subject.

3 If there be equal conjectures each way (for a real and a personal pact), the result must be that favourable pacts are to be believed real, odious ones, personal. Treaties of peace or commerce are favourable: those made with a view to war, not all odious, as some think, since *epimachies*, engagements of support in defensive war, are nearer to favour; *symmachies*, engagements to war in general, nearer to burthens. Add to which, that in a treaty looking to any war, it is presumed that account is had of the prudence and piety of the person treated with, as one who will not undertake a war unjustly, nor even rashly.

4 The maxim, that partnerships are separated by death, I do not here adduce: for that belongs to private partnerships, and is a maxim of Civil Law. Whether the Fidenates, Latins, Etruscans, Sabines, were right or wrong in renouncing their league with the Romans when Romulus, Tullus, Ancus, Priscus and Servius were dead, we cannot judge, not having the words of the treaties extant. Not unlike this is the controversy in Justin, whether the cities which had been tributaries of the Medes, when the empire was changed, had changed their condition. For the argument of Bodinus is by no means to be accepted, that treaties do not pass to the successors of kings, because the force of an oath does not go beyond the person. For the obligation of the oath may bind the person only, while the obligation of the promise may bind the heir.

5 Nor is it true, as he assumes, that treaties depend entirely upon oaths; for the promise of itself gives force to the treaty, and the oath is added only for the sake of religious reverence. So when the Roman people had sworn that they would make a treaty under direction of the Consul, and Valerius the Consul died, some of the Tribunes held that the people was not bound: but Livy judges otherwise: *As yet*, he says, *men had not become, as now, careless of oaths.*

XVII. If a treaty be made with a king, and he or his successor be expelled by his subjects, the treaty remains valid: for the right of the kingdom remains with him, though he have lost possession. So Lucan, speaking of the Roman Senate in exile.

XVIII. On the other hand, if an Usurper of the kingdom be

attacked by its ally with the consent of the true king; or if the oppressor of a free people be so attacked, before the sufficient consent of the people can be obtained; nothing is done against the treaty: for such persons have possession, but not right. As Quintius said to Nabis, *We made no alliance with you, but with Pelops, the just and legitimate king of the Lacedæmonians.* And these qualities, (just and legitimate,) in treaties, refer to the right of the king and his successors: the cause of Usurpers is an *odious* cause.

XIX. Chrysippus had treated this question, Whether a prize proposed to him who reaches the goal first should, if both arrive there at the same time, be given to both or to neither. And in fact, the word *first* is ambiguous: it means either him who gets before all others, or whom none gets before. But because the prizes of excellence are matters of favour; the sounder opinion is, that the two should share the prize: though Scipio, Cæsar, Julian, more liberally gave a full prize to both of those who had mounted the walls at the same time.

And so much of the interpretation which is adapted to the proper or improper signification of words.

XX. 1 There is also another kind of interpretation, from Conjectures extraneous to the signification of the words in which the promise is made: and this interpretation is twofold, either extending or restricting the meaning. But the interpretation which extends, proceeds more difficultly, that which restricts, more easily. For as in all things, in order that the effect may not follow, it is enough if one of the causes be wanting; and in order that it may take place, it is necessary that all conspire; so in obligation also, a conjecture extending the obligation is not lightly to be admitted; and in this case it is much more difficult than in the case which we spoke of before, to assign to words some large but unusual signification. For here, besides the words of promise, we have to look for some conjecture, which ought to be very certain, which may induce an obligation; nor does analogy suffice, we must have identity of reason: nor is it always enough that we can say the words are to be extended for existing reasons: for, as we have said, reason often so operates, that nevertheless, the will may be a sufficient cause, without any reason.

2 Therefore, in order that such an extension may be rightly made, it is necessary that it should be apparent that the reason under which the case comes which we wish to comprehend, should be the sole and efficacious cause which moves the promiser; and that that reason was considered by him in its generality; because otherwise the promise would have been unjust or useless. This is also treated by Rhetoricians in their sections on *What is said and what is meant;* of which one kind which they mention is, when we always utter the same sentence. But also another section, *On reasoning,* belongs to the subject: namely, when from what is written we deduce what is not written, as Quintilian says: and also what is delivered by the Jurists as to what is done fraudulently.

3 Take an example in an agreement made that no place shall be walled round, made at a time when there was no other way of fortification. That place cannot even have an earth-work made round it, if it appear that the only cause for prohibiting walls was that the place might not be fortified. An example is often taken in the conditions introduced in the will of a testator in case his posthumous child die, the testament being made by one who fully expected a posthumous child; and the rule is used to extend the dispositions of the testament to the case in which the posthumous child is not born: because it is evident that the will of the testator was moved by the consideration of a progeny which never came into existence: which example we find not only in the Jurists, but also in Cicero and Valerius Maximus.

4 See Cicero in the oration *pro Cœcina*. And hence the form of interdict, *Unde tu me vi dejeceris hominibus coactis armatisve*, will hold against all force endangering life, though there may not be a body of armed men. As Cicero says, the legal effect is the same. So Quintilian says, *Murder* seems to imply steel weapons and blood; but if any one is killed in any other way, we still recur to that law: for instance, if the man be thrown from a precipice. So Isæus, because by the Attic Law a testament could not be made [by a father having no son] against the will of a daughter, infers that an adoption could not be made without her consent.

XXI. And on these principles is to be solved that celebrated question which we have in Gellius, about a commission; whether it may be fulfilled, not by the identical thing directed, but by another equally useful or more useful than that which was enjoined by him who gave the commission. For it is lawful to do so, if it be clear that what was prescribed was not prescribed under its special form, but under a more general purpose, which might also be obtained in some other way: thus, he who was ordered to give security for a loan to be made to a third person, might, instead, give an order to the lender to make the payment to the third person; as Scævola held. [*Dig.* XVII. 1.] But when that is not clear, we must hold, as Crassus says, in Gellius in that place, that the demand of the superior is disregarded, if any one, in place of discharging his commission as directed, respond by advice which was never asked for.

XXII. An interpretation restricting a promise, extraneously to the signification of the words which contain the promise, is derived either from original limitation of the will [of the promiser], or from the repugnance with such will which comes to view in some occurring case. A limitation of the original will is understood—from the absurdity which would evidently follow, if it were not so limited;—from the cessation of the reason which alone fully and efficaciously moved the will;—and from the defect of the matter.

The first restriction has its ground in the consideration, that no one is supposed to intend what is absurd.

XXIII. The second in this, that what is contained in the promise, when such a reason is added, or the reason is certain, is not considered nakedly, but so far as it comes under that reason.

XXIV. The third in this, that the matter which is dealt with is always supposed to be present to the mind of the speaker (the promiser), although the words have a wider signification. This way of interpretation also is treated by writers on Rhetoric in the Section, *Of what is said and what is meant;* and has for its Title, *When the same words are used, but not in the same sense.*

XXV. 1 But with regard to the reasons [of promisers, as here applied], it is to be noted that there are comprehended therein many things, not as to whether they exist, but as to their power morally considered; and when this holds, the restriction is not to be introduced. Thus if it be stipulated that an army or a fleet is not to be moved into a certain place, it must not be moved thither, though it be done with no purpose of attack. For in the compact, it was not a certain damage, but a danger of any kind which was considered.

2 This also is often disputed, whether promises have in themselves this tacit condition, If things remain in their present state. And this is to be denied, except it be quite clear that the present state of things was included in that sole reason of which we have spoken. Thus we constantly read in history of ambassadors who gave up their commission and returned home, because they understood that the state of things was changed, so that the whole matter or cause of the embassy ceased.

XXVI. 1 The repugnance of an occurring case with the will [of the promiser] is commonly, in writers on oratory, referred to the Section of which I have spoken, *Of what is said and what is meant.* It is twofold: for the will is either collected from natural reasons, or from some other sign of the will. Aristotle, who has most correctly treated this part, ascribes to the intellect a peculiar power for judging of the will, which he calls γνώμη, or εὐγνωμοσύνη, that is *equitable insight;* and to the will he ascribes a corresponding power, ἐπιείκεια, *equity,* which he ably defines, The correction of the law, when it is defective from the universality of its expression[*]. And this equity is also to be applied to testaments and compacts in an appropriate manner. For since all cases can neither be foreseen nor expressed, there is a necessity for some liberty for excepting cases which he who has spoken would except if he were present. But this is not to be done rashly; (for that would be for the interpreter to determine the acts of another); but on sufficient indications.

2 The most certain indication is, if in any case to follow the words would be unlawful, that is, at variance with the precepts of Natural or Divine Law. For such cases, since they cannot impose an obligation, must necessarily be excepted. *Some things,* says Quintilian the father, *though they are not comprehended in any terms of the law, are by their nature excepted.* Thus he who has received a sword

[*] See *E. M.* 401.

as a deposit, promising to give it up on demand, is not to give it up to a madman, in order that he may not create danger to himself or to other innocent persons. Tryphoninus says, *I agree that it is justice to give to each his own, but in such a way that it may not be again demanded on a better claim by some other person.* The reason is, because, as we have elsewhere noted, the force of ownership once introduced, is such that not to restore a thing to the owner, when known, is altogether unjust.

XXVII. 1 A second indication of a reason for deviating from the words of the promiser, in our interpretation, is, if to follow the words will be, not indeed quite unlawful, but to a person fairly estimating the matter, grievous and intolerable : either looking absolutely at the condition of human nature, or comparing the person and thing in question with the end of the act. Thus he who has lent a thing for a few days, may demand it back again within that time, if he himself have great need of it : because this [lending] is an act so beneficial in its nature, that it is not to be supposed that any one would thereby bind himself to his own great inconvenience. Thus he who has promised assistance to a federate ally, will be excused as long as he is in danger at home, so far as he has occasion for his powers. And a concession of immunity from tax and tribute must be understood with reference to daily and yearly taxes, not to those which some extreme necessity requires, and which the State cannot do without.

2 Whence it appears that Cicero spoke too laxly, when he said that your promises are not to be kept which are useless to those to whom they are made ; nor if they harm you more than they advantage them. For whether the thing will be useful to him to whom it is promised, the promiser is not the judge, except perhaps when the promisee is mad, of which case we have spoken above : and in order that a promise may not oblige the promiser, it does not suffice that it brings some harm to the promiser ; but it must be such harm as according to the nature of the act must be supposed to be excepted in the promiser. Thus he who has promised his neighbour so many days' labour, is not bound if a critical and dangerous disease of his father or his son keeps him away. So Cicero in his *Offices.* (I. 10.)

3 What Seneca says is to be taken in the same sense, and not to be pushed further : *I must keep my promise if all things are the same : but if anything be changed, I am at liberty to revise my decision. Thus I promised to advocate a cause ; but it appears that the cause is intended to injure my father : I promised to accompany one on a journey ; but it appears that the road is infested with robbers : I was to come at a certain time ; but my son is ill, my wife is in childbirth. All must be the same as it was when I promised, to oblige me to keep my word.* Understand, *all things* according to the nature of the act in question, as we have just explained.

XXVIII. We have said that there may also be other signs of the will, which shew that the case is to be excepted. Among these signs, nothing is more decisive than words used in another place; not when they directly oppose the promise, which is *antinomy*, as mentioned above; but when unexpectedly and by the very event of things they are in conflict, which the rhetoricians call *circumstantial contradiction*.

XXIX. 1 In the discussion, Which part of a document ought to prevail in case of such a collision, Cicero has given certain rules from ancient authors; and these, though not, in my ·judgment, to be rejected, seem to me not to be placed in due order. We shall arrange them in this way:

Permission gives way to command, or, as the writer to Herennius says, command outweighs permission *:

What is to be done at a certain time, is to be preferred to what may be done at any time: and hence a prohibitive pact outweighs an imperative one: except either the time be expressed, or the command contains a tacit prohibition:

Between those pacts which are equal in the above qualities, that is to be preferred which is more peculiar, and comes nearer to the thing: for special expressions are commonly more efficacious than general:

In prohibitions, that which has a penalty added is to be preferred to that which has not, and that with the greater penalty, to that with the less:

That is to be preferred which rests upon causes more honourable or more useful:

Lastly, that which was last said has most weight†.

2 We must repeat that some pacts are to be understood according to the most received propriety of language, repudiating all tacit and unnecessary restrictions. Whence if a sworn pact be at variance with an unsworn one in a certain event, that is to be preferred which has the sanction of an oath.

XXX. It is also made a question, Whether in a doubtful case a contract is to be held perfect before it is committed to writing and delivered. So Murena argued against the convention of Mithridates and Sylla. It appears plain to me that, except it be agreed otherwise, it must be supposed that writing is adopted as a monument of the contract, not as a part of it. If this is not so, it is expressed, as, *From the day when the conditions are written and delivered.*

XXXI. I do not admit, what many writers have held, that the contracts of kings and peoples are to be interpreted according to Roman Law; except when the Roman Law has been accepted as belonging to the Law of Nations; which is not lightly to be presumed.

XXXII. As to the question which Plutarch discusses in his *Sympo-*

---

* Barbeyrac says, not always: a universal command gives way to a particular permission.

† Barbeyrac observes that this last rule is out of place here.

sium, Whether the condition of the offerer or the words of the acceptor
are more to be attended to; it appears that, since the acceptor is the promiser, his words must give force to the business, if they are absolute and
perfect.   If by affirmation (as by saying *yes*) they respect the words
of the offerer, then, from the nature of relative words, these are to be
understood as repeated.   But before the condition is accepted, the
offerer is not bound; till then, the other part acquires no right, even
in a promise; and an offer is less than a promise.

CHAPTER XVII.

Of Damage done wrongfully and consequent Obligation.

I. WE have said above that there are three sources of debts due to us; Pact, Wrong, Law. Of pacts we have sufficiently treated: we come to what by Natural Law is due on account of Wrong. We have given the name of *wrong* to every fault, either of doing or of omission, which is at variance with what men ought to do, either on the ground of their common connexion, or of some special quality. From such fault arises by Natural Law an obligation, if the wrong be accompanied with damage: namely, the obligation of repairing the wrong.

II. 1 Damage, *damnum* (perhaps from *demo*,) is when a man has less than what is *his*, whether it be *his* by mere nature, or by some human act in addition, as ownership, pact, law. Things which a man may regard as *his* by nature are life, not indeed to throw away, but to keep, his body, limbs, fame, honour, his own acts. What is his by ownership and pact, and how, we have shewn above, both as to things, and as to right over others' acts. In like manner the law determines for each what is his, for the law can do more for a man than he can do for himself. Thus a ward has a right to a certain care and diligence from his guardian; the State, from a magistrate; and not only the State, but each citizen, as often as the law expressly, or by clear implication, marks such a consequence.

2 But a mere Moral Claim, which is not properly a Right, and belongs to distributive or assignatory justice, does not produce true ownership, and the consequent obligation of restitution: for that is

not any one's to which he has merely a moral claim. *A man does not wrong any one when he refuses to give from illiberality*, says Aristotle. So Cicero.

III. But here we must take care not to confound things of diverse kinds: for he who has to appoint a magistrate is bound to the republic to elect one who is worthy; and the republic has a right to demand this: and therefore, if by an unworthy election he has produced damage to the republic, he is bound to make it good. So any citizen, not unworthy, although he has not a right to any office, yet has a right to be a candidate along with others; and if he is disturbed in this right by fraud or violence, he may demand, not the whole value of that which he sought, but the estimated value of his loss. So in the case of him to whom a testator was by force or fraud prevented from leaving a legacy; for the capacity to receive a legacy is a certain right, which has for its consequence this, that to impede the liberty of the testator as to that right, is a wrong.

IV. A person may have less than his own, and so, have suffered loss, not only in the thing which belongs to him, but in the produce of the thing, whether he has collected such produce, or only would have collected it: and his loss consists in that produce, *minus* the expense of improving the thing, and of collecting the produce.

V. Also the hope of gain from a thing which is ours may be estimated, not as what it is simply, but according to its prospect; as the hope of the harvest in the sower.

VI. Besides him who immediately causes the loss, others may be bound, either by doing or not doing.

By doing, some primarily, others secondarily: Primarily, he who commands it, who gives the requisite consent, who helps, who receives what is taken, or who participates in the crime in any other way.

VII. Secondarily, who advises, praises, approves. See Cicero.

VIII. Also by not doing, primarily and secondarily. Primarily, when one who by his proper right ought to forbid the act, or help the person wronged, does not.

IX. Secondarily, he who does not dissuade when he ought, or keeps silence about a fact which he ought to make known. And this *ought*, in all these cases, we refer to proper rights and expletory justice, whether arising from law or quality. For if he ought by the law of charity only, he sins indeed in not doing it, but is not held to reparation; for this has its origin in a proper right, as we have said.

X. It is to be noted also, that all those of whom we have spoken are bound if they were really the cause of the damage, that is, if their influence shared in producing either the whole loss or a part of it. For it often happens in agents or *negligents* of the secondary order, and sometimes in those who are of the first order, that even without their act or neglect, the person who committed the damage was certain to commit it: in which case they will not be liable. Which answer is not so to be understood as, that if others would not have been wanting to persuade or assist, those who did persuade or assist are not liable; if without suasion or assistance the author of the damage would not have done it. For those others who should have persuaded or assisted would have been liable.

XI. Those are liable in the first place, who, by command, or in any manner, impel any one to the act: failing these, the perpetrator of the deed; after him, the rest in any way concerned; and those jointly who gave cause to the act, if the whole act proceeded from them, though not from them alone.

XII. They who are liable for the act, are also liable for the natural consequences of the act. Seneca puts a case of a man setting fire to a plane-tree, by which a house was burnt, and holds him liable. [See.] Ariarathes, having wantonly stopped the course of the river Melanus, caused a flood of the Euphrates, which produced great damage in Galatia and Phrygia: and the matter being referred to the Romans, paid 300 talents to make good the loss.

XIII. Take these examples: A person who unlawfully kills another is bound to pay the expenses of physicians, if any, and of those who depended for subsistence on the person killed, his parents, wives, children, as much as their hope of support was worth, considering the age of the person killed. So Hercules paid a fine for the death of Iphitus. So Michael Ephesius on Aristotle. We say *unlawfully* kills; for if a person was acting lawfully, as if he was assailed and did not run away, though he may have sinned against charity, he is not liable. The life of a free man cannot be valued: it is different in a slave, who may be sold.

XIV. If a person maims another, he is similarly liable to the expenses, and to the estimated value of how much less the maimed man can earn. But as the free man's life, so his wound, is not capable of estimation. The same is to be said of unjust imprisonment.

XV. The adulterer and adulteress are liable not only to indemnify the husband for the expenses of rearing the progeny, but also to repay the legitimate offspring what loss they suffer from the concourse of the offspring so arising in the inheritance.

He who deflowers a virgin by force or fraud is bound to pay her as much as she loses by the diminished hope of marriage; and even to marry her if it was by such a promise that he became master of her person.

XVI. The thief and the robber are bound to restore the thing subtracted, with its natural increase, and with the consequent loss, or consequent cessation of gain; and if the thing have perished, its estimated value, not the highest, nor the lowest, but the medium value. In this class are to be placed those who defraud the lawful taxes. Also those are liable who by false testimony have occasioned damage in an unjust sentence, or an unjust accusation.

XVII. Also he who has caused a contract or promise by fraud, trick, or violence, is liable to restore to his original condition him who has been thus dealt with: because he had a right not to be deceived, and not to be forced: the former, from the nature of a contract, the latter from natural liberty as well. To these are to be reckoned those who would not do, except for money given, what they were bound to do for their office.

XVIII. He who gave cause why he should suffer force, or be compelled by fear, has himself to blame for what happens: for an involuntary act arising from a voluntary one is held morally for a voluntary one.

XIX. As, by the consent of nations, a rule has been introduced, that all wars, conducted on both sides by authority of the sovereign power, are to be held just wars; so this also has been established, that the fear of such a war is held a justly imposed fear, so that what is obtained by such means cannot be demanded back. And here the distinction appears between an enemy and pirates or robbers*. For what these take, may be demanded back, except an oath have been introduced to prevent it; what those take, not so. Wherefore, what appears to Polybius to be a just cause for the Carthaginians beginning the second Punic war, that the Romans had before made war upon them when they were engaged with the mutiny of their mercenaries, and had wrung from them the island of Sardinia, and a money payment, has some shew of natural equity, but is at variance with the Law of Nations, as we shall elsewhere explain.

XX. 1 Kings and magistrates are liable for neglect, who do not apply the remedies which they can and ought, to restrain robbery and piracy: on which ground the Scyrians were in ancient times condemned by the Amphictyons. I recollect the question being proposed to me,—from the fact that the rulers of our country had given several persons letters of privateering and authority to make captures, and some of these persons had captured the property of friends, and, leaving their country, led a life of sea-rovers, not returning even when summoned home;—Whether the rulers were bound to restitution; either as having used the agency of bad men, or as not having demanded caution-money. I gave my opinion, that they were bound to nothing more than to punish and surrender the guilty persons, if they could be found; and, besides, to make the goods of the plunderers liable: for that they had not been the cause of the unlawful spoliation, nor had in any way shared in it; and had forbidden by law the plunder of friends: that there was no law obliging them to demand caution-money, since they might, if they chose, give all their subjects the right of capturing enemy's goods, which in former times had been done: and that such permission was not the cause why friends had been damaged, since private persons, even without such permission, could arm vessels and go to sea. And that whether those who went would turn out good or bad men, could not be foreseen; nor was it avoidable to use the

* And so the connexion between "private war" and public war disappears. W.

agency of bad men as well as good, since otherwise no army could be got together.

2 Nor, if either soldiers or sailors, contrary to command, do any damage to friends, are the kings liable; which has been proved by the testimony both of France and England: that any one, without any fault of his own, is bound by the acts of his agents, is not a part of the Law of Nations, by which this controversy must be decided, but a part of the Civil Law; nor of that in general, but introduced against sailors, and certain others, for peculiar reasons. And sentence was given to that effect by the Judges of the Supreme Court, against certain Pomeranians; and that, according to the precedent of a similar cause, adjudged two centuries ago.

XXI. It is to be noted also that the Rule, that if a slave, or any animal, cause any damage or loss, it creates a liability in the master, is also a creation of Civil Law. For the master, who is not in fault, is not liable by Natural Law; as also he is not whose ship, without any fault of his, damages another's ship: although by the laws of many nations, and by ours, the damage in such case is commonly divided, on account of the difficulty of proving where the fault lay.

XXII. Damages also, as we have said, may be inflicted on a man's honour or reputation; as with blows, insults, abusive language, calumny, ridicule, and the like. In which cases, no less than in theft, and other offenses, the badness or malice of the act must be distinguished from the damage. For the badness of the act is a ground for punishment, the loss, for reparation: which, in this case, is made by confession of the fault, manifestation of respect, testimony of the innocency of the calumniated person, and the like: though such damage may also be recompensed by money, if the injured person choose; because money is the common measure of valuable things.

P

CHAPTER XVIII.

Of the Right of Legation.

I. HITHERTO we have spoken of things which are due to us by Natural Law, adding only a few points which belong to the instituted Law of Nations, in so far as, by that, any thing was added to the Law of Nature. It remains to speak of the obligations which that which we call the Instituted Law of Nations has of itself introduced: in which class, the principal head is the Right of Legation. For we everywhere read of the reverence for Embassies; the sacredness of Ambassadors; the Rights of Nations lodged in them by Divine and Human Law; all which belong to those Instituted Laws; with other the like phrases. [See other phrases in the text. Papinius Statius; Cicero.] To violate this is not only unjust, but impious, by the confession of all; as Philip says.

II. 1 But, in the first place, this Law of Nations, whatever it be, applies to those Ambassadors only who are sent by Sovereign Powers to one another. For those who are sent as representatives of provinces, towns and others, are not governed by the Law of Nations, that is, by International Law, but by the Civil Law. An Ambassador, in Livy, calls himself the Public Messenger of the Roman People. And again, the Senate says that the Right of Legation belongs to a foreigner, not to a citizen. And Cicero, arguing that ambassadors should not be sent to Antony, says, *For we have not to deal with Hannibal, an enemy of the State, but with a citizen of the State.* Virgil explains clearly who are strangers (*Æn.* VII. 369).

2 Those states which are joined by an unequal league, when they do not cease to be their own masters, will have the Right of Legation: and also those who are only partly subject, for the part in which they are not subject. But kings who have been conquered in a formal war, and deprived of their kingdom, along with their other possessions, lose the right of legation. So P. Æmilius retained the negotiators who came from Perseus, whom he had conquered.

3 But in civil wars, necessity sometimes makes room for this right,

extra regulam : for instance, when the people is divided into nearly equal parties, so that it is doubtful with which party the right of the supreme authority is: or when two claimants for the succession contend with very balanced pretensions.   For in such an event, one nation is, for the time, two nations. Thus Tacitus accuses the Flavians, that the right of Legation, which is sacred even between strangers, they had savagely violated in the case of the Vitellians.   Pirates and robbers, who do not make a State, cannot claim the right of legation. Tiberius, when Tacfarinas sent ambassadors to him, was disturbed that a deserter and a robber gave himself the air of an open enemy, as Tacitus says.   But sometimes such persons obtain a right of legation by promise given them on good faith, as was the case with a band of fugitives in the Pyrenees.

III.   1 There are two points with regard to ambassadors which we everywhere find referred to the Law of Nations : that they be admitted, and that they be not violated.

Of the first point; Hanno inveighs against Hannibal, that, not admitting the ambassadors of the allies, he had violated the Law of Nations.   Which however is not to be understood so absolutely; for the Law of Nations does not prescribe that all ambassadors are to be admitted; but that they are not to be excluded without cause.

The cause may be, on the part of him who sends, of him who is sent, or in the fact that he is sent.

[Examples of the first case.]

2 Melesippus, the ambassador of the Lacedæmonians, was dismissed beyond the borders of the Attic territory, by the advice of Pericles, because he came from an armed enemy [within the territory].   So the Roman Senate declared that no embassy of the Carthaginians could be received while their army was in Italy.   The Achæans did not admit the ambassadors of Perseus, when he was organizing a war against the Romans.   So Justinian rejected the embassy of Totila, who had often broken his faith; and the Goths at Urbino sent back the ambassadors of Belisarius.   So Polybius relates that the ambassadors of the Cynethenses, as being those of a wicked race, were every where expelled.

Of the second case, we have an example in Theodorus, who was called the Atheist, and whom Lysimachus would not hear, when he was sent by Ptolemy; and the same happened to others on account of some peculiar odium.

The third case occurs when the cause of the mission is either suspected, as when Rabshakeh was sent to Hezekiah : or is not conformable to the dignity of the receiver, or to the time.   So the Romans forbad the Etolians to send any embassy, except by permission of the Emperor; commanded Perseus to send, not to Rome, but to Licinius; and ordered the ambassadors of Jugurtha to quit Italy within ten days, except they came to surrender the king and the kingdom.   The embassies which may be with the best right excluded, are those resident embassies which are now common, but which are not necessary; as we learn from ancient custom, to which they were unknown.

IV.   1 The question of the inviolability of ambassadors is more difficult, and variously treated by the able men of our time.   We must first consider the persons of the ambassadors, and then their suite and property.

With regard to the persons of ambassadors, some are of opinion that they are protected only from unjust violence: for that their privileges are to be interpreted by common Law.   Others think that force may be put upon an ambassador, not for any cause, but only if he violate the Law of Nations ; which is a very wide expression ; for in the Law of Nations, Natural Law is included: and so, according to this, an ambassador might be punished for any offense, except those which arise from mere Civil Law.   Others restrict this to what is done against the state or dignity of the commonwealth to which the ambassador is sent : and others think that even this is dangerous, and that complaints against the ambassador are to be transmitted to him who sent him, and that he is to be left to be judged by him.   Some, again, think that kings and nations who are not interested in the question, should be consulted ; which may be a matter of prudence, but cannot be a matter of right.

2 The reasons which each of these parties adduce do not conclude anything definitely ; because this Law of Nations is not like Natural Law, which flows in a sure way from certain reasons ; but this takes its measure from the will of nations.   For nations might either altogether refuse to entertain ambassadors, or with certain exceptions. For on the one side stands the utility of punishment against grave delinquents, [even if they be ambassadors,] and on the other, the utility of ambassadors, the sending of whom is facilitated by their having all possible security.   We must consider, therefore, how far nations have agreed ; and this cannot be proved by examples alone. For there are many each way.   We must recur therefore to the judgments of good authorities, and to conjectures, that is, probable arguments.

3 There are two judgments of great note, that of Livy, and that of Sallust.   Livy's is about Tarquin's ambassadors, who stirred up a treasonable design at Rome : *Though they had behaved so that they might have been treated as enemies, the Law of Nations prevailed :* here we see that the Law of Nations is extended even to those who act as enemies.   The dictum of Sallust pertains to the subordinate members of the legation, of whom we shall have hereafter to speak, not to the ambassador : but the argument proceeds rightly, from the greater, that is, the less credible, to the less, that is, the more credible.   He says thus : *Bomilcar, his companion, who had come to Rome on the public faith, is put under accusation, rather on the ground of equity, than of the Law of Nations.*   Equity, that is, mere Natural Law, allows penalties to be demanded when the delinquent can be got hold of ; but

the Law of Nations makes an exception in favour of ambassadors and those who come under the public faith. Hence to put ambassadors under accusation is contrary to the Law of Nations, which forbids many things which Natural Law permits.

4 Conjecture also is on this side. For it is the sounder opinion that privileges are so to be understood, that they give something beyond common rights. But if ambassadors were only protected from unjust violence, there would be in that nothing great, nothing distinguished. Add that the security of the ambassadors may preponderate over the utility which involves a penalty. For punishment may be had through his means who sent the ambassador; and if he will not afford it, may be demanded by war of him as the approver of the crime. Others object that it is better that one should be punished than many involved in war: but if he who sent the ambassador approve of what he did, his punishment will not save us from war.

On the other side, the safety of ambassadors is in a very insecure position, if they have to render account of their acts to other persons than him who sent them. For since the views of those who send the ambassador, and those who receive him, are generally diverse, often contrary, it is scarcely possible that something may not be said against the ambassador which may take the form of an accusation. And though some things of this kind are so manifest that they admit of no doubt, the universal danger suffices to establish the equity and utility of the universal rule.

5 Wherefore I quite think thus: that the common rule, that he who is in a foreign territory is subject to that territory, does, by the common consent of nations, suffer an exception in the case of ambassadors; they being, by a certain fiction, in the place of those who send them: [see Cicero:] and by a similar fiction they are, as it were, *extra territorium;* and thus, are not bound by the Civil Law of the People among whom they live. Hence, if there be any delict which can be treated lightly, either it is to be overlooked, or the ambassador ordered beyond the borders, as Polybius relates was done to him who, at Rome, had aided the escape of the hostages. On which occasion, in passing, we are given to understand that at another time, the ambassador of the Tarentines, who had committed the same offense, was scourged; but that was done, because the Tarentines had begun to be subject to the Romans. If the crime be more atrocious, and tending to public mischief, the ambassador must be sent back to him who sent him, with a demand that he be punished or surrendered; as the Gauls asked that the Fabii should be given up to them.

6 But, as we have said above, that all human rights are so conditioned, that they do not bind in cases of extreme necessity, so is this true in this doctrine of the inviolability of ambassadors. But that extreme of necessity does not occur in the requirement of punishment; which may also be suspended in other cases by the Law of Nations; as will appear below, where we treat of the established effects of war:

still less does this necessity operate in the place, time, and manner of taking punishment; but it does hold in precautions against graver evil, especially public evil. Wherefore in order to obviate imminent danger, if there be no other effectual course, ambassadors may both be detained and interrogated. Thus the consuls of Rome apprehended the ambassadors of Tarquin, looking first to the letters which they carried, as Livy says, that *they* might not escape them.

7 If the ambassador use armed force, he may undoubtedly be killed, not in the way of punishment, but in the way of natural defense. Thus the Fabii, whom Livy calls the violators of human law, might have been killed by the Gauls. So in Euripides, Demophon threatens the Herald. The name of this Herald was Copreus, and because he used violence, he was put to death by the Athenians, as Philostratus relates. Cicero solves, by a not dissimilar distinction, the question, whether a son ought to accuse a father who is betraying his country. For he decides that he may do so, to avert the imminent danger, but not to invoke punishment when the danger is past.

V. 1 But the law which I have stated, of the inviolability of ambassadors, is to be understood to bind him to whom the embassy is sent; and more particularly, if he has received the ambassador, as if from that time a tacit compact had been introduced. But prohibitions may be and are often delivered, that ambassadors are not to be sent; and that if sent, they will be treated as enemies: as notice was given to the Ætolians by the Romans; and as it was in old times announced by the Romans to the Veians, that except they quitted the city, they would be treated as Lars Tolumnius had treated their ambassadors; [who put them to death:] and as was announced to the Romans by the Samnites, that if they presented themselves at any public meeting in Samnium, they would not depart inviolate. This law does not affect those through whose territory the ambassadors pass without having received permission: for in so far as they go to their enemies, or come from their enemies, or in any other way appear as enemies, they may be put to death. As the Athenians dealt with the ambassadors between the Persians and Thebans, and the Illyrians with those between the Essii* and the Romans: and much more may they be thrown into bonds, as Xenophon did to certain persons, and Alexander to those who were sent from Thebes and Lacedæmon to Darius, and the Romans to the ambassadors of Philip to Hannibal, and the Latins to those of the Volsci.

2 If there be no such cause, and ambassadors [passing through the territory] are ill treated, it is not the Law of Nations, of which we are speaking, which is violated, but the friendship and dignity, either of him who sent them, or of him to whom they go, which is conceived to be violated. Justin says of the letter of Philip, king of Macedon, that his ambassador to Hannibal being carried to Rome, he was dismissed in safety by the Senate, not out of honour to the king, but in

---

* The inhabitants of Issa, an island on the coast of Illyria. *Gronov.*

order that he, as yet doubtful, might not be made an indubitable enemy.

VI.   But the embassy, once admitted, has, even with enemies, and much more with a party merely unfriendly, the protection of the Law of Nations.   Heralds and negociators are at peace in the middle of war, says Diodorus.   The Lacedæmonians who put to death the ambassadors of the Persians, are said thereby to have *thrown into confusion the rights of mankind.*   So Pomponius, Tacitus, Cicero, Seneca, Livy, Curtius. [See the passages.] And with great reason; for in war, many things happen which cannot be transacted except by ambassadors; and peace itself can scarcely be attained in any other way.

VII.   It is also made a question, whether by the law of retaliation, an ambassador may be put to death or ill treated, who comes from a person who has perpetrated something of that kind.   And certainly there are in histories many examples of such revenge.   But histories relate not only what was rightly done, but what wrongly, angrily, passionately.   The Law of Nations not only provides for the dignity of the Sender, but for the security of the Sent; and therefore there is a contract with the latter also.   Wrong, therefore, is in such case done to him, though none be done to him who sent him. Therefore it was not only magnanimously done of Scipio, but also according to the Laws of Nations, when, after the ambassadors of the Romans had been illtreated by the Carthaginians, he had the Carthaginian ambassadors brought before him, and being asked, What was to be done with them, answered, Nothing like what the Carthaginians had done.   Livy adds, that he said that he would do nothing unworthy of the institutions of Rome.   Valerius Maximus, in a similar but more ancient fact, ascribes to the Consuls this saying, *From such fear, Hanno, the faith of our city liberates you:* for there also Cornelius Asina, contrary to the rights of legation, had been thrown into chains by the Carthaginians.

VIII.   1 The suite and the furniture of the ambassadors have also their own sacredness; and so the ancient formula of the Feciales ran: *King, do you make me the royal messenger of the Roman People, with my company and equipments?*   And by the Julian Law, those are held to be guilty of unlawful violence who have done injury, not only to ambassadors, but also to their companions.   But these are sacred, in an accessory manner only, and so far as the ambassador chooses: and the ambassador may be required to give them up.   But they are not to be taken by force.   When this was done by the Achæans to some Lacedæmonians who were in the company of the Roman ambassadors, the Romans exclaimed loudly that the Law of Nations was violated.   To this may be referred the judgment of Sallust concerning Bomilcar, which we have quoted above.   But if the ambassador will not give them up, the course is to be taken which we have pointed out in speaking of the ambassador.

2 Whether the ambassador has jurisdiction over his own family

and suite, and whether his house is to be an asylum for all who take refuge there, depends on the concession of the party with whom he resides: for it is not a part of the Law of Nations.

IX. Also the moveable property of an ambassador, which is regarded as an appendage to his person, cannot be taken or impounded for debt; neither by order of a court, nor (as some think) by the royal hand. For all compulsion ought to be removed from an ambassador; that which touches things necessary to him, as well as his person, that he may have full security. Therefore, if he have contracted any debt, and, as may easily happen, has no real property in that country, he is to be asked for it in a friendly way; and if he refuse, he who sent him is to be applied to: and at last, he may be proceeded against in the manner of debtors who are without the territory.

X. 1 Nor is it to be feared, as some think, that on such terms no one will contract with an ambassador. For kings also, who cannot be compelled, do not fail to find creditors: and in some peoples it has been the custom, that he who had given credit on a contract should not have a sentence in his favour by a court: any more than if he brought an action for ingratitude; so that men would be compelled either to receive ready money, or to trust to the naked good faith of the debtor. Seneca expresses a wish for such a state of things. So Appian says this was the Persian practice.

2 Elian relates the same thing of the Indians. Charondas made the like rule; and Plato approves. Aristotle remarks the same. [See.] The arguments against this from the Roman Law do not pertain to ambassadors such as we speak of, but to representatives of provinces and towns.

XI. Wars engaged in on account of ambassadors being ill used, are found in all parts of profane history. Also Scripture mentions the war which, on this account, David undertook against the Ammonites. Cicero says, there is no juster cause of war.

CHAPTER XIX.

Of the Right of Sepulture.

I. 1 THE Laws of Nations voluntarily instituted, direct also the sepulture of dead bodies. Dio Chrysostom, among the *usages*, which he opposes to *written law*, mentions, after the rights of legation, the usage of not refusing burial to the dead. So Seneca the father, Philo, Josephus, Isidore of Pelusium, who calls this *a law of nature*, the general natural habits of man being included in the term *nature*, as elsewhere noticed. So Euripides, Aristides, Lucan, Papinius [Statius], Tacitus. He who prevents it, puts off humanity, as Claudian says; disgraces humanity, as Leo; insults decency, as Isidore says.

2 This right, as being common to all civilized men, was referred to the gods as its authors. So in the *Supplices* of Euripides; the *Antigone* of Sophocles. [See.]

3 So Isocrates in several places*, Herodotus, Diodorus, Xenophon, Lysias and Aristides†.

4 And names implying Virtue are given to this office, as *humanity*‡, *mercy, compassion, religion, a feeling for our common nature, a recollection of our human condition, a work of kindness.* [See the authors.] The Donatists who refused burial to the bodies of Catholics are accused of *impiety*. So Papinius [Statius]. Spartian says that such are *without reverence for humanity.* So Livy, Homer, Lactantius. [See.]

II. 1 There are different opinions as to the origin of this practice of burying bodies; either first embalming them, as the Egyptians did; or burning them, as among the Greeks mostly; or without preparation, which Cicero notes as the oldest practice. Moschion thought the custom intended to be a memorial of the abolition of the practice of eating human bodies. [See.]

2 Others regard it as a willing payment of a debt to Nature, which, if not given, she will take. That man is made from earth, was not only told to Adam by God. Cicero also quotes from Euripides, *Earth to earth;* and in Eccl. xii. 7, we read, *Then shall the dust return to the earth as it was, and the spirit shall return to God who gave it.* See

---

* The passage about the Thebans is wrongly applied. J. B.

† The passage of Aristides in wrongly applied. J. B.

‡ An expression which, in this sense, Grotius wrongly ascribes to Cicero. J. B.

Euripides; Lucretius; Cicero, from Xenophon. Pliny says that the earth receives us when we are born*, nourishes us as we grow up, feeds us at every age, and at last receives us into its bosom as a mother, when the rest of nature rejects us.

3 Others think that the hope of the resurrection was intended to be marked by this practice, and transmitted to posterity. So Democritus seems to have thought†. The Christians often refer the practice of burial to this hope. So Prudentius; *What mean hollowed stones, what mean sculptured tombs, save that what we trust to them is not dead, but sleepeth?*

4 It is more simple to say, that considering the superiority of man to other animals, it was deemed unworthy of him that other animals should feed on him, and that sepulture was invented to obviate this. The pity of men protects the body from birds and beasts, says Quintilian. To be devoured by beasts was considered shocking. So Cicero, Virgil, Jerem. xxii. 19, 1 Kings xxi. 19, Lactantius, Ambrose.

5 And even without regarding such insults, it seems unfit for the dignity of man's nature that his body should be torn and crushed. So Sopater, Gregory Nyssen.

6 Hence the office of burial is conceived as rendered, not so much to the man, that is, the particular person, as to Humanity, that is, to Human Nature. So Seneca and Quintilian call it *public humanity,* Petronius, *transferred humanity.* And hence it follows, that sepulture ought not to be withheld, either from our friends or from enemies. See this thought in the *Ajax* of Sophocles: in Euripides: in Virgil, and the writer to Herennius, who quotes him‡. So Papinius [Statius] and Optatus speak of death terminating all enmity.

III. 1 Hence all agree that sepulture is due to public enemies; and is a right of war. So Appian, Philo, Tacitus, Dio Chrysostom, Lucan, Sopater, Dio Chrysostom again.

2 And examples occur in abundance. Enemies were buried by Hercules, Alexander, Hannibal; of the latter case Silius says, *You might have supposed the dead man a Sidonian leader.* So the Romans buried Hanno; Pompey, Mithridates; Demetrius, several: Antony, Archelaus. The oath of the Greeks who marched against the Persians included this§. And we constantly read in history that the vanquished obtained permission to bury their dead. So Pausanias says the Athenians buried the Medes.

3 The Hebrew High Priest, though on other occasions forbidden to have anything to do with a funeral, was yet commanded to bury a dead body if he found it by accident. Christians thought the burial of the dead so important, that in order to do it, as in order to relieve

---

* Referring to the practice of laying a new-born child on the ground. *Gronov.*

† The passage is wrongly quoted, and misunderstood. J. B.

‡ A mistake of Grotius, which Barbeyrac has ingeniously traced.

§ A mistake of Grotius, as Barbeyrac shews.

the poor, or to ransom captives, they thought it lawful even to sell the consecrated vessels of the church.

4 There are examples of burial denied, but they are condemned by the common judgment. See Virgil, Claudian, Diodorus.

IV. 1 With regard to great criminals, there seem to be doubts. The Hebrew law directed the bodies of those who were publicly executed to be taken away and buried before sunset: and the commentators note this as an evidence of reverence for the divine image in which man is made. Egisthus was buried by Orestes. Among the Romans, the bodies of those executed were not denied to their relatives; or even to any who asked for them, as Paulus thought. So Diocletian and Maximian directed.

2 Examples of bodies thrown out unburied, are more common in civil than in foreign wars. And at this day, some criminals are gibbeted and left in public view: but whether this be a laudable practice, is disputed both by politicians and by theologians.

3 On the other hand, we find persons praised, for ordering the bodies of those to be buried who had themselves refused the rite to others, as Pausanias. So Statius makes Theseus act to Creon. So the Pharisees buried Alexander Jannæus. If God punished some by denying them sepulture, he did this by his own right. David's proceeding with Goliath's head was no general case.

V. 1 The Hebrews, however, made one exception, in the case of those who had died by their own hands. And this is fit; for there can be no other punishment, for those to whom death is no punishment. So the Milesian virgins, and the Plebs at Rome were deterred from suicide. So Ptolemy ordered the body of Cleomenes to be hung. And it is, says Aristotle, a common practice, as Andronicus explains him. And on this ground, Dion lauds Demonassa, queen of Cyprus. And it is no objection, that, as the poets sometimes say, the dead feel nothing, and are not affected by loss or shame. For it is enough if what is done to the dead deters the living.

2 The Platonists argued well, against the Stoics and others who thought that the need of a refuge from slavery and disease, and the hope of glory, were just causes of a voluntary death. They replied, that the soul must remain at its post in the body, and that we must not quit this life without His leave who placed us in it: as we find in Plotinus, Olympiodorus, Macrobius. On this ground, Brutus, at an earlier period, condemned the act of Cato, which he afterwards imitated. See Plutarch. And Megasthenes noted that the act of Calanus, [who burnt himself in the presence of Alexander and his army,] was blamed by the wise men of the Indians; for that their doctrine did not approve of such impatience of life. So Darius said, *I would rather die by another's crime than my own.*

3 Hence the Hebrews called death *dissolution* and *departure*, not only Luke ii. 29, but also in the Greek version of Gen. xv. 2, Num.

xx. 29; which mode of speaking was also used by the Greeks. See Themistius, and Plutarch.

4 Some of the Hebrews make one exception to the rule against suicide, in a case of a *laudable retirement,* if any one foresees that he will in future live to the dishonour of God. For since God, not man, has a right to our lives, they think that the presumed will of God is the only thing which excuses the purpose of anticipating death. To this they refer the examples of Samson and of Saul. The former saw that in his person the true religion was scorned. The latter was restored to a right way of thinking, after the shade of Samuel had predicted to him his death; and though knowing that this was at hand, he did not refuse to fight for God and his country; and fell on his sword to avoid the insults of the enemy: thus obtaining eternal praise, even from David. The third example is that of Razis, in the history of the Maccabees, 2 Macc. xiv. 37. In Christian history also, we read similar examples of persons who have killed themselves, lest under the pressure of torments they might renounce the Christian religion: and of virgins who have drowned themselves to save their chastity, and whom the Church places amongst its martyrs. But it is worth while to see what Augustine says of these cases.

5 I find that another exception obtained among the Greeks; which the Locrians objected to the Phocians: *It was the common usage of Greece that sacrilegious persons should be cast forth unburied.* So Dio Prusæensis. So traitors were treated at Athens, as Plutarch says.

But to return to my subject; the ancients were generally agreed in holding that war might justly be undertaken on account of sepulture denied; as appears by that history of Theseus which Euripides treats in the *Supplices,* and Isocrates in the Oration quoted.

VI.   There are some other things which are due by the instituted Law of Nations; as possession by prescription, succession to intestates, and the results of contract, even if unequal. For all these, although in a certain way they have their origin in Natural Law, yet received from human law a certain firmness, both against the uncertainty of conjecture, and against exceptions which otherwise natural reason seems to suggest: as we shewed above in passing.

CHAPTER XX.

Of Punishments.

I. 1 WHEN above we began to speak of the causes for which wars are undertaken, we said that facts might be considered in two ways, either with a view to reparation, or to punishment. We have now finished the former part of the subject, and proceed to the latter, Punishment. And this must be the more carefully treated by us, because its origin and nature, not well understood, have given rise to many errors.

Punishment, in its general signification, is *An Evil of suffering which is inflicted on account of* (ob) *an evil of doing*. For though labour [not pain] may be the sentence of persons as a punishment, yet such labour is considered as it is disagreeable, and therefore is a sort of suffering. But the inconveniences which some persons have to suffer on account of an infectious disease [Lev. xiii.], or a mutilation of the body [Deut. xxiii. 1], or other uncleanness [Lev. xv.]; such as, to be excluded from public assemblies, or from certain functions, are not properly punishments; although on account of a certain resemblance, and by an abuse of language, they may be called by that name.

2 Among the things which nature herself dictates as lawful and not unjust, this stands; that he who has done evil should suffer evil; which the philosophers call the ancient and Rhadamanthean law, as we have elsewhere said [I. ii. 3.] So Plutarch; Plato. [See.] So Hierax defined justice by this as its noblest element; and Hierocles called it *the medicine of wickedness*. So Lactantius.

3 And this characteristic of Punishment, that it is the return for transgression, is noticed by Augustine; [see]; which belongs also to punishments inflicted by God; though in these sometimes it appears, through human ignorance, as he says, that *the transgression is hid while the punishment is apparent*.

II. 1 Whether Punishment belongs to attributive or to expletory justice there are different opinions. For inasmuch as those who transgress more gravely are more heavily punished, and those who sin less gravely, more lightly; and because punishment is assigned by the whole to a part, therefore they ascribe punishment to attributive justice.

But the principle on which they proceed, that attributive justice obtains wherever an equality is introduced between more than two terms, we have proved, in the beginning of this work, not to be true [I. i. 8]. And in the next place, that greater offenders are punished more severely, smaller ones more lightly, that only happens by consequence, and is not what is looked to in the first place and *per se*. For the thing first looked at is the equality between the offense and the punishment, as Horace says. [See.] And in like manner Deut. xxv. 2, 3; and the *Novella* of Leo.

2 Nor is their other principle more true, that all punishments come from the whole to a part, as will appear by what we have hereafter to say. But further: it is shewn above that the true notion of attributive justice does not properly consist, either in such equality, or in the process from the whole to a part; but in taking account of that claim which does not include right strictly taken, but gives occasion to it. And although he who is punished ought to have a moral claim, or to be worthy, to be punished, still that does not go to prove that he has such a quality as attributive justice requires.

But neither do they who hold that expletory, or, as it is commonly

called, commutatory justice, is exercised in Punishment, explain themselves better. For they regard the transaction as if something were
paid to the offender, as is commonly done in contracts. They are
deceived by the vulgar expression in which we say that Punishment is
the due of him who has transgressed; which is plainly an improper
expression, for he to whom anything is properly a due, has a right
over another. But when we say that punishment is any one's due, we
mean nothing else than that it is just that he should be punished.

3 Still, however, it is true, that in punishment the justice which is
exercised is, in the first place and *per se*, expletory justice: because he
who punishes, in order to punish rightly, ought to have a right to
punish, which right arises from the delinquency of the offender. And
in this matter, there is another thing which approaches to the nature of
contracts; that as he who sells, although he say nothing particularly,
is conceived to have obliged himself to all the things which are natural to selling; so he who has wilfully offended, seems to have obliged
himself to undergo punishment; because grave crime cannot be otherwise than punishable: so that he who directly wills to offend, must
also by consequence have willed to incur punishment. And in this
sense, the emperors say to such a person, *You have subjected yourself
to this punishment;* as those who take wicked counsels are said to have
already incurred punishment in their own thoughts: and in Tacitus,
a woman who had joined herself to a slave is said to have consented
to her own slavery, because that was the punishment for such persons*.

4 Michael Ephesius on Aristotle illustrates this.

III. 1 Of such punishment, the subject, that is, the person *to
whom* it is due, is not determined by nature itself. Nature dictates
that evildoing may be punished, but not who ought to punish:
except that nature sufficiently indicates that it is most suitable that
it be done by one who is superior: yet not in such way as to shew
that this is necessary; except the word *superior* be taken in this sense,
that he who has done wrong has, by that very fact, made himself
inferior to any other, and has thrust himself out of the class of men
into that of the inferior brutes, as some theologians hold. See Democritus, Aristotle.

2 It follows, as a consequence of this, that the offender ought not
to be punished by one who has offended equally, as Christ said, Joh.
viii. 7, *He that is without sin among you* (that is, such sin) *let him cast
the first stone.* And this he said, the Jews being very wicked and
adulterous at that time, Rom. ii. 22; where the Apostle says what
Christ had said. Seneca says the same; and Ambrose, in the apology
of David.

IV. 1 Another question is of the End of punishment. For what
has been said hitherto only proves that transgressors have no wrong

---

* Tacit. *Annal.* xii. 53. The passage, rightly used, is nothing to the purpose,
as Barbeyrac remarks.

done them if they are punished. But from that, it does not necessarily follow that they must be punished. Nor is it necessary; for many offenders are pardoned for many things both by God and by men, and these are often praised on that account. Plato's saying is celebrated (in his Laws), which Seneca translates, *No wise man punishes because wrong has been done, but in order that wrong be not done:* and so elsewhere; and in Thucydides.

2 This is true in human punishments; for men are so bound together by their common nature, that they ought not to do each other harm, except for the sake of some good to be attained. In God the case is different, and Plato does ill in extending this doctrine to him. For the actions of God may depend on his right of Supreme Authority, especially when there is some special merit [or demerit] of man in addition, although he propose to himself no extrinsic end: and so the Hebrew commentators explain Prov. xvi. 4: *The Lord hath made all things for himself, yea, even the wicked for the day of evil.* But even if we take the more common interpretation, it comes to the same thing: that God has done all things by the right of his supreme liberty and perfection, seeking and requiring nothing beyond himself; as he is said to be self-existent. Certainly the words of Scripture testify, that the punishments of very wicked men are inflicted on this account, when they speak (Deut. xxviii. 63) of God's *rejoicing over them to destroy them:* of his mocking and laughing at them (Prov. i. 26. Isai. i. 24). And that what we have said against Plato is true, is proved by the last judgment, after which no amendment is to be expected: as also by the infliction of some inconspicuous punishment, as the hardening of the sinner's heart, in this life.

3 But man, when he punishes a being of the same nature as himself, ought to have some object in view. And this is what the Schoolmen say, that the mind of him who inflicts punishment ought not to rest in the evil inflicted on any one. Plato had said the same before. [See.] And Seneca; so also Aristotle.

V. 1 Therefore what has been said by various writers, that the pain of the offender is a remedy of the pain of the injured person, (Publius Syrus, Plutarch, Cicero,) does indeed agree with the nature which man has in common with brutes; for anger is, in brutes as in man, a heat of the blood arising from the desire of revenge, which appetite is irrational; so that it is often directed against objects which have done them no harm, as against the offspring of the creature which did the harm, or against things which have no sense, as in a dog against the stone which hit him. But such an appetite, considered in itself, does not correspond to our rational part, of which the office is to control the passions; and consequently, not to Natural Law, because that is the dictate of our rational and social nature as such. But reason dictates to man that nothing is to be done by him so as to harm another man, except it have some good purpose. But in the pain of an enemy, so nakedly regarded, there is no good, but a false and imaginary one; as in superfluous riches, and many other things of that kind.

2 And in this sense revenge is condemned, not only by Christian doctors, but also by heathen philosophers. So Seneca, Maximus Tyrius, Musonius. In Plutarch, Dio, who converted the Platonic wisdom into acts, says that vengeance proceeds from the same disease of the soul as injurious aggression. [See.]

3 It is therefore contrary to the true nature of man acting on man, to find satisfaction in the pain of another person, as pain. See Juvenal on Revenge. [Sat. XIII. 180.] So Lactantius.

4 Therefore man is not rightly punished by man merely for the sake of punishing: let us see then what utility makes punishment right.

VI. 1 To this subject pertains the division of punishment stated in Plato's *Gorgias*, and Taurus on the place, as quoted by Gellius: which division is taken from the end of punishment; except that while Plato mentions two ends, *amendment* and *example*, Taurus adds a third, *retribution*. So Clemens Alexandrinus. Aristotle takes the two latter ends. Plutarch recognizes retribution. And this is properly what Aristotle refers to *synallactic* justice.

2 But this must be more minutely examined. We shall say then that in punishment is regarded either the utility of the offender, or of him who suffers by the offense, or of persons in general.

VII. 1 To the first of these ends, pertains punishment which is called reformatory: of which Paulus, Plutarch, and Plato speak; the object of which is to make a better man of the offender. For as repeated acts beget habits, vices are to be cured by taking away the pleasure which they bring, and putting pain for their sweetness. So Plato and Tacitus.

2 That punishment which answers such an end, is lawful to every one of sound judgment, who is not implicated in that or the like vices, appears from what is said of verbal castigation. It is *an unofficial Duty.* [See Plautus.] In stripes and inflictions, which contain anything of compulsion, the difference between the persons to whom it is, and to whom it is not lawful, is not made by nature, (nor could be, except that nature commends to parents the office of correcting their children,) but by the laws, which, for the sake of avoiding quarrels, have restricted that general relation [of correctors and corrected] to the nearest family relatives, as we may see in the Codex of Justinian, Title *De emendatione propinquorum.* So also in Xenophon, Lactantius.

3 But this kind of punishment cannot extend as far as death, except in what they call a reductive way, in which negations are reduced to the opposite class. For as Christ said, it would have been better for some if they had never been born, that is not so ill: so for incurable dispositions, it is better, that is less evil, to die than to live, since by living they are sure to become worse. Seneca says they must

Q

perish, in order that they may not perish.   So Jamblichus, Plutarch, Galen.

4 Some think that these are those whom St John speaks of as sinning unto death. But this is doubtful, and charity requires that we should not lightly hold any one's condition for desperate ; and so we must rarely punish in such a view.

VIII. 1 The utility of him whose interest it was that the fault should not have been committed, consists in this, that he do not in future suffer anything of the same kind from the same person or from others. Gellius, from Taurus, says of this case : *When the dignity or authority of him against whom the offense is committed is to be protected, lest punishment omitted produce contempt thereof, and diminish its honour ;* but what is said of injury done to authority, is true of injury done to liberty, or to any other right. As Tacitus says of a person, *That he might consult his security by just punishment.*

That he who has been injured may not suffer evil from the same person, may be provided for in three ways : first, by the removal of the delinquent ; secondly, by taking away his power of doing harm ; thirdly, by teaching him, by suffering, not to offend ; which is connected with the amendment of which we have spoken. That the person offended shall not be injured by another, is to be procured, not by any casual punishment, but by a punishment open and conspicuous, of the nature of example.

2 Up to these limits then, if vindicative punishment be directed, and be kept within the bounds of equity, even if inflicted by a private hand, it is not unlawful, if we look at the naked law of nature, that is, abstracting divine and human law, and conditions which are not necessary concomitants of the thing itself ; whether it be inflicted by him who is injured, or by another ; since for man to help man is consentaneous to nature. And in this sense, we may admit what Cicero says, when he declares the law of nature to be that which is given us, not by opinion, but by an innate power ; and then places among the examples thereof, vindicative punishment, which he opposes to mercy. And that no one may doubt how much he would have understood by that term, he defines vindicative punishment to be *that by which we repel force and contumely from us and ours, by defending or revenging, and by which we punish offenses.* So Mithridates, in Justin, speaks of our *drawing the sword against robbers, if not for safety, yet for revenge.* And so Plutarch calls this *the law of defense.*

3 On the ground of this Natural Law, Samson reasoned when he said (Judg. xv. 3), *Now shall I be more blameless than the Philistines though I do them a displeasure,* after they had injured him ; and again, v. 11, *As they did unto me so have I done unto them.* So the Platæans in Thucydides said. So Demosthenes against Aristocrates. So Jugurtha in Sallust against Adherbal. Aristides the orator proves from the poets, legislators, orators, and from proverbs, the right of taking revenge on those who attack. Ambrose praises the Macca-

bees, who, even on the sabbath-day, avenged the death of their innocent brethren. And he too, arguing against the Jews who complained
of their synagogue as having been burnt by the Christians, says, *If I
went upon the law of nations, I should say how many Christian houses
of worship the Jews burnt at the time of Julian:* where the law of
nations to which he refers is, returning like for like. So Civilis in
Tacitus.

4 But because in things which concern us and ours, we are misled
by affection, therefore many families were brought together in one
place, judges were constituted, and to these alone was given the
power of righting those that were injured, the liberty which nature
had given to other persons being taken away. So Lucretius of the
origin of civil society: Demosthenes against Conon: Quintilian ; the
emperors Honorius and Theodosius; and king Theodoric. [See.]

5 Yet the old natural liberty remains; first, in places where there
are no tribunals, as at sea. And to this perhaps we may refer the
proceeding of Cæsar when, as a private man, having been taken by
pirates, he collected ships, and partly put theirs to flight, partly sunk
them; and then, when the proconsul was slow in punishing those
who were taken, he himself gibbeted them. The same holds in
deserts, or where men live a Nomadic life. So among the Umbrici,
as Nicholas Damascenus relates, every one is his own avenger; which
is also the custom among the Muscovites, after a certain time has
elapsed from the application to the judge. And this was the origin
of the duels which, before the introduction of Christianity, were common among the German nations, and are not yet sufficiently gone
out of use. And so, as Paterculus relates, the Germans when they
became acquainted with the Roman jurisdiction, admired to see
injuries concluded by judicial proceedings, which they were accustomed to see terminated by an appeal to arms.

6 The Hebrew Law permitted the relative of the person slain to
kill the slayer, anywhere without the places of refuge: and the Hebrew
commentators rightly note, that retaliation for a person slain might
be executed by personal force; but for the person himself, for
example, for a wound, no otherwise than before a judge ; because
moderation is more difficult when the pain comes nearer ourselves.
That a like mode of avenging murder by the hands of a private
person prevailed among the Greeks of old, appears in Homer. But
the examples of this are most frequent among those who have not a
proper judge. *Just wars,* says Augustine, *are commonly defined to be
those which avenge injuries;* and Plato approves battles on such
ground.

IX. 1 The utility of persons in general, which was the third
end of punishment, offers the same divisions as the utility of the
injured man. For either the object is that he who has done harm
to one may not do harm to others; which is secured, either by taking
him away, or by taking away his power of mischief, or by constrain-

ing him so that he cannot do harm, or by amending him : or else the
object is to prevent others from being tempted by impunity to do
harm to any others, which is provided for by conspicuous punishments, examples. These are employed, that the punishment of one
may produce the fear of many; that others may be deterred by the
kind of punishment, as the laws speak; that others may be compelled to look forward and fear, as Demosthenes says.

2 The right of inflicting such punishment, is also, by Natural Law,
in the hands of every man. So Plutarch says that a good man is by
nature pointed out as a perpetual magistrate; for by the law of
nature, authority is given to him who does just things. So Cicero
proves that a wise man is never a private man, by the example of
Scipio Nasica. And Horace calls Lollius, Consul not for his year
alone; so Euripides: which however must be understood with reference to the laws of the State.

3 Of this Natural Law Democritus speaks; first, of the right of
killing harmful beasts; and certainly it is not improbable that good
men did this before the deluge, before God had delivered his
will to man, that other animals should become his food. And then
he extends this to man: and afterwards says that whoever kills a
thief or robber, by his hand, command, or vote, is innocent. And
Seneca seems to have referred to this. [See the passages.]

4 But since the proof of the fact often requires great care, and
the estimate of punishment requires great prudence and great equity,
communities of men have chosen, for this office, those whom they
thought to be, or hoped to find, the best and most prudent. So
Democritus.

5 But as in punishment vindicative, so in punishment exemplary, there remain vestiges of the original law, in those places and
between those persons who are not under fixed judgments; and besides, in some excepted cases. So amongst the Hebrew customs, a
Hebrew apostatizing from the true God and joining idolatrous worship, might be at once put to death by any person. The Hebrews
call it a judgment of zeal, of which they say Phineas set the first example. (Numb. xxv.) So in the Maccabees (1 Macc. ii. 24), Mattathias
slew a Jew polluting himself with Greek rites; and so in 3 Maccab.
[vii. 15.] 300 Jews were killed by their countrymen. And the stoning
of Stephen, and the conspiracy against Paul, were on the same pretext,
as well as many other examples in Philo and in Josephus.

6 So also among many peoples, masters retained the right of punishing their servants, and parents their children, even to death. So
at Sparta, the Ephori could put a citizen to death without trial.

From what we have said, we may see what is the Law of Nature
with regard to punishment, and how far it continued.

X. 1 We must now consider whether the Gospel Law has limited
this liberty more narrowly. Certainly, as we have elsewhere said, it
is not to be wondered at, that some things which are permitted by the

Natural and the Civil Laws, are forbidden by the Divine Law; that being both the most perfect of Laws, and one which promises rewards beyond the discovery of mere human nature; and to obtain which, very reasonably, virtues are required which go beyond the mere precepts of nature. But punishments or castigations which neither leave behind them infamy nor permanent damage, and which are necessary, according to the age or other quality of the offender, if they are inflicted by those to whom human laws give such permission, as parents, tutors, masters, teachers, have nothing which is at variance with the evangelical precepts. These are remedies of the soul, as innocent as bitter medicines are.

2 With regard to revenge, the case is different. For so far as it is a mere satisfaction of the mind of the person offended, it is unlawful, not only by Gospel Law, but by Natural Law. The Hebrew Law too, not only forbids persons to bear malice against their neighbour, that is, their countryman, but even commands them to bestow certain common benefits on such enemies. And therefore the name of *neighbour* being by the Gospel extended to all men, it is required of us, not only that we do not do harm to our enemies, but that we do them good; which is also directly commanded, Matth. v. 44. The Hebrew Law permitted men to revenge the graver injuries, not by their own hand, but by recourse to the judge. Christ, however, does not permit the same to us; as appears by the opposition, *Ye have heard it said— But I say unto you.* For though what follows properly refers to the repelling of injury, and in some degree restricts even the liberty of doing that, these precepts are much more to be understood as condemning revenge; for they reject the ancient permission as suitable only to a more imperfect time. So the Clementine Constitutions.

3 Tertullian comments on Christ's teaching, as an addition to that of the Old Testament, that vengeance is to be left to God. They who believe in Him, are to expect that He will punish; they who do not, are to fear retaliation.

4 Christ, he adds, did not destroy the teaching of the Old Law. God has provided judges of injury. Without this, forbearance loses its reward: for it is by the fear of punishment that injury is controlled. Without this, violence would go to extremes.

5 Thus Tertullian thinks that revenge was permitted to the Hebrews, not as a thing blameless, but to avoid a greater evil. And this is undoubtedly the case, with such demand of satisfaction as proceeds from wrath; and so the purpose of the law was understood, as appears in Philo. And this is the point to which Christ's precepts tend, when he enjoins forgiveness of injuries. We are not to procure or wish ill to men from the feeling of the ill which they have done us. So Claudian: and so Lactantius and Ambrose correct Cicero.

6 But what are we to say of revenge, as it respects, not the past, but protection for the future? Here also Christ enjoins us to for-

give, if he who has injured us shews any signs of penitence; [see the passages;] in which he speaks of a plenary remission of injury, which may restore the offender to his former place in our good will; whence it appears that nothing is to be required of him in the way of punishment. And even if signs of such penitence be wanting, we are not to take it too severely, as the precept, of giving our coat also, shews. And even Plato said something like this. An Action for contumely (such as Christ indicates in speaking of one striking us on the cheek), Musonius said he would neither promote nor authorise, it being better that such things should be pardoned.

7 But if such forbearance bring great peril, we are to be content with such precaution as shall do the least harm to the offender. So among the Jews, the person offended accepted a pecuniary fine; which was also practised at Rome. So Joseph, the husband of Mary, and the educator of our Lord Jesus, when he conceived his wife to be guilty of adultery, was minded to put her away, not to bring her before a public tribunal; and this, because he was a just, that is, a merciful man. And on this account Ambrose and Lactantius praise him. So Justin, of the accuser of the Christians, says, We do not wish our calumniators to be punished: their depravity and ignorance are punishment enough.

8 There remain punishments which provide, not for private but for public good; partly by coercion of the mischievous, partly by the effect of example. And that these are not taken away by Christ, we have elsewhere clearly proved, in that while he gave his precepts, he declared that he did not destroy the Law. The Law, as long as it continued, rigidly required the magistrates to punish homicide and some other crimes. And if the precepts of Christ could stand along with the law of Moses when it pronounced even capital punishments, they may also stand along with human laws, which in this respect imitate the Divine Law.

XI. 1 There are some, who in defense of the contrary opinion, adduce the great mercy of God in the New Covenant, which they conceive must be followed by men, and even by magistrates, as the vicars of God: and that this is in some degree true, we do not deny, but it does not extend so far as they wish. For the great mercy of God in the New Covenant especially regards offenses against the primeval law [given to Adam], or the law of Moses, committed before the knowledge of the Gospel was received. [See the passages quoted.] For transgressions committed after this, especially if there be added contumacy, have a threatening of a much more severe judgment than that which was instituted by Moses. [See the passages.] And not in another life only, but in this also, God frequently punishes such transgressions. And such offenses are not commonly pardoned, except man punish himself, by serious contrition, 1 Cor. xi. 31, 2 Cor. ii. 7.

2 They urge that at least they who are penitent ought to receive

impunity. But, not to say that true penitence is a matter of which men can hardly be assured, and that any one may obtain impunity, if it be sufficient to profess penitence in any way he chooses; God himself does not always remit the whole of the punishment to those who are penitent, as appears by the example of David. As therefore God could remit the punishment of the law, that is, violent or untimely death, and yet inflict evils not at all slight upon the offender; so now also, he may remit the punishment of eternal death, and yet give up the offender to untimely death, either inflicted by himself, or, in conformity with his will, by the magistrate.

XII. 1 Again, others use this argument, that when life is taken, the time for penitence is cut off. But they know that pious magistrates take careful account of this view, and that no one is hurried to capital punishment without giving him time to see and seriously to detest his sins: and that such penitence, although works corresponding do not follow, being intercepted by death, may be accepted by God, the example of the thief crucified with Christ proves. But if it be said that a longer life might have been profitable for a more serious repentance, there may also be found those to whom may deservedly be applied what Seneca says, *The only good thing which you can now furnish is the spectacle of your death:* and again: *Let them cease to be bad men by death, the only way they can.* As Eusebius the philosopher also says, *Since they can do it no other way, let them at least in this · escape the bonds of wickedness, and find that refuge.*

2 This then, in addition to what we said at the beginning of the work, is our answer to those who hold that either all punishment, or at least capital punishments, are without exception forbidden to Christians: which is contrary to what the Apostle teaches us, who includes the use of sword in the royal office, as the exercise of divine vengeance; and who elsewhere bids us to pray that kings may be Christian, and, as kings, be a protection to the innocent. And this, seeing the wickedness of great part of men, even after the propagation of the Gospel, cannot be secured, except, by the death of some, the boldness of others be repressed; since even now, when capital punishments and gibbets are so common, there is scarcely safety for innocence.

3 Still it will not be improper for Christian rulers, at least in some degree, to propose for their imitation the example of Sabaco, king of Egypt, who is reported by Diodorus to have commuted capital punishments for condemnation to the public works, with the happiest success. And Strabo says, that even the peoples about Caucasus *punished no crimes with death, not even the greatest.* Nor is that of Quintilian to be despised : *None will doubt that if guilty men can be brought to a good way of thinking in any way, as it is granted that sometimes they can, it would be better for the State that they should be preserved than capitally punished.* Balsamon notes that the Roman laws which enacted the punishment of death, were, by the Christian emperors, changed for

the most part into other punishments, that both the condemned might be more thoroughly driven to penitence, and their punishment being prolonged, might be more profitable as example.

XIII.   1 But in the enumeration of the ends of punishment by Taurus, it appears that something was overlooked. Gellius thus quotes him: *When therefore there is either great hope that the offender will without punishment correct himself; or, on the other hand, there is no hope that he can be amended and corrected; or, there is no reason to fear that the dignity which is offended will suffer; or, the offense be not such as requires exemplary fear to correct it; then the offense does not seem to be one for which a punishment need be devised.* For he speaks as if when one end of punishment is taken away, the punishment should be removed; while on the other hand, all the ends must cease to exist, in order that there may be no ground for punishment. And moreover he omits that end, when a man who is unamendable is removed from life, that he may not commit more or greater crimes : and what he says of loss of dignity, is to be extended to other evils which are to be feared.

2 Seneca spoke better when he said : *In punishing wrongs, the law has had these three objects, which the prince also ought to aim at; either to amend him who is punished; or to make others better by the punishment; or to make the rest of mankind more secure by removing the bad.* For here, if by *the rest*, he means not only those who have been injured, but others who may hereafter be so, you have a complete division of the subject, except that to *removing* you should add *or repressing*. For both imprisonment, and any other way of diminishing their power, tends the same way. He has another less perfect partition in another place; as has Quintilian.

XIV.   From what has been said, it may be collected, how unsafe it is for a private Christian man to inflict punishment, and especially capital punishment, either for the sake of his own or of the public good, upon a guilty person; although, as we have said, that is sometimes permitted by the Law of Nations. And hence we must approve of the usage of those peoples by whom navigators are provided with commissions from the public power to suppress pirates, if they find any upon the seas; on which commissions they may act, not as of their own motion, but by public command.

XV.   Of much the same kind is the provision which prevails in many places, that not any body who chooses can take up the accusation of crimes, but only certain persons on whom that office is imposed by the public power; so that no one shall do any thing to shed the blood of another, except by the necessity of his office. Accordingly the canon of the Council of Seville provides, that if any one of the faithful shall turn informer, and by his means any one shall be proscribed or put to death, he shall not receive the Communion, even when dying.

XVI.   And this too follows from what has been said, that it is not advisable for a truly Christian man, nor is even decent, that he should of his own accord mix himself with public business which involves capital punishment, and seek for a power of life and death, as if he were a sort of God among men. For certainly what Christ says, applies here, that it is dangerous to judge others, since as we judge them, God will judge us.

XVII. 1 It is a noted question, whether the human laws, which permit the slaying of certain men, really justify the slayers in the sight of God, or only give them impunity among men. Covarruvias and Fortunius hold the latter, which opinion Vasquius calls shocking. It is not doubtful, as we have said, that, in certain cases the Law can do both the one and the other. But whether the law had that intention, is to be understood partly from the words of the law, and partly from the matter. For when the law gives indulgence to human feeling, it takes away the punishment of the law, but not the sin, as in the case of a husband who kills the adulterous wife or the adulterer.

2 But if the law look to future danger from the delay of punishment, it is to be conceived to give right and public power to the private person, so that he is no longer a private man.

Of this kind is the law in the Codex under the rubric, *When it is lawful for any one without a judge to do justice for himself or for the public service;* [Cod. III. 27] where any one is allowed to suppress by force soldiers who plunder; where too the reason is added, putting such soldiers on the footing of robbers. And a similar law is given respecting deserters. As Tertullian says: *Against traitors and public enemies every one is a soldier.*

3 There is a difference in the right of killing exiles, outlawed persons: namely, that there, a special opinion has preceded, but in this case, a general edict, which is combined with the evidence of the fact, and has the force of a judicial sentence.

XVIII. Let us now consider whether all vicious acts are such that they may be punished by men. It is certain that they are not all such. For, in the first place, mere internal acts, even if they come to be known, for instance by confession, cannot be punished by men; because, as we have said, it is not congruous to human nature that mere internal acts should give rise to right or obligation. And so the Roman law. But that does not prevent that internal acts, so far as they influence external, may not be taken into account in estimating, not themselves properly, but the external acts which receive from them their character of desert.

XIX. 1 In the next place, acts unavoidable to human nature cannot be punished by man. For though nothing is sin which is not done freely, yet to abstain from all sin and always, is above the condition of humanity; and hence sin is said to be natural to man by some of the philosophers, and by many of the Christians. See Seneca, Sopater, Philo, Thucydides, Diodorus.

2 It may even be doubted whether those acts can properly be

called sin, which, though they have an appearance of liberty, are not free, when considered in their generality. So Plutarch in *Solon*. Then again there are other acts which are inevitable, not to human nature properly, but to this particular person at this moment, on account of the constitution of the body affecting the mind, or inveterate habit; which is commonly punished, not in itself, but on account of precedent fault; because either the remedies were neglected, or the diseased thoughts willingly admitted into the mind.

XX. 1 Thirdly; those offenses are not to be punished, which neither directly nor indirectly regard human society or any other man. The reason is, that there is no cause why such sins should not be left to God to punish, who can both know them best, and judge them most justly, and punish them most effectually. Wherefore if such a punishment were instituted, it would be useless, and therefore blameable. From this remark are to be excepted punishments for amendment, which have for their object to make the man better, though the interest of others is not concerned. Also punishments are not to be inflicted on acts opposed to those virtues of which the nature rejects all compulsion, as mercy, liberality, gratitude.

2 Seneca treats this question, Whether ingratitude ought to meet with impunity; and gives many reasons why it ought not [to be punished]; but this as the principal one, which may be extended to other like cases : *Since gratitude is a most graceful thing, if it be necessary it ceases to be graceful :* that is, it loses its degree of gracefulness, as appears by what follows: *We praise a grateful man only as one who returns a deposit or pays a debt without being forced :* and again, *It could not be a glorious thing to be grateful except it were safe to be ungrateful.* As Seneca the father says, *I do not want to have* [*such*] *a person praised who is accused, but to have him acquitted.*

XXI. We must now discuss whether it is ever lawful to excuse or pardon : The Stoics denied it, but with a poor argument: *Pardon is the remission of a due penalty, but the wise man does what is due.* Here the fallacy is in the word *due.* For if you understand that he who has transgressed owes the penalty, that is, may be punished without wrong, it will not follow that he who does not punish him, does not do what he ought. But if you say that the punishment is due on the part of the wise man, that is, that he ought by all means to require it, we deny that that is always the case, and therefore say that the punishment in that sense is not due, but only lawful. And that may be true, both before and after the penal law.

XXII. 1 Before the penal law is instituted, it is not doubtful that punishment may have place; because by Natural Law he who has transgressed is in that state in which he may be lawfully punished; but it does not follow that punishment ought to be exacted: because this depends upon the connexion of the ends for which punishment is instituted with punishment itself. Wherefore if those ends are, in moral estimation, not necessary, or if there are, opposed to those,

other ends not less useful or necessary, or if the necessary ends of
punishment can be obtained in another way, it follows that there
is nothing which precisely obliges to exact punishment. We may
take an example of the first case in a sin known to few, and of which
the public notice is not necessary, or is even hurtful. As Cicero says
of a certain Zeuxis, *Being brought to trial perhaps he ought not to
be dismissed, but it was not necessary to bring him to trial.* An
example of the second case is one who puts forward his own merits
or those of his parents, as a set-off against his fault; so Seneca: an
example of the third case, we have in him who is reformed by remon-
strance, or who has satisfied the injured person by a verbal acknowledgment, so that punishment is not necessary for those ends.

2 And this is one part of the clemency which liberates the
offender from punishment, of which the Hebrew wise man says,
Clemency becomes the just man. For since all punishment has in
it something opposed not to justice, but to charity, reason easily
permits us to abstain from it, except some greater and juster charity
oppose insurmountable obstacles. So Sopater, Cicero, Dio Prusæensis, Favorinus.

XXIII. These cases may occur: that punishment may require
absolutely to be exacted, as in crimes of very bad example;—or may
be fit not to be exacted, as if the public good require it to be omitted;—or either course may be allowable: when, as Seneca says, *Clemency has free will.* Then, say the Stoics, the wise man spares, but
does not pardon: as if we might not, with common usage, call that *pardon*, which they call *sparing*. In fact, here and elsewhere, as Cicero,
Galen and others have noted, a great part of the disputations of the
Stoics is about words, which a philosopher ought carefully to avoid.
So the writer to Herennius, and Aristotle say.

XXIV. 1 There seems to be a greater difficulty, after the
penal law is instituted; because the author of the law is, in a certain
way, obliged by his own law; but this, as we have said, is true; so
far as the author of the law is considered as a part of the State, but
not, so far as he bears the character and authority of the State. For
in that capacity, he may rescind the whole law, because the nature of
human law is, that it depends on human will, not only in its origin,
but in its duration. But yet the author of the law ought not to
abolish it, except for a probable cause, since otherwise he offends
against the rules of governmental justice.

2 But as he may take away the whole law, so may he remove
its obligation with regard to a particular person or fact, the law for
the rest remaining; following the example of God himself, who, as
Lactantius says, *when he established the law did not deprive himself of
the power of pardon.* So Augustine, and Seneca in the character of
Nero.

3 But this also is not to be done except there be a probable
cause. What are probable causes, although it cannot be precisely

defined, yet we must hold by this, that they ought to be greater after the law, than were regarded before the law; because the authority of the law, which it is important to preserve, has been added to the other causes of punishment.

XXV. The causes of liberating any one from the punishment of the law, are commonly either intrinsic or extrinsic : an intrinsic cause is when the punishment, though not unjust, is severe compared with the fact.

XXVI. An extrinsic cause of remission of punishment is that which arises from some merit or other thing commending the offender to mercy; or from a great hope of him in future ; which kind of cause will then be of most avail, if the reason of the law, at least in a particular point, ceases as to the fact in question. For although to sustain the efficacy of the law, the universal reason suffices, there being no repugnant contrary reason ; yet the cessation of the reason for the particular case, effects that the law may be more easily, and with less loss of authority, loosened. And this happens most in those offenses which are committed through ignorance, though not free from all fault; or through infirmity of mind, superable indeed, but yet difficultly superable. To these, the Christian ruler ought mainly to look, that he may imitate God, who in the Old Testament gives testimony by word and by deed that he is indulgent in forgiving such. [See the passages.] And that by those words of Christ, *Father, forgive them ; for they know not what they do*, Theodosius was moved to pardon the Antiochians, is noted by John Chrysostom.

XXVII. And hence it appears how ill Vasquius said, that a just cause of dispensing with, that is of relaxing the law, was such alone as one about which, if the author of the law had been consulted, he would have said that it was not in his mind to have it observed. Here he has not distinguished between the *equity* which interprets the law, and a relaxation of it. And on this ground he elsewhere reproaches Thomas Aquinas and Sotus, for saying that the law obliges, even though the cause in particular ceases, as if they had thought that the law was only the written word, which never came into their minds. For so far is it from being the case that any relaxation of the law, which may often be freely either given or omitted, is to be referred to *equity*, that even that relaxation which is due to charity or to governmental justice is not to be referred to that principle. For it is one thing to take away the law for a probable, or even for an urgent cause, and another to declare that the fact was from the beginning not comprehended in the mind of the law.

We have spoken hitherto of taking away punishments, let us now consider their apportionment.

XXVIII. From what has been said above, it appears that two things are regarded in punishments; for what, and on account of whom. For what, is a question of merit; on account of whom, is a question of the use of the punishment. No one is to be punished beyond his desert, as Horace and Cicero say: accordingly, Papinian calls punishment the valuation [of an offense]. Aristides says that it is suitable to nature that there should be some point beyond which punishment shall not proceed; Demosthenes says that equality of punishment [and crime] is not to be regarded nakedly as in weights and measures, but with estimation of the purpose and intention of the offender. Within the limit of this desert, crimes may be punished more or less, according to utility.

XXIX. 1 In examining desert, these points come under consideration; the cause which impelled, the cause which ought to have withheld, and the fitness of the person to each. [First, of the impelling cause.] Scarce any one is wicked for nothing: if there be any person whom wickedness delights on its own account, he has gone beyond the limits of humanity. The greater part of persons are led to sin by the affections: *When desire hath conceived it bringeth forth sin*, James i. 15. Under the name of desire, I include also the impulse to shun evil, which is the most natural, and therefore the most decent of the appetites. Hence what is done wrongly to avoid death, imprisonment, pain, or extreme want, is commonly held most excusable.

2 And so Demosthenes, Polybius, Aristotle, Porphyry.

3 Other appetites tend to some good, either imaginary or real. True good, is, besides the virtues and their actions which do not tend to sin, either things which delight, or the cause of delight, which is called utility, as abundance of possessions. Imaginary goods, not real, are superiority over others, so far as it is separate from virtue and utility, and revenge. These three appetites St John calls *the lust of the flesh, the lust of the eyes, and the pride of life.* The first comprehends the desire of pleasure, the second, cupidity of having, the third, the pursuit of vain glory, and anger. Philo says that all evil comes of the desire of wealth, glory, or pleasure. So Lactantius.

XXX. 1 [Second, of the withholding cause.] The general cause which ought to withhold men from offending is justice. [Hence injustice is a measure of punishment.] The injustice is the greater as the greater damage is done to any one. Therefore the first place belongs to consummated crimes; the next, to those which have proceeded to some acts, but not to the last; and among these, everything is the more grievous in proportion as it has gone further. In each class, that injustice has an eminent place which disturbs the common order, and therefore hurts the greatest number; that comes after, which affects individuals. The greatest offense here is that which affects life; the next, family, of which the foundation is matrimony; the last, desirable objects, either directly by subtracting them, or by producing damage through wrong doing.

2 These matters might be divided more subtilly; but the order which we have indicated is that which God has followed in the Decalogue. [The fifth commandment includes duties to governors]; for by

the name of parents, who are natural magistrates, other rulers also must be understood: then follows the interdiction of homicide; then the sanction of matrimony by the prohibition of adultery; then theft; then false witness; in the last place, sins unconsummated.

Among the withholding causes, ought to be put, not only the character of that which is directly done, but of that which will probably follow: as in setting fire to a house, or breaking down a dam, great calamity, and even deaths, are to be looked for.

3 To the injustice which we put as the general cause, there is often added some other vice, as impiety towards parents, inhumanity towards neighbours, ingratitude towards benefactors; which increases the offense. Also there appears a greater pravity, if any one has often offended: because bad habits are worse than bad acts. And hence it may be understood how far that was by nature equitable, which was practised among the Persians, that the anterior life was taken into account along with the offense. That may be applied, where a person, not otherwise bad, has been overcome by some sudden temptation: but not in those who have changed their whole course of life, in whom God says he will not regard the former life (Ezek. xviii.*). So Thucydides.

4 The ancient Christians, in assigning punishment by the canons, rightly directed, not the naked delict to be regarded only, but at the same time the preceding and succeeding life. A law directed against a special sin, if violated, adds a degree of depravity to that which the sin by itself would not have. So Augustine, Tacitus.

XXXI. 1 [Third, as to the aptitude of the person.] The aptitude of the person, either to consider the withholding causes, or to feel the power of the impelling affections, may be considered as to his constitution, age, sex, education, and the circumstances of the act. For children, women, persons of dull intellect, ill educated persons, are less able to perceive the differences of just and unjust, of lawful and unlawful: those in whom bile prevails are irascible; those in whom blood, lustful; and youth tends to one of these ways, age, the other. Andronicus speaks of such palliations. Then again fear is augmented by the thought of imminent danger; anger, by recent and still smarting vexation; so that they scarce suffer reason to be heard: and transgressions which thus arise are deservedly less odious than those which spring out of the desire of pleasure, which is both slower in its impulses, and may more easily be put off and led to seek other matter. Aristotle discusses this question, *Eth. Nicom.* VII. 7.

2 This also is to be held, that in proportion as the judgment of the person choosing his course is more impeded, and by mere natural causes, the offense is less. So Aristotle in the same place. Antiphanes; and old men in love, in comedies. And by these principles

---

* The principal part of the passage rather refers (see v. 10) to the son being bad when the father has been a good man. W.

we must estimate the limiting amount of punishment according to desert.

XXXII.   1 We must remark that the doctrine of the Pythagoreans, that justice is *a reciprocal proportion,* is not to be so understood as if he who has deliberately and without extenuating causes, injured another, should himself receive so much harm, and no more.   That this is not so, the Hebrew law shews, when it directs thefts to be punished by forfeit to four or five times the amount.   By the Attic Law, the thief, besides a fine of the double, was kept in bonds some days.   So Ambrose, Aristides, Seneca.

2 Among the Indians, as Strabo notes, he who had maimed any one, besides retaliation, had his hand cut off.   In Aristotle's *Magna Moralia, If any one strike out the eye of another, it is just that he suffer not so much only, but more.*   For it is not just that the danger of the guilty and of the innocent should be the same, as Philo shews, in treating of the punishment of homicide.   And this may be estimated also by considering that some delicts not consummated, and therefore less than if they were consummated, bring down, as punishment, an evil equal to that meditated: as we read of the Hebrew law of false witness, and the Roman law against him who went about with a weapon to kill a man.   From which it follows, that to the crime when consummated, a heavier punishment will correspond: but because nothing is heavier than death, and that cannot be reiterated, as Philo notes, the punishment is necessarily confined within those limits, sometimes adding tortures according to the desert.

XXXIII.   But the magnitude of the punishment is to be regarded, not nakedly only, but with respect to the patient.   For the fine which will press down a poor man will sit lightly on a rich one: and to a disreputable person, ignominy as a punishment will be a small evil, but a great one to a man in honour.   The Roman law often uses this kind of diversity; whence Bodin constructed his harmonic proportion: although in reality the proportion is simple, and resembles numerical equality: the punishment is to be equal to the desert, as, in contracts, the money to the goods: although the same goods are in one place worth more, in another less, and money in like manner.   But it must be confessed that this, in the Roman law, is often not done without too much respect of persons and qualities not pertaining to the fact; while the law of Moses is always quite free from this fault.   And this, as we have said, is the intrinsic apportionment of punishment.

XXXIV.   But a tenderness for him who is punished, leads us to the minimum of punishment, except a juster tenderness for the greater number persuade us to some other course for an extrinsic cause; which cause is, sometimes, great danger from him who has offended, but more frequently, the necessity of example.   And this necessity usually arises from the general incitements to sin, which cannot be repressed without sharp remedies.   The principal incitements are custom and facility.

XXXV. On account of the *facility*, the divine law given to the Hebrews punishes more heavily theft from the field than from the house; Exod. xxii. 1 and 7. So Justin says the Scythians account theft a most heinous crime, in consequence of its facility among their uninclosed herds. So Aristotle.

The *custom* of an act, though it subtracts something from the fault (so Pliny), yet on one side it demands severity, to meet the prevailing evil. But in particular judgments, we must more lean to leniency, in making laws, to severity; taking account of the time when the laws or the judgments are delivered, because the utility of the punishment is most considered in the general case; but the fault is greater or less in individual cases.

XXXVI. 1 What we have said, that when great and urgent causes cease, we should be prompt rather to diminish the punishment, is the direction in which the other part of clemency is seated: the former part consisting in taking away the punishment altogether. So Seneca speaks of *tempering* punishment when we cannot pardon; so Diodorus Siculus, Capitolinus, describing M. Antoninus, Isocrates, speak of punishment below the requirement of the laws.

2 Augustine admonishes Count Marcellinus of his duty, urging clemency.

XXXVII. We hope we have omitted nothing important in this obscure and difficult argument. We have taken account of the four things which Maimonides says are chiefly to be regarded in punishments; the greatness of the sin, its frequency, the amount of desire, the facility of the deed; and also the seven points which Saturninus very confusedly considers in punishments; the person who did the deed, the person who suffers, the place, the time, the quality, the quantity, the event;—all the seven belong to one or other of our heads.

XXXVIII. That wars are undertaken not unfrequently to demand punishment, we have shewn above, and history everywhere teaches: but mostly this cause is conjoined with that other, the reparation of the damage, when the same act was both vicious and produced damage: from which two qualities two different obligations arise. That wars are not to be undertaken for every fault, is obvious enough; for even the laws do not apply their vindictive operation to all faults, though they only harm the guilty. This is right, as we have said. So Sopater.

XXXIX. 1 What Cato said for the Rhodians, that it was not just that a person should be punished for the evil which he was alleged only to have wished to do, was not ill put in its own place, because no decree of the Rhodians [declaring war against the Romans,] could be adduced, but only conjectures of a fluctuating mind: but this is not universally to be received. For the will which has proceeded to external acts, is commonly obnoxious to punishment. So Seneca, senior and junior. Not the event of things, but the intent, are treated by the laws, says Cicero. So Periander. So the Romans decreed the second war against king Philip, except he gave satisfaction concerning the designs he had entertained of making war against Rome; inasmuch as he had collected arms, soldiers, and a fleet. And this is noted in the oration of the Rhodians in Livy; that neither is it established by the laws nor by the customs of any nation, that if any one wished his enemy to perish, but did nothing to bring such a result to pass, he should be capitally condemned.

2 But again, it is not every perverse will, which comes to be indicated by a fact, that gives occasion for punishment. For if we do not punish all perpetrated crimes, much less shall we punish those only thought of and conceived. In several places we may say what Cicero says; *I do not know whether it is not enough that the person who has done wrong should repent.* The Hebrew law did not provide specially against most offenses against piety merely preconceived, or even against the life of man (except by means of judicial proceedings); since error about divine things, which are obscure to us, is easily committed, and the impulse of anger may be pardoned.

3 But in matrimony, where so many matches are to be had, to attempt to disturb the married life of another; or in property, when the division is so equal, to contrive devices by which one may enrich himself at the expense of another, was not to be borne. That command, *Thou shalt not covet,* in the Decalogue, although if you look at the object of the law, that is, the spiritual object, it is of wide extent; for the law desires all to be pure even in mind; yet as to the external precept, the carnal commandment, it refers to the affections of the mind which are disclosed by deeds; as appears by St Mark, who gives that same precept, *Defraud not;* having before given, *Do not steal* (Mark x. 19). And the Hebrew word and the Greek one corresponding are found in that sense in Micah ii. 2, *And they covet fields, &c.* And elsewhere.

4 Therefore inchoate delicts are not to be punished by arms, except either the matter be grave and have gone so far that, from such act, a certain evil, though not that which was intended, has ensued; or at least, great danger; so that the punishment be conjoined with protection against future mischief, or be a defense of offended dignity, or a remedy to a pernicious example.

XL. 1 It is to be understood also that kings, and they whose rights are of the nature of royal rights, have the right of requiring punishment, not only for injuries committed against them and their subjects, but for those also which do not peculiarly touch them, but which enormously violate the law of nature and nations in any persons. For the liberty of providing for human society by punishment, which at first, as we have said, was in the hands of individuals, did, when states and tribunals were instituted, fall to the share of the supreme authorities, not properly as commanding others, but as being themselves subject to none. For subjection took away the right from others. Indeed it is more honourable to punish the injuries of

R

others than your own, in proportion as, in your own, it is to be feared lest a person may, by the sense of his own pain, either exceed due measure, or vitiate his mind with malice.

2 And on this account Hercules is praised by the ancients for having freed the land from Antæus, Busiris, Diomedes, and similar tyrants; having, as Seneca says, passed through the land not in concupiscence, but in just indignation, and thus being the author of great good to man. So Lysias, Diodorus, Dio Prusæensis, Aristides. Theseus is praised in like manner for removing the robbers Sciron, Sinis, and Procustes. See Euripides, Valerius Maximus.

3 Thus we do not doubt that war is just against those who are impious against their parents; such as the Sogdians were, before Alexander cured them of this barbarity; against those who kill strangers; against those who feed on human flesh, which usage Hercules compelled the Gauls to give up, as Diodorus narrates: and against those who practise piracy. Seneca says, that *though he does not do any harm to my country, yet such depravity cuts him off [from the tie of humanity]*: Augustine says that *there are things which if any state on earth have decreed, or should decree, that state would require to be overthrown by a decree of the human race.* Of such barbarians, and wild beasts, rather than men, we may say what Aristides previously said of the Persians, (who were really no worse than the Greeks,) that war against them is natural; and what Isocrates said, that war against brute beasts was most just, and next to that, war against men who are like brutes.

4 And so far we follow the opinion of Innocentius, and of others who say that war may be made against those who sin against nature; contrary to the tenets of Victoria, Vasquius, Azorius, Molina, and others; who seem to require, in order to justify a war, that he who undertakes it should be either injured in his own person, or in the country to which he belongs, or that he should have jurisdiction over him whom he attacks. For they hold that the power of punishing is the proper effect of Civil Jurisdiction; while we conceive that it comes also from Natural Law. If the opinion of those from whom we dissent be admitted, an enemy will not have the power of punishing an enemy, even after war has been justly begun, if it be for another cause than to inflict punishment: which right, however, most authors concede, and the usage of all nations confirms, not only after the war has been finished, but even while it is going on; and this right is claimed, not from any civil jurisdiction, but from that natural right which existed before states existed, and is still in force in places in which men live, distributed into families and not into states.

XLI. But here some cautions are to be applied; first, we are not to take instituted usages of states, though received among many nations, and not without reason, for the laws of nature; of which kind mostly were those things in which the Persians differed from the Grecians; to which we may refer what Plutarch says: *that to profess to civilize barbarous nations, was a pretext to cover mere cupidity.*

XLII. In the second place, we must take care that we do not rashly reckon, among the things forbidden by nature, those, with regard to which this is not clear; and which are rather interdicted by the divine will: in which class we must place concubinage, and some of the offenses called incest, and usury.

XLIII. 1 In the third place, we must carefully distinguish between general principles,—such as that we must live virtuously, that is, according to reason, and some which approach to them and are so manifest that they admit of no doubt, as, for instance, that we are not to take by violence what belongs to another;—and inferences from these; of which some are easy to know, for instance, that assuming matrimony, we are not to allow adultery; but others not so easy, as that the revenge which has for its ultimate object the pain of others is vicious. We have here nearly the same case as in mathematics, where there are certain primary notions, or truths immediately connected with these, [axioms], and some demonstrations which are forthwith understood and obtain assent; and again, certain propositions which are true but not apparent to all.

2 As then, with regard to civil laws, we excuse those who did not know, or did not understand the law; so also with regard to the law of nature, it is reasonable to excuse those who are embarrassed, either by weakness of reason or by a bad education. For ignorance of the law, as, when it is invincible, it takes away the sin, so too, even when mixed with some negligence, it diminishes the offense. And therefore Aristotle compares barbarians who, being educated in a depraved manner, commit offenses in such cases, to those who have appetites corrupted by disease. Plutarch says: *There are certain diseases which throw the mind out of its usual balance.*

3 In the last place, that also is to be added, which I say once for all, that wars undertaken on the ground of punishment, must be very suspected, except the crimes are very atrocious and very manifest; or except some other cause concur. Perhaps Mithridates was not very wrong when he said of the Romans, that *they did not really attack the vices of kings, but their power and majesty.*

XLIV. 1 Our order has led us to the offenses which are committed against God. For it is made a question whether war may be undertaken to punish these; and this is treated at sufficient length by Covarruvias. But he, following others, thinks that there is no punitive power without jurisdiction properly so called; which opinion we have already rejected. Whence it follows, that as bishops are said, in a certain way, to have received the care of the catholic or universal Church, so kings, besides the care of their particular state, have incumbent upon them a general care for human society. The sounder reason for the doctrine that such wars are not just, is this, that God is sufficient to punish offenses against himself; whence it is commonly said, that *wrongs against the gods are the business of the gods,* and that, *perjury has a sufficient avenger in God.*

2 But it is to be recollected that this may be said of other offenses also. For God is no doubt sufficient to punish these also; and yet they are rightly punished by men, no one dissenting. Some pursue the argument, and say, that other offenses are punished by men, so far as men are by them hurt or injured. But it is to be noted, on the other hand, that offenses are punished which not only hurt others directly, but those also which do so by consequence, as self-murder, and bestiality, and others.

3 For though religion of itself is efficacious in conciliating the favour of God, yet it has in human society its especial effects, and those very important ones. For Plato, with great reason, called religion the bulwark of virtue, and the bond of the laws and of honest discipline; and Plutarch similarly, the cement of society, and the foundation of laws. So Philo calls it the most potent love-charm, and indissoluble bond of benevolence. And the reverse of all this is said of impiety. All false persuasion concerning divine things is pernicious, and if passions are combined with it, is most pernicious. In Jamblichus we have a dictum of Pythagoras: *The knowledge of God is virtue and wisdom and perfect happiness.* Hence Chrysippus called Law the Queen of divine and human things, and Aristotle held, that among public cares, the first was that of divine things; and the Roman jurisprudence was described as the knowledge of things human and divine: and in Philo, the royal art is the *care of things private, public and sacred.*

4 All these things are to be considered, not only in one state, as when Xenophon makes Cyrus say, that his subjects would be more attached to him in proportion as they feared God more; but also, in the common society of the human race. *If we take away piety,* says Cicero, *good faith and the fellow-feeling of mankind and justice are taken away.* And again: *We learn what justice is when we know the authority of the supreme Governor and Lord, what is his design, what his will.* And an evident proof of this is, that Epicurus, when he had taken away divine providence, left nothing but the empty name of justice, saying that it arose from convention only, and lasts so long only as the common utility continues; that we must abstain from every thing which would turn others, solely from the fear of punishment. See his words in Diogenes Laertius.

5 Aristotle also saw this connexion, as where he says of a king, that *the people will the less fear to be unjustly treated by the prince, if they believe him to be religious.* And Galen says that many discussions are carried on, about the world and the divine nature, without any moral use; but he acknowledges the question concerning providence to be of the greatest use, both in its bearing upon private and upon public virtues. So Homer opposes, to wild and unjust men, those who have a

religious mind. So Justin praises, in the ancient Jews, their justice mixed with religion: and so Strabo. So Lactantius says that he who is not religious does not know what justice is.

6 And religion is even more useful in that larger society [of the human race] than in civil society; since in the latter, its place is supplied by laws, and the easy execution of laws; while on the contrary, in that wider community, the execution of law is very difficult, since it can only be carried into effect by arms, and the laws are very few. And these too have their sanction mainly from the fear of the divine power: and hence, they who transgress the Laws of Nations, are everywhere said to violate the divine laws. And hence the Emperors have rightly said that the infraction of religion is a wrong against all.

XLV. 1 To examine the whole matter, we must remark that true religion, common to all ages, rests mainly on four principles; of which the first is, that God exists, and is one: the second, that God is not any visible object, but something higher: the third, that God cares for human affairs, and judges them with perfect justice: the fourth, that God is the creator of all other things. These four points are delivered in the first four commandments of the Decalogue.

2 For in the first, the unity of God is plainly delivered: in the second, his nature, as invisible; for on this account it is forbidden to make any image of him. So Antisthenes; Philo; Diodorus, speaking concerning Moses; Tacitus, of the Jews; Plutarch, of Numa.

By the third commandment is indicated God's knowledge and care of human things, even of human thoughts; for that is the foundation of oaths. For God is a witness even of the heart; and if any one swear falsely, He is invoked as the punisher: and by this is declared both the justice and the power of God.

By the fourth, the origin of the whole world in the act of God, in memory of which the sabbath was instituted, and hallowed with a peculiar sanction above other rites. For if any one transgressed other rites, the penalty of the law was arbitrary, as concerning forbidden meats: but for the violation of the sabbath, it was death; because the violation of the sabbath implied the denial of the creation of the world by God. And the world, as created by God, contains a tacit indication of his goodness, wisdom, eternity, and power.

3 From these contemplative notions follow active precepts; as that God is to be honoured, loved, worshipped, and obeyed. Hence Aristotle says that he who denies that God is to be honoured, or parents to be loved, is to be brought to reason, not by arguments, but by punishment. And elsewhere he says that other things are reckoned right in one place or another, but to honour God, in all places.

The truth of those contemplative notions, as we have called them, may doubtless be demonstrated by arguments taken from the nature of things; among which arguments, that is the strongest; that our senses shew us that some things are made; and that the things which are made lead us to something not made. But because all

cannot take in this reason and similar ones, it is sufficient that all
ages, and all countries, with very few exceptions, have given their
consent to these notions : and those, some too dull to intend to
deceive, and others too wise to be deceived.   And this consent, in so
great a variety of other laws and other opinions, shews sufficiently
a tradition propagated from the first race of men to us, and never
solidly refuted ; which of itself is sufficient to produce belief.

4 The points which we here mention concerning God are
brought together by Dio Prusæensis, when he says that our conception
of God is partly internal, partly acquired by tradition.   So Plutarch
speaks of *the ancient faith, than which no more evident proof can be
found, the common foundation and basis of piety.*   So Aristotle and
Plato.

XLVI. 1 Wherefore they are not blameless who, although
they are too dull either to discover or to understand the solid arguments for these points of belief, reject them ; since there exist, for
them, guides to the right way, and the opposite opinion has no
arguments to rest upon.   But since we are speaking of punishments,
and of human punishments, a difference is to be taken between the
notions themselves, and the mode of departing from them.   These
notions, that there is a deity (I do not here say whether one or
many), and that he cares for human affairs, are most universal, and
absolutely necessary to constitute all religion, true or false.   *He
that cometh to God* (that is he who is to be religious) *must believe
that he is, and that he is a rewarder of them that seek him.*   Heb. xi. 6.

2 So Cicero ; Epictetus ; Elian ; Plutarch ; Lactantius.   To deny
that God exists, and to deny that he attends to human affairs, comes
to the same thing, as to its moral effect.

3 Wherefore these two points of belief have been preserved, as
if by necessity, among almost all nations of which we know anything.   Hence Pomponius describes religion towards God as a part
of the law of nations ; and Socrates in Xenophon says that to worship
the gods, is a rule among all men.   So Cicero ; Dio Prusæensis ;
Xenophon in the *Symposium.*

4 Therefore those who first begin to take away these convictions,
as they may, in well constituted states, be coerced by punishment,
as was done to Diagoras Melius, and to the Epicureans, who were
ejected from well-governed states ; so may they be coerced, as I
conceive, in the name of human society, which they violate without
probable reason.   So Himerius pleading against Epicurus : *Do you
then demand that mere doctrines be punished ? By no means, but that
impiety should.   Men may deliver doctrines ; they may not oppose piety.*

XLVII. 1 Other points of religion are not so evident ; as, that
there are not more gods than one : that God is not any visible
object ; not the world, not the sky, not the sun, not the air ; that the
world does not exist from eternity ; not even matter, of which it is
made, but that matter was created by God.   Therefore, as to these

points, the knowledge has been, among many peoples, obliterated by the lapse of time, and as it were extinct; and the more easily because the laws gave less attention to this point, as being that without which at least some religion might subsist.

2 Even the law of God, given to the Jewish people, who were imbued with a knowledge of these things, neither obscure nor uncertain, by the prophets, and by miracles, partly seen by themselves and partly delivered by clear tradition, still does not punish with death all who are convicted of this offense; but only those in whom there is some particular circumstance to aggravate the fact, or who have seduced others; as Deut. xiii. 1, 6; or the city which begins to worship strange gods, ver. 12, 13; or that worships the sun, or the moon, or the host of heaven, Deut. xvii. 3; (which St Paul calls serving *the creature, and not the Creator,* Rom. i. 25; and which also was at one time punished among the posterity of Esau, Job xxxi. 26, 27, [*If I beheld the sun when it shined, or the moon walking in brightness, and my heart hath been secretly enticed, or my mouth hath kissed my hand;*]) or that gave his children to Moloch, Lev. xx. 2; that is, to Saturn.

3 The Canaanites and the neighbouring peoples, who fell away to depraved superstitions, God did not straightway punish, but only at last, when they had accumulated great wickedness upon this transgression, Gen. xv. 16. [God says to Abraham, *In the fourth generation they shall come again; for the iniquity of the Amorites is not yet full.*] So in other nations also, God winked at the times of this ignorance, Acts xvii. 30. Philo says truly, that each one thinks his own religion the best, judging mostly, not by reason, but by affection; as Cicero says of philosophical doctrines. He adds, that most are involved in their religious belief, before they can use their judgment.

4 As, then, those are excusable, and certainly not to be punished by men, who, not having received any law delivered by God, worship the influences or spirits of the stars, or of any other natural bodies, either in images, or in animals, or in other things; or even the souls of those who have excelled in virtue, and in benefits bestowed on the human race; or some incorporeal minds; especially if they have not themselves invented this worship, and therefore have not deserted for it the worship of the supreme God; so, on the other hand, they are to be reckoned impious rather than erroneous, who appoint divine honour and worship for evil demons, whom they know to be such, or for names of vices, or for men whose life was marked by wicked deeds.

5 Nor are they less to be reckoned impious, who worship gods with the blood of innocent men; which custom Darius of Persia and Gelo of Syracuse compelled the Carthaginians to discontinue, and are therefore praised. Plutarch relates that some barbarians, who worshipped the gods with human victims, were on the point of being punished by the Romans; but, having excused themselves by the antiquity of the

custom, no harm was done them; but they were commanded not to do the like in future.

XLVIII. 1 What shall we say of making war on certain peoples because they will not embrace the Christian religion when offered to them? I will not now enquire whether it be proposed to them such as it ought to be, and in such manner as it ought to be. Suppose this : we have then two remarks to make. The first is, that the truth of the Christian religion, in so far as it adds not a few points to natural and primitive religion, cannot be proved by mere natural arguments, but rests both on the history of the resurrection of Christ, and on that of the miracles done by him and the apostles; which is a matter of fact, proved of old by irrefragable testimonies, but only of old; so that this also [the ancient testimony] is a matter of fact, and of very old fact. Hence this doctrine cannot be received by those who now hear it for the first time, without the assistance of secret help from God; and as this, when given, is not given as the reward of any work, so if it be denied, or given less largely, this is done for causes, not unjust indeed, but mostly unknown to us, and hence not punishable by human judgment. To this the canon of Toledo has respect. The Synod enjoins that henceforth no one suffer violence, to make him believe : For God will have mercy on whom he will have mercy, and whom he will he hardeneth. It is the manner of the scriptures, to ascribe to the divine will the things of which the causes are hid from us.

2 Another remark is, that it was the will of Christ, the author of the new law, that none should be urged to receive his law by the punishments of this life, or by their fear. [See the passages, Rom. viii. 15, *Ye have not received the spirit of bondage again to fear.* So Heb. ii. 15, *subject to bondage.* John vi. 67, *Will ye also go away?* Luke ix. 55, *Ye know not what manner of spirit ye are of.* Matt. xiii. 29, *Nay, lest while ye gather up the tares,* &c.] In this sense, that saying of Tertullian is most true, *The new law does not assert its rights with the sword.* So in the Clementine Constitutions : Athanasius. Chrysostom, on the passage, John vi. 67, says that it removes all compulsion.

3 The parable of the wedding, Luke xiv. 23, *Compel them to come in,* is not against this. For in that parable, the expression signifies the urgency of the invitation; and in like manner, in the interpretation, in which sense words of the like signification are used, Luke xxiv. 29, *They constrained him.* So Matt. xiv. 22, *Jesus constrained his disciples,* &c., and in the parallel passage, Mark vi. 45. So Gal. ii. 14, *Why compellest thou the Gentiles,* &c. Procopius says, that Justinian was blamed by wise men for compelling the Samaritans by force to become Christians : and adds the inconveniences which resulted, which you may find in his book.

XLIX. 1 They who teaching or professing Christianity, add punishments on that account, doubtless act against reason; for there is nothing in the scheme of Christianity (considered by itself, and not

with impure mixtures,) which can hurt human society; indeed nothing
which does not profit society.   The thing itself speaks, and strangers
are compelled to acknowledge it.   Pliny says, that the Christians
bound themselves by a common sacrament not to commit theft, robbery, or fraud.   Ammianus says, that nothing is taught in that religion except justice and mercy.   And it was a common saying, *Caius
Sejus is a good man, only he is a Christian.* [Therefore persecution is
inconsistent with Christianity*.]

Nor can we admit the excuses for persecution, that all novelties
are dangerous, and especially assemblies ; for doctrines, although new,
are not dangerous, if they lead to all virtue, and to obedience towards
superiors : nor are assemblies of virtuous men to be feared, who do
not seek to meet in secret, except they are compelled.   I may here
adopt what Augustus said, as recorded by Philo, respecting the assemblies of the Jews ; that they were not bacchanalian meetings, or assemblies for disturbing the peace, but schools of virtue.

2 Those who persecute such, are themselves justly punishable, as
also Thomas Aquinas holds.   And on that account, Constantine made
war on Licinius, and other emperors upon the Persians ; though these
wars belong rather to the defense of the innocent, of which we shall
hereafter speak, than to the exaction of punishment.

L. 1 But those act most unjustly, who persecute and punish
those who, while they hold the law of Christ as true, only doubt or
err concerning some things which are either extraneous to the law,
or being in the law, seem to have an ambiguous sense, and are not
always expounded by the ancient Christians in the same way.   And
this appears both by what we have said, and by the ancient example
of the Jews.   For they, though they had a law which was sanctioned
by the punishments of this life, never penally assailed the Sadducees,
who rejected the doctrine of the resurrection ; a doctrine most true,
but not delivered in the old law, except obscurely and in images.

2 But what are we to say, if the error be more grave, and one
which may easily be refuted before an impartial tribunal, by sacred
authority, or the consent of the ancients ? Here also we are to reflect
how great is the force of inveterate opinions, and how much the
party-feeling of each sect impairs their judgment; a disease, as Galen
says, worse than the itch.   So Origen.   Add that the amount of this
fault depends upon the manner in which a person is enlightened,
and other dispositions of the mind, which it is not given to man to
know.

3 He, and he only, is a heretic, according to Augustine, who either
devises or follows false and new opinions, for the sake of his own
advantage, and especially of his own glory and power.

---

* This is the thesis which suits the argument : but some of the examples rather
seem to imply that Grotius was thinking of the thesis : "Therefore those act unreasonably who persecute Christians." W.

Salvian urges the duty of toleration towards the Arians, on the ground of their sincerity. [See the passage.]

4 Augustine argues for toleration of the Manicheans, in whose errors he had long shared.

5 Athanasius inveighs against the Arians, because they first called in the judicial power against their adversaries; *This shews*, he says, *that their way is not pious;* referring, I think, to Gal. iv. 29: *As then, he that was born after the flesh persecuted him that was born after the spirit, even so it is now.* In Gaul, the bishops were condemned who used the sword against the Priscillianists; and in the east, the Synod which agreed to the burning of Bagomilus. (Plato says wisely, that the proper punishment of him who is wrong*, is to be taught right).

LI. 1 Those may be more justly punished who are irreverent and irreligious towards those whom they believe to be gods. This cause among others was adduced for the Peloponnesian war between the Athenians and Lacedæmonians, and by Philip of Macedon against the Phocians: of whose sacrilege Justin says, that *it required to be expiated by the arms of the whole world.* Jerome says, on Daniel v. *As long as the sacred vessels* [of the Hebrews] *were in the idol-temple at Babylon, God was not angry, (for they still seemed to be devoted to divine worship, though accompanied with perverted opinions;) but after that they were polluted by human uses, the punishment straightway follows the sacrilege.*

Augustine thinks that the Roman Empire was favoured by God, because, though their religion was false, they were in earnest about it†; and as Lactantius says, they held to the main duty of man, though not in truth, yet in purpose‡.

2 We have already said that even imaginary deities when appealed to by perjured persons, have their cause taken up by the true God. He is punished, says Seneca, because he did it, as to God; his own opinion binds him to punishment. And so I take that other passage of Seneca: The punishment of violating religion is different in different places, but some punishment there everywhere is. So Plato condemns those who do not believe in the existence of the gods, to imprisonment or death (Laws, b. x. end).

---

* Plato says, *of ignorance.* J. B.

† Augustine says that the Roman Empire was favoured by divine Providence on account of their civil virtues, *De Civit. Dei,* Lib. v. c. 12. J. B.

‡ Lactantius is speaking of idolatry in general: *Instit. Div.* Lib. ii. c. 3. The passage from Seneca is not appropriate. J. B.

CHAPTER XXI.

Of the Communication of Punishments.

I. 1 WHEN we speak of the extension of punishment from one person to others, we speak either of those who are partakers in the delict, or of others. Those who are partakers in the delict are not punished so much for another's delict as for their own. Who these are, may be understood from what has been said above concerning damage wrongfully inflicted. For generally, a person comes to be a sharer in the delict, in the same way in which he comes to be a sharer in the damage done; yet it is not always true that when a person is bound for the damage, he is also liable to punishment; but only when there has been, besides, some notable malice; whereas to make a person bound for the damage, any fault whatever often suffices.

2 Therefore they who command a vicious act, they who give the consent which is requsite, they who assist, who receive the things, or in any other way participate in the crime itself; they who give their counsel towards it, who praise it, who assent to it; those who being bound by their special rights to forbid it, do not forbid it; or being bound by similar rights to give aid to the person who suffers wrong, do not do so; those who do not dissuade when they ought to dissuade; who keep silence with regard to a fact which they were bound by some right to make known; all these may be punished, if there be in them such malice as suffices for penal desert, according to what has already been said.

II. 1 The thing will be made clearer by example. A Civil Community, like any other Community, is not bound by the act of an
individual member thereof, without some act of its own, or some omission. Augustine says well, *There is a difference between the fault that,
in a people, each person has of his own; and a fault common to all,
which is committed with one mind and one will.* And accordingly, in
Treaties the formula is, [Liv. i. 24,] *If he violate this by public
act.* The Locrians in Livy plead to the Roman Senate that their de-
fection was by no means a public act. So again Zeno, pleading for
the Magnesians, begged with tears *that they would not ascribe to the
whole city the insanity of one man: that each one's madness must be at
his own risk.* And the Rhodians, before the Senate, separate the public
cause from that of private persons, saying that there is no city which
has not often wicked citizens, and always a senseless mob. So the
father is not bound by the delict of the son, nor the master by that
of the servant, except there be some cause of blame in themselves.

2 But of the ways in which rulers come to share in the crime of
others, there are two which are most common, and require diligent
consideration: their allowing and their receiving.

With regard to *allowing*, it is to be held that he who knows of
the commission of the offense, who can, and is bound to prevent it,
and who does not, does himself offend. So Cicero against Piso;
Brutus, in a letter to Cicero; Agapetus to Justinian; Arnobius; Salvian; Augustine.

3 So he who allows his slave to be prostituted when he could prevent her, is held by the Roman Law to have prostituted her. If a
slave commit homicide with the knowledge of his master, the master
is equally liable, for he is considered as guilty of the homicide. And
by the Fabian law, the master is punished if his servant, with his
knowledge, has drawn away and secreted another servant.

4 But as we have said, there is required, to produce this liability,
not only knowledge, but the power of prevention. And this is what
the Laws say; that knowing, when it is directed to be punished, is taken
for allowing; so that he who could have prevented, is held bound if he
did not do so; and that the knowing here spoken of is considered as
combined with willing; and that knowledge is taken along with purpose;
and therefore, that the master is not bound if the slave has asserted
and appealed to the laws for his liberty; or, if he have disregarded
his master; for he is blameless who knows, but cannot prevent.

5 When Hesiod says,

> Often the whole of the city is punished for one man's injustice,

Proclus says well, *As having had it in their power to prevent him, and
not having done so.* So Horace of Agamemnon,

> Though 'tis the kings that are mad, the Achaians suffer the evil.

For they might have compelled him to restore the priest his daughter.
And so after the Greek fleet was burnt,

> All for the fault of one, for the madness of Ajax Oïleus.

As Ovid says on the same subject,

> One constrained the maid, but the penalty spread to the many:

because the others did not prevent the sacred virgin from suffering
violence. So Livy about the Laurentian ambassadors, repelled by
Tatius. So Salvian speaks of kings. And Thucydides says, *He
who could prevent it does it.* So in Livy, the Veientes and Rutulians
excuse themselves to the Romans, in that their subjects had assisted
the enemies of the Romans, they having no knowledge of the fact.
And on the other hand, the excuse of Teuta, the queen of the Illyrians, is not accepted, when she said that piracy was not practised by
her, but by her subjects; for she did not prevent it. And in ancient
times the Scyrians were condemned by the Amphictyons because they
allowed some of their people to practise piracy.

6 It is easy to know, so far as presumption goes, acts which are
conspicuous and which are frequent. What is done by many, can be
ignored by none, as Dio Prussæensis says. Polybius heavily blames
the Etolians, because, when they were desirous of not being deemed
the enemies of Philip, they allowed their people to commit hostile
acts, and gave distinguished honours to those who had been prominent
in such proceedings.

III. 1 Let us come to the other question, of *receiving,* as a subject of punishment. Punishment, as we have said, according to Natural
Law, may be inflicted by any one who is not open to a like charge;
though no doubt it is in conformity with civil institutions, that the
delicts of individuals, which regard their own community, should be
left to that community, and to its rulers, to be punished or passed
over as they choose.

2 But there is not the same full power left to them in delicts
which in any way pertain to human society in general: for these,
other states and their rulers may prosecute, as in particular states
there is a prosecutor of certain offenses which any one may put in
motion: and much less have they such a power in offenses by which
another state or its ruler are especially assailed; and in which, consequently, the state or the ruler have, on account of their dignity or
security, a right of exacting punishment, as we have said. This right
is not to be impeded by the state in which the offender lives, or its
ruler.

IV. 1 But since states are not accustomed to permit another
state to enter their territory armed for the sake of exacting punishment,
nor is that expedient; it follows that the city, where he abides who is
found to have committed the offense, ought to do one of two things:
either itself, being called upon, it should punish the guilty man, or it
should leave him to be dealt with by the party who makes the demand: for this is what is meant by *giving* him *up,* so often spoken of
in history.

2 Thus the Israelites demand of the Benjamites, that they give up

those who have committed the crimes; Judges xx. The Philistines require from the Hebrews that they give up Samson as an evil-doer; Judges xv. So the Lacedæmonians made war upon the Messenians because they did not give up a man who had killed Lacedæmonians: and, at another time, because those were not given up who had done violence to virgins sent to perform a sacred office. So Cato advised that Cesar should be given up to the Germans, for wrongfully making war upon them. So the Gauls demanded that the Fabii should be given up to them, because they had fought against them. The Romans required those who had plundered their land to be given up to them by the Hernici; and Amilcar, by the Carthaginians, not the celebrated general, but another, who stimulated the Gauls: they afterwards demanded Annibal; and Jugurtha from Bocchus, that, as Sallust puts it, *you may relieve us from the painful necessity of punishing at the same time, you who are in error, and him who is most criminal.* The Romans themselves gave up those who had done violence to the ambassadors of the Carthaginians; and again, of the Apolloniates. The Achæans required the Lacedæmonians to give up those who had attacked the town of Las, adding, that if they did not do so, the league was violated. So the Athenians proclaimed by a herald, that if any one practised secretly against Philip, and then fled to Athens, he would be liable to be given up. The Beotians required of the Hippotians that those who had slain Phocus should be given up.

3 All which passages, however, are so to be understood that the people or the king are not strictly bound to give up the person, but, as we have said, to punish him. For thus we read that the Eleans made war on the Lacedæmonians, because they had not punished those who had done injury to the Eleans; that is, they neither punished them nor gave them up. It is a disjunctive obligation.

4 Sometimes the option is given to those who demand the guilty, that the satisfaction may be more complete. The Cærians, in Livy, signify to the Romans that the Tarquinians passing through their land with a small force, though they had asked for nothing but a passage, had drawn along with them some of the country people to join them in the marauding practices of which they were accused: that if it were wished that they should be given up, they were ready to give them up; if it were wished that they should be punished, they were ready to punish them.

5 In the second league of the Carthaginians and Romans, which is extant in Polybius, there is this passage (if rightly read): *If not, let each pursue his own right by private proceedings: if this does not succeed, let it be considered a public delict.* Eschines, in his answer to the accusation of Demosthenes respecting his embassy to Philip, relates that when they discoursed with Philip on the peace of Greece, he said, among other things, that it was just that the punishment of the crimes which were committed should fall, not on the cities, but on

the offenders: and that the cities who should bring to judgment the persons accused, ought not to be harmed. (Quintilian says, *Those are next door to deserters who harbour deserters* *.*)

6 Among the evils which arise from the discords of states, Dio Chrysostom puts this: *It is possible that those who have injured one city, to fly to another.*

7 There occurs the question, of persons given up, if they are given up by one state, and not accepted by the other, do they remain citizens?

P. M. Scævola held that they did not: since when the people had given up a person, it was as if they had expelled him from the city, as if they had interdicted him from fire and water. Brutus, and after him Cicero, defend the opposite opinion. And this is the sounder opinion; not, however, properly for the reason which Cicero gives, that a surrender, like a donation, cannot be understood without acceptance. For the act of donation is not complete without the consent of two: but the giving up or surrender of which we have spoken is nothing more than leaving a citizen of ours to the power of another people, so that they may determine about him what they will. But this permission does not give or take away any right: it may take away an impediment to the execution of punishment. Therefore if the other people do not use the right which is conceded to it, the person so surrendered will be in a condition to be punished by his own nation, (as happened in the case of Clodius, surrendered to the Corsicans and not accepted by them;) or he may not be punished, as there are many delicts in which the one or the other may take place. And the rights of a citizen, like many other rights and possessions, are not lost by a mere fact, but by some decree or sentence; except there be some law which directs the fact to be considered as a judicial act, which cannot be said in this case. And in the same way, if goods are surrendered but not accepted, they remain whose they were. But if the surrender of a person is accepted, and afterwards he who had been surrendered happens to return, he is no longer a citizen, except by some new concession of citizenship to him: and in this sense the opinion which Modestinus gave respecting a person surrendered, is true.

8 What we have said of surrendering or punishing criminals, applies not only to those who have always been the subjects of him under whose rule they are now found; but also to those, who, after committing a crime, have fled to any place.

V. 1 Nor is this doctrine impeached by the rights of suppliants, and the cases of asylum, which are so much spoken of. These arrangements are for the advantage of those who are persecuted without deserving to be so; not of those who have committed what is injurious to human society or to other men. So Gylippus says of this right of suppliants. [See.] Menander very properly distinguishes

---

* This passage is not quite to the purpose. W.

misdeed from misfortune; the former, he says, happens by will, the latter by chance. So Demosthenes, and Cicero after him, say that *the proper objects of pity are those who are in distress through fortune, not through malice.* And so that of Antiphon*, and that of Lysias. [See.] So in the Hebrew law, he who had killed a man by chance, might take to the city of refuge: but they who had deliberately killed an innocent man, or disturbed the state of the city, were not to be protected, even by the altar of God. So Philo. And the more ancient Greeks had the same rule. The Chalcidians would not give up Nauplius to the Achaians; but the cause is added, because he had sufficiently cleared himself from the accusations of the Achaians.

2 There was at Athens an Altar of Mercy, mentioned by Cicero†, Pausanias, Servius, Theophilus, and described at length by Statius in his *Thebaid.* But to whom was it accessible? The poet says, *The miserable made it sacred:* and adds, that *those who came together there, were those conquered in war, those driven from their country, those who had no state to which they belonged.* So Aristides, in praise of the Athenians, says that Athens was the refuge for the wretched. In Xenophon, Patrocles the Phliarian says the same. So Demosthenes; and Sophocles in the *Œdipus Coloneus;* and Demophon, [rather the Chorus, in Euripid. *Heracleid.* v. 330, &c. J.B.] And this is the point for which Callisthenes especially praised the Athenians.

3 On the other hand, in the same tragedy‡, one of the characters says that he knows no piety which withholds him from dragging guilty men from the altar to the tribunal. And the same author, in the *Ion,* says, that guilty men should not go to the gods for refuge, but that the temples should be open to the pious to protect them from injury. Lycurgus the orator relates that a certain Callistratus, who had committed a capital offense, having consulted the oracle, received for answer that if he went to Athens, *he would have the benefit of the law:* that accordingly, he took refuge at the most sacred altar at Athens, depending upon impunity; but that he was nevertheless put to death by the city, strictly careful of its religious observances; and thus the oracle was fulfilled. Tacitus blames the custom which was in his time prevalent, of protecting, in the Greek cities, the crimes of men as the ceremonies of the gods. The same writer says, that *Princes are indeed like gods; but that even the gods hear only the just prayers of suppliants.*

4 Such persons, therefore, are either to be punished, or surrendered, or at least, removed. So the Cymeans, not being willing either to give up Pactyas the Persian, or to retain him, allowed him to go to Mitylene. Demetrius of Pharos, who, when defeated, had fled to

* *Orat.* xiv. xv. p. 134. Ed. Wech. not Antiphanes. J. B.

† Quoted by the Scholiast on Statius, *Theb.* xii. 481, where he refers it to the Tusculans: but in that work there is nothing about such an altar. J.B.

‡ Not the same, but an uncertain tragedy of Euripides in Stobæus: *Germ.* xiv. Tit. 46. J. B.

Philip, king of Macedon, the Romans demanded from the king. Perseus, king of Macedon, in defending himself to Martius, and speaking of those who were said to have laid wait for Eumenes, said that he had commanded them to depart from his kingdom, and never to return. The Samothracians denounced to Evander, who had practised secretly against Eumenes, the necessity of freeing their temples from pollution.

5 But this right of demanding, for the sake of punishing, those who have fled out of the territory, is, in this and the last preceding ages, in most parts of Europe, used only with regard to those crimes which affect the public good, or have some peculiar features of atrocity. It has become the custom to overlook on both sides smaller offenses, except there be a treaty with some especial provisions on this subject. It is to be remarked, however, that robbers and pirates who have made themselves strong and formidable, may be received and defended [on condition of desisting from their evil practices, G.] so far as punishment goes; because it is the interest of the human race, that if they cannot be reformed in any other way, they may be so by the assurance of impunity for the past; and any people or any ruler may negotiate such a matter.

VI. 1 It is to be remarked that it sometimes happens that suppliants are defended [provisorily], till their case can be fairly judged. So Demophon says to the messenger of Eurystheus, that if he has any charge against the refugees, he will obtain justice, but that till then, they will not be given up. And in another tragedy [the *Œdipus Coloneus* of Sophocles, v. 904]. Theseus says to Creon that it is against the practice of Athens to give up refugees. Your attempt, he says, is an act unworthy of Thebes and of you*.

2 And then, if that of which the refugees are accused is not a matter against the law of nature or of nations, it must be judged by the civil law of the people from whom they come; as Æschylus assumes in his *Suppliants*, where Danaus addresses the persons who came from Egypt to that effect.

VII. 1 We have seen how the fault passes to the rulers from the subjects, either ancient or recently acquired; in like manner the fault will pass from the rulers to the subjects, if these have consented to the crime, or if they have done anything by the command or the suasion of their superiors, which they could not do without guilt: on which point it will be more correct to treat hereafter, when we have to speak of the duties of subjects. There is even a participation of punishment by communication between the general body and individuals; for, as Augustine says, *The general body consists of individuals,* &c.

2 But the fault lies at the door of the individuals who have consented to the act, not of those who were outvoted by the others. For the punishments of individuals and of the general body are different.

* In the Greek, ἐμοῦ, but Grotius translates it *te*, both here and in his extracts from the Greek Tragedies and Comedies. J. B.

S

As the punishment of individuals is sometimes death, so it is the punishment of a city to be destroyed, which is done when the civil body is dissolved; of which case we have spoken elsewhere.   And if a city or state cease to exist in this manner, Modestinus rightly said, that the life-interest which any persons have in it ceases.   Individuals are reduced to slavery in the way of punishment, as the Thebans under Alexander of Macedon: excepting those who had voted against the proposal of making the alliance [with the Macedonians, G.]   So also a city or state undergoes civil slavery, by being reduced into the condition of a province.   Individuals lose their goods by confiscation. But [in punishing a city] the things which are taken from the city are the public property; as walls, arsenals, fleets, arms, elephants, its treasury, and its public lands.

3 But that individuals should lose what is their own property, on account of a delict of the general body, committed without their consent, is unjust: as Libanius rightly shews on the sedition of Antioch. The same writer approves an act of Theodosius, who punished a public offense by interdicting the theatre, the public baths, and the title of *metropolis*.

VIII. 1 This important question occurs, whether punishment may always be exacted for the delicts of the general body.   So long as the constitution of the body continues, it would seem that it can, because the same body remains, though preserved by a succession of different particles, as we have elsewhere shewn.   But, on the contrary side, it is to be observed that some things are asserted of the body primarily and *per se*, as to have a treasury, laws, and the like; others only derivatively from its members.   Thus we call a body learned and brave, which has many learned and brave members.   And desert [of punishment, G.] is of this kind; for, in the first place, it belongs to individuals, as having a spirit and intelligence which the body by itself has not.   Therefore if these persons be extinct, from whom desert was deduced and carried to the account of the body, the desert is extinct, and also the desert of punishment; which, as we have said, cannot exist without desert.   So Libanius says: *It must suffice you as to punishment, that no one is left of those who offended.*

2 We must therefore approve the opinion of Arrian, when he condemns* the revenge of Alexander upon the Persians, since those who had wronged the Greeks were long ago dead.   Concerning the destruction of the Branchidæ by the same Alexander, the judgment of Curtius is similar, *that it was not justice, but cruelty, to punish those who could not betray Xerxes, and had never seen Miletus.*   And of the same kind is the judgment of Arrian respecting the burning of Persepolis, that there was no true punishment in it, since the offending Persians had long ceased to be.

* Arrian, Lib. ii. c. 14, does not condemn this plea of Alexander: the author was thinking of Arrian's judgment on the burning of Persepolis, which occurs immediately after in the text, but was not mentioned in the first edition. J.B.

3 Every one sees the absurdity of Agathocles' answer to the complaints of the Ithacans, of damage done by the Sicilians; that the Sicilians had received more damage from Ulysses. And Plutarch, in his book against Herodotus, says, that it is very unlikely that the Corinthians should have wished to avenge an injury received from the Samians after three generations. Nor is the defense of such cases satisfactory, which we find in Plutarch *On the delayed punishments of the gods*. For the justice administered by God is one thing, that by men, another, as we shall shew hereafter. Nor again can we argue that, because descendants receive honours and rewards for the merit of their ancestors, therefore it is just that they should be punished for their crimes. For benefits are of such nature, by their matter, that they may be bestowed upon any without injury, but punishments are not.

IX. We have spoken of the ways in which a participation in the punishment takes place in consequence of a participation in the crime. It remains that we consider whether, when there is not a participation in the offense, there may be in the punishment; and here, that we may not be misled by the similarity of words when the things are different, we must make a few remarks.

X. 1 First, that a damage directly caused is one thing, and a damage caused by consequence, another. I call that a damage directly caused, by which any one is deprived of a proper right which he has; a damage by consequence, that by which any one has not that which he would have had: namely, by the cessation of the condition, without which his right cannot subsist. We have an example in Ulpian: If in my ground I have opened a well, by which the springs which would have come to you are cut off: he denies that, by the effect of my operations, a wrongful damage is done to you, since I was using my own right in my own property. And in another place, he says it makes a great difference, whether any one suffer a loss, or be prevented in a gain which he was going on to enjoy. And so Paulus says, that it is preposterous that we should be supposed to have possessions before we have acquired them.

2 So when the goods of the parents are confiscated, the children feel the loss; but that is not properly a punishment, because those goods were not to become theirs, except their parents kept possession of them till their last breath. Which is rightly noted by Alphenus, when he says that by the punishment of the parent, the children lose that which from him would have come to them; but that which was given them by the nature of things, or from any other source, they do not lose. So Cicero says, that the children of Themistocles were in absolute want, and he does not think it unjust that the children of Lepidus should bear the same lot. And this, he says, was the ancient custom, and common to all cities; though this custom was much limited and tempered by the later laws of Rome. So when by the delict of the general body, which, as we have said, stands for the whole body, the whole body is in fault, and on that ground loses, as we have

said, civil liberty, city walls, and other advantages, innocent individuals also feel the inconveniences; but they feel it in those things which only belonged to them through the general body.

XI. 1 It is further to be remarked, that sometimes a person has harm imposed upon him, or loses good, by the occasion indeed of another's fault, yet not so that the fault is the proximate cause of the action, so far as pertains to the right of acting. Thus he who has promised something on occasion of another's debt, suffers damage, as the old proverb says, *Suretyship is next door to mischief;* but the proximate cause of the obligation is his promise. For as he who is surety for a buyer, is not properly bound by the sale, but by his promise; so he who is bound for a delinquent, is not bound by the delict, but by his own engagement. And hence the loss which he has to bear is measured, not by the other's delict, but by the power which he had in promising.

2 From which it follows, that according to the opinion which we hold for the sounder, no body can be put to death in virtue of suretyship; because we hold that no one has such right over his own life, that he can himself take it from himself, or bind himself to have it taken: though the ancient Romans and Greeks thought otherwise on this point: and therefore held sureties to be bound to undergo capital punishment for their principal, as it is in the verse of Ausonius: [*Who takes death as a substitute for another? The Surety. Quis subit in pœnam capitali judicio? Vas.* Gronov.], and as appears in the well known story of Damon and Pythias*: and hostages have often been put to death, as we have elsewhere stated. What we have said of life, may also be said of limb: for man has no right to sacrifice that, except for the sake of preserving the whole body.

3 But if the promise included the expatriation of the promiser, or the payment of a sum of money, and the condition be not fulfilled by the fault of another, the person who gives such security must bear the loss; which, however, properly speaking, is not a punishment. Something similar occurs in any right which a person has in such a way that it depends on the will of another; such as a right granted to be held during the pleasure of the grantor, and even the right of private property, which is liable to be interfered with by the *dominium eminens*, which the state has for public purposes. If any thing of this kind is taken away from any one on account of the fault of another, it is not properly a punishment, but the execution of a pre-existing right, which was in the hands of him who takes the precarious right away. And inasmuch as brutes are not capable of punishment, when a beast is put to death, as in the case provided for in the law of Moses, this is not really punishment, but the exercise of human dominion over the beast.

XII. Having premised these distinctions, we say that no one innocent of delict can be punished for the delict of another. But the

* The right name is Phintias, Cic. *Off.* iii. 10. *Gronov.*

true reason of this, is not that which is given by Paulus, that punishment is instituted for the amendment of men: for it would seem that an example may be made even extraneously to a man's own person, in a person whose welfare affects him, as we shall soon have to shew: but because liability to punishment arises from desert: and desert is a personal quality, since it must have its origin in the will, than which nothing is more peculiarly ours: it is, as we may say, *self-causing.*

XIII.   1 *Neither the virtues nor the vices of parents,* says Jerome, *are imputed to the children:* and Augustine, *God would be unjust if he condemned an innocent person.*   Dio Chrysostom says of the law of God, speaking on the occasion of Solon's law, by which the children were stigmatised; *this law does not, like that, punish the children of criminals; in this, every one is his own cause of suffering.*   And hence the rule, *Noxa caput sequitur, Punishment is personal.*   So the Christian Emperors direct.

2 It is just, says Philo, that those should have the penalty who had the sin: reprehending the manner of some nations which punished with death the children of traitors or tyrants.   The same custom is blamed* also by Dionysius, who shews that the reason sometimes given is fallacious, that the children will probably be like their parents; since that is uncertain, and an uncertain fear ought not to cause any one's death.   Some Christian did venture to advise the emperor Arcadius, that those ought to suffer the same punishment as their parents, in whom the repetition of their parents' crime was feared: and Ammianus relates that a family was put to death, even at an early age, *that they might not grow up to be like their parents.*   Nor is fear of revenge a more just cause of such proceeding, notwithstanding the Greek proverb, *Who kills the sire and spares the son is mad.*

3 Seneca on the other hand says, Nothing is more unjust than to make a man the heir of his father's odium.   When Attagines was the means of the Thebans deserting to the Medes, Pausanias did not harm his children: *they had had nothing to do with Medizing,* he said.   M. Antoninus, in an epistle to the senate, wrote, *You will pardon the wife and the son-in-law of Avidius Cassius* (who had conspired against him). *But why do I say pardon, when they have committed no offense?*

XIV.   1 God indeed, in the law which he gave the Hebrews, threatens that he will visit the impiety of the fathers upon their posterity.   But God has the most plenary right of dominion, as over our goods, so over our lives, as his gift; which he may take away from any one, whenever he will, and without any cause.   If, therefore, he takes away, by an untimely and violent death, the children of Achan, Saul, Jeroboam, Ahab, he uses towards them his right of dominion, not of punishment; but by the act, he more grievously punishes the parents.   For if they outlive their children, which is the case that the divine law principally regards; (and therefore the law

* No, says Barbeyrac: Dionysius leaves the matter undecided.   See the place, Lib. VIII. c. 80.

does not extend its threatenings beyond great grandchildren, Exod. xx. 5: because the common age of man allows him to see them;) it is certain that then they are punished by such a spectacle; for that is more grievous to them than what they themselves suffer, as Chrysostom says; or if they do not live so long, still, to die with such a fear hanging over them, is a great punishment. *The people's hardness of heart,* as Tertullian says, *led to such remedies, that they might obey the divine law, even out of regard for their posterity.*

2 But it is to be noted, at the same time, that God does not make use of this heavier kind of punishment, except towards offenses especially tending to his dishonour, as false worship, perjury, sacrilege. Nor did the Greeks judge otherwise; for the crimes which were supposed to entail a curse on posterity, are all of this kind; as Plutarch learnedly shews in his book On the procrastinated anger of the gods. In Elian, we have an oracle which says that the guilty cannot escape, but that vengeance follows them and their posterity. But there, sacrilege was in question, as is proved by the history of the Tholosan gold. We have above adduced similar opinions concerning perjury. Moreover, though God has threatened this, he does not always use his power, especially if the children turn out eminently virtuous; as see Ezek. xviii., and as Plutarch proves by examples.

3 And since, in the New Testament, the punishments are declared more clearly than before, which await the wicked after this life; therefore in that law there is no threatening of punishment which goes beyond the persons of the offenders: to which especially, though less openly, as the manner of the prophets is, that prophecy of Ezekiel looks. But this fact on the part of God is not to be imitated by men; nor is the reason alike: because, as we have said, God has a right over men's lives without regarding their faults: but men have such a right only on the ground of a graver fault, and one which belongs especially to the person.

4 Wherefore the same divine law, as it forbids parents to be capitally punished for their children, so does it forbid children to be so punished for their parents. And this law pious kings have observed, even with regard to their open enemies; and the rule is greatly praised by Josephus and Philo, as also a similar law of Egypt by Isocrates, and one of Rome by Dionysius*. And it is one of Plato's Laws, that the ignominy and punishment of the father are not to fall upon the children. So Callistratus the Jurist, adding the reason, that a man does not succeed to the crimes of another. *Would any city,* asks Cicero, *have a law condemning the son or grandson for the delinquencies of the father or grandfather?* Hence to put to death a pregnant woman was held inadmissible by the laws of the Egyptians, Greeks, and Romans.

XV. But if those human laws are unjust which put to death children for the offenses of their fathers, still more unjust was the law of

* See Barbeyrac's corrections of these references.

the Medes and Persians, which devoted to destruction the lives of the relatives of the criminal, in order that death might be more bitter to those who had offended against the king, as Curtius speaks; a law which surpasses all others in cruelty, as Ammianus Marcellinus says.

XVI. This, however, is to be noted, that if the children of enemies have anything which is not their own, but of which the right belongs to the people or the king, that may be taken from them by the right of dominion, the exercise of that right operating collaterally to the punishment of the criminal. To this we may refer the case of the children of Antiphon, who, as the children of a traitor, were excluded from honours; as at Rome were the children of those proscribed by Sulla. So in the law of Arcadius, that rule concerning children is not intolerable: *Let them be admitted to no honours nor public offices.* How far slavery may pass to children without wrong, we have treated elsewhere.

XVII. 1 What we have said of evil inflicted upon children for the delicts of fathers, may be applied also to a people really subject to their ruler: (for he who is not subject may be punished for his own fault, as we have said, that is, for neglecting to control the offender:) if it be asked whether such a people may be eviltreated on account of the crimes of the ruler or king. We do not now inquire if the People's consent has been obtained, or if they have done anything which is by itself worthy of punishment; but we inquire concerning the connexion which naturally arises between that body of which the king is the head, and of which others are the members. God, on account of the sin of David, wasted the people with a pestilence; the people being innocent, as David judged: but God had a plenary right over their lives.

2 In the mean time, this was not the punishment of the people, but of David; for as a Christian writer says; *The sharpest punishment of offending kings is the punishment of their people.* It is, as the same writer says, as if one who has sinned with his hand were to be punished with strokes on his back: as Plutarch says, it is no otherwise than when a physician cauterizes the thumb to cure the hip. Why men may not lawfully do the same, we have already said.

XVIII. The same may be said of the evil inflicted through their property, or the like, upon individuals who have not consented to the crime, on account of the delict of the general body.

XIX. If we ask why, since the heir is bound to the other debts of the deceased, he is not bound to his punishment, as Paulus says the commentators* have decided, this is the true cause; that the heir

---

* *Commentitio jure*] Difficile satis est definire, quid intelligat Paullus, dum illud *jus commentitium* vocat. Vide A. Fabrum, *Jurispr. Papinian. Tit.* I. *Princip.* II. Illat. 5. Marc. Lycklamam, *Membran.* I. 9. Jac. Gothofred. in *L.* 1. *De Regg. Jur.* pag. 5. Cl. Schulting. *Jurisprud. Ante-Justin.* pag. 675. col. 1. init. Expendi etiam potest nova interpretatio, quæ legitur in *Actis Eruditorum Lipsiensibus*, ann. 1714. pag. 555. ubi vult Auctor Clar. Wæchtlerus, jus *commentitium* esse, quod ex notione quadam communi oritur. *J. B.*

represents the person of the deceased, not in his deserts, which are matters merely personal, but in his possessions; and with them are inseparably connected his debts; and accordingly this rule came in as soon as ownership came in. So Dio Prusæensis.

XX. And hence it follows that if, besides desert, some new cause of obligation should arise, that which was a part of the punishment may become debt, though not as a punishment of the heir. Thus, after the sentence of a court, or after the decision of a lawsuit, to which events the power of a contract is given, the pecuniary penalty will be due from the heir, as also matters which were agreed to be so decided. For these events are a new cause of a debt being due.

CHAPTER XXII.

Of Unjust Causes of War.

I. 1 WE have said above, when we began to treat of the causes of war, that some are justificatory or justifying, some suasory or impelling. Polybius, who first noted this difference, calls the former *pretexts*, the latter, *causes;* Livy sometimes calls the former *titulus* *.

2 Thus in the war of Alexander against Darius, the *pretext* was revenge for the injuries which the Persians had done to the Greeks; the *cause* was the desire of glory, empire, wealth, added to a great hope of the facility of the conquest, proved from the expeditions of Xenophon and Agesilaus. So the *pretext* of the second Punic war was the controversy concerning Saguntum, the *cause* was the indignation of the Carthaginians excited by the terms which the Romans had imposed upon them in their evil times, and their courage exalted by their successes in Spain; as Polybius notes. In the same way Thucydides judges that the true cause of the Peloponnesian war was the strength of the Athenians, increasing and drawing the suspicion of the Lacedæmonians; the pretext, the controversy of the Corcyreans, of the Potideans, and others things: where however he uses the terms *pretext* and *cause* (πρόφασις and αἰτία) indiscriminately. [See Lib. v. c. 53. Gron.] The same distinction occurs in the oration of the Campanians to the Romans, when they say that they fought against the Samnites, nominally for the Sidicini, really, for themselves; because they saw that when the Sidicini were consumed, the conflagration would spread to them. So Livy says that Antiochus made war upon the Romans, having, as a pretence, the death of Barcillas, and other matters, but really, because he had conceived great hope from the relaxed discipline of the Romans. So Plutarch notes that it was not truly objected to Antony by Cicero that he was

* For example, Lib. xxxvii. c. 54. num. 13. J. B.

the cause of the civil war; since Cæsar was already resolved upon war, and only took his pretext from Antony.

II.   Some there are who rush into war not actuated by either of these kinds of cause, being, as Tacitus says, greedy of danger for its own sake*.   These men are of a temper which does not lie within the proper limits of humanity, of a ferine nature.   So Seneca, *On Clemency*, says, it is not mere cruelty but a ferine disposition, which delights in human blood and butchery.   So Aristotle says that that is a sanguinary character, which makes a man break with his friends for the sake of fighting and shedding blood; and Dio Prusæensis says it is mere madness.   So Seneca, Epist. xiv.

III.   1 However, most parties, when they go to war, have impelling causes, either with or without justifying causes.   There are some who frankly do not trouble themselves about justificatory causes; to whom we may apply the maxim of the Roman jurists, that he who, when he is asked by what claim he possesses a thing, can assign no other than that he does possess it, is a robber.   Aristotle speaks of those who give no care to the question whether it is just to enslave unoffending neighbours.

2 Such a man was Brennus, who said that everything belonged to the stronger: such is Annibal in Silius, whose *sword is the measure of right and justice:* such Attila; and those who say, as in Seneca, *Our thought the fortune not the cause of war;* or as in Lucan, *This day will make the conquered part the guilty;* or as in Tacitus, that *In the highest fortune what is strongest is most just.*   Yet as Augustine says, *To make war on unoffending neighbours and to harass and subjugate them out of mere love of honour, what name does it deserve, except that of a huge robbery?*   Of such wars, Velleius says they are wars *not entered into for justice, but for gain.*   So Cicero says that *Courage without justice not only is not a part of virtue, but is an inhuman extravagance.*   And Andronicus Rhodius speaks to the same effect.

IV.   Other parties, in going to war, allege justificatory causes, which, when brought to the standard of right reason, turn out unjust; and then it appears, as Livy says, that what is aimed at is, not a trial of right, but of strength.   Most kings, says Plutarch, use the two names, *peace* and *war,* only as coins, to procure, not what is just, but what is expedient.   What are unjust causes, may be known in some measure from the just causes which we have been explaining: the straight line is the index of what is oblique.   But for the sake of perspicuity we shall make some general remarks.

V.   1 That fear from a neighbouring power is not a sufficient cause, we have said above.   For, that defense may be just, it must be necessary; and it cannot be this, except there be clear evidence,

---

* As Barbeyrac shews, Grotius has put together two phrases of Tacitus: *Periculorum avidi, Hist.* III. 41, and v. 19; and *Non tam præmiis periculorum, quam ipsis periculis lætus, Hist.* II. 86.

not only of the power, but of the *animus* of the party; and such evidence as amounts to moral certainty.

2 Hence we can by no means approve the opinion of those who hold it to be a just cause of war, if a neighbour, being prevented therefrom by no pact, establish a fortress on his own ground, or any other munition of war, which may possibly at some time be mischievous to us. For the proper remedies against such fears are opposing munitions, and the like, not force of arms. Therefore unjust were the wars of the Romans against Philip of Macedon, and of Lysimachus against Demetrius, except there were some other reason. I am much pleased with what Tacitus says of the Chauci: *The most noble people among the Germans, and a people that prefers to secure its greatness by its justice; not greedy, not passionate, but quiet and retired. They provoke no wars, they practise no robbery or plunder of their neighbours; and the great proof of their virtue and their strength is, that it is not by wrong-doing that they preserve their superiority. Yet they can promptly use arms, and if need be, raise armies: they are numerous in infantry and cavalry, and retain their reputation even in inaction.*

VI.   Nor does utility generate a right, in the way in which necessity does.

VII.   Thus when there is no want of opportunity of marriage, any marriage denied cannot supply a cause for war; though Hercules formerly took occasion to make war on Eurytus on such grounds, and Darius on the Scythians.

VIII.   Neither is the desire of migrating from one place to another a just ground of war; that a nation leaving marshes and deserts, may become possessed of a more fertile soil; which Tacitus mentions as the reason of making war among the old Germans.

IX.   It is no less unjust to claim lands on the ground of having discovered them, when they are occupied by another, even though the possessors be bad men, with wrong notions of God, and dull intellects. For those lands only can be discovered which belong to nobody.

X.   1 Nor is there required for ownership [to exclude such claim] either moral virtue, or religion, or perfection of intellect: except that this may, it would seem, be defended; that if there be any people altogether destitute of the use 'of reason, such may not have ownership, but out of charity those things ought to be given them only which are necessary to life. For what we have said above, concerning the sustentation of ownership, which the law of nations performs for infants, and persons out of their mind, pertains to those peoples with whom others have an intercourse of pacts; and if there be any people altogether irrational, they are not such: but I much doubt the fact.

2 Therefore it was unjust on the part of the Greeks to say, that the Barbarians were their natural enemies, merely on account of the diversity of manners, or because they seemed to be inferior in intel-

lect. How far dominion may be taken away from a people on account of grave offenses, impugning nature or human society, is another question, and must soon be treated by us, when we speak of the right of punishing.

XI. Nor again can we say of the liberty, either of individuals, or of cities, or states, (that is, *autonomy* or self-government,) that it is either by natural law, and at all times, an attribute of all, or that in the cases in which it is, it furnishes just ground for war. For when we say that liberty by nature belongs to men or to peoples, we are to understand that, of a natural right preceding all human pacts; and of liberty by negation of slavery, not of liberty in opposition to slavery; so that man is not a slave by nature, but he is not by nature a creature that cannot be a slave. For in this latter sense, no one is free. And to this view pertains what is said by Albutius, that *No one is born free, and no one is born a slave;* these names came afterwards to belong to men by their fortune. So Aristotle says, that it is a result of law that one man is free, another a slave. Therefore they who have, by a legitimate course, come into slavery, either personal or civil, ought to be content with their condition; as St Paul teaches, *Art thou called being a servant? Care not for it.* 1 Cor. vii. 21.

XII. Nor is it less unjust to wish to subjugate any by arms, as being worthy to be slaves, or as philosophers sometimes speak, naturally slaves. For even if there be anything which is fit for me, it does not follow that any one has a right to impose it on me by force. For those who have the use of reason, ought to have a free election left them of what is useful to them and what is not, except another have a right over them. The case is plainly different with infants, the government of whom, since they themselves have not the right of independent action and self-direction, nature gives to those who have a claim to it, and can exercise it.

XIII. 1 It would hardly be necessary to notice that the title given by some to the Roman Emperor is absurd, as if he had the right of ruling over the most remote and hitherto unknown peoples; except Bartolus, who was long held the prince of jurists, had ventured to pronounce every one a heretic who denies it; namely, because he sometimes calls himself the Lord of the World; and also, because in scripture, the empire is called the empire of the whole inhabited earth, an *œcumenical* empire, according to the Greek word; *Romania* in some later writers. And so Petronius speaks of the victor Roman having *orbem totum,* the whole globe. And many the like things are said, when we use comprehensive, or excessive, or emphatic expressions: as when in the same scripture, Judæa is called *the inhabited earth:* in which sense we are to understand the saying of the old Jews, that Jerusalem is in the middle of the earth, that is, in the midst of Judæa; as Delphi was called the navel of the world. Nor should any one be moved by the argument of Dante, in which he tries to prove that such a right belongs to the emperor, because it is for the advantage of the human race. For the advantages which he adduces are outbalanced by disadvantages. For as a ship may be so large that it cannot be steered, so the number of subjects and the distance of places may be so great that they cannot subsist under one government.

2 But even if we grant that such a government is expedient, there does not follow any right of empire, for that can arise only from consent or from punishment. The Roman emperor has not now any right over even all those places which were formerly under the Roman people; for many of these, as they were won by war, so have they been lost by war; some have passed by compacts, and some by dereliction, under the authority of other nations or kings. Again, some cities, formerly entirely subject, have since become subject in part only, or have become merely federate parts of the empire. For all these ways either of losing, or of changing the rights of rulers, are valid against the Roman Emperor, as against any other party.

XIV. 1 There have also been persons who have asserted the right of the Church, even over the peoples who occupy the hitherto unknown parts of the earth. And yet St Paul plainly says, that he does not judge those who are outside the boundary of Christianity. *What have I to do to judge them that are without?* 1 Cor. v. 12. And the right of judging which pertained to the Apostles, though in its own way it pertained to the things of earth, yet was, as I may say, of a heavenly not of an earthly character; it was to be exercised, not by arms or by scourges, but by the word of God generally set forth, and adapted to peculiar circumstances; by the exhibition or denial of the seals of divine grace [communion and excommunication, G.] according to each one's case: and in short, by a mode of punishment not natural, but super-natural, and proceeding from God; as appeared in the cases of Ananias, Elymas, Hymenæus, and others.

2 Christ himself, from whom all Ecclesiastical power flowed, and whose life is proposed as the pattern of the Church, so far as it is the Church of Christ, said that his kingdom was not of this world; that is, of the same nature as other kingdoms; adding, that if it had been, it would, like other kingdoms, have been defended by its fighting men. But no: if he had asked for legions, they would have been legions of angels. And what he did on the part of his authority, he did, not by human, but by divine agency, even when he drove the money-changers out of the temple. For the scourge which he then used was a sign, not an instrument, of divine wrath; as in other cases, the oil and the spittle was not the remedy, but the sign of cure. And to this purpose Augustine speaks on that passage of St John.

3 A bishop is required by St Paul, among other things, not to be a striker. So Chrysostom says, that to rule by force, that is human force, belongs to kings, not to bishops. And elsewhere, such power is not given to us that we can constrain men from offending by the

authority of our judgments, (such, that is,) as include a right of execution of the judgment by the hands of kings, or soldiers, or by the deprival of any human right: and he says also, that a bishop discharges his office, *not by coercing, but by persuading*: From this it appears sufficiently, that bishops, as such, have no right of ruling men in a human manner.   So Jerome, comparing a king and a bishop, says, that *the king rules unwilling subjects, the bishop, willing ones.*

4 Whether Christian kings may make war on kings who reject Christianity, on that ground, as a punishment, we have sufficiently discussed above.

XV.   I will also give a warning not superfluous, but because, comparing old speculations with new, I foresee a great evil if it be not averted.   A just cause of war cannot be derived from any explanation of the divine prophecies.   For besides that unfulfilled prophecies can hardly be interpreted with certainty without the spirit of prophecy, even if the events are certain, we may be wrong as to the time.   And lastly, the prediction, except there be an absolute command of God, gives no right, since the events which are predicted by God are often brought to pass by wicked men or wicked actions.

XVI.   This also must be observed; that if any one has a claim upon him, which is not a claim of justice, but of some other virtue, as liberality, kindness, mercy, charity; as this claim cannot be prosecuted in a court of justice, so also it cannot be asserted by arms. For neither the one nor the other of these can be resorted to, in order that what is demanded may be done for a moral reason: it is requisite besides, that there be in us some right to that very thing: which right sometimes divine and human laws give with respect to the claims which rest upon other virtues [than justice]; and when this happens, then there is introduced a new reason of obligation, and the matter belongs to justice.   When that is wanting, the war is unjust for that reason: as was, for instance, the war of the Romans against the king of Cyprus, because he was ungrateful.   For he who has bestowed a benefit has no *right* to require a return: if he had, it would be a contract, not a benefit.

XVII.   1 We must remark also that this often happens; that there is a just cause really existing for the war, but that the putting it in action becomes vicious from the intention of the agent: either because something else, not in itself unlawful, incites him more than the right, as for instance, the desire of honour, or some advantage, public or private, which is expected from the war, distinct from the justificatory cause; or because there is introduced some affection plainly unlawful, as a pleasure in doing mischief to another without respect of good. So Aristides says that the Phoceans were deservedly destroyed; but that Philip was not in the right when he destroyed them, as not being really in earnest in defense of religion, but seeking to increase his empire.

2 *An eminent and ancient cause of war,* says Sallust, *is a deep-seated desire of empire and of wealth.* So Tacitus, *Gold and riches, a principal cause of war.* And so in Seneca's tragedy of the *Hippolytus.* And so Augustine.

3 But these causes, in which a justifying cause of the war is not wanting, do indeed imply a fault in him who makes the war; but yet the war itself is not thereby unjust: and, therefore, for such a war, no restitution is due.

CHAPTER XXIII.

Of Doubtful Causes of War.

I. WHAT Aristotle wrote is most true, that certainty is not to be found in morals as it is in mathematics: of which the reason is this, that mathematics separate the forms of things altogether from matter: and that the forms are of such a nature that there is nothing intermediate between two of them; as between a straight line and a curve there is no medium. But in moral matters, circumstances, even the least, often vary the matter; and the forms that are treated have often intermediate degrees, of such latitude that the case sometimes approaches nearer to the one extreme, sometimes to the other. Thus between that which ought to be done, and that which is entirely unlawful, there is a medium which is allowable, nearer sometimes to the one, and sometimes to the other: whence an ambiguity often takes place, like twilight between day and night, or cold water gradually heated. And this is what Aristotle says, that it is often difficult to decide which of two things is to be preferred: and so Andronicus Rhodius.

II. 1 In the first place, this is certain [as a point of morality], that if anything be just in itself, yet if it be done by him who, having deliberately weighed, thinks it unjust, the act is vicious: as St Paul says, that whatsoever is not of faith is sin; in which place *faith* signifies the judgment of the mind concerning the act. For God has given us the power of judging, as the guide of human actions; and if this be despised, the mind is brutified.

2 It often happens that the judgment does not pronounce a certain decision, but hesitates: and if this hesitation cannot be cleared off by an attentive consideration, Cicero's rule must be followed; those advise well who direct you not to do anything of which you doubt whether it is just or unjust: and so the Hebrew masters say, *Abstain from doubtful things.* But this does not apply in cases where we absolutely must do one of two things: in that case we must choose the part that seems least unjust. For in all cases in which the elec-

tion cannot be avoided, the less unjust assumes the character of good. The least of evils is to be chosen. So Aristotle, Cicero, Quintilian.

III. But in most cases, in dubious matters, the mind after some examination, does not remain undecided, but is drawn this way or that, by arguments derived from the subject, or by the opinion which it has of other men who deliver their sentiments on the subject. For what Hesiod says is true, that the best thing is to be wise one's self, the next best, to be guided by others. Arguments from the subject are taken from the causes, effects, and other adjuncts of it.

IV. 1 But to know them well, a certain practice and skill is necessary: and those who have not this, in order rightly to frame their active judgment, are bound to listen to the counsels of wise men. For the probable opinion, as Aristotle says, is that which is held by all, or by the greater part, or the most eminent. And this is the way of judging which kings mostly use, who have not leisure to peruse or to weigh the technical descriptions of such matters. *The king is wise by the multitude of wise counsellors*, as an old proverb says*. So Aristides. And so the ancient Romans undertook wars only after they had consulted the College of *Feciales*, instituted for that purpose, and the Christian Emperors rarely without consulting the bishops; that if there were any impediment which religion interposed, they might be warned thereof.

V. 1 It may happen, in many controversies, that probable arguments are adduced on both sides, either intrinsic to the subject, or derived from the authority of others. When that happens, if the things in question are of moderate importance, the choice, it would seem, is free from blame, on whichever side it falls. But if there is question of a matter of great moment, as of a capital punishment, then, on account of the great difference between the two sides of the choice, the safer part is to be preferred. It is better to acquit a guilty man than to condemn an innocent.

2 The writer of the Problems which go under the name of Aristotle's, says this: and adds the reason just given. So Antipho.

VI. War is a very weighty matter, being a thing from which great calamities fall upon the innocent. Therefore when opinions are balanced, peace must have the preference. So Silius Italicus praises Fabius.

But there are three ways in which controversies may be prevented from breaking out into war.

VII. 1 The first is, Conference. *There are two ways of settling disputed questions*, says Cicero; *one by discussion, the other by force: and the first being the character of man, the second of brutes, we are to have recourse to the latter, only if the former fails.* So Terence, Apollonius Rhodius, Euripides in several places; and Phæneas in Livy

---

* Quoted by Aulus Gellius, *Noct. Attic.* XIII. 18. J. B.

T

goes further; saying, *In order to avoid war we are to yield many things which cannot be gained by war.* And Mardonius in Herodotus blames the Greeks for not trying negociation before war, being of the same language.

2 Coriolanus in Dionysius says, *If a man asks only for his own, and betakes himself to war only when he cannot get that, all allow that it is just.* And in the same writer, Tullus says, that *what cannot be settled by discussion must be decided by arms.* So the Vologeses in Tacitus: and so king Theodoric.

VIII. 1 Another way is Compromise, or Arbitration, between parties who have no common judge. As Thucydides says, It is wicked to proceed against him as a wrong doer, who is ready to refer the question to an arbitrator. So Adrastus and Amphiaraus referred the question concerning the kingdom of Argos to the judgment of Eriphyle. So to decide the question concerning Salamis between the Athenians and the Megareans, five Lacedæmonian judges were chosen. So the Corcyreans signify to the Corinthians that they are ready to discuss their respective claims before the cities of Peloponnesus which they might agree to appoint. And Aristides praises Pericles, because to avoid war, he was willing to appoint arbiters. And so Æschines praises Philip for being willing to submit his controversies with the Athenians to any city equally just to both parties.

2 So the Ardeates and the Aretians in old time, and the Neapolitans and the Nolans later, referred their controversies to the decision of the Roman people. And the Samnites in controversy with the Romans appeal to common friends. So do the Carthaginians in their controversies with Masinissa to avoid war: and the Romans themselves concerning their controversy with the Samnites, refer to their common allies. Philip of Macedon in his controversy with the Greeks, says that he will take the judgment of Peoples who are at peace with both. At the request of the Parthians and Armenians, Pompey gave arbiters to settle their boundaries. Plutarch says that this was the main office of the Roman Feciales, not to allow recourse to be had to arms till all hope of a peaceable decision was gone. And Strabo says of the Druids of the Gauls, that formerly they were arbiters between hostile parties, and often made them part without fighting, who were drawn up in warlike array against each other. The same writer testifies that the priests in Iberia had the same office.

3 But especially are Christian kings and states bound to try this way of avoiding war. For if, in order to avoid being subject to the judgments of persons who were not of the true religion, certain arbiters were appointed both by the Jews and by the Christians, and the practice is commanded by Paul; how much more is this to be done, in order to avoid a much greater inconvenience, namely, war. So in one place Tertullian argues that a Christian must not go as a soldier, since he may not even go to law; which latter, however, as we have already shewn, is to be taken with a certain limitation.

4 And both for this reason and for others, it would be useful, and indeed it is almost necessary, that certain Congresses of Christian Powers should be held, in which the controversies which arise among some of them may be decided by others who are not interested; and in which measures may be taken to compel the parties to accept peace on equitable terms. This was the office of the Druids of old among the Gauls, as Diodorus and Strabo tell us: and we read that the Frankish kings left to their nobles the judgment of questions concerning the division of the kingdom.

IX. The third way is by Lot; which method is commended for this purpose by Dio Chrysostom, and much earlier by Solomon, Prov. xviii. 18. [*The lot causeth contentions to cease, and parteth between the mighty.*]

X. 1 Closely related to the practice of casting Lots, is the practice of Single Combat: of which the use does not appear to deserve altogether to be repudiated, if two persons whose controversies would otherwise involve two peoples in great evils are prepared to decide the question by arms, as formerly Hyllus and Echemus fought for Peloponnesus; Hyperochus and Phemius for the region on the Inachus; Pyræchma the Etolian and Degmenus the Epean for Elis; Corbis and Orsua for Ibas. For we may grant that if that be not done by the parties without blame on their part, yet that it may be accepted by the states in question as the lesser evil. So in Livy Metius says to Tullus, *Let us take a course by which we may decide without great bloodshed in each people which shall govern the other*. Strabo says that this was an ancient custom of the Greeks, and in Virgil, Eneas says it was right that the question between him and Turnus should be so decided.

2 Among the other customs of the Franks, this is especially the object of Agathias's praise. He says that if their kings have any quarrel, the armies on each side are assembled and brought face to face, and then the kings are told to fight the matter out between themselves, and the two armies lay down their arms and mix like friends.

XI. But though in a doubtful case, both parties are bound to seek for conditions of compromise by which war may be avoided, the party which makes a claim is more bound than the party which is in possession. For that in parity of case, possession is a presumption, to be accepted as favourable, is a matter which agrees not only with civil but with natural law: of which we have given the reason from the Problems ascribed to Aristotle, [cap. v. § 12.] And we may here add, that he who knows himself to have a good cause, but has not sufficient documents to convince the possessor of the injustice of his possession, cannot lawfully make war; because he has not the right of compelling the other to give up possession.

T 2

XII. But when the right is ambiguous, and neither is in possession, or each is equally so, then if one of the parties refuse to divide the matter in question, he is to be reckoned unjust.

XIII. 1 From what we have said, we may decide the question moved by many writers, whether a war, regarded in reference to those who are the principal movers of it, can be just on both sides. We must distinguish various acceptations of the word *just*. A thing is called just from its cause, or from its effect. And again, from its cause, either in the special acceptation of justice, or in that general acceptation in which all rectitude or rightness comes under that name. Again, the special acceptation is divided into that which belongs to the act itself, and that which belongs to the agent; of which the former may be called positive, the latter negative. For the agent is sometimes said to act justly, when he does not act unjustly, although what he does be not just; as Aristotle rightly distinguishes, *to act unjustly*, and *to do an unjust thing*.

2 In the special acceptance of justice, as bearing upon the thing itself, a war cannot be just on both sides, as a lawsuit cannot. Because a moral claim to two contrary things, to act and to prevent the action, by the nature of the subject, cannot exist. But it may be that neither of the belligerent parties act unjustly: for no one acts unjustly except he who knows that he is doing an unjust thing: and many persons do not know this when it is so. Thus persons may carry on a lawsuit justly, that is, *bona fide* on both sides. For many points both of law, and of the facts from which the law arise, escape the notice of the parties concerned.

3 In a general acceptation, that is called *just* which is free from all fault of the agent. Many things are done without right, or done without fault, on account of inevitable ignorance; of which we have an example in those who do not observe the law, being ignorant of it without any fault of theirs, though it has been promulgated, and a sufficent time for their becoming acquainted with it has elapsed. So in litigation it may happen that both parties are free not only from injustice, but from all other vices; especially when both parties, or at least one, litigates not on his own account, but on that of another; as for instance, in consequence of the office of guardian or trustee, whose business it is not to desert a right which is only doubtful. So Aristotle says that in a doubtful question of law, neither side is bad; and Quintilian, that there are cases in which a good man may speak as an advocate on either side. Aristotle says too, that there are two senses in which we may say the judge judges rightly; the one, in which he judges as he ought according to the case, not making allowance for ignorance; the other, in which he judges sincerely as he thinks. To do this, as he says in another place, is not to judge unjustly.

4 But in war it cannot easily happen that there is not, on one side

at least temerity and a lack of charity, the matter being so grave, that we ought not to be content with probabilities, but should require evident causes.

5 If we take *just* as to some legal effects, it is certain that in this sense a war may be just on both sides; as will appear by what we shall have to say hereafter of a penal public war. So a sentence of a judge, though given not according to law, and possession without right, have certain legal effects.

CHAPTER XXIV.

Warnings not to go to War rashly, even for just causes.

I. 1 ALTHOUGH it might seem that we who profess to write about the Rights of War, that is, its justice, have nothing to do with the consideration of what other virtues besides justice commend or recommend; yet we must try to obviate the error which would be committed if any one were to think that when the right was once established, it is forthwith either proper that war should be undertaken, or even that it is always lawful to undertake it. For on the contrary, it is mostly more right and more pious to give up one's rights. For as we have already said, we may even sacrifice our life in order to further, as much as is in us, the life and eternal salvation of another. And this is especially suitable to a Christian's character; who in doing this, imitates the perfect example of Christ, who was willing to die for us when we were yet ungodly and hostile. Which is a reason why we should not prosecute our rights or our dues to the inconvenience of others, to so great an extent as war occasions.

2 That war is not to be undertaken for every such cause, both Aristotle and Polybius teach us. Hercules is not praised[*] by the ancients for that he took away the arms of Laomedon and Augias, because they did not pay him for his labour. Dio Prusæensis says that the question is to be asked, not only whether an injury has been received from those with whom we think of going to war, but also at what amount it is to be estimated.

II. 1 To pass over offenses without punishment, is a course to which many reasons exhort us. See how many things parents overlook in children: on which Cicero in Dio Cassius treats; so Seneca; and Phineus in Diodorus; and Andronicus Rhodius.

2 Now whoever undertakes to punish another, assumes in a certain degree the character of a governor, that is, of a parent; as Augustine says to Count Marcellinus, *Christian judge, fulfil the office of a pious parent.* The Emperor Julian praises a speech of Pittacus; *who*

---

[*] But neither is he blamed, at least in the passage of Pausanias quoted. J. B.

prefers pardon to punishment. So Libanius says, that he who wishes to be like God, rejoices more in forgiveness than in punishing.

3 Sometimes the circumstances of the case are such, that to abstain from exercising one's right is not only laudable, but a duty; taking account of the kindness which we owe even to enemies, either considered in itself, or in the way in which the holy law of the Gospel requires it of us. And thus, we have said that there are some cases in which, even when we are attacked, we ought to prefer the salvation of the assailant, even to our own life, because we know him to be either necessary or extremely useful to the general interests of humanity. If Christ enjoins that some things are to be given up only to avoid strife, we must still more believe that he would have us give up greater things rather than go to war, since war is so much more hurtful than mere strife.

4 So Ambrose says, that *for a good man to relax somewhat of his rights, is not only a point of liberality, but often of convenience.* So Aristides persuades cities to pardon and concede, if it be any moderate matter; adding the reason, *that even in private persons this is laudable.* So Xenophon, and Apollonius in Philostratus.

III. 1 With regard to punishments, it is, in the first place, our duty, if not as men, at least as Christians, to forgive willingly and freely offenses against us, as God in Christ forgives our offenses. Eph. iv. 32. So Josephus.

2 So Seneca characterizes a prince, that he forgives his own injuries more easily than those of others; so Quintilian; and Cicero of Cæsar, that he forgot nothing but injuries. So Livia in her address to Augustus in Dio: Antoninus the philosopher: Ambrose to Theodosius; Themistius in praise of the same Theodosius.

3 Aristotle makes it a character of the magnanimous man, not to remember evil done to him; which Cicero copies. The Scripture gives us great examples of this virtue in Moses and David. [See.] This holds especially when we are ourselves conscious of some wrong; or when the wrong done us proceeds from some human and excusable infirmity; or when it is evident that he who has done the wrong is penitent. So Cicero, and Seneca. And so far, of the causes of abstaining from war, which arise from the kindness which we either owe to enemies, or rightly bestow upon them.

IV. 1 Often also it is a duty which we owe to ourselves, and those who depend upon us, not to recur to arms. Plutarch, in the life of Numa, says that when the Feciales had decided that war might be undertaken justly, he consulted the Senate whether it was advantageous to enter upon it. In one of Christ's parables, we are told that when a king, going to make war, finds that his forces are inferior to those of his enemy, he desires conditions of peace. Luke xiv. 31.

2 So the Tusculans, bearing everything and refusing nothing, obtained, by their merit, peace from the Romans. So Tacitus says of the Eduans, that a cause of war against them was sought in vain, for

they did more than was demanded of them. So queen Amalasuntha told the ambassadors of Justinian that she would not contend with him in arms.

3 There may be also a moderation exercised in such cases, as Strabo relates of Syrmus king of the Triballi, who forbad Alexander of Macedon to enter the island of Peuce, and at the same time sent presents to him; shewing that what he did was done from a reasonable fear of the consequences, not from dislike or contempt of him. What Euripides said of the Greek cities, you may apply to any other parties; that if men could foresee the evils which war produces to themselves, they would avoid such a course. So Livy, and Thucydides.

V. 1 Those who deliberate in such cases, deliberate partly concerning the ends, not the ultimate, but the intermediate ones, and partly, concerning the means which lead to the ends. The end is always some good, or at least the avoidance of evil, which may stand in the place of good. The means which lead to ends are not sought on their own account, but as they lead to the end. Therefore in our deliberations we must compare ends with one another, and the efficacy of the means to produce the end: as Aristotle says of the motions of animals.

There are three rules for such comparisons.

2 The first rule is, if the thing in question seems, in moral estimation, to have an efficacy both for good and for evil; it is to be chosen only if there is more of good in the good consequences than of evil in the evil. So Aristides and Andronicus Rhodius.

3 The second rule is, if the good and the evil which may proceed from the thing be equal; it is to be chosen if the efficacy be greater for the good than for the evil.

The third rule is, if the good and the evil be unequal, and the efficacy to the one and the other also unequal; the thing is to be chosen, if the efficacy to good compared with the efficacy to evil be greater than the evil is compared with the good; or if the good compared with the evil be greater than the efficacy of the means for evil compared with its efficacy for good.

4 We have stated this somewhat formally. Cicero comes to the same result by a plainer way, when he says, that we are to avoid incurring danger without cause, than which nothing can be more foolish; wherefore, in incurring dangers, we are to imitate the practice of physicians, who, when men have a slight disease, cure them by slight means; but in more grave diseases, are compelled to apply dangerous and doubtful remedies. Whence, he says, the wise man must watch the occasion, and the more so, if you gain more good by the plain way than you can avoid evil by the doubtful way.

5 So Cicero in an Epistle to Atticus, Dio Prusæensis, Aristides.

VI. 1 Let us take an example from a deliberation which, as Tacitus relates, was held among the cities of Gaul, *whether they would try for Liberty or for Peace:* where, by Liberty, we are to understand Civil Liberty, that is, the right of governing themselves : which right is plenary in a popular state, limited in an aristocracy, especially in one in which no one of the citizens is excluded from honours; and by Peace, we are to understand such a one as is the alternative of an internecine war, or as Cicero says, quoting Greek, where the question is about endangering the whole fortunes of the State; where nothing less than the destruction of the whole people is portended; as was the condition of Jerusalem besieged by Titus. In such a case, what Cato would have said, who chose to die rather than submit to the rule of one man, every one knows: as Lucan says in that case, *It is an easy exercise of virtue to escape slavery by our own hand;* and many other things in the same strain.

2 But right reason dictates another course; namely, that life, which is the foundation of all temporal and the occasion of eternal good, is of more value than liberty; whether you take the alternative in a single man or in a people. And so God himself speaks of it as a benefit, that he does not destroy men, but delivers them into slavery; 2 Chron. viii. 7, 8, [of the remnant of the Canaanites spared by Solomon.] And in another place he, by the Prophet, persuades the Jews to submit to servitude under the Babylonians, that they may not die of famine and pestilence, Jer. xxvii. 11. And therefore the act of the Saguntines [who destroyed themselves in their city rather than yield it], though praised by the ancients, is not to be praised by us; nor the courses which lead to it.

3 For the destruction of a people, in questions of this kind, is to be held as the greatest of evils. Cicero puts this as an example of necessity, that it was necessary for the Casilinenses to surrender to Annibal; although they had the alternative of perishing by hunger. We have this judgment of Diodorus, concerning the Thebans of the time of Alexander of Macedon, that they were more brave than prudent, in bringing destruction upon their country.

4 Concerning Cato, of whom we have spoken, and Scipio, who after the victory of Pharsalia would not yield to Cæsar, we have Plutarch's judgment, that they were to be blamed for having caused the destruction of many brave and excellent men in Egypt, for no valuable purpose.

5 What I have said of liberty, I would have understood also of other desirable objects, if the expectation of a greater opposite evil be more just, or be equal. As Aristides said, men are accustomed to save the ship by throwing overboard, not the passengers, but the cargo.

VII. Again, in exacting punishment, that is especially to be observed; that we are never on such ground to engage in war with one who is as strong as ourselves. For as a civil judge ought to be much more powerful than the criminal, so must he be who undertakes to punish crimes by arms. And not only does prudence and charity for those who are dependent upon us require us to abstain from a perilous war, but often justice also, that is, rectorial justice; which, from the very nature of government, binds the superior to care for the inferiors, no less than the inferiors to obey the superior. From which it follows, as theologians have observed, that a king who undertakes wars for light causes, or for the purpose of exacting punishments which are not necessary, and which bring great danger with them, is bound to his subjects for reparation of the loss thence arising to them; for if he do no injury to the enemy, he does one to his own subjects, when, for such causes, he implicates them in so great evils. As Livy says, war is just, when it is necessary; *their* arms are pious, who have no hope left except in arms. This is what Ovid wishes:

> No arms be borne save those which put down arms.

VIII. Thus the cases are rare, in which war either may not or ought not to be avoided; in cases only when, as Florus speaks, the enforcement of rights is worse than arms. Seneca says, *We may run into danger, when we have as much to fear if we sit still:* so Aristides. This Tacitus puts, by saying that *A miserable peace is well changed for war;* where, as he also says, *Liberty may crown the attempt, and defeat will leave them no worse.* So Livy: but not when the pretence is as Cicero describes it; If you are conquered you are proscribed; if you are victorious you are a slave.

IX. Then only is the time for war, when we have right on our side, and, what is of the greatest consequence, strength also. This is what Augustus said, that war was not to be undertaken except when there could be shewn more hope of gain than fear of loss. What Scipio Africanus and Emilius Paulus said of a battle, may be applied to war in general; that *We ought never to fight except there were either the greatest necessity or the greatest occasion.* And this is especially true, when there is a hope that the matter may be brought to an issue merely by terror and by the reputation of strength, with little or no danger. Pliny says, *He gained the most brilliant kind of victory, conquering by terror.*

X. 1 War, says Plutarch, is a dire business, and brings with it an accumulation of injuries and cruelty. And Augustine says wisely, that this being so, the wise man will not be satisfied merely if the war is just; he will grieve that there should be a necessity for just wars; since, except they were just, he would not go to war; and in this very way, there would be no wars. The iniquity of men may make wars just, and even necessary; but this iniquity is a thing to be lamented, even if it did not lead to war. Whoever considers the evils of war, must confess the miseries of the case; who suffers it without grief, is more miserable in his joy, because he has lost the sense of humanity. And in another place, *The bad think war a pleasure, the good, a necessity.* So Maximus Tyrius.

2 To which we must add what Seneca says, that man is not to use man prodigally. Philiscus admonished Alexander, that he might

consult his glory, but on condition that he did not make himself a pestilence or a plague : meaning that he must not bring about the destruction of populations and the desolation of cities, such as a pestilence produces : while nothing more becomes a king, than to provide for the safety of all, as peace does provide.

3 When we consider that by the Hebrew law he who had slain a man, even without intending it, was obliged to fly; that God forbade his temple to be built by David, who is related to have carried on pious wars, because he had shed much blood; that even among the ancient Greeks, those who had stained their hands with manslaughter, even without fault, had need of expiation; how can any one fail to see, especially any Christian, what an unhappy and disastrous thing, and how strenuously to be avoided, is a war, even when not unjust? Certainly among the Greeks who professed Christianity, the Canon was long observed, by which those who had killed an enemy in any war whatever, were for a time excluded from participation in sacred offices.

CHAPTER XXV.

Of the Causes of going to War for others.

I. 1 WHEN we above spoke of those who make war, it was said and proved by us that, by Natural Law, not only each person has an executive power to assert his own right, but also the rights of others. Whence it follows, that the causes which justify him whose interest is concerned, do also justify those who help him.

2 The first and closest of such relations is, the care which we are bound to exercise for those who are under us, whether as members of a family or of our civil community; for these are, in a way, a part of him who is at the head of the body, as we there said. Thus the Gibeonites having put themselves under the Jewish people, that people took up arms for them, with Joshua for their leader. *Our ancestors,* says Cicero, *often undertook war, because merchants and sailors belonging to them were treated with injury.* And elsewhere, *How many wars did our ancestors undertake because Roman citizens were injured, their navigators detained, their merchants despoiled!* The same Romans, though they would not take up arms for their allies, yet when the same peoples had become their subjects, thought it necessary to do so. The Campanians say to the Romans, *Since you will not allow us to defend our property against force and injury by our own just force, you will certainly defend it by yours.* Florus, as ambassador of the Campanians, says that the league which existed before had become more sacred by the surrender of all his country-men. *It was considered a point of good faith,* says Livy, *not to desert those who had surrendered to us.*

II. But yet it is not always, even if the cause of a subject be just, that it obliges the rulers to enter upon a war; but then only, if it can be done without the damage of all, or the greater part, of the subjects. For the office of the ruler is concerned more with the whole than with the parts; and in proportion as the part is greater, it approaches nearer to the nature of the whole.

III. 1 Therefore if one citizen, though innocent, be demanded by the many, in order to be put to death, it is not doubtful that he may be given up*, if it appear that the state of which the demand is made is much too weak to contend. Vasquius disputes against this opinion ; but if we look, not so much at his words, as at his purport, he seems to come to this, that such a citizen is not lightly to be deserted, when there is a hope that he may be defended. For he adduces the history of the Italic infantry, which deserted Pompey when his cause was not yet desperate, being assured of their safety by Cæsar; which he blames, and deservedly.

2 Whether an innocent citizen may be delivered into the hands of the enemy to avoid the otherwise imminent destruction of the city, the learned dispute, and the dispute existed also in ancient times; as when Demosthenes narrated the clever fable of the wolves requiring the sheep to give up their dogs for the sake of peace. That it is not lawful to do so, is maintained not by Vasquius only, but Sotus also, whose opinion Vasquius condemns as approaching to perfidy. Yet Sotus holds that such a citizen is bound to surrender himself to the enemy: this Vasquius denies, because the nature of civil society which every one enters into for his own advantage, does not require such a step.

3 But from this, nothing follows but that a citizen is not bound to this step, by any law properly so called; but it does not follow that charity allows him to do otherwise. For there are many duties, not of justice properly so called, but of good will, which it is not only laudable to perform, but which it is blameable to omit. And of such nature appears this to be, that each person should prefer the life of an innocent multitude to his own. So Euripides. And so Phocion exhorted Demosthenes and others that they should rather submit to death, after the example of the daughters of Leos and the Hyacinthids, than bring an irreparable calamity on their country. Cicero, pleading for Sextius, says, that if he were in a ship attacked by pirates who demanded him in particular, and would destroy the ship if he were not given up, he would rather throw himself into the sea than bring upon all the rest, not only certain death, but even extreme danger of death. And again, he says that a wise and good man will rather consult the safety of all than of any one in particular, even of himself. In Livy we read: I have often heard of men who would die for their country, but I never heard of any who thought it reasonable that their country should perish for them.

4 But, this being assumed, there remains this doubt, whether,

---

* This is an example of the evil of laying down rules for cases of necessity. If a city under the terror of destruction from a cruel enemy, should give up an innocent person to death, we might excuse them when the thing was done; but we can hardly look upon it as a speculative opinion which they may morally hold beforehand, that men are right in doing so. The certainty of saving themselves by such means must be doubtful, as Barbeyrac says: and no protest could be strong enough to express the horror which the Rulers of a State ought to feel towards such a step. W. W.

what they are thus bound to do, they can be compelled to do.   Sotus
denies this, adducing the example of a rich man who is bound to give
alms to a needy man by the rule of mercy, but cannot be compelled
to do so.   But it is to be remarked that the relation of such parties
is different from that of superiors compared with subjects.   For an
equal cannot compel an equal, except to that which he has a right to,
speaking strictly.   But a superior can compel him to other things also
which any virtue prescribes; because in the peculiar right of a superior as superior, this is comprehended.   Thus in a great scarcity of
corn, the citizens may be compelled to contribute to the common
stock what each one has; and thus, in this question before us, it seems
to be sound doctrine that the citizen may be compelled to do that
which charity requires*.   And thus Phocion, whom I have already
mentioned, pointed out a very intimate friend of his, Nicocles by
name, and said that matters were come to such a miserable condition
that if Alexander demanded *him*, he would be of opinion that he
ought to be given up.

IV.   As parties whom we are bound to defend, next to our subjects, come our allies.   This is comprehended in our engagement
with them, whether they have put themselves under the authority
and protection of others, or have contracted for mutual aid.   *He who
does not repel an injury for an ally, if he can, is in the wrong as much
as he who does the injury,* says Ambrose.   That such contracts are
not to be extended to wars, where there is no just cause for the war,
we have elsewhere said.   And this is the reason why the Lacedæmonians, before they began their war with the Athenians, put the matter to the judgment of all their allies; as also the Romans did with
regard to the Greeks, respecting the war with Nabis.   We will further
add, that even in such a case, the ally is not bound, if there be no
hope of a good result.   For such alliances are contracted, not for
the sake of evil results, but of good.   An ally however is to be
defended even against another confederate, except there be some
special stipulation to the contrary in some previous convention.
Thus the Corcyreans, if their cause was good, might have received
defensive aid from the Athenians, even against the Corinthians, who
were their old allies.

V.   The third cause [in which we may undertake war on account
of others, subjects and allies being the first two cases,] is the cause
of friends, to whom we have not promised aid, but to whom it is in a
manner due on the ground of friendship, if it can be given easily and
without inconvenience.   Thus Abraham took arms for Lot, his relative;
the Romans commanded the Antiates not to exercise piracy against

---

* It is quite extravagant to place the sacrifice of one's own life on a level with
other offices of charity.   As Grotius himself has just said, (chap. xxiv. 6,) life is
the foundation of all enjoyment in this world, and the occasion of all the happiness of another: and it must be only under peculiar circumstances that a man
can dispose of these possessions, as if they resembled other possessions.   W.

the Greeks, as being related to the Italians. The Romans too, often took up arms for their allies, not only when they were bound to do so by treaty, but also for their friends; or threatened to take up arms in such cases.

VI. The last and widest reason for taking up arms, is the connexion of men with men as such, which alone is often sufficient to induce them to give their aid. *Men are made for mutual help*, says Seneca, and the like; so Euripides and Ambrose.

VII. 1 Here the question is raised, whether man be bound to defend man, and people to defend people, from wrong. Plato thinks that *he* ought to be punished who does not repel force offered to another; and this was also provided by the laws of the Egyptians. But, in the first place, if the danger be manifest, it is certain that he is not so bound; for he may reasonably prefer his own life and possessions to those of others. And in this sense, as I conceive, we are to interpret what Cicero says, that *he who does not repel and resist an injury when he can, is as much in fault as if he were to desert his parents, or his country, or his allies: when he can*, we are to understand, with convenience to himself: for the same writer elsewhere says, *Perhaps we cannot defend men without incurring blame.* So Sallust says that *when we are asked to assist allies, it is to be considered whether we may abstain from war; and then, whether what is required is sufficiently pious, safe, glorious; or on the other hand, unbecoming.*

2 And the warning of Seneca is not to be despised: *I am willing to help a man who is perishing, but so that I myself do not perish; except I am to be the ransom of a great man or a great cause.* And even then, he will not be bound, if the person oppressed cannot be extricated without the death of the assailant. For if he may in some cases prefer the life of the assailant to his own, when he is attacked, as we have elsewhere said, he will not be wrong who either thinks or desires that another person so attacked has the same preference: especially when there is a greater danger of irreparable and eternal loss on the part of the invader.

VIII. 1 There is also another question, Whether a war for the subjects of another be just, for the purpose of defending them from injuries inflicted by their ruler. Certainly it is undoubted that ever since civil societies were formed, the rulers of each claimed some especial right over his own subjects. Euripides makes his characters say that they are sufficient to right wrongs in their own city. And Thucydides puts among the marks of empire, the supreme authority in judicial proceedings. And so Virgil, Ovid, and Euripides in the *Hippolytus*. This is, as Ambrose says, that *peoples may not run into wars by usurping the care for those who do not belong to them.* The Corinthians in Thucydides say that it is right that each state should punish its own subjects. And Perseus says that he will not plead in defense of what he did against the Dolopians, since they were under his authority and he had acted upon his right. But all this applies when the subjects have really violated their duty; and we may add, when the case is doubtful. For that distribution of power was introduced for that case.

2 But the case is different if the wrong be manifest. If a tyrant like Busiris, Phalaris, Diomede of Thrace, practises atrocities towards his subjects, which no just man can approve, the right of human social connexion is not cut off in such a case. So Constantine took arms against Maxentius and Licinius; and several of the Roman emperors took or threatened to take arms against the Persians, except they prevented the Christians being persecuted on account of their religion.

3 But if we should grant that subjects cannot rightly take up arms even in extreme necessity, (which, we have seen, has been doubted even by those whose purpose was to defend the royal power,) it would not follow that others may not take up arms for them. For when the impediment which exists to an action is in the person, not in the thing itself; in such cases, what is not lawful to one person may be lawful to another for him, if it be a case in which one can help another. Thus for a ward or minor, who is not capable of legal acts, the guardian or trustee sustains the suit; and for an absent person, an agent even without a special commission. Now the impediment which forbids the subject to resist, does not arise from the cause, which is the same in the subject and the non-subject; but from the quality of the person, which does not pass over to others.

4 Thus Seneca thinks that I may attack in war him who, though he is a stranger to my nation, persecutes his own; as we said when we spoke of exacting punishment: and this is often joined with the defense of innocent subjects. We know indeed, both from ancient and from modern histories, that the desire to appropriate another's possessions often uses such a pretext as this: but that which is used by bad men does not necessarily therefore cease to be right. Pirates use navigation, but navigation is not therefore unlawful. Robbers use weapons, but weapons are not therefore unlawful*.

IX. 1 But, as we have said, that leagues made with a view to mutual help in all wars alike, without distinction of the cause, are unlawful; so no kind of life is more disreputable than that of those who act as soldiers for pay merely, without regard to the cause; whose motto is, *the right is where the best pay is:* as Plato proves from Tyrtæus. This is the reproach which Philip cast upon the Etolians, and Dionysius of Miletus upon the Arcadians; saying, that *there was a market where the Arcadians made a profit of the misfortunes of the Greeks.* As Antiphanes says, It is a wretched life to be ready to die in order to live. So Dio Prusæensis.

2 But that they sell their own lives is little, if it were not that they sell too the lives of other innocent men: and in this way they are worse than the hangman, in proportion as it is worse to kill men without a cause than for a cause: as Antisthenes says that executioners

* See Barbeyrac's happy verification of these and the following quotations.

are more respectable than tyrants, for they kill guilty, these, innocent men. Philip of Macedon (the greater) said that for those whose gain was in a soldier's life, peace was war, and war, peace.

3 War is not one of the arts of life. On the contrary, it is a thing so horrible, that nothing but the highest necessity or the deepest charity can make it be right: as may be understood from what we have said in the last chapter but one. Augustine says, *to be a soldier is not a sin, but to be a soldier for plunder, is.*

X. And not for plunder only, but for pay, if that be regarded solely or principally; though in the other case, it is allowable to receive pay. St Paul says, *Who goeth to warfare at his own charge?*

U

CHAPTER XXVI.

Of just Causes for War in those who are under another's jurisdiction.

I. WE have treated of those who are their own masters. There are others who by their condition are under authority, as sons of families, servants, subjects, even individual citizens, as compared with the whole body of their city.

II. These, if they are either called to counsel, or if a free option is given them of war or peace, ought to follow the same rules as they who by their own decision undertake wars for themselves or others.

III. 1 But if they are commanded to join in a war, as often happens, if they are quite clear that the war is unlawful, they ought to abstain. That God is to be obeyed rather than men, not only the Apostles have said, but Socrates also: and the masters among the Hebrews have a saying indicating that even the king, if he command anything against the law of God, is not to be obeyed. That our obedience is to be limited by our duty to God, is declared by Polycarp at the point of death; Jerome on St Paul, Eph. vi. 1; Tertullian; Sylvanus the martyr; Antigone in Euripides; Musonius.

2 That a father or master is not to be obeyed if he command a crime, as treason, the murder of his mother, false sentence, and the like, is asserted by Gellius, Quintilian, Seneca, Sopater. Stratocles was laughed at in Athens for proposing a law that whatever was thought good by Demetrius, should be reckoned right and pious. Pliny somewhere says that he had laboured to prove that to be ministerial in a crime was a crime.

3 Even the Civil Law, which is facile in giving pardon to excusable offenses, is favourable to those who are under the necessity of obeying, but not to all. It excepts cases of great atrocity, crimes which are naturally abominable, not condemned by the opinion of lawyers only, but by natural feeling.

4 Josephus relates that the Jews, under Alexander the Great, would perform other military works, but could not be compelled to pile up earth to restore the temple of Belus. But we have a closer exception

in the Theban legion under Julian, who were willing, as Ambrose says, to use their arms for the State, but not against Christians; when required to do this, they obeyed the King of heaven, not the emperor of earth. So we read that, of the soldiers whose office it was to execute the condemned, those who had been converted died rather than lay their hands on the Christians.

5 The rule is the same, if any one be falsely persuaded that what is commanded is unjust. The thing is unlawful for him, as long as he retains that opinion, as appears by what is said above.

IV. 1 But if the subject doubts whether the matter be lawful or not, must he remain quiet or obey [and assist in war?] Most writers think that he ought to obey. And they hold that the rule does not apply, *If you doubt do not do it*. Because he who doubts speculatively, may not be in doubt in his practical judgment. He may believe that in a doubtful matter he ought to obey his superior. And certainly, that this distinction of a twofold judgment, a speculative and a practical, holds in many actions, cannot be denied. Civil Laws, not those of the Romans only, but of other nations also, in such circumstances, not only grant impunity to those who obey, but also refuse a civil action against them. They say, he does the damage who orders it to be done; he is in no fault who is obliged to obey; the necessity imposed by authority excuses; and the like.

2 So Aristotle enumerates, among those who do an unjust thing, but do not act unjustly, the servant of the master who commands it; he says that he who in such case acts unjustly, is he in whom the origin of the action is. For in the servant, the power of deliberation is not complete. As in the proverb, and in Homer, *The day that makes man a slave takes half his worth away*. And so Philo, *You are a slave, what have you to do with reason?* So Tacitus. And the same writer narrates that Tiberius forgave the crime of Piso's son, who engaged in the civil war: because his father commanded, and the son could not refuse. So Seneca says, *The slave is not the critic, but the minister of the command.*

3 And especially in this question of acting as a soldier, Augustine so thought. He says, *A just man acting as soldier, even under a sacrilegious king, may rightly take a part in war at his command, if he be certain that what is commanded is not against the precepts of God, or if he be not certain that it is so; the iniquity of the command may make the king guilty, but the rule of obedience may make the soldier innocent.* And elsewhere, *A soldier, when he kills a man, obeying legitimate power, is not guilty of homicide. If he had done so without command, he would be liable to punishment; if he do not so under command, he is also liable to punishment.* And hence the opinion is everywhere received, that so far as subjects are concerned, there may be wars which are just on both sides, that is, free from injustice. So Lucan.

4 But this matter is not without difficulties of its own. Adrian

our countryman, who was the last Cisalpine Pope, defends the contrary opinion. And it may be supported, not precisely on that ground which he adduces, but on this, which is more satisfactory, that he who doubts speculatively ought in practice to choose the safer side. And the safer side is, to abstain from war*. The Essenes are praised for swearing that *they would not harm any one, even if they were commanded.* And so are their imitators the Pythagoreans, who abstained from war, as Jamblichus says, adding for cause *that war produces bloodshed.*

5 Nor is it a sufficient objection to this, that on the other side there is the danger of disobedience. For when the right and wrong is uncertain (for if the war be unjust, there is no [moral] disobedience in declining it,) then disobedience is free from sin, and this is the less of two evils. Disobedience in such a case is a less evil than homicide, and especially, than the homicide of many innocent persons. So the ancients say that the gods would not absolve Mercury for the death of Argus, though done by the command of Jupiter†. And so Martial condemns Pothinus the attendant of Ptolemy, who put him to death, as worse than Antony who commanded the act. Nor is that of much weight which is alleged on the other side; that if such a rule were adopted, the state would often be damaged, since generally it is not expedient to publish to the people the grounds of public acts. For however true this may be of the impelling causes of war, it is not true of the justificatory causes, which should be clear, and such as both may and ought to be openly expounded.

6 What Tertullian says, somewhat indistinctly, of laws in general, is very just with regard to laws or edicts for making war: *A citizen does not obey the laws faithfully if he be ignorant at what crime the punishment of the law is aimed. The law may not be content with its own conscience; it owes a justification to those for whom it claims obedience. A law is suspected, which does not seek moral approbation; it is bad, if, being examined, it is not approved.* So in the *Achilleïs* of Statius, Achilles requires Ulysses to instruct him of the justice of the Greek cause. And in his *Thebaïs,* Theseus bids his followers to go forwards, confiding in their just cause. So Propertius had said that the soldier's courage rises and falls with his cause; and that if that be not just, his arms are blunted. And so that Panegyrist says, that conscience has so great a power in arms, that victory depends more upon integrity than upon courage. And so some learned men interpret what is said of Abraham's arming his servants, to imply that he instructed them of the justice of his cause, Gen. xiv. 14.

7 And in fact, declarations of war used to be made, as we shall have to say hereafter, accompanied by a declaration of the cause of the war; that the whole human race, as it were, might judge of its

---

* Barbeyrac says the safer side may be to obey: but Grotius is speaking of the danger of being morally wrong, not of danger to outward fortunes. W.

† Barbeyrac remarks, that the example is not pertinent.

justice. And as Aristotle says, prudence is properly the virtue of a ruler, but justice is a virtue which belongs to man as man.

8 But undoubtedly the opinion of Adrian which we have mentioned seems fit to be followed, if the subject not only doubts of the justice of the cause, but, induced by probable arguments, rather inclines to believe the war unjust: especially if the question be of attacking others, not of defense.

9 It is also a probable opinion that an executioner who is to put a man to death, ought to know that there is a cause in his deserts for doing so; either as having been aware of the trial and proofs, or by the confession of the criminal. And this is observed in some places; and to this the laws of the Hebrews seem to have regard, when, in the stoning of a condemned person, it directs the witnesses to begin the execution.

V. 1 But if the minds of the subjects cannot be satisfied by the exposition of the cause, it will by all means be the part of a good magistrate rather to impose extraordinary contributions upon them, than military service; especially as it is to be supposed that persons willing to serve as soldiers will not be wanting; whose acts, not only if they are morally good, but even if they are bad, a just king may use; even as God makes use of the spontaneous acts of the devil and of impious men; and as he is free from fault, who being in pecuniary distress, takes money from a wicked usurer.

2 And even if there can be no doubt as to the justice of the war, it does not seem at all equitable that Christians who are unwilling should be compelled to act as soldiers; when we consider that to abstain from military service, even when such service is lawful, is the course directed by especial holiness, such as was long exacted of ecclesiastical persons and penitents, and strongly recommended to all others in many ways. Origen, answering the objection of Celsus to the Christians, that they declined military service, says: *Those who require this, we remind of the priests of the heathens, who were bound to keep themselves pure from the shedding of human blood; and this ought still to be the rule for those who are all priests of God. They in their prayers to God wrestle for them who fight justly, and for him who reigns justly:* where he calls all Christians *priests,* following the Scriptures, Rev. i. 6; 1 Pet. ii. 5.

VI. 1 I think however that it may happen, that in a war not doubtful, but even manifestly unjust, there may be a just defense of the subjects who take a part in it. For since the enemy, though carrying on a just war, has not a true and intrinsic right to kill innocent subjects, who have nothing to do with the fault of the wars, except either for necessary defense, or by consequence and extrinsically to his purpose; (for they are not liable to punishment;) it follows that if it be clear that the enemy comes with such a purpose that though he could save the lives of the subjects of his adversary, he will not; those subjects may defend themselves by the law of nature, which they are not divested of by the law of nations.

2 Nor shall we then say that the war is just on both sides; for the question is not concerning the justice of the war, but concerning a certain and definite action of the enemy. And this action, though it be the action of a person having in other respects a right of making war, is unjust, and therefore may be justly repelled.

OF THE

RIGHTS OF WAR AND PEACE.
BOOK III.

CHAPTER I.

General Rules as to what is lawful in War by Natural Law; and herein of deceit and falsehood [in War].

I. WE have seen who may carry on war, and from what causes they may do it lawfully. It follows that we consider what is lawful in war, and to what extent; and this is to be considered either nakedly, or as depending on antecedent promise: and nakedly, first by Natural Law, and next by the Law of Nations. Let us then see what is allowed by Natural Law.

II. 1 First, as we have already repeatedly said, the means which lead to an end in a moral matter receive their intrinsic value from the end: wherefore the steps that are necessary [to a lawful end], *necessity* being taken not in physical exactness but morally, we have a right to use.　By Right, I mean Right taken strictly, such as implies a competence to act in respect of society alone.　Wherefore, if I cannot otherwise preserve my life, I may, by any force which I can use, repel him who assails it, even if he be without fault; as we have elsewhere noted : because this right does not properly arise from the fault of another, but from the right which nature gives me for my own preservation.

2　Further, I may take possession of a thing belonging to another, from which a certain danger impends over me, without consideration of another's fault: not however so as to become the owner of it, (for that is not a step suitable to the end,) but to keep it till sufficient provision is made for my security: which question we have also elsewhere treated.　So by Natural Law I have a right to take from another a thing of mine which he detains ; and if that is too difficult, another thing of the same value: and the like I may do for the sake of recovering a debt: and in this case my ownership also is consequent, because the equality which has been disturbed cannot be restored in any other way.

3　So also when punishment is just, all force is just without which punishment cannot be attained: and every thing which is part of the punishment, as the destruction of property by burning or otherwise; that is, within just limits, corresponding to the offense.

III.　It is to be noted in the second place, that these rights are not only to be regarded with reference to the origin of the war, but also with reference to causes *subnascent,* that is, growing up during the progress of the war : as also in civil suits, after the point in dispute is dealt with, there often arises a new right to the party.　Thus those who join themselves to the party which attacks me, whether as allies or as subjects, give me a right of defending myself against them.　So again those who mingle themselves in a war which is unjust, especially if they may know and ought to know that it is unjust, become bound to make good the expense and damage, because they occasion damage with fault.　Thus too, those who join in a war undertaken without a plausible reason, incur the desert of punishment, in proportion to the injustice which belongs to their act.　So Plato approves a war carried on *till those who are guilty are compelled to undergo penalties to the satisfaction of the innocent who suffer by it.*

IV.　1 It is to be observed in the third place, that upon the right of thus acting, many consequences follow indirectly and extraneously to the intent of the actor, to which of themselves he would not have a right.　How this holds in self-defense we have elsewhere explained.　Thus in order to recover what is ours, if we cannot take exactly so much, we have a right to take more; under the obligation however of restoring the excess of value.　Thus a ship occupied by pirates, or a house by robbers, may be battered to pieces, although there may be in the ship or in the house a few infants or women, or other innocent persons who may thus be put in danger.　*He is not guilty of the death of another,* says Augustine, *who has walled round his own possessions, if any one be injured or killed by the wall falling.*

2 But as we have often warned the reader, that which is agreeable to strict right is not always lawful in all respects: for often goodwill to our neighbour does not permit us to use rigorous rights. Wherefore the events which take place extraneously to our intent, and which we see to be likely, are to be provided against, except the good to which our action tends be much greater than the evil which is apprehended; or except, the good and the evil being equal, the hope of the good is much greater than the fear of the evil; a point which is to be left to the decision of prudence; with the caution that we are always, in a doubtful case, to regard the interest of others rather than our own, as the safer course. *Let the tares grow,* says the best of Teachers, *lest you pull up the wheat with them.* So Seneca says that to cause conflagration and ruin, is to destroy many without distinction. We learn from history, with how grave a remorse Theodosius, on Ambrose's admonition, expiated such an unmeasured course of punishment, [when he had sacked Thessalonica for a sedition, A.C. 390. Gronov.]

3 And if God sometimes does something of this kind, we are not to draw that into an example for us; for he has unlimited dominion over us, but he has not given us such dominion over others, as we have elsewhere explained. And even God himself, who is the supreme Lord of men, often spares the whole body, though large, for the sake of a few good men; and thus manifests his equity as a judge; as the dialogue of God with Abraham concerning Sodom plainly shews.

From these general rules we may see what is lawful against an enemy by Natural Law.

V. 1 But the question often arises, what is lawful against those who are not enemies, or will not allow themselves to be so called, but who provide our enemies with supplies of various kinds. This has been a point sharply contested, both anciently and recently; one party defending the rigorous rights of war, the other, the freedom of commerce.

2 In the first place, we must make a distinction as to the things supplied. For there are some articles of supply which are useful in war only, as arms; others which are of no use in war, but are only luxuries; others which are useful both in war, and out of war, as money, provisions, ships and their furniture. In matters of the first kind, that is true which Amalasuintha said to Justinian, that they are of the party of the enemy who supply him with what is necessary in war. The second class of objects is not a matter of complaint. So Seneca says that he would do kindnesses even to a tyrant, if the service so rendered neither gave him greater power for the common mischief, nor confirmed the power which he had, but was only what might be given him without any public evil: *I will not give him money to pay his satellites; but there is no reason why I should*

*not furnish him with marbles and tapestries for his luxury. I will
not supply him with soldiers and armour; but if he pressingly asks
for stage-players who may soften his disposition, I will willingly give
them. I would not send him ships of war, but I will send him ships
of pleasure, barges, and other playthings of kings who amuse themselves at sea.* So Ambrose judges, that to give money to him who
is conspiring against his country is not a laudable liberality. [This
last quotation belongs to the first, not to the second case.]

3 In the third class, objects of ambiguous use, the state of the war
is to be considered. For if I cannot defend myself except by intercepting what is sent, necessity, as elsewhere explained, gives us a right
to intercept it, but under the obligation of restitution, except there
be cause to the contrary. If the supplies sent impede the exaction
of my rights, and if he who sends them may know this; as if I were
besieging a town, or blockading a port, and if surrender or peace were
expected; he will be bound to me for damages; as a person would who
liberates my debtor from prison, or assists his flight to my injury; and
to the extent of the damage, his property may be taken, and ownership thereof be assumed for the sake of recovering my debt. If he
have not yet caused damage, but have tried to cause it, I shall have a
right, by the retention of his property, to compel him to give security
for the future, by hostages, pledges, or in some other way. But if,
besides, the injustice of my enemy to me be very evident, and he confirm him in a most unjust war, he will then be bound to me not only
civilly, for the damage, but also criminally, as being one who protects
a manifest criminal from the judge who is about to inflict punishment:
and on that ground it will be lawful to take such measures against him
as are suitable to the offense, according to the principles laid down
in speaking of punishment; and therefore to that extent he may be
subjected to spoliation.

4 On this account, belligerents[e] commonly issue manifestos to other

---

[e] There are examples of rules on this subject in the Roman Law. [See the
quotations.] In modern times, the book *Consolato del Mare* was published in
Italian, and contains the constitutions of the Emperors of Greece and Germany, the
kings of the Franks, of Spain, Cyprus, the Balearic Isles, of the Venetians, and of the
Genoese. In Title 274 of this book, controversies of this kind are treated; and the
rule given is this, That if the ships and the lading both belong to the enemy, the
matter is plain, and they become the property of the captors. If the ship belong
to a neutral, the goods to an enemy, the belligerent may compel the ship to go into
a port of his own, paying the navigators for the freight. If, on the other hand, it
is an enemy's ship, with the goods of a neutral, the ship is to be ransomed, and if
the navigators refuse this, they may be taken into a port of the captors, and the
captor must be paid for the use of the ship.

In the year 1438, when the Hollanders were at war with Lubeck and other
cities on the Baltic and the Elbe, they decided in full Senate, that goods of neutrals
found in the enemy's ships were not good prize, and that law was afterwards maintained. So also in 1597, the king of Denmark judged, when he sent an embassy to
the Hollanders, and their allies, asserting for his subjects the right of carrying

nations, to make known both the justice of the cause, and also the probable hope of exacting their rights.

goods into Spain, with which the Hollanders were then in fierce war. The French always permitted neutrals the right of carrying on commerce with those who were the enemies of France; and so indiscreetly, that their enemies often covered their goods with neutral names; as appears by an edict of 1543, chap. 42, which was copied again in an edict of 1584, and the following year. In those edicts, it is plainly declared that the friends of the French shall be allowed to carry on commerce during war, provided that they do it with their own ships and their own men; and that they may land where they please, provided the goods are not munitions of war; but if these are carried, it is declared to be lawful for the French to take such goods, paying a fair price for them. Here we note two points, that even munitions of war were not declared prize; still less goods of a peaceful character.

I do not deny that the northern nations asserted other rules, but variously, and rather for an occasional purpose than as a permanent rule of equity. For when the English, under pretence of their wars, had interfered with the Danish commerce, a war arose between those two nations, of which the event was that the Danes imposed a tribute on England, which, under the name of the *Danes' penny*, remained, though the alleged reason was changed, to the time of William the Conqueror, the founder of the present dynasty in England, as Thuanus notes in the history of 1589. Again, Elizabeth, the sagacious queen of England, sent in 1575, Sir William Winter, and Robert Beal, secretary of state, to Holland to complain that the English could not allow the Dutch, in the heat of the war, to detain, as they had done, English ships bound to Spanish ports. So Reidan relates in his Batavian history, at the year 1575, and Camden, at the following year. But when the English had themselves gone to war with the Spanish, and interfered with the right of the German cities to sail to Spain, how doubtful the right was by which they did this, appears from the adverse arguments of both nations, which deserve to be read for the purpose of understanding this controversy. And it may be noted that the English themselves acknowledge this; since the two main arguments which they allege are, that what the Germans carried into Spain were munitions of war, and that there were old conventions which prohibited such an act. And conventions of this kind were made by the Hollanders and their allies, with the Lubeckers and their allies in the year 1613; to the effect that neither party should permit the subjects of an enemy to traffic in their country, nor should assist the enemy with soldiers, ships or provisions. And afterwards, in 1627, a convention was made between the kings of Sweden and of Denmark, to the effect that the Danes should prevent all commerce with the Dantzickers, the enemies of the Swedes; and should not allow any merchandize to pass the Sound, to the other enemies of the Swedes; for which terms the king of Denmark stipulated in turn certain advantages to himself.

But these were special conventions, from which nothing can be inferred which is binding upon all. For what the Germans said in their declarations was, not that all merchandize was prohibited by this convention, but that only which was once carried to England or made in England. Nor were the Germans the only party who refused to acknowledge the doctrines of the English, forbidding commerce with their enemy. For Poland complained by her ambassador that the Laws of Nations were infringed, when, on account of the English war with Spain, they were deprived of the power of trafficking with the Spanish; as Camden and Reidan mention under the year 1597. And the French, after the peace of Vervins with Spain, when Elizabeth of England persisted in the war, being requested by the English to allow their ships going to Spain to be visited, that they might not

[The note of Grotius respecting the cases in which the rights of belligerents against neutrals had then been enforced is so important, that I will give the substance of it below. I may observe that the rules which he has here laid down agree with the Rules of International Law, as laid down by modern authors: namely (see *E. M.* 1087, 1088), That Neutrals have no right of carrying *Munitions of War*, (Grotius's first class of supplies, called *Contraband of War*,) to one of the belligerents; and that they have no right of carrying anything to a place in a *state of Blockade*.]

5 We have referred this question to Natural Law because we have not been able to find in history [f] anything on the subject as deter-

privily carry munitions of war, would not permit this; saying that the request, if granted, would be made a pretext for spoliation and disturbance of commerce.

And in the league which the English made with the Hollanders and their allies in the year 1625, a convention was indeed made, that other nations, whose interest it was that the power of Spain should be broken, should be requested to forbid commerce with Spain; but if they would not agree to this, that their ships should be searched, to see whether they carried munitions of war; but that beyond this, neither the ships nor the cargo should be detained, nor that any damage should be done to neutrals on that ground. And in the same year it happened, that certain Hamburghers went to Spain in a ship laden for the most part with munitions of war; and this part of the lading was claimed by the English; but the rest of the lading was paid for. But the French, when French ships going to Spain were confiscated by the English, shewed that they would not tolerate this. Therefore we have rightly said that public declarations are required. And this the English themselves saw the necessity of. For they made such public declaration in 1591 and 1598, as we see in Camden.

Nor have such declarations always been obeyed, but times, causes, and places have been made grounds of distinctions. In 1458 the city of Lubeck refused to obey a notice given to them by the Dantzickers, that they were not to trade with the people of Malmoge and Memel. Nor did the Hollanders in 1551 obey, when the Lubeckers gave them notice to abstain from traffic with the Danes with whom they were then at war. In the year 1522, when there was a war between Sweden and Denmark, when the Danes had asked the Hanseatic cities not to have commerce with the Swedes, some of the cities who had need of their friendship conformed to this, but others did not. The Hollanders, when war was raging between Sweden and Poland, never allowed their commerce with either nation to be interdicted. The French always restored the Dutch ships which they took either going to or coming from Spain, then at war with them. See the pleading of Louis Servinus, held in 1592, in the case of the Hamburghers. But the same Dutch did not allow the English to carry merchandize into Dunkirk, before which they had a fleet; as the Dantzickers in 1455 did not allow the Dutch to carry anything into Königsberg. [See the authorities.

See also the subsequent views entertained on this subject, *E. M.* 1085—1091, and the authorities there quoted.]

[Grotius's note.] [f] There is much on this subject in Meursius's *Danish History*, B. I. and II. There you will see that the Lubeckers and the Emperor are for commerce, the Danes against it. Also see Crantzius, Thuanus, as quoted, Camden, besides the passages already quoted, on the years 1589 and 1595; where that controversy between the English and those Germans whom they call the Hanse towns is treated of.

mined by Instituted Law. When the Romans carried provisions to the enemies of the Carthaginians, they were sometimes taken prisoners by the Carthaginians, and then given up by the Carthaginians to the Romans on being demanded. When Demetrius held Attica with an army, and had taken Eleusis and Rhamnus, neighbouring towns, intending to reduce Athens by famine, and when a ship attempted to introduce corn into the city, he hung the captain and the pilot of the ship, and thus, deterring others, became master of the city.

VI. 1 As to the mode of acting in war, force and terror are the appropriate means. Whether it is allowable to use stratagem also, is a common question. It is assumed that it is, by Homer, Pindar, Virgil, Solon, Silius. [See the passages quoted.]

2 Ulysses in Homer, the example of a wise man, is full of stratagems towards the enemy; and Lucian praises those who deceive the enemy. Xenophon said that in war nothing was so useful as deceit; so in Thucydides, Brasidas; and in Plutarch, Agesilaus. Polybius and Silius say that in war fraud is better than force; so the severe Lacedæmonians thought, as Plutarch says: and so he praises Lysander and Philopemen.* So Ammianus.

3 The Roman Jurists call it good deceit (*bonus dolus*) which a man practises against an enemy, and say that it makes no difference whether any one elude the enemy by force or by fraud. So Eustathius. Among the Theologians, Augustine says the same; and Chrysostom, that the generals who had conquered by deceit were most praised.

4 But there are not wanting opinions which bear the other way, of which we will adduce some. The determination of this question depends on this, whether deceit in its kind be always a bad thing: if so, we are not to do evil that good may come: or whether it be a thing of that kind which is not universally bad by its nature, but which may happen to be good.

VII. It is to be noted, therefore, that deceit may be of two kinds, as it consists in a negative or in a positive act. I extend the term *deceit* to acts of a negative kind, on the authority of Labeo, who refers the act to deceit not evil, when any one by dissimulation defends his own or another's goods. Undoubtedly Cicero spoke too generally, when he said that simulation and dissimulation are to be entirely removed from our scheme of life. For since we are not bound to disclose to others all that we know or all that we wish, it follows that we may dissemble, that is, conceal and keep secret, some things from some persons. As Augustine says, *It is lawful to conceal in prudence the truth under a certain dissimulation.* And Cicero himself repeatedly acknowledges that this is necessary and inevitable, especially for those who have to administer public affairs. We have an example of this, Jeremiah, chap. xxxviii. 24, 25; where the prophet, having been consulted by the king as to the event of the siege of the city, gave to the princes another reason for the conference. And of the same kind was Abraham's dissembling that Sarah was his wife.

VIII. 1 Deceit which consists in a positive act, if it be perpetrated by things, is called *simulation*, if by words, a *lie*. Some lay down this distinction between these two, that they say that words are naturally the signs of notions, but that things are not so. But the contrary is true, that words, by nature, and extraneously to the will of man, have no signification; except inarticulate sounds, as of grief; which, however, may rather be called actions than words. But if it be said that this is the peculiar nature of man, that he can convey the conceptions of his mind to other men, and that words were invented for that purpose; this is truly said; but then it ought to be added, that such indications are not made by words alone, but also by nods, as among dumb persons, whether those nods have by their nature anything in common with the thing signified, or have their signification by institution. And of the same nature with these nods, are those written characters which do not express words as they are pronounced, but things; whether in virtue of some agreement between the character and the thing, as in hieroglyphics, or by arbitrary appointment, as among the Chinese.

2 We must, therefore, have recourse to another distinction, of the kind of that which we adopted to get rid of the ambiguity in speaking of *jus gentium*. For we said that the term was applied both to that which had been established by separate nations without mutual connexion, and to that which contains a common mutual obligation. Words then, and nods, and the written characters which we have mentioned, have been invented to signify a meaning with mutual obligation, or by convention; but other things, not so. Hence we may use other things although we foresee that another person will therefrom form a false opinion. I speak of what is intrinsic, not of what may happen. Therefore we must take an example where no damage follows; or where the damage, setting aside the consideration of deceit, is lawful.

3 Of the former kind we have an example in Christ, who, having accompanied the disciples to Emmaus, *made as if he would go further :* he pretended to intend to do so : except we prefer to say that he did intend to go further except he were detained by urgency : as God is said to intend many things which do not come to pass. And in another place Christ, it is said, (Mark vi. 48) *would have passed by* the disciples : that is, if he had not been urgently entreated to come into the ship. We may give another example in Paul, who circumcised Timothy, knowing that the Jews would take this as if the command of circumcision, though the necessity thereof was really abolished, still bound the Israelites, and as if Paul and Timothy so thought : while Paul's purpose was not this, but only to obtain for himself and Timothy the means of living on familiar terms with the Jews. The act of circumcision, when the divine law was taken away, no longer implied by institution such a necessity ; and the evil which thence followed, of error for a time, which error was afterwards to be rectified, was not of so great moment, as the good to which St Paul

tended; that is, the communication of evangelical truth. This simulation the Greek fathers often call *Economy;* and so Clemens Alexandrinus says, that *a good man will do for the advantage of his neighbours some things which he would not do of his own motion.* Such an act was that of the Romans in war, who threw loaves from the capitol into the stations of the enemy, that they might not appear to be distressed by famine.

4 An example of the latter (where the damage to the other party is lawful) we have in the feigned flight which Joshua advised his men to execute in order to take Aï; and which other generals have often practised. For here the damage is approved to be lawful in virtue of the justice of the war. And the flight itself means nothing by institution, though the enemy takes it as a sign of fear, which the other is not bound to prevent, using his liberty of going one way or another, quickly or slowly, with gestures and movements such or such. To the same head we must refer the cases in which soldiers have used the arms, standards, uniforms, rigging, of the enemy*.

5 All these things are of such kind that they may be used by any at his own choice, even contrary to custom: because the custom was introduced by the arbitrary choice of individuals, not as it were by common consent, and is such a custom as binds no one.

IX. 1 More grave is the question concerning those signs which belong to the usual intercourse of men, and to which, when used deceitfully, lies properly belong. There are many passages against lying in the Scriptures, Prov. xiii. 5; xxx. 8; Psalm v. 7; Coloss. iii. 9. And Augustine is rigid on this side, as are some of the philosophers and poets. So Homer, Sophocles, Cleobulus [rather Menander, J. B.], Aristotle.

2 There are, however, authorities on the other side; first, examples of persons in Scripture who told lies, and who are not blamed: and next, opinions of the old Christians, Origen, Clemens, Tertullian, Lactantius, Chrysostom, Jerome, Cassian; indeed almost all, as Augustine himself confesses.

3 Among the philosophers, we have evidently on this side Socrates, and his disciples Plato and Xenophon; and in some places Cicero, and if we believe Plutarch and Quintilian, the Stoics, who, among the gifts of the wise man, place that, to know how and when to lie. Aristotle in some places appears to be of the same opinion. Andronicus Rhodius, speaking of a physician who tells a lie to his patient, says, *he deceives, but is not a deceiver;* and adds the reason, that *his object is not to deceive, but to save the man.*

4 Many others defend lies for good purposes: Quintilian, Diphilus, Sophocles, Pisander, Euripides, Quintilian again, Eustathius, who brings testimonies from Herodotus and Isocrates.

* Quere: Whether the standards or colours of each party have not an instituted meaning; and whether a party which deceives the enemy by simulating them is not liable to a severity beyond the usual rules? W.

X.   1 Opinions so widely differing, perhaps we may in some measure conciliate, by a larger or stricter acceptation of the term *lie*. For we do not here use the term *lie*, so as to apply where it is unintended; we may distinguish a *falsehood* and a *lie*. We mean that which is knowingly uttered with a meaning which is at variance with the conception of the mind, either as to what it understands or as to what it wills. For that which is primarily and immediately indicated by words and the like signs, is the conception of the mind; and therefore he does not lie who says a thing which is false, but which he believes to be true; and he does lie who says a thing which is true which he believes to be false. Therefore the falsity of the meaning is what we require to the common notion of a lie. From which it follows that if any word or phrase have several significations, either by common usage, or technically, or figuratively, then if the conceptions of the mind conform to one of these significations, there is no lie, though he who hears it takes it in another.

2 But still it is true that such a mode of speaking, lightly used, is not to be approved of; although, from accidental causes, it may become proper : as for instance, if it be used in instructing him who is committed to our care, or to evade an unfair question. Of the former kind Christ himself gave an example, when he said, *Our friend Lazarus sleepeth :* which the Apostles received as if he had spoken of ordinary sleep. And what he said of rebuilding the temple, intending his own body, he knew that the Jews would accept of the temple, properly so called. So when he promised his disciples that they should sit upon twelve thrones and judge the twelve tribes of Israel; and when he spoke of drinking new wine in his Father's kingdom; he appears to have known that they would take his words as implying some kingdom and authority to be given him in this life, of which hope they were full to the very moment of Christ's ascension. And in other places he teaches the people by fables and parables, that hearing they might not understand; that is, except they brought to the work of listening proper attention and docility.

An example of the latter kind (to avoid unfair questions) we may take from profane history in the case of L. Vitellius, whom Narcissus urged to explain the plot and tell the truth; but only got him to use doubtful expressions which might be drawn either way. There is a Hebrew proverb, that if any one cannot talk without saying anything decided, he had better hold his peace.

3 On the other hand, it may happen that to use such a mode of speech is not only unbecoming, but wicked; for example, when the honour due to God or the love due to our neighbour, or the reverence due to a superior, or the nature of the matter, requires us to say what we have in our mind : as in contracts, we have said that all is to be disclosed which the nature of a contract is understood to require; in which sense we very properly understand that of Cicero, that lying must altogether be taken away from contracts : in which

case *lying* is, it would seem, to be understood so laxly as to include even obscure language; which however we have excluded from our notion of a lie.

XI. 1 To the common notion of a lie, then, it is required that what is said, written, conveyed by signs or gestures, cannot be understood otherwise than in that sense which differs from the mind of the utterer. But to this laxer notion of a lie in general, must be added some stricter proper difference, to define a lie, as unlawful by Natural Law: and this difference, if we examine the matter, can be no other, according to the common estimation of nations, than a discrepancy with some existing and permanent right of the person to whom the words or signs are addressed: for that no one lies to himself, is sufficiently evident. By *right*, I do not here mean any right extrinsic to the matter, but something proper and cognate to the matter in hand. But this right is no other than the liberty of judging of my future acts, which I, speaking with other men, am understood to owe to them. This is merely that mutual obligation which men wished to introduce when they instituted the use of speech and the like signs. For without such an obligation the invention of such means of communication would be useless.

2 We desire then, that while speech is thus used, this right should subsist and remain: for it may be that the right may have existed, but may have been taken away, or may be taken away by some supervenient right, as a debt is taken away by an acknowledgment of payment, or by the cessation of the condition. It is also required that the right which is violated, be a right of the person with whom we speak, not of another, (as in contracts, injustice does not arise, except from the violation of the right of the contracting parties). To this view you may properly apply what Plato says, after Simonides, referring veracity to justice; and also that lies, that is, forbidden lies, are often described in Scripture as false witness, or speaking against our neighbour; and that Augustine makes the essential nature of a lie consist in the intention to deceive. Also Cicero wishes the question of speaking truth to be referred to justice as its principle.

3 Now the right of which we have spoken, may be taken away, either by the express permission of him with whom we deal; as if any one have announced that he would tell falsehoods, and the other have permitted it; or by tacit permission, or permission presumed on fair reason; or by the opposition of another right, which, by the common opinion of all, is of much more importance.

These principles, rightly understood, will give us many consequences, which will be of great use in reconciling the dissentient opinions above mentioned.

XII. The first result is, that though any thing be said to an infant, or a person out of his mind, which has a false signification, it does not involve the guilt of a lie. The common sense of mankind

X

permits the thoughtless age of childhood to be deluded.   So Quintilian.   The reason is, that they have no liberty of judgment, and therefore they cannot be wronged with regard to such liberty.

XIII.   1 The second remark is, that so long as our speech is directed to him who is not deceived, it is no lie, although a third person should thereby imbibe a false persuasion.   It is not a lie with regard to him whom we address, because his liberty of judging is not disturbed; as in the case of those to whom a fable is told, which they know to be such, or to whom figurative language is used, or irony, or hyperbole; which figure, as Seneca says, arrives at the truth by a lie, and which Quintilian calls an allowable exaggeration.   Nor is it a lie with regard to him who accidentally hears it: because we have nothing to do with him, and therefore have no obligation to him.   If he form an opinion from what is said to another, and not to himself, he must take the responsibility of his opinion on himself, and not throw it on another.   For properly speaking, the speech is, with regard to him, no speech, but a mere thing which may signify any thing.

2 Therefore Cato the Censor was not guilty of a lie when he falsely promised assistance to his allies; nor Flaccus, who related to others that the enemy's city was taken; though the enemy was thus deceived; and Plutarch relates a similar act of Agesilaus.   For in these cases nothing was said to the enemy: and the damage to them which followed is extrinsic to our act, and is in itself not unlawful to be wished or procured.   To this head Chrysostom and others refer the discourse of Paul, in which at Antioch he reprehended Peter as judaizing too far: for they conceive that Peter sufficiently understood that that was not seriously done; and in the mean time, that the infirmity of the bystanders was consulted.

XIV.   1 A third case [in which there is no lie] is when it is certain that he who is addressed will not be dissatisfied with the disturbance of his liberty in judging, but rather will be gratified at the course taken, on account of some advantage which follows therefrom. In this case there is not a lie strictly so called, that is, a wrongful lie; just as he would not be guilty of theft who, presuming the consent of the owner, should consume some small matter, and so procure him great gain.   For in matters which are thus certain, a presumed will is held equivalent to an expressed will; and to a willing man, no wrong is done.   So he is not guilty of lying who consoles a sick friend with a false persuasion; as Arria did Pætus when his son was dead, which history we have in Pliny's Epistles; nor he who, when the battle is wavering, gives courage to his party by false news, and so incites them to obtain the victory; and thus catches them that they may not be caught, as Lucretius says.

2 That we may deceive our friends for their good, is asserted by Democritus, Xenophon, Clemens Alexandrinus, Maximus Tyrius, Pro-

clus. [See.] Such cases are Xenophon's declaration that the allies were at hand: and that of Tullus Hostilius, that the Alban army was making a circuit by his order: and that of Quintius the consul, a wholesome lie, as the historians speak, that the other wing of the enemy was in flight; and numerous other passages in historians. And it may be remarked, that the disturbance of the power of judging is in this case of the less consequence, inasmuch as it is momentary only, and the truth very soon comes out.

XV. 1 A fourth case of the same kind [in which a falsehood is not a lie] is when he who has a supereminent right over the rights of another, uses that right either for his private good or for the public good. And this Plato seems to have had in view, when he allows the governors of a state to deceive. And when Plato sometimes seems to allow and sometimes to disallow this practice in physicians, it would seem that this difference is to be taken; that in the former case he means physicians who are publicly called to this office of giving false hopes; in the latter case, those who arrogate such an office to themselves. But God, though he have the supreme right over men, cannot use lies, as Plato rightly acknowledges; because it is a mark of our weakness to take refuge in such means.

2 We have an example of falsehood, which even Philo praises, in Joseph; who, acting with royal power in Egypt, accuses his brothers first of being spies, and then of stealing, knowing that it was not so. And again in Solomon, when he gave orders to slay the child, about which the mothers disputed, though he never intended this to be done. So Quintilian.

XVI. A fifth case may be, when the life of an innocent person, or something of like value, cannot otherwise be preserved, and when another person cannot otherwise be withheld from the perpetration of a wicked act: as in the case of Hypermnestra, *nobly false*. (Hor.)

XVII. 1 What learned men commonly lay down, goes further than what we have said;—namely, that we may utter falsehoods to an enemy. Thus to the rule *not to lie*, an exception, *unless to an enemy*, is added by Plato, Xenophon, Philo among the Jews, Chrysostom among the Christians. And to this case you may refer the promise of the men of Jabesh (1 Sam. xi. 10), that they would come out on the morrow; and the act of Elisha when he misled his pursuers (2 Kings vi. 19); and the saying of Valerius Lævinus who boasted that he had killed Pyrrhus.

2 To the third, fourth and fifth of the preceding remarks belongs a passage of Eustratius on Aristotle's Ethics. And Quintilian says, that a lie to prevent a murder, or the destruction of one's country, though at other times a thing blameable in a slave, is then commendable in a free man.

3 These doctrines are not approved of by the school of Theologians of more recent times, who have followed Augustine almost

exclusively in all points.   But this same school allows of tacit interpretations, which are so repugnant to common usage, that we may
doubt whether it would not be better to admit false speaking towards
some parties, in the cases of which we have spoken, or some of them,
(for I do not here pretend to give accurate rules,) rather than thus
make such indiscriminate exceptions as to *what is* false speaking:
thus when they say, *I do not know,* they hold that it may mean, *I do
not know that I shall tell you;* when they say, *I have not,* they hold
that it may mean, *I have not to give to you;* and others of this
kind, which the common sense of mankind repudiates; and which, if
they are admitted, there is no reason why he who affirms may not be
held to deny, and he who denies to affirm.

4 For it is undoubtedly true, that there is no word which does
not admit of an ambiguous sense, since all words have, besides
their primary meaning, or signification of first notion, another meaning, the signification of second notion, and that, various according to
the various technical applications, and other meanings from metaphor
or other figures.   Nor do I more approve the device of those who,
as if they were afraid of the word only and not the thing, call those
expressions *jests,* which are uttered with the most serious countenance and manner of delivery.

XVIII.   But it is to be observed that what we have said of false
speaking in assertory discourses, applied so that it can damage none
except a public enemy, is not to be referred to promissory declarations.   For from a promise, as we have partly said, a new and
special right is conferred on him to whom the promise is made;
and this holds even between enemies, without any exception as to
hostility existing at the moment; and not only in express promises,
but also in tacit ones, as we shall shew in speaking of parley,
when we come to that part which concerns the keeping of faith in
war.

XIX.   Further, we must again apply what we have said in our
former discussion concerning Oaths, whether assertory or promissory;
that they have force to exclude all exceptions which may be taken
on account of the person with whom we are dealing: since in these,
we have to do, not with men only, but with God also, and are bound
by our oath to Him, although there should no right accrue to any
man.   And we have there said also, that in an oath, it is not as in
other discourse, that to excuse us from the guilt of a lie, unusual
interpretations of words may be admitted; but that by all means
truth is required in that sense which the hearer is in good faith conceived to understand: so that we must detest the impiety of those
who say that men are to be deceived with oaths as boys with toys.

XX.   1 We know that some of the kinds of fraud which we
have said are allowed by Natural Law, have been repudiated by some
people, or some individuals.   But that does not proceed from an

opinion that such frauds are iniquitous, but from a certain eminent loftiness of mind, and sometimes from a confidence in the strength of the speaker. In Elian we have a saying of Pythagoras, that men approach to the gods principally by two things; by always speaking the truth, and by doing good to others; and in Jamblichus veracity is called the leader to all divine and human good things. So Aristotle says that the *magnanimous man loves to speak truly and freely;* Plutarch, that *to lie is slavish.* So Arrian of Ptolemy and of Alexander; Mamertinus of Julian; so Plutarch of Aristides, and Probus of Epaminondas, that they would not lie even in jest.

2 And this is still more to be observed by Christians, to whom not only simplicity is commanded, Matt. x. 16, but also vain speaking interdicted, Matt. xii. 36; and He proposed as an example, in whose mouth was found no guile. So Lactantius says that we must not be content with telling truth to our friends, but also to strangers and enemies. So Neoptolemus is described in Sophocles, *excellent in simplicity and noblemindedness;* as Dio Prusæensis notes. See his answer to Ulysses in the *Philoctetes,* and see Euripides in the *Rhesus.*

3 So Alexander said that he would not steal a victory. And Polybius relates that the Achæans abhorred all fraud towards enemies; thinking victory then only firm when, as Claudian says, it subjugates the minds of the enemy. Such were the Romans till the end of the second Punic war. It is their virtue, Elian says, not to seek victory by art and cunning. And accordingly when Perseus was deceived with the hope of peace, the older senators said that they did not recognize the arts of Rome; that their ancestors had never in war boasted of cunning instead of courage; not of the tricks of the Carthaginians, not of the subtlety of the Greeks, among whom it was more glorious to deceive an enemy than to overcome him by force. And then they added that sometimes, for the present moment, success might be obtained by deceit more than by valour; but that his mind only was thoroughly conquered, who was compelled to confess that he was subdued, not by art or by chance, but in a close trial of strength in a just and pious war. So even later in Tacitus. Such too were the Tibarenians, who announced beforehand the time and place of battle. And Mardonius in Herodotus says that the Greeks of his time did the same.

XXI. As to what concerns the mode of acting, this is to be noted; that what it is not lawful for another to do, it is not lawful for us to impel or solicit him to do. We may take such examples as these: it is not lawful for a subject to kill his king, nor to give up towns without public authority, nor to despoil his fellow-citizens. Therefore it is not lawful to move a citizen, continuing in that character, to do such things. For in all cases, he who gives another cause to sin, does himself sin. Nor is it enough to reply that to him who impels such a man to such a deed, say to kill an enemy, the deed is lawful. It is lawful, but not in that manner. Augustine says well, *It makes no difference whether you yourself commit a wickedness, or make another man commit it for you.*

XXII.   The case is different, if any one use the help of a person who does wrong of his own accord, and not at his impulse; which we have proved elsewhere, by the example of God himself, not to be unjust. *We receive a deserter by the laws of war,* says Celsus; that is, it is not against the laws of war to receive him who leaves the enemy and comes over to us.

CHAPTER II.

How far by the Law of Nations the goods of Subjects are liable for the debt of the Rulers; and herein, of Reprisals.

I. 1 LET us come to the results which in war flow from the Law of Nations. These belong partly to any war, partly, to certain kinds of war. We begin with the general case.

By the mere Law of Nature, no one is bound by the act of another, except he who is the successor to his property : for the rule that property passes with its burthens, was introduced when property was introduced. The emperor Zeno says that it is contrary to natural equity that one person should be molested for the debts of another. Hence the Roman Law provides that the wife is not responsible for the husband, the husband for the wife, the son for the father, the father or mother for the son.

2 Nor do individuals owe what the general body owes, as Ulpian plainly says: that is, if the general body have property; for otherwise, they are bound, not as individuals, but as parts of the general body. Seneca says, *If any one lends money to my country, the debt is not mine : but I will give my share towards the payment.* He had before said, *Individuals will owe, not as a part of their own debt, but a part of the public.* Hence it was specially provided by the Roman Law that the members of a village should not be responsible for the debts of others of the same village; and elsewhere, no possession can be made responsible for other persons' debts, not even public debts. And in a law of Justinian, securities for others are forbidden; it being stated as the reason, that the debtor is one person, and the person distrained, another, which is stated to be unreasonable and odious. And so king Theodoric calls this liberty of suretyship disgraceful.

II. 1 But though this is so, a rule may be introduced by the instituted Law of Nations, and it appears, has been introduced, that for a debt due from any civil society or its head, either on his own account or as bound for another, all the goods, corporeal and incorporeal, of the members of the society, are bound and liable. And this rule has been established by a certain necessity, in that otherwise

there would be great licence for the commission of injury, since the
goods of the rulers often cannot so easily be got at, as those of private persons, who are more numerous. And therefore this is one of
the rights which, Justinian says, were instituted by nations on the
exigency of usage and to meet human necessities.

2 And this is not in any way so repugnant to nature that it may
not be introduced by usage and tacit consent, since sureties become
bound for debts without any cause, by consent alone. And it was to
be hoped that the members of the same society would be able to exact rights from one another, and to consult their own indemnity, more
easily than strangers, who in many cases are little attended to: and
moreover there was, by such an obligation, an advantage to be gained
by all peoples, so that they upon whom in one case it presses heavily,
in another would find their relief in it.

3 That this usage is received, appears not only from the wars on
a large scale which one people carries on against another : for in these
the rule that is followed appears in the formulæ by which war is declared ; as in Livy, *I declare war against the people of the Latins and
against the Latian men* : and in the proposal, *Whether they wished that
war should be declared against Philip of Macedon and those who are
under his rule* : and in the decree itself, *The Roman people order that
war should be with the Hermundulan people, and with the Hermundulan
men ;* in Cincius on military affairs, and elsewhere, *Let him be an enemy
and those who are under his protection* : but also, when war on this full
scale has not yet taken place, but where some violent exaction of rights,
that is, an imperfect war, has been found necessary, we see the same
usage prevail. Agesilaus said to Pharnabazus, *When we were friends to
the king we behaved in a friendly manner to his people : and now that we
are enemies, we shall behave hostilely to the same : and therefore as you
choose to belong to the king, we shall attack him through you.*

III. 1 A kind of the exaction of rights of which we speak was
what the Athenians called *androlepsy,* or man-taking ; and the Attic
law was, that *if any one was violently killed, his neighbours and relatives
had the right of taking men till either the murderer was punished, or the
murderers given up ; but three men only may be taken, and not more.*
Here we see that for a debt of the city which is under an obligation
to punish those of its subjects who have injured others, a certain incorporeal right of the subjects is held bound, namely, their personal
liberty ; so that they are enslaved till the city punishes the guilty.
The Egyptians, as we learn from Diodorus, held that a man's body or
liberty were not to be bound for a debt : but yet there is nothing in
such a usage repugnant to nature : and the contrary practice has prevailed not only among the Greeks, but also other nations.

2 Aristocrates, a contemporary of Demosthenes, had proposed a
decree that if any one slew Charidemus, he might be taken wherever
he was, and if any one resisted he should be held as an enemy. In
this, Demosthenes finds much to reprehend ; first, that Aristocrates had

not distinguished between killing justly and unjustly, though it might happen that he was killed justly: and next, that he does not require that first a trial should be demanded: and thirdly, that he requires those to be bound who have received the homicide, and not those among whom the act was committed. And he then refers to the *androlepsy* just mentioned, saying that *The law made them responsible among whom the homicide took place; but that Andronicus left these untouched, and punished those who received the homicide; though the usage of all nations was to protect refugees.* The fourth objection is, that Aristocrates makes the matter forthwith a case of public war, the law being content with the man-taking.

3 Of these, the first, second, and fourth arguments are not without weight. But as to the third, except it be restricted to the case of slaying by accident or in self-defense, is said rather oratorically than according to truth and justice: for the law of nations that suppliants are to be received and defended, applies to those, as we have said, who have been unfortunate, not criminal.

4 Moreover the case is the same as to those among whom the crime was committed, and those who refuse to punish or to give up the guilty person. And therefore the law which Demosthenes quotes either receives from usage that interpretation which I have given, or was afterwards expressly made valid against such evasions. That one of these two was the case will not be denied by any one who attends to what is said by Julius Pollux of this androlepsy, referring it to those who receive the homicide. So Harpocration on androlepsy.

5 A like practice it is, when, to recover a citizen made captive by manifest wrong, citizens of the state by which this has been done are detained. Thus at Carthage some interfered to prevent Aristo of Tyre being taken, saying that if this was done, *the same would be done to Carthaginians at Tyre, and in other mercantile cities whither they went in numbers.*

IV. Another kind of the violent exaction of rights is taking security of the people of the offender; which the more recent jurists call the *Right of Reprisals;* the Saxons and Angles, *Withernamium;* and the French, among whom it is granted by the king, *Letters of Marque.* And this has place, as the jurists say, when Rights are denied.

V. 1 This is understood to be permitted by custom, not only if judgment against a criminal or a debtor cannot be obtained within a reasonable time; but also in a very clear case, (for in a doubtful case the presumption is for the established judges,) if judgment be given plainly against right. Even among subjects, a wrong sentence does not abolish a true debt. *A true debtor though absolved remains a debtor,* says Paulus. And when by the wrong doing of the judge the creditor takes a thing which was not the property of the debtor, as being liable; and when it was inquired *if when the debt was paid this ought to be restored to the debtor,* Scævola decided that it was. There is this difference [between a question among subjects of the same state and a question with foreigners], that the subjects of the same state cannot lawfully impede by force the execution even of an unjust sentence, on account of the authority of the law over them; but foreigners have the right of compelling: a right however which they may not lawfully use, so long as they can obtain by judgment what is their own.

2 The rule then that, for such a cause, either the bodies or the moveables of the subjects of him who does not grant me justice, may be taken by me, is not indeed introduced by nature, but is everywhere received as usage. The oldest example is in Homer, where Nestor says that he took the flocks and herds of the Elidians as reprisals for his father's horses. He goes on to say that he summoned all those to help him who had any debts owing from the Elidians. There is another example in the Roman history, where Aristodemus, the heir of the Tarquins, detained the Roman ships at Cumæ, as security for the goods of the Tarquins. And Aristotle, in his *Œconomics*, mentions the decree of the Carthaginians for taking the ships of strangers *if any one has a claim.*

VI. That the life of innocent subjects should be held bound for such cause, was perhaps believed among ancient peoples; and on this ground, that they conceived that every man had a plenary right over his own life, and that this might be transferred to the state; but that this is not good doctrine, nor agreeable to sound theology, we have elsewhere said. It may however take place, not intentionally, but by accident; as if they are killed who attempt to impede the exaction of rights. But if such a result be foreseen, by the law of charity the promotion of right is rather to be omitted, as we have elsewhere shewn; since by that law, the life of a man ought to be of more value to us, especially being Christians, than our goods.

VII. 1 In this matter, no less than in others, we are to distinguish what things are properly *juris gentium*, parts of the Law of Nations, and what is constituted by Civil Law or by Compact.

2 By the Law of Nations, all the subjects of him who does an injury are liable to be security for satisfaction, being subjects from a permanent cause, whether indigenous or immigrants; but not they who are there in passing, or making a short stay. For such liability is introduced according to the example of the burthens which are laid on subjects for paying public debts: to which those are not liable who are subject to the laws of the place only for a time. From the subjects, are excepted, by the Law of Nations, ambassadors not sent to our enemies, and their property.

3 But by the civil or instituted Law of Nations, there are often excepted from this liability the persons of women and children; and the property of literary classes, and of merchants. By the Law of Nations any one may take surety for satisfaction, as in the *androlepsy* of the Athenians. By the instituted law of many places, such satisfaction is to be sought from the supreme authority; and in other

places, from the judges. By the Law of Nations, the ownership of things taken is *ipso facto* acquired to the extent of the debt and expenses, the residue being to be returned. By instituted Law, they are to be cited who are concerned, and then their property sold or seized by public authority for the benefit of those who have a claim. Such and other rules are to be sought in those who treat of the Civil Law, and especially, in this matter, from Bartolus, who has written on Reprisals.

4 I will add, because it is a point which tends to the softening of the right of which we are speaking, which of itself is sufficiently harsh, that they who, by not paying what they owed, or by withholding any right, have given occasion for this seizure of securities, are, by Natural and Divine Law, bound to make good the loss to those who have thereby suffered.

CHAPTER III.

Of a Just or Formal War by the Law of Nations; and herein of Declaration of War.

I. 1 WE have above begun to say that a *just* war is often so called in respectable authors, not from the cause in which it originates, nor from the scale of the movements, but on account of certain peculiar jural effects. What kind of war this is, is best understood from the definition of an enemy in the Roman Jurist: *Those are our enemies who publicly declare war against us or we against them: others are robbers or pirates,* says Pomponius. And so Ulpian, adding: *therefore he who is taken prisoner by robbers is not subject to them, nor is postliminium necessary for him. But he who is taken prisoner by enemies, suppose Germans or Parthians, becomes their slave, and recovers his former state by postliminium.* So Paulus. Ulpian adds that, in civil wars, the opposite parties are not formal enemies, and therefore the captives taken do not lose their free condition.

2 We may note that which is said by the Roman jurists, of the Roman People, is to be understood of him who has the supreme power in any state. *He is our enemy,* says Cicero, *who has the government, the council, the treasury, the consent and agreement of the citizens, and the power of making war and peace.*

II. 1 A State or Commonwealth does not cease to be such by perpetrating an act of injustice, even in common: nor is a band of robbers or pirates a State, although they preserve a sort of equal rule among them, without which indeed no body of men can hold together. For such a body is associated for the purpose of crime: but the others, though they are not free from fault, are associated by mutual rights, and acknowledge certain rights in others; if not rights according to Natural Law (which is often much obliterated), yet rights according to certain conventions or usages.   Thus the Greeks, while they held it lawful to plunder at sea, abstained from murder, from night-attacks, and from seizing oxen and ploughs, as the Scholiast to Thucydides notes.   Other nations, as mentioned by Strabo, who lived by plunder at sea, were in the habit, when they had carried their plunder home, of sending to the owners to ransom it at a fair price.   So Homer.

2 But in morals, the principal part is taken as the characteristic; so Cicero and Galen.   Wherefore Cicero spoke too widely, when he said (in the third book of the *Republic*) that when the king is unjust, or the aristocracy, or the people itself, the commonwealth is not so much to be called vicious, as non-existing: which opinion, Augustine correcting, says, *We are not to say that the people does not exist, or that its common concerns are not those of a commonwealth, so long as there remains a body of any reasonable number, associated by a common participation in its interests.*   A body which is diseased is still a body; and a state, though grievously out of health, is a state, as long as there remain the laws, the tribunals, and other things which are necessary in order that strangers may there obtain justice, as well as private persons in their affairs one with another.   Dio Chrysostom speaks more rightly when he says that Law, (especially that which realizes the Law of Nations,) exists in a state, as the soul in the body; and that when that is taken away, the state no longer exists.   And Aristides, in the oration in which he exhorts the Rhodians to concord, shews that many good laws may subsist even under a tyranny.   Aristotle in his *Politics* says, if any one carry too far the violent proceedings either of the Few or of the People, the commonwealth first becomes vicious, and by going on, becomes non-existent.   We will illustrate this by examples.

3 That a person taken prisoner by robbers is not subject to them, we have above quoted from Ulpian.   He says also that those who are taken by the Germans do lose their liberty.   Yet among the Germans, robberies which were exercised out of the boundaries of each state were subject to no infamy; which are the words of Cæsar.   Tacitus says of the Venedi, *In the woody and mountainous region which occupies the whole space between the Peucini and the Fenni, they drive their booty freely.*   The same writer elsewhere says that the Catti, a noble people of Germany, practise plunder.   The same author calls the Garamantes a nation habituated to plunder, but still a nation. The Illyrians were accustomed to plunder at sea without distinction: yet a triumph over them was celebrated, as over an hostile nation; though Pompey had no triumph for conquering the Pirates.   So great is the distinction between a people, though wicked, and those who, not being a people, associate for the sake of crime.

III.   But a transition may take place from one condition to the other; not only in individuals, as Jephtha, Arsaces, Viriatus, from being leaders of bands of robbers, became regular rulers; but also in societies, so that they who had been only robbers, embracing another mode of life, become a state. Augustine, speaking of bands of robbers, says, *If this evil, by the accession of bad men, grows to such a height that they keep possession of their ground, establish a seat of residence, occupy cities, subjugate peoples, it assumes the name of a kingdom.*

IV. Who have sovereign authority, we have discussed above: from whence it may be understood that if any have it partially only, they may, so far as that part goes, carry on a just war: and much more they who are not subjects, but bound by an unequal league; as under the Romans, we learn that the Volsci, Latins, Spaniards, Carthaginians, though inferior in the federation, all maintained just wars.

V. But that a war may be just in this sense, it is not sufficient that it be carried on between the supreme authorities on each side; but it is requisite also, as already said, that it be publicly decreed; and in such manner publicly decreed, that signification of that fact is made by the one party to the other, as Ennius [Cicero, J. B.] speaks of *promulgated wars.* So Cicero, in his *Offices,* says that by the Fecial Law, no war was just except one preceded by a demand for redress, or by a declaration of war. So in Isidore. So Livy: and where he narrates that the Acarnanians wasted Attica, he adds, *This was the first irritation of the minds of the parties; afterwards a just war was decreed and declared by the states.*

VI. 1 In order to understand these passages concerning the declaration of war, we must distinguish what is done by Natural Law, and what is, by nature, not due, but only decent: what by the Law of Nations is required for the jural effects of that Law, and what, besides, follows from the peculiar institutions of certain peoples.

By Natural Law, when either violence is to be resisted, or punishment is to be exacted from an offender, no declaration is required. This is what Sthenelaidas the Ephor says in Thucydides: *We have not to wrangle in words and pleadings, being wronged in more than words.* And Latinus in Dionysius: *He who begins a war may be repelled by the sufferer.* So Elian from Plato. Hence Dio Chrysostom says that *most wars are begun without declaration of war.* And on the same ground Livy objects to Menippus, the prefect of Antiochus, that he had slain certain Romans, war being neither declared, nor so far existing, that they had heard of swords drawn and blood shed; thus shewing that either of these two cases would have sufficed for the defense of the act. Nor is declaration of war any more necessary, if the owner attempts to lay hands upon his own property.

2 But whenever one thing is taken as security for another, or the property of the debtor is seized for the debt, and still more, if any one sets about taking the property of those who are subjects of the debtor, a formal demand is requisite, by which it may appear, that in no other way can we obtain our property or our debt. For this right of so taking is not a primary right, but a secondary and substitutive right, as we have elsewhere explained. And in like man-

ner, before he who has the supreme power can be attacked for the debt or delict of his subject, there ought to be interposed a formal demand which may put him in the wrong, so that he may be either supposed to be the author of a damage, or to have himself committed a delict according to the principles already laid down.

3 And even when Natural Law does not require such a formal demand to be made, yet it is decent and laudable that it be interposed; in order, for instance, to avoid offense, or to give room for making atonement for the delict by repentance and satisfaction, as we have said in speaking of the ways of avoiding war; so that extremes are not to be tried in the first place. And to the same purpose is the precept which God gave the Hebrews, that before besieging a city they should invite it to make peace. This command, however, was specially given to the Hebrew people, and therefore is wrongly by some confounded with the Law of Nations. Cyrus, when he had come into the country of the Armenians, before he did any harm to any one, sent persons to the king to ask for the appointed tribute and soldiers; *thinking that more humane than to march upon him without notice*, as Xenophon says in the *Cyropœdia*. But by the Law of Nations, a declaration of war is requisite in all cases to give occasion for these peculiar effects; not on both sides, but on one.

VII. 1 But such a declaration is either conditional or pure; conditional, when it is conjoined with a demand for the restoration of the things in question. But under the demand of restoration of things, the Fecial Law comprehended not only demands by the right of ownership, but also the promotion of anything which was due for civil claims or criminal acts; as Servius rightly explains. Hence the formula requiring that the things be *restored, satisfied, given up:* where *given up*, as we have elsewhere explained, is to be understood that the persons summoned may be allowed to prefer themselves punishing the guilty person. This demand was called *clarigation*, as Pliny testifies. We have in Livy a conditional declaration: that *this injury, except it were remedied by those who had done it, they themselves would repel:* and in Tacitus, *except they exact punishment of the offenders, he would make a promiscuous slaughter.* And in the same way in the *Supplices* of Euripides; and Statius in his narration of the same matter in the *Thebais*. Polybius calls this *demanding satisfaction;* the old Romans, *condicere.*

A pure declaration is what is especially called *indictio.*

2 But a conditional declaration is [often] followed by a pure declaration, though this is not necessary, but is done *ex superabundanti*. And the formulæ are given, accusing the enemy of injustice. But that in this case, as we have said, such declaration is not necessary, appears from this, that it might be made to the nearest town occupied by troops, as the Feciales announced, when they were consulted about the case of Philip of Macedon, and afterwards of Antiochus, since the first declaration of war was to be made by him who

was attacked. In the war with Pyrrhus, the declaration was made to one of the soldiers of Pyrrhus, and this was done in the Circus of Flaminius, where the soldier was compelled formally to purchase his place in order to be a party to the cause, as Servius relates on the ninth book of the *Æneid*.

3 That the formality is unnecessary, is also proved by this, that war is often declared on both sides, as the Peloponnesian war by the Corcyreans and Corinthians, though it was sufficient that it should be declared on one side only.

VIII. There are some things which belong to the institutions of certain nations, not to the Law of Nations in general; as the Caduceus, or Herald's rod among the Greeks; the *sagmina* (sacred herbs,) and bloody spear, among the Equicolæ at first, and the adoption of this by the Romans; the renunciation of friendship and alliance, if any had existed; the thirty appointed days after the demand of restitution; the sending of the spear a second time; and other observances of the same kind, which are not to be confounded with things which belong to the Law of Nations in general. For Arnobius informs us that the greater part of those things had ceased to be practised in his time; and even in the age of Varro some were omitted. The third Punic war was declared and commenced at the same time. And Mæcenas in Dio holds that some of these belong especially to a popular state.

IX. A war declared against him who has the supreme authority in a people is conceived as declared, at the same time, not only against all who are his subjects, but also against all who join themselves to him, as accessories to him; and this is what the [feudal] jurists say, that he who defies the prince defies his adherents; for to declare war they call *to defy*. This is to be understood of that especial war which is carried on against the person mentioned in the declaration: thus when war had been declared against Antiochus, it was not thought proper to declare it against the Etolians separately, because they openly joined Antiochus; the Feciales answered that *the Etolians had of themselves declared war against themselves*.

X. But if, when that war is over, a people or a king are to be attacked on account of aid supplied, then, in order to obtain the effects of the Law of Nations, there is need for a new declaration of war. And therefore it was rightly said that those were not just wars according to the Law of Nations, which Manlius carried on against the Gallo-Grecians, or Cæsar against Ariovistus: for they were then attacked, not as accessories in another's wars, but as principals; and to this effect, by the Law of Nations, a declaration of war was required, and by the constitution of Rome, a new edict of the people. For what had been said in the decree against Antiochus: *Do you decree that war should take place with Antiochus and his followers?* which form was also used with regard to Perseus, seems to require to be understood, as long as the war with Antiochus or with Perseus continued, and with regard to those who really joined in the war.

XI.   The cause why nations require a declaration of war for that
kind of war which we call *just* by the Law of Nations, is not that given
by some, that nothing may be done clandestinely or fraudulently; for
that is a matter rather of bold frankness than of right; as some
nations are related to have announced beforehand the day and place
of battle: but that it might be clearly known that the war was
undertaken, not as a venture of private persons, but by the will of
the two peoples, or their heads: for from this public character arise
peculiar effects, which do not take place either in a war carried on
against pirates, or in one which a king makes against his subjects.
And so Seneca speaks with a distinction, of *war declared against neigh-*
bours, or carried on against our own citizens.

XII.   For what some remark, and illustrate by examples, that
even in such wars, what is captured becomes the property of the captors, is true, but on one side only, and that by Natural Law, not by
the instituted Law of Nations; since that regards only nations and
their dealings with nations, not those who are without nation, or are
only part of a nation.   They err in this, that they think that a war
undertaken for the purpose of defending one's self or one's property,
does not need to be preceded by a declaration of war; for it by
all means needs such an introduction: not indeed simply, but for
the sake of leading to the effects we have already partly explained, and
shall explain further.

XIII.   Nor is it true even that a war may not be begun immediately after it has been declared: which Cyrus did in Armenia, and
the Romans towards the Carthaginians, as we have already said.   For
a declaration of war does not, by the Law of Nations, require any
definite time after it.   But it may be requisite that, by Natural
Law, some time may be required, in consequence of the quality of
the business: as for instance, if property is required to be restored,
or criminals to be punished, and this is not refused.   For then,
so much time is to be given as may conveniently suffice for doing what
is asked.

XIV.   But even if the rights of legation be violated, it does not
follow that a declaration of war is not needed for the effects to
which I refer: but it is sufficient if it be made in such way as it
may safely be made, that is, by letter: as also it is usual to make
summonses and denunciations in unsafe places.

Y

CHAPTER IV.

Of the right of killing enemies in formal War, and of other violence against the person.

I. ON the line of Virgil, *Æn.* x. 14, in which he says that after the declaration of war it will be lawful to ravage the enemy, Servius Honoratus gives an account of the origin of the Feciales, and the mode of claiming what had been taken from the Romans, and if satisfaction were not given by restoration, declaring war by throwing a spear. *Rapere,* to ravage, and *satisfacere,* to restore, were words of a technical comprehensiveness. And thus we learn that a war declared between two nations, or their heads, has certain peculiar and appropriate effects, which do not follow from the nature of war itself: and this agrees with what we have already adduced from the Roman lawyers.

II. 1 But Virgil said *licebit,* it will be lawful; let us see what that implies. For sometimes *that* is said to be lawful which is every way right and pious; though something else might be done which is more laudable; as St Paul says, *all things* (of a certain kind) *are lawful for me, but all things are not expedient.* Thus it is lawful to marry, even when celibacy is better; it is lawful to marry a second time, though once only is better; it is lawful for a Christian husband to leave his pagan wife (in certain circumstances), but he may keep her: as Augustine says, both are lawful before God, but not alike expedient. Ulpian says, that a seller, after the day appointed for delivering the wine, may let it run away; *but though he may thus shed it, if he do not, he is rather to be praised.*

2 In other cases a thing is said to be lawful, not which is agreeable to piety and duty, but which is not liable to punishment. So among some people fornication is, in this sense, lawful; and among the Egyptians and Lacedæmonians, theft also. So the right of dividing the debtor's body was lawful by the Twelve Tables. But this use of the word *licere*, to be lawful, is less proper, as Cicero says: *it is not lawful to commit a sin, but we are deceived by an erroneous phrase; for we say that is lawful which is allowed by law:* and in another place he says to the judges, *you are not to consider what is lawful or allowed, but what is decent and proper.* So to kings who are irresponsible everything is said to be *lawful.* But Claudian rightly says to a king, *You are not to consider what is lawful, but what becomes you.* And so Musonius.

3 And in this sense, what is lawful is often opposed to what is right (*oportet*), as in Seneca repeatedly. So Ammianus, Pliny, Cicero. And Cicero opposes *fas esse*, what is right by nature, to *licere*, what is allowed by law. And Quintilian opposes *jura*, lawful rights, to justice.

III. In this latter sense, it is lawful to harm an enemy, both in person and in property; and this, not only for him who is making a just war and who harms the enemy in the way which is allowed by Natural Law, as we have explained; but on both sides, and without distinction: so that he cannot for this reason be punished, if caught in another territory, as a homicide or a thief, nor can war be made on him on the ground of such an act. So Sallust says, *All being lawful to the victor by the laws of war.*

IV. The reason of this rule among nations was this: that for other nations to offer to pronounce on the right of war between two peoples, would be dangerous for those who interfered, and who might thus be involved in a war belonging to others; as the Massilians said, in the case of Cæsar and Pompey, that they had neither jurisdiction nor power to discern which side was most in the right. And in the next place, it can scarcely be known by external indications, in a just war, what is the proper limit of self-defense, of recovery of property, or of exaction of punishment; so that it is by all means better to leave this to the conscience of the belligerents, than to appeal to extraneous decision. So the Achæans in their oration to the Senate*, ask, *In what manner are things done by the laws of war to be called under discussion?* Besides this effect of this allowable character of acts, there is another, as regards ownership, of which we shall have to speak hereafter.

V. 1 This right of doing harm to the enemy, extends, first to their persons, as we have many testimonies in Greek authors. *He is pure who slays enemies,* according to the Greek proverb in Euripides.

---

* Not to the Senate, but to Appius the legate in the Achæan Council. J. B.

And therefore by the usages of the Greeks, though it was not lawful to wash, or to eat, or to drink, and still less to join in sacred offices, with those who had slain a man not in war; yet it was lawful to do so with those who had slain in war.   And perpetually, to slay, is called the right of war.   So in Livy, Marcellus, and Alorcus, and so of the Astapenses slain by the laws of war.   So Cicero for Deiotarus and for Marcellus; Cæsar to the Hædui; Josephus; Statius; speak of persons slain, or liable to be slain, by the right of war.

2 That when these writers speak of the right of war, they do not mean a right free from all blame, but such an impunity as I have mentioned, appears from other places.   So Tacitus says, *In peace, men's case and desert is regarded; when war comes, the guilty and the innocent fall alike.*   And elsewhere, *The justice of men did not permit them to honour that slaughter, nor the right of war to avenge it.*   And in the same way we must understand the right of war which Livy says the Achivi did not exercise against Eneas and Antenor, because they had always advised peace.   So Seneca, in his epistles, says that *The things which, if men did privately, would subject them to capital punishment, when they are done in the general's cloak, we praise;* and Cyprian, *When individuals commit homicide, it is a crime; it is called a virtue when done publicly.   Impunity is acquired not by innocence, but by the greatness of the mischief done.*   And again, *Rights were accommodated to the convenience of the offenders, and that became lawful which was public.*   So Lactantius says that the Romans inflicted injuries legitimately, and Lucan speaks of *right given to wickedness.*

VI.   And this right to do such things as allowable, is very comprehensive.   For in the first place, it comprehends not only those who actually bear arms, or who are the subjects of him who makes the war, but all who are within the hostile boundaries; as appears by the formula in Livy: *Let him be an enemy, and those that are under his protection.*   This is held, because such persons also may give occasion for fear, which in a continued and extended war, suffices to establish the right of which we speak.   This case is different from that of securities [of individuals for the state], which, as we have said, were introduced after the example of burthens imposed to pay the debts of the state; wherefore it is not to be wondered at that much more is allowable in war than in the law of securities.   And this is not a matter of doubt as concerns strangers who enter the enemy's confines when war has been begun and is known.

VII.   But those who had gone thither before the war, may, it would seem, by the law of nations, be held for enemies after a moderate time within which they could depart.   And thus the Corcyreans, when about to besiege Epidamnus, first gave allowance to strangers to depart, and announced that if they did not, they would hold them for enemies.

VIII.   1 As to those who are truly the subjects of the enemy, that is, from a permanent cause, it is allowable to attack them where-ever they are, by this right of nations, if we regard their persons. For when war is declared against any people, it is declared against the men of that people, as we shewed above; and so in the decree against Philip. And he who is an enemy may be attacked every-where, as Euripides says. So Marcion, of deserters.

2 Therefore we may slay such persons on our own soil, on the hostile soil, on ground which is no one's, and on the sea. That it is not lawful to slay them, or do them violence, in a peaceful neutral territory, is a consequence, not of their personal rights, but of the rights of the lord of the territory. For civil societies may establish a rule that, against those who are in any territory, nothing shall be done by violence, except when judicial proceedings have been tried; as we have already quoted from Euripides. And when judicial proceedings are in force, then the deserts of persons are regarded, and there is an end of that promiscuous right of doing harm, which, as we have said, has been established between enemies. Livy relates that seven ships of war of the Carthaginians were in a port belonging to Syphax, who was then at peace both with the Carthaginians and the Romans; and that Scipio came with two ships and might have been destroyed by the Carthaginians before they entered the harbour; but that coming with a brisk wind they struck into the port before the Carthaginians could raise their anchors; and then, in the port belonging to the king, the Carthaginians did not venture to attack them.

IX. 1 To return to the subject; how wide this allowance of doing harm to enemies extends, may be understood from this; that the slaughter of infants and women is allowed to have impunity, as comprehended in that right of war. I will not here adduce the slaying of the women and the little ones of Heshbon (Deut. ii. 34); and what they did to the Canaanites and their allies; for these are the doings of God, who has a more absolute right over men than men have over brutes. But a passage which approaches more nearly to a testimony of the common usage of nations, is that in the Psalms, cxxxvii. 9, *Happy shall he be that taketh and dasheth thy little ones against the stones.* So Homer.

2 When the Thracians took Mycalessus they put to death the women and children. So the Macedonians did when they took Thebes; the Romans when they took Ilurgis in Spain; Germanicus ravaged the Marsi with fire and sword without mercy to sex or age. Titus exposed the children and women taken at Jerusalem to fight with wild beasts in the public spectacles*. And yet Germanicus and Titus are considered as humane men; so much had that kind of cruelty become customary. And hence we are the less to wonder that old men were slain, as Priam by Pyrrhus.

X. 1 Even captives were not exempted from this liability. No

---

* Barbeyrac shews that this assertion is not supported by good authors, and is apparently taken from a declamation of Cardan against Titus.

law spares or protects a captive. So Pyrrhus in Seneca, Scylla in the Ciris of Virgil; and so in the case in Seneca, where the captive was a woman, Polyxena. So Horace. Donatus says that *servi* were so called because they were preserved when the law of war was that they should be slain. So the captives at Epidamnus were slain; and five thousand captives by Annibal: and by M. Brutus not a few. So Cæsarianus in Hirtius speaks.

2 Nor is the power of killing such captives excluded by any lapse of time, so far as the Laws of Nations are concerned; though by the Laws of States, this right is restricted, in some places more, in some, less.

XI.   We have even examples constantly of persons who offer themselves as suppliants, and are put to death; as seen in the act of Achilles in Homer, and Mago and Turnus in Virgil: which are narrated so as to imply a defense of the right of war which I have mentioned. And Augustine, praising the Goths who had spared those who begged for their lives, and those who took refuge in temples, says, *What would have been allowable by the right of war, they held not allowable for them.*   Nor are those who surrender always received, as in the battle of the Granicus, those were not who were serving under the Persians *; and in Tacitus, the Uspenses praying for pardon for the free persons; *which prayer*, he says, *the victors rejected, that they might rather fall by the right of war.*   Here again note *the right of war.*

XII.   Even those who have surrendered unconditionally and been received, you may find, in history, put to death; as the rulers of Pometia by the Romans; the Samnites † by Sulla, the Numidians, and Vercingentorix himself, by Cæsar. Indeed this was almost the constant practice of the Romans towards the leaders of their enemies, whether taken or surrendered, that they should be put to death on the day of the triumph: as Cicero tells us, and Livy, Tacitus, and others. Tacitus also relates that Galba ordered a body of men to be decimated whom he had received begging for their lives: and Cecina, having had Aventicum surrendered to him, put to death Julius Alpinus, as the instigator of the war: but left the others to the clemency or cruelty of Vitellius.

XIII.   1 Historians sometimes mention, as the cause of putting to death enemies, especially captives or suppliants, the rule of retaliation, or their obstinacy in resisting: but these causes, as we have elsewhere explained, are rather suasory than justificatory. For *retaliation*, which is just, and properly so called, must be exercised against the same person who has offended: as may be understood from what we have said of the punishment of accessories. But on the other hand, it commonly happens that what is called retaliation, falls upon those

---

* This is not supported by the historians of Alexander, as Barbeyrac shews.

† This is not supported by good historians: J. B. who explains the error.

who have no share in the blame which is charged. The practice is, that those who are defeated, are made to suffer what they had intended to inflict; and that by such inflictions, the enemy are restrained from overbearing severities. So Diodorus.

2 As for obstinacy in defending one's own side, no one can think that a case for punishment, as the Neapolitans replied to Belisarius; and this is especially true when the part of each side in the war is either assigned by nature, or by choice for honourable reasons. Indeed this obstinacy is so far from being a crime, that it is a crime if any one leave his post; especially by the old military law of Rome : which admitted no excuse of fear or danger. *To quit one's post is with the Romans a capital crime,* says Livy. And therefore it is for his own utility, that a person uses this extreme rigour when he thinks it good: and this rigour is defended by that part of the Laws of Nations of which we now speak.

XIV. The same right has also been used towards hostages; and not those only who have bound themselves by some sort of convention, but those who are delivered up by others. By the Thessalians there were put to death on one occasion two hundred and fifty : by the Romans, the Volsci Aurunci, to the number of three hundred. It is to be noted also, that it was the custom to give boys as hostages, as by the Parthians; and this was done by Simon the Maccabee; also women were given up by the Romans at the time of Porsena; and by the Germans, as Tacitus relates*.

XV. 1 As the Laws of Nations permit many things, (in this way of permitting which we have explained,) which are forbidden by Natural Law; so they forbid some things which are permitted by Natural Law. For him whom it is lawful to put to death, whether we put to death by the sword or by poison, it makes no difference, if we look to Natural Law. It is doubtless more generous to kill, so that he who is killed has the power of defending himself; but this is not due to him who has deserved to die. But the Laws of Nations, if not of all, at least of the best, have long been, that it is not lawful to kill an enemy by poison. This consent had its rise in common utility, that the dangers of war, which are numerous enough, may not be made too extensive. And it is probable that this rule proceeded from kings, whose life may be defended from other causes, better than the lives of other persons; but is less safe than that of others from poison, except it be defended by the scruples of conscience, and the fear of infamy.

2 Livy, speaking of Perseus, calls these clandestine atrocities : so Claudian and Cicero use like expressions. The Roman consuls say that it is required, as a public example, that nothing of the kind be admitted, in the epistle to Pyrrhus which Gellius gives. So Valerius. And when the prince of the Catti offered to procure the death of

* J. B. corrects this reference.

Arminius by poison, Tiberius rejected the offer; thus gaining a glory like that of the ancient generals. Wherefore they who hold it lawful to kill the enemy by poison, as Baldus, following Vegetius, regard mere Natural Law, and overlook the Instituted Law of Nations.

XVI. 1 Somewhat different from poisoning, is the use of poisoned arrows or missiles, as approaching to open force: doubling the means of death, as Ovid says. This was practised by the Getæ, Parthians, Africans, Ethiopians. This, however, is against the Law of Nations, not universal, but of European nations, and those which share in European culture, as John of Salisbury has rightly observed. So Silius speaks of *making the weapon infamous with poison.*

2 To poison fountains, which must be discovered before long, Florus says, is not only against old rule, but also against the law of the gods; as the Laws of Nations are often ascribed to the gods; nor is it to be wondered, if to diminish dangers, there be some such tacit conventions of belligerents; as formerly in the permanent war of the Chalcidians and Eretrians, it was agreed not to use missiles*.

XVII. But the same is not true of making waters foul and undrinkable without poisoning them; which Solon and the Amphictyons are said to have justified towards barbarians: and Oppian mentions as customary in his time. For that is the same thing as turning away a stream, or intercepting a spring of water, which is lawful both by Natural Law and by consent.

XVIII. 1 It is often made a question, whether it be consistent with the Laws of Nations to send an assassin to put to death an enemy. But we must make a marked distinction between assassins who violate express or tacit faith; as subjects towards a king, vassals towards a seigneur, soldiers towards their general; those received as suppliants or as guests or as deserters, towards those who have received them; and on the other hand, those who are not bound by any such tie of good faith; as Pepin, the father of Charlemagne, with one attendant passed the Rhine and slew his enemy in his chamber; and Polybius relates that Theodotus the Etolian attempted the like against Ptolemy king of Egypt, *a manly deed of daring.* Such also is the attempt of Mutius Scævola, praised by historians, which he himself defends, saying, *An enemy I sought to slay an enemy.* And Porsena himself saw nothing but courage in the act: Valerius Maximus calls it a brave and pious deed; Cicero praises it.

2 In peril it is lawful to kill an enemy anywhere, not only by Natural Law, but by the Laws of Nations, as we have said above; nor does it make any difference how many they are who do or who suffer in such case. The six hundred Lacedæmonians with Leonidas entered the enemies' camp, and sought their way to the royal tent. A smaller number might have done the same with equal right. Those were few who laid an ambush for Metellus the consul and slew him: and those

---

* Of such acts in war, see *E. M.* 1062, &c.

who were very near stabbing Petilius Cerialis in his bed. Ambrose praises Eleazar because he attacked an elephant which was eminent above the rest, thinking that it carried the king. And not only they who do such acts, but they who procure others to do them, are held blameless by the law of nations. The persons who impelled Scævola to his deed were the old Roman Senators, so admired for their sanctity in war.

3 Nor ought any one to be moved by recollecting, that such persons, when taken, are put to the torture; for that happens, not because they have offended against the Laws of Nations, but because by the same Laws of Nations anything is lawful against an enemy; and each person inflicts on his enemy a heavier or a lighter ill according to his own utility*. And thus spies, whom undoubtedly it is lawful by the laws of nations to send, such as Moses sent, of whom Joshua was one, if taken are subject to the severest inflictions: (as Appian says, *It is the custom to kill spies*): and this is just in some cases, on the part of those who have a just cause of war; in others, is justified by the allowance which the right of war gives. And if any have been found who would not stoop to use such means, that is to be referred to their magnanimity, and trust in the open force which they can use, not to an opinion of what is just or unjust.

4 But with regard to the assassins whose deed includes perfidy, we are to judge otherwise. For not only do the perpetrators of such deeds act contrary to the Laws of Nations, but also they who use their services. For though in other cases, they who use the services of bad men against enemies are held to offend in the eye of God, but not in the sight of man, that is, not to act against the Laws of Nations; for in these cases, as Plautus says, *Custom has drawn law to its side;* and as Pliny says, *To deceive according to the manner of the time is called prudence;* yet this custom has stopped short of the right of murder. For they who make use of the perfidy of others for such purposes, are held to have violated, not only Natural Law, but also the Laws of Nations. This is conveyed in the letter of Alexander to Darius: *You carry on an impious war; and though you act with arms in your hands, you bargain for the heads of your enemies.* And again: *You who have not even observed the rights of war towards me.* And elsewhere, *He is to be followed to his destruction, not as a regular enemy, but as an assassin or a poisoner.* To the same rule is to be referred what is said of Perseus; that *he did not make arrangements for a regular war with a royal mind; but used all the clandestine acts of assassins and poisoners.* So Marcius Philippus, referring to the same acts of Perseus, that *all those acts which were hateful to the gods, he would feel in the sequel of his fortunes.* And to the same point tends what Valerius Maximus says: that *the killing of Viriatus brought on a double accusation of perfidy:—against his friends, in that he was taken off by their*

* See *E. M.* 1064.

hands:—against Servilius Cœpio the consul, because he was the author of this crime, by granting impunity to the perpetrators, and thus did not earn, but buy, a victory.

5 The reason why, in this case, a different rule was made, from that which prevails in other things is, that the dangers which beset eminent persons may not be too extreme. Eumenes said, that *he did not believe that any general wished to conquer in such a way that he should establish a very bad example against himself,* as Justin relates. And the same writer says that when Bessus had killed Darius, it was considered an example of what might happen to kings, and therefore a common cause of kings. So Œdipus in Sophocles; and Seneca in his tragedy on the same subject. The Roman Consuls wrote to Pyrrhus, *It seemed suitable to common example and to good faith that we should not be accessary to your death.*

6 And thus in a regular war, or between those who have the right of declaring a regular war, such a practice is not lawful. But out of regular war it is held lawful, also by the Laws of Nations. Thus, when such a plot was laid against Gannascus the traitor, Tacitus will not allow that it was degrading. Curtius says that the treachery of Spitamenes might be deemed less odious, because nothing that was done against Bessus, the murderer of his own king, could seem wrong. Thus also violation of faith in dealing with pirates and robbers is not blameless; but by usage, in consequence of the evil character of those against whom it is committed, it is unpunished.

XIX. 1 The violation of women in war you may perpetually find both allowed and disallowed. Those who allowed it, looked only at the injury done to the person, and judged that it was not incongruous to the laws of war that what belonged to the enemy should be subject to such injury. But others have judged better, who regarded, not only the injury, but the act of uncontrolled lust; and that the act has no tendency either to security or to punishment; and therefore ought to be no more unpunished in peace than in war: and this latter rule is the Law of Nations, not of all, but of the best. Thus Marcellus, before he took Syracuse, is recorded to have provided for the security of chastity, even in the enemy. Scipio says that it concerns both him and the Roman people that *nothing which is held sacred anywhere should be violated by them,* that is, by the more civilized people. Diodorus says of the soldiers of Agathocles, that they did not abstain from wicked violence against the women; and Elian, when he had related that the women and virgins of Pellene were violated by the victorious Sicyonians, exclaims, *Savage is this, O gods of Greece, and shocking even among barbarians, so far as I recollect.*

2 And it is fit that this rule should be observed by Christians, not only as part of military discipline, but as part of the Law of Nations: that is, that he who violates a woman, even in war, shall be everywhere liable to punishment. By the Hebrew law, no one could have

committed such an act with impunity; as may be understood from
what is said, Deut. xxi. 14, of marrying a captive and then not selling
her, on which place, Bechai, a Jewish master, observes: *God willed that
the camp of the Israelites should be holy, not given up to fornication
and other abominations, like the camps of the heathen.* Arrian, when he
has narrated that Alexander was captivated with the love of Roxana,
adds, that *he would not humble her as a captive, but take her in marriage;*
and praises the deed. Plutarch says of the same act, *He did not
humble her, but took her to wife like a philosopher.* Plutarch relates also
that by a decree of the Romans, a certain Torquatus was banished to
the island of Corsica for violating a virgin of the enemy.

CHAPTER V.

Of Ravaging and Pillaging Property.

I. CICERO says it is not against nature to despoil him whom it is honourable to kill. Wherefore it is not to be wondered at if the Laws of Nations permit the property of enemies to be destroyed and ravaged, when it has permitted them to be killed. Polybius says that by the Laws of War, all munitions of the enemy, ports, cities, men, ships, fruits, and anything of like kind, may be either plundered or destroyed. And in Livy we read; *There are certain rights of war which may be exercised and must be submitted to; as to burn crops, to destroy buildings, to drive off booty of cattle and men.* Indeed you find in every page of history, whole cities destroyed, walls levelled with the ground, lands depopulated, conflagrations raised. And it is to be noted that these measures are allowed also against those who have surrendered. *The townsmen,* says Tacitus, *opened their gates and put themselves at the mercy of the Romans, which was their safety; Artaxatœ was burnt.*

II. 1 The mere Law of Nations, setting aside the consideration of other duties, of which we shall afterwards speak, does not except sacred edifices, that is, those which are dedicated to God or to gods. *When places are taken by the enemy, all ceases to be sacred,* as Pomponius the Jurist says. *The sacred places of Syracuse were desecrated by victory,* as Cicero says. The cause of this is that the places which are called sacred are not really abstracted from human uses; but are called sacred in consideration of the end to which they are destined. A sign of this is that when a people gives itself up to another people or king, it gives up also what are called sacred edifices, as appears by the formula which we have elsewhere cited from Livy. So Plautus in the *Amphitruo.*

2 And therefore Ulpian says that public law includes sacred things also. Pausanias says that it is a practice common to Greeks and barbarians, that sacred things should be at their disposal who have taken the city. So when Troy was taken, the image of Hercæan Jove was granted to Sthenelus; and Thucydides mentions many examples of this usage: *that they who rule the land possess the temples.* And Tacitus's account is not really different, that in the Italic towns all the ceremonies, temples, images, are under the Roman authority.

3 Wherefore the people may change its will, and make a sacred building into a profane one; as Paulus and Venuleius not obscurely

imply; and we see that, by the necessity of the times, sacred things are sometimes converted to the use of war by those who had consecrated them; as by Pericles, under the promise of restoring as much; by Mago in Spain; by the Romans in the Mithridatic war; by Sulla, Pompey, Cæsar, and others. In Plutarch, Tiberius Gracchus says; *Nothing is so sacred as what is dedicated to the honour of the gods; yet this may be used and removed by the people.* So Seneca says, that *for the service of the public, temples are stripped, and dedicated objects turned into money.* So Trebatius in the time of Cæsar. And Germanicus used this right of war, when in his war against the Marsians he destroyed the celebrated temple at Tanfana. So Virgil. And Pausanias notes that objects dedicated to the gods are taken by the victors; and Cicero calls this the law of war, speaking of P. Servilius. So Livy, speaking of the ornaments of the temples brought by Marcellus from Syracuse to Rome. So C. Flaminius in Livy, and Fulvius in Polybius, and Cæsar in Sallust.

4 It is however true, that if there be any image in which a divine virtue is supposed to exist, it is wicked that it should be violated or destroyed by those who agree in that persuasion. And in this sense they who commit such acts are accused of impiety, or even of breaking the Laws of Nations; that is, on the assumption of such an opinion. It is another matter if the enemies do not so think. Thus the Jews were not only permitted, but commanded to destroy the idols of the Gentiles. For their being forbidden to take and keep them was for this reason; that the Hebrews might the more defeat the superstition of the Gentiles, being warned that there was defilement in the very touch of them; not as if they spared the sacred objects of other nations, as Josephus expounds the fact; no doubt speaking with a view to gain favour with the Romans: as he does also in the explanation of another precept, the prohibition of naming the gods of the Gentiles: which he explains as if they were forbidden to speak evil of them; whereas in reality the law did not permit Jews to speak of them with honour or without abomination. For the Hebrews knew, by the undoubted instruction of God, that these idols were not occupied either by the Spirit of God, or by good angels, or by astral influences, as the misguided heathen thought, but by evil demons, the enemies of the human race: as Tacitus said rightly in describing the institutions of the Jews; *All things are profane to them which are sacred to us.* Thus when Xerxes destroyed the images of the Greeks, he did nothing contrary to the laws of nations, although the Greek writers greatly exaggerate his acts for the sake of throwing odium upon him. For the Persians did not believe that there was any divinity in idols, but that the Sun was God, and that fire was a portion of him.

5 By the Hebrew Law, as Tacitus also rightly says, *All except the priests were excluded from the threshold of the temple.* But Pompey, as the same writer relates, entered the temple by the right of victory,

or, as Augustine says, *not with the devotion of a worshipper, but with the claim of a conqueror:* and he did well in sparing the temple and the things therein, although, as Cicero plainly says, not through religion, but shame and the fear of obloquy; but ill in that he entered, doing so out of contempt for the true God; as also the Chaldeans are condemned by the prophets for doing. And some think that it was on this account that, by a peculiar providence of God, Pompey was slain almost within sight of Judea, at Casius, a promontory of Egypt. But if you regard the opinion of the Romans, there was in what he did nothing contrary to the Law of Nations. So the same temple was consigned to destruction by Titus, as Josephus says, by the Laws of War.

III. What we have said of sacred places is also to be understood of burial-places; for these do not belong to the dead but the living, either a people or a family. And thus as sacred places taken by the enemy cease to be sacred, so do places of burial; as Paulus and Pomponius write: *The sepulchres of enemies are not objects of religion to us; and therefore we may convert to any use stones therein taken.* Which however is to be understood in such a way that the bodies of the dead are not to be ill-treated; for that is against the rights of burial, which is part of the Law of Nations, as we have elsewhere shewn.

IV. I will briefly again notice that by the Law of Nations, our property may not only be rescued from the enemy's hands by force, but also that deceit which involves no perfidy is allowed, and even the procurement of perfidy in others. In fact the Law of Nations has begun to connive at these smaller and frequent offenses, as the Civil Laws connive at prostitution and usury.

CHAPTER VI.

Of the right of acquiring things captured in War.

I. 1 BESIDES the impunity of certain acts among men, which we have hitherto noticed as one of the effects of war, there is another effect peculiar to a war regular according to the Law of Nations: namely, acquisition.

By Natural Law we acquire in a just war such things as are equivalent to a debt due to us which we cannot otherwise obtain, or such things as inflict on a guilty person a reasonable measure of punishment, as we have explained elsewhere. By this right Abraham gave of the spoil which he had taken from the five kings, a tenth to God, as the narrative in Gen. xiv. is explained by the writer to the Hebrews, vii. 4. And in the same way the Greeks, the Carthaginians, and the Romans, consecrated a tenth of their booty to their gods, Apollo, Hercules, and Jupiter Feretrius. And Jacob, leaving to Joseph his legacy, says, *I give thee a portion above thy brethren which I took from the hand of the Amorite with my sword and with my bow*: Gen. xlviii. 22. In which place the word *took* seems to be used by a prophetic

mode of speaking for *shall take;* and that is ascribed to Jacob which
his posterity were to do: as if the progenitor and his descendants
were the same person.   For this is a better explanation than to refer
it to the plunder of the Shechemites, which had been already perpetrated by the sons of Jacob: for that deed Jacob, as a pious man,
always condemned.   Gen. xxxiv. 30; xlix. 6.

2 That the right of taking booty within the natural boundaries
which I have mentioned was approved by God, appears from other
places also.   God, in his law, speaking of a city taken after it had
refused peace, says, Deut. xx. 14: *All the spoil thereof shalt thou take
to thyself; and thou shalt eat the spoil of thine enemies which the
Lord thy God hath given thee.*   So 1 Chron. v. 20, the Reubenites,
Gadites, and half tribe of Manasseh, made war upon the Hagarites
and their neighbours, and took much spoil; there being added as a
reason, that they cried to God in the battle and he was entreated of
them.   Also 2 Chron. xiv. 13, the pious king Asa is related to have
cried unto the Lord, and to have conquered the Ethiopians who
attacked him unjustly, and to have carried away very much spoil:
which is the more to be noted, because in that case arms were not
taken up by a special mandate, but on the ground of the common
Laws of Nations.

3 Also Joshua, (xxii. 8) when he sent away the Reubenites, and
blessed them, said, *Divide the spoil of your enemies with your brethren.*
And David, (1 Sam. xxx. 26) when he sent to the Hebrew elders
part of the spoil of the Amalekites, said, *Behold a present to you of
the spoil of the enemies of the Lord.*   Indeed as Seneca says, it is a
graceful thing for a military man to enrich a friend with the spoil of
an enemy.   There are also divine laws concerning the division of the
spoil, Num. xxxi. 27.   And Philo says that it is among the curses of
the law, that the land be plundered by the enemy, whence want to
friends and abundance to enemies.

II. 1 But by the Laws of Nations, not only he who for just
cause carries on a war, but any one, in a regular war, may without
limit or measure take and appropriate what belongs to the enemy,
to this effect, that both he and those who derive their title to the
property from him are to be defended in possession thereof.   So
Xenophon and Plato say that in war all the property of the conquered becomes the right of the conqueror : and the latter in another place enumerates among the natural modes of acquisition that
by war, contest, or strong hand ; and in this Xenophon agrees with
him, as where Euthydemus is made to allow that it is not unjust
to despoil an enemy.

2 So Aristotle says the law is a sort of convention by which
what is taken in war becomes the property of the captors.   So Antiphanes, Plutarch, Xenophon, Philip, Eschines.

3 Marcellus in Livy speaks of what he took from the Syracusans
as taken by the laws of war.   So the Romans to Philip, Masinissa,

Mithridates in Justin, Cicero, of Mitylene. So he says, that private property began when men took possession of what was vacant, or won it in war. So Dio Cassius, and Clemens Alexandrinus.

4 *What is taken from the enemy becomes the property of the captor,* says Caius the Jurist. This Theophilus calls *natural acquisition ;* so Aristotle. For in this case the naked fact of possession is looked at, and right arises from that. So Nerva, as Paulus quotes him, said that ownership arises from natural possession ; and that a vestige of this right appears in things which are taken in hunting, and also in war, which forthwith are the property of the captors.

5 Those things are supposed to be taken from the enemy which are taken from his subjects. So Dercyllides reasons in Xenophon, that since Pharnabazus is the enemy of the Lacedæmonians, and Manias the subject of Pharnabazus, the goods of Manias are in a condition in which they may be fairly captured as prize of war.

III. 1 But in this question of war, it has been established as a rule of nations, that he is understood to have captured a thing who detains it in such a manner that the other has lost probable hope of recovering it ; or so that the thing has escaped from his grasp, as Pomponius says. And in moveables, this is applied so that things are considered as captured when they are brought within the boundaries, or *intra præsidia,* under the protection of the enemy. A thing is lost in the same way in which it is recovered by postliminium : and it is recovered when it comes again within the boundaries of the empire, which is elsewhere explained as *intra præsidia.* Indeed Paulus expressly says of a man, that he is lost when he goes out of our boundaries ; and Pomponius explains a man taken in war to be one of ours whom the enemy has taken and brought *intra præsidia sua :* and that till then he is a citizen.

2 A man and a thing in this part of the Law of Nations are under the same rule. Hence it is to be understood that when it is said that things captured forthwith become the property of the captors, is to be understood with a certain condition, namely, that the possession continues till they are thus brought *intra præsidia.* Whence it seems to follow that at sea, ships and other things captured are understood to be captured when, and not till, they are brought into dock or harbour, or to the place where the fleet is ; for then recovery becomes desperate. But we find that it has been established by the more recent law of nations among Europeans that such things are understood to be captured when they have been twenty-four hours in the possession of the enemy.

IV. 1 But lands are not understood to be captured as soon as they are occupied. For though it be true that the part of the land which an army has entered upon with a great force is for the time in its possession, as Celsus notes ; yet for the effect of which we speak, possession of every kind is not sufficient, but firm possession is required. Thus the Romans were so far from judg-

Z

ing the land on which Annibal had planted his camp to be lost, that at that very time it sold for no less than it had sold for before. That land then is conceived to be captured, and no other, which is included in permanent defenses, so that it is evident there is no access to it till these are carried.

2 And this origin of the word *territory, a terrendis hostibus,* from terrifying the enemies from it, given by Siculus Flaccus, appears no less probable than that given by Varro, *a terendo,* from ploughing it; or that of Frontinus*, from *terra,* the land; or that of Pomponius the jurist, from the right which the magistrates had *terrendi,* of going out with the lictors before them (Gronov.). So Xenophon says that possession in the time of war is held by muniments.

V. This also is plain, that in order that a thing may become ours by the right of war, it is requisite that it should have belonged to the enemy. The things which are in the hands of the enemy, as in their houses or under their protection, but of which the owners are neither subjects of the enemy nor hostile in intention, cannot be acquired by war; as Eschines shews that Amphipolis, which city belonged to the Athenians, could not become the property of Philip by his war against the Amphipolitans. For the reason why it should do so is wanting; and this right of changing the ownership by mere force is too odious to be extended beyond the strict meaning of the rule.

VI. Wherefore what is said, that goods found in enemies' ships are to be treated as enemies' goods, ought not to be accepted as a settled rule of the Law of Nations, but as indicating a certain presumption which may be rebutted by valid proofs to the contrary. And so it was judged in full senate by our Hollanders in 1333, when a war was raging with the Hanse towns; and the judgment has become law.

VII. 1 But this is beyond controversy, if we look at the Laws of Nations, that those things which we take from our enemies cannot be reclaimed by those who possessed them before the enemy, and lost them in war; because the law of nations first made them owners *prima facie,* and then us. And on this ground, among others, Jephtha defends himself against the Ammonites, because the land which the Ammonites claimed had passed by the law of war from the Ammonites, as also another part from the Moabites to the Amorites, and from the Amorites to the Hebrews. So David takes as his own and divides what he had taken from the Amalekites, and the Amalekites before from the Philistines.

2 Titus Largius, when the Volsci reclaimed in the Roman Senate what they had formerly possessed, declared that the Romans held the right of possession of land by conquest to be good, and would not recede from it. So the Romans in their answer to the Aurunci; and again to the Volsci; and to the Samnites.

3 Livy, after relating that the land near Luna was divided by the

---

* Frontinus is here misquoted: see Barbeyrac.

Romans, remarks, *This land had been taken from the Ligurians, and had at a still previous period belonged to the Etruscans.* On this ground they retained Syria, and did not restore it to Antiochus Pius, from whom Tigranes, an enemy of the Romans, had won it. And so Pompey replied to the same Antiochus [Antiochus Magnus, *J. B.*], that *he had not taken it from him, and would not give him what he did not know how to defend.* So those parts of Gaul which the Cimbri had taken from the Gauls, the Romans kept as their own.

VIII. It is a more serious question, who becomes the owner of things of the enemy taken in a public and regular war; whether the people itself, or particular persons of the people, or in the people. On this point the recent interpreters of the law greatly vary. The greater part of them, having read in the Roman Law that things captured become the property of the captors, and in the body of canons, that the booty was distributed by public order, have followed one another, as is usual in such cases; and have said that in the first place, and by law, the captures become the booty of the persons who actually take them, but that they are to be assigned to the general to distribute among the soldiers. As this opinion, though generally received, is false, it must be carefully refuted by us, as a specimen how little safety there is in such authority on such subjects. For it cannot be doubted that by the consent of nations either rule might be established; that captures might go, either to the people which makes the war, or to the individuals who actually take them. But we inquire what they really have established, and we say that they have ruled that the property of enemies should be, for enemies, in the same condition as *res nullius*, that which is no one's property, as we have already explained from the dictum of Nerva (§ II. Art. 4).

IX. 1 Now *res nullius* do indeed become the property of those who take them, but of those who take them by the agency of others, as well as by their own. Thus, not slaves only, or sons who are under their fathers, but also free men, if they work for others in fishing, fowling, hunting, pearl-fishing, acquire their captures for those who employ them. So Modestinus says that *the possession which we can acquire by natural law, we may acquire by any one whom we appoint:* and Paulus, in a well known maxim: *We acquire possession by bodily or mental act: the mental act is our own; the bodily act may be ours or another's;* which he explains to mean, if others give their labour to us. Thus, among the Greeks, the prizes at the Olympian Games were gained by those who sent the combatants. The reason is, that by Natural Law, a man who wills it, may be the instrument of another who wills it, as we have elsewhere said.

2 Wherefore the distinction which is delivered between free persons and servile, as to acquisitions, belongs to the Civil Law, and properly pertains to civil acquisitions, as appears from the passage quoted from Modestinus. And even these civil acquisitions, the emperor Severus afterwards brought nearer to the example of natural acquisi-

tions, not only for the sake of utility, as he professes, but also of jurisprudence. Hence, setting aside Civil Law, the rule holds, that what a person can do by himself he may do by another, and it is the same thing whether he do it by himself or by another.

X. But in our question, we must distinguish between acts really public done in a war, and private acts done on the occasion of a public war: and by these private acts, things are acquired by private persons primarily and directly; by those public acts, they are acquired to the public. And by this law of nations Scipio deals with Masinissa: *Syphax was conquered and taken under the auspices of the Roman people; therefore he and all that was his is the booty of the Roman people.* In the same way Antiochus the Great argued that Cœle-Syria became the property of Seleucus, not of Ptolemy, because the war was the war of Seleucus, and Ptolemy had only acted as an auxiliary.

XI. 1 Landed property cannot be taken except by a public act, by leading in an army, and establishing strong places. Therefore, as Pomponius gave his opinion: *Land which is taken from an enemy becomes public property:* that is, as he explains, does not become private booty. So Salomo the *præfectus prætorii* said: *That captives and other things should become private booty is not unreasonable,* (that is, if it be done by the public consent,) *but land belongs to the prince and people of Rome.*

2 So among the Hebrews and Lacedæmonians [*Qu.* Athenians, *J. B.*], land taken in war was divided by lot. So the Romans, when they took land in war, either kept it and let it for rent, sometimes leaving a small portion to the ancient possessor, *honoris gratia;* or sold it; or assigned it to settlers; or imposed a ground-rent upon it; as we have perpetual evidence in the laws, and histories, and in the commentaries of the *agrimensores.* So Appian. Cicero, in his *Oratio pro Domo sua,* notes that sometimes lands taken from the enemy were consecrated by the Imperator, but by order of the People.

XII. 1 Things moveable and self-moving are either taken in the public service or extraneously to it. If extraneously to it, they are the property of the individual captors. To this we must refer what Celsus says, *The things which, belonging to the enemy, are in our hands, are not public property, but the property of those who take possession:* the things which are in our hands, that is, which are found with us when war arises. The same rule was observed with regard to men, at the time when men were reckoned among things captured. There is a noted passage of Typho on the subject: *Those who in peace come to another nation, if war between the nations suddenly breaks out, become the slaves of those enemies among whom their destiny has thrown them.* He speaks of *destiny* because they are reduced to slavery by no desert of their own. So Nævius, *It is the destiny of the Metelli to be consuls* at Rome.

2 It follows from the same view, that what soldiers capture, when

not on duty or on service to which they are ordered, but in the course of what they do by promiscuous right or by permission, is forthwith their own: for they do this not as public servants. Such are spoils which they win from any enemy in single combat; and such as they take in free excursions not made by order, at a distance from the enemy; (the Roman rule was ten miles, as we shall see). This kind of capture the Italians at present call *correria, plunder,* and distinguish it from *butina, booty.*

XIII. But when we say that by the law of nations such things are acquired directly by individuals, we are to understand that this is the law of nations previously to all civil law. For any nation may establish a different rule with regard to its own subjects; and anticipate the ownership of individuals, as we see in many places done with regard to wild beasts and birds [by game-laws]. And so a rule may be introduced by law that all things which are taken from the enemy shall be public property.

XIV. 1 But with regard to the things which any one takes by a regular military process, the case is different. For then individuals bear the character of the State and act on its behalf; and therefore the people, if the civil law do not otherwise direct, obtains through them both possession and ownership, and transfers it to whom it will. And as this is directly at variance with public opinion, we must adduce proofs more largely than usual, from the examples of the most eminent peoples.

2 I begin with the Greeks. Homer speaks of the cities being divided which had been taken: he makes Achilles say that he gave to Agamemnon all that he won in war. In which case Agamemnon is to be regarded partly as the prince of all Greece, and as representing the people; and partly as holding the office of general, and therefore having a larger share than the rest. So in another place Achilles says to him. [See.] And in another place, Agamemnon offers to Achilles, by the public consent, a ship full of brass and gold and twenty female slaves. So Virgil, speaking of the capture of Troy, describes the plunder under the custody of Phœnix and Ulysses. So at a later period, Aristides guarded the booty taken at Marathon. After the battle at Platæa there was a severe edict that no one should privately take any part of the booty. Afterwards, when Athens was conquered, the booty was made public property by Lysander: and the Spartan officers who had to deal with this measure were called *prize-sellers.*

3 If we go to Asia, the Trojans were accustomed, as Virgil teaches, *to draw prize-lots,* as is done in dividing common property. In other cases the decision of the matter was with the general: and by this right, Hector promises Dolon the horses of Achilles when he stipulates for them; by which you may see that the right of prize-treasure was not in the captor alone. So when Cyrus was victor, the booty was taken to him; and when Alexander, to him.

If we look at Africa the same custom recurs. Thus what was

taken at Agrigentum, and in the battle of Cannæ, and elsewhere, was sent to Carthage.

Among the ancient Franks, as we learn from Gregory of Tours, what was captured was divided by lot; and the king had nothing of the booty but what the lot gave him.

4 But in proportion as the Romans were eminent above other nations in military matters, they are the most worthy examples to refer to. Dionysius of Halicarnassus, a most diligent observer of Roman manners, thus teaches us on this subject: *Whatever is captured from the enemy, the law directs to be public property; so that not only private persons are not the owners of it, but even the general is not. The Questor takes it, sells it, and carries the money to the public account.* These are the words of those who accuse Coriolanus, somewhat turned to the purpose of making him odious.

XV. For, that the people was the owner of the prize-treasure was true; but it was not less true that the office of deciding on its distribution had been left with the General while the republic was free; with the condition that he was responsible to the people. So L. Emilius, *Cities taken not surrendered, are plundered; but in these cases the decision is with the general, not the soldiers.* But this decision which usage gave to the general, they sometimes, in order to avoid all suspicion, threw upon the Senate, as Camillus: and they who retained it, in proportion as they were actuated by conscience, reputation, or ambition, are found to have used it diversely.

XVI. 1 They who wished to be, or to appear, most scrupulous, did not at all touch the booty, but if the prize were money, directed it to be received by the questor; or, if it were other objects, ordered them to be sold by auction (*sub hastâ*) by the questor: and on this account the money thus raised was called *manubiæ.* This money was transferred by the questor into the treasury: being in the first place however, if there was a triumph, publicly shewn. So Livy of C. Valerius; Velleius of Pompey; Cicero of himself. And this was the common custom in the good old times. So Plautus.

2 But other generals sold the booty themselves without the intervention of the questor, and transferred it to the treasury, as is to be collected from the words of Dionysius. So when king Tarquin had conquered the Sabines, he sent the booty and the captives to Rome. So Romilius and Veturius the consuls are related to have sold the booty on account of the low state of the treasury, the army being much discontented with the proceeding. But inasmuch as this occurs perpetually, there is no need to accumulate examples, how much each general carried to the treasury from Italian, African, Asiatic, Gallic and Hispanic triumphs. That is rather to be noted, that the booty, or a part thereof, was sometimes given to the gods, sometimes to the soldiers, and sometimes to others. To the gods either the captured things themselves were given, as the spoils which Romulus hung up to Jupiter Feretrius, or the money produced from them, as Tarquinius

Superbus from the Pometine spoil built the temple of Jupiter in the Tarpeian mount.

XVII. 1 To give the plunder to the soldiers appeared to the ancient Romans an act savouring of ambition or popularity-hunting: as Sextus the son of Tarquin the Proud, while an exile at Gabii, is said to have distributed the booty among the soldiers, as a mode of gaining influence. Appius Claudius in the senate condemned a similar liberality as new, lavish, and imprudent.

Booty which is given up to the soldiers is either divided or scrambled for. It may be divided either in the proportion of the pay, or of the deserts of individuals. That it should be divided in proportion to the pay, was the direction of Appius Claudius; and if he could not carry that, that the money raised from it should be transferred to the treasury. Polybius explains accurately the whole scheme of such a division; namely, that one part of the army, the lesser portion, was commonly sent to collect the booty; and that what each found he was ordered to bring into the camp, that it might be equally divided by the tribunes; those being summoned to take their share who had guarded the camp, (which also was ordered by David among the Hebrews, and thence, as we learn, passed into a law,) and those who had been absent from sickness, or any sent off on service elsewhere.

2 But it was not the booty itself, but the money raised from it, which was given to the soldiers in the place of the booty, which was often done in the triumph. I find this proportion in Livy; one share to a foot-soldier, twice as much to a centurion, three times as much to a horseman or knight. Sometimes one share to each of the foot, two to the horse. Again, one share to the foot-soldier, two to the centurion, four to the tribune and the horsemen. Often account was taken of desert, as Marcius, in consideration of his bravery, was rewarded out of the spoils of Corioli by Posthumius.

3 In whatever way the division was made, it was allowed to the general to take a *first choice*, some principal thing, of what value he chose, that is, what he thought fair: and this was sometimes awarded to others on account of their valour. So Euripides in the *Troades*, speaking of the noblest of the Trojan women, says, that they were given to the leaders of the army. And of Andromache, that in this way she became the property of Pyrrhus. So Ascanius says, in Virgil, that the shield and the helmet he will exclude from the division by lot. Herodotus tells us that after the battle at Platæa, Pausanias had, given to him, the most eminent objects, women, horses and camels. So king Tullius received Ocrisia, the principal person of the Corniculanæ. Fabricius in Dionysius, in his oration to Pyrrhus, says, *Of those things which were taken in war, it was allowed me to take what I chose.* Isidorus, referring to this passage, when he speaks of military law, says, *the distribution of the spoil is, a just division according to the qualities and performances of persons, and*

the prince's portion. Tarquin the Proud, as it stands in Livy, both wished to enrich himself and to win the minds of the people with the distribution of prize-money. Servilius in his oration for L. Paulus, says that he might have made himself rich by dividing the shares of booty *. And there are writers who think that the prince's portion was rather what was really meant by *manubiæ*, as Asconius Pedianus.

4 But those persons are more praised who, giving up their right, took no part of the booty to themselves; like Fabricius, of whom I have spoken, *Who in his love of glory put aside even just gain*, as Dionysius says; which he said he did according to the example of Valerius Publicola, and a few others. And these, M. Porcius Cato also imitated in his Spanish victory; asserting that nothing should come to him from the spoils of war, except what he had spent in meat and drink: adding however, that he did not blame the generals who had accepted the advantages usually granted; but that he would rather contend for the prize of virtue with the best, than for the pre-eminence in wealth with the richest. Nearest to this praise come those who have taken to themselves a moderate share of the prize-treasure; as Pompey in Lucan is praised by Cato, for having given up more than he kept.

5 In the division, there is sometimes account taken of those who have been absent; as Fabius Ambustus directed when Anxur was taken. And sometimes for some special reason account is not taken of some of those who were present, as of the Minutian army, by the dictator Cincinnatus.

6 The right which, under the old republic, the Imperator had, was after the extinction of the republic, transferred to the *magistri militum*, as appears by the Codex of Justinian; where, in speaking of reports to be made to the emperor, of the proceedings of the military authorities, an exception is made with regard to donations of moveables which the *magistri militum* make to the soldiers out of the spoils of the enemy; whether in the occupation of war, or in the places where they are known to live.

7 But this division, from an early period, gave opening to calumny, as if the generals had in this way sought private favour; on which ground accusations were brought against Servilius, Coriolanus, Camillus, as having lavished the public treasure upon their friends and clients. And they defended themselves by alleging the public good, *that they who had had a share in the service, by receiving the reward of their labour, might be more prompt to other expeditions*, as Dionysius says.

XVIII. 1 I come now to speak of indiscriminate pillage. This was granted to the soldiers, either when a country was to be ravaged; or, after a battle or the taking of a town, it was allowed that pillage

---

* Not *himself*, but Servius Galba, who was discontented that he was not allowed to make the division. *J. B.*

was to begin at an appointed signal. This was rare in early ages, but still, not without example. Tarquinius gave up Suessa to be pillaged by the soldiers; Q. Servilius the Dictator gave up the camp of the Equi to the same fate: Camillus the city of Veii; Servilius the consul, the camp of the Volsci; L. Valerius permitted pillage in the country of the Equi; Q. Fabius did so when the Volsci had been dispersed, and Ecetra taken; and others frequently on subsequent occasions. When Perseus was conquered, Paulus the consul gave the spoils of the army which was defeated to the infantry, the plunder of the surrounding country to the cavalry. The same leader, by a decree of the senate, gave up the cities of Epirus to pillage by the soldiers. When Lucullus conquered Tigranes, he long restrained the soldiers from taking spoil, but at last, when the victory was certain, he gave permission to pillage. Cicero puts, among the ways of acquiring property, if we take anything from the enemy which is not liable to be divided and sold on the public account.

2 They who condemn this practice say, that greedy hands, active in pillage, are so forward as to snatch the prizes which ought to fall to the share of the bravest; for it commonly happens that they who are slowest in fight are quickest in plunder, while the bravest soldiers commonly take the main share of danger and toil; as Appius says in Livy. And so in Xenophon. On the other hand it is said that what each takes from the enemy with his own hand and carries home, is more grateful and valued than a thing of many times the value, which he receives at the will of another.

3 Sometimes again, pillage is allowed, when it cannot be prevented. In the storming of Cortuosa, a town of the Hetrusci, Livy says, *The Tribunes directed that the booty should be public property; but the command was too slow for the intention. The soldiers had already taken the booty, and it could not be taken from them without doing a very odious thing.* So the camp of the Gallo-Græcians was plundered by the troops of C. Helvius contrary to the general's wish.

XIX. What I have said, that booty or prize-money is sometimes given to others than soldiers, generally happens, in order that those who have contributed to the expenses of the war should be remunerated; we may also sometimes read of public spectacles provided out of the spoils.

XX. 1 But not only have different usages prevailed in different wars, but in the same war the same booty has often been applied to different uses, either by dividing it into parts, or by distinguishing the kind of objects. Thus Camillus dedicated the tenth part of the spoil to Pythian Apollo, following the example of the Greeks, which however, came originally from the Hebrews: and at that time, the dedication of a tenth of the spoil was held by the priests to include, not moveables only, but the lands and the city. By the same general, when victorious over the Falisci, the greater part of the booty was transferred to the questor, and a small part only given to the soldiers. So L. Manlius, *either sold the spoil, that part of it which was to go to the public, or divided it among the soldiers, taking care that the division should be exactly fair,* as Livy says.

2 The classes of objects into which spoil may be divided, are these: men, captives, herds and flocks, which the Greeks, when they speak strictly, call λεία; money and other moveables, either precious or common. Q. Fabius, when he had conquered the Volsci, ordered the λεία and spoils to be sold by the questor; he himself managed the money. The same, when the Volsci and Æqui were conquered, gave to the soldiers the captives, except the Tusculans; and in the land of Ecetra, gave up men and cattle to pillage. L. Cornelius, when Antium was taken, transferred to the treasury the gold, silver, and brass; the captives and spoil he sold by the questor; he gave up to the soldiers what pertained to food and raiment. Nor was the rule of Cincinnatus dissimilar, who, when he became master of Corbio, a town of the Æqui, sent the more precious parts of the spoil to Rome, and divided the rest according to centuries. Camillus, when Veii was taken, assigned nothing to the public except the money from the sale of the captives. When the Hetrusci were conquered, and the captives sold, out of the money he repaid to the matrons the gold which they had contributed, and placed three golden pateræ in the Capitol. When Cossus was dictator, all the prey of the Volsci, except the bodies of the free men, was given up to the soldiers.

3 When Fabricius had conquered the Lucani, Brutii and Samnites, he enriched the soldiers, restored the tributes to the cities, and carried forty talents to the treasury. Q. Fulvius and Appius Claudius, when the camp of Hannibal was taken, sold the booty and divided it, giving donations to those who had performed eminent services. Scipio, when Carthage was taken, gave up to pillage what was in the city, excepting the gold, silver, and donations. Acilius, when Lamia was taken, partly divided and partly sold the spoil. Cn. Manlius when the Gallo-Græcians were conquered, burnt their arms from a Roman superstition, and ordered all to bring in the rest of the spoil; and either sold that part of it which was to go to the public, or divided it with care that the division should be fair*.

XXI. 1 From what we have said, it appears that among the Romans, as well as among most other nations, the spoil belonged to the people, but that some discretion in dividing it was allowed the general; but, as we have said, in such way that he was responsible to the people. This appears, among other instances, by the example of L. Scipio, who was condemned for peculation, as Valerius Maximus tells us, as having received four hundred and eighty sesterces of silver more than he had transferred to the treasury; and of others whom we have mentioned.

* He had quoted this before, Art. 1, of this section, but had by mistake called the general L. Manlius instead of Cnæus Manlius. (Gronov.)

2 M. Cato, in an oration concerning prize-treasure, written, as Gellius says, in vehement and brilliant language, complained of the impunity and licence of peculation. Of that oration this fragment is extant: *Private robbers are put in prison and in bonds: public robbers are seen in purple and gold.* He had elsewhere said that *He marvelled that any one could set up in his house images which were taken in war.* So Cicero makes it a point to inflame the odium against Verres, that he had appropriated an image, and that one taken as spoil from the enemy.

3 And not the generals only, but the soldiers also, were held accountable for peculation of prize-treasure; that is, if they did not transfer it to the public. For all were bound by the military oath, as Polybius says, not to appropriate any part of their booty, but to keep their good faith as sworn. And to this perhaps we may refer the formula of oath in Gellius, by which the soldier is commanded not to take anything, within ten miles of the army, of more value than a silver *nummus* (sesterce), or if he did take it, to bring it to the consul, or to announce it within three days. Hence we may understand what Modestinus says; *He who secretes booty taken from the enemy is guilty of peculation;* and this passage alone might satisfy juristical interpreters, that they are not to suppose that what individuals take from the enemy becomes their own: since peculation can only apply to property public, sacred, or religious. All these cases concur to make it appear, as we have said above, that setting aside the Civil Law, and primarily, things taken by military operations become the property of the people or king who are carrying on the war.

XXII. 1 I have added "setting aside the Civil Law, and primarily," that is, directly. The first clause, because concerning things not yet actually acquired, the law may regulate according to public utility; whether the law be made by the people, as among the Romans, or by the king, as among the Hebrews and elsewhere. And under the name of "law," I also include custom rightly introduced. The other clause, "primarily," tends to this: that we mean that spoil, like other things, may be conceded by the people to others, not only after acquisition, but also before; so that when the capture follows, the two events may be conjoined *brevi manu,* so as to be one, as the jurists speak. And such concession may be made, not only naming each person, but by classes; as in the times of the Maccabees, a part of the spoil was given to widows, old men, and needy orphans; or even to uncertain persons, as in a scramble, in which the Roman consuls gave things to those who caught them.

2 And this transfer of right (from the public to private persons,) which is made by law or concession, is not always a mere donation, but sometimes a contract, sometimes a payment of what is due, or a remuneration for losses suffered, or expenses incurred in the war, either in the way of payment or of work done; as when allies and

subjects serve in the war without pay, or with pay insufficient to the work. For we see cases in which the whole booty, or a part of it, is assigned for such causes.

XXIII. And this we find that our jurists note as almost universally introduced by custom ; that what is captured by allies or subjects who carry on the war without pay, at their own risk, becomes theirs. The reason in the case of allies is evident ; because, by Natural Law, ally is bound to ally for the reparation of losses which occur in the course of a common or public transaction. Add, that work is seldom done gratis. *Physicians are paid,* says ´Seneca, *because they leave their own business to attend to ours.* Quintilian thinks the same thing is reasonable in advocates, because by spending their time and strength on that office, they are prevented from making gain in other ways. So Tacitus. It is therefore presumable, except some other cause appear, for instance mere good will or antecedent contract, that this hope of getting gain from the enemy was looked to, as the compensation for loss and labour.

XXIV. 1 In the case of subjects the argument is not equally obvious, because they owe their labour to the state. But on the other hand, when it is not all, but only some, who serve in war, these have a claim to retribution for the labour and expense which they incur beyond others, and still more, for the loss. And in the place of such certain retribution, it is not unreasonable to concede to them a hope either of the whole spoil, or of an uncertain part thereof. So the Poet Propertius.

2 We have an example, as to allies, in the Roman league, in which the Latins are admitted to an equal share of the spoil in the wars carried on under the auspices of the Roman people. So in the war which the Etolians carried on, the Romans helping them, the cities and lands were given to the Etolians, the captives and moveables to the Romans. After the victory over king Ptolemy, Demetrius gave a part of the spoil to the Athenians. Ambrose, in treating of the history of Abraham, shews the equity of this custom : *He gives to those who had been with him and helped him, a part of the gain as a reward of their labour.*

3 With regard to subjects, we have an example in the Hebrew people, among whom half of the spoil went to those who were in service in the army. Thus also the soldiers of Alexander had for their use the booty taken from private persons, except that there was a custom of transferring to the king any object of peculiar value ; and accordingly, we find that those who were said to have conspired at Arbela, were accused of intending´ to appropriate the whole of the spoil, and to give nothing to the treasury.

4 But what had been with the enemy, public property or king's property, was exempted from this licence. Thus we read that the Macedonians, when they stormed the camp of Darius at the river Pyramus, plundered a great mass of gold and silver, and left nothing.

untouched except the king's tent: *according to the established usage,* says Curtius, *that the conquered party should receive the conqueror in the king's tent.* And the usage of the Hebrews was not different, who put the crown of the conquered king on the head of the conqueror, and assigned to him (as we read in the Talmudic Collections) the royal furniture which was taken in the war. So, in the history of Charlemagne, we read that when he had conquered the Hungarians, the private treasure went to the soldiers, the royal, to the treasury. Among the Greeks there were two different words for public and private spoil, λάφυρα and σκῦλα. The latter implies what was taken from the enemy during the contest; the former, what was taken afterwards; which distinction was also made by some other nations.

5 But among the Romans, there was not so much allowed to the soldiers under the old republic; as sufficiently appears from what we have said above. In the civil wars, they began to be more indulged. Thus we read that Equulanum was plundered by the soldiers of Sulla. And Cæsar, in Lucan, gives up the camp of Pompey after the battle of Pharsalia to be plundered. The soldiers of Octavius and Antony plundered the camp of Brutus and Cassius. In another civil war, the Flavians being led to Cremona, though night was at hand, hasten to storm that rich colony; fearing lest otherwise the wealth of the Cremonese should fall into the lap of the prefects and legates; knowing in fact, as Tacitus says, that *when a city is stormed, the booty belongs to the soldiers; when it is surrendered, to the general.*

6 In the decay of discipline, this concession to the soldiers was the more willingly made, lest they should, before the fight was over, turn away from the enemy to fall on the spoil, and so have their hands ill employed; a turn by which many victories were frustrated. When Corbulo stormed the strong place Volandum in Armenia, *the common people,* says Tacitus, *was sold by auction, the rest of the booty was given to the soldiers.* In the same writer, Suetonius, in the Britannic battle, exhorts his men to continue the slaughter of the enemy without regarding the spoil; adding that when the victory is gained, all will be theirs; and the like you find in many other places. Add what we have just adduced from Procopius.

7 Some matters of booty are so small that they are not worth giving to the public. These are commonly allowed to belong to the captor by the permission of the people. Such, in the old republic of Rome, were the spear, javelin, firewood, food, water-bottle, scrip, link, and small money. For we find these exceptions added in Gellius to the military oath. And something similar was allowed sailors when serving in war: the French call this *spoil* or *pillage*, and comprehend in it clothing, and gold and silver within ten crowns. In some places, a certain fraction of the booty is given to the soldiers, as in Spain; sometimes a fifth, sometimes a third: in other cases, a half goes to the king; and a seventh, sometimes a tenth, to the general; the rest to the captors; except the ships of war, which go altogether to the king.

8   In some cases the partition is made, taking account of trouble, danger, and expense; as among the Italians, the third part of a captured ship goes to the captain of the victorious ship, a third part to the merchants to whom the cargo belonged, and a third part to the sailors.   Also in some cases, those who fight at their own danger and expense do not take the whole booty, but are obliged to give a part to the public, or to those who derive their right from the public.   So with the Spaniards, if ships are sent out at private expense, part of the prize goes to the king, part to the High Admiral.   By the custom of France, the Admiral has a tenth; and so with the Hollanders; but here a fifth part of the booty is taken by the State.   By land, the common use everywhere now is, that in pillage of towns, and in battles, every one makes his own what he takes; but in expeditions for booty, the captures are common to those who are in the company, and are divided according to their rank.

XXV.   The tendency of these remarks is, that if, in a neutral nation, a controversy arises concerning things captured in war, they are to be adjudged to those to whom they belong by the laws and customs of the people by whose party the capture is made.   And if there is no proof on this point, then, by the common Laws of Nations, the thing is to be adjudged to the nation itself, provided it be taken in war.   For from what we have said, it appears that the assertion of Quintilian is not exactly true, pleading for the Thebans; that in a matter which can be brought into a court of justice, the right of war goes for nothing; and that which is taken by arms can only be kept by arms.

XXVI.   1 Things which do not belong to the enemy, though they are found with the enemy, do not belong to the captors; for that, as we have said, is neither congruous to natural law nor established by the Laws of Nations.   So the Romans say to Prusias, *If the land had not belonged to Antiochus, it would thence follow that it did not become the property of the Romans.*   But if the enemy had any right over these objects, such as is connected with possession; as a right of pledge, retention, servitude, there is no reason why that should not pass to the captors.

2 This also is often made a question, whether things taken outside the territory of both belligerents become the property of the captors; which is controverted, both with regard to persons and things.   If we regard only the Laws of Nations, I think the place is not to be considered; as we have said, that an enemy may be lawfully slain anywhere.   But he who has authority over the place, may by his law, prohibit such an act; and if it be done against the law, may require satisfaction.   It is like the case in which a wild creature taken in another's land is said to be the property of the captor: but our access to it may be prohibited by the owner of the land.

XXVII.   This external right*, however, of becoming the owner of things captured in war, is peculiar to a regular war according to the Laws of Nations, so that it does not obtain in other wars.   For in other wars between strangers, a thing is not acquired by force of the war, but as a compensation for a debt which cannot otherwise be obtained.   But in wars between citizens, whether they be great or small wars, there is no change of ownership without the authority of a judge.

* A right which exists between persons of different nations.

CHAPTER VII.

Of the right over Prisoners of War.

I. 1 BY nature, that is, in the primeval state of nature, and without the act of man, no men are slaves, as we have elsewhere said; and in this sense we may assent to what the jurists say, that slavery is against nature. But that slavery should have its origin in human act, that is, in convention or delict, is not repugnant to natural justice, as we have also shewn.

2 But by the laws of nations, of which we now speak, slavery is more comprehensive, both as to persons, and effects. For, if we regard the persons, it is not those only who surrender themselves, or promise slavery, who are reckoned slaves; but all persons whatever who are taken in a regular war, as soon as they are brought *intra præsidia*, as Pomponius says. Nor is delict requisite; the lot of all is alike: even of those, as we have said, who by their destiny are found within the enemies' boundaries when war breaks out.

3 So Polybius says, *What punishment have these justly incurred? some one may say, when he sees men sold with their wives and children, when they have been conquered in war. These calamities are by the laws of war to be borne by those who have done no wrong.* And hence, as Philo notes, *many good men have, by various misfortunes, lost the liberty to which they were born.*

4 Dio Prusæensis, after reciting some modes of acquiring ownership, adds, When a person, having acquired another as a captive in war, holds him as a slave. So to carry off boys captured in war Oppian calls the Law of War.

II. And not only do they themselves become slaves, but their posterity for ever; that is, those who are born of a slave-mother in slavery. And this is what Martianus says, that by the Law of Nations, those are born our slaves, who are born of our slave-servants. The womb was subjected to slavery, says Tacitus, speaking of the wife of a German leader: [Arminius, whose wife was pregnant when she came into the power of the Romans. *Gronov.*]

III. 1 The effects of this right are unlimited, so that the master may do any thing lawfully to the slave, as Seneca says. There is no suffering which may not be inflicted on such slaves with impunity; no act which may not in any manner be commanded or extorted; so that even cruelty in the masters, towards persons of servile condition, is unpunished; except so far as the Civil Law imposes limits and punishments for cruelty. *In all nations alike*, says Caius, *we may see that the masters have the power of life and death over slaves.* He adds afterwards, that by the Roman Law, limits were set to this power, that is, on Roman ground. So Donatus on Terence, *What is not lawful from a master to a slave?*

2 And all the property which is taken becomes the right of the master, along with the person. The slave who is under the power of another, can have nothing of his own, says Justinian.

IV. Hence the opinion is refuted, or at least restricted, of those who say that incorporeal things are not acquired by right of war. For it is true that such property is not primarily and *per se* acquired, but it is acquired by the intervention of a person to whom it had belonged. We must except however rights which flow from a peculiar character of the person, and are therefore inalienable, as the paternal right. If these can remain at all, they remain with the person; if not, they are extinguished.

V. 1 All these powers are introduced by the Laws of Nations, for no other cause than this; that the captors, induced by so many advantages, may willingly abstain from the extreme rigour by which they were allowed to put captives to death, either immediately or after any delay, as we have said. *They are called servi*, says Pomponius, *because the conquerors commonly sell them, and so preserve them from being killed.* I have said that they may *willingly* abstain: for it is not a compact by which they are compelled to abstain, if you look at the Laws of Nations; but a mode of persuading them to adopt a more useful course.

2 For the same reason, this right is allowed to be transferred to others, like the ownership of things. And this right is extended so as to apply to the offspring, on this account; that otherwise, if the captors had used their extreme right, they would never have been born. From which it follows, that those born before the calamity, if they are not captured, do not become slaves. And therefore it was established that the children should follow the condition of the mother, because the cohabitation of slaves was not guarded, either by law or by sure custody, so that there could be no sufficient presumption to indicate the father. And in this sense we must take the dictum of Ulpian: *The law of nature is this, that he who is born out of legitimate matrimony follows the mother*: that is, the law of general custom, drawn from a natural reason; as we have shewn that the phrase *the law of nature* is elsewhere improperly used.

3 That these rights were not introduced in vain by the nations,

A A

we may understand by the example of civil wars, in which we commonly find the captives put to death, because they could not be reduced to slavery; as Plutarch and Tacitus note.

4 Whether those who are captured belong to the people or to individuals, is to be determined by what we have said of prize: for the laws of nations have put men on the footing of things, in this point. So Caius says, *What is taken from the enemy becomes forthwith*, jure gentium, *the property of the captors; and thus free men also are reduced to slavery.*

VI. 1 But what some theologians hold, that they who are captured in an unjust war, or born of such captives, have no moral right to escape, except to their own people, I do not hesitate to pronounce a mistake. There is indeed this difference; that if they escape to their own people while the war is still going on, they obtain their liberty by the right of *postliminium*: if they escape to others, or even to their own people after peace is made, they are to be restored to their master on his claiming them. But it does not thence follow that they are under a bond of conscience: for there are many rights which only regard an external judgment; and such are those rights of war which we are now expounding. Nor is it a valid objection that such a bond arises from the nature of ownership. For I reply that there are many kinds of ownership; and that thus there may be ownership which is valid only in a human judgment, and that, a coactive one: and this occurs also in other kinds of rights.

2 Such also, to a certain extent, is the right of annulling testaments, for defect of some formality which the Civil Law prescribes. For the more approved opinion is, that what is left me by such a testament, I may retain with a good conscience: at least as long as it is not contradicted. And nearly the same is the case of one who, according to the Civil Law, occupies a thing by prescription *malâ fide*, knowing that he had no right to it: for he too is protected in his ownership by the Civil Law. And by this distinction, we easily solve the knot which Aristotle proposes, *It is right that each one should have his own. But what the judge decides sincerely, even if wrong, is law. And thus the same thing would be right and not right.*

3 But in our question, [whether a captive may escape,] no cause can be devised why nations should have imposed any bond beyond the external one. For the right of claiming a slave, of coercing him, even of putting him in chains, and of keeping his property, was sufficient to induce captors to spare their captives; or if they were so savage as not to be moved by these advantages, they would certainly not be moved by that mental bond; and even this, if they judged it necessary, they might demand as a promise or oath.

4 Nor are we lightly, in a law which is established, not upon natural equity, but for the sake of avoiding a greater evil, to assume an interpretation which would make unlawful an act otherwise lawful. So the Florentine Jurist; *It makes no difference how a cap-*

tive returns, whether he has been set at liberty or escaped by art or force.
For in fact, this right of captivity is a right, in such a sense that in
another sense it is commonly a wrong: as it is called by Paulus
the jurist. It is a right, so far as certain effects are concerned;
it is a wrong, if you look at the intrinsic nature of the thing.
Whence this also appears; that if any one, captured in an unjust
war, comes into the power of the enemy, he is not morally guilty of
theft if he carries away his own property, or the reward of his
labour, if there is any due beyond his aliment; provided that he
do not owe any thing to his master, either on his own or on the
public account, or to him whose right the master has received. Nor
does it prove any thing, that such flight and subduction of property
is commonly severely punished. For these and many like things
are done by the more powerful, not because they are just, but because they are expedient.

5 The precepts in some of the Canons, forbidding persons to persuade a slave to leave the service of his master, if you refer them to
slaves who are bearing a just punishment, or have made themselves
slaves by a voluntary compact, are just precepts. But if you refer
them to those who are captured in an unjust war, or born of such
captives, the precepts tend to shew that Christians ought rather to
encourage Christians to patience, than to a course which though lawful, may offend minds strangers to Christianity, or otherwise weak.
And in the like spirit we must receive the exhortations of the Apostles
to slaves, except that these seem rather to exhort them to obedience
while they are slaves, which is agreeable to natural equity; for aliment
and work done have a natural correspondence.

VII. But I think that another precept of the theologians whom I
have begun to speak of is right: that a slave cannot, without violating
the duty of justice, resist the master in the execution of that external
right. For between this case and the other, there is a manifest dis-
crepance. The external right, which consists not only in the impunity of the act, but in the protection of the right by the judicial tribunals, is void if the right of resisting on the opposite side remain. For
if it be lawful to resist the master by force, it will be lawful to resist
the magistrate who protects the master; and yet the magistrate, by
the Law of Nations, ought to defend the master in his ownership and
its exercise. This right, therefore, resembles that which we have elsewhere ascribed to the supreme authority in each state, that to resist
them by force is not lawful or morally right. And so Augustine joined
the two, when he said, *The common people must bear with princes, and
slaves with their masters, that by the exercise of longsuffering, temporal
things may be borne, and eternal things looked to.*

VIII. This also is to be noted; that this Law of Nations respecting captives, has neither been received always, nor among all nations;
although the Roman jurists speak universally, pointing at the more
known part by the name of the whole. Thus among the Hebrews,

who were separated by special institutes from the common rules of other nations, there was a refuge for slaves (Deut. xxiii. 15): that is, as the commentators rightly note, for those who had fallen into that calamity by no fault of theirs. And from a like cause appears to have arisen the right which, in the Frankish land, was given slaves, of claiming to be free; although at present that is given not only to captives taken in war, but to slaves of every kind.

IX. 1 It has also been established among Christians in general, that in cases of war, the captives are not to be made slaves so as to be sold, forced to work, or to suffer other things which belong to the condition of slaves: and most rightly: since they have been, or ought to be, better taught by the great teacher of all charity, than to be incapable of being withheld from killing wretched men except by the concession of some smaller cruelty. And we are told by Gregoras that this custom long ago passed from one generation to another of those who professed the same religion: nor was it peculiar to those who lived under the Roman empire, but common to them with the Thessalians, Illyrians, Triballians and Bulgarians. And this advance, at least, a small advance though it be, was produced by a reverence for the law of Christ, which, when Socrates formerly urged upon the Greeks, as a rule among themselves, he produced no effect.

2 The rule which the Christians follow in this matter, the Mahomedans also follow among one another. But there has remained among Christians the usage of keeping captives till a price is paid for them, of which the appointment is in the will of the victor, except there be some certain convention. The right of retaining captives is usually given to those who have captured them, except persons of the highest rank: for with regard to them, the custom of most countries gives the right to the State or its Head.

CHAPTER VIII.

Of Lordship over the Conquered.

I. 1 SINCE the victor can subject individuals to personal servitude, it is not surprizing that he should be allowed to reduce a body of men, whether they be a State, or part of a State, to a servitude, either civil or domestic, or mixed. This is the argument used by some one in Seneca: *That he is my slave whom I have bought by the laws of war, is a rule expedient for you Athenians; otherwise your empire which has been gained by war is reduced within its ancient limits.* And accordingly, Tertullian says that empire is sought by arms and extended by victories: and Quintilian, that kingdoms, peoples, the boundaries of nations and of cities, are defined by wars. Alexander, in Curtius, says, that laws are given by the conquerors, and accepted by the conquered. So Minio in his speech to the Romans: *Why do you send to Syracuse and the other Greek cities of Sicily every year your prætor with the ensigns of office? You can only say that you have imposed those laws on conquered peoples.* So Ariovistus in Cesar.

2 Justin, from Trogus, relates, that those who made war, before Ninus, *did not seek empire but glory; and, content with victory, abstained from empire;* that Ninus was the first who extended the bounds of empire, and reduced other nations to his authority by war; and that thenceforth it became a custom. So Bocchus in Sallust, says, that *he had taken arms to defend his government; for that the part of Numidia from which he had expelled Jugurtha was his by the right of war.*

3 But authority may sometimes be acquired by victory, only so far as it exists in the king or other ruler: and in that case, the conqueror succeeds only to his rights, and no more: or as far as it is in the people; in which case the victor has the authority, in such a way that he may alienate it, as the people could have done. And hence it comes to pass, that some kingdoms are patrimonial, as we have elsewhere said.

II. 1 But more may sometimes be effected by the right of conquest; namely, so that what was a state may cease to be a state; so that it may become an accessory part to another state, as the Roman provinces; or may be attached to no state, as if a king, carrying on a war at his own expense, subject a people to him in such a way, that he may direct it to be governed mainly to the advantage, not of the people, but of the governor; which is a character, not of civil government, but of a master over servants. So Aristotle: *Government is sometimes for the advantage of the governor, sometimes, of the governed: the latter has place among freemen: the former is the government of servants by a master.* The people which is so governed is, from the time of conquest, not a state, but a large family. For it was well said by Anaxandrides, that *slaves do not make a state.*

2 And Tacitus opposes these conditions to one another: *Not masters and slaves, but a governor and citizens.* So Xenophon of Agesilaus, that *he governed the cities which he reduced not as slaves under a master, but as free men obey their rulers.*

III. And hence we may understand what is that mixed government, compounded of mastership and civil rule, of which we have spoken; namely, when servitude is combined with a certain personal liberty. Thus we read of peoples whose arms were taken from them, and who were commanded not to possess any iron except for agriculture; and of others who were compelled to change their language and habits of living.

IV. 1 For, as the things which had belonged to individuals, do, by the laws of war, become the property of those who conquer them, so also the property of the general body becomes the property of the victors, if these so choose. What Livy says of persons who surrender, that *all things are surrendered to the conqueror, and that it is for him to decide what they may keep and what they must forfeit,* holds with regard to the conquered in war. For surrender gives up what would otherwise be taken by force. So Scaptius in Livy, of the land of Corioli. Annibal in his oration to his soldiers in the same historian, told them that all that the Romans had won would be theirs. So Antiochus said of the possessions of Seleucus. So Pompey took all that belonged to the empire of Mithridates.

2 And hence incorporeal rights also, which had belonged to the general body, become the rights of the victor, so far as he chooses. Thus when Alba was conquered, the Romans claimed what had been the rights of the Albans. Whence it follows that the Thessalians were altogether liberated from the obligation of a hundred talents, claimed by the Thebans; which sum Alexander the Great, having conquered Thebes, gave to them by the right of victory; nor is that true which is alleged for the Thebans in Quintilian: that that only belongs to the victor which he himself has in his hands; and that an incorporeal right cannot so be taken possession of: that the condition of an heir is different from that of a victor, because to the former the right passes, to the latter the thing only. For he who is lord of the persons, is lord of the things also, and of all things which belong to the person. He

who is in the possession of another, has no possession for himself; and he who is not his own master, can be master of nothing else.

3 Even if any victor leave to the conquered people the rights of their state, he may take to himself some things which belonged to the state: for it depends on his own will what limit he chooses to fix to the benefits which he gives. Cesar imitated the act of Alexander, in remitting to the Dyrrachians the debt which they owed to some of the adverse party. But here it might be objected that the war of Cesar was not of that kind for which this law of nations was established.

CHAPTER IX.

Of Postliminium.

I. 1 THOSE who in previous ages have treated of *jus*, as they have given no sound rules concerning captures from the enemy, so have they given no sound rules concerning *postliminium*. This subject was treated more accurately by the old Romans, but often too confusedly; so that the reader was not able to distinguish what belonged to the Laws of Nations, and what to the Civil or Roman Law.

2 With regard to the word *postliminium*, we must reject the opinion of Servius, who thinks that the latter part of the word is a lengthening of the former, without signification. We must follow Scævola, who taught that the word was compounded of *post*, implying a return, and *limen*. For *limen*, a *threshold*, and *limes*, a *boundary*, differ in their ending and declension, but otherwise are the same in their primitive notion and origin; for they come from the old word *limo*, which signifies *transversum, across*: like *materia* and *materies; pavus* and *pavo; contagio* and *contages; cucumis* and *cucumer;* although in later usage, it came to pass that *limen*, a *threshold*, was referred more to private things, *limes*, a *boundary*, to public. So the ancients used *eliminare*, meaning to expel from the bounds of the state, and exile they called *eliminium*.

II. 1 *Postliminium*, then, is the right which arises from returning *in limen*, that is within the boundaries of the state. Thus Pomponius says, *he* is returned by postliminium who has begun to be within our *præsidia;* Paulus, when he has entered our boundaries. But by parity of reason, the consent of nations led to the rule that postliminium should hold, if any man or any thing to which civil rules apply, comes to our friends or allies, as the same two jurists also say. And here our friends and allies are to be understood, not simply those with whom we are at peace, but those who are of our party in the war. Those who come to such are safe, as if they, man or thing, came to their own people.

2 Coming among those who are friendly, but not of the same party, prisoners of war do not change their condition, except by special compact. As in the second league made between the Romans and Carthaginians, it was agreed that those of the peoples, friends of Rome, who were taken prisoners by the Carthaginians, if they came into ports subject to the Romans, might claim their liberty; and that the friends of the Carthaginians should have a like right. Therefore those of the Romans in the second Punic war, who, being prisoners, came into Greece on commercial designs, had not there the right of postliminium, because the Greeks, in that war, had taken part with neither side: and therefore it was necessary for them to be ransomed, in order to regain their liberty. In Homer too we see prisoners of war sold in neutral places, as Lycaon, *Iliad* xx. Eurymedusa, *Odyssee* viii.

III. The old phraseology of the Romans spoke of free men also as received by *postliminium*, namely, if a man went to another city and then returned to his own. Also servants, horses, mules, ships which fell into the enemy's hands, and were then retaken, were recovered by postliminium. The later jurists made two kinds of postliminium: that by which we ourselves return, and that by which we recover anything.

IV. 1 The right exists in war and in peace. In peace, it belongs to those who, when the war breaks out, are among the enemy. Other prisoners of war have not postliminium, except that be agreed upon. So Tryphoninus, emended; and Zonaras. Pomponius says, *If a prisoner of war, being allowed by treaty to return, chooses to remain with the enemy, he loses postliminium.* Paulus says, *If a captive of war, after peace is made, escapes to his home, by postliminium he returns to the master to whom he was captive during the war, except there be a convention that captives are to be returned.*

2 The reason why captives taken in war are thus allowed to remain in the enemy's hands, is given by Tryphoninus; *That they might place their hope of returning rather in valour than in peace, was the wish of the Romans:* the city having little indulgence for captives, as Livy says. This reason being peculiar to the Romans, could not be the reason for the law of nations: but it might be among the reasons why the Romans took such a rule from other nations. But the truer reason is, that the belligerents are regarded as if their wars were just,

and neutrals cannot safely interpose, and must therefore acquiesce; and so, must reckon actual captives as justly captives.

3 But with regard to those who were caught among the enemy when the war broke out, the same could not be said: for they could not be conceived to have done any wrong. Yet to diminish the strength of the enemy, they were retained while the war lasted. These then, by the consent of nations, were to be liberated, on the arrival of peace, as innocent; but other prisoners to be regulated by laws of war, except so far as regulated by compact. And for the same reason, slaves and other property are not restored at peace, except by compact; for they are supposed to be taken by right, and to deny this, would be to make wars grow out of wars. Whence it appears that what is alleged by Quintilian for the Thebans, is ingenious, but not true.

4 By postliminium in war, those who were free men before their capture, *return;* slaves and things are *recovered.*

V. A free man returns by postliminium, if he comes to his own party with this intent: inasmuch as, in order that a slave [or a captive] may become free he must, so to speak, acquire himself, which cannot be done without his will. But whether he be recovered from the enemy by warlike force, or make his escape, makes no difference, as is noted by Florentinus. The same follows if he be spontaneously given up by the enemy.

But what is the result if he be sold by the enemy in the usual way of traffic, and so come to his own people? This controversy is treated by Quintilian, with reference to the Olynthian, whom Parrhasius had bought. For a decree having been made by the Athenians that the Olynthians should be free, he enquires whether this means that they should become free, or should be adjudged to be free: of which the latter is the more true opinion.

VI. 1 Moreover a free man, after he has returned to his own people, acquires, not only himself, but all the property which he had in a neutral State, both corporeal and incorporeal. For the neutral State, as they took the fact for law in the case of captivity, must do the same in the case of liberation, to shew themselves impartial to both parties. Therefore the right, which he who possessed him by the law of war, had over his property, was not altogether without conditions: it was liable to cease without his consent, if he who had been captive made his way to his own people. He therefore loses the property, as he loses the man to whom it was an accessary.

2 But what if he had alienated this property? Will he who derives his title from him who, at the time, was owner, by the right of war, be safe by the law of nations; or may the property be recovered from him? I speak of the property which he had in a neutral state. Here, it seems, we must make a distinction between things which are of such a nature that they return by postliminium, and things not of that nature: which difference we shall soon explain. The former class of things are, it would seem, alienated with their cause, the per-

son, and under condition : the latter are simply alienated.   By alienated, I mean given away, or acknowledged as received.

VII.   And as the person who returns by postliminium recovers his rights, so also rights against him are restored, and are held the same as if he had never been in the power of the enemy, as Tryphoninus says.

VIII.   To this rule concerning free men, Paulus rightly annexed this exception.   Those who surrender themselves, lose postliminium, namely, because conventions made with an enemy are valid by the law of nations, and against these, postliminium does not hold.   So the Romans captured by the Carthaginians, say, in Gellius, that they have no right to postliminium, since they were captives by right.   Whence during a truce, there is no postliminium, as Paulus rightly notes; but those who are surrendered to the enemy without any compact, return by postliminium, as Modestinus gave his opinion.

IX.   1 What we have said of individuals, I conceive holds also for a people; so that they who have been free, recover their liberty, if it happen that the force of their friends extricate them from the power of their enemies.   But if the multitude which had constituted the state or city be dissolved, I conceive it to be more true that it is not to be reckoned the same people, and that their condition is not restored by postliminium, by the law of nations : for a people, like a ship, by the dissolution of its parts, perishes outright; since its whole nature consists in the continuity of its composition.   And therefore that which had been the city of Saguntum was no longer the same city, when the same place was restored to the old inhabitants eight years later : nor was Thebes the same city when the Thebans had been sold as slaves by Alexander.   Hence it appears that what the Thessalians owed the Thebans was not restored to the Thebans by postliminium, and that, for two reasons : because it was a new people; and because Alexander could and did alienate this right; and because a credit is not of the number of the things which return by postliminium.

2 What we have said of a city, is not dissimilar from the old Roman law, according to which, marriages being dissolvable, the marriage state was not considered to be restored by postliminium, but required to be renewed by a new agreement.

X.   1 Such is the Law of Nations, as to postliminium for free men : the Civil Law modifies and extends this.   So deserters had not this privilege; nor sons under the Quirital *patria potestas :* for, as Paulus says, the discipline of the camp outweighed the love of children : as Cicero says of Manlius, that he preferred discipline and loyalty to paternal affection.

2 Again, there was this restriction of the privilege, by Attic and Roman laws, that he who was ransomed must serve his ransomer, till he had remunerated him.   This however was to encourage the practice of ransoming.   And this servitude was afterwards mitigated, and, by Justinian, reduced to five years : and extinguished by the death

of the person ransomed; as also remitted by marriage contracted between the ransomed and the ransomer; and lost by the prostitution of a woman so redeemed; and other laws of Rome there were on this subject. [See the text.]

3 Again, the privilege was extended by the Roman and Attic law, so that all rights were restored to the person. So a person, calling himself the son of Callias, who had been a slave in Thrace, having been taken in the defeat at Acanthus, returned to Athens, and claimed the inheritance of Callias from the possessors of it; and, in the trial, no enquiry was made, except whether he were the son of Callias. So the Messenians, after long servitude, recovered their liberty and their country. Even what had been lost by usucaption, or otherwise, might be recovered.

4 The Cornelian law provided for the heirs of those who died while in the enemies' hands. If this had not been so, any one might have seized their property, for they were reckoned as nullified; and if they returned, had no right, except to postliminium *jure gentium*. The confiscation of the property of captives, if there is no heir, is a special Roman law.

So much of those persons who return: now of the things which are recovered.

XI. 1 Such are men and women slaves, even when repeatedly alienated, or manumitted by the enemy: for such manumission cannot prejudice the right of the citizen owner. But that a slave be recovered, he must be in a condition to be got at by his master; not only returned within the empire, but known of; it is not enough if he be hidden in Rome. And as a slave in this differs from inanimate things, in another point he differs from a free man; it is not necessary he should have come with a view of staying with us.

2 Runaway slaves are not excepted from this rule. The owner recovers his former right to them. To punish them, would injure the master rather than the slave. The rule with regard to slaves recovered by the army, is that *they are recovered, not captured: the soldier is their defender, not their owner.*

3 Slaves ransomed from the enemy, become the property of the ransomer, or may be recovered by postliminium, on paying the price. But the details of this belong to the juristical commentators: and were afterwards changed.

XII. Another question belongs more to us; whether a people, who have been subjected to a foreign authority, return to their ancient condition: which may be treated, if not he to whose government they had belonged, but some of his allies, have delivered them from the enemy. I conceive we must here decide as we do concerning slaves, except there be some other convention in the alliance.

XIII. 1 Among things, land first occurs. This is recovered by postliminium, when the enemy are expelled: that is, when the enemy can no longer openly approach the land. So the Lacedæmonians, when they had taken Egina from the Athenians, restored it to its ancient owners. Justinian gave the lands taken from the Goths and Vandals to the heirs of the old possessors, not admitting contrary prescriptions.

2 What is true of lands, is true of all rights adhering to the soil. So places which had been consecrated as religious, if liberated, resume their former state: as Cicero argues against Verres, of the Diana of Segeste. Marcion compares the right of postliminium to that by which, when a house tumbles down, the soil is restored to the shore. And therefore the usufruct of recovered land is to be restored: as was ruled, if it had been inundated. So the Spanish law directs that counties, and hereditary jurisdictions, are restored by postliminium; the major ones, absolutely; the minor, if they are claimed within five years from their recovery; except that a fort, lost and regained, the king has the right of retaining.

XIV. 1 Concerning moveables, on the other hand, the contrary rule in general holds: that they do not return by postliminium, but become prize. Hence objects of traffic, wherever bought, become the property of him who buys them: and if found among neutrals, or brought home, cannot be claimed by the old owner. But from this rule, were excepted formerly munitions of war; the reason being, apparently, that men might be more active in recovering these. For many states have their laws made especially with a view to war. We have already stated what are munitions of war. [See also Cicero, &c.]

2 Arms and clothing have their use in war, but had not the privilege of postliminium; because they who lost them were little favoured, indeed were disgraced. And so a horse is different in this respect from arms; for the horse may be lost without fault of the rider. Boethius seems to imply that the distinction held up to his time, under the Goths.

XV. But at a later period, if not sooner, this distinction was abolished; for those who speak of customs, always say that moveables have not postliminium; and we see this, in many places, practised as to ships.

XVI. Things which are not yet brought *intra præsidia*, though seized by the enemy, do not need postliminium, because they have not changed their master *jure gentium*. So, what things pirates and robbers take from us, do not need postliminium; for such persons, *jure gentium*, cannot change the ownership. And on this ground, when pirates had taken Halonesus from the Athenians, and Philip had taken it from pirates, the Athenians wished him not to give, but to restore it to them. Things taken by such persons may be claimed wherever they are found: except, as elsewhere said, that by natural law, we must pay the possessor who has acquired them at his own expense, as much as the owner would pay to recover them.

XVII. But other rules than this may be established by Civil Law: as by the Spanish law, ships become theirs who regain them from pirates; nor it is unreasonable that private interests should yield to public utility; especially, the difficulty of recovery being so great. But such a law does not prevent strangers from trying to recover what is theirs.

XVIII. 1 It is more remarkable, that, as the Roman Laws testify, the right of postliminium had place, not only between enemies, but between the Romans and foreign nations. But, as we have elsewhere said, these traits were relicks of the nomade age of mankind, in which barbarous manners had blunted the natural sense of the natural society which ought to bind men to men. And thus, even between nations which had not a public war between them, there was a kind of licence of private undeclared war: and in order that this licence might not go to the length of putting strangers to death, there was introduced a right of making prisoners between nations; from which it followed, that there was also occasion for postliminium, in a different way than with robbers and pirates; because that force, used in such cases, led to fair compacts; which are commonly held in no regard by robbers and pirates.

2 It appears formerly to have been a matter of controversy whether those members of a people, allied to us, who are slaves in our country, do, if they return home, return by postliminium. For so Cicero proposes this question; and Gallus Ælius says, that with free and with allied people, and with kings, we have postliminium, as with enemies. On the other hand, Proculus says, that *federate peoples are externi, and that there is not postliminium with them.*

3 I conceive that a distinction must be taken between different leagues of alliance. If these were entered into merely for the purpose of settling or preventing a public war, these would not prevent either captivity or postliminium: but if the leagues contained a provision that those who came from one party to the other should be safe on the public security, then, captivity being removed, postliminium would cease also. So Pomponius: *If we have, with any nation, neither friendship, hospitality, nor league of friendship, these are not enemies; but if anything of ours goes to them it becomes theirs; and a free man of ours, made captive there, is their slave; and so from them to us. In this case, then, postliminium exists.* By saying "a league of friendship," he shews that there may be other leagues, which do not give the right of hospitality or friendship. So Proculus sufficiently implies that he means, by "federate peoples," those who have promised friendship or safe hospitality, by saying, *For what need is there of postliminium in such a case; since they retain their liberty and ownership in our territory equally as in their own; and we in theirs?* Wherefore what follows in Gallus Ælius: *With the nations which are under our authority, there is no postliminium,* is to be understood with the addition, nor with those with whom we have a league of friendship.

XIX. 1 In our own time, not only among Christians, but also among most Mahometan nations, the right, both of making prisoners out of war-time, and the right of postliminium, have vanished ; the necessity of both having disappeared, by the restoration of that relationship which nature intended to exist among men.

2 But that ancient Law of Nations may have place, if we have to do with a nation so barbarous, that it is accustomed, without cause or declaration, to treat all foreigners and their property in a hostile manner.

And at the very time that I am writing, a judgment to this effect is given in the High Court of Paris, under the presidency of Nicolas Verdun : that goods which had belonged to French citizens, and had been taken by the Algerines, who are accustomed to send sea-rovers, and to attack all nations, had changed their owner by the right of war : and consequently, being recovered by others, became the property of those who had recovered them.   And in the same cause, this also was adjudged, that ships are not, at the present day, in the number of the things which are recovered by postliminium.

CHAPTER X.

Warnings concerning things done in an unjust War.

I. 1 I MUST now tread back my steps, and take from belligerents nearly all, which I have seemed to grant them; and yet have not really granted; for when I began to explain this part of the Law of Nations, I testified that many things were said to be *law*, or *lawful*, because they are done with impunity; partly also, because coactive judgments of tribunals accommodate their authority to them: while the things themselves either deviate from the rule of right, (whether that rule be regulated by strict justice, or by the precepts of other virtues,) or at least, may more righteously and laudably be omitted.

2 We have often *pudor, shame,* referred to as moderating strict rights: *pudor* meaning, not so much a regard to reputation and men's opinion, as a regard to what is equitable and good, or at least, more equitable and better. So Seneca. So in Justinian's *Institutes,* Trusts (*fidei commissa*) are said to have for their bond the *pudor* of the Trustees. So Quintilian says the creditor cannot go to the surety, *salvo pudore,* except the debtor fails him. And in this sense *pudor* is often conjoined with justice, as in Ovid. So Hesiod conjoins δίκη and αἰδώς. And Plato says that αἰδώς is the assessor of δίκη. And in the Protagoras, he says that the two, δίκη and αἰδώς, a feeling of justice and of mutual reverence, were given to man to hold society together. So Plutarch also, and Dionysius of Halicarnassus. So Josephus, and Paulus the Jurist. Cicero arranges the offices of justice, and *verecundia,* so that the former prevents us wronging men, the latter, offending them.

3 So Seneca says: *How much wider is duty than law!* and the like. Justice is distinguished from *jus,* law; for *jus* is what holds in external judgments. And elsewhere, he explains this by the example of a master's right over his servants. *We are not to consider what you may do, but what is required by justice and fairness, which require us to spare even captives and slaves.* And again: *Though everything is lawful towards a slave, there are things which common humanity declares not to be lawful.* Whence note the two different uses of *lawful,* referring to external and to internal justice.

II. 1 The same distinction is made by Marcellus speaking to the

Senate: by Aristotle, when he says that slavery, though lawful, may be unjust: by the Thebans in Thucydides.

2 So the Roman jurists, though they speak of the right of captivity, also call this right a wrong, *injuria*. So Seneca. So Livy says the Italians were obstinate in injury, because they retained what they had in war taken from the Syracusans. So Dio Prusæensis speaks of captives taken in war, as unjustly enslaved. So Lactantius says that philosophers, discussing the rights of war, do not regard justice and virtue, but the customs of states: and he speaks of the *legitimate wrongs* inflicted by the Romans.

III. First, then, we say, that if the cause of war be unjust, though the war be regular in manner, all acts thence arising are unjust, according to internal injustice. And all who operate knowingly in such acts, or co-operate, are in the number of those who cannot enter into the kingdom of heaven without repentance for their acts. Now repentance, if time and opportunity be granted, requires restitution. And therefore, God declares that the fastings of those who (Isaiah lviii. 6) do not unloose unjust bonds are not grateful to him. And (Jonah iii. 8) the king of Nineveh proclaimed a fast, that the people might cease from violence: acknowledging, by a natural impulse, that repentance was idle without such amendment. And such we find the judgment, not only of Christians and Jews, but of Mahomedans.

IV. The restitution is due, from the authors of the war, for all evils inflicted: and for anything unusual which they have done, or not prevented when they could. So the generals are responsible for what is done by their order; and the soldiers severally and jointly who have joined in any act; as the burning of a city: and in separable acts, each for what he did, or aided in doing.

V. 1 Nor do I conceive that the exception is to be admitted, of those who act for others, if they have committed any fault [with deceit, *J. B.*]; for to make restitution be proper, fault is enough without deceit. There are some who seem to think that things taken in war, even if there were no just cause of the war, are not to be restored, because the belligerents are understood to have given such things to the captors. But no one can be lightly presumed to set his property on a cast: and war of itself is far removed from the nature of a contract. And in order that neutral parties might have a clear rule to follow, and might not be involved in a war against their will, the introduction of that external ownership, of which we have spoken, was enough; which may consist with the internal obligation of restitution. So the Samnites, in Livy, give up what they had taken; *which*, they say, *seemed ours by the right of war: seemed,* because the war was unjust, as the Samnites had confessed.

2 It is a case of the same kind, that an unequal contract, made without deceit, gives, by the Law of Nations, a right of compelling the fulfilment of the compacts; and yet he who has the advantage, is bound by the duty of an honest and pious man, to reduce it to equality.

B B

VI. 1 But also, he who has not caused any damage, or has caused it without any fault, but who has in his possession a thing taken in war from another, is bound to restore it, because there is no cause, naturally just, why the other should be deprived of it; not his consent; not his ill desert; not compensation. There is a story to this effect in Valerius Maximus: *When P. Claudius had taken and sold the people of Camerina, although the money and the conquest were very advantageous, the Roman people sought them out and redeemed them, because the justice of the proceeding did not seem clear; and gave them a dwelling in the Aventine, and restored their property.* So, by a decree of the Romans, the Phocenses had their liberty and land restored. So the Ligurians who had been sold by M. Popilius, were redeemed and restored to liberty, and their property given back. So with regard to the Abderites, the Senate decreed the same thing, adding the reason, that the war had been unjust.

2 But he who holds such property, if he have spent anything upon it, may deduct as much as it was worth to the owner to recover possession, as we have elsewhere explained. If the possessor have without fault consumed or alienated the thing, he is not bound, except so far as he is made richer.

[This and the succeeding chapters point out the Restraints which morality and religion impose on the exercise of Rights. That the exercise of rights will be restrained by morality and religion, wherever these prevail among men, is so obvious, that it does not need any large array of authorities to prove it: and the application of such views has, in some measure, modified the received usages of war among Christian nations. I shall, therefore, considerably abridge the illustrative matter in this part. Of the Laws of War so modified, see *Elements of Morality*, 1061, &c.   W. W.]

CHAPTER XI.

Restraints as to the Right of killing in War.

I. 1 [WE have been speaking of the restraints which the injustice of a war imposes;] but even in a just war, we are not to say with Lucan, *He who denies justice, gives everything.* Better Cicero, *There are duties even against those who have injured us. There is a limit to punishment and revenge.* And he praises the old times of Rome, when the event of a war was either mild or necessary. So Seneca. So Aristides says that over-punishment makes a new injury; and so Ovid.

2 So the Plateans in Isocrates, and so Aristides, speak of a measure of punishment proportioned to the offense. So Propertius and Ovid.

II. What killing is just in war, according to internal justice, we may see from what has been said. A man may be killed of purpose, or not of purpose. No one can be justly killed of purpose, except either as a just punishment, or so far as we cannot otherwise defend our life and property. And even this step, of killing a man for perishable human property, is at variance with the law of charity. In order that punishment may be just, it is necessary that he who is killed should have himself offended, and so offended, that a just judge would think death a fit punishment. Of this we have spoke, in treating of punishment.

III.   1 Above, in speaking of suppliants (for there are such in war as in peace, namely, those who ask for mercy,) we distinguished misfortune and misdeed.   So Gylippus considers to which class the Athenians belong, and says they were not men unfortunate, but unjust, and must therefore bear the evils of war.   Of unfortunate persons, examples are those who are with the enemy, without being hostile in mind, as the Athenians at the time of Mithridates.   So Paterculus describes them, applying what Livy says, of Indibilis the Spaniard, that his body was with the Carthaginians, his mind with the Romans.

2 So Cicero speaks of faults of necessity, as opposed to those of will: so Julianus, the commentator on Thucydides, says, that according to the mild spirit of the Greeks the Corcyrean captives were spared on this ground.   The Plateans plead the same excuse in Isocrates; and the other Greeks.   So Herodotus of the Phocians.   So Alexander spared the Zelites.   So Nicolaus of Syracuse, pleading for the captives.   So the Syracusans in Livy.   So Antigonus said that he made war on Cleomenes, not on the Spartans.

IV.   1 But we must note that, between a clear injury and a mere misfortune, there is a middle case, composed of both; so that the act can neither be said to be that of one simply knowing and willing, nor of one ignorant or unwilling.

2 This is what Aristotle calls ἁμάρτημα, and we may call *culpa*, a fault.   The passage is in *Eth.* v. 10.   *There are three cases in which damage may be done to men: by misfortune, by fault, and by injury. But injury may be done, willingly indeed, but not deliberately, as when it is done through sudden anger.*

3 *Anger at supposed wrong is some excuse.*

4 *What is done through ignorance is excusable.*

5 Michael Ephesius comments, and explains, this passage.   So Aristotle in his *Rhetoric*.   And the ancients quote Homer to the same effect.

6 A similar division is given in Marcian, of delicts *proposito, impetu, casu*.   The first two are distinguished by Cicero.   So Philo says, that without purpose prepense, the deed is reduced to half.

7 The principal examples are those which necessity, if it do not justify, at least excuses.   So Demosthenes; Thucydides; the Cærites for themselves; Justin for the Phocians; Isocrates; Aristides; Philostratus for the Messenians.   So Aristotle speaks of a man *half wicked, not unjust, for the act was not deliberate*.   Themistius uses this difference in praise of Valens.

8 The same writer elsewhere presses it upon the young Emperor. So in Josephus, Titus makes a difference.

Mere misfortunes neither deserve punishment, nor oblige to recompense of loss: unjust actions do both.   The intermediate case, fault, is liable to restitution, but often does not merit punishment, especially capital punishment.   So Valerius Flaccus.

V. Themistius, in the passage above quoted, praises Valens for making a difference between the authors of the war, and their followers: and this is often exemplified in history. So the Greeks, in dealing with the Thebans for joining the Medes. So the leaders of the sedition at Ardea were put to death: so at Agrigentum, Atella, and Calasia; and elsewhere. So Eteocles is praised in Euripides; and the Athenians, for this reason, repented of their decree against the Mitylenians. So Demetrius acted at Thebes.

VI. 1 But also, in the authors of the war, the causes of the act are to be distinguished; for there are some which, though not just, may impose on those who are not bad men. The writer to Herennius puts this as a strong ground of excuse. So Seneca; so the Cærites plead in Livy; so the Phocians and others were pardoned by Rome; so Aristides pleads for the Thebans.

2 Cicero says that those are to be spared, who have fought without cruelty; and that wars for glory should be carried on less bitterly. So Ptolemy tells Demetrius that they were to fight, not for existence, but for glory and empire. So Severus says of Niger.

3 Often, as Cicero says of the war between Cæsar and Pompey, the case was obscure, and that many doubted which was the better side. And of himself he says, *We may not be free from human fault, but we are free from wickedness.* So he says also of Deiotarus. So Sallust says of the multitude. What Brutus wrote of the civil wars, may be applied to other wars: *That they who raised them were more proper objects of anger than they who were conquered in them.*

VII. 1 Even when justice does not require us to spare men's lives in war, it is often agreeable to goodness, to moderation, to magnanimity. So Sallust says of one, that he *increased the greatness of the Roman people by mercy.* Tacitus recommends keenness against the enemy, kindness towards the suppliant. Seneca says that it is only the baser wild beasts which tear them that are down; elephants and lions pass them by. So Virgil, of the Trojan feeling.

2 There is a passage to this effect in the book *ad Herennium,* which praises the Romans for sparing those they had vanquished. But to this, other passages may be opposed, as the panegyric of Constantine. But this again is too lax. Josephus gives a like example of the Roman severity, speaking of putting to death Simon Barjoras: but he speaks of leaders like Pontius the Samnite, not of kings. Cicero, in his Verrine Oration, says the same. .

3 With regard to this putting to death leaders, there are everywhere examples. Some there are of kings, as Aristonicus, Jugurtha, Artabasdus, [Gronovius notes that the two former were spurious kings; and that the last was put to death at Alexandria, *M. Antonii scelus,* as Tacitus says]. But besides Perseus, others, as Syphax, Gentius, Juba, and at the time of the Cæsars, Caractacus, escaped this punishment; so that it appears that the Romans regarded the cause of the war, and the mode of conducting it by the enemy: and yet they

were too harsh in victory, as Cicero and others acknowledge. And M. Æmilius Paulus, in pleading for Perseus, warns the Roman Senators to fear Nemesis, the divine vengeance, if they use victory insolently. Plutarch notes that, in the Greek wars, even the enemies did no violence to the Lacedæmonian Kings, out of reverence for their dignity.

4 An enemy, therefore, who considers, not what human laws permit, but what is his duty, what is righteous and pious, will spare hostile blood: and will never inflict death, except either to avoid death, or evils like death, or to punish crimes which are capital in desert. And even to some who have deserved that, he will remit all, or at least, capital punishment, either out of humanity, or for some other plausible causes. So Diodorus says that *victory depends on fortune, but mercy in victory on virtue.* So Curtius, of Alexander.

VIII. With regard to those who are killed without its being intended, we must hold that if justice do not require, at least mercy does, that we should not, except for weighty causes tending to the safety of many, undertake anything which may involve innocent persons in destruction. So Polybius.

IX.   1 Having settled these principles, it will not be difficult to lay down more special rules.

Children are excused by their age, women by their sex, as Seneca says, in the books in which he writes, angrily, *Against Anger.* God himself, even when peace had been offered and refused, directed that women and infants were to be spared, except in a few cases, in which the war was the war of God, not of men, and was so called. And when he directed the Midianitish women to be slain for their crime, he excepted the virgins. And when he had threatened Nineveh with destruction, he was moved to change his purpose, (Jonah iv. 11,) by the consideration that there were so many persons who could not distinguish right from wrong. So Seneca and Lucan speak of children. And if God did and directed thus, the Giver and Lord of life, what should men do, to whom he has given no authority over men, except what is necessary to preserve the safety and society of men?

2 With regard to Children, we are supported by the judgment of the most moral times and peoples. So Camillus, in Livy; Plutarch, who says *there are, among good men, certain laws of war:* where note *apud bonos,* among good men, that you may distinguish those laws from the customary rights of war, which only mean impunity. So Florus: and Livy again.

3 The rule of mercy which obtains always in infants, obtains mostly in Women, (except they have incurred punishment by some special act, or assumed masculine offices). For the sex is unfit for arms: *Does enemy apply to women?* is asked in the tragedy. So Alexander in Curtius; Gryphus in Justin; and another in Tacitus, *neque adversus feminas:* [but it is *feminas gravidas* in the passage. J. B.]

4 Valerius speaks of the savage cruelty of Munatius Flaccus to women and children, intolerable to hear of. So the Carthaginians

are said to have put to death old men, women, children, *without feeling*. This is *cruelty*. So Pacatus and Papinius.

X.   1 The same rule is to be laid down generally, for Men whose kind of life is repugnant to arms. *Slaughter of men armed and resisting is the law of war*, says Livy; that is, by Natural Law. So Josephus says, that it is reasonable that they who have taken arms should be punished in battle, but that Non-combatants are not to be hurt.   So Camillus, in storming Veii, directed the unarmed to be let alone.

In this class, first we must place Those who perform sacred offices. For that these abstain from arms, is an ancient custom of all nations; and in old time, they were not molested.   So the Philistines did not hurt the school of the prophets (1 Sam. x. 5 and 10) at Gaba, where they had a garrison. And so (1 Sam. xix. 18) David and Samuel took refuge at Naioth, where there was also a school of the prophets. Plutarch relates that the Cretans, in their intestine wars, abstained from injuring the priests, and the buriers of the dead. Hence the Greek proverb, *not even the pyre-lighter was left*, when all were killed. Strabo notes that in ancient times, when all Greece was in disturbance with arms, the Eleans, as sacred to Jupiter, and they who were under their hospitality, lived in profound peace.

2 Along with Priests, are properly ranked in this matter, all who have chosen a similar course of life, as Monks, and Novices, that is, Penitents; and these, the Canons direct, are to be spared, as well as priests; following, in this, natural equity.   Add to these, Those who give their labour to honourable literary studies, useful to mankind.

XI.   Next add Husbandmen, whom also the Canons include. Diodorus, praising the Indians, says that in their wars, the warriors fight, but they leave the cultivators unmolested, as the common benefactors of both sides.   So Plutarch, of the old Corinthians and Megareans. So Cyrus proposed to the king of Assyria. So Belisarius acted, as Suidas says.

XII.   The Canon adds Merchants, which is to be understood, not only of those who make a temporary residence in the hostile country, but also of permanent subjects.   For their life also is foreign to arms.   And under this name are included Artisans, and Workmen, whose gain requires peace, not war.

XIII.   1 To come to those who have borne arms, we have already quoted the speech of Pyrrhus in Seneca, who says that we are prevented, *pudore*, by decency, from putting a captive to death. We adduced a similar opinion expressed by Alexander, who conjoins captives with women.   We may add Augustine, Xenophon, Diodorus Siculus.

2 When Sallust says, that all the men were slain after the surrender, he adds, *contrary to the Laws of War*: that is, contrary to the manner of humane nations.   So Lactantius.   So Tacitus of Antonius and Varus.   So Aristides.

Elisha the prophet says to the king of Samaria, 2 Kings vi. 22:

Wouldest thou smite those whom thou hast taken captive with thy sword and with thy bow? So in Euripides. So the Byzantines and Chalcedonians are said to have done acts of extraordinary cruelty, in killing captives. And to spare captives, is a common law. So Seneca, already quoted. And when a general, embarrassed by the number of his captives, dismisses them, he is praised in history.

XIV. 1 Hence surrender on condition of life is accepted, both in a battle and in a siege. Hence Arrian says that the slaughter of the Thebans, who had surrendered, was an *un-Greek* massacre. So Thucydides, *You received us, holding out our hands as surrendering: to kill such is not the Greek custom.* So the Syracusans in Diodorus; and Sopater.

2 In besieging towns, the Romans did this, before the battering-ram had struck the walls. So Cæsar announces to the Aduatici. And this rule holds at the present day for weak places, before the fire of artillery begins; in strong places, before a storm is ordered. Cicero, looking at equity, says, those who surrender are to be received, even if the ram have struck the wall. The Hebrew commentators note that their countrymen, in their sieges, were wont not to carry the works quite round the city, but to leave an opening for escape, to avoid the shedding of blood.

XV. The same equity commands us to spare those who surrender unconditionally, or ask their lives. *To massacre those who surrender, is savage,* says Tacitus. So Sallust of Marius; and Livy.

And pains are to be taken to make them rather surrender through fear, than be slain. Brutus is praised that he ordered his adversaries to be turned in flank, not charged in front, as being soon his own.

XVI. 1 Exceptions, by no means just, to these precepts of equity and natural justice are often alleged:—Retaliation:—the necessity of striking terror:—the obstinacy of the resistance. It is easily seen that these are insufficient arguments. There is no danger from captives or persons willing to surrender; and therefore, to justify putting them to death, there should be antecedent crime, of a capital amount. And when this can be urged, surrender on condition of life is sometimes not accepted; or they are put to death after surrender: for instance, those who, though convinced of the injustice of the war, remained in arms; or attacked the reputation of their enemies with monstrous calumnies; or violated faith; or other laws, such as the rights of legation; or were deserters.

2 But as to Retaliation, nature does not allow it, except against the offender himself. Nor is it sufficient, that the enemy is, by a sort of fiction, conceived as forming one body; as appears from what we have said above of the punishment of accessories. Aristides speaks of *blaming what others do, and yet imitating it.* Plutarch accuses the Syracusans on this ground, as having put to death the wives and children of Hicetas, because he had killed the wife, sister, and son of Dion.

3 The advantage which is expected by striking terror, cannot give a right to kill men: but if we have a right, it may be a reason for not remitting it.

4 An obstinate adherence to one's own party, if their cause be not indecently bad, does not deserve punishment: [so in Procopius:] or at least, not a punishment extending to death; for no impartial judge would so decide. When Alexander ordered the men to be put to death, in a town which had resisted obstinately, the Indians thought him a ruffian; and he, in fear of such a reputation, afterwards used his victory more temperately. To the Milesians he was more generous, sparing them for their fidelity to their friends. When Phyto the governor of Rhegium was led to death with torture by Dionysius, for defending his city obstinately, he exclaimed that the gods would revenge his case; his unjust punishment, as Diodorus calls it. Cæsar, in Lucan, wishes well to him who can think that his citizens have done well, though they carried arms against him; which I admire, including, in *citizens*, the citizens, not of one nation, but of all.

5 Still less is such killing justified by grief for calamity suffered; as when we read that Achilles, Æneas, Alexander, marked the funerals of their friends with the blood of captives, or persons who had surrendered. Homer calls such a purpose κακὰ ἔργα, *evil deeds*.

XVII. Even when the offenses are such that they may seem to deserve death, it is the office of mercy to remit the extreme of right, on account of the number of offenders. We find an example of this clemency in God himself, who allowed that the Canaanites and their neighbours should have the offer of peace, on condition of tribute. So Seneca, *Pardon is necessary, when the whole army has deserted. What takes away the wise man's anger? the offenders' number.* So Lucan. Cicero speaks of lot in such a case. So Sallust to Cæsar.

XVIII. 1 What is to be the rule of hostages, we have already suggested. Formerly, when it was believed that every one had a right over his own life, and that he had transferred this to the state, it is not so surprizing, if we find hostages, without any private crime, put to death, for the fault of their city; either as by their own consent, or by the public consent, in which their own was included. But when a better wisdom has taught us that our life is not put in our power by God, it follows that no one can by mere consent give a right over his own life, or that of his fellow-citizen. And so Narses thought it atrocious to punish innocent hostages: and Scipio said he would not punish the hostages, but the offenders: not the unarmed, but the armed.

2 What is said by recent writers, that such conventions are valid if authorized by custom, I allow, if they mean that they obtain impunity, which often passes for right; but if they mean that *they* are free from sin, who take away life on a mere convention, I am afraid they are both wrong themselves, and mislead others. If, however, a person who comes as a hostage, is or has been a grave criminal, or griev-

ously violates his faith given, it may be that the punishment may be right.

3 But Clelia, who was sent as a hostage, not by her own consent but by command of the city, and who escaped by swimming the Tiber, was praised by the Etruscan king, as Livy says.

XIX.   We must add, that all combats by challenge, which are of no use in obtaining rights, or in ending the war, but are merely for the sake of shewing valour or skill, are at variance with Christian duty and with humanity.   Rulers ought decisively to forbid such, since they must render an account to him, in whose stead they bear the sword, of blood shed uselessly.   So Sallust praises leaders who conquer bloodlessly.   So the Catti, a people of known valour, are praised by Tacitus, because, *with them, champions stepping out of the ranks, and chance fights, are rare.*

CHAPTER XII.

Restraints as to Wasting, and the like.

I. 1 IN order that any one may destroy the property of another without wrong, one of these three things is necessary:—either such a necessity as must be supposed to be accepted in the first institution of property: (as if any one, to save himself, threw into the river the sword of another, which a madman was going to use; in which case, however, the better opinion is, that the obligation of restitution remains:)—or some debt remaining unpaid, in which case the thing destroyed is to be reckoned as received, otherwise the right does not exist:—or some ill desert, to which such punishment is suited, and so that the loss does not exceed the desert: for, as a sound theologian rightly notes, it is not equitable that for some cattle driven away, or some houses burnt, a kingdom should be laid waste; as Polybius also said; who would not allow that in war punishment should go on to an indefinite extent, but only so far that the offenses may be equitably expiated. And for these causes, and within these limits, to damage another's property is not to do a wrong.

2 But except there be some motive of utility, it is foolish, for no good of your own, to harm another. Therefore wise men are commonly moved by their advantages, of which the principal is, that which Onosander notes: *Let the general waste, burn, and ravage the enemy's country; for the want of money and provision breaks down a war as abundance holds it up.* And so Proclus, *It is the part of a good general to cut off the enemy's resources.* So Curtius, of Darius.

3 Such ravage is tolerable (to the moralist) as in a short time reduces the enemy to seek peace: which was the kind of war that Halyattes carried on against the Milesians, the Thracians against the Byzantines, the Romans against the Campanians, Capenates, Spaniards, Ligurians, Nervians, Menapians. But if you weigh the matter well, you will find that such practices are admitted, rather through spite than prudence. For it generally happens, either that these motives cease, or that other motives which act the other way are more powerful.

II. 1 That will be the case, in the first place, if we are in possession of the country which yields provisions, so that it cannot avail the enemy for their supply. And to this point properly tends the divine law (Deut. xx. 19, 20), which forbids the cutting down fruit-trees for bulwarks and other warlike uses, and points out trees which do not supply food, as proper to be used for such purposes; and adds the reason, that " the tree of the field is man's life," and that they cannot war against man, as man can. And this Philo extends to fields which have fruit; adding, that they minister food and comfort to the victors: they pay tribute. Josephus adds, on the same place, that if the trees could speak, they would complain of the injustice of their bearing the penalty of the war, of which they are not the cause. And on the same ground rests the Pythagorean dictum in Jamblichus, that it is unlawful to hurt a fruit-bearing tree.

2 Porphyry, in his book Against Eating Animals, speaking of the manners of the Jews, being guided, as I conceive, by custom, extends this to animals used in agriculture: for he says that Moses commanded to spare these also. And the writers of the Talmud, and the Hebrew Commentators, say that this law is to be extended to anything which is destroyed without cause, as when buildings are burnt, or victuals spoiled. And with this law, agrees the prudent moderation of Timotheus, the Athenian general, who *did not allow a house or city to be burnt, or a fruit-tree to be cut down,* as Polyænus relates. In Plato's *Laws* we have this, that *the land is not to be ravaged nor houses burnt.*

3 Much more will this hold after a complete victory. Cicero does not approve of Corinth being destroyed; where, nevertheless, the Roman ambassadors had been shamefully treated. The same writer elsewhere says, that a war made against walls, roofs, columns, and posts, is horrible, wicked, and stained with all spite. Livy praises the clemency of the Romans, when Capua was taken, that there were no severities exercised, by conflagration and ruin, against harmless roofs and walls. So Agamemnon, in Seneca, declares he wished of Troy.

4 The Sacred History tells us of some cities, which were given up to destruction; and that, even against the sacred law which we have mentioned; the trees of the Moabites were commanded to be cut down (2 Kings iii. 19); but this was not done in hostile spite, but in detestation of wickednesses, which were either publicly known, or were, in the judgment of God, worthy of such inflictions.

III. 1 In the second place, the rule which we mention will hold, even when the possession of the land is doubtful, if there be strong hope of a speedy victory, of which the reward will be, both the land and its fruits. So Alexander restrained his soldiers from wasting Asia, telling them not to destroy what was to be their own. So Quintius exhorted his soldiers to march through Thessaly, as a country already their own. So Crœsus said to Cyrus, to dissuade him from wasting Lydia, *You will not destroy my possessions, but your own.*

2 To those who do otherwise, we may apply what Jocasta says in Seneca: *You destroy your country while you try to win it, &c.* So Cur-

tius, *What they spoiled they acknowledged to belong to the enemy.* So Cicero argues against Pompey's design, of reducing his country by famine. And on this ground Alexander Isius blames Philip, as Livy translates from Polybius.

IV. 1 In the third place, this holds if the enemy can support himself from other quarters; as if the sea, or boundaries on another side, be open. So Archidamus exhorting the Lacedæmonians from war with the Athenians, asks if they depend on wasting Attica, when the Athenians have other territories (Thrace and Ionia), and can obtain supplies by sea. In such a state of things, then, it is best that agriculture should be secure, even in the contested region, which we have lately seen practised in the war in Germanic Belgium*, on paying a tribute to both parties.

2 This is agreeable to the practice of the ancient Indians, among whom the cultivators worked undisturbed close to the camps, as a race sacred from injury, and beneficial to all.

3 Xenophon says that a convention was made between Cyrus and the Assyrians, that *there should be peace with the cultivator, war with the soldiers.* So Timotheus let the most fertile part of the land to husbandmen, as Polyænus relates, and even, as Aristotle adds, sold the produce to the enemy, to raise money to pay his soldiers; and so Viriatus did in Spain. And the same was done in the Belgico-Germanic war of which we have spoken, with great reason, and great advantage, to the admiration of foreigners.

4 These practices are proposed for imitation by the Canons, the teachers of humanity, to all Christians, as owing and professing a humanity greater than other men. And therefore these Canons direct, not only that cultivators should be out of danger of war, but animals for the plough, and the seed for sowing. And this is for the same reason for which the Civil Laws forbid the instruments of ploughing to be taken in pledge; and among the Phrygians and Cyprians of old, and among the Athenians and Romans, it was reckoned abominable to kill the ox that drew the plough.

V. In the fourth place, it happens that some things are of such a nature that they are of no effect in making or carrying on war; and these, it is reasonable should be spared during the war. To this case belongs the pleading of the Rhodians to Demetrius the City-taker, in favour of the painting of Ialysius, which Gellius gives. They tell him that if he destroy that part of the city, he will be supposed to make war upon Protogenes the great painter. So Polybius says, that it is a mark of a savage mind to make war on things which neither weaken the loser nor strengthen him who destroys them; as temples, porticos, statues, and the like. So Cicero says, that Marcellus *spared the build-*

---

* The War of the United Provinces against Spain. Gronovius says that this was not only done with regard to lawful Articles under Licenses (*Licenten*), but that ships of war were furnished out at Amsterdam for the enemy with the connivance of the magistrates.

*ings of Syracuse, public and private, as if his army had come to defend,
not to destroy them.* And again, that *Our ancestors left to them what is a
gratification to the conquered and a trifle to us.*

VI.   1 And as this is true in all ornamental works, for the reason
which we have mentioned, there is, besides, an especial reason in things
dedicated to sacred uses. For though these, as we have said, are
public in a peculiar way, and therefore may be violated with impunity
by the laws of nations; yet if there be no danger from them, there
is a motive for sparing them, besides those which have been mentioned,
in the reverence for divine things: and especially, among those who
worship the same God by the same law, even though they differ in
some rites and doctrines.

2 Thucydides says that this was the rule of the Greeks. Livy
says, that when Alba was destroyed, the temples were spared. When
Capua was taken, Silius speaks of the religious feeling which led the
Romans to preserve the temples. Livy says that it was objected to
Q. Fulvius the Censor, that he built temples with the ruins of temples,
as if the gods were not everywhere the same; and thus involved the
Romans in religious irreverence. When Marcius Philippus came to
Dius, he ordered the tents to be pitched under the temple, that
nothing in the sacred place might be violated. Strabo relates that
Tectosages, who had plundered the treasures at Delphi, did, in order
to appease the offended deity, consecrate them at his home with
additional offerings.

3 To come to Christians: Agathias relates that the Franks spared
the temples; being of the same religion as the Greeks, whom they
conquered. And even men were commonly spared on account of the
temples, as (not to adduce examples of heathen nations, which are
numerous, inasmuch as writers call this *the common usage of the
Greeks,*) by the Goths, when they took Rome; which Augustine
praises.

VII.   1 What has been said of sacred places, may be applied also
to burial-places, and to the monuments of the dead: for these, though
the Law of Nations allows wrath to do its work on them with impunity, cannot be violated without trampling on humanity. Jurists say
that that is the highest Reason, which is on the side of religion. So
Euripides, speaking both of temples and of tombs. Apollonius
Tyanæus interpreted the war of the giants against the gods to mean,
that they violated the temples. In Statius, Annibal is called *sacrilegus,*
for that he *Deum face miscuit aras,* put the torch to the altar.

2 Scipio, when Carthage was taken, gave donations to the soldiers,
except those who had transgressed against Apollo's temple. Cæsar would
not venture to destroy the trophy erected by Mithridates, as being
consecrated to the gods. Marcellus, withheld by religion, did not touch
what victory only had made profane, as Cicero says; and adds, that
there are enemies who, even in war, respect the rights of religion and
custom. And elsewhere, he calls the violence of Brennus, done to the

fane of Apollo, nefarious. The act of Pyrrhus, in despoiling the treasure of Proserpine, is called, by Livy, foul and contumacious against the Gods. So Diodorus speaks of Himilco; Livy, of Philip. Florus, of the same, calls it wickedness and madness. Polybius, touching on the same history, says the like, as already quoted; and does not admit the excuse of retaliation.

VIII. 1 Although it is not a part of our purpose to speak of the *advantages* of any course of conduct, but rather to restrain the loose license of war to that which is lawful by nature, or among the lawful ways, the better; yet even Virtue, in this age often little esteemed on her own account, ought to pardon me, if I try to make her value apparent by her utility. First, then, this moderation in preserving things which do not affect the course of war, takes away from an enemy that great weapon, despair. So Archidamus says, that the enemy's land is a hostage, to be spared that despair may not give them strength. So Agesilaus advised to let the Acarnians sow their land; saying, that they would be all the more desirous of peace. So Juvenal, *spoliatis arma supersunt*, when men have lost all they find arms. So Livy says the Gauls judged, when they took the city.

2 Add, that such a course, during war, presents the appearance of a great confidence of victory; and that clemency is apt to bend and conciliate men's minds. So Annibal, in his conduct towards the Tarentines, does not waste the land; not from moderation, but to conciliate them. So Augustus acted towards the Pannonians. So Timotheus, in the case already mentioned, obtained the good will of the enemy. So Quintius and the Romans, in the case above given, found that, as the fruit of their conduct, the cities of Thessaly and the others came over to them. The city of the Lingones, *which escaped the apprehended ravage in the war against Civilis, was reduced to obedience, and supplied seventy thousand armed men;* as Frontinus relates.

3 The opposite cause leads to an opposite result. Livy gives an example in Annibal, when he committed ravage in his retreat, and alienated the minds, both of those who suffered, and of those who feared.

4 It is also most true, as some theologians have noted, that it is the duty of rulers and leaders, who wish to be reckoned Christians by God and by men, to abstain from storming of cities, and other like violent proceedings; which cannot take place, without great calamity to many innocent persons, and often do little to promote the ends of the war: so that Christian goodness almost always, justice mostly, must inspire a repugnance to them. The tie of Christians amongst each other is closer than was that of the Greeks formerly; and yet there was a decree of the Amphictyons, that in their wars, no Greek city should be destroyed. And the ancients relate, that Alexander the Great never repented of anything, so much as he did of the destruction of Thebes.

CHAPTER XIII.

Restraints respecting Captures.

I. 1 EVEN the capture of what belongs to the enemy in a just war, is not to be conceived to be free from fault, or relieved from all burthen of restitution. For if you look at what is right, it is not lawful to take or have anything, beyond what rests on the enemy's debt to you; except that beyond this, things necessary to your safety may also be detained, but are to be restored when the peril is over, either in themselves or in their price; as we have explained, B. II. C. ii. For what would be lawful in things belonging to those with whom we are at peace, is still more clearly lawful in the case of an enemy. This is the right of taking, without the right of keeping.

2 As a debt may be due to us, either to rectify an existing inequality, or as a punishment; so a thing belonging to the enemy may be acquired either way, but with a difference. For as we have said above, in virtue of the former kind of debt, the property, not only of the debtor himself, but of his subjects also, is bound by the Instituted Law of Nations, as under a kind of suretyship. And this Law of Nations we hold to be of another kind from that which consists only in impunity, or the compulsion of tribunals. For, as he with whom we deal, does, by our private consent, acquire, not only an external right to our property, but an internal also; so also is such a right acquired from a kind of common consent which contains in itself by a peculiar force the consent of individuals; in which sense, the Law is called *the Common Pact of the State.* And that such an appointment was intended by nations, in this case, is the more probable, inasmuch as this Law of Nations is introduced, not only for the sake of avoiding a greater evil, but in order that each one may obtain his own right.

II. But in the other kind of debt, which is debt as penalty, I do not see that such a right over the property of subjects is established by the Law of Nations. For such an obligation, imposed on the property of another, is an odious rule, and therefore ought not to be carried further than it appears to be actually settled; nor is the utility of the extension on a parity, in this, and in the other kind of debt: for the other is a part of my property, but this is not; and therefore the exaction of it may be omitted without wrong. Nor is there any objection, in what we have said above of the Attic law. For in that case, men were obliged, not properly because the city could be punished, but only in order to compel the city to do what it ought to do, that is, to pass judgment on a guilty person; which official debt is to be referred to the former kind of debt, not to the latter.   For it is one thing to owe the duty of punishing, another, to owe or to be liable to a punishment; although, from the omission of the former, the latter often may follow; but still, so that they are distinct, the former as the cause, and the latter as the effect.   Therefore the property of subjects cannot be acquired on the ground of penalty, but that of those only who have offended; among whom are included also the magistrates, who do not punish offenses.

III.   But the property of subjects may be both taken and kept, not only for the exaction of the primary debt, from whence the war arose, but also of a debt which grows up during the process, as we said at the beginning of this Book.   And in this sense, we are to take what is said by some theologians, that captures in war are not to be reckoned only in the way of compensation for the principal debt. For this is to be understood until, according to a sound judgment, satisfaction is made for the damage which has been inflicted in the war itself.   Thus the Romans in their dispute with Antiochus, thought it a reasonable demand that the king should repay all the expenses of the war, since by his fault the war took place.   So, of the expenses of the war, in Justin, Thucydides; and elsewhere frequently.   And what is justly imposed on the conquered, is justly extorted by war.

IV.   1 But here too, we must recollect what we have elsewhere said, that the rules of charity are wider than those of justice.   He who abounds in wealth, is guilty of want of clemency, if he wring a needy debtor with stringent rules, and exact the uttermost farthing: and still more, if that debtor have run into the debt by his own goodness, as for instance, by being security for a friend, without having turned any of the money to his own profit.   *The danger of a surety is to be pitied,* as Quintilian says.   And yet even so hard a creditor does nothing against strict right.

2 Wherefore humanity requires that we should leave, to those who are not in fault in the war, and who are only bound as sureties, the things which we can do without, better than they can: especially if it appear that they will not recover from their city what they thus lose. So Cyrus, when Babylon was taken, said to his soldiers, *What ye do not take from the enemy, they will owe to your humanity.*

3 This also is to be noted, that so long as we have a hope of receiving our debt from the original debtor, or from those who have made themselves debtors by not yielding our right, to come upon those who are free from fault, although it may not be at variance with strict law, is contrary to humanity.

4 Examples of this humanity are everywhere extant in history, especially that of Rome: as when, on the conquest of a country, the lands were granted, on condition that they should belong to the con-

C C

quered city: or when a portion of the land was left *honoris gratia* to the old possessors. Thus the Veientes were mulcted of part of their land by Romulus. So Alexander of Macedon gave the Uxii their lands, on the payment of tribute. So you often read that cities which surrendered, were not plundered. And we have said above, that not only persons, but the lands themselves of the cultivators, were often spared, with general approval, and according to the pious precept of the Canons, at least under tribute; and that, under a like tribute, merchants have been accustomed to receive protection in war.

CHAPTER XIV.

Restraints respecting Prisoners.

I. 1 IN those places in which the captivity and servitude of men is usual, it must, if we regard internal justice, be limited in the same way as property; so that we may have such acquisitions, only so far as is permitted by the amount of a debt, either primary or subnascent; except there should be some peculiar delict, which equity allows to be punished by the loss of liberty. So far, therefore, and no further, has a belligerent right over captive enemies, and the power of a valid transfer of such right to others.

2 It will moreover be the duty of equity and goodness, to apply, here also, those distinctions which we noted before, with regard to killing enemies. Demosthenes praises Philip, because he did not make slaves of all who had been his enemies, but weighed their deserts.

II. 1 But first, this is to be noted; that the right which arises from citizens being a sort of surety for the State, is by no means to be extended so widely as the right which arises *ex delicto* against those who are penal slaves. And thus, a certain Spartan said, that he was a captive, but not a slave. For if we rightly look at the matter, this general right against captives, is on a like footing with the right of a master over those who have sold themselves into slavery under the compulsion of want; abstracting the heavier part of their calamity, that they have come into that case, not by any special act of their own, but by the fault of the rulers. *It is the bitterest lot, to be a captive by the laws of war,* as Isocrates says.

2 This servitude, then, is the perpetual obligation of working for perpetual aliment. The definition of Chrysippus here exactly applies; *A slave is a perpetual labourer for hire.* And the Hebrew law plainly compares him who, under the compulsion of need, has sold himself, to a labourer for hire; and directs that, in redeeming him, his labour

shall be reckoned in the same way, that the produce which has been gathered from land sold, is to be reckoned to the former owner. Deut. xv. xviii.

3 There is a great difference between that which may be done with impunity towards a slave by the Law of Nations, and that which natural reason suffers to be done. We have before cited Seneca to this effect. So Philemon says, *A slave does not cease to be a man.* Seneca adds that *Slaves are not only men, but fellow-lodgers, humble friends, fellow-servants:* agreeing plainly with what St Paul says, Colos. iv. 1. And elsewhere, Eph. vi. 9, he directs masters to do good to their slaves, forbearing threatening, on the same ground, knowing that their Master also is in heaven, who does not regard such differences. In the Clementine Constitutions we have the same. So Clemens Alexandrinus bids us use our slaves as our other selves, since they are men no less than we; following the saying of the Hebrew wise men.

III. The right of life and death over a slave, then, gives the master a domestic jurisdiction; which, however, is to be exercised with the same regard to conscience, as a public jurisdiction. So Seneca, as before; and again, he compares a slave to a subject, and says that, though by a different title, the same things only are lawful in the one case as in the other; which is especially true with regard to this right of taking away life, and what approaches to it. *Our ancestors, says Seneca, regarded a house as a small republic:* so Pliny. Cato the Censor, if any slave was supposed to have committed a capital offense, did not punish him, till he had been condemned by the judgment of his fellow-servants. See Job xxxi. 13, *If I did despise the cause of my man-servant,* &c.

IV. And even with regard to smaller punishments, as stripes to servants, we must apply equity, and even clemency. The Hebrew law says, Deut. xv. 17, 45, 53, *Thou shalt not oppress him nor rule him harshly,* of their servants; which must now by analogy be extended to all servants. And on this Philo comments. So Seneca says, *Is it not savage and foolish to treat servants worse than brute animals?* &c. Hence by the Hebrew law, *If a man smote out the eye or tooth of a servant, he obtained his liberty.* Exod. xxi. 26.

V. 1 There is, moreover, to be moderation and regard to the servant's health, in the work required of him. And this, among other things, is aimed at in the institution of the Hebrew Sabbath; that there may be a breathing time from labour. So Pliny, to Paulinus, speaks of their common kindness to their slaves; quoting Homer, who speaks of Priam being *always kind as a father;* and saying that he always recollects the Roman word *Paterfamilias.*

2 So Seneca judges of lessons contained in this word *paterfamilias,* and in the name for slaves, *familiares.* So Dio Prusæensis says that a good king will not like the term *master,* not only of freemen, but even of slaves. Ulysses, in Homer, says that the slaves who have been faithful, shall be as if they were brothers of Telemachus his

son. Tertullian says, *fathers rather than masters.* Jerome or Paulinus exhorts Celantia to be a mother rather than a mistress of her family. So Augustine says that masters help their servants to worship God.

3 There is a similar lesson of piety in the word *puer* for *servant,* as Servius notes. So the Heracleotes called their slaves *gift-bearers.* Tacitus praises the Germans whose servants were as tenants. Theano says that slaves should not suffer from over-labour or want.

VI. 1 In return for labour, sustenance and clothing are due to the slave. So Cicero, Aristotle, Cato, Seneca. The food allowed was four bushels of wheat a month. Martianus the jurist speaks of the things which the master is bound to provide the slave, as clothing and the like. The cruelty of the Sicilians, who starved the Athenians, is branded in history.

2 Moreover Seneca proves that, for some purposes, the slave is free; and that he has the means of conferring benefits on his master; as, if he do anything which exceeds the measure of a slave's duty, and which proceeds, not from command, but from good-will, where there is a transition from service to the affection of a friend. With this agrees what Terence says, (in the *Phormio*) that if a slave has saved anything by living sparely, or working over-hours, it should be in a way his own. Theophilus defines the *physical means* of a slave to be a natural patrimony, as we might define *contubernium,* the cohabitation of slaves, to be a natural matrimony: and Ulpian says the *peculium,* the slave's private store, is a little patrimony. Nor does it make any difference, that the master may, at his pleasure, take away or diminish this peculium; for if he do this without cause, he will not do what is just. And by *cause,* I here understand, not only punishment, but also the need of the master; for the advantage of the slave is subordinate to the advantage of the master, even more than the advantage of the citizens to that of the State. So Seneca, *We are not to say that the slave has nothing, because he will have nothing if the master refuse his permission.*

3 And hence it is, that the master cannot recover from the slave a debt which was due to him during his servitude, and which he paid after manumission; because, as Tryphoninus says, the distinction of indebted and not indebted, is understood according to Natural Law, and not according to Civil Law, in such an action for debt; and the master may owe a debt to the slave by Natural Law, though not by Civil Law. And accordingly, we find, that as clients have made contributions for the use of their patrons, and subjects for the use of kings, so slaves have done the same for the use of their masters; for instance, for the dowry of a daughter, the ransom of a son, or any similar object. Pliny, as he tells us in his *Epistles,* allowed his servants to make wills, and to dispose of their property within his family. In some nations, we have read of a larger right of acquiring property being conceded to slaves; as we have elsewhere said, that there are several degrees of slavery.

4 In many nations, the laws have reduced that external right of masters to this internal justice which we are expounding. For among the Greeks, when slaves were harshly treated, they were allowed *to demand their sale :* and at Rome, to fly to the statues for refuge, or to implore the help of magistrates against cruelty or starvation, or intolerable wrong. This is a matter, not of strict law, but of humanity and kindness : and sometimes this makes the slave's liberty his due, after long or very great labours.

5 When Slavery was introduced by the Law of Nations, the benefit of Manumission was added, says Ulpian. So in Terence, the slave is made a freedman, for serving liberally. Salvian says that slaves have often their liberty given, and are allowed to take with them their property. Of this kindness, we have many examples in the martyrologies. And here, we must praise the kindness of the Hebrew law ; which directed that the Hebrew slave was, after a certain time, to be absolutely manumitted, and "not empty," Deut. xv. 13: of the neglect of which law the prophets complain heavily. Plutarch condemns Cato the Elder, because he sold his slaves when past work, thus disregarding the common bond of human nature.

VII. The question here occurs, whether he who is taken prisoner in war may justifiably make his escape. We do not here speak of him who has merited such punishment by crime, but who has been brought into the condition by some public event. The truer opinion is, that the step is not justifiable ; because, as we have said, by the common convention of nations, he owes his labour on the part of the State. Which, however, is to be understood, with the provision that intolerable cruelty do not impose on him such a necessity. See on this subject the Response of Gregory XVI.

VIII. 1 We have elsewhere discussed the question, whether, and how far, children, born of slaves, are bound to the master by internal justice ; and this question ought not to be omitted in its especial bearing on prisoners of war. If the parents had, by crime, deserved the penalty of death, their prospective posterity might be bound to slavery, as a condition of life spared, because otherwise they would not have come into existence : for parents may sell their children into slavery, on account of the want of sustenance which would otherwise fall upon them, as we have said. Such was the right which God granted to the Hebrews over the posterity of the Canaanites.

2 And those who were already born, might be liable for the debt of the State, as being part of the State, no less than their parents. But this cause does not seem sufficient, in those who are not yet born ; some other seems necessary ; either the express consent of the parents, added to the necessity of providing sustenance for them, and that, for ever ; or the actual supply of sustenance, and that holds only till they have worked off the whole expense of their maintenance. If any right beyond this is given to the master, it seems to proceed from a Civil Law, too liberal to masters.

IX. 1 Where this right of servitude arising from war is not established by use, it will be the best course to exchange the prisoners; and next to that, to let them be ransomed at a reasonable rate. What this is, cannot be precisely defined: but humanity teaches us that it should not be stretched so far that it leaves the prisoner without the necessaries of life. For even the Civil Law grants this indulgence to many who have come into debt by their own act. In other cases, this is determined by law or custom; as anciently, among the Greeks, the ransom was set at a mina, and among soldiers, at a month's pay. Plutarch says that the Corinthians and Megareans carried on war humanely. Captives were reckoned as the guests of their captors, and dismissed on their promise.

2 More lofty in spirit is what Cicero quotes of Pyrrhus (*Off.* I. 12); so Cyrus; Philip, after Chæronea; Alexander, towards the Scythians; Ptolemy and Demetrius contending in generosity to prisoners, as in arms. Dromichætes, king of the Getæ, made Lysimachus his prisoner, his guest, and a witness of the poverty and equity of the Getæ, and thus gained him as his friend.

CHAPTER XV.

Restraints respecting Conquest.

I. EQUITY, which is required, and humanity, which is praised, towards individuals, are the more requisite and praiseworthy, towards nations and parts of nations, inasmuch as the injury or kindness is greater with the number. Now as other things may be acquired in a just war, so may imperial authority over a people, and the right which the people itself has in the government: but only so far as is limited, either by the nature of a penalty arising from delict, or by the nature of some other debt. To which is to be added, the reason of averting extreme danger. This last cause is commonly mixed up with others; but is, in reality, to be much regarded for its own sake, both in establishing peace and in using victory. For other things may be remitted out of compassion; but in a public danger, a disregard of the danger which goes beyond the just limit, is want of compassion. Isocrates tells Philip that he must master the barbarians, so as to place his own territory in security.

II. 1 Sallust says of the old Romans: *Our ancestors, the most religious of men, took from the vanquished nothing but the licence of wrong-doing;* words worthy of having been said by a Christian: and with them agrees what is also said by the same writer: *Wise men bear labour in the hope of rest, and make war for the sake of peace.* So Aristotle also says: and so Cicero, in several places.

2 To the same effect is the teaching of Christian theologians, that the end of war is to remove the hinderances to peace. Before the time of Ninus, as we before said, following Trogos, it was rather the habit to defend than to extend the boundaries of empires: every one's rule ended with his own country; kings did not seek empire for themselves, but glory for their peoples, and content with victory,

abstained from empire. And to this point, Augustine brings us back, when he says: *Let them consider that it is not the part of good men to rejoice in the extent of empire;* and again: *It is a greater felicity to have a good neighbour at peace, than to conquer a bad neighbour in war.* The prophet Amos severely rebukes the Ammonites who had committed atrocities *that they might enlarge their border.* Amos i. 13.

III. To this pattern of ancient innocence, the nearest approach was made in the prudent moderation of the old Romans. *What would our empire be at this day,* says Seneca, *except a wholesome prudence had mixed the conquered with the conquerors?* And, *Our founder Romulus,* Claudius says in Tacitus, *carried his wisdom so far, that most of the peoples with whom he had to do were, on the same day, first his enemies, and then his citizens.* He adds, that nothing was more destructive to the Lacedæmonians and Athenians, than that they treated as strangers those they conquered. So Livy says that the Roman power was increased, by taking enemies into the composition of the state. There are, in history, the examples of the Sabines, Albans, Latins, and others in Italy: until at last *Cesar triumphed over the Gauls; and he who did this gave them votes.* Cerialis says, in his oration to the Gauls, in Tacitus, *You yourselves for the most part command our legions; you govern those provinces; nothing is kept from you or barred against you;* and further: *Do you then further and cultivate peace and safety which we conquerors and conquered alike hold by the same right.* At last, by a very remarkable law* of the Emperor Antonine, all the inhabitants of the Roman empire were made Roman citizens, as Ulpian tells us; and so, as Modestinus says, Rome was the common country of all.

IV. 1 Another kind of moderated victory is, to leave to conquered kings or peoples the authority which they had. So Hercules professes, in Seneca, to have done to Priam; so he gave Neleus the kingdom of his father Nestor; so the Persian kings let conquered kings keep their kingdoms: so Alexander did to Porus. Seneca praises this *taking from conquered kings nothing but glory.* And Polybius celebrates the goodness of Antigonus, who, having Sparta in his power, left them the constitution and liberty of their forefathers; and on this account obtained great praise through all Greece.

2 So the Romans allowed the Cappadocians to have what constitution they liked; so Carthage was left free; so Pompey left some conquered nations free. And Quintius, when the Etolians said that peace could not be lasting except Philip were deprived of his kingdom, told them they forgot the Roman habit of sparing the vanquished: and added that great men were mild to conquered enemies. So Zorsines is treated in Tacitus.

V. Sometimes, while authority to govern is granted, provision is

---

* A very bad law, says Gronovius; as if any one were to declare all rustics to be nobles.

made for the security of the conquered.   So Quintius restored Corinth to the Achæans, but with the reservation, that there should be
a garrison in Acrocorinthus: and that Chalcis and Demetrias should
be kept, till the anxiety about Antiochus was past.

VI. The imposition of a tribute often has reference, not so much
to the restitution of the expenses incurred, as to the future security
both of the victor and the vanquished. So Cicero says of the cities of
Asia, that they owe their security to the Roman empire, and ought
to be content to pay taxes for its support, as the price of peace and
ease. So Cerialis, in Tacitus. tells the Gauls, that *the Romans, though
so often provoked, had only taken the means of keeping peace: for there
is no quiet among nations without armies; no armies without pay;
no pay without taxes.* To this pertains what we have elsewhere said
of unequal leagues, where one party gives up fleets, fortresses, &c.

VII. 1 That the vanquished should retain their power of governing, is often, not only a measure of humanity, but of prudence. Numa
directed that the rites of Terminus should not include blood in their
celebration: implying, that to keep our own boundaries, is the way to
live in peace. So Florus says, *It is more difficult to retain provinces
than to make them; they are gained by force, they are kept by right.*
So Livy: *It is easier to gain them one by one than to keep all.* And so, the
saying of Augustus in Plutarch; that *ordering a great government is a
greater work than acquiring it.* So the ambassadors of Darius to
Alexander.

2 This was what Calanus, and before him Œbarus, expressed
by the similitude of a dried hide, which rises in one part, when you
tread down another: and T. Quinctius, in Livy, by the comparison of
a tortoise, which is secure against blows when gathered within its
shell, but exposed and tender when it puts out any member. So
Plato applies Hesiod's *half greater than the whole.* And Appian notes
that many peoples, which wished to be under the Roman empire,
were rejected: while others had kings set over them. At the time
of Scipio Africanus, in his judgment, the possessions of Rome were so
wide, that it was greedy to wish for more; and happy if they lost
nothing. And he altered the lustral lay which was sung on the
taking of each census, and which prayed the gods to make Rome's
fortunes better and greater; so that the prayer was made to be,
that they might be kept ever free from harm.

VIII. The Lacedæmonians, and at first the Athenians, claimed
no authority over the cities which they had conquered: only they
required them to have a constitution like their own; the Lacedæmonians, an aristocracy, the Athenians, a democracy, as we learn from
Thucydides, Isocrates, Demosthenes, and Aristotle. Of these two
characters who constantly disturbed Greece, Aristocracy and Democracy, an old comedian, Heniochus, speaks, as women. So Artabanus,
in Tacitus, established an aristocracy at Seleucia. Whether such

changes add to the victor's security, is not a matter for our consideration.

IX. In the cases in which it is not safe to abstain from all authority over the conquered, still the portion assumed may be limited, so that some authority may be left to them, or their kings. Tacitus speaks of it as the custom of the Romans *to have kings as the instruments of their rule*: and calls Antiochus *the richest of subject kings*. So Musonius [in Stobæus, see J. B.'s note], Strabo, Lucan. So among the Jews, the sceptre remained in the Sanhedrim, even after the confiscation of Archelaus. So Evagoras of Cyprus was willing to obey the Persian king, as one king another. And after Darius was conquered, for some time Alexander offered him the condition that he should govern others and obey Alexander. We have spoken elsewhere of mixed empire. In some cases, a part of the kingdom is left to the vanquished, as a part of the lands to the old possessors.

X. Even when all authority is taken from the vanquished, they may be allowed to retain their own laws with regard to public and private property, their own customs and magistrates. So in Bithynia, which was a proconsular province, Apamea had the privilege of governing itself in its own way: as we learn from Pliny: *the Bithynians have their own magistrates, their own senate*. So the Amiseni in Pontus, by the good office of Lucullus [from Appian, J. B.] The Goths left to the conquered Romans the Roman law.

XI. 1 It is a part of this indulgence, to permit the use of their own religion to the conquered, except so far as they are persuaded to change. And that this is both a great boon to the conquered, and no harm to the conqueror, is proved in the oration of Agrippa to Caius, given by Philo. And both Josephus and Titus object to the rebellious Jews, that they were allowed the practice of their own religion, so far as to be authorized to exclude strangers from the temple, even on pain of death.

2 But if the vanquished profess a false religion, the victor will do well to take care that the true religion be not subjected to oppression: which Constantine did, when he had broken the party of Licinius; and after this, the Frank kings and others.

XII. 1 The last caution is this: that even in the most absolute and despotic government, the conquered are treated with clemency, so that their utility be joined with the utility of the victor. So Cyrus told the conquered Assyrians to be of good cheer, for they had only changed their king, and would keep all their rights and property, and be protected therein. So Sallust, of the Roman treatment of those they vanquished. So Tacitus says, that the Britons in his time paid their tribute readily, if no injury was added to it: they would be subjects, but not slaves.

2 The Privernate ambassador, when asked what peace the Romans might expect from them, answered, *If you give us a good one, you will*

have a faithful and perpetual one; if a bad one, a short one.   And the reason was added, that nobody will stay longer than he can help, in a condition which he thinks bad. So Camillus said, that the firmest government was that which the subjects were glad to obey. The Scythians told Alexander, that between master and slave, there is no friendship: even in peace, the rights of war are kept up. Hermocratus says, *The glorious thing is, not to conquer, but to use victory clemently.*   The maxim of Tacitus is wholesome with reference to the use of victory: *Those endings of wars are to be admired which are brought about by granting pardon.*   In the epistle of the Dictator Cesar, we read, *Be this a new way of conquering; to protect ourselves with mercy and liberality.*

CHAPTER XVI.

*Restraints as to things which, by the Laws of Nations,
have not the right of Postliminium.*

I. 1 HOW far things, which are captured in a just war, become the
property of the captor, we have stated above. Of these
things, those are to be excepted, which are resumed by right of Postliminium; for these are held as not captured. But what is captured
in an unjust war is to be restored, as we have said; and not only by
the captors, but by others, into whose hands it has anyhow come.
For no one can transfer to another more of right than he himself possesses; as the Roman Jurists say: which Seneca briefly explains, *No
one can give what he has not.* The first captor had not internal
ownership, [just ownership;] and therefore, that *he* cannot have, who
had his title from him. Therefore the second or third possessor
took an ownership which, for the sake of distinction, we will call *external;* that is, he took this advantage, that he is everywhere to be
protected as owner, by the sentence and authority of the judge: but
if he use this right against him who lost the property by an unjust
act, he will not do rightly.

2 The answer which was given by illustrious jurists, respecting a
slave who, captured by robbers, had afterwards made his way to the
enemy, [and was then captured from them, and exposed for sale.
Gronov.] namely, that it was true, that he had been stolen, and that
his having been in the hands of the enemy, or having returned by
postliminium, was no obstacle to that view; is the same answer which
we must give respecting him who, being captured in an unjust war,
afterwards by just war, or in any other way, comes into the possession
of another: for in internal justice, an unjust war does not differ from
a robbery. And to this effect responded Gregory of Neocesarea,
being consulted in reference to the case, when certain men of Pontus
had received into their possession property of the citizens captured
by barbarians.

II. 1 Such property, then, is to be restored to them from whom
it was taken: and we see that this has often been done. Livy, after
mentioning that the Volsci and Equi were conquered by L. Lucretius

Tricipitinus, says that the booty was exposed three days in the Campus Martius, that each person might know and take his own.   And when he has related that the Volscians were defeated by Posthumius the dictator; he adds, *The part which belonged to the Latins and Hernici was given them back on their recognizing it: a part was sold by auction;* and elsewhere, *Two days were given for owners to know and recover their property.*   And when he has related the victory of the Samnites [no, the Romans, J. B.] over the Campanians, he adds, the most joyful part of the victory was, that 7500 captives were recovered; and a great booty of the allies: and by a public notice, owners were summoned to take back their own property.   And soon after he relates a similar act of the Romans, at Interamna, when they had conquered the Samnites.   So at Ilipa in Lusitania.   So T. Gracchus at Beneventum gave the owners of cattle thirty days to recognize their stock in the booty.

2 So Polybius says that L. Emilius, when he had conquered the Gauls, restored the spoil to those from whom it had been taken.   So Scipio did, when, having taken Carthage, he found there many presents which had been made by the cities of Sicily and others, and carried thither.   Cicero, in his oration against Verres, speaking of the Sicilian jurisdiction, says that *Scipio when he had taken Carthage, restored to the Sicilian allies what had been taken by the Carthaginians at Himera, thinking it right that, by the Roman victory, they should recover their property.*   And he follows out this subject, this deed of Scipio's, in his oration against Verres on the works of art.   The Rhodians restored to the Athenians four ships of theirs, which had been taken by the Macedonians.   So Phaneas the Etolian thought it just that there should be restored to the Etolians what they had had before the wars.   And T. Quinctius did not deny that this would have been right, if the question had been of cities captured in war, and if the Etolians had not broken the truce.   Even the treasures consecrated to the gods at Ephesus, which the kings had appropriated, the Romans restored to their ancient state.

III.   1 But if such an article of property should have come into any one's possession by traffic, can he charge the person from whom it had been taken with the price which he has paid?   It is agreeable to the principles which we have elsewhere laid down, that it may be charged, at such a rate as the recovery of the possession would be worth, considering that he may have despaired of such recovery.   But if such expenses may be charged, why not also the estimated value of the labour and danger; just as if any one should, by diving, recover a treasure belonging to another, which had been lost in the sea?   Apposite to this question seems to me the history of Abraham, when he had conquered the five kings and returned to Sodom: Moses says (Gen. xiv. 16), *He brought back all the goods,* namely, those which he had before spoken of as being taken by the four kings, Chedorlaomer, &c., and from the five kings of Sodom, &c. (v. 11).

2 And to the same practice we must refer the conditions which the king of Sodom proposes to Abraham, that he should give up the captives, and keep the goods for his labour and danger (v. 21). Abraham indeed, a man not only pious but magnanimous, refused to take anything for himself (v. 23): but from the property restored (for those are the goods spoken of) he gave a tenth to God, he deducted the expenses of the young men, and requested a portion to be given to his allies.

IV. As property is to be restored to its owner, so too are peoples and parts of peoples to be restored to those who had rightful authority over them; or to themselves, if they had been their own masters, before the unjust violence. Thus Sutrium was recovered and restored to the allies, at the time of Camillus. The Eginetans and Melians were restored to their cities by the Lacedæmonians: the Greek cities which had been invaded by the Macedonians were restored to liberty by Flaminius. And the same general, in his conference with the ambassadors of Antiochus, urged that it was just that the cities in Asia which were of the Grecian race, and which Antiochus had recovered, should be made free; for that *Greek colonies were not sent into Æolia and Ionia to be slaves to the king, but to extend the race, and to diffuse over the earth the Greek nation.*

V. A question is sometimes raised, concerning the length of time by which the internal obligation of restoring a thing may be extinguished. This question, between citizens of the same government, is to be determined by their own laws: (provided such laws recognize an internal [that is, an equitable] as well as an external [or strictly legal] right; which is to be collected from the words and design of the laws, by a careful consideration of them:) but between those who are foreigners to each other, it is to be determined by a probable judgment as to dereliction: on which subject we have elsewhere said as much as is necessary for our purpose.

VI. If the right of war be very ambiguous, it will be best to follow the counsel of Aratus of Sicyon; who in part persuaded the new possessors to accept money and give up the possessions; and partly induced the old owners to be paid for what they gave up, as more convenient than to attempt to recover it.

CHAPTER XVII.

Of Neutrals in War.

I. IT may appear superfluous for us to treat of those who are ex-traneous to the war, since it is evident that there are no rights of war against them. But since many liberties are often taken with them, especially when they are neighbours, on the pretext of neces-sity, we may here briefly repeat what we have already said:—that Necessity, in order to give a person a right to another's property, must be of the extremest kind;—that it is further requisite, that there be not a similar necessity on the part of the owner;—that even when the necessity is plain, more is not to be taken than it requires; that is, if keeping the thing is sufficient, it is not to be used; if using it is sufficient, it is not to be destroyed; if destroying it is requisite, the price is to be repaid.

II. 1 When Moses was under an extreme necessity of passing with the people through the land of the Edomites, (Num. xx. 17,) he says, first, that he will go by the king's highway, and will not turn aside into the fields or vineyards; and that even if he have to drink of the water of the wells, he will pay the price of it. The same was done by Greek and Roman generals, who are mentioned with praise. So the Greeks, in Xenophon, who were with Clearchus, promise the Persians that they will pass without doing any mischief: and that if they supply them with food to purchase, they will not take by force meat or drink.

2 So Dercyllides acted, according to Xenophon: Perseus in Phthio-tis, &c.; Agis in Peloponnesus; Sulla in Calabria and Apulia; Pom-peius in Asia; Domitian in the country of the Ubii; Severus in his Parthian expedition; the Goths, Huns, and Alans of Theodosius's army, of which latter the Panegyrist says; *There was no tumult, no confusion, no plunder, as you might expect from barbarians. If the supply of provisions was at any time more difficult, they bore the defici-ency with patience, and made up for the scarcity by spare diet.* Claudian ascribes the same merit to Stilico, and Suidas to Belisarius.

3 This was brought about by an exact care in the supply of neces-saries, punctual pay, and vigorous discipline, of which you find the rule in Ammianus: *The lands of neutrals are not to be trampled:* and in Vopiscus: *Let no one take a fowl which is not his, or touch a sheep;*

or pluck a bunch of grapes; or cut the corn, or demand oil, salt or wood. So the same writer in Cassiodorus: *Let the soldier live with the provincials according to the civil law, and shew no military insolence. The shield is for the protection of the countrymen.* So Xenophon, in the *Anabasis.*

4 And hence we see the meaning of that which was said to soldiers by a prophet, and one that was greater than a prophet (Luke iii. 14): *Do violence to no man, neither accuse any falsely, and be content with your wages.* And so Aurelian said, *Let them live on the spoil of the enemy, not on the tears of the provincials.* And we are not to think that this is fair talking, but what cannot be done in fact: for the inspired man would not exhort to such a course, and wise expositors of law enjoin it, if they thought it could not be done. And in short, we must allow that *that* can be done, which we see is done. And on this account, we have adduced examples; to which we may add that eminent case which Frontinus mentions, of Scaurus; that an apple-tree which was included within the lines of the camp, was found next day, when the camp was broken up, with its fruit untouched.

5 When Livy speaks of the Romans, in the camp at the Sucro, behaving irregularly [in the absence of S. Scipio], and some of them going on plundering expeditions into the neighbouring neutral ground, he adds, that everything was given up to a licentious and greedy soldiery, nothing done according to military rule and discipline. And again, in the same writer, where the passage of Philip through the land of the Denthelatæ is described, it is said that *The army, being in great want, treated the country as if it had been an enemy's, plundering towns and villages; much to the king's mortification, who heard his allies imploring him and the gods for help in vain.* In Tacitus, the fame of Pelignus is tarnished by his preying upon friends rather than foes. The same writer speaks of the Vitellians, as, in all the towns of Italy, idle, and formidable to their friends only. So in Cicero against Verres; *You authorized the insulting and plundering of friendly towns.*

6 And here I cannot omit the opinion of theologians, which I think perfectly true; that a king who does not pay his soldiers their wages, is not only bound to satisfy the soldiers for the damage so done them, but also to make compensation to his subjects and neighbours, whom the soldiers, under the impulse of want, have treated ill.

III. 1 On the other hand, it is the duty of neutrals to do nothing which may strengthen the side which has the worse cause, or which may impede the motions of him who is carrying on a just war, as we have said above; and in a doubtful case, to act alike to both sides, in permitting transit, in supplying provisions, in not helping persons besieged. The Corcyreans say, that it is the duty of the Athenians, if they will be neutral, either to prevent the Corinthians from raising soldiers in Attica, or to allow them to do so. To Philip king of the Macedonians it was objected, that the league was doubly violated by him: inasmuch as he had done injury to the allies of the Romans, and helped their

enemies.   The same is urged by T. Quinctius, in his conference with
Nabis.

2 In Agathias, we read, that he is an enemy, who does what the
enemy wishes: and in Procopius, that he is reckoned to be in the
army of the enemy, who helps the enemy's army in matters which are
properly of military use. So Demosthenes had said before. M. Acilius,
in speaking to the Epirotes, who were accused of sending money to
Antiochus, says that he does not know whether he is to regard them
as enemies or neutrals. L. Emilius, Pretor, condemns the Teians, because they had supplied the enemy's fleet with provisions, and had
promised it wine; adding, that except they did the same to the Roman
fleet, he should hold them as enemies. So Augustus said that *A city
lost the rights of peace when it received an enemy.*

3 It may be of use for a neutral party to make a convention with
each of the belligerents; so that it may be allowed, with the good will
of both, to abstain from war, and to exercise towards both the common duties of humanity. So in Livy. So Archidamus king of Sparta,
when he saw that the Eleans inclined to the Arcadians, wrote to them,
It is well to be quiet.

CHAPTER XVIII.

Of acts done by Private Persons in a Public War.

I. 1 WHAT we have hitherto said, pertains, for the most part, to those who either have the supreme authority in war, or hold public offices. We must now consider what is lawful for private persons, according, respectively, to Natural Law, Divine Law, and the Law of Nations.

Cicero relates that Cato's son served in the army of Pompilius till his legion was dismissed: that he then remained with the army as a volunteer: and that Cato wrote to Pompilius, that if he wanted to keep him in the army, he must make him take the military oath again; because the former oath being cancelled, he could not lawfully fight with the enemy. He adds also the very words of Cato's letter to his son, warning him not to take part in the fighting. So we read that Chrysas, a soldier of Cyrus, was praised, because, when he had raised his sword to cut down an enemy, he lowered it on hearing the signal for a retreat. So Seneca.

2 But they are mistaken, who think that this rule comes from the external Law of Nations: for if you look at that, as any one has a right to seize an enemy's property, as we have shewn above, so has he a right to kill the enemy: for in the eye of that law, enemies are held for nobodies. And therefore Cato's doctrine comes from the military discipline of the Romans: of which the rule was, as Modestinus has noted, that he who did not obey orders, should be capitally punished, even if the act turned out well. And he was understood not to have obeyed orders, who had, out of the regular ranks, without the command of the general, fought with the enemy; as the orders issued by Manlius prove to us: on this account namely; that if such conduct were permitted, either posts would be deserted, or even, as the license went further, the army, or a part of it, would be implicated in casual combats, which was by all means to be avoided. So Sallust, speaking of the Roman discipline, says, *In war those are often punished who, contrary to orders, have fought the enemy, or who, being ordered to*

retreat, have been slow in doing so. The Lacedæmonian who, when about to cut down an enemy, lowered his sword, on hearing the signal for retreat, gave the reason, *It is better to obey a commanding officer than to kill an enemy.* And Plutarch gives, as a reason why he who has left the army cannot lawfully kill an enemy, that he is not bound by that military law by which persons who engage in battle should be bound. And Epictetus, in Arrian, referring to the act of Chrysas just mentioned, says, *So much better did he think it to do his officer's will than his own.*

3 But if we look to Natural Law and internal right or justice, it seems to be conceded, in a just war, to any one, to do any thing, which he considers will benefit the innocent party, within the just limits of warfare: but not to make captured property his own, because there is nothing owing him, except in the case in which he is exacting a just punishment by the common right of war. Which last, in what manner it is restricted by the Gospel Law, may be understood by what has been already said.

4 A mandate of a commanding officer may be either general or special: general, as in a tumult among the Romans, the Consul said, *Who are for the safety of the republic follow me.* And sometimes, even individual subjects have the right given of killing an enemy, even when not in self-defense, when it is expedient on public grounds.

II. 1 A special command may be given, not only to those who receive pay, but also to volunteers, who serve at their own charge, and who, what is more, support part of the charge of the war; as for instance, those who fit out ships, and support them at their own expense; and who are allowed, instead of pay, to appropriate their own captures, as we have elsewhere said. But how far this may be done without violating internal justice and charity, is a question not unworthy of discussion.

2 The justice of the case has respect, either to the enemy, or to the state with which such contract is made. We have already said that from an enemy, any possession which may feed the war, may be taken away for the sake of security; but this, under the *onus* of restoring it: and that the ownership may be taken, so far as compensation for what was either owing at the beginning of the war, or has become owing by some subsequent pact, to a state carrying on a just war; whether such possession belong to the hostile state, or to individuals, even innocent ones: and that the goods of guilty parties may, in the way of penalty, be taken from them and acquired by the captors. And thus, so far as the rights of the enemy are concerned, hostile property will become the property of those who carry on a part of the war at their own expense [Privateers], so far as the limit which has been stated is not exceeded; which must be estimated by an equitable opinion.

III. The internal justice of the case, with regard to the state for which the privateer acts, is satisfied if the contract be an equal one: that is, if the expense and danger be equal in value to the chance of prizes. For if this chance is much more valuable, the surplus ought to be given to the state; as if any one had beforehand purchased a haul of fish at an unusually low price.

IV. But even if justice strictly speaking be not violated, there may be an offense against the loving our neighbour, especially in a Christian view: as if it appear that such privateering will not hurt the general body of the enemy, or their king, or the guilty portion of them, but the innocent; and will inflict upon them calamities which it would be cruel to inflict, even on those who are personally indebted to us. And if, besides this, such a privateering warfare is not likely to conduce, either to the termination of the war, or to any notable damage of the enemy's public power, then it must be considered unworthy a right-minded man, and especially a Christian, to make a gain in this way out of the unhappiness of the times.

V. It sometimes happens, that a private war grows out of a public one; as, for instance, if any one fall in with the enemy, and incur danger of life or goods; in which case the rules are to be observed which we have elsewhere stated, as to the lawfulness of defending one's self. Also public authority is often conjoined with private utility; as if any one, having suffered some great loss from the enemy, should obtain authorization to reimburse himself out of the enemy's property: and the right, in this case, is to be defined by what we have said above of *pignoration*.

VI. But if any one, soldier or other, even in a just war, sets fire to buildings of the enemy, wastes the land, and inflicts damage of that kind, without orders, and we must add, when there is neither any existing necessity nor any just cause, he is bound to make good the damage, as is rightly laid down by theologians. But I have, for good reason, added a condition omitted by them, *If there be not any just cause;* for if there be such a cause, he may perhaps be responsible to his own state whose laws he has violated, but not to the enemy to whom he has done no wrong. On this, hear what a Carthaginian replied to the Romans, when they asked to have Annibal given up to them: *Whether Saguntum was taken by public or by private act, is not the point, but whether it was taken rightfully or wrongfully. The question between us and our citizen is, whether he acted by his own motion or by our direction: the question between you and us is, whether what was done was lawful under our convention with you.*

CHAPTER XIX.

Of Faith between Enemies.

I. 1 WHAT is lawful in war, and to what extent, we have said, is to be considered, partly absolutely, partly with reference to antecedent promise. Having finished the former part of the subject, there remains the latter, namely the question of the faith of enemies to one another. The rule of keeping such faith inviolate, is praised by Silius Italicus, Xenophon, Aristides, Cicero.

2 Public faith, as the elder Quintilian says, makes truces between armed enemies, and preserves the rights of surrendered cities. It is the supreme tie, as he elsewhere says. So Ambrose; Augustine. In fact, those who are enemies do not cease to be men: but all men (who have the use of reason) are capable of having rights given them by promise. So Camillus in Livy.

3 Out of the common use of reason and language, arises the obligation from promise, of which we speak. Nor are we to think that, because to tell a falsehood to an enemy may either be lawful, or at least, allowable, according to the opinion of many (as stated above), that by parity of reason this may also be true of faith given. For the obligation of speaking the truth arises from a cause which was anterior to the war, and may perhaps, in some degree, be taken away by the war; but a promise of itself confers a new right. Aristotle saw this difference when he said, *In speaking of Truth at present we mean Sincerity, which is opposed to Pretence; not Truth or Good Faith, which applies to contracts, for this belongs to another Virtue. Eth. Nic.* IV. 13.

4 Pausanias says of Philip of Macedon, that he could not be called a great general, for he was in the habit of breaking his promises on every occasion. So Valerius Maximus of Annibal. The Trojans in Homer reproach themselves with having broken their oaths.

II. 1 We have above said, that we are not to accept that maxim of Cicero, that *with Tyrants we have no community of intercourse, but the most entire separation;* and also, *a Pirate is not a regular enemy; with him we can neither have faith nor oath in common.* So Seneca speaks of the society of human right being cut off with a tyrant. And from this source, flowed the error of Michael Ephesius, who, in his *Commentary on Aristotle,* says, that with the wife of a tyrant, adultery cannot be committed. And some of the Jewish masters, by a like error, hold this of strangers, whose marriage they reckon as nothing.

2 And yet Pompeius wound up the war of the pirates, in a great degree, by conventions, in which he promised them their lives and a settlement in which they might live without rapine. And tyrants have sometimes restored liberty to their subjects, bargaining for impunity. Cesar writes that the Roman generals treated with the bands of robbers and fugitives who were in the Pyrenean mountains: and who will say that, if a convention had been made, no obligation would have followed from it? It is true, such persons have not that special community of rule, which the law of nations has introduced between enemies, in a regular and complete war: but, inasmuch as they are men, they are under a common tie of Natural Law, as Porphyry explains; whence it follows, that conventions with them are to be observed. So Lucullus kept faith with Apollodorus, the leader of the fugitives. And Augustus paid to Crocotas the robber, when he surrendered himself, the reward which had been promised on his being taken, that faith might be kept.

III. 1 But let us see whether any arguments, more specious than those which Cicero gives, can be adduced against such a rule. The first reason which suggests itself is, that atrocious criminals, who are not part of any state, may be punished by any man, if we merely regard Natural Law, as we have elsewhere explained: and they who may be punished by loss of life, may be deprived of property and other rights; as Cicero rightly says. Now among other rights, is this Right bestowed by a Promise; therefore this right may be taken from him as a penalty. To this I answer, that the argument would hold, if the convention with him had been on the supposition of his not being a criminal. But when the treating with such a one has gone on with him as being such a one, we must suppose that the treaty included the remission of the penalty, so far as this matter is concerned: because, as we have elsewhere said, we must suppose such an interpretation, as provides against the whole act being null and void.

2 In Livy, Nabis well says, when Q. Flaminius objects to him his being a tyrant: *With regard to that name, I can answer, that whatever I am, I am the same with whom you, T. Quintius, have made a league of*

alliance. And again: *I had already done those things, whatever their character be, when you made an alliance with me.* He adds, *If I had changed in anything, I should have had to give account of my inconsistency; as it is, you owe an account of yours.* There is a similar passage in Pericles's speech to his citizens in Thucydides: *We shall suffer the cities in alliance with us to be free, if they were so when the treaty was made.*

IV. Again, it may be objected that, (as we have said already,) he who, by means of fear, caused the promise, is held to free the promiser, because he inflicted damage by injustice; that is, by an act which is at variance with the nature of human liberty, and with the nature of an act which ought to be free. But though we allow that this may sometimes hold, it does not apply to all promises made to robbers. For, that he to whom a promise has been made, should be bound to liberate the promiser, it is necessary that he should have caused the promise by unjust fear. If, then, any one have promised a payment in order to extricate a friend from captivity, he is bound by his promise; for he has not been put in fear, but comes and makes the contract of his own free will.

V. Add to this, that even he who, under the influence of unjust fear, has made a promise, may be bound if the sanction of an oath be added. For then, as we have elsewhere said, man is not bound to man only, but to God also, towards whom fear is not an exception. It is however true, that, by such a bond of itself, the heir of the promiser is not bound; because what passes to the heir is only what belongs to human commerce, from the primeval law of ownership: and the right which belongs to God, as such, is not included among such things. And moreover we must again repeat what we have said above; that if any one violate his faith given to a robber, either with or without an oath, he is not on that account liable to punishment at the hands of other nations; inasmuch as, on account of the hatred borne to robbers, nations have agreed to overlook what is done against them, even by vicious acts.

VI. What shall we say of the wars of subjects against kings and other supreme authorities? That these, even when they have a cause in itself not unjust, still have not the right of acting by force, we have shewn elsewhere. But sometimes, in such cases, the injustice of the cause, or the wickedness of the resistance, may be so great, that it may be liable to heavy punishment. And yet if a treaty be conducted with persons, as with deserters or robbers, such liability cannot be opposed to the promise, as we have just said. Even to slaves, faith must be kept, according to the piety of the ancients; and it was believed that the Lacedæmonians were visited by the divine anger, because, contrary to convention, they had put to death the Tænarians, who were slaves. And it is noted by Diodorus, that faith pledged to a slave in the temple of the Palici was never violated by a master. And the exception of fear imposed, may here also be cancelled by interposing an oath; as M. Pomponius, tribune of the people, under the obligation of an oath, kept the promise which L. Manlius had made under fear.

VII.   But beyond these difficulties a special difficulty arises from the right which the State possesses to make laws, and from its right of eminent dominion over the goods of the subjects; which rights are exercised in its name by the supreme authority. For if that right extend to all the possessions of the subjects, why should it not extend to the right arising from a promise made in war? And if this be granted, it would seem that all conventions must be of no force, and consequently, that there is no way of terminating a war but by victory. But on the other side, it is to be noted, that that eminent right does not extend to everything promiscuously, but so far as it is expedient, as a part, not of a master's authority, but of civil or royal authority. And in general, it is expedient that such conventions should be observed; to which point pertains what we have elsewhere said, of maintaining the present state of things. Add to this, that when the case requires the exercise of this eminent dominion, compensation is to be made, as will be explained more at length below.

VIII.   1 Moreover, compacts may be sanctioned by oath, not only by a king or a senate, but by the state itself; as Lycurgus made the Lacedæmonians swear to observe his laws, and Solon, the Athenians, his; and that the force of the oath might not be broken down by the change of persons, the oath to be repeated every year. For if that be done, there must be no going back from the promise, not even for the sake of public utility. For the state may give up what is clearly its own, and the words may be so plain as to allow no exception. Valerius Maximus says to the Athenians, *Read the Law to which you are bound by oath.* The Romans called such laws *leges sacratæ:* and by such, the Roman people itself, as Cicero for Balbus explains, was in conscience bound.

2 There is a somewhat obscure dissertation on this subject, in the third Book of Livy, in which he says that, according to the opinion of many jurists, the tribunes were *sacrosanct*, but not the ediles, judges, decemvirs; though if harm was done to any of them it was unlawful. The cause of the difference is, that the ediles and others were defended by the law only; and while the law lasted, no one might act against it; but the tribunes were defended by the public religious engagement of the Roman people: for an oath had been administered, which those who had taken it could not set aside with a safe conscience. So Dionysius relates the rule established by L. Junius Brutus. And hence this law was called *sacrata.* And therefore good men condemned the act of Tiberius Gracchus, when he abrogated the tribuneship of Octavius; and said that the tribunitian power has its sacredness from the people, not against the people. And therefore, as we have said, a state or a king may be bound by an oath, even in the case of subjects.

IX.   But also, in such a case, a valid promise may be made to a third person, who has not imposed fear. Nor, so far as this rule is concerned, shall we inquire closely what are the subtilties of the Roman law. For by nature, it is the interest of all men, that regard should be had to other men besides the parties. Thus when Philip made peace with the Romans, he was deprived of the power of punishing the Macedonians, who had revolted from him.

X. But also, since we have proved elsewhere, that mixed states sometimes exist; as we may pass from one pure state to another, so we may pass into a mixed state by compacts; so that they who had been subjects, may begin to have the supreme authority, or at least a part of it; and even with the liberty of defending that part by force.

XI. 1 A regular war, that is, one, on both sides public and declared, as it has other peculiarities which exist in external rights, so has it this; that what is promised in the course of such a war, or for the purpose of ending it, is of such validity, that it cannot be rendered void by the allegation of fear unjustly impressed, contrary to the will · of the promiser. For as many other things, although not free from blame in general, are, in such a war, made lawful by the Law of Nations, so among them, is the fear which is in such a war impressed by each side upon the other. If this were not the acknowledged rule, such wars, which are very frequent, could neither be moderated nor ended; while yet it is the interest of the human race that they should be so. And this is to be understood to represent the rights of war, which, Cicero says, are to be kept with enemies; who too says elsewhere, that an enemy in war has his rights; that is, not only natural rights, but others arising from the agreement of nations.

2 But yet it does not follow from hence, that he who has extorted such promise in an unjust war can retain what he has received, with no violence to piety and the duty of a good man: nor even that he can compel the other to stand by his compacts, made with or without an oath. For internally, and by the nature of the thing, it remains unjust; and this internal injustice of the act cannot be taken away, except by a new and truly free consent.

XII. But when I say that the fear which is impressed in a regular war is held to be just, I must be understood to speak of such fear as the Law of Nations does not condemn. For if anything be extorted by the fear of having the chastity of women violated, or by any other terror contrary to good faith, it is more true that the matter remains subject to Natural Law; for the Law of Nations does not extend its countenance to such fear.

XIII. 1 We have above said, that faith is to be kept even with the perfidious; and Ambrose teaches the same. And this is undoubtedly to be extended also to perfidious enemies; such as were the Carthaginians, to whom the Romans religiously kept their faith. *The Senate looked to itself, not to those to whom the performance was made,* says Valerius Maximus. And Sallust says the like.

2 Appian says of the faith-breaking Lusitanians, whom Sergius Galba deceived by a new convention, and so put to death, that *he avenged perfidy by perfidy, and, in a way contrary to the Roman dignity, imitated the barbarians.* And on that ground, this Galba was afterwards brought under accusation by Libo, the tribune of the people; and then, as Valerius Maximus remarks, *The question was not determined by justice but by mercy; and the acquittal which could not be given to his innocence, was granted out of regard to his children.* Cato, in his *Origines,* had written, on this occurrence, that except he had had recourse to tears and children, he would have been condemned.

XIV. But at the same time it is to be remarked, that there are two ways in which the promiser may be blameless of perfidy, though he does not perform what he had promised; namely, by defect of the condition, and by compensation.

By defect of condition, the promiser is not truly liberated from a promise, but the event shews that there was no obligation, since it was contracted only under the condition. And to this head is to be referred the case in which the other party has not fulfilled what, on his part, he was bound to fulfil. For in a contract of that kind, each article implies the others in the way of condition; as if it had been expressed by saying, I will do so and so if the other does what he has promised. So Tullus, answering the Albans, says that he calls the gods to witness that, *Whichever people shall first reject and dismiss the ambassadors who come and ask for restitution, on it shall fall all the calamities of the war.* Ulpian says, *He is not to be held as an ally who renounced the treaty because some condition on which the alliance was agreed to was not performed.* On this account, if the intention of the treaty be different from this, it is usually clearly expressed, that if anything be done contrary to this or that part, the other parts still remain valid.

XV. Compensation, as to its origin, we have elsewhere explained; when we said that if there be anything which is ours, or which is owing to us, and which we cannot otherwise obtain from him who has it, or owes it, we may take a thing of equal value in any other shape. From whence it follows, that we may, still more, retain what we have in our hands, whether corporeal or incorporeal. Therefore, that which we have promised, we may be excused from giving, if it be not of more value than our property which is unjustly detained by another. Seneca says, *So the creditor is often brought in debtor to his debtor, when he has taken away more in another shape than he seeks as a debt. The judge does not merely look at the single debt; but says, You lent him money; what then? you have plate* of his which you never paid for. Let a balance be struck, and you go away as a debtor, who came as a creditor.*

XVI. The same will be the case, if he with whom the question is, owes me more, or as much, from another contract, and I cannot

* Grotius reads *agellum,* Gronovius, *argentum.*

get it any other way.   In the court of justice indeed, as Seneca also
says, actions at law are kept separate, and the mode of claiming one
and the other are not mixed together.   But such examples, as he
there explains, are limited by certain rules, which it is necessary to
follow.   We must go the way the law points.   But the Law of
Nations does not acknowledge those distinctions, that is, when there is
no other hope of getting our own.

XVII.   The same must be said, if he who urges our promise has
not made a contract with us, but has inflicted a damage upon us.
So Seneca, in the same place, *The landowner is not to have the right
of binding the farmer to him, even if the agreement be uncancelled, if he
trample down his corn, if he cut down the plants; not because he has
received what he agreed for, but because he has himself been the means of
his not receiving it.*   And he adds other examples: *You have driven off
his cattle, you have killed his slave.*   And then: *Let me compare what
benefit any one has produced me, and what harm, and then pronounce
whether more is owing to me or from me.*

XVIII.   Finally, that which is due as penalty may be balanced
against that which has been promised, which is explained at length in
the same place, thus: *Benefit demands recompense; injury, satisfaction;
where both occur, I neither owe him recompense, nor he me satisfaction.
We are quits with one another.   Balancing the benefit and the injury, I
shall see whether anything more is due to me.*

XIX.   1 But, as in the case where any agreement has been made
between the two parties to a lawsuit, they cannot, during the suit, set
against what was promised, either the original ground of action, or
the loss and expense of the suit; so while the war goes on, we cannot
bring into the balance, either the original ground of the war, or anything which has resulted from the exercise of the usual belligerent
rights.   For the nature of the business shews that the convention, in
order that it may not be without any effect, must have been made
setting aside the controversies belonging to the war itself.   For otherwise there could be no convention which might not be eluded.   To
this we may apply a passage of Seneca: [which however is not very
closely to the purpose. W.]

2 What then are the matters, which may be balanced against that
which was promised?   This for instance; if the other, though from
another contract, made during the war, owes us a debt; or if he have
committed damage during a time of truce; or if he have violated the
rights of ambassadors; or done anything else which the Law of Nations condemns as between enemies.

3 But it is to be observed, that compensation must take place
between the same persons who are so bound to each other, and so
that the right of a third party be not injured; but still, so that the
goods of subjects are understood to be bound for what the state owes,
as we have elsewhere said.

4 We must add this also; that it is the part of a generous mind

to stand to agreements, even after an injury has been received; on which grounds Iarchas, the wise Indian, praised a king who, having been injured by a neighbour who was under league to him, did not swerve from the faith which he had sworn, saying that *he had sworn so solemnly that he could not hurt the other even after receiving the injury.*

5 The questions which commonly occur with regard to keeping faith with enemies, may almost all be solved, by applying the rules given above, concerning the force, both of promises in general, and of oaths in particular, the effect of conventions and securities, the rights and obligations of kings, and the interpretation of ambiguities.   But that the use of what has been said may be the more manifest, and that, if there be any remaining controversies, they may be discussed, we shall not hesitate to take the trouble of touching upon the more frequent and more celebrated of special questions.

CHAPTER XX.

Of the public Faith by which Wars are terminated; and herein, of Treaties of Peace; of Lot; of Combat by Agreement; of Arbitration; of Surrender; of Hostages; and of Pledges.

I. CONVENTIONS between enemies depend either on express engagements, or on tacit ones. An express engagement is either public or private. A public engagement is either one made by the supreme powers, or by inferior powers. An engagement made by the superior powers either puts an end to the war, or is of force while the war goes on. In those which end the war, we are to look at the principal matters, and at the accessories. The principal pacts are those which end the war either by their own act, as convention, or by consent having reference thereto, as lot, the event of a combat, the decision of an arbiter: of which the first is merely casual; the other two, temper chance with the powers of the body or the mind, or with the exercise of judgment.

II. To make conventions which terminate the war, is the office of those who make the war; for each person is the manager of his own affairs. Whence it follows, that in a war public on both sides, this is the office of those who have the right to exercise supreme authority. In a monarchical state, it is therefore the office of the monarch, provided he be a monarch who has a right not impeded in such acts.

III. 1 For a king who is not of the age which implies maturity of judgment, (which age is, in some kingdoms, defined by law, in others, is to be estimated by probable conjecture,) or who is of weak intellect, cannot make peace. The same is to be said of a king in captivity, provided he received his sovereignty from the people; for it is not to be supposed that they would bestow the power, to be used by a person who was not free. Hence, in this case, the sovereignty, not indeed as to its whole rights, but as far as exercise and guardianship, will be with the people, or him to whom the people commits it.

2 But as to things which belong to himself, if a king, even in captivity, make any compact, it will be valid, according to the example of private conventions, of which we have spoken. But if the king be an

exile, can he make peace ?   Yes, if he is under no constraint; otherwise, his condition differs little from that of a captive: for the custody of a captive is often lax.   Regulus refused to deliver his opinion in the Senate, saying that so long as he was under an oath to the enemy, he was not a senator.

IV.   In an aristocratical or democratical state, the right of making treaties will be with the majority, respectively, of the Council, and of the Assembly of citizens who have a vote, as we have elsewhere said.   Therefore conventions so made, bind them also who dissented. So Livy; Dionysius; Appian; Pliny.   And those who are bound by the peace, also may share its advantages.

V. 1 Let us now consider what things may be the subjects of convention. The royal authority, or any part of it, cannot be alienated by convention by kings, such as most kings now are, having their authority not as a patrimony, but as a life estate.   Indeed before they received the royal authority, at which time the people was superior to them, there might have been a law made to render such acts invalid in all future time, so that they should not produce any obligation at all, even for compensation for non-fulfilment.   And it is to be believed that the people intended this ; since, if the action was valid to the contractor for compensation, the goods of the subjects might be taken for the debt of the king; and thus, the provision against alienating the royal authority might be defeated.

2 Therefore, that the whole royal authority may pass in a valid manner, it is necessary to have the consent of the whole people ; which may be effected by the representatives of different classes, whom they call the Orders or the Estates of the realm.   That any part of the empire may be alienated, there is need for a double consent ; both of the general body, and of that special part which is under question ; since it cannot, without its own good-will, be separated from the body of which it was a part.   But the part itself may transfer to itself the sovereign authority, without the consent of the people, in an extreme and otherwise inevitable necessity ; because it is to be supposed that that power was excepted from the compact in such a case, when civil society was formed.

3 But in patrimonial kingdoms, there is nothing which prevents the king alienating his kingdom.   Still, it may be, that such a king has not power to alienate any part of the empire ; namely, if he had received the kingdom as his property, with the *onus* of not dividing it.   As to the valuables which are called the Property of the Crown, they may come into the king's patrimony in two ways ; either separably, or inseparably with the kingdom itself.   If in the latter mode, they may be transferred, but only with the kingdom ; if in the former, they may be transferred separately.

4 As to kings whose kingdom is not patrimonial, they can hardly have the right of alienating the property of the crown ; except it appear plainly to be so, from a primeval law or uncontradicted custom

VI. How far the king's successors, and the people, are bound by his promise, we have also stated elsewhere; namely, so far as the power of so obliging was included in the royal authority; which is neither to be infinitely extended, nor too much narrowed; but regulated by fair reasons. It is plainly another matter, if the king be the absolute master of his subjects, and have received a domestic rather than civil authority; as in the case of those who reduce a conquered people to slavery; or if, without having such dominion over their persons, they have it over their goods; as Pharaoh king of Egypt, by purchase; and others, who have received new comers into their private property. For here, another kind of right, added to the regal rights, produces a result which the regal rights of themselves could not produce.

VII. 1 This is also a common question; what may be done for the sake of peace, with the goods of individuals, by kings who have no other right over the property of subjects than the regal right. We have elsewhere said, that the property of subjects is under the eminent dominion of the state; so that the state, or he who acts for it, may use, and even alienate and destroy such property; not only in case of extreme necessity, in which even private persons have a right over the property of others; but for ends of public utility, to which ends those who founded civil society must be supposed to have intended that private ends should give way.

2 But it is to be added, that when this is done, the state is bound to make good the loss to those who lose their property; and to this public purpose, among others, he who has suffered the loss must, if need be, contribute. Nor is the state relieved from this *onus*, if, for the present, it be unable to discharge it; but at any future time, when the means are there, the obligation which had been suspended revives.

VIII. Nor do I admit, without distinction, what Vasquius says; that the state is not bound to acknowledge the damage which is inflicted by war, because the right of war permits such damage. For that right of war has regard to other peoples, as we have elsewhere explained; and, partly at least, affects enemies in their mutual relations, not citizens in theirs; for since these are socially bound together, it is just that they bear in common the losses which happen for the sake of society. It may however be established by the Civil Law, that a thing lost in war shall not give a citizen a right of recovery against the State; in order that each person may the more strenuously defend his own property.

IX. There are some writers who make a broad distinction between things which belong to the citizens by the Law of Nations, and things which belong to them by the Civil Law: so that with regard to the former, they allow a looser right to the king, so that he may take them without cause and without compensation; but not so with regard to the latter. Wrongly. For ownership, from whatever cause it

E E

arises, has always its effects by Natural Law; in so far that it cannot be taken away, except either from causes which belong to the very nature of ownership, or arise out of the act of the owners.

X.   But this consideration, that the property of private parties is not to be given up, except on the ground of public utility, regards the king and his subjects; the other consideration, respecting compensation for loss, regards the state and individuals. For as regards strangers who contract with the king, the act of the king is sufficient; not only on account of the presumption of due authority which the dignity of the person implies; but also from the Law of Nations, which allows the goods of subjects to be bound by the act of the king.

XI.   1 With regard to the interpretation of conventions of peace, we must observe what has been delivered above that; in proportion as any condition is more favourable, it is to be taken more loosely: in proportion as it is the contrary, more restrictedly. If we regard mere Natural Law, the most favourable condition seems to be, that each shall obtain his own: and therefore the interpretation of doubtful expressions is to be drawn to that sense; that he who has taken up arms justly, shall obtain that for which he went to war, and recover his losses and expenses; but not that he shall obtain anything under the plea of penalty; for that is more odious.

2 But since parties will hardly come to peace by one side confessing to being in the wrong, therefore that interpretation is to be taken which puts the parties, as much as possible, on an equality with respect to the justice of the war. And this is done mainly in two ways; either that the possession which has been disturbed by war should be restored, as expressed by the formula *in statu quo ante bellum;* or that matters remain as they are, which is expressed by *uti possidetis.*

XII.   1 Of these two rules, the latter is, in a doubtful case, to be preferred, as being the easier, and inducing no change. Hence the rule of Tryphoninus; that in peace, those prisoners only shall have *postliminium* for whom such a compact was made; which, as we have shewn above, is the true reading. And thus, deserters are not to be given up, except this be agreed upon; for we receive deserters by the laws of war: that is, by the laws of war it is lawful for us to admit and enrol in our numbers him who changes his side.   Other things, on such agreement, remain with the person who is in possession.

2 But this *possession* is taken not according to Civil but to Natural Law; for in war, the fact of possession suffices, and nothing else is attended to. And we speak of lands, as in possession, if they are protected by fortifications; for a temporary occupation, or an encampment, is not here regarded. Demosthenes says that Philip made haste to occupy what places he could, knowing that when peace was made, he would keep what he held. Incorporeal possessions are not held, except by means of the thing to which they adhere; as the servitudes of lands; or by the persons to whom they belong, provided they are

not such as are to be exercised in the soil which had been the enemy's; [for then they go with the soil].

XIII.   In the other kind of pacification, the *status quo ante bellum*, it is to be noted that the last possession which preceded the war is meant; but in such a way, that private encroachments are to be set aside by an order of court, or sentence of a judge, when it can be had.

XIV.   But if any people, which is its own master, has, of its own free will, subjected itself to one of the belligerent parties, the restitution is not to be extended to it, since the restitution applies to those things which are done by force or fear, or by some stratagem lawful towards an enemy.   So when the Greeks made peace, the Thebans retained Platæa; saying, that *they had not taken it by force, nor by treachery, but by the free will of those whose it was.*   And on the like grounds, Nisæa remained in the possession of the Athenians.   T. Quinctius used the like distinction towards the Etolians, saying, that *this was the law of captured cities: the Thessalian cities have by their own will come under our authority.*

XV.   If no other convention is made, in every war it is to be supposed to be settled, that the losses which have been caused by the war are not liable to be recovered.   And this is to be understood also of losses to private persons; for these are the effects of war.   For in a doubtful matter, the contracting belligerent parties are to be supposed to have intended that neither should be condemned as unjust.

XVI.   But debts which were due to private persons at the time of the war breaking out, are not to be supposed cancelled; for these are not acquired by the right of war, but only prevented by war from being exacted.   And therefore, when the impediment is removed, they retain their force.   But though the right which existed before the war, is not lightly to be supposed to be taken from any one, (for on this account mainly were states established, that each person might have his own, as Cicero rightly says), yet this is to be understood of rights which result from an inequality which requires to be balanced.

XVII.   Not therefore of a public right to a penalty.   For that right, as far as it concerns the relations of kings and peoples, must be conceived to be remitted, on this account; that a peace will be no peace, if the old causes of war are left standing.   And here, demands which were not known of, will be included in the general words: as with respect to the Roman merchants who had been drowned by the Carthaginians, without the Romans knowing it.   *The best pacifications are those which obliterate anger and the memory of offenses,* as Dionysius says.   So Isocrates.

XVIII.   The rights of private persons to a penalty, do not offer the same reason for being supposed to be remitted; because they might be exacted without the arbitrament of war.   But still, since this right is not ours in the same way as one which arises from an inequality, and punishment has always in it something odious, a slight implication of words will suffice to make it understood that such penalties also are to be remitted.

XIX. What we have said, that the right which existed before the war is not lightly to be supposed to be taken away, is to be firmly held with regard to the rights of private persons. In the rights of kings and peoples, we may more easily suppose some condonation to take place, if there be any words, or fair conjecture, to countenance the suppositions: and this especially, if the right in question be not clear, but controverted. For it is gracious to suppose that to have been done, which plucks up the seeds of war. So Dionysius Halicarnassus, whose concluding words are nearly taken from Isocrates in his oration on the Peace.

XX. What is taken after the treaty is made, is to be restored; for the right of war was previously extinguished.

XXI. In agreements concerning the restitution of captures made in war, in the first place, those articles are to be interpreted more widely, which are mutual, than those which are one-sided; in the next place, those which treat concerning men are to be taken more favourably than those concerning things; and amongst those concerning things, those concerning lands, more favourably than those concerning moveables; and those concerning things in public possession, more favourably than those which are in private; and among those which are in private possession, those which direct the restitution of things possessed by a lucrative title, more favourably than by an onerous title; and those which have been acquired by purchase, more favourably than those by donation.

XXII. If a possession is conceded to any one in a pacification, there are conceded to him the fruits of the possession from the time of concession, but not backwards; a rule which Augustus rightly defends against Pompeius; who, when Peloponnesus was granted to him, claimed, at the same time, the tribute which was due for the years which had elapsed.

XXIII. The names of countries (provinces and the like) are to be taken according to the use of the present time; and the use of the learned, rather than of the vulgar; for these matters are commonly treated by learned men.

XXIV. These rules also are often applicable:—that as often as reference is made to an antecedent or ancient convention, so often the qualities or conditions expressed in the former convention are to be understood as being repeated;—and that a party is to be understood as having done what he wished to do, if his not doing it was occasioned by the other party with whom the controversy is.

XXV. What some say, that for a short time an excuse for delay is to be admitted, is not true, except an unforeseen necessity prevents the fulfilment. That some canons favour such excuses is not surprizing, since it is their office to move Christians to such courses as are suitable to mutual charity. But in this question concerning the interpretation of conventions, we do not now require what is best, nor even what religion and piety demand of each party; but what he can be compelled to: and the whole of this question belongs to what we call external right.

XXVI. In a doubtful sense, the interpretation is rather to be made against the party which drew up the conditions, which is commonly the more powerful party; (as Annibal says, *He who gives, not he who asks, must prescribe conditions of peace:*) as in a sale, the interpretation is against the seller; for he has himself to blame for not speaking more plainly: and the other party, if there are several senses to an expression, may fairly receive it in the way most useful to himself. Aristotle says, *Where there is a friendship for the sake of utility, the utility of him who receives the advantage is the measure of what is due.*

XXVII. Also the dispute constantly occurs, When a peace is to be supposed to be broken: for which occasion the Greeks have a special name; for it is not the same thing to give a new occasion to war, and to break the peace. There is a great difference between the two, both as to the penalty incurred by the transgressor, and as to relieving from his engagements the other party. Peace is broken in three ways: either by acting against rules which are involved in every peace; or against that which was distinctly said in this peace; or against that which ought to be understood from the nature of each peace.

XXVIII. A person acts against rules involved in every peace, if he use warlike force; that is, no new cause having arisen. If such a cause can be alleged with probability, it is better to presume that the injustice was committed without perfidy, than with it. (Thucydides says, *They break the peace not who resist force, but who use force*).

This being laid down, we must see by whom, and to whom, force employed breaks the peace.

XXIX. If those who have been allies in the war do anything of the sort, the peace is held by some writers to be broken. Nor do I deny that it may be agreed that it shall be so: not, properly, that one person shall be liable to penalty for another person's act; but under a condition of the peace, partly potestative and partly casual. But a peace ought not to be assumed to be made in this way, except it manifestly appear; for such an interpretation is irregular and contrary to the common intention of those who make the peace. Therefore if any have used force, the others not helping them, against them there is a right of war, but not against the others. This is contrary to what the Thebans said against the allies of the Lacedæmonians on a certain occasion. (Paus. ix. 1.)

XXX. If subjects do anything by armed force without public command, it will have to be seen whether the private act can be said to be publicly approved. And to this, three things are requisite, knowledge, power of punishing, and neglect; as may appear from what we have already said. Knowledge is proved by the facts being manifest, or being denounced. Power is presumed, except some reason for its defect appears. Neglect is proved by the lapse of such a time as, in each state, is commonly taken for punishing offenses. And such neglect is equivalent to a positive decree; as Agrippa says in Josephus, that the Parthian king will think that peace is broken, if his subjects proceed in arms against the Romans [without being restrained by him.]

XXXI. It is often made a question, whether this holds, if the subjects of any sovereign do not take arms on their own account, but act in military service under others who are making war. Undoubtedly the Cerites in Livy excuse themselves, by saying that their citizens had joined the army by no public act: and the same defense was alleged by the Rhodians. And the better opinion is, that such service is not permitted, except it appear by probable arguments that some other line was agreed on; as we sometimes see in our days; [that persons of another country serve in armies which are carrying on war;] following the example of the old Etolians, who took service and gathered booty on both sides in any war, as Polybius and Livy say. In former times, the Etruscans, though they would not send aid to the Veientes, did not prevent any of their young men going as volunteers to the war.

XXXII. 1 Again, the peace must be supposed to be broken, if armed force be used, not only against the general body of the state, but against its subjects; that is, without new cause. For peace is concluded, that all the subjects may be in safety: peace is the act of the state for the whole and for the parts. And even if a new cause do arise, it will be lawful, notwithstanding the peace, for the persons attacked to defend themselves and their property. For it is natural, as Cassius says, to repel arms by arms: and therefore we are not readily to believe that this right is abdicated between equals. But in such case, to exercise vindictive acts, or to recover by force what has been taken away, will not be lawful, except after judgment has been denied. For satisfaction and recovery admit of delay, but self-defense does not.

2 But if there be any portion of the subjects, whose malpractices are so perpetual, and so contrary to the laws of nations, that what they do, they must by all means be supposed to do contrary to the approval of their rulers; and if they cannot be called before a proper tribunal, as for instance, Pirates; from them it is lawful to exact satisfaction, and to recover property, as from persons surrendered to us. But to attack other innocent persons on that ground, is a breaking of the peace.

XXXIII. 1 Also armed force, exerted against allies, breaks the peace: but against those allies only who are comprehended in the peace, as we shewed in examining the Saguntine controversy. So the Corinthians urge, *We all have sworn to you all.* But if the allies themselves have not made the treaty, but others for them, the same rule must be laid down, as soon as it appears that those allies hold the peace to be good. For so long as this is uncertain, they are to be considered as enemies.

2 With regard to other allies, and other parties, in any way related to the principals, but who are neither subjects, nor nominated in the peace, the case is different; nor can force used towards them be regarded as an infraction of the peace. But still, it does not follow, as we have also said before, that war may not be undertaken on that ground; but that will be a war from a new cause.

XXXIV. The peace is broken, as we have said, by doing against that which is set down in the peace: but under *doing* we include, *not* doing what we ought, and when we ought.

XXXV. Nor can I admit the distinction of articles of peace, of greater, and of less importance. For everything which is put in the treaty is of importance enough to be kept. But yet goodness, and especially Christian goodness, will the more readily pardon the lighter faults, especially if there be penitence for them. But in order the better to provide for the permanence of the peace, it may be added to the less important articles, that if anything is done against them, the peace is not broken: so that arbitration is to be had recourse to, rather than arms; which was the case in the Peloponnesian league, as Thucydides relates.

XXXVI. And I conceive that this must be understood to be settled, if any special penalty be added: not that I am ignorant, that a contract may be made, on this condition, that it shall be at the election of him who receives injury, whether he will have the penalty, or will recede from the transaction; but that the nature of the business rather requires what I have stated. It is apparent, however, and has already been said by us, that he does not break the peace, who does not stand by covenants made simply [that is, without a penalty,] when the other party has set him the example. For he was only bound conditionally.

XXXVII. But if any necessity be the cause why one party has not fulfilled what was promised; for instance, if the thing demanded have perished, or been taken away, or the act have become impossible by any event; the peace indeed shall not be broken; for, as we have said, it does not commonly depend on a casual condition. But the other party must have the option, whether he will rather wait, if there be any hope that the promise can be fulfilled at a later period; or receive the estimated value of his loss; or be liberated by mutual concessions corresponding to that article, or of the like value.

XXXVIII. Undoubtedly even after faith has been violated, it is open to the blameless party to observe the peace; as Scipio did, after many perfidious acts of the Carthaginians; because no one, by acting against his obligation, exempts himself from his obligation: and if it be added in the treaty, that in such a case the peace is to be understood to be broken, this is to be supposed added only for the benefit of the innocent party, if he choose to use the liberty given.

XXXIX. Lastly, we have said that the peace is broken, by doing that which the special nature of the peace repudiates.

XL. 1 Thus, acts which are against friendship, break a peace which was contracted under the law of friendship : for what, between others, the office of friendship only would require, is here also to be performed by the covenanted right. And to this case, but not to every peace whatever, (for there are leagues not for the sake of friendship, as Pomponius teaches us,) I refer many discussions which occur in lawyers, about injuries not by arms, and insults, and the like ; and especially that of Cicero : *After the return into goodwill, if any wrong is committed, that must be considered, not as a neglect but as a violation, and assigned not to oversight but to perfidy.* But here also we must divest the fact of an odious character as much as possible.

2 And hence an injury done to a person connected with or subject to another, shall not be supposed to be done to him with whom the peace was made, except it be openly done to insult him. And this rule of natural equity is followed by the Roman laws, in weighty injuries done to another person's servants : so that adultery or violation shall be imputed rather to lust than to enmity : and the seizure of another person's goods rather constitutes an act of new cupidity, than of broken faith.

3 Atrocious threats, without any new cause preceding, are at variance with friendship : and to this head I refer fortresses built on the border of a territory, for the sake, not of defense but of offense ; and unusual raising of troops, if it appear, by sufficient indications, that these are intended against the person with whom peace was made.

XLI. 1 It is not against friendship to receive individual subjects, who wish to migrate from the authority of one party to that of the other. For such liberty is not only natural, but advantageous also, as we have elsewhere said (B. II. Ch. v. § 24. No. 3). Under the same head, I place refuge granted to exiles. For, as we have before said, the state has no right over exiles. So Perseus in Livy ; and Aristides says, *It is the common right of men to receive exiles.*

2 Towns, or large bodies of men, which make an integral part of a state, it is not lawful to receive, as we have elsewhere said : nor those who, under an oath or otherwise, owe ministerial offices or obedience. With regard to those who are slaves by the fortune of war, the same rule has been introduced by the Law of Nations, among some peoples, as we have said. Concerning the extradition of those who, not being exiled, fly from just punishment, we have spoken elsewhere.

XLII. The practice of submitting the event of the war to the result of Lot, cannot always be lawfully adopted ; but then only, when the matter in question is one over which we have plenary dominion. For the state is bound to defend the life, chastity, and like possessions of its subjects, and the sovereign, to defend the good of the state, by ties too close, to allow him to pass by those reasons which are most natural, for the defense of himself and others. But if, in a reasonable estimation, he who is attacked in an unjust war is so far inferior that there be no hope of resisting, it seems that the chance of Lot may be offered, that he may avoid a certain danger by an uncertain one: for this is the less of the evils.

XLIII. 1 Then follows a much agitated question, concerning Combats agreed upon to take place between a definite number, for the sake of ending the war ; for example, between one on each side, as Eneas and Turnus, Menelaus and Paris ; between two on each side, as between the Etolians and the Eleans ; [a mistake, J. B.] between three on each side, as the Horatii for Rome, and the Curiatii for Alba ; between three hundred on each side, as between the Lacedæmonians and Argives.

2 If we only look at the external Law of Nations, it is not to be doubted that by it, of itself, such combats are lawful ; for that law permits the killing of all the enemy without distinction. And if the opinion of the old Greeks, Romans, and other nations were true, that each person is supreme master of his own life, then also internal justice would not be wanting in such combats. But we have already said, more than once, that this opinion is at variance with right reason and the precepts of God. That he sins against the love of his neighbour, who kills a man in order to keep things which he can afford to go without, we have elsewhere shewn, both by reason and by the authority of the sacred writings.

3 We have now to add, that he sins against himself and against God, who holds cheap the life that was given him by God as a great boon. If a matter worthy of a war be at stake, as the safety of many innocent persons, for it we must contend with all our powers. To have recourse to a set combat, as a testimony of a good cause, or an instrument of divine justice, is a vain fancy, and foreign to true piety.

4 There is one circumstance, which may render such a combat just and pious on one side only; if otherwise it is to be confidently expected that he who maintains an unjust cause, will be victorious with a great slaughter of innocent persons. For there is then no blame imputable to him who, in such a case, prefers the combat which gives him the best hope which is to be had. But this also is true, that some things which may be done without blame, cannot without blame be approved by others; though they may be permitted that graver evils, which cannot otherwise be avoided, may be avoided : as in many cases, usury and prostitution are tolerated.

5 Therefore what we have said above, when we spoke of preventing war; that if two persons between whom lies the dispute concerning a kingdom, are ready to fight it out in a combat, the people may allow it to be so decided, that the greater calamity which otherwise impends may be avoided; may be said here also, when the question is

about terminating the war. In this way, Cyrus challenged the Assyrian king: and in Dionysius, Metius says that it would not have been unjust, that the leaders of the two peoples should themselves decide the matter by a combat, if the controversy were concerning their own power or dignity, and not that of the peoples. So we read that Heraclius the emperor fought Cosroes, the son of the king of the Persians, in a single combat.

XLIV. But they who thus set the issue of the dispute on the result of a combat, may indeed forfeit their own right, if they have any, but they cannot so give to another what they themselves have not, in those kingdoms which are not patrimonial. Therefore that such a covenant may be valid, it is necessary that there should be obtained also the consent, both of the people, and of those who are in existence, who have a right to the succession: and, in fiefs which are not free, the consent also of the lord or seignior of the fief.

XLV. 1 In such combats, it is often a question which party is to be esteemed the conqueror. A party can be reckoned vanquished, only when either all its combatants have fallen, or have been put to flight. In Livy it is a mark of being conquered, when the party are driven into their own boundaries or towns.

2 In the three great historians, Herodotus, Thucydides, and Polybius, there are three controversies concerning victory; of which the first refers to a set combat. But if any one examines well, he will find that in all the three, the parties separated without a real victory. The Argives, in Herodotus, were not put to flight by Othryades, but went away on night coming on, thinking themselves victorious, and carried that news to their friends. Nor did the Corcyreans in Thucydides put to flight the Corinthians; but the Corinthians, when they had carried on the combat successfully, seeing the fleet of the Athenians approach in force, retreated without trying their strength with it. In Polybius, Philip of Macedon took indeed the ship of Attalus when it had been deserted by its crew, but was very far from having put to flight his fleet; and therefore, as Polybius says, he rather bore himself as victor, than thought himself victorious.

3 Those proceedings, of collecting the spoils, granting the bodies of the dead for sepulture, provoking the adversary to renew the battle, which, in the places just quoted, and in Livy, you sometimes find put forwards as signs of victory, of themselves prove nothing; except so far as they go along with other indications to prove the flight of the enemy. Certainly he who has left the field may, in a case of doubt, be supposed to have run away. But when there is no clear proof of victory, the matter remains in the condition in which it was before the battle; and recourse must be had either to war, or to new agreements.

XLVI. 1 Of Arbitrations there are two kinds, as Proculus teaches us: one, in which, whether the decision is just or unjust, we must submit to it; which is the rule, he says, when we come to arbitration by a compromise; another, in which the matter is reduced to the decision of a fair man. Of this we have an example in the response of Celsus. *If a freedman*, he says, *has sworn to give as many days' work as his master shall judge right, the master's decision is not valid except he judge fairly.* But this mode of interpreting an oath, though it may be introduced by the Roman laws, is not in agreement with the simple meaning of the words. Still it is true that an arbitrator may be taken in two different ways, either as a mediator only, as we read that the Athenians were between the Rhodians and Demetrius; or as one whose decision is to be absolutely obeyed. And this latter is the kind of which we here speak, and of which we have already said somewhat, when we spoke of the means of obviating war.

2 For although, with regard to arbiters who are referred to by compromise, the Civil Law may direct, and does in some places direct, that it shall be lawful to appeal from them, and to complain of their wrong; this cannot have place between kings and peoples. For in their case, there is no superior power, which can either bar or break the tie of the promise. And therefore they must stand by the decision, whether it be just or unjust; so that, as Pliny says, *When you choose a person your umpire, you make him your supreme judge.* For the discussion of the office of an arbiter is one thing, and that of the duty of persons who make a compromise is another.

XLVII. 1 In considering the office of an arbiter, we must consider whether he be elected into the place of a judge, or with some laxer power, which Seneca speaks of as the proper power of an arbiter: *The judge is limited by rules of law: the umpire is left quite free, and can soften law and justice by kindness and mercy.* So Aristotle says, *That a fair man will rather go to an arbiter than to a judge, because the arbiter looks to equity, the judge to law.*

2 In this place, *equity* does not mean, as elsewhere, that part of justice which interprets the law by its general tendency and real purpose, (for this part also is committed to the judge;) but it means everything which is better done than not done, even extraneous to the rules of justice, properly so called. Such arbiters are frequent, in cases between private persons and citizens of the same empire; and are especially commended to Christians by St Paul, 1 Cor. vi. ; but in a doubtful case, we are not to suppose that so much power is assigned to them. For in doubtful cases, we assume as little as may be. And this especially holds, between parties who have supreme authority; for these, since they have no common judge, are to be supposed to have bound the arbiter by the rules by which the office of a judge is commonly bound.

XLVIII. This however is to be remarked, that arbiters chosen by peoples or sovereigns ought to decide concerning the principal point, [right of ownership, for instance,] not about possession: for judgments concerning possession belong to the Civil Law. By the Law of Nations, the right of possession follows the right of ownership.

Therefore while the case is undergoing investigation, no innovation is to be made [in the possession], both to avoid prejudice, and because recovery of things so taken is difficult. So Livy says, between the Carthaginians and Masinissa, *the commissioners did not change the right of possession.*

XLIX. 1 The reference to an arbiter is of another kind, when a person gives himself up to the enemy as his arbiter. This is a pure surrender, making him who so gives himself up a subject, and giving supreme power to him to whom the surrender is made. So the Etolians were asked, in the senate, whether they gave themselves to the Roman people as arbiters concerning them. And P. Cornelius Lentulus, about the end of the second Carthaginian war, demanded that the Carthaginians should give themselves up entirely to the Romans, not as by treaty, but as by pure surrender.

2 But here also we must make a distinction, as to what the vanquished party ought to suffer; what the victorious party may do by right; what other duties require of him; and finally, what becomes him. The vanquished, after surrender, is liable to suffer everything: he is already a subject; and if we look at the extreme right of war, is in such a condition that everything may be taken from him; even his life; even his personal liberty; much more, goods not only public, but even private property. So in Livy, *the Etolians, having surrendered at discretion, (permisso libero arbitrio,) were afraid that even their persons would not be spared.* We have elsewhere cited expressions, to the effect that the conqueror may take all: to the same effect is the passage of Livy, where he says that, of old, the Romans were not satisfied with anything short of a complete surrender on the part of their enemies. And we have shewn that those who have surrendered may sometimes lawfully be put to death.

L. 1 But the victor, in order not to do anything unjustly, ought first to consider that he is not to put any one to death except such a fate be deserved by his own act. And within this limit, as far as our own safety permits, it is always praiseworthy to incline to clemency and liberality; and sometimes, from circumstances and rules of manners, even necessary to do so.

2 We have elsewhere said, that a war is well ended, when it is finished by a pardon. So Nicolaus of Syracuse says, *They have surrendered, relying upon our clemency, wherefore it would be a shame that they should be mistaken.* And afterwards, *Who ever of the Greeks put to death those who gave themselves up to the clemency of the victor?* And Cesar says to L. Antonius, *If you had come to treat, you would have found me a victor who has received wrongs; but since you give yourself up entirely, you take away my anger and my power. I must consider, not only what you have deserved, but what is fit for me to do, and must prefer the latter.*

3 We find, in the Roman historians, mention of surrendering to the faith, or the faith and clemency, of the adversary. See Livy,

concerning Perseus. But all these expressions mean nothing but mere surrender. *Faith*, in such cases, means only the probity of the victor to whom the vanquished party commits himself.

4 There is a celebrated history, in Polybius and Livy, of Phaneas, the ambassador of the Etolians; who, in his oration to Manlius the consul, went so far as to say that the Etolians gave themselves up to the faith of the Romans. Then, when the consul asked again, and he had repeated the assertion, the consul asked that certain persons who had been the movers of the war should be given up. When Phaneas had objected, *We give ourselves up to your faith, not to slavery,* and that what was demanded was not according to Greek usage, the consul replied that he did not care for Greek usage; that by Roman usage he had authority over those who had surrendered deliberately; and ordered forthwith the ambassadors to be thrown into chains. *Do you*, he said, *talk of duty and decorum, when you have given yourselves up to our faith?* From which words, we see how much may be done with impunity, and without violating the Laws of Nations, by him to whose faith an adversary has surrendered himself. For the Roman consul did not use this power; but dismissed the ambassadors, and allowed the Etolian council to deliberate afresh on this subject. So the Roman people answered to the Falisci, that it had learnt, that they had committed themselves, not to the power, but to the faith of the Romans; and of the Campanians, we read that they came into faith with the Romans, not by league, but by surrender.

5 But with reference to the duty of him to whom the surrender is made, we may apply what Seneca says: *Clemency is not governed by the rules of law, but judges fairly, and can absolve the offender, or tax the contest at what rate it pleases.* Nor do I conceive that it makes any difference, whether he who surrenders, professes to give himself up to the wisdom, or moderation, or mercy of the victor. All these are merely soft words: the fact remains, that the victor is the arbiter.

LI. There are also conditional surrenders, which secure the interests of individuals; so that their lives, or liberties, or goods, are excepted; or of the whole body; and some such conventions may even give rise to a mixed authority between the parties; of which we have elsewhere spoken.

LII. Hostages and Pledges are accessories to conventions. Hostages, as we have said, are given either by their own will, or the will of him who has authority over them. For in a supreme civil sovereignty, is comprehended a right over the actions of subjects, as well as their goods. But the state, or its ruler, will be bound to make compensation for the inconvenience to the person who suffers, or his near relations. And if there are several persons, among whom it makes no difference to the state which is the hostage, it appears proper that the matter should be settled by lot. A vassal, except he be a subject also, is not liable to such a right on the part of the seignior: for the reverence and obedience which he owes his lord do not go so far as this.

LIII. The putting to death a hostage is, as we have said, lawful by the external Law of Nations; but not by internal rightness, except there be a corresponding crime on his side. Also hostages do not become slaves: but on the contrary, by the Law of Nations they can hold property and leave it to their heirs; though by the Roman law, it is provided that their goods shall go into the public treasury.

LIV. It is made a question, whether it is lawful for a hostage to make his escape. And it appears plainly that it is not lawful, if, either at first, or afterwards, he have given his word, in order to be in looser custody. Without such a condition, it would seem that the state had not the intention of binding its citizen not to escape, but of giving the enemy the power of keeping him as they chose. And in this way, the act of Clelia may be defended. But although she had not been in fault, the city could not receive and keep the hostage. So Porsenna: *If the hostage were not given up, he would hold the treaty broken:* and so *the Romans gave up the pledge of peace according to the treaty.*

LV. However, the obligation of hostages is odious; both because it is against liberty, and because it punishes a person for what another has done. Therefore, in such cases, a strict interpretation is applicable. And thus, persons given up on one account cannot be retained on another: which is to be understood with this condition, If anything else be promised without the stipulation of hostages. But if, in the other cause, faith have been violated, or a debt contracted, the hostage may then be retained; not as a hostage, but by that part of the Law of Nations by which subjects may be detained for the act of their rulers. But it may be provided that this shall not be done, by adding a covenant, that the hostages shall be given up, when that, on account of which they were given, has been fulfilled.

LVI. He who is given as a hostage, only to redeem another who is a prisoner or a hostage, is liberated, on the death of that other. For in him, when he dies, the right of the pledge is extinguished; as Ulpian said of a prisoner who is ransomed [and dies before the ransom is paid]. Wherefore, as in Ulpian's question, the price is not due, so here too, the person of the vicarious hostage is not bound. Thus Demetrius justly demanded of the Roman senate to be set free, as having been given up for Antiochus, and Antiochus being dead. This being so, he said he did not know whom he was hostage for.

LVII. When the king is dead who made the convention, whether the hostage be still bound, depends on the question which we have elsewhere treated, whether the convention is to be held personal or real: for accessory circumstances, such as hostages, cannot be a reason for receding from the rule, in the interpretation of the main articles. The accessories must follow the nature of the main business.

LVIII. This however may be added in passing: that sometimes the hostages are not an accessory part of the obligation, but really a principal part; as when any one, by contract, promises something to be done by another; and, that not being performed is held to the amount of interest involved in the agreement; then his hostages are bound in his place; which was the doctrine held in the Caudine convention, as we have elsewhere stated. The opinion of those who hold that hostages are bound for one another's acts, even without their own consent, is hard and unjust.

LIX. Pledges have some points in common with hostages, some, peculiar. It is common to the two, that being given for one thing, they may be retained for another, except a stipulation to the contrary have been made. And it is peculiar to Pledges, that the covenant which is made concerning them, is not to be taken so strictly as that concerning hostages: for things are made, to be held as property; men are not.

LX. We have also said elsewhere, that no period of time can supersede the obligation of restoring the pledge, if that be done to secure which the pledge was deposited. For an act which has an old and known cause is not to be believed to come from a new one. Therefore the forbearance of the debtor [who deposited the pledge] is to be ascribed to the old contract, not to derelict; except well-founded conjectures point to another interpretation: as if when any one wished to resume the pledge, and was prevented, he had passed it over for so long a time as to give room for a presumption of consent.

CHAPTER XXI.

*Of Faith while war continues ; of Truce ; of Safe Passage ;
of Ransom.*

I. 1 EVEN during war, the supreme authorities are wont to grant
certain kinds of intercourse among the hostile parties; as
Truce, Safe Passage, Ransom.   Truce is a convention, by which, the
war remaining, the parties are for a time to abstain from warlike acts.
I say, the war remaining; for as Cicero says, between war and peace,
there is no medium; and war is the name of a state or condition which
may exist, even when it does not exhibit its operations: according to
Aristotle's distinction, of virtues or qualities which may continue to
exist, even while they are not exerted. And so his commentators, as
Andronicus, speak of a habit which exists without the act; and Eustratius, who exemplifies it by a geometer in whom geometry resides,
though he be asleep.   And so Horace.

2 And thus, as Gellius says: *A truce is not peace; for the war remains, though the fighting ceases.* And in another: *A truce is a suspension of war.* Which I mention to shew that if any convention be made which is to be valid in time of war, it is valid also during a truce, except it plainly appear that, in the convention, it is not war which is looked to, but the operations of war. And on the other hand, if anything is said of peace, that will not hold for the time of truce: although Virgil calls a truce *a sequestral peace,* which Servius, on the passage, explains as a temporary peace. As also the Scholiast on Thucydides, *an occasional peace,* or *a war in labour.* Varro calls it *a camp-peace, a peace of a few days;* but all these are not definitions, but descriptions, and metaphorical descriptions. So too is that of Varro, when he calls a truce *the holiday* or *vacation of war.* He might have called it *a slumber of war.* So the holiday produced by the forensical ceremonies is called a peace by Papinius. Aristotle calls sleep *the chain of the senses;* and adopting that image, you might call a truce *the chain of war.*

3 In the exposition of Varro's words which Donatus follows, Gellius rightly reprehends his having added, "a peace *of a few days;*" and he shews that truces were granted for hours. And I add further, that truces have been made for years, as twenty, thirty, forty, even a hundred; of which we have examples in Livy, which shew the error of that definition of Proclus the Jurist: *A truce is, when for a short and present time, a convention is made, that the parties are not to attack each other.*

4 It may however happen, that if it appear that the sole moving reason of any convention was the cessation of warlike acts, that then, what is said of the time of peace shall hold for a time of truce; not from the force of the word, but from the clear inference of intention, of which we have elsewhere spoken.

II. The name *Induciæ* does not come, as Gellius would have it, from *inde uti jam;* nor as Opilius holds, from *endoitu,* that is, introgression; but from *inde otium,* because from a certain time there is a cessation of acts. It appears also, from Gellius and Opilius, that the ancients wrote this word with the letter *t,* not *c;* and that though now it is plural only, it formerly had a singular. The old form was *indoitia,* for *otium* was then written *oitium,* from the verb *oiti,* which later became *uti;* as from *poina* (afterwards *pœna*) came *punio,* and from *Poino* (afterwards *Pœnus*) came *Punicus.* And as from *ostia* in the plural, *ostia, ostiorum,* a door, came the singular *ostia, ostiæ;* so from the plural *indoitia, indoitiorum,* came *indoitia, indoitiæ,* and thence *indutia,* of which, as I have said, the plural only remains in use, though the singular formerly was used, as Gellius tells us. Donatus is not far from this etymology, when he says that *Induciæ* were so called because they give *in dies otium,* cessation for days. *Induciæ,* or Truce, then, is a cessation of acts in war, not a peace; and therefore the

F F

historians speak accurately, when they say that peace was denied, but truce granted.

III.   And therefore there is no need of a new declaration of war after a truce : for the temporary impediment being removed, the state of war comes into play, as a matter of right; it was not dead, but only sleeping; and revives, as the right of ownership or of paternal power revives, in a man who recovers from a state of lunacy. Still we read in Livy, that in pursuance of the opinion of the Feciales, when the truce was over, war was declared: but in fact, the old Romans wished to shew, by those superfluous cautions, how much they loved peace, and by how just causes they were drawn into arms. Livy implies this : *Truce was granted, not peace made ; the last day of the truce had passed, and before that day, they had resumed hostilities ; yet the Feciales were sent, and when they made their formal application, they were disregarded.*

IV.   1 The time of a truce is commonly defined by its length, as, for a hundred days ; or by fixing the end of the term, as, till the first of March.   In the former case, the reckoning is to be made even to minutes : for that is the natural way.   The cessation by civil days comes from law, or the customs of peoples.   In the other case, it is often a doubt, whether the day or month or year to which the truce was to last is excluded or included in the truce.

2 Certainly in natural things there are two kinds of boundary; the one, within the thing, as the skin is the boundary of the body: the other without the thing, as a river is the boundary of the land.   And so, boundaries which are made by the will of man, may be settled either the one way or the other.   But it seems more natural, that a boundary should be taken which is a part of the thing : *a terminus is the last part of a thing*, as Aristotle says : nor is use against this.   The lawyers say : *If any one says that a thing is to be done before the day of his death, the day on which he dies is reckoned in.*   Spurina predicted to Cesar a danger which would not be protracted beyond the Ides of March.   And when he was interrogated on the Ides themselves, he said the Ides were come, but not gone.   And therefore this interpretation is much the rather to be taken, when the prolongation of the time has a favourable effect; as in a truce which spares human blood.

3 But the day from which any measure of time is said to begin is not included; because the force of the preposition *from* is to disjoin, not to conjoin.

V.   I will add this by the way, that a truce or any similar transaction binds the contracting parties immediately, as soon as the contract is made: but that subjects on both sides begin to be obliged, when the truce has taken the form of a law, in which is involved some external publication: and this being done, it immediately begins to have force to oblige subjects : but that force, if the publication is made at one place only, does not operate through the whole government at the same moment; but in a time sufficient to carry the knowledge to each place. Wherefore, if anything be in the mean time done by the subjects against the truce, they will not be liable to punishment: but nevertheless the contracting parties will be bound to make good the damage.

VI.   1 What is lawful during the truce, and what is not, is given to be understood by the terms themselves which are employed. All acts of war, whether against persons or against things, are unlawful; that is, everything that is done against an enemy. Everything of that kind is, in time of truce, against the Law of Nations; as L. Emilius says in his speech to the soldiers in Livy.

2 Even things belonging to the enemy, which have, by any chance, come into our hands, are to be restored; and this, even if they had previously been ours: because, so far as regards external right, by which such things are to be judged, they have become theirs. And this is the purport of what Paulus the jurist says, that in time of truce, there is no postliminium; because postliminium requires that the right of capture in war should precede; which, in time of truce, cannot be.

3 It is lawful to go and return on either side, but with such apparatus only as shews that there is no danger. This is remarked by Servius upon Virgil, *Mixtique impune Latini:* where he also relates, that when the city was besieged by Tarquin, and truce was made between Porsenna and the Romans, when the Circensian games were celebrated in the city, the leaders of the enemy entered and contested in a chariot-race, and were crowned as victors.

VII.   To retire into the interior of our own territory, as we read in Livy that Philip did, is not at variance with a truce; nor to repair the walls of fortified places; nor to raise soldiers, except there be some more special convention.

VIII.   1 To corrupt the garrisons of the enemy, and so to obtain possession of places which they hold, is undoubtedly in contravention of a truce; for such an acquisition cannot be just, except by the right of war. The same is to be held, if subjects wish to revolt to the enemy. We have an example in Livy. *Those of Corona and Haliartus being inclined to kings, sent ambassadors into Macedonia to ask for a garrison to defend them against the Thebans; to whom the king answered, that on account of the truce with the Romans he could not send a garrison.* In Thucydides, Brasidas took possession of Menda, which revolted from the Athenians to the Lacedæmonians during the time of truce: but there is added the excuse, that he had things to complain of in return against the Athenians.

2 It is lawful in time of truce to occupy what is derelict; provided it is truly derelict, that is, left with the intention of not being resumed by those to whom it had belonged; not if it is merely unguarded; whether the custody were withdrawn before the truce, or after the

truce was concluded. For the ownership remaining, makes the possession of the other party unjust. And by this rule, the false plea of Belisarius against the Goths is refuted ; for he, on such a pretence had seized in time of truce places stripped of their garrisons.

IX. 1 It is made a question, whether he who, being prevented by major force* from retreating, is caught within the boundaries of the enemy after the period of the truce has expired, has the right of returning. If we regard the external Law of Nations, I do not doubt that such a person is in the position of one who, having come in peace, is, by the sudden breaking out of war, caught by accident among enemies; and we have noticed before that such a one remains a prisoner till a peace. Nor is internal justice wanting for such a proceeding; so far as the goods and actions of enemies are bound for the debt of the state, and are taken towards its payment. Nor has such a person more ground to complain, than so many other innocent persons upon whom the calamities of war fall.

2 Nor ought there to be urged, on the other side, the cases of merchandises which, by stress of weather, are carried past the place where dues are to be paid, and which nevertheless are excused†; nor the case mentioned by Cicero, of a ship of war, forced by stress of weather into a port, where its entering was contrary to the law, and which the questor wanted to confiscate. For in these cases, the operation of major force excuses the party from the penalty : but in our case, the question is not properly concerning penalty, but concerning a right [of war], which was quiescent only during a certain interval of time. But that to remit such rights is more humane, and also more generous, admits of no doubt.

X. There are also some things which are unlawful during a truce, in consequence of the special nature of the convention: as if a truce is granted, only for the sake of burying the dead, nothing is to be changed; and if a truce is given to a besieged place, only that they are not to be assaulted, it will then not be lawful to admit aid and provisions : for since such a truce is given as an advantage to one of the parties, it ought not to damage the position of him who granted it. Sometimes also it is stipulated, that it shall not be lawful for persons to pass between the parties. Sometimes such passage is granted to persons, but not to things; in which case, if persons are hurt in resisting the passage of things, the truce is not broken. For since it is lawful to oppose the passage of things, the security of persons is to be referred to that which is principal, not to that which is a matter of consequential result merely.

XI. If the faith of the truce be broken on one side, there is no ground for doubting whether it be open to the other party to return to the employment of arms, even without a declaration; for the Articles of the convention are parts of the convention, in the way of

---

* *Force majeure :* force which cannot be effectually resisted.

† So Gronovius understands the case.

condition, as we said a little while ago. You may indeed find in history examples of persons who have continued to bear wrongs even to the end of the truce. But on the other hand, war was made against the Hetruscans and others, because they did acts against the truce; and this diversity is an argument that the right is as we say; but that, to use or not to use such right, is at the option of the injured party.

XII. This is certain, that if the penalty agreed upon is demanded and paid by him who has acted against the truce, there is then no right of going to war; for the penalty is paid that everything else may remain unviolated. And on the other hand, if the war is resumed, it is to be considered that the claim of penalty is abandoned, since the option is given.

XIII. Private acts do not touch a truce, except a public act be added; for example, an act of commanding the thing to be done, or of accepting it as valid when it is done; and these public acts are understood to be adjoined, if those who have offended are neither punished nor given up; or if the things seized are not restored.

XIV. The right of Safe Passage out of the time of truce, is a privilege; and therefore in the interpretation of this right, the rules are to be followed which are given for privileges. This privilege, however, is neither hurtful to a third person, nor very burthensome to the giver; and therefore within the propriety of the words, a lax rather than a strict interpretation is to be admitted; and still more, if it be not a boon given on asking, but voluntarily offered: and more still, if, besides private convenience, some public utility is involved in it. Therefore the strict interpretation is to be rejected, even when the words imply it, except some absurdity would otherwise follow, or very probable conjectures of intention point that way. And on the other hand, a laxer interpretation, even not included in the propriety of the words, will be applicable, to avoid a similar absurdity, or upon very urgent conjectures.

XV. Hence we collect, that Safe Passage, granted to soldiers, is extended, not only to subaltern officers as well as to common soldiers, but also to the highest in command: because the propriety of the words admits of that signification; though there is another stricter limitation of the expression. So under the title of Clerks, comes also a Bishop. Also sailors who are in fleets are included; and all who are under the oath of military obedience.

XVI. 1 In granting free passage for going, is included also returning; and this, not from the force of the word, but to avoid an absurdity: for the boon ought not to be useless. And safe departure is understood to extend till the person comes to a place where he is in safety. And hence, Alexander is accused of bad faith, who, having granted safe departure to certain persons, ordered them to be put to death on the way.

2 But he who is allowed to depart, is not, necessarily, allowed to return: and he who is allowed to come himself, cannot send another: nor on the contrary, can he who is allowed to send, come himself. For these are different things, nor does reason compel us in this case to wander beyond the words; but yet so that a mistake on this subject, though it do not give a right, yet relieves the person from the penalty if any be added. Also he who is allowed to come, is allowed to come once, not repeatedly; except by the addition of time, ground is given to conjecture otherwise.

XVII. The son is not allowed to accompany the father, nor the wife the husband, any otherwise than is allowed in the right of dwelling in the enemy's territory: for we are used to dwell with our families, but to travel without them. But one or two servants, even if it be not expressed, will be supposed to be comprehended in the case of a person who cannot with decorum travel without such accompaniment: for he who concedes any favour, concedes its necessary consequences: and necessity is here to be understood morally.

XVIII. In like manner, goods of any kind are not comprehended in such a grant, but only such as you usually take on a journey.

XIX. If companions be expressed, those are not to be understood, whose case is more odious than the person himself to whom the grant is made. Such are pirates, robbers, deserters, refugees. The expression of the name of the nation of the companions permitted, shews sufficiently that the permission does not extend to others.

XX. The right of Safe Passage, since it proceeds from the force of power, in a dubious case is not extinguished by the death of the grantor; as we have said elsewhere of grants made by kings and other governors.

XXI. Disputes often arise on the point of grants made with the expression, *As long as I shall think proper.* And theirs is the sounder opinion, who hold that such a grant continues, even if a new act of willing do not intervene; because in a dubious case, that is presumed to continue to operate, which is necessary to the effect of right; but this is not so, when he who made the grant has ceased to be able to will, as happens by death. For the person being taken away, that presumption of duration falls to the ground along with it, as an accident ends with the substance.

XXII. Safe Passage implies safety beyond the territory of the grantor, as well as within it: for it is given against the right of war, which is not limited to the territory; as we have elsewhere said.

XXIII. The Ransom of Prisoners is very favourably looked upon, especially among Christians, to whom the divine law especially commands this kind of mercy. *The Ransoming of Captives is a great and excelling office of justice,* are the words of Lactantius. So Ambrose. And he defends the act of himself and the Church in breaking up, even the consecrated vessels of the church, in order to redeem captives. *The ornament of the sacraments is the redeeming of captives;* and much to the same effect.

XXIV.   1 These considerations prevent me from approving, without distinction, of those laws which forbid the ransom of captives, as we learn that the old Roman laws did.   *No city holds its captive citizens more cheap than we do,* says some one in the Roman Senate. And the city is called, by Livy, little indulgent to its captives, from early time.   So Horace calls the ransom of captives a foul condition, and an example leading to evil, loss added to shame.   But in fact, the blame which Aristotle casts upon the Lacedæmonian institution is also ascribed to the Roman; that everything has reference to war, as if the safety of the state depended on that alone.   But if we consider the interests of humanity, it would often be better that the right which is sought in war should be lost, than that a great number of men, our relations or fellow-countrymen, should be left in a condition of the deepest calamity.

2 Therefore such a law does not appear to be just, except it appear that there is need of such rigour, that more or greater evils, otherwise inevitable, may be averted.   For in such a necessity, as the prisoners themselves should, by the law of charity, bear their lot patiently, so may this be enjoined them; and others may be directed not to do anything to the contrary; according to what we have elsewhere said of surrendering a citizen for the public good.

XXV.   According to our habits, those taken in war do not become slaves: but I do not doubt that the right of exacting the amount of the ransom may be transferred, by the person who has the possession of the prisoner, to another person: for nature permits even incorporeal things to be alienated.

XXVI.   And the same person may owe the amount of ransom to more persons than one, if, when he has been let go by one, and the price is not yet paid, he is captured by another: for these are different debts from different causes.

XXVII.   The agreement concerning the amount of ransom, cannot be rescinded on account of the prisoner being discovered to be richer than he was supposed to be; because, by the external Law of Nations, which is the subject of our present enquiry, no one is compelled to give more than he promised in a contract, at a price different from the current price, if there has been no deceit: as may be understood from what we have said about Contracts.

XXVIII.   From what we have said, that prisoners with us are not slaves, it follows that there is an end of that acquisition of a right over all that belongs to the person, as well as the person; for that this is a mere accessory to the power over the person, we have elsewhere said.   Therefore nothing else becomes the property of the captor, but what he specially takes possession of.   And therefore, if the prisoner has anything secreted with him, that is not acquired by the captor, because it was never in his possession. So Paulus the jurist gave his opinion against Brutus and Manilius, that he who came into possession of a piece of land, did not acquire possession of a treasure which he did not know to be there; because not knowing of it, he could not be the possessor of it. From which it follows, that property so concealed may be applied to furnish the amount of ransom; the ownership having been retained by the prisoner.

XXIX. 1 This is also a frequent question: whether the ransom agreed upon, and not paid before death, be due from the heir. The answer appears to me to be obvious, if the prisoner die in captivity, that it is not due: for the promise was, on the condition that the prisoner should be liberated, and a dead man is not liberated. On the other hand, if he dies when he is at liberty, it is due; for he had already got the thing for which the price was promised.

2 I undoubtedly confess that the agreement may be made otherwise, so that, from the moment of the contract, the price may be absolutely due, and the prisoner may be retained, not now as a prisoner of war, but as a pledge given by himself: and on the other hand, that it may be covenanted that the payment of the price shall take place, if on a certain appointed day, he who is captive, be alive and free. But such conditions, as being less natural, are not to be presumed, except upon manifest evidence.

XXX. This question also is propounded: whether *he* ought to return into captivity, who was set free, on the compact that he should cause another to be liberated, who, by dying, prevented that being done. We have elsewhere said that the liberal promise of a third person is fulfilled with sufficient exactness, if nothing be omitted on the part of the promiser; but that in onerous promises, the promiser is obliged to an equivalent. And therefore in the question proposed, the person liberated will not be bound to return himself into captivity; for that was not the agreement, and the favour which is to be shewn to liberty, does not allow us to suppose it tacitly understood; nor ought he to take his liberty, as a gain, without a consideration; but he must give the estimated value of the thing, which itself he cannot give. For this is more agreeable to the simplicity of nature, than the rules which the Roman jurists give, in speaking of an action on a promise made in formal terms; or a suit when a thing is given for a cause, and the cause does not follow.

CHAPTER XXII.

Of the Faith of subordinate Powers in a War.

I.   AMONG Public Conventions, Ulpian places this class: *When Generals make agreements.* We have said that, after faith is pledged by the supreme powers, we must consider that which the subordinate powers pledge to one another or to others: whether those subordinate powers are those nearest to the supreme, as Generals properly so called, (with regard to whom we must understand the expression of Livy, *We know no General except him who conducts the war;*) or those farther removed, of whom Cesar thus speaks, *A Brigadier has one duty, a General another; the former is to execute his orders; the latter to act freely with regard to the whole posture of affairs.*

II.   The promises of Officers of this kind give rise to two kinds of considerations: Whether they bind the supreme authority; and whether they bind themselves. The former question is to be decided by what we have said; that we are bound by his acts whom we have selected as the minister of our will, whether that will be specially expressed, or be collected from the nature of the command committed to him. For he who gives the means of acting, gives, as far as depends on him, the means which are necessary to such action: which, in moral matters, is to be understood in a moral manner. Therefore there are two ways in which subordinate authorities bind the supreme authority by their acts: either by doing that which, on probable grounds is conceived to be included in their office; or beyond that, committed to them by some special assignment of authority, known to those whose interests are dealt with.

III.   There are also other ways in which the supreme authority is bound, in virtue of an antecedent act of its ministers, but so that that act is not, properly speaking, the cause of the obligation, but the occasion; and that, in two ways; either by consent of the superior, or by the thing itself. Consent appears by sanction of the act; not express only, but tacit also; that is, when the supreme authority knew what was done, and allowed it to be done; and in this case, if no other reason [besides consent] can be probably assigned, we have elsewhere stated what course the matter must take. The superior authority are obliged by the thing itself to this extent; that they are not to be made better off by the loss of other persons; that is, that they are either to fulfil the contract by which they wish to obtain an advantage, or are to give up the advantage; a case of equity which we have elsewhere discussed. And so far, and no further, acts which are performed so as to bring utility to us, are to be said to be *valid*. On the other hand, they cannot be excused from the charge of injustice, who, while they condemn the compact, retain that which without the compact they would not have: as when the Roman Senate neither could approve the act of Cn. Domitius, nor would rescind it: of which kind of occurrence we have many in history.

IV.   1 We must also repeat what we have said before, that he who placed a person in a command, is bound, even though the person so placed acts against secret orders; at least, within the limits of his public function. This rule of equity was rightly followed by the Roman Prætor, in the action against an Agent; for it is not everything done by the Agent which obliges the Principal, but such things only as are contracted in the matter for which his agency was employed; but he concerning whom public notice was given, that contracts with him would not be held good by the Principal, does not stand in the place of the Principal. But if notice were given, and were not publicly known, the Principal is bound. Also the condition of the agency is to be observed; for if the Principal directed the contract to be made on certain rules, or by the intervention of a certain person, it is just that the contract should be valid on these conditions.

2 From which it follows, that some kings and peoples may be more, and others less bound, by the contracts of their generals, if their laws and rules are sufficiently known. If these are not commonly known, the interpretation must be followed which conjecture dictates; in such a way that that is understood to be conceded without which the functions which belong to a person's duty cannot be conveniently carried out.

3 If a subordinate authority has exceeded the bounds of his commission, he will be bound, if he cannot perform what it has promised, to an estimated equivalent: except some law sufficiently known prevent that also. But if deceit be added, that is, if he pretended to an authority greater than he had, he will then be bound, both for the damage done by his fault, and as a criminal, to the penalty corre-

sponding to his guilt. On the first ground, his goods are liable, and if they are insufficient, his labour, or his personal liberty: on the second ground, his person also is liable, or his goods, or both, according to the quantity of the transgression. What we have said of deceit, will hold, even if the person so acting made an attestation that he did not intend himself to bear the obligation; because the debt due for the damage, and the penalty due for the crime, are connected therewith, not by a voluntary, but by a natural tie.

V.   And since, in all cases, either the supreme power is bound, or its minister, it is therefore certain that the other party is bound also: nor can it be alleged that the contract is one-sided.

We have considered the relation of subordinates to superiors; let us now see what power they have over inferiors.

VI.   I have no doubt, that a General can bind soldiers, and a Magistrate, citizens, within the limits of those acts which are customarily done at their command: in other cases, consent is necessary. On the other side, the compact of a general or magistrate will give advantages to their inferiors absolutely, in things simply useful; for that was sufficiently comprehended in their power: also in those things which have an *onus* annexed to the utility, within the limits of their customary command, absolutely: and out of those limits, if they accept the compact; which agrees with what we have delivered concerning stipulations for a third party on grounds of Natural Law. These general principles will become plainer by examining specific cases.

VII.   To negociate concerning the causes and consequences of the war, does not belong to the general of the army; for it is not a part of the conduct of the war, to end the war.   Even if he be appointed to the command with the greatest powers, those are to be understood as relating to the conduct of the war.   The answer of Agesilaus to the Persians was, that, *To make peace was a matter for the State.*   Sallust says, *The peace which A. Albinus had made with Jugurtha, without the authority of the Senate, the Senate rescinded.*   And in Livy: *How can that peace be valid which we have made without the authority of the Senate, and the command of the Roman People?* So the convention of Caudæ, so that of Numantia, did not bind the Roman People, as we have elsewhere explained.   And so far that dictum of Posthumius is true, *If the people can be bound to anything, it can be bound to everything;* that is, of those things which do not pertain to the conduct of the war: for that this is the application of the words, is shewn by what precedes; of surrender; of engagements with regard to giving up or burning a city; of change of the state.

VIII.   To grant a Truce, is the business of a general; and not only of the supreme general, but also of subordinate ones; namely, to those whom they besiege or blockade, as far as concerns themselves and their forces.   For such truces do not bind other generals of equal authority; as the history of Fabius and Marcellus in Livy declares.

IX. 1 In the same way, it is not the business of generals to give up men, conquests, lands, obtained in war. By this rule, Syria was taken from Tigranes, though Lucullus had given it to him. Of Sophonisba, who had been taken prisoner in war, Scipio says that the judgment and decision of the Senate and People of Rome was to determine; and that therefore Masinissa, though the general by whom she was taken, could not give her liberty. That over other things which are taken as prize of war, a certain disposal is conceded to persons in authority, we have seen; not so much from the force of their power, as from the customs of each people: on which subject we have already spoken sufficiently.

2 It is however in the power of generals to grant the possession of things not yet acquired: because towns sometimes and men often surrender themselves in war, on condition of lives being spared, or liberty, or property; among which concessions generally, the state of things does not allow the decision of the supreme authority to be asked. And by parity of reason, this right is also given to commanders who are not the highest, within the limits of the matters which are committed to them to execute. Maharbal had given to some Romans who had escaped from the battle at Trasimenum, Annibal being absent for so long a time as to leave room for this, not only his pledge for their lives, but, if they gave up their arms, the liberty of departing each with a single suit of apparel. But Annibal retained them, alleging that *it was not in the power of Maharbal to pledge himself, without consulting him, to those who surrendered, that they should be free from harm and penalty.* The judgment of Livy respecting this act follows: *This pledge was observed by Annibal with Punic faith.*

3 And therefore we must take what Cicero says, in the case of Rabirius, as coming from an advocate, not a judge. He maintains that Saturninus was lawfully put to death by Rabirius, having been drawn from the Capitol by C. Marius on his faith given. *How,* he says, *could faith be given without a decree of the Senate?* And he reasons as if Marius alone were bound by such a pledge. But C. Marius had received from the Senate the commission of acting so as to preserve the empire and the majesty of the Roman people: and in that power, which was the highest, according to Roman custom, who can deny that there was comprehended the right of granting impunity, if in that way all peril might be averted from the commonwealth?

X. But in these pacts of generals, because they act concerning the affairs of others, so far as the nature of contracts allows, the interpretation is to be limited; namely, so that the supreme power is not bound by their act more than it intended, and so that they do not suffer damage by undertaking their office.

XI. And thus he who is admitted to a pure surrender by the

general, is understood to be accepted on the condition that the victorious people or king is to determine his fate: of which examples are to be found in Gentius the Illyrian, and Perseus the Macedonian, of whom the former surrendered himself to Anicius, and the latter to Paulus.

XII.   The condition added, *This to be valid if the Roman People so judge,* which you often find in conventions, will produce the effect, that if that sanction do not follow, the general is held to nothing, except so far as he is himself bettered by the transaction.

XIII.   Also they who have promised to give up a town may dismiss the garrison; as we read that the Locrians did.

CHAPTER XXIII.

Of Private Faith in War.

I. THE dictum of Cicero is sufficiently well known;—*Even if individuals under the pressure of the time have promised anything to the enemy, faith also is to be observed in that:* individuals meaning either solders or civilians: for it makes no difference which they be, as to the obligation of good faith. It is strange that there should have been found masters of law who taught that pacts made publicly with enemies, bind us to good faith; but that those which are made by private persons, do not. For since private persons have private rights which they can subject to obligation, and since enemies are capable of acquiring rights, what can there be to impede the obligation? Add, that except we establish this rule, there is given occasion of bloodshed, and impediment to liberty; for if the faith of private persons be removed, the former can often not be prevented, nor the latter obtained by prisoners.

II. Indeed, not only is our word binding when given to an enemy whom the Law of Nations acknowledges as such, but even to a robber or a pirate; as we have said above, in speaking of public faith. There is this difference, that if an unjust fear, impressed by another, has been the force impelling to the promise, he who made the promise may seek restitution; or if the other will not give it, may take it by his own power. This does not hold in the case of fear proceeding from a war public according to the Law of Nations. But if an oath be added, he who promised must by all means perform what he has promised, if he wishes to escape the crime of perjury. Yet such a perjury, if committed towards an enemy, is commonly punished by men; if it be committed against robbers or pirates, it is commonly overlooked, in consequence of the hatred borne to such persons.

III.   In this case of private faith we do not except a Minor, who is in such a condition that he understands the act. For the allowances which are made to minors are made by the Civil Law. And we are now considering the results of the Law of Nations.

IV.   With regard to Error, we have elsewhere said that there is a right of receding from a contract, if that which was by error given in trust have, in the mind of him who entrusted it, the force of a condition.

V.   1 How far the power of private persons, to make agreements, extends, is a more difficult question. That what is public property cannot be alienated by a private person, is sufficiently plain: for if that was not even permitted to generals, as we have proved just now, much less is it to private persons. But it may be questioned concerning their own actions and property; because it may seem that these also cannot be conceded to the enemy without some damage of the party: whence it may seem that such pacts with the enemy are unlawful for citizens, on account of the eminent jurisdiction of the state; and for regular soldiers, on account of their military oath.

2 But it is to be considered that those pacts which are made in order to avoid a greater or certain evil, ought to be reckoned more useful than hurtful to the public also; because the lesser evil assumes the nature of a good. Nor does fidelity to the state or his superior, since by this the person does not abdicate his power over himself and his property; nor does the public utility alone, without the authority of law; produce such an effect, that what is done, even if it be done against duty, shall be void and destitute of jural effect.

3 Law indeed may take from subjects, either perpetual or temporary, their power: but the law does not always do this; for it is tender of the interests of citizens. For human laws, as we have elsewhere said, have then, and then only, a binding force, if they are made in a humane manner, not if they impose burthens which are repugnant to reason and nature. And therefore special laws and precepts which have, upon the face of them, anything of this kind, are not to be held as laws: and general laws are to be interpreted indulgently, so as to exclude cases of extreme necessity.

4 If an act, which was interdicted by a law or precept, and deprived of its validity by prohibition, could be interdicted with reasonable right, the act of the private person will be void; but at the same time he is liable to punishment for having promised what was not in his power, and especially if he did it under oath.

VI.   The promise of a prisoner to return into captivity is rightly allowed: for it does not render the condition of the prisoner worse than it was. And therefore Regulus, in doing what he did, acted not gloriously only, as some think, but also as he ought. *Regulus*, says

Cicero, *ought not to disturb the conditions and covenants belonging to the laws of war, by an act of perjury.* Nor is it a sound objection, that, as Horace says, he knew the tortures which awaited him: for when he gave the promise he knew how likely this was. And so with regard to the ten prisoners, as Gellius tells the story out of old authors; *Eight said that they had no right to postliminium, for they had by their oaths lost the character of citizens.*

VII. 1 Also prisoners often promise not to return to a certain place, or not to bear arms against him who has them in his power. We have an example of the former case in Thucydides; when the Ithomians promise the Lacedæmonians that they will quit Peloponnesus, and never return. The latter kind of engagement is now common. We have an old example in Polybius, when the Numidians are dismissed by Amilcar, on condition of never bearing arms against the Carthaginians. Procopius in his Gothic history has a similar pact.

2 Some moralists pronounce this pact void, because it is against the duty which a person owes to his country. But what is against duty, is not necessarily and of course void; as we have already explained. And in the next place, it is not against duty to obtain one's liberty by promising that which is already in the enemy's power. For the cause of the country is not worsened by such an act; for he who is a captive has ceased to be of any value to that cause.

VIII. Also some promise not to make their escape. They are bound by this promise, even though they were under restraint when they promised; contrary to the opinion of some moralists. For in this way, men's lives are saved, and their captivity made less harsh. If, however, a person, having made such a promise, is afterwards put in chains, he will be liberated from his promise, if he made it to avoid being put in chains.

IX. A question is raised, idly enough, whether he who is captured can surrender himself to another than the captor. For it is abundantly certain that no one can by a compact of his take away a right from another. And the captor has already acquired a right, either by the right of war, or partly by the right of war, partly by the concession of the superior authority which makes the war; as we have explained above.

X. With regard to the effects of compacts, there is a noted question, whether private persons, if they are negligent in fulfilling their engagements, can be compelled by their own authorities. And the sounder opinion is, that they are compellable only in a regular war, on account of the Law of Nations, by which the belligerents are bound to fulfil the rules of justice to each other, even with regard to the acts of private persons; as for instance, if ambassadors had been violated by private persons. So Cornelius Nepos, as Gellius informs us, had written, that many of the senators were of opinion, that those of the ten captives who were unwilling to return, should be sent to Hannibal under guard.

XI. With regard to Interpretation, the rules are to be observed in this case also, which we have several times mentioned; that we are not to recede from the propriety of the words, except in order to avoid an absurdity, or for some other good probable reason: that in a doubtful case we are rather to interpret the words against him who gave the law: and the like.

XII. He who has covenanted for his life, has not a right to his liberty also. Under the name of clothes, arms are not included: for they are different in kind. Aid is said to have arrived, if it be in sight, though it be doing nothing; for the presence of it has an efficacy.

XIII. But he cannot be said to have returned to the enemy according to his promise, who returned secretly in order to go away again immediately: for he was to be understood to mean by *return*, that he was again to be in the power of the enemy. The contrary quibbling interpretation is called by Cicero silly cunning, involving fraud and perjury. And this interpretation is called by Gellius a fraudulent cunning; and those who had employed it were noted as ignominious by the censor, and made incapable of giving evidence, and disreputable.

XIV. When an agreement is made for surrendering a city except proper aid arrive, such aid is to be understood as makes the danger cease.

XV. This also is to be noted, that if any covenant is made as to the mode of executing the convention, that does not become a condition of the agreement: as, if it were said that it is to be discharged in a certain place, which place afterwards changes its master.

XVI. With regard to Hostages, what we have said above is to be observed, that in general, they are accessories to the principal act: but it may be covenanted that the obligation shall be disjunctive; that either something shall be done, or the hostages retained. But in a doubtful case, we must hold to the most natural supposition, that they are only accessories.

CHAPTER XXIV.

Of Tacit Faith.

I. IT is well said by Javolenus, that some things are agreed upon in silence. This happens in public conventions, and in private, and in mixed. The cause is this; that consent, however indicated and accepted, has the force of transferring right. But there are other signs of consent, besides words and letters, as we have more than once indicated.

II. Some are by nature inherent in certain acts. For an example, take him who coming from the enemy, or from strangers, gives himself into the hands of another people or king. For that such a person tacitly binds himself not to do anything against that state in which he seeks refuge, cannot be doubted. Wherefore they are not to be followed, who say that the act of Zopyrus was free from blame: for his fidelity to his king does not excuse his perfidy towards those to whom he fled. The same must be said of Sextus; the same of Tarquin who went over to Gabii. Virgil speaks of Sinon's treachery and crime.

III. So he who either asks for or grants a parley, tacitly promises that it shall be without damage to the parties parleying. When enemies are harmed under pretence of a colloquy, Livy says that the law of nations is violated: adding, *Colloquium perfide violatum.* So Valerius Maximus, of Cn. Domitius, who had drawn in Bituitus, king of the Arverni, under pretence of a colloquy, and had then thrown him into chains: *Too great greediness of glory made him perfidious.* And hence we must wonder why the writer of the eighth Book of Cesar's Gallic War, whether it be Hirtius or Oppius, relating a similar act of Labienus, adds: *He judged, that his* (Comius's) *faithlessness might be suppressed without perfidy;* except we are to look upon this as the judgment of Labienus, not of the writer.

IV. But this tacit will [or promise] is not to be drawn beyond the limits which I have stated: for provided the collocutors suffer no harm, to turn away the enemy from warlike measures by the appearance of

a colloquy, and in the mean time to push on our own designs, has no
perfidy in it, and is reckoned among good stratagems.   And thus
they who complained that Perseus was deceived by the hope of
peace, took account, not so much of right and of good faith, as of
magnanimity and glory : as may be understood by what we have said
of stratagems.   Of the same kind was the trick by which Asdrubal
saved his army from the Ausetanian jungle; and by which Scipio
Africanus Major learnt the situation of the camp of Syphax: both
which stories are told in Livy.   And these examples are imitated by
L. Sylla, in the social war at Esernia, as we read in Frontinus.

V.   There are also certain mute signs which have a signification
from custom, as formerly fillets and olive-branches; among the Macedonians the raising of spears; among the Romans the placing the
shields on the head, the sign of a suppliant surrender; which immediately obliges the persons to lay down their arms.   As to him who
signifies that he receives the surrender, whether he be obliged, and
how far, is to be determined by what we have said above.   At present
a white flag is a tacit sign of asking for a parley; and binds the askers
as much as if they used words.

VI.   How far engagements made by generals are to be supposed
tacitly approved by the people or the king, we have also discussed
above; namely, that it is so to be understood, when the act is known,
and anything is done, or not done, of which no other reason can be
assigned but the will to approve the convention.

VII.   The remission of a penalty cannot be collected merely from
silence.   It is necessary that there be added some act, which either
of itself shews friendship, or a league on the ground of friendship, or
an opinion of the existence of virtues which may give rise to a condonation of previous acts; whether that opinion be expressed in words,
or by means of things which by custom are appointed to convey such
meaning.

CHAPTER XXV.

The Conclusion, with admonitions to Good Faith and Peace.

I. 1 AND here I think that I may make an end; not that I have said all that might be said, but that enough has been said to lay the foundations; on which, if any one will erect a fairer superstructure, he will be so far from being the object of any grudging on my part, that I shall be grateful to him. Only before I dismiss the reader, as when I spoke of undertaking a war, I added admonitions on the duty of avoiding war as much as possible, so now I will add a few admonitions which may tend in war, and after war, to the preservation of good faith and peace; and of good faith, both on other accounts, and that the hope of peace may not be destroyed. For not only is each commonwealth kept together by good faith, as Cicero says, but that greater society of which nations are the members. If Faith be taken away, as Aristotle says, *the intercourse of men is abolished.*

2 Therefore Cicero rightly says, that it is atrocious to break that faith which holds life together; *the holiest good of the human heart*, as Seneca speaks. And this, the supreme rulers of mankind ought to be more careful of preserving, in proportion as they have more impunity for their violations of it: so that if faith be taken away, they will be like wild beasts, whose strength is an object of general horror. And in other parts of its sphere, justice has often somewhat that is obscure; but the bond of good faith is manifest of itself, and indeed is used to remove obscurity from all other matters.

3 And therefore it is especially the office of kings, to cherish good faith; first, for the sake of conscience, and then, for the sake of good opinion, by which the authority of kingdoms stands. Let them be certain therefore that they who instil into them acts of deceit, are themselves the deceivers they would make *them*. Doctrines cannot long work well, which make man unfit for society with man; and we may add, hateful to God.

II. In the next place, a mind serene and trusting in God cannot be retained in the whole administration of a war, except it always look to peace.   As Sallust most truly says, *Wise men carry on war for the sake of peace:* and to this the opinion of Augustine agrees; and of Aristotle.   It is a ferine force which is prominent in war; and must be tempered with humanity, that we may not cease to be men, by imitating brutes.

III.   If therefore a peace sufficiently safe can be had, it is not ill secured by the condonation of offenses, and damages, and expenses: especially among Christians, to whom the Lord has given his peace as his legacy.   And so St Paul, his best interpreter, exhorts us to live at peace with all men.   As Sallust says, A good man takes up the beginning of war reluctantly, and does not follow its extremes willingly.

IV.   This of itself ought to be enough; but often human Utility draws men the same way: those first who are the weakest; for a long struggle with a more powerful adversary is perilous; and as in a ship, we must avert a greater calamity by some loss, putting away anger and hope, fallacious advisers, as Livy says.   So Aristotle.

V.   But also this is for the benefit of the stronger: for as Livy also says, To them peace, if they grant it, is bounteous and creditable, and better than a victory merely hoped for.   For they must recollect that Mars is on both sides.   So Aristotle.   And so in the oration for peace in Diodorus.   And there is much to be feared from the courage of despair, like the dying bites of a wild beast.

VI.   If the two parties reckon themselves equal, then, as Cæsar holds, is the best time for treating of peace, since each trusts in himself.

VII.   Peace made on any conditions whatever is, by all means, to be kept, on account of the sacredness of good faith, of which we speak; and care must be had to avoid, not only perfidy, but anything which may exasperate the mind of the other party.   For what Cicero says of private friendships, you may adapt also to public ones; that as all such connexions are to be maintained with the utmost conscience and good faith, so especially those in which a reconciliation has taken place of a previous enmity.

VIII.   May God write these lessons—He who alone can—on the hearts of all those who have the affairs of Christendom in their hands: and may he give to those persons a mind fitted to understand and to respect Rights, divine and human; and lead them to recollect always that the ministration committed to them is no less than this; —that they are the governors of Man, a creature most dear to God!

LATIN AND GREEK INDEX

OF SUBJECTS AND WORDS CONTAINED IN THE WORK.

The first Number marks the Book; the second, the Chapter; the third, the Section; the fourth, the Article or Division of the Section: except '&' be inserted, for then the following Number is also the Section: *prol.* denotes the Prolegomena.

A.

ABDICARI regnum an possit. ii. 7, 26

Abdicato filio an quid debeatur. ii. 7, 7

Abitus tutus quomodo sumatur. iii. 21, 16

Abrahamus bello adjuvit extraneos a fide. ii. 15, 9, 6

Abrahamus res hostiles sibi acquisitas judicat et dedicat. iii. 6, 1, 1

Abrahami filii ex Cethura non habuerunt partem hereditatis. ii. 7, 8, 3

Absentes an partem prædæ ferant. iii. 6, 17, 5

Absentium jus præsentibus accrescit. ii. 5, 20

Absolvere cur satius quam condemnare. ii. 23, 5, 1

Absolutio a juramento, unde vim habeat. ii. 13, 20, 2

Abstinentiæ in solo pacatorum exempla. iii. 17, 2

Absurda nemo credendus est velle. ii. 16, 22

Absurdus intellectus, vitandus. ii. 16, 2, & 5, & 6

Acceptatio pro altero facta quid operetur. ii. 11, 14, & 17

Acceptatio an præcedere alienationem possit. ii. 6, 2

Accessionis jus quale. ii. 8, 11, et seqq.

Accipi plus potest quam quod nostrum est, sed sub onere restituendi quod excedit. iii. 1, 4, 1

Accusare an Christiano conveniat. ii. 20, 15, 16

Accusatores ex officio publico constitui melius. ii. 20, 15

Achæi dolis abstinebant. iii. 1, 20, 3

Acquiri bello non possunt quæ penes hostes sunt. Sed non hostium. iii. 6, 5, & 26, 1.

Acquiruntur bello quoad jus externum quæ hostis noster bello acquisiverat. iii. 6, 7, 1

Acquisitio naturalis in bello. iii. 6, 1, 1, 2. Rerum originaria. ii. 3, 1. Acquisitiones improprie dictæ juris gentium. ii. 8, 1

Actio injuriæ an Christiano conveniat. ii. 20, 10, 1, 2

Actionum injustarum gradus. ii. 20, 29, 1, 3 ———— forensium et belli iidem fontes. ii. 1, 2, 1

Actor ut bellum vitetur re dubia potius cedere debet. ii. 23, 11

Actus homini inevitabiles an puniri possint. ii. 20, 19. Qui humanam societatem non spectant, puniendi non sunt. ii. 20, 20. Ex more communes nemini prohibendi. ii. 3, 22. Interni an punibiles inter homines. ii. 20, 18. Imperfecti an puniantur jure gentium. ii. 20, 39. Contra conscientiam illiciti. ii. 23, 2. Publici et privati in bello publico. iii. 6, 10. Benefici. ii. 12, 2. Permutatorii. ii. 12, 3. Diremtorii. *ibid.* Communicatorii. ii. 12, 4. Mixti. ii. 12, 5. Positivi et negativi quantum differant. ii. 15, 17, 2. Communes a dividuis distinguendi circa restitutionem. iii. 10, 4. Contra juramentum factus quando sit vitiosus tantum, quando et irritus. ii. 13, 19. Humani quotuplices. ii. 12, 1.

Ἀδέσποτα. ii. 8, 7

Admiralitatis natura. ii. 12, 25. Contractus. ii. 12, 4

Consiliarii Regum quomodo obligentur ex bello injusto. iii. 10, 4

Consita an solo cedant. ii. 8, 22

Constantiæ debitum quale. ii. 11, 3

Constantinopolitani nullum jus ad eligendum Imperatorem habuerunt, quod non dependeret a populo Romano. ii. 9, 11, 2

Constituens non semper superior constituto. i. 3, 8, 13

Consuetudo quomodo introducatur. ii. 4, 5, 2. Pro consensu populi in jure concedendarum jurisdictionum. ii. 6, 10

Consuetudo horum temporum de mobilibus bello captis. iii. 9, 15. De recipiendis deditis. iii. 11, 14, 2

Consumens nummos furtivos ad restitutionem tenetur. ii. 10, 2, 2

Consortia impiorum vitare, sapiens monitum. ii. 15, 9, 10

Contrahendum (ad) nemo metu impellendus. ii. 12, 10

Contractus quid. ii. 12, 7. Contractuum divisio. ii. 12, 2, 3. Contractus innominati qui, et unde dicti. ii. 12, 3, 3

Contractu populi facto cum liber esset, Rex postea factus tenetur. ii. 14, 12, 2

Contractus vergens ad perniciem publicam an obliget. ii. 14, 12, 4

Contractus Regum secum ferentes alienationem pecuniæ populi, regni, partis regni, patrimonii regalis an valeant. ii. 14, 12, 5. Contractus regis an actionem pariant. ii. 14, 6, 2; & §§ 4, 5, 9. Subditis jus cogendi non dant. ii. 14, 6, 2 & 2, 2. An leges dicendi. ii. 14, 9, 1

Contractus et leges misceri possunt. *ibid.*

———— perfectus sine scriptura. ii. 16, 30

———— regum et populorum an interpretandi ex jure Romano. ii. 16, 31

Contractui extrinseca non sunt indicanda. ii. 12, 9, 2

Contractibus (in) vitium rei indicandum et quare. ii. 12, 9, 12

———— (de) leges Romanorum et Hebræorum. ii. 12, 13, 2

———— invasorum sive tyrannorum populi non tenentur. ii. 14, 14

Contractuum natura repudiat ambiguas locutiones. iii. 1, 10, 3

Contumelia quo sensu ab injuria distinguatur. i. 2, 8, 7

Conventio de redemptione an rescindi posset ob læsionem. iii. 21, 27

Conventionum divisio in publicas et privatas. ii. 15, 1; iii. 20, 1. Publicarum divisio. ii. 15, 2

Conventiones. *Vide* Contractus et Fœdera.

Convictus cum impiis et contumacibus quatenus sit illicitus, qualis prohibeatur. ii. 15, 9, 10, & 10, 3

Cornelius mansit Centurio post baptismum. i. 2, 7, 9

Cornelia lex pro heredibus eorum, qui postliminio redierunt. iii. 9, 10, 4

Corpus ad servitutem obligari potest. ii. 15, 16, 4

———— naturale idem quamdiu dicatur. ii. 9, 3, 1

———— ex terra ortum terræ debetur. ii. 19, 2, 2

———— humanum bestiis dari miserandum. ii. 19, 2, 4

Corpora hominum debent dissolvi extra conspectum. ii. 19, 2, 5

Corcyrensis controversia inter Athenienses et Corinthios. ii. 16, 13, 3

Corraria quid. iii. 6, 12, 2

Credens pecuniam patri ad alendum filium actionem habet in filium. ii. 10, 2, 3

Creditor tenetur de perceptis fructibus supra usuram. ii. 10, 4

Culpa sine dolo sufficit ad restitutionis obligationem. iii. 10, 5, 2

———— media inter injuriam et infortunium. iii. 11, 4, 1

Curatores regni summum imperium habere possunt. i. 3, 11, 2

Curæ clericis interdictæ. i. 2, 10, 10

Cyri et Arsicæ controversiæ. ii. 7, 28

D.

Damnum quid, et unde dictum. ii. 17, 2, 1. Contra honorem et famam datum. ii. 17, 22. Faciendo quomodo detur. ii. 17, 6, 7. Non faciendo quomodo detur. ii. 17, 8, 9. Damni directe dati, et in consequentiam distinctio. ii. 21, 10, 1. Causa qui dicantur. ii. 17, 10. Dati consequentia quæ censeantur. ii. 17, 11. Damna in dubio pace remissa censentur. iii. 20, 15. Damnum datum ob causam turpem retineri potest. ii. 10, 12. Datum ob rem honestam, sed alioqui debitam, an retineri possit. *ibid.*

David quomodo et quatenus Sauli restitit. i. 4, 7, 4, 6

———— res acquirit jure belli. iii. 6, 7, 1

Jehu factum quale. i. 4, 19, 4

Jephthis controversia cum Ammonitis. ii. 4, 2, 1

Ignoscere an liceat interdum. ii. 20, 21. An liceat posita lege pœnali. ii. 20, 24

Ignorantia quæ delictum minuat. ii. 20, 43; ii. 26, 1

Illicita eximenda verborum universalitate. ii. 16, 27, 1

Illyrii prædari soliti, triumphati. iii. 3, 2, 3

Immemoriale tempus. *Vide* Tempus immemoriale. ii. 4, 7

Immunitas rerum ad agriculturam pertinentium. iii. 13, 4, 4

Impediens aliquem a petendo munere quando teneatur. ii. 17, 3

Impendens in rem alienam receptu difficilem sumptus servat. ii. 10, 9

Imperator Romanus an imperium habeat in omnes. ii. 22, 13. Qua talis, unde jus suum habeat. ii. 9, 11, 4. Vicarium ei quis dare possit. *ibid.* Germaniæ qua talis, unde jus suum habeat. *ibid.*

Imperium acquiri quatenus possit. iii. 15, 1. In victos accipi recte ad sui tutelam. iii. 15, 2, 1. Bello acquiritur. iii. 8, 1. Ut in rege imperante alio est bello acquiritur. iii. 8, 4, 1, 2. Alienari potest a rege consensu populi. ii. 6, 3. Romanum distinctum ab Imperio Francorum, et regno Longobardorum. ii. 9, 11, 3. A Germania magna. ii. 9, 11, 1. Et majestatem conservare, quid? i. 3, 21, 2

Imperii Romani nunc non sunt omnia quæ olim fuerunt. ii. 22, 13, 2. Summi jus tam populo, quam regi longa possessione acquiritur. ii. 4, 11. Subjecta personæ et territorium. ii. 3, 4, 1. Pars pignori dari non potest. ii. 6, 9. Proprii exempla. i. 3, 12, 3, 4. Summi partitio quomodo fiat. i. 3, 17, 1, 2. Vox improprie sumta pro ductu, et pro postulato. i. 3, 21, 8

Imperio partito singuli imperantes pro sua parte jus belli habent. i. 4, 13

Imperia magna difficulter custodiuntur. ii. 22, 13, 1; iii. 15, 7, 2. Successiva non semper summa. i. 3, 10, 5. Non summa plene haberi, et in patrimonio esse possunt. i. 3, 14. Electiva quædam summa. i. 3, 10, 5. Quædam in patrimonio, et alienabilia. i. 3, 14. Quomodo intereant sublato subjecto. ii. 9, 1. Profanorum sponte non subeunde. ii. 15, 10, 4

Impietatis auctores jure gentium punibiles. ii. 20, 47, 2, 4, & 50, 3, & 51, 1.

Impossibilitas facti promissi excusat, ne pax rumpatur. iii. 20, 37

Inæqualitas, quæ inest contractui, jure gentium non resarcitur. ii. 12, 26, 1

Incarcerans alterum injuste ad quid teneatur. i. 17, 14, 16

Incestum jure gentium. ii. 5, 12, 3

Incorporalia cum persona acquiruntur. iii. 7, 4, & cap. 8, 4, 2

Indefinita pro universali quando sumenda. ii. 16, 12, 1

Indi plures uxores habebant. ii. 5, 9, 4

Indictum bellum principi, simul indictum subditis et sociis. iii. 3, 9

Indictio belli. iii. 3, 5, & 6, & 7. Utrinque facta. iii. 3, 7, 3. Specialis requiritur, si socii per se, et apud se bello impetantur. iii. 3, 10

Indirecte licent quædam quæ directe non licent. iii. 1, 4, 1

Induciæ quid et unde dictæ. iii. 21, 2. Quando incipiant obligare. iii. 21, 5. Ad certum finem; et earum effectus. ii. 21, 6, & 13. A ducibus dantur. iii. 23, 8

Induciarum tempus an veniat sub belli an pacis nomine. iii. 21, 2. Tempus quomodo computandum. iii. 21, 4

Induciis finitis nova indictione non opus. iii. 21, 3. Earum tempore quid liceat. iii. 21, 6, 11. An deficientes et relictos recipere liceat. iii. 21, 8, 1. Elapsis, qui sine culpa penes hostem reperitur an capi possit. iii. 21, 9. Ab altera parte ruptis indictione non opus. iii. 11, 11

Inermibus parcendum. iii. 11, 10

Infans promittendo non obligatur. ii. 11, 5

Infantis dominium unde. ii. 3, 6

Infantium dominium quale. ii. 3, 6; ii. 5, 2, 2

Infantibus parcendum. iii. 11, 9, 1, 2

Infeudatio est alienatio. ii. 6, 9

Infeudationes regnorum irritæ sine consensu populi. *ibid.*

Infortunium et injuria quo distent. ii. 21, 5, 1; 3, 11, 3, 1

Infortunii et injuriæ distinctio. iii. 11, 3, 1, 4

Ingrati non puniuntur. ii. 20, 20, 1, 2

Inimici sepeliendi. ii. 19, 3

Injuria quando alteri in persona alterius facta censeatur. iii. 20, 40, 2

Injuriæ, culpæ, et infortunii discrimen. iii. 11, 4, 1, 5, 6. Quædam ferendæ, et quales. i. 2, 8, 7

Injustitia committi potest in bello justo. iii. 11, 1, 1

Injustum quid. i. 1, 3, 1

capta sua faciant. iii. 18, 1, 3. De bello captis, quando hosti, quando civitati teneantur. iii. 18, 2, 2

Privatis Christianis an liceat punire maleficos. ii. 20, 16

Privata causa cum publica in bello conjungi potest. i. 5, 1

Privatæ interfectionis exempla. ii. 20, 9, 5

Privilegia quomodo interpretanda. ii. 18, 4, 4. Quæ late interpretanda. iii. 21, 14

Prohibita non semper etiam irrita. ii. 5, 16, 1

Promissa multa, quæ natura valent, lex civilis irrita facit. ii. 11, 8, 3. Quæ plus nocent promittenti quam alteri prosunt, an præstanda. ii. 11, 1, 1; & cap. 16, 27, 2. Favorabilia, odiosa, mixta vel media. ii. 16, 10. Regum. Vide Reges.

Promissi onus in commodum tertii adjunctum, quid operetur. ii. 11, 19

Promissio non omnis tollit summum imperium. i. 3, 16, 1. Ut valeat acceptanda. ii. 11, 14. Illius acceptatio quomodo fiat: et an innotescere debeat promissori, ut perfectam vim habeat promissio. ii. 11, 15. An revocabilis ante acceptationem : et mortuo ante acceptationem promissario. ii. 11, 16. An revocari possit mortuo internuntio : item mortuo tabellario. ii. 11, 17. Per ministrum facta quando revocabilis. ii. 11, 17, 1. Facti alieni quid operetur. ii. 11, 22. Requirit usum rationis in promittente. ii. 11, 5. In errore fundata quando dicatur, et quid operetur. ii. 11, 6. Rei illicitæ non valet. ii. 11, 8, 1. Facti, quod nunc in potestate promittentis non est, quid valeat. ii. 11, 8, 2. Ex metu. ii. 11, 7. Ob causam ante debitam an obliget. ii. 11, 10. Perfecta quid, et quam vim habeat. ii. 11, 4, 1. Novum jus confert. iii. 18, 1. De non fugiendo a vincto facta valet. iii. 23, 8. Redeundo in certum locum, et de non militando, hosti facta valet. iii. 23, 7

Promissiones causam expressam non habentes naturaliter valent. ii. 11, 21

Promissioni onus adjici quando possit. ii. 11, 19

Promissionis materia qualis esse debeat. ii. 11, 8, 1. Vis. ii. 11, 1, 3, 4

Promissum ob causam turpem an præstandum. ii. 11, 8, 1, 9

Promittendi modus quis. ii. 11, 11

Promittens metu an teneatur. ii. 11, 7

Prophetarum dicta de pace sub Evangelio quem sensum habeant. i. 2, 8, 1

Proportio Arithmetica et Geometrica an proprie distinguant justitiam expletricem et attributricem. i. 1, 8, 2

Propositi, impetus, et casus distinctio. iii. 11, 4, 6

Proprietatis exordium. ii. 2, 1, 2, 5

Προστάγματα. ii. 15, 7, 1

Πρόθυρα maris quorum sint. ii. 3, 10, 1

Provisi et improvisi distinctio. iii. 11, 4, 5

Provocatio non datur ab arbitris lectis inter summas potestates. iii. 20, 46, 2

Proximi nomine venit etiam qui per repræsentationem consequitur jus gradus superioris. ii. 7, 30, 2

Proximus quis in lege Hebræa : et quis in lege Evangelica. i. 2, 8, 10

Ψεύδεσθαι in sacris literis quid. ii. 13, 3, 4

Ψευδορκεῖν. ii. 13, 13, 2

Publica utilitas ad alienanda, etc. Vide Utilitas publica.

Pudicitiæ conservandæ causa interfectio licita. ii. 1, 7

Pudor quid, ubi de jure agitur. iii. 10, 1, 2

Pueri, id est, servi. iii. 14, 5, 3

Pugnare in hostem qui miles non sit, quo jure vetetur. iii. 18, 1, 1

Punici belli secundi controversia. ii. 17, 19

Puniri an possint qui in falsos Deos impie agunt. ii. 20, 51

Punitio exemplaris. ii. 20, 9, 1

Pupillus ex commodato tenetur in quantum locupletior. ii. 10, 2, 2

Q.

Quintii Consulis salubre mendacium. iii. 1, 14, 2

Quiritari unde dictum. ii. 1, 2, 1

R.

Rabirii factum. iii. 22, 9, 2

Rami olivarum. iii. 24, 5

Ratam rem haberi, obligatio qualis. ii. 15, 3, 3

Ratihabitione summa potestas quomodo obligetur. iii. 22, 4, 1

Ratio juris fundamentum. i. 1, 11, 1. Adæquata quæ. ii. 16, 20, 2. Sæpe consideranda secundum potentiam, non secundum existentiam. ii. 16, 25, 1. Legis non plane idem cum mente. ii. 16, 8. Adæquata quæ, et quid operetur. *ibid.*

Rationis identitas quando inducat extensivam interpretationem. ii. 16, 20, 2

Razis mors. ii. 19, 5, 4

Redempti ex captivitate redemptori quomodo teneantur. iii. 9, 10, 2

Rediisse ad hostem quis dicendus. iii. 23, 13

Redimi captivos et servos factos, æquum. iii. 21, 24

Regimen non omne ejus causa qui regitur. i. 3, 8, 14

Regna media inter absolutum et Laconicum. i. 3, 20, 1. A populo delata in dubio individua. ii. 7, 14. Non deferuntur ad eos, qui a primo rege non descendunt. ii. 7, 15. Non veniunt ad naturales nec ad adoptivos. ii. 7, 16. Ad mares veniunt potius quam ad fœminas. ii. 7, 17. Quomodo deferantur per successionem ab intestato. ii. 7, 10, 2, & § 11, 2. Patrimonalia pervenire possunt ad eos, qui a primo rege non descendunt. ii. 7, 12

Regni et principatus voces significatu proprio et improprio. i. 3, 10, 1, 2. Pleni sive absoluti exempla. i. 3, 8, 8. A populo delati successor non tenetur ad onera hæreditaria. *ibid.*

Regnum. *Vide* Imperium. Quomodo dividatur, et quo effectu. ii. 9, 10. Patrimoniale, si sit individuum, debetur maximo natu. ii. 7, 23. A populo delatum est hæreditas separata cetera hæreditate. ii. 7, 19. Italiæ. ii. 9, 11, 4, 3

Regula, secundum naturam esse, ut quem sequuntur incommoda et commoda sequantur, quomodo intelligenda. ii. 8, 16

Regulæ de eo quod licet in bello. iii. 1, 2, 3, 4. Super deliberationibus politicis. ii. 24, 5, 1, 4

Relatum in referente. iii. 20, 24

Religio quo sensu juris gentium. ii. 20, 45, 3, & § 46, 3. Christiana, qua talis proprie, naturalibus argumentis non nititur. ii. 20, 48, 1, 2

Religionis publicæ status apud Hebræos a rege pendebat. i. 4, 6, 3, 4. Jus ad societatem humanam. ii. 20, 44, 3

Religionem multi affectu non judicio sequuntur. *ibid.*

Religiosa belli jure destruuntur. iii. 5, 2, 4. Loca hostibus religiosa non sunt. iii. 5, 2, 6

Religiosis locis parcendum in bello. iii. 12, 7

Renuntiare. *Vide* Abdicare.

Renuntiatio de regno an noceat liberis natis, et an nascituris. ii. 7, 26

Repetere (non) aliud quam dare. ii. 13, 5

Repræsentatio apud Hebræos. ii. 7, 6. Germanis sero cognita. ii. 7, 30, 1. In dubio admittenda. *ibid.* Non surrogat in privilegium, quod sexus aut ætatis erat proprium. ii. 7, 18, & ii. 30, 2

Repræsentationis jus unde. ii. 7, 6

Repressaliæ quid. iii. 2, 4

Repressaliarum facultas impetrari a principe solet. iii. 2, 7, 2. Jura alia sunt juris gentium, alia juris civilis. iii. 2, 7, 2, 3

Repressaliis qui culpa sua causam dederunt, tenentur eos, qui damnum passi sunt, indemnes præstare. iii. 2, 7, 4. Obnoxii qui sint. iii. 2, 5, 2. Non subsunt legati et res eorum. iii. 2, 7, 2. Eximi lege civili solent mulieres, infantes, res studiosorum, aut ad nundinas missæ. *ibid.*

Res repetita quid significet. iii. 3, 7, 1. Rapere quid veteribus Latinis. iii. 4, 1, 1. Reddere pro quavis satisfactione. *ibid.* Possunt capi, etiam in compensationem debiti in bello subnascentis. iii. 1, 3, & cap. 13, 3, 1. Hostium perdere quousque liceat justitia interna. iii. 12, 1. Amicorum, quæ reperiuntur in navibus hostium, an belli jure acquirantur. iii. 6, 5, 6. Et modus circa imperium distinguuntur. i. 3, 11, 1. Non perductæ intra præsidia dominium non mutant. iii. 6, 3, & cap. 9, 16, 1

Rebus ad bellum non facientibus parcendum. iii. 14, 5

Rerum defensio an jus det occidendi. ii. 1, 11. Servandarum causa vis per Evangelium an et quatenus licita. ii. 1, 13

Reipublicæ bonum an nostri tantum causa desideremus. ii. 1, 9, 2. Forma mutata apud victos, et an recte. iii. 15, 8

Rescissoria actio ex postliminio apud Romanos. iii. 9, 10, 3

Resistere an liceat superiori in summa necessitate. i. 4, 7, 2, 4

Resistentia obstinata non sufficit ad jus internum occidendi resistentem. iii. 12, 16, 1. Aliqua in delatione imperii reservari interdum solet. i. 4, 12

Respublica non tenetur ex facto subditi. ii. 22, 2, 1

Restituere qui teneantur faciendo, aut non faciendo. ii. 17, 6

Restitutio non debetur ex bello justo ob vitiosam intentionem. ii. 22, 17, 3. Rerum cap-

4, 3. Jus de captivis redemptis. iii. 9, 11, & 3, 10, 2. Jus pro iis, qui postliminio redierunt. iii. 8, 10, 3. Lex circa res captas. iii. 13, 4, 4. Mos circa reges captos. iii. 11, 7, 2, 3 Ruben exheredatus a jure primogenituræ. iii. 7, 25

S.

Sabbathi lex pro servis. iii. 14, 5, 1. Cujus rei symbolum. ii. 20, 45, 2. Violati pœna cur capitalis. *ibid.*

Sacerdotibus et eorum asseclis parcendum in bello. iii. 11, 10, 1

Sacra corrumpi an possint jure belli. iii. 5, 2, 1, 3. Quo sensu publica. iii. 5, 2, 2. In deditione comprehenduntur. iii. 5, 2, 1, & i. 3, 8, 3. Hosti sacra an sint. iii. 5, 2, 4. Populi voluntate profana facta. iii. 5, 2, 3, 5, & cap. 12, 7, 2

Sacramentum militare post Constantinum. i. 2, 10, 4, & ii. 13, 11, 3

Sacris parcendum in bello. iii. 12, 6

Sagmina. iii. 3, 8

Saguntina controversia inter Romanos et Carthaginienses. ii. 16, 13

Samsonis mors. ii. 19, 5, 4

Sapiens natura magistratus, quo sensu. ii. 20, 9, 2

Satisfactio offerenda ab eo qui deliquit, antequam justum bellum gerere possit. ii. 1, 18, 2

Saul an in impietate mortuus. ii. 19, 5, 4

Sciens, præsens et tacens quando consentire credatur. ii. 4, 5, 1

Scientia quando præsumatur. ii. 21, 2, 6

Scholasticorum sententia de mendacio et æquivocatione. iii. 1, 17, 3

Scripti et sententiæ locus apud Rhetores. ii. 16, 4, 2

Scriptura in dubio ad monumentum contractus adhibita censetur. ii. 16, 30

Scripturæ et picturæ eadem ratio. ii. 8, 21, 1

Σκυθισμός. ii. 15, 5, 1

Σκῦλα. iii. 6, 24, 4

Semipravi. iii. 11, 4, 6

Senatus Romanus aliquo tempore partitus summum imperium cum populo. i. 3, 20, 6

Sententia jus proprie non dat. iii. 2, 5, 1

Sententiæ quæ dividendæ aut conjungendæ. ii. 5, 19. Quomodo numerandæ inter eos, qui dispares partes in re habent. ii. 5, 22

Sententiarum pari numero reus absolvitur et possessor vincit. ii. 5, 18

Sepeliendi jus quale. ii. 19, 1, 5. Mos unde ortus. ii. 19, 2, 1, 4. Hostes et inimici. ii. 19, 3, 1, 2, 3

Sepeliendos (ob) mortuos bella. ii. 19, 3, 6

Sepultura an debeatur his, qui se occiderunt. iii. 19, 5, 1, 3

Sepulturam prohibere furor dicitur. iii. 19, 3, 4

Sergius Paulus in magistratu manet factus Christianus. i. 2, 7, 10

Servitus ex voluntate. ii. 5, 26, 27. Neutiquam pugnat cum jure naturali. ii. 5, 27, 2. Ex pœna. ii. 5, 3. Perfecta, et imperfecta quæ. ii. 5, 27, 1, & 30, 1. Quo sensu contra naturam dicatur. iii. 7, 1, 1

Servitutis imperfectæ genera. ii. 5, 30. Bellicæ causa. iii. 7, 5, 1

Servus mercedem laboris sui an sumere possit. iii. 7, 6, 4. Resistere an licite possit domino. iii. 7, 7. Cognosci debet, ut postliminio recipiatur. iii. 9, 11, 1. Recipitur, etiamsi animum res nostras sequendi non habet. iii. 9, 11, 1. Mercenario comparatur. iii. 14, 2, 2

Servum (in) quidvis licet. iii. 7, 3, 1

Servi fratres nostri. iii. 14, 2, 3. Naturaliter philosophis qui. ii. 22, 12. Ad operas urgendi moderate. iii. 14, 5, 1. Quo casu fugere possint. ii. 5, 29, 2, & iii. 7, 6, 1, & i. 4, 7, 1. Transfugæ recipiuntur postliminio. iii. 9, 11, 1. Quando postliminio recipiantur. iii. 9, 11, 3. Etiam manumissi postliminio recipiuntur. *ibid.* Redemti quod jus apud Romanos. iii. 14, 5, & 10, 2. Dicuntur populi subjecti. i. 3, 12, 1. Pro dominis bellant. i. 5, 3. Res fiunt domini. iii. 7, 3, 2

Servis Romæ licebat ad statuas confugere. iii. 14, 6, 4

Servo Dominus quæ præstare debeat. iii. 14, 5, 1, 3

Servorum nati matrem sequuntur. iii. 7, 2. Deliberatrix facultas imperfecta. ii. 26, 4, 2. Filii an naturaliter servi, et quatenus. ii. 5, 29

Servos (in) lenitas adhibenda. iii. 14, 4. Jus vitæ et necis in eos quale. iii. 14, 3. Dominorum quale. ii. 5, 28, & 3, 7, 3, & cap. 14, 3, 1

Servos Romana lex bello arcebat. i. 5, 4. (circa) Francorum jus et Hebræorum. iii. 7, 8

Severitas laudabilis Dei, Mosis, Christi, et Apostolorum. i. 2, 8, 11

I I

Victis eripere nihil nisi quod pacem impedit, landabile. iii. 15, 2, 1. Relictum suum imperium. iii. 15, 7. Imperium relinquere generosorum est, iii. 15, 4. Imperium relingui solet, locis quibusdam deteritis. iii. 15, 5. Imperii pars relicta, iii. 15, 9. Permissæ suæ leges, et magistratus, iii. 15, 10.

Victor curare debet, ut religio vera libere prædicetur. ibid. Quis dicendus. iii. 20, 45. Ejus officium in eos, qui se dedunt, iii. 20, 49, 2

Vindex sanguinis apud Hebræos, ii. 20, 8, 6, & i. 2, 5, 4

Vindicatio. Vide Ultio.

Vindictæ privatæ exempla, ii. 20, 8, 3

Virtuti moderatio. iii. 12, 4, 3

Virtutis actus quos jus Hebræorum exigit, exiguntur et nunc a Christianis. i. 1, 17, 5

Vis injusta naturaliter quæ, i. 2, 1, 6. Justa naturaliter quæ. i. 2, 1, 7. Testimonii probatur. i. 2, 1, 5, 7. In bestiis, quo sensu. 1, 2, 1, 5, 2. Pœnæ ergo licita, iii. 1, 2, 3

Vi hominibus armatis, coactive, quid significet. ii. 16, 20, 4

Vita in statu innocentiæ, ii. 2, 1, 2. Populi præferenda libertati, ii. 14, 6, 2. An obligari possit, iii. 2, 6. Tota reorum an examinanda. ii. 20, 30, 4

Vitam valide obligari, antiquorum sententia. ii. 15, 16, 4

Vitæ tuendæ causa mentiri an liceat, iii. 1, 16. Pactio libertatem non comprehendit. iii. 23, 12

Vitia qualia impunita esse debeant, ii. 20, 18, 20, 1

Vitiositas actus ab effectu discernenda. ii. 17, 22

Vitium rei in contractibus indicandum, et quare. ii. 12, 9, 1

Vittæ. iii. 24, 5

Ultio an juri naturæ conveniat, ii. 20, 5, 1, 3. Licita jure naturæ et gentium, ii. 20, 8, 2. 3. Christianis permissa, ii. 20, 10, 5

Ultionis restrictio unde. ii. 20, 8, 4

Unio populorum, aut regnorum, quid operetur. ii. 9, 9

Universitas obligat singulos, ii. 5, 17

Universitatis debito singuli an obligentur, et quatenus. ii. 14, 7

Voces an naturalia signa, iii. 1, 8, 1

Vocibus (de) meris disputatio cavenda. ii. 20, 23

Volenti mentiendo an injuria fiat, iii. 1, 14, 1

Voluntas defuncti pro lege, ii. 7, 3. Quæ punibilis. ii. 20, 18. Dei nominatur, ubi causæ non apparent. ii. 20, 48, 1. Jure mutabilis. ii. 11, 2

Ὑπερβολὴ figura qualis. iii. 1, 13

Ὑπόκρισις. ii. 13, 21

Urbes quædam a Deo excidio damnatæ: quare. iii. 12, 3, 4. A Salomone Hieromo datæ quales. i. 3, 12, 3

Urbium matricum jus in colonias apud Græcos. i. 3, 21, 1

Usucapio locum non habet inter duos populos aut reges. ii. 4, 1. Imo. ibid. § 3, 4

Usuræ quo jure vetitæ. ii. 12, 20, 1, 3. Vetita lege Hebræa. ibid. Not 3. Christianis illicitæ. ibid. Crimen quibus casibus non admittatur. ii. 12, 21

Usuras (circa) legum civilium efficacia. ii. 12, 22. Hollandicum jus circa ipsas. ibid.

Usus auctoritas in explicandis legibus. i. 2, 9, 1. Rerum naturalis. ii. 2, 1. Rei in abusu consistens æstimabilis extra rem. ii. 12, 20, 2

Uti opera oblata licet, etsi offerenti illicita. iii. 1, 21, 22, & 2, 26, 5, 1

Utilitas publica alienando bona subditorum pacis causa, quo sensu requiratur. iii. 20, 7, 1, & 10, 1

Utilitas belligeranti ex abstinentia populationum. iii. 12, 8, 1

Utilitatis innoxiæ jus. ii. 2, 11

Uxor in corpus mariti jus habet ex lege evangelica. ii. 5, 9, 2. Rem vindicat, emtam pecunia sua, quam repetere potuisset. ii. 10, 2, 2

Uxores, an plures habere licitum sit: qui plures habuerint, qui una contendi; et an licitum sit eas deserere. ii. 5, 9, 1, 2, 4

X.

Xerxis et Artabazanis controversia. ii. 7, 29

Ξύμμαχία. ii. 15, 6, 2

Z.

Zelandorum jus circa alluviones. iii. 8, 15, 1